For teaching—
372
392
393

Carol Bly
1668 Juno Ave.
Saint Paul, MN 55116-1415

Carol Bly
St. Paul,

——NOVEMBER 1998

Praise for

An Anthology of Russian Literature

from Earliest Writings to Modern Fiction

"An astonishing anthology: an attempt, through a sampling of a saint's life, epic, narrative poem, parodic spoof, drama, lyric, and prose, to communicate some of the literary bedrock of Russian national consciousness. The translations are everywhere persuasive and the selection uncannily good. When the Soviet period passes wholly into history and Russian culture reassembles on the far side of the millennium, Rzhevsky's volume will be a major resource for English-language readers interested in a vivid, diversified introduction to one of the world's most provocative cultures."

—Caryl Emerson, Princeton University

"This is an excellent anthology that can serve as the basis for a variety of college courses on Russian literature and culture, and as a splendid introduction to these subjects for a general reader. A highly original and appealing feature of the collection is that the works in it were selected because of their varied resonances in Russian culture, including adaptations and translations into other artistic forms such as opera, theater, and film. Professor Rzhevsky traces these and other links in a series of concise and illuminating essays and provides references that would allow the motivated reader or instructor to pursue connections throughout Russian culture from the earliest period to the present day. The illustrations echo the anthology's focus on an 'inter-representational' history of Russian culture."

—Vladimir Alexandrov, Yale University

"Rzhevsky's concept of selecting literary texts on the basis of their relevance to other art forms and their quality of being representative of Russian culture (the 'spirit of Russia') seems most appropriate. The selection strikes a good balance between 'Russianness' and accessibility to an American reader."

—Victor Terras, Brown University

"Rzhevsky's anthology makes all the Russian literary texts one needs to teach a culture course available in a single, affordable volume. His choice of literary texts that resonate to other arts (music, film, painting—primarily Russian but also European) is excellent. The introductory essays are interdisciplinary and wide-ranging in scope, and have something to say to undergraduates at all levels. The multidisciplinary bibliographies after each work are also useful."

—Maria Carlson, The University of Kansas

An Anthology of RUSSIAN Literature

An Anthology of RUSSIAN Literature

from Earliest Writings to Modern Fiction

INTRODUCTION TO A CULTURE

Edited by

Nicholas Rzhevsky

M.E. Sharpe

Armonk, New York
London, England

Permission to reprint the following is gratefully acknowledged:

"The Narrative, Passion, and Encomium of Boris and Gleb," from *Medieval Slavic Lives of Saints and Princes*, trans. and ed. Marvin Kantor, Michigan Slavic Translations Series No. 5, Michigan Slavic Publications, 1983, pp. 163–97 (abridged).

Archpriest Avvakum: The Life Written by Himself, ed. and trans. Kenneth N. Brostrom, Michigan Slavic Translations Series No. 4, Michigan Slavic Publications, 1979 (abridged).

Alexander Pushkin, "The Bronze Horseman," from *Narrative Poems by Alexander Pushkin and by Mikhail Lermontov*, trans. Charles Johnston, London, 1984. © The Literary Executor of Charles Johnston.

Mikhail Lermontov, "Taman." The translation from Lermontov's *A Hero of Our Time* by Vladimir and Dmitri Nabokov by permission of the Estate of Vladimir Nabokov. All rights reserved.

Anton Chekhov, *The Cherry Orchard*, trans. and ed. E.J. Czerwinski, in *Chekhov Reconstructed*, a special issue of *Slavic and East European Arts*, vol. 4, no. 2 (1986), pp. 143–55 (Act 1).

Library of Congress Cataloging-in-Publication Data

An Anthology of Russian literature from earliest writings to modern fiction : introduction to a culture / edited by Nicholas Rzhevsky.
p. cm.
Includes bibliographical references.
ISBN 1-56324-421-7 (alk. paper).—ISBN 1-56324-422-5 (pbk. : alk. paper)
1. Russian literature—Translations into English.
I. Rzhevsky, Nicholas, 1943–
PG3213.A56   1996
891.708—dc20
95-42684
CIP

Printed in the United States of America

The paper used in this publication meets the minimum requirements of the American National Standard for Information Sciences— Permanence of Paper for Printed Library Materials, ANSI Z 39.48-1984.

♾

BM (c) 10 9 8 7 6 5 4 3 2 1
BM (p) 10 9 8 7 6 5 4 3 2 1

The editor dedicates this book to the women who brought
Russian culture into his life:

Irina Aleksandrovna Rzhevskaya
Vera Georgievna Karsanova
Sofia Savvichna Rzhevskaya

Alla Djakova, Anastasia Rzhevskaya, Svetlana Rzhevskaya,
Lidia Zhuravskaya, Nadezhda Martinjuk, Natalie Slocum, Irina Fedorova,
Tatiana Rzhevskaya, Natalia Rzhevskaya, Alexandra Fedorova,
and Kyra Rzhevskaya

~Contents~

~Introduction~

Russian Literature and Culture

Literature's centrality in culture is sometimes obvious—when a composer and librettist shape an opera out of fictional narrative, when a theater director picks up a dramatic text or novel to create a performance, or when a painter takes inspiration from literary subjects and myths. Such aesthetic events reflect a more general role played by works of literature in interpreting experience and serving as cultural mileposts for readers. The concepts, images, and emotions literature generates resonate throughout the arts—in music, film, performance, and other forms of representation—and, by indicating recurring values and ideas, serve as an entry to central issues of culture. These are the basic judgments that inspired the present anthology of Russian literary texts. Each work offered below has an explicit inter-representational history, reflected most often in adaptations to opera, theater, or film but also in significant cultural resonances other than adaptations as such.

The act of placing emphasis on literature as a central form of cultural definition has the virtue of addressing several common dilemmas. One of the greatest difficulties of introducing Russian culture is the issue of focus—where to begin, where to end, what to emphasize, and what to neglect out of a huge and unwieldy body of disparate examples. This collection offers one solution to such problems of organization and initial definition, whether for the typical college course or for the interested reader outside the classroom who yearns for some depth of understanding when listening to a Russian opera, visiting an exhibition of icons, or viewing the latest film adaptation of a Russian novel. Literature, for such purposes, provides cultural memory, a favorable vantage point from which to initiate our own exploration of the arts.

The various musical compositions, paintings, and performances mentioned below are also manifestations of the intellectual function literary texts have served for Russian artists and performers. Although Russian culture did not produce a strong philosophical tradition until the end of the nineteenth and beginning of the twentieth century, its contribution to the exploration of ideas is hardly questionable when one looks to the works of Russian writers. Whatever may be the differences between analytical modes of philosophy and the imaginative modes of fiction, it can be argued that Dostoevsky, when measured by the common goal of insight into ultimate issues of existence, holds up his end in the world of ideas inhabited by thinkers like Feuerbach or Kant, and Tolstoy his in the realm of intellectual discourse and imagination occupied by Herder and Rousseau.

Russian intellectual engagements can be seen to follow a much-repeated pattern. What begins as eager and at times unquestioning imitation—of ideas originating in Greece or France, for instance—rapidly turns into original literary inquiry and intellectual creativity. Generalizations in cultural and intellectual histories about the "silence" of Russian culture, or the related observations of sympathetic and perceptive readers—such as Sir Isaiah Berlin, Father Georges Florovsky, and James Billington—about the Russian propensity to be overly engaged by the intellectual accomplishments of other cultures and to take on ready-formed ideas and values, underestimate the actual cultural situation when uninformed by the literary transformations those ideas and values undergo. The works of Berlin, Florovsky, and Billington, in fact, themselves provide some of the most perceptive interpretations available of the strong intellectual roles of Russian literary texts.

Literature, then, has served the Russians as a testing ground—through the imagined situations writers have created—for measuring insights and hypotheses. At times, of course, imagination has fallen short or overextended itself; in other instances, imagination has served as historical prophecy. Some Russian readers, for example, overextended Nikolai Chernyshevsky's popular novel *What Is to Be Done?* by turning the lure of utopia into the tragedy of Soviet totalitarianism. Dostoevsky's *Notes from the Underground* and *The Devils*, on the other hand, were immediately available (and very evident in the late Soviet period of glasnost) as indications of the dangers of playing out such fictions. In any case, both instances demonstrate, as do Pushkin, Gogol, Tolstoy, Chekhov, and Bulgakov, a passionate engagement with ideas and values that have profoundly influenced the ways in which Russian men and women have looked at and reacted to the world both in social-political action and in aesthetic representation.

The collection is organized chronologically, except for the early nineteenth century, when the progression is briefly interrupted in order to arrange texts by topic. The introduction to each section places the literary works in their historical context and notes later cultural resonances. Following each text is an introductory guide to primary and secondary sources, including available aesthetic transformations of the work, its subjects, and its motifs in film, video, musical recordings, and art collections. As indications of an ongoing cultural process, these listings emphasize Russian rather than non-Russian responses in the arts—for example, Sergei Bondarchuk's film adaptation of *War and Peace* rather than the popular American version with

Audrey Hepburn and Henry Fonda. On the same principle, the bibliographies include Russian criticism and scholarship, alongside English-language commentary.

The cultural juxtapositions and broad chronological leaps in the editor's introductions reflect conditions of creative work in which artists roam freely through past centuries as well as their own time. This free and broad perspective does not mean that the artists themselves stand outside of history, of course, but it does suggest that readers must be prepared to follow their sometimes unexpected creative journeys and to assess their discoveries alongside more reductive approaches to history. A writer such as Alexander Pushkin has insight to offer regarding certain ethical and political issues raised by the sixteenth century (the time of Boris Godunov) which carries weight and significance for Russian culture as important as the generalizations of historians, such as Nikolai Karamzin, from whom he borrowed. The efficacy of Pushkin's aesthetic imagination is evident in its becoming Russian cultural history in its own right. To rephrase T.S. Eliot, although we might think we know more about the Russian past than Pushkin did, he is often what we know.

The present collection selects certain texts because they influence the cultural process more than other texts do. Such discriminations are invariably conditioned by personal bias, particularly when considerations of space require the drastic and highly questionable discriminations *within* texts known as excerpts. In some instances, such as Aleksandr Solzhenitsyn's works, the widespread availability of reliable editions suggested choosing different authors altogether; in other instances, texts that profoundly affected and reflected popular culture—such as Lermontov's "Borodino," or Mikhail Sholokhov's *Virgin Soil Upturned*—were given preference over texts by the same authors usually favored by critics. The decision to go no further than the concluding years of the Soviet presence in Russian culture, in spite of all the fascinating works written in the early postcommunist period, seemed most prudent because this literature had not yet had time to develop a lasting cultural presence when this anthology was being prepared. There is little defense—outside of printing parameters—for omitting any number of other worthwhile works or complete versions. There are, however, solid arguments to be made for the texts and parts of texts that are included, and those arguments are made in the introduction to each section.

This gesture of bowing to the inevitability of subjective choice, so fashionable in the intellectual world of the late twentieth century, need not turn into an exaggerated relativism. Judgments of literary merit usually can be traced past political, social, or aesthetic agendas to the rock-bottom ethical views of a particular critic or editor. Such views are inevitably a response to other views and are always relative—Kant forgive us—to the time and space in which they were formulated. But although each individual responds to particular personal contingencies, she or he can join others in honoring specific values and texts so that they continue to exist over time and beyond a particular space. Empathy and agreement of this sort make possible traditions that transcend relativism. At the time of the compilation of this collection and in the space of the Western humanities it occupies, there has been a considerable erosion of such cultural centers, accompanied by the collapse of political centers such as the government of the Soviet Union. The editor, however, has chosen to answer the challenges of history by suggesting that centers of Russian culture *do* exist in the basic values and ideas that artists have turned to again and again.

One leitmotif of this sort that has attracted the attention of even jaded postmodern readers—thanks, in part, to the works of the Russian philosopher Mikhail Bakhtin—is respect for the self, viewed in terms of its broadest realities and interactions. Notions of the self's properties and intricate engagements are very much a particular Russian concern, and the related values of empathy, humility, compassion, and optimism in regard to the self's ability to make choices in spite of historical and social contingencies are expressed throughout this collection. The Russians bring to these fairly common cultural emphases complex and sometimes unique explorations of the linkages and separations between the self and the other that underlie perennial concerns, including those based on ethnic, gender, social, and political considerations.

The significant contributions of the literary works gathered here at such fundamental levels of cultural discourse suggest that the magnificent cultural tradition Russian writers represent and invigorate will continue to find an audience. The reader is invited to join their prospective and existing company, from the anonymous bards and priests to the highly visible personalities who have helped shape the course of the modern arts. Behind the products of literary imagination lie individual sensibilities, different in talent, choices of subject, and opinion but joined in responding to the crucial issues, and joined as well in creating and stimulating the best works Russian culture has to offer.

Acknowledgments and a Few Words on Translation

Without indulging in too much polemic at the expense of existing translations, it can be noted that work on this anthology was stimulated by a critical appraisal of English texts based on Russian originals. There are good translations—although often rendered in antediluvian English—but there are also many examples of ignorant or dishonest ones that throw up a wall of misunderstanding between English-speaking readers and Russian cultural endeavors. This judgment led to the inevitable conclusion that new translations were needed, although an extended search of the available literature not surprisingly brought forward a number of admirable translations that were added to those newly done. Particular recognition is due Marvin Kantor, Kevin Brostrom, Edward Czerwinski, Sir Charles Johnston, and Vladimir and Dmitri Nabokov for work that would have been difficult to duplicate in sensitivity and talent.

In regard to the methodology of the new translations, the attempt was made to remain faithful to original texts by semantic doubling and reversal. That is, each English equivalent was measured by retranslation into Russian. The continued presence of the original Russian word, phrase, expression, or nuance would suggest the felicity of the English version, its absence a new effort. In difficult cases, colloquial English was given preference on the whole, although in some instances, following Vladimir Nabokov's example, awkward English was allowed in an attempt to stretch the reader's imagination (and one hopes not the reader's patience) in the direction of the Russian meaning.

Poetry is a special case, and amid the passionate debates over translation of poetry one keeps coming back to unquantifiable matters of taste. Issues such as whether or not to rhyme, how far to follow rhythm, and how closely to render metaphor were all dealt with by the same attempt to remain faithful to the original while striking a balance with suitable English. In instances such as Derzhavin's "Felicity," the original meter and rhyme were not followed closely because of the awkwardness of initial results. In other cases, usually of shorter poems, an attempt was made to at least hint at the original rhythm and sometimes rhyme. In one important text, that of "The Bronze Horseman," the poetic talent of the translator himself made it possible to offer a version that combines grace in English with a close approximation of Pushkin's technical achievement. In all these cases, the best that can be hoped for is that the force and beauty of the Russian poems might be sensed if not duplicated.

Igor is the only instance in which earlier translated versions—in modern Russian, English, and French—were consulted from the outset. In regard to this text, translation in itself has become an important cultural process in Russia, and the offered variant continues rather than breaks with the work of Dmitry Likhachev, Vladimir Nabokov, and Roman Jakobson. The text and annotations that most directly affected the present version are found in Likhachev's edition, which comments extensively on past textual and translation history. Jakobson, Nabokov, and other readers of *Igor*, however, are not in agreement with a number of Likhachev's suggestions or with each other in choices made. The translators joined this creative dialogue by offering their own specific strategies and interpretations of a text in which each and every word has a critical history.

The translation of *Boris Godunov* was begun during rehearsals of the 1982 Taganka Theater production and was inspired by the evidence, clearly apparent then, that Pushkin's play should be performed as well as read. No attempt was made to render Pushkin's blank verse in a precise equivalent; close attention to the caesura and a mixture of blank verse and prose—permissible, I would suggest, in light of Pushkin's own sense of style—suggested a way of making the rhythm and meaning of the original both recognizable and suitable for English-language performance. As with the other texts of dramatic literature included here, such translation work is never complete until it finds another voice—the actor's—to fulfill it.

Finally, it is a pleasure to acknowledge the students who have passed through the seminar on literary translation given in Stony Brook. They suffered many of the problems noted above along with me, and they provided challenges to find the right solution or often the solution itself that helped the work to its conclusion. In addition to the colleagues and friends noted earlier, Christina Bethin gave intelligent advice for dealing with *The Tale of Igor*, and Vera Dunham and Timothy Westphalen contributed sensitive translations of texts that lightened the burden in no small way. Victor Terras, who has set the standard for collegiality among scholars of Russian literature in recent years, gave freely of his advice and unique erudition in suggesting improvements. Additional thanks are due to Patricia O'Brien, Debbie DeBellis, and the Italian Center at Stony Brook, directed by Mario Mignone, for help with computer chores. Richard Kramer, Dean for Humanities and Fine Arts in Stony Brook, offered concrete encouragement by way of a grant to cover research and typing costs, as did the NYS/UUP PDQWL Committee in two Continuing Faculty Awards. Therese M. Malhame, Marian Schwartz, and Dobrochna Dyrcz-Freeman skillfully edited an unwieldly manuscript, and they were joined by Rama Sohonee in preparing the bibliographies and in translating some of the texts. Last of all, the staunch support and ever-gentle prodding of Patricia Kolb, Ana Erlić, and Elizabeth Granda of M.E. Sharpe helped greatly in advancing a large and difficult job to its conclusion.

A Note on Transliteration

Except in the case of previously published texts, transliteration has been based on the Library of Congress system with adjustments made for common usage.

Nicholas Rzhevsky
Stony Brook, March 1996

An Anthology of RUSSIAN Literature

~ I ~

Cultural Beginnings

In 1185, the armed forces of Igor, prince of Novgorod-Seversk and son of Prince Sviatoslav of Chernigov, were soundly defeated by Polovtsian (Kuman) nomads. This historical event prodded an anonymous author to write one of the first literary masterpieces of Russian culture. In result of his efforts, Igor, an otherwise minor historical figure, gained immortality in the aesthetic world of Ulysses, Beowulf, Roland, and King Arthur.

Since its discovery in the latter part of the eighteenth century, *The Tale of Igor* has attracted the attention of a broad range of writers, historians, translators, critics, and men and women of the arts. Igor's travails are probably most familiar to the Western public through an opera composed by Alexander Borodin, *Prince Igor*, one of the best-known works in the Russian musical repertoire. Borodin was inspired by a professional man of letters, the critic Vladimir Stasov, who gave him a scenario based on the original text. Work began in 1869 but was completed after Borodin's death in 1887, when a member of the "Mighty Group," Nikolai Rimsky-Korsakov, and the young composer Alexander Glazunov finished the necessary orchestrations.

The musical response to *Igor* in turn inspired another art form, the dance. In 1909, under Sergei Diaghilev's leadership, the master choreographer Mikhail Fokine and the artist Nikolai Roerich, using Borodin's music, gave visual form to the Polovtsian dances as part of the Ballets Russes season in Paris. The course of twentieth-century ballet—a slightly disreputable art form before the arrival of Diaghilev's Russians in the West—was strongly influenced by this production. Borodin's music became a familiar part of Western culture, entering America in one well-known instance through Robert Wright and George Forest's Broadway hit *Kismet* and the immensely popular

The Literary Museum, Pushkin House

Boyan, a 1950 woodcut by V.A. Favorsky depicting the *Igor Tale* bard.

song "Stranger in Paradise." Wright and Forest freely acknowledged their debt to Borodin; much more typical of the hidden musical voyages of Igor was the camouflaged borrowing of Claude-Michel Schonberg's *Miss Saigon*, which began a long run on Broadway in 1991.

In other cultural meanderings, translation of the text into German was undertaken by Rainer Maria Rilke, and an English variant, complete with the brilliant insights and awkward idiosyncracies readers learned to expect from Russia's greatest English-writing novelist, was provided by Vladimir Nabokov in 1960.

Needless to say, before becoming part of Western aesthetic tradition in such forms, *Igor* influenced a broad range of cultural endeavors in Russia, notably including the work of nineteenth- and twentieth-century painters. Vasily Perov created his well-known study *Yaroslavna's Lament* in response to the literary text, and Viktor Vasnetsov contributed a popular painting titled *After Igor Sviatoslavich's Battle with the Polovtsians*. Nikolai Roerich produced a masterly stage design for Borodin's opera, Vladimir Favorsky provided illustrations for a printed edition of the work, and the talented Palekh artist Ivan Golikov used the typical naive style of his school to create a memorable (and often repeated) example of the folk genre of miniature lacquer boxes.

But the primary response to *The Tale of Igor* has been in written texts. Russian men and women of letters have kept this work active in Russian culture by an ongoing tradition of translations, adaptations, and borrowings reserved for the most basic works of literature. It is curious that a pervasive insecurity about sources—the original manuscript is lost and our version of *Igor* is a copy of a copy probably made in the sixteenth century and itself destroyed during Napoleon's invasion in 1812—has resulted not in neglect but in creative engagement. The various transcriptions, retellings, and archaisms of the versions we do have make it very difficult to reproduce a definitive text, but the very obscurity of language, combined, it is true, with a rare display of literary talent in the passages that *are* decipherable, has attracted Russia's most talented writers to the riddle of *Igor*.

After the initial well-meaning but uninformed translation by Count Aleksei Musin-Pushkin, the man who discovered the manuscript and printed it in 1800 in collaboration with two coeditors, new versions or retellings were provided by the Ukrainian poet Vasily Kapnist (1757–1823); the writer Nikolai Karamzin (1766–1826), who included passages in his *History of the Russian State*; the paterfamilias of Russian Romanticism, Vasily Zhukovsky (1783–1852); the poet Apollon Maikov (1821–1897); the great Ukrainian writer of the nineteenth century, Taras Shevchenko (1814–1861); and the major Belarusian writer Ianka Kupala (1882–1942). Alexander Pushkin (1799–1837) worked on the Zhukovsky translation and left remarks testifying to the anonymous writer's talent. The symbolist poet Konstantin Balmont published a translation in emigration in 1930, and Nikolai Zabolotsky, who stayed very much a Soviet poet, created another verse version in 1946. In the West, in addition to Nabokov, the famous linguist and philologist Roman Jakobson provided a translation informed by his pioneering research in language.

The direct influence of *The Tale of Igor* on literary texts was manifested relatively quickly in terms of cultural history in a thirteenth-century work, *The Tale of the Destruction of the Russian Land*. This text was followed in the fifteenth century by the better-known *Zadonshchina* (Beyond the Don), or *The Tale of the Great Prince Dmitry, Son of Ivan, and His Brother Vladimir, Son of Andrei*. The latter work eventually set off a storm of literary controversy in the twentieth century, when some critics (notably the French scholar André Mazon) claimed that *Zadonshchina*'s aesthetic superiority to *The Tale of Igor* suggested that *Igor* was a later imitation. The great majority of informed readers argued that *Zadonshchina*'s obvious inferiority indicated precisely the reverse process of imitation. Although the debate has continued among Slavic scholars, the weight of evidence is with those who view *Igor* as an early masterpiece. Their conclusion allows an obvious generalization about history and literature: tragic historical events, marked by bloodshed and the destruction of great cities or armies, are more readily suited to great works of art than more cheerful moments (such as the defeat of the Tatars commemorated in *Zadonshchina*), which often prod awkward aesthetic responses influenced by sentiment and optimism.

In any case, Igor's defeat continued to inspire Russia's best literary talents. The amazingly long-lived poet Fedor Glinka (1786–1880); the short-lived but more talented Nikolai Yazykov (1803–1846); the blind Ivan Kozlov (1799–1840); the historical novelist and imitator of Sir Walter Scott, Mikhail Zagoskin (1789–1852); Russia's most famous dramatist after Pushkin and before Chekhov, Aleksandr Ostrovsky (1823–1886); the first Russian Nobel Prize winner in literature, Ivan Bunin (1870–1953); the Symbolist philosopher Vladimir Soloviev (1853–1900); the symbolist poets Valery Briusov (1873–1924) and Alexander Blok (1880–1921); the twentieth-century poets Maksimilian Voloshin (1877–1932), Sergei Gorodetsky (1884–1967), Eduard Bagritsky (1897–1934), and Georgy Adamovich (1884–1972)—all honored *The Tale of Igor* with direct imitation, the most sincere form of literary flattery.

Igor's popularity in Russian cultural history was encouraged by its continued, if unfortunate, relevance to historical events. Since Igor's defeat by the invading Kumans, the Russians have faced military invasions in each century. As in *Igor*, it is true, they have responded with their own invasions; the moral justifications for such counteraggression—based in religious principles suggesting that the last shall be first and the defeated will reign victorious—form a leitmotif of Russian culture. Those readers who remember seeing Sergei Eisenstein's film *Alexander Nevsky* and hearing Prokofiev's marvelous score will recognize how another medieval ruler was used to justify militarism before the threat of one more German invasion joining this century with the past.

Fortunately, the text before us goes beyond a reflexive patriotism to question aggression from the perspective of poetic vision. It does so by contrasting values of humility with military bravado and of fraternity with individual power. Igor, like other epic heroes such as Achilles, Beowulf, and Roland, directly reflects broadly based cultural concerns. Like Homer, the anonymous author is more a singer of his time than a critic maintaining the distance between a writer's point of view and society that the modern perspective entails. Igor's epic qualities of strength, valor, and honor carry ironic tonalities, therefore, but they are not a vehicle for the author's isolated voice responding in opposition to generally held truths and values.

The irony and pathos of Igor's story reflect, rather, widespread concerns repeated over and over again in other genres such as chronicles, saints' lives, and sermons. Igor's courage, search for honor, and call to arms— meritorious as they may be—were recognized by the culture of his time to be the origins of his army's destruction and of the greatest disservice to Russia. Personal courage without political agreement can be ruinous, the events of *Igor* suggest, and honor untempered by humility can lead to personal and general disaster. Such conclusions reflect complex cultural sensibilities engaging moral dilemmas and private and public issues and provoking subtleties of pro and contra in aesthetic tradition.

In light of the later historical context of the Russian Empire in which Borodin wrote his opera, it is tempting to look to obvious and long-standing ethnic enmities and to take their retelling in literary text and opera to indicate the crude ambitions of imperialism. It is possible, for instance, to interpret the romantic passion expressed by Igor's son Vladimir and the khan's daughter Konchakovna as a cautionary tale of sexual-political seduction in which the young man is rendered impotent by sinister Oriental charm. Their music, as in its use in *Miss Saigon*, can be taken to be a form of imperialistic stereo-typing intended to entrap the opera's audience.

In terms of the original narrative, however, it is a strange sort of imperialism indeed when offered in the person of a military commander who fails due to excessive zeal and aggressiveness. In terms of the opera's libretto, it takes similar ingenuity to see an ethnically hostile or colonizing function in the text. Vladimir is more easily seen as a victim of love than of imperialistic ambitions; indeed, the character who would best serve a program of coloni-zation, the converted Christian Ovlur, is depicted as a morally ambiguous traitor initially rejected by Igor. Igor's own key moment in the opera is not a cry to dominate or educate savages but an impassioned aria asking for freedom—again more nineteenth-century Romantic than imperial in its origin. Defined in terms of Romanticism's political motifs, Igor's experience is directly opposite—as Byron, Mickiewicz, Lermontov, and Pushkin would argue—to the enslavement of neighboring tribes.

Rather than a drive to dominate, or the ethnic hostility postulated frequently as an a priori condition in multicultural relations, *Prince Igor*'s success, then, is more profitably viewed in terms of a cultural process of engagement and openness. Borodin and his colleagues demonstrated that without the capacity to accept and learn the music of other cultures, Russian culture itself would have been poorer. Without minimizing historical and ethnic differences or the tragic failures to resolve them, both the opera and the original literary *Igor* ultimately suggest an attempt to mediate engagements with others as a fundamental source of cultural vitality.

The anonymous "Boris and Gleb" and "Life of Alexis, Holy Man of God" address some of the same basic issues as *The Tale of Igor*. Unlike *Igor*, however, both narratives appear in numerous versions throughout the entire course of Russian medieval literature as well as in the early retellings of other aesthetic genres—the architecture of churches named after Boris and Gleb, icons, and popular woodcuts.

Both texts depend heavily on Russian culture's Byzantine heritage, particularly in its emphasis on kenotic values of humility, suffering, and depreciation of material concerns. The spiritual heroism they advocate is one possible measure postulated for Igor and neglected by him in the pursuit of political glory. Alexis's "Life" is part of the translated literature—the common heritage of Western civilization but emphasizing the Greek civilization of Asia Minor—that became Russia's own and that marks the origins of its literacy. Alexis served as a prototypical image of the holy fool present throughout the course of Russian culture; Boris and Gleb, judged to be saints because of their recognition of higher standards than earthly political aggrandizement, ultimately served on the banners of Russian armies to provide moral justification for wars imposed by the necessity of foreign invasion.

Both texts indicate particular Russian emphases on common and basic concerns present in the West, from the life of St. Francis of Assisi to the humble heroism of Forrest Gump. In Russian literature they prod the creation of Tolstoy's Platon Karataev, Dostoevsky's Sonia Marmeladov, Solzhenitsyn's Matryona, and a host of other touchstones of humility and transcendence. Their influence is so pervasive as to be unexpected at times, as in the twentieth-century theater adaptation of Alexis's *vita* in Mikhail Kuzmin's *The Comedy of Alexis, Man of God* (published 1908). The text

Icons of Sts. Boris and Gleb in St. Vladimir's Cathedral, Kiev, painted by Mikhail Nesterov in the early 1890s.

allowed a full display of Kuzmin's varied talents as composer, lyricist, and writer. It combined, in what might appear to be strange juxtaposition, Kuzmin's Beardsley sensibility with the long-standing values of piety and physical forbearance. The result was one of Kuzmin's best theatrical efforts, judged by D.S. Mirsky to be his most refined work.

The multirepresentational combinations of performance, painting, music, and narrative were present in Russian culture at its beginning in religious worship. The humility and martyrdom of Alexis, Boris, and Gleb were founded in Christ's Passion and death, kenotic imperatives for the aesthetic strategies of church rituals. The Russians were fortunate in that they had one of the most talented theologians of Christianity, St. John of Damascus (born early eighth century, died c. 753), to defend rituals and icons as ways of worship and to create two religious services, the Requiem and the Hours of Easter, for believers to participate in Christ's humble passage and spiritual victory over death. The services celebrate transcendence of the ultimate humiliation and do so in terms of aesthetic affinities that continue to be active to the present day.

N. R.

1

~Anonymous~

The Tale of Igor
The Tale of Igor's Campaign,
of Igor, Son of Sviatoslav, Grandson of Oleg

Would it not become us, brothers, to begin in ancient words the mournful tales of Igor's campaign, of Igor, son of Sviatoslav? Let this song begin in keeping with the real events of our time, and not according to Boyan's fancy.[1]

For he, prophetic Boyan, if he wished to compose a song for someone, ranged in thought through the woods—a gray wolf on the ground, a blue-gray eagle beneath the clouds. He recalled, it is said, the feuds of bygone years. Then he would send out ten falcons after a flock of swans, and the one overtaken would be first to sing a song—to old Yaroslav, to brave Mstislav, who slew Rededia before the Kasog troops, to handsome Roman, son of Sviatoslav.[2] That was Boyan, brothers, not sending out ten falcons after a flock of swans but placing his own prophetic fingers upon the living strings, and they themselves would ring out with glory to the princes.

So let us, brothers, begin this tale, from old Vladimir[3] down to the Igor of today, who strengthened his mind with his fortitude and honed his heart with manliness and, filled with martial spirit, led his valiant host against the land of the Polovtsians on behalf of the Russian land.

And so it was that Igor glanced at the bright sun and saw it cover his warriors in darkness. And Igor said to his armed company: "Brothers and retinue! Better to be killed than to be a prisoner; so let us, brothers, mount our swift steeds and let us look upon the blue Don." Passion gripped the prince's mind and his longing for the great Don blocked out the omens. "For I want," he said, "to break a lance at the border of the Polovtsian field; with you, Russians, I want either to lay down my head or to drink from the Don with my helmet."

O Boyan, nightingale of times of old! You would have sung of these campaigns, skipping, nightingale, on the tree of thought, your mind flying

11

beneath the clouds, weaving glory for both sides of this time, racing on Troyan's path across fields onto hills.[4]

A song would have been sung then for Igor, grandson of Oleg: "It is not a tempest that has driven falcons over the wide fields; flocks of jackdaws rush to the Great Don." Or thus would you sing, prophetic Boyan, grandson of Veles:[5] "Horses neigh beyond the Sula—glory rings out in Kiev. Trumpets blare in Novgorod, banners fly in Putivl." Igor waits for his dear brother Vsevolod. And Bui Tur[6] Vsevolod says to him, "One brother, one bright light—you, Igor! We are both Sviatoslav's sons. Saddle, brother, your swift horses, and mine are ready—saddled near Kursk. And my men of Kursk are experienced warriors—swaddled under trumpets, cared for under helmets, fed from the point of a lance; the roads are known to them, the ravines familiar, their bows are stretched tight, quivers are open, sabers sharpened, they race like gray wolves in the field, seeking for themselves honor and for the prince glory."

And so it was that Prince Igor mounted golden stirrups and rode into the open field. The sun blocked his way with darkness, night awoke birds with the tempest's moaning, a beastly whistling arose; Div stirred, calling out on the treetop, commanding the attention of an unknown land—the Volga, and Pomorye, and Sula, and Surozh, and Korsun,[7] and you, idol of Tmutorokan![8] And the Polovtsians hastened by untrodden ways to the Great Don. The carts screech at midnight like frightened swans.

And Igor leads warriors to the Don. Birds in the oak grove already await his misfortune; wolves conjure up a thunderstorm in the ravines; the eagles by their screeching call beasts to bones; foxes yelp at the dark red shields.

O Russian land! You are already beyond the hill!

The night is slow in falling. Dawn flared light, mist covered the fields, the nightingale's twitter died out, a jackdaw's chatter rose up. Russians have blocked off great fields with dark red shields, seeking for themselves honor and for the prince glory.

Early in the morning on Friday they trampled the pagan Polovtsian troops, and, scattering like arrows over the field, they carried off the fair Polovtsian maidens and with them gold, and brocades, and precious samites. With covers and mantles, and clothing of sheepskin, and with rich Polovtsian attire they began to lay bridges to bridge swamps and marshes. A dark red standard, a white banner, a dark red pennant, a silver pole—for the brave son of Sviatoslav!

Brave Oleg's[9] brood slumbers in the field. Far has it flown! It was not begotten to be offended, neither by the falcon, nor by the gyrfalcon, nor by you, black raven, pagan Polovtsian! Gzak races like a gray wolf, Konchak shows him the way to the Great Don.[10]

Very early next day the bloody dawn foreshadows light; black clouds come from the sea, they want to cover the four suns, and blue lightning flickers in them. There will be mighty thunder, a rain of arrows will come from the Great Don! Here lances shall break, here sabers shall strike against Polovtsian helmets, on the river Kaiala,[11] by the Great Don.

O Russian land! You are already beyond the hill!

And the winds, Stribog's[12] grandsons, blow arrows from the sea upon Igor's brave troops. The earth rumbles, the rivers flow turbid, dust covers the fields, banners announce: the Polovtsians come from the Don and from the sea; and they have surrounded the Russian columns from all sides. The Devil's children fenced off the fields with their shouts, while the brave Russians blocked it off with their dark red shields.

Yar Tur Vsevolod! You fight in the front ranks, shower arrows upon the warriors, thunder down on helmets with steel swords. Wherever, Tur, you gallop, your golden helmet shining, there lie pagan Polovtsian heads. Avar helmets are splintered with your tempered sabers, Yar Tur Vsevolod! What do wounds matter, dear brothers, to one who has forgotten honors and life, and his father's golden throne in the city of Chernigov,[13] and the habits and customs of his dear wife, the beautiful daughter of Gleb!

There were the ages of Troyan; past are the years of Yaroslav; and there were the wars of Oleg, Oleg, son of Sviatoslav. That Oleg forged sedition with his sword and sowed arrows throughout the land. He mounts golden stirrups in the city Tmutorokan, and that clanging would be heard by ancient Yaroslav the Great; while Vladimir, son of Vsevolod, every morning stopped up his ears in Chernigov. And glory brought death to Boris, son of Viacheslav,[14] and spread on the Kanin a green shroud for him for the offense to Oleg, the brave young prince. From the same Kaiala Sviatopolk too carefully brought his own father between Hungarian pacers to St. Sophia in Kiev.[15] Then at the time of Oleg, son of Woe-Glory, sown and over-grown by feuds, the life of Dazhbog's[16] grandson wasted away, the ages of men grew short in the feuds of princes. The plowmen would call out rarely in the Russian land, but the ravens would croak often, dividing corpses among themselves; and the jackdaws would chatter in their own tongue, wanting to fly to the feeding.

So it was in those battles and in those campaigns, but such a battle has never before been heard of! From early morning till evening, from evening till dawn, tempered arrows fly, sabers thunder against helmets, steel lances rattle in the unknown field of the Polovtsian land. Under hooves the black earth was sown with bones and watered with blood: like grief they sprouted throughout the Russian land!

What sounds, what rings out from far away, early before dawn? Igor turns back his troops: he has pity for his dear brother Vsevolod! They fought one day, they fought another, on the third day, toward noon, Igor's banners fell. Here the brothers parted on the bank of the swift Kayala; here the bloody wine ran dry; here the brave Russians ended the feast. They satiated the guests with drink and themselves lay down for the Russian land. The grass droops with pity, and a tree in sorrow bends to the ground.

For already, brethren, a joyless time has come, already desert has covered the army. Resentment came over the forces of Dazhbog's grandson, like a maiden stepped into Troyan's land, splashed together swan wings on the blue sea by the Don, and, splashing them, disturbed the times of abundance. The princes' strife with pagans ended, for brother said to brother, "This is mine, and that is mine, too." And the princes began to say, "This is important," of small things and to forge sedition among themselves, while pagans from all sides came with victories to the Russian land.

O, far the falcon flew, slaying birds: to the sea! But Igor's brave troops cannot be resurrected! After him Karna cried, and Zhlia galloped over the Russian land, spreading fire to the people from her flaming horn.[17] The Russian women began to lament, saying: "No more shall we have our loved ones to think of in thinking, nor to contemplate in contemplation, nor to see with our eyes, nor shall we hold gold and silver with our hands." And Kiev, brothers, groaned from grief, and Chernigov from attacks. Anguish spilled through the Russian land, munificent woe flowed in the land of the Russians. And the princes forged sedition among themselves, while the pagans for their part victoriously invaded the Russian land and took tribute of a squirrel from every home.

So those two brave sons of Sviatoslav, Igor and Vsevolod, awoke the evil that had been lured to sleep by their father, Kiev's fierce great Sviatoslav, that had been subdued by his ferocity, by his strong troops and steel swords. He came to the Polovtsian land, trampled hills and ravines, muddied rivers and lakes, dried up streams and marshes. And like a whirlwind he snatched the pagan Kobiak[18] from the curved seashore, out from the mighty iron Polovtsian troops; and Kobiak fell in Kiev city in Sviatoslav's hall. Here Germans and Venetians, Greeks and Moravians sing the glory of Sviatoslav and reproach Prince Igor, for he sank riches to the bottom of the Kaiala, the Polovtsian river, pouring out Russian gold. Now Prince Igor exchanged his golden saddle for the saddle of a wanderer. Ramparts of the cities are downcast, and joy has been subdued.

And Sviatoslav saw a troubled dream in Kiev on the hills. "Early this night they dressed me," he said, "in a black shroud on a bed of yew; they ladled out for me dark blue wine, mixed with sorrow; from the empty quivers of pagan foreigners they poured large pearls on me and caressed me. Already the beams of my gold-roofed palace are without girding. All night, since evening, gray ravens were croaking near Plesensk on the meadow, they were in the forest of Kisan [Kiian], and they rushed toward the dark blue sea."

And the boyars said to the prince, "Already, prince, grief has seized the mind. Two falcons have flown from their father's golden throne to gain the city of Tmutorokan, or at least to drink of the Don from a helmet. Already the falcons' wings have been clipped by the pagans' sabers, and they have been enmeshed in tangles of iron. For it was dark on the third day: Two suns grew dark, both crimson pillars extinguished and plunged into the sea, and with them two young moons, Oleg and Sviatoslav, were enveloped in darkness. On the river Kaiala darkness has covered the light; Polovtsians have scattered over the Russian land like a brood of panthers and woke great rejoicing among the Hins. Already shame has come down upon glory; already violence has struck freedom; already Div has thrown himself to earth. And already fair Gothic maidens have begun to sing on the shores of the dark blue sea, jingling Russian gold, singing about the time of Bus; cherishing revenge for Sharukan.[19] And already we, a company of warriors, thirst for joy."

Then great Sviatoslav let fall a golden word, mixed with tears, and said, "O my brethren, Igor and Vsevolod! You began early bringing grief to the Polovtsian land with your swords and seeking glory for yourselves. But you have conquered without honor, for without honor you shed pagan blood. Your brave hearts are forged of hard steel and tempered in boldness. What have you done to my silver-gray hairs!

"I no longer see the power of my brother Yaroslav, mighty and wealthy and rich in warriors, with Chernigov boyars, with Moguts, and with Tatrans, and with Shelbirs, and with Topchaks, and with Revugs, and with Olbers.[20] For they, after all, without shields, with boot knives, with war cries, vanquish armies, ringing in their forefathers' glory. But you said, 'Let us be valiant alone. Let us alone uphold the glory of the past, and alone share the glory of the future.' Is it strange, brothers, for an old man to grow young? If a falcon is molting, he strikes birds on high, he does not allow his nest to be harmed. But here is the evil; the princes are no help to me: the times have taken a bad turn. Now at Rimov they scream under Polovtsian sabers, as does Vladimir covered with wounds. Woe and sorrow for the son of Gleb!"[21]

Great Prince Vsevolod![22] Do you not think of flying from afar to protect your father's golden throne? You can, after all, scatter the Volga into drops with oars and with helmets scoop dry the Don. If you were here, a female slave could be bought for one *nogata* and a male slave for a *rezana*.[23] For you can shoot live bolts, Gleb's bold sons, over dry land.

You, bold Rurik, and David![24] Was it not your warriors who swam in blood with gilded helmets? Does not your courageous armed company roar, like bulls wounded by tempered sabers in an unknown field? Then step, my lords, into golden stirrups, in response to the affront of our time, for the wounds of Igor, brave son of Sviatoslav!

Osmomysl Yaroslav of Galicia![25] You sit high on your gold-forged throne, you support the Hungarian mountains with your iron troops, blocking the king's way, closing the gates of the Danube, hurling weights through the clouds, dispensing justice to the Danube. Your thunder flows over the lands, you open Kiev's gates, from your father's golden throne you shoot saltans beyond lands.[26] Shoot then, lord, at Konchak, the pagan Polovtsian, for the land of Russia, for the wounds of Igor, brave son of Sviatoslav!

And you, brave Roman, and Mstislav![27] Courageous thought brings your minds to a great deed. High you soar to a great deed of courage, like a falcon fluttering on the winds, intent through boldness to overpower a bird. For you have iron breastplates beneath Latin helmets. Because of them the earth trembled, and many nations—Hins, Lithuanians, Yatviagians, Deremelians, and Polovtsians—dropped their lances and bowed their heads beneath those swords of steel. But already, prince, sunlight has dimmed for Igor, and a tree has shed its foliage not to the good; the towns have been divided along the Ros and Sula.[28] And Igor's brave troops cannot be resurrected! The Don, prince, calls to you and summons the princes to victory. The descendants of Oleg, courageous princes, have been prompt to the battle . . .

Ingvar and Vsevolod, and all three sons of Mstislav, six-winged ones of no mean nest![29] Have you not by fortune of victory seized properties for yourselves? Where, then, are your golden helmets and Polish lances and shields? Bar the gate of the field with your sharp arrows, for the Russian land, for the wounds of Igor, brave son of Sviatoslav!

No longer indeed the Sula flows with silvery streams toward the city of Pereiaslavl,[30] and the Dvina flows like a swamp for the once dreaded men of Polotsk,[31] under the pagans' shout. Only Iziaslav, son of Vasilko,[32] rang his sharp sword against Lithuanian helmets, maintained the glory of his grandfather Vseslav,[33] and himself was cut down by Lithuanian swords, beneath the dark red shields, on blood-stained grass with his beloved. And said: "Prince, birds have overcome your armed company with their wings, and beasts have licked their blood." Neither brother, Briachislav nor the other—Vsevolod—was there. Thus, alone you dropped a soul of pearl out of your brave body through the golden necklace. Voices have grown melancholy, joy is muted, the trumpets of Gorodensk sound out.

Yaroslav and all the grandsons of Vseslav! Lower now your banners, sheathe your dented swords, for you have lost already the glory of your grandfathers. With your sedition you began to draw the pagans to the Russian land, the domains of Vseslav. For it was because of feuds that violence came from the Polovtsian land!

In the seventh age of Troyan, Vseslav cast lots for the maiden he loved. That one cunningly used steeds and galloped to the city of Kiev and with a staff touched the golden throne of Kiev. Like a wild beast he leapt away from them, out of Belgorod[34] at midnight, hanging on a blue cloud, snatched good fortune in three attempts, opened the gates of Novgorod, shattered Yaroslav's glory, leapt like a wolf to the Nemiga from Dudutki.[35]

On the Nemiga they are laying out sheaves of heads and threshing with flails of steel, laying down lives on the threshing floor, winnowing soul from body. The blood-soaked banks of the Nemiga were not sown with good things: they were sown with the bones of Russian sons.

Prince Vseslav gave justice to the people, gave cities to the princes, and himself at night roved like a wolf. From Kiev to Tmutorokan he would rove before cock-crow, as a wolf would cross the path of great Hors.[36] In Polotsk on his behalf in the early morning they rang the bells of St. Sophia for matins, and he heard the ringing in Kiev. Although he had a prophetic soul in a valiant body, yet he often suffered calamities. Prophetic Boyan the Wise long ago spoke a refrain for him: "Neither the cunning man, nor the agile one, nor the agile bird shall escape God's judgment."

Oh, the Russian land shall moan, recalling former times and the first princes! That Vladimir of yore could not be nailed to the Kievan hills; while now his banners have become Rurik's, and others, David's, but separate their standards fly. The lances are singing.

On the Danube, the voice of Yaroslavna is heard; like an unknown cuckoo, she cries early. "I will fly," she says, "like a cuckoo along the Danube, I will dip a silken sleeve in the river Kaiala, I will wipe clean for the prince his bleeding wounds on his mighty body."

Yaroslavna early laments in Putivl on the rampart chanting: "Oh wind, wind! Why, Lord, do you blow perversely? Why do you hurl Hinnish arrows on your light wings against my beloved's warriors? Was it not enough for you to flow beneath clouds, caressing ships on the blue sea? Why, Lord, have you strewn my happiness over the feather grass?"

Yaroslavna laments on the rampart of Putivl town, chanting: "O Dnieper Slovutich! You have broken through rocky mountains across the Polovtsian land. You have nurtured Sviatoslav's boats as far as Kobiak's camp. Nurture, Lord, my beloved, bring him to me, so that I may not send him tears on the sea, early in the morning."

Yaroslavna early laments in Putivl on the town wall, chanting: "Bright and thrice-bright Sun! For all you are warm and beautiful, but why, Lord, did you spread your burning rays upon the warriors of my beloved? In the arid field you weakened their bows with thirst, sealed off their quivers with grief."

The sea splashed at midnight, clouds move like whirlwinds. God points the way to Prince Igor out of the Polovtsian land to the Russian land to his father's golden throne. Dawn has faded in evening. Igor sleeps and does not sleep, Igor, thinking, measures the plains from the Great Don to the little Donets. At midnight Olvur[37] whistled for a steed from beyond the river—he bids the prince to heed: Prince Igor shall disappear! He called out, the earth rumbled, the grass rustled, the Polovtsian tents stirred. But Igor, the prince, sped like an ermine into the rushes, like a white duck on the water; he jumped on a swift steed, leapt from it like a barefoot wolf, and sped on the Donets water meadow, and flew like a falcon beneath clouds, slaying geese and swans for morning fare, and for dinner, and for supper. If Igor flew as a falcon, Olvur ran like a wolf, shaking off the freezing dew: they drove their steeds to exhaustion.

The Donets said: "Prince Igor! Is there not enough glory for you, and detestation for Konchak, and joy for the Russian land!" Igor said: "O Donets! Is there not enough glory for you nourishing the prince on waves, spreading him green grass on your silver banks, clothing him in warm mist beneath the shade of the green tree? You guarded him as a golden-eye duck on the water, as gulls on the stream, as black ducks in the air." Not so, it is said, is the river Stugna, endowed with an evil stream, having swallowed up alien brooks and streams, having widened at its delta and imprisoned a youth, Prince Rostislav,[38] on the bottom by a dark bank. Rostislav's mother weeps for the youth, Prince Rostislav. Flowers have withered in commiseration, and a tree in sorrow has bent to the ground.

These are not magpies chattering: it is Gzak and Konchak riding on Igor's trail. Then the ravens did not croak, the jackdaws fell silent, the magpies did not chatter, only the crawlers crawled. The woodpeckers by their knocking show the way to the river, the nightingales with their joyous songs announce the dawn.

Says Gzak to Konchak, "If the falcon flies toward its nest, we will shoot the falconet with our gilded arrows."

Says Konchak to Gzak, "If the falcon flies toward its nest, we will entangle the falconet with a fair maiden."

And said Gzak to Konchak, "If we entangle him with a fair maiden, we shall have neither the falconet nor the fair maiden, and the birds will strike at us in the Polovtsian field."

Boyan, of the age of Sviatoslav, songmaker of Yaroslav, of Oleg's ancient times, said: "O, Kogan, it is hard for a head to be without shoulders as it is grievous for the body to be without a head"—and so it is for the Russian land without Igor.

The sun shines in the sky, Prince Igor is in the Russian land. Maidens sing on the Danube, voices twine across the sea to Kiev. Igor rides along Borichev, to the Holy Virgin of Pirogoshch.[39] The lands are happy, the cities are joyful.

Having sung a song for the old princes, then we shall sing for the young. Glory to Igor, son of Sviatoslav, Bui Tur Vsevolod, Vladimir, son of Igor! Hail princes and the princes' armed company defending Christians against pagan troops! Glory to the princes and to the princes' armed company! Amen.

Translation by Nicholas Rzhevsky and Tatiana Shamkovich

Notes to the translation begin on page 553.

RESOURCES

Primary Text

Dmitriev, L.A., and D.S. Likhachev, eds. *Slovo o polku Igoreve.* Leningrad: Sovetskii pisatel', 1967, pp. 43–56.

Secondary Sources

Literary and Cultural Studies

Adrianova-Peretts, V.P., ed. *Slovo o polku Igoreve.* Moscow–Leningrad: Akademiia nauk SSSR, 1950.

Bulakhov, M.G. *"Slovo o polku Igoreve" v literature, iskusstve, nauke.* Minsk: Universitetskoe, 1989.

Dianin, Sergei. *Borodin.* Trans. Robert Lord. London: Oxford University Press, 1963.

La geste du Prince Igor'. Épopée russe du douzième siècle. Ed. Henri Grégoire, Roman Jakobson, and Mark Szeftel. Annuaire de l'Institut de philologie et l'histoire orientales, et slaves. Vol. 8. New York, 1948.

Likhachev, D.S. *"Slovo o polku Igoreve"—Istoriko-literaturnyi ocherk.* Leningrad: Akademiia nauk SSSR, 1955.

———. *"Slovo o polku Igoreve" i kul'tura ego vremeni.* Leningrad: Khudozhestvennaia literatura, 1985.

Nabokov, Vladimir, trans. *The Song of Igor's Campaign: An Epic of the Twelfth Century.* New York: Vintage, 1960.

Orlov, A.S. *Slovo o polku Igoreve.* Moscow–Leningrad: Akademiia nauk SSSR, 1946.

Rothstein, E. "When Worlds Collide, on the Operatic Stage." *The New York Times,* October 9, 1994, p. 31.

Rybakov, B.A. *"Slovo o polku Igoreve" i ego vremia.* Moscow: Nauka, 1985.

———. *Russkie letopisi i avtor "Slova o polku Igoreve."* Moscow: Nauka, 1972.

Slovar'-spravochnik "Slovo o polku Igoreve." Compiled by V.L. Vinogradova. Leningrad: Nauka, 1965–73.

Taruskin, R. "Sex and Race, Russian Style." *The New York Times*, September 4, 1994, p. 1.

Worth, Dean. "*Slóvo o polkú Ígoreve* (The Tale of Igor's Campaign)." In *Handbook of Russian Literature*, ed. Victor Terras. New Haven: Yale University Press, 1985, pp. 425–27.

Literature

Rilke, Rainer Maria. *Collected Works*. Trans. and ed. Stephen Mitchell. New York: Random House, 1982.

Art

Favorsky, Vladimir. *The Lay of Igor's Campaign*. Trans. Irina Petrova. Moscow: Progress, 1981.

Koromyslov, Boris. *Mstera*. Moscow: Planeta, 1968.

See also, Bulakhov, *"Slovo o polku Igorev" v literature, iskusstve, nauke.*

Dance

Beaumont, Cyril. *Complete Book of Ballets*. London: Putman, 1956, pp. 684–88.

Borodin, A.P. *Polovetsian Dances from the Opera Prince Igor*. New York: Edwin F. Kalmus, 1933. Score.

Classic Kirov Performances (for a 1983 version of Fokine's Polovetsian dances). Produced by Castle Communications and Kultur, 1992. Videocassette.

Music

Borodin, A.P. *Prince Igor*. Opera in a prologue and four acts. Text by the composer after a play by Vladimir Stasov; completed by Rimsky-Korsakov and Glazunov. Cast: Ivan Petrov, Tatiana Tugarinova, Vladimir Atlantov, Artur Eizen, Elena Obraztsova, Aleksandr Vedernikov. Orchestra and Chorus of the Bolshoi Theater. Conductor, Mark Ermler. Melodiia/Angel, 1977.

Tishchenko, B. *Yaroslavna*. Ballet in Three Acts. Choreographed meditations. Leningrad, Maly Ballet Theater, n.d., 2 records.

Film

Aleksandr Nevskyii. Director, Sergei Eisenstein. Mosfilm. 1938. Distributed by Hollywood Home Theater, 1980.

Kniaz' Igor' (Prince Igor). Director, Roman Tikhomirov. Music, A.P. Borodin. Kirov Opera and Ballet. Lenfilm. 1969.

~Anonymous~

Boris and Gleb

The Narrative and Passion and Encomium of the Holy Martyrs Boris and Gleb[1]

Bless Us Lord, Our Father

The generation of the righteous shall be blessed, said the prophet, and their seed shall be blessed.[2] Thus, these things came to pass before the time when the autocrat of the entire land of Rus' was Volodimir, son of Svjatoslav and grandson of Igor, he who enlightened this entire land of Rus' with holy Baptism.[3] Of his other virtues we shall speak elsewhere, there is not time now, but of such things we shall speak in due course.

Now this Volodimir had twelve sons, not by one wife, but by their several mothers.[4] Among these sons Vyšeslav was the eldest, and after him came Izjaslav. The third was Svjatopolk, who conceived this evil murder. His mother, a Greek, was formerly a nun, and Jaropolk, Volodimir's brother, took her, and because of the beauty of her face he unfrocked her and begot of her this accursed Svjatopolk. But Volodimir, who was still a pagan, killed Jaropolk and took his wife who was pregnant; and of her was born this accursed Svjatopolk. And he was of two fathers who were brothers, and for this reason Volodimir loved him not for he was not of him. And by Rogneda he had four sons: Izjaslav, Mstislav, Jaroslav, and Vsevolod; and by another he had Svjatoslav and Mstislav; and by a Bulgarian woman, Boris and Gleb. And he placed them all in different lands as rulers: . . . the accursed Svjatopolk as ruler in Pinsk, and Jaroslav in Novgorod, Boris in Rostov, and Gleb in Murom. But I will cease speaking of this at length, lest we lose ourselves through prolixity in forgetfulness. But let us speak about what I began.

Now after many days had passed and Volodimir's days were drawing to a close—for twenty-eight years had passed since the holy Baptism—he fell gravely ill. At that same time Boris was coming from Rostov. The Pechenegs[5] from that region were waging war against Rus'. And Volodimir was in great sorrow because he could not march against them, and he sorrowed much. And summoning the blessed Boris—who was named Roman in holy Baptism and was quick in obedience—and turning over many troops to him, he sent him against the godless Pechenegs. And rising with joy he went, saying, "I am prepared to do before your eyes as much as the will of your heart commands." For of such did the author of the Proverbs say: "I was my father's son, obedient and beloved in the sight of my mother."[6]

But after setting out and not finding his adversaries, he turned back. And a messenger came to him, informing him of his father's death: how his father Vasilij—for such was the name give him in holy Baptism—had passed away,[7] and how Svjatopolk had concealed the death of his father, and at night in Berestovo,[8] after taking up the floor and wrapping him in a rug, they lowered him to the ground with ropes, took him by sledge,[9] and placed him in the Church of the Holy Mother of God.

And when the saintly Boris heard this he grew weak in body and his entire face was covered with tears. And being choked with tears, he could not speak, but in his heart he began to speak thusly: "Woe unto me, light of my eyes, radiance and dawn of my face, bridle of my youth, admonition of my foolishness! Woe unto me, my father and lord! To whom shall I turn, to whom shall I look, where shall I sate myself with the good instruction and admonitions of your understanding? Woe unto me, woe unto me! How could you vanish, my light, while I was not there? If only I myself had prepared your venerable body for burial with my own hands and committed it to the grave. But I neither carried the manly beauty of your body, nor was I worthy of kissing your resplendent gray hair. But, O blessed one, remember me in your peace! My heart burns, my soul confuses my mind, and I know not to whom to turn and to whom to extend this bitter sorrow. To the brother whom I would have in place of a father? But he, methinks, has learned worldly vanities and contemplates my murder. If he sheds my blood and attempts to slay me, then a martyr shall I be unto my Lord. For I shall not resist, because it is written: 'God resisteth the proud, but giveth grace unto the humble.'[10] And the Apostle says: 'He who says, I love God, and hateth his brother, is a liar.'[11] And again: 'There is no fear in love; perfect love casteth out fear.'[12] Therefore what shall I say or what shall I do? Lo, shall I go to my brother and say, 'Be a father to me. You are my brother and elder. What is your command, my lord?' "

And musing thus in his mind, he set off to his brother, and he said in his heart: "Were I at least to see the face of my younger brother Gleb, as Joseph did Benjamin."[13] And considering all this in his heart, he said:[14] "Thy will be done, my Lord." And in his mind he thought: "If I go to my father's house, many tongues there will incline my heart toward banishment of my brother, just as my father acted before holy Baptism for the sake of glory and princely power in this world, all of which passes away being less than a cobweb. So whither must I go upon departure from this place? And how shall I return then? What will an answer be for me?

"Where shall I conceal the multitude of my sins? For what did my father's brothers or my father heretofore acquire? Where are their lives and their worldly glory, the purple robes and silks, the silver and gold, the wines and meads, the fine food and swift steeds, the great and beautiful homes, the many possessions, the tribute and countless honors, and the pride in their boyars? All this already is for them as though it had never been. Everything has vanished with them,[15] and there is no help from any one of them or from their possessions, from a multitude of slaves or from the glory of this world. For Solomon, having passed through all things, having seen all things, having acquired and accumulated all things, did say after casting his eyes about: 'Vanity of vanities; all is vanity!'[16] Help comes only from good deeds, from true belief, and from unfeigned love."[17]

Continuing on his way, he considered the beauty and goodliness of his body and was completely choked with tears. And wanting to restrain himself, he could not. And all who saw him thus wept for his virtuous body and the venerable understanding of his age. And each in his soul groaned with heartfelt grief, and all were troubled in their sorrow. For who would not bemoan that grievous death upon drawing it before the eyes of his heart! For his countenance and gaze were downcast, and his holy heart was broken. For this blessed one was just and compassionate, serene, gentle, humble, merciful to all, and solicitous of all. And the divinely blessed Boris meditated in his heart and said: "I know my brother is incited by men of evil intent to slay me, and he will destroy me. If he sheds my blood, then a martyr shall I be unto my Lord, and the Lord will receive my spirit." Then, forgetting his deathly sorrow, he comforted his heart with the divine words: "Whosoever shall lose his soul for My sake and for the sake of My words, shall find it and keep it in life eternal."[18] And he went on with a joyful heart, saying: "O most merciful Lord, despise not me, who trusts in Thee, but save my soul."

Now after his father's death, Svjatopolk had settled in Kiev. Upon summoning the people of Kiev and giving them many gifts, he dismissed them. Then he sent to Boris, saying: "Brother, I wish there to be love between us and shall add to your share of father's possessions."[19] But he spoke deceitfully and not the truth. He came secretly at night to Vyšegorod,[20] summoned Put'ša and the men of Vyšegorod, and said to them: "Tell me in truth, are you loyal to me?" And Put'ša said: "We all are ready to lay down our lives for you."

But the Devil, that hater of man's goodness from the beginning of time, upon seeing the saintly Boris had placed all his hope in the Lord, began to be even more active. And as once before he found Cain ablaze with fratricide, so now he found in truth a second Cain in Svjatopolk and snared his thought, that he should kill all his father's heirs and seize all power for himself alone. Then the thrice-accursed Svjatopolk summoned to himself the counselors of all evil and the chiefs of all untruth, and upon opening his lips most foul he emitted an evil voice, saying to Put'ša's people: "Since you promise to lay down your lives for me, go in secret, my friends, and where you find my brother Boris, watch for an opportunity and slay him." And they promised to do so. For of such the prophet said: "They make haste to shed blood unjustly: for they pledge blood and gather evil unto themselves. Their ways are those of gathering iniquity; and they embrace their souls with impurity."[21]

Now, upon returning, the blessed Boris pitched his tents on the L'to.[22] And his retinue said to him: "Go, settle in Kiev on your father's throne, for all the troops are in your hands." But he answered them: "It is not for me to raise my hand against my own brother, and especially against an elder one whom I would have as a father." And when they heard this, the troops departed from him, and he remained with only his retainers.

On the Sabbath day he was in distress and grief, and his heart was oppressed. And he entered his tent and wept with a broken heart but a joyful soul, sorrowfully lifting his voice: "Despise not my tears, O Lord. For as I have my hope in Thee, so shall I, together with Thy servants, accept my portion and lot with all Thy holy ones, for Thou art a merciful God, and unto Thee shall we render praise forever. Amen." He thought of the martyrdom and passion of the holy martyr Nikita and of Saint Vjačeslav, whose murders were similar to this, and how the murderer of Saint Barbara was her own father.[23] And he thought of the word of the wise Solomon: "The righteous live for evermore; their reward also is with the Lord, the care of them is with the Most High." And only with this word was he comforted, and he rejoiced.

Then evening came. And he commanded that Vespers be chanted, and he himself entered his tent and began to say the evening prayer with bitter tears, frequent sighs, and much groaning. Afterward he lay down to sleep. And his sleep was troubled by many thoughts and a great, heavy, and terrible grief: How to give himself up to the martyr's passion; how to suffer and end the course[24] and keep the faith so as to receive the predestined crown from the hands of the Almighty.

Upon awakening early, he saw it was the time of morning: it was holy Sunday. He said to his presbyter: "Arise, begin Matins." And having put shoes on his feet and having washed his face, he himself began to pray to the Lord God.

But those sent by Svjatopolk had arrived on the L'to during the night, and drawing near they heard the voice of the blessed martyr chanting the morning psalter. And since he had knowledge of his murder, he began to chant: "Lord how are they increased that trouble me! Many are they that rise up against me," and other psalms in their entirety. And he began to chant the psalter: "Many dogs have compassed me and fat bulls have beset me round";[25] and also, "O Lord my God, in Thee do I put my trust: save me." After this he chanted the canon in the same way. And when he finished Matins, he began to pray, gazing upon the icon of the Lord and saying: "O Lord Jesus Christ, Who in this image didst appear upon earth, having by Thy will chosen to be nailed to the cross, accepting Thy passion for the sake of our sins, make me worthy of accepting my passion."

And when he heard evil whispers near the tent, he was atremble and began to shed tears from his eyes, and he said: "Glory be to Thee, O Lord, for all things; for Thou hast made me worthy of accepting this bitter death, prompted by envy, and to suffer all things for the love of Thy word. I desired not[26] to seek for myself alone and have chosen nought for myself, according to the Apostle: 'Charity beareth all things, believeth all things, and seeketh not her own,'[27] and also: 'There is no fear in love; but perfect love casteth out fear.' Therefore, O Lord, my soul is ever in Thy hands, for the law I have not forgotten. As it pleaseth the Lord, so be it." And when the priest and the retainer who served him looked and saw their lord downcast and overwhelmed by grief, they began to mourn greatly and said: "O dear and precious lord of ours, how filled with goodness you are that for the sake of the love of Christ you desired not to resist, though many were the troops you held in your hands." And having said this, they were saddened.

And at that moment he saw those running toward the tent, the flash of weapons and the unsheathing of swords. And the venerable body of the most merciful Boris, Christ's holy and blessed martyr, was pierced without mercy. Those who stabbed him with lances were the accursed Put'ša, Tal'ts, Elovič, and Ljaš'ko. Upon seeing this, his retainer threw himself upon the body of the blessed one, saying: "I shall not leave you, my precious lord; where the beauty of your body withers, there too will it be granted me to end my life." He was a Hungarian by birth named George, and upon him was placed a golden necklace, and he was loved by Boris beyond measure. And they ran him through on that spot.

And as he was wounded, Boris ran out of the tent in haste. And those standing around him began to say: "Why do you stand gazing? Let us end what was begun and do as we were commanded."

Hearing this, the blessed one began to pray and ingratiate himself to them, saying: "My dear and beloved brethren, grant me a little time that I may at least pray to my God." And upon glancing tearfully up at the heavens and sighing bitterly, he began to pray with these words: "God of many mercies, my merciful and most merciful Lord! Glory be to Thee, that Thou hast made me worthy to flee from the deception of this deceitful life. Glory be to Thee, most compassionate Giver of life, that Thou hast made me worthy of the suffering of the holy martyrs. Glory be to Thee, O Lord. Lover of man, that Thou hast made me worthy to fulfill the desire of my heart. Glory be to Thee, my Christ, to Thy great Compassion, that Thou hast directed my worldly feet onto the right way, running to Thee without fault. Look down from Thy holy heights and see the sickness of my heart, which I caught from my kinsman, that for Thy sake I am killed this day.[28] I am counted as a sheep for the slaughter. For Thou knowest, my Lord, that I shall neither resist nor speak contrarily. Though I had all my father's troops in my hands and all whom my father loved, yet I plotted nought against my brother. But he has found it possible to rise up against me so greatly. If an enemy reproached me, I could have borne it; if he that hated me did magnify himself against me, I would have hid myself.[29] But, Thou, O Lord, behold and judge between me and between my brother;[30] and, Lord, lay not this sin to their charge, but receive my spirit in peace.[31] Amen."

Then, looking at them with tender eyes and a downcast face, and bathed in tears, he said: "Brethren, end the service you have begun; and peace be unto my brother, and unto you, my brethren."

And all those hearing his words were unable to utter a single word because of tears and fear, and bitter grief, and much weeping, but with bitter sighs they wept, and each groaned in his soul and said mournfully: "Woe unto us, our dear and precious prince, guide for the blind, clother of the naked, staff for the aged, teacher for the untaught! Who will do all these things now? For surely he did not desire the glory of this world; he did not desire revels with venerable nobles; he did not desire the grandeur found in this life! Who does not marvel at his great humility; who is not humbled, seeing and hearing of this humility!" And at that moment he passed away and delivered his soul into the hands of the living God, in the month of July, on the twenty-fourth day, the ninth day before the calends of August.[32]

And they also slew many retainers. But since they could not remove the necklace from George, they cut off his head and tossed him aside, and for that reason his body could not be recognized later. Upon wrapping the blessed Boris in a tent flap and laying him in a wagon, they drove off. And when they were in a pine forest he began to raise his holy head. Learning of this Svjatopolk sent two Varangians, and they pierced him through the heart with a sword. Thus he expired and received a crown everlasting. After having brought him to Vyšegorod, they laid his body in the earth and buried it near the Church of Saint Vasilij.

And the accursed Svjatopolk stopped not with this murder but rabidly began to crave even greater ones. And as it was evident his heart's desire had been gained, he immediately forgot his evil murder and great offense and did not, therefore, give himself over in the least to repentance. But it was at this moment that Satan entered his heart[33] and began to spur him to commit greater, crueler, and more numerous murders. For he said in his accursed soul, "What shall I do? If I abandon the matter of this murder of mine now, I must expect two things. If my brothers find me out, then they, anticipating me, will deal with me even more bitterly. And if not this, they will drive me out, and I will be a stranger to my father's throne, and the sorrows of my land will devour me, and the scorn of the scorners will fall upon me; another will receive my principality, and none will dwell in my courts, for I have persecuted the one the Lord did love and added a wound to grief. Thus I shall add iniquity to iniquity. Let not the sin of my mother be expiated, and let me not be recorded with the righteous, but let my name be expunged from the book of the living."[34]

And so it came to pass, as we shall relate later; there is no time for this now. But let us return to the foregoing.

Having put this in his mind, that evil counselor the Devil summoned the blessed Gleb, saying: "Come quickly, your father summons you and is very sick." He quickly mounted his horse and set off with a small retinue. And when he came to the Volga, the horse beneath him stumbled over a rut in the field and slightly injured its leg.[35] And he came to Smolensk and went on from Smolensk, and within viewing distance therefrom he boarded a small vessel on the Smjadin'.[36]

At that time news of his father's death reached Jaroslav from Predslava.[37] And Jaroslav sent a message to Gleb, saying: "Do not go, brother, your father has died. And your brother has been murdered by Svjatopolk."

Upon hearing this, the blessed one cried out with bitter weeping and heartfelt grief, saying: "O woe unto me, my Lord! With twofold weeping I weep and moan, with twofold grief I grieve and groan. Woe unto me, woe unto me! I weep greatly for my father, but I weep even more and have despaired for you, my brother and lord Boris. How is it that you have been run through! How is it that you have been delivered to death without mercy! How is it that you have received your ruin not from an enemy but from your own brother! Woe unto me! Better it would have been for me to die with you than to live on in this life, alone and orphaned without you. I thought soon to see your angelic face, and behold, such distress has overtaken me.

In hopeless grief I would have died with you, my lord! And now what shall I do, wretched and separated from your goodness and from the great wisdom of my father? O, my dear brother and lord! If you received courage from the Lord, pray for me in my grievous hopelessness, that I may be made worthy to receive the same passion and to abide with you rather than in this deceitful world."

And so, as he was groaning and weeping and wetting the earth with his tears, and calling upon God with frequent sighs, those sent by Svjatopolk suddenly arrived—those evil servants of his, merciless bloodsuckers, the fiercest of fratricides, having the souls of savage beasts. The saintly one had set off in a small vessel, and they met him at the mouth of the Smjadin'. And when he saw them, he rejoiced in his soul; but they, upon seeing him, were covered with gloom and rowed toward him. And he expected to receive greetings from them. But when they drew alongside, the evil ones began to leap into his boat with bared swords, which glittered like water in their hands. And immediately the oars fell from all hands, and all were numb with fear.

When the blessed one saw this, he understood they wished to kill him. He gazed at them with tender eyes, his face bathed in tears, broken in heart, humbled in mind, frequently sighing, choked with tears, and weakened in body, and he lifted his voice in sorrow: "Let me be, my dear and precious brethren, let me be, for I have done you no evil! Leave me alone, brethren and lords, leave me alone! What wrong have I done my brother and you, my brethren and lords? If there be some wrong, take me to your prince, to my brother and lord. Have mercy on my youth, have mercy, my lords! You are my lords, I your slave. Reap me not from a life unripened; reap not the ear of grain still unripe but bearing the milk of innocence! Cut not the shoot still less than fully grown but bearing fruit. I implore you and humble myself before you, fear that spoken from the mouths of the Apostles: 'Be not children in understanding: howbeit in malice be ye children, but in understanding be men!' I, brethren, both in malice and maturity am still a child. This is not murder but butchery!³⁸ What evil have I done? Witness to it, and I shall not complain if you wish to sate yourselves with my blood. I am in your hands already brethren, and my brother's, your prince."

But not a single word of this shamed them in any way, and like savage beasts they seized him. Seeing they did not heed his words, he began to speak thus: "Save yourself my dear father and lord Vasilij! Save yourself, my mother and lady! Save yourself also brother Boris, elder of my youth! Save yourself also, brother and helpmate Jaroslav! Save yourself also, brother and enemy Svjatopolk! Save yourselves also, brethren and retinue! All save yourselves! I shall no longer see you in this life, for I am parted from you by force."

And weeping he said: "Vasilij, Vasilij, my father and lord! Incline your ear and hear my voice, look and see what is happening to your child, how I am being slaughtered without guilt. Woe unto me, woe unto me! Hearken, O heaven, and attend, O earth! And you, brother Boris, hear my voice! My father Vasilij have I summoned, and he obeyed me not. Do you not wish to obey me as well? See the sorrow of my heart and the wound of my soul! See my tears flowing like a river! And no one heeds me. But you remember me and pray for me to our Lord as one possessing courage and standing by his throne."

And bending his knees, he began to pray thus: "Most compassionate and most merciful Lord! Turn not from my tears but have pity on my grievous hopelessness, see the crushing of my heart. For lo, I am being slaughtered and know not why, nor understand for which wrong. Thou knowest, O Lord, my Lord! I know Thee, Who to Thy Apostles said: 'For My name, for My sake, they shall lay their hands on you, and ye shall be betrayed by kinfolk and by friends; and brothers shall betray brother unto death and they shall cause you to be put to death for My name's sake.'[39] And also: 'In your patience you possess ye your souls.' See, O Lord, and judge! For behold, my soul is prepared before Thee, Lord, and we lift up our praise unto Thee, the Father, the Son, and the Holy Spirit, now and always and forever more. Amen."

Then, looking at them, he said with a dejected voice and choking throat: "You have already done this in your thoughts; now that you have come, do what you were sent for."[40] Then the accursed Gorjaser ordered them to slay him quickly. Gleb's cook, Torčin by name, drew a knife and, seizing the blessed one, slaughtered him like a meek and innocent lamb. It was in the month of September, on the fifth day, on Monday.[41] And a pure and fragrant sacrifice was brought to the Lord; and he entered into the dwelling places of heaven, and came to the Lord, and saw the brother whom he desired, and both received the heavenly crown they had desired, and they rejoiced in the great ineffable joy they had attained.

But they, the accursed murderers, returned to the one who had sent them, just as David said: "Sinners shall be turned to hell, and all those that forget God."[42] And again: "The sinners have drawn out the sword and have bent their bow, to slay the upright of heart. And their sword shall enter into their own heart, and their bows shall be broken, for the sinners shall perish."[43] And they told Svjatopolk, "We have done what you have commanded." And hearing this he exalted in his heart. And that which was said by the psalmist David came to pass: "Why boastest thou in mischief, O mighty man? Thy tongue deviseth lies and iniquity all the day long. Thou lovest evil more than good, lying rather than to speak righteousness. Thou lovest all devouring words, and a deceitful tongue. For this reason God shall destroy thee forever. He shall take thee away and pluck thee out of thy dwelling place, and root thee out of the land of the living."[44]

After Gleb had been slain, he was cast in a deserted place between two hollowed-out tree trunks.[45] But the Lord does not forsake His servants, as David said: "The Lord keepeth all their bones: and not one of them is broken."[46] And though the saintly one lay there a long time, he remained entirely unharmed, for He left him not in oblivion and neglect but gave signs: now a pillar of fire was seen, now burning candles. Moreover, merchants passing by on the way would hear the singing of angels; and others, hunters and shepherds, also saw and heard these things. It did not occur to anyone to search for the body of the saintly one until Jaroslav, unable to bear this evil murder, moved against that fratricide, the accursed Svjatopolk, and fought many battles with him and was always victorious, with the aid of God and the help of the saintly ones. And as many battles as he waged, the accursed one always returned shamed and defeated.

Finally this thrice-accursed one attacked with a horde of Pechenegs. And having gathered troops, Jaroslav went forth against him, to the L'to River, and he halted at the place where the saintly Boris was slain. Lifting up his hands to heaven, he said: "Behold, the blood of my brother crieth out unto Thee O Lord, just as the blood of Abel did in times past. Avenge him too; afflict him with sorrow and fear, just as Thou didst the fratricide Cain. Yea, I beseech Thee, O Lord, may they receive accordingly. And though ye are departed in body, yet in grace ye live and stand before the Lord: Help me with your prayer."[47]

After this was spoken, they advanced against one another, and the field of the L'to was covered with a multitude of troops. As the sun rose, they met in battle, and the fighting was extremely fierce. They clashed three times and fought throughout the entire day.[48] Toward evening Jaroslav triumphed, and the accursed Svjatopolk fled. A demon fell upon him, and his bones became weak so that he was unable even to sit on his horse; so they carried him on a litter. They fled to Brest with him, but he said: "Flee! O behold, they are pursuing us!" They sent out troops to meet them, but there was no one pursuing or chasing after him.[49] And lying in a faint, he would start and say, "Let us flee, they are still pursuing, O me!" And he could not endure being in one place and fled through the land of the Ljakhs, pursued by the wrath of God. He fled into the wilderness between the lands of the Czechs and Ljakhs and there forfeited his life in an evil manner. And he received his reward from the Lord. And just as the fatal wound was visited upon him, so after death eternal torment. Thus was he deprived of both lives. Here he lost not only his princedom but also his life, and there he was not only bereft of the kingdom of heaven and life with the angels but was given over to torment and fire. And his grave exists even to this day, and from it issues an evil stench for the edification of men.[50]

Whoever acquits himself so after hearing of such things will receive the same, and even more than this. Just as Cain, who knew not the retribution he would receive, received one wound, but Lamech, because he knew of the punishment visited upon Cain, was punished seventyfold.[51] Such are the retributions for evildoers. For just as the Emperor Julian,[52] who spilled much blood from the holy martyrs, received a bitter and inhuman death, stabbed in the heart with a lance, not knowing by whom he was run through, so too did this one, fleeing not knowing from whom, receive a vile death. And from then on discord ceased in the land of Rus', and Jaroslav assumed all power over it. . . .

Translation by Marvin Kantor

Notes to the translation begin on page 554

RESOURCES

Primary Text

Kniazevskaia, O.A., V.G. Dem'ianov, and M.V. Liapon, eds. *Uspenskii sbornik. XII–XIII vekov.* Moscow: Nauka, 1971.
"Skazanie o Borise i Glebe." In *Khrestomatiia po drevnei russkoi litereature,* ed. N.K. Gudzii. Moscow: Prosveshchenie, 1973, pp. 40–51.

Secondary Sources

Literary and Cultural Studies

Fedotov, G.P. *The Russian Religious Mind.* New York: Harper Torchbooks, 1960.
Kantor, Marvin, trans. and ed. *Medieval Slavic Lives of Saints and Princes.* Ann Arbor: Michigan Slavic Publications, 1983. For the full text and commentary of the life, pp. 163–254.
Lenhoff, Gail. *The Martyred Princes Boris and Gleb: A Socio-cultural Study of the Cult and the Texts.* Columbus, OH: Slavica, 1989.
Likhachev, D.S., ed. *Vzaimodeistvie literatury i izobrazitel'nogo iskusstva v drevnei Rusi.* Moscow–Leningrad: Nauka, 1966.
Ziolkowski, Margaret. *Hagiography and Modern Russian Literature.* Princeton: Princeton University Press, 1988.

Art and Architecture

Brumfield, W.C. *A History of Russian Architecture.* New York: Cambridge University Press, 1993, pp. 137–38, plate 46, for Church of Sts. Boris and Gleb, in Ziuzino, Moscow (1688–1704).
Dembo, H.G., ed. *Gosudarstvennyi Russkii Muzei. Al'bom reproduktsii.* Moscow–Leningrad: Izobrazitel'noe iskusstvo, 1959, plate 1.

Russian Icons and Objects of Ecclesiastical and Decorative Arts from the Collection of George R. Hann. Introduction by A. Avinoff. Pittsburgh: Carnegie Institute Press, 1944, plate 95.

Talbot Rice, Tamara. *A Concise History of Russian Art*. New York: Praeger, 1967, p. 57. For a seventeenth-century icon of the Stroganov school.

Volodarsky, V., comp. *The Tretyakov Gallery Painting*. Leningrad: Aurora, 1981, plate 4. For a fourteenth-century icon of Boris and Gleb.

Literature

Fedotov, G.P., ed. *A Treasury of Russian Spirituality*. New York: Harper & Row, 1965.

Music

The Russian Orthodox Requiem and Hymns to the Virgin. The Russian Orthodox Cathedral Choir of Paris. Conductor, P.V. Spassky. New York: Monitor, n.d.

Tysiacheletie Kreshcheniia Rusi (988–1988). Pesnopeniia Russkoi Pravoslavnoi Tserkvi, Velikii Post i Sviataia Paskha. Conductor, Nikolai Matveev. Moscow: Moscow Patriarchate, 1987.

3

～Anonymous～

The Life of Alexis, Holy Man of God

There was a man in Rome, a devout man named Ephimianos whose wife's name was Aglais, who lived in the reign of the renowned Emperors of Rome, Honorius and Arcadius.[1] He was mighty, noble, and very rich. Ephimianos had three hundred young male servants, all of whom wore golden belts and precious garments. But he had no child, for his wife was barren. They lived piously and obeyed God's commandments. Every day he fasted until the ninth hour,[2] and he prepared three tables in his house: one for orphans and widows, another for wayfarers and travelers and the sick, and the third for his household. Thus, at the ninth hour, he tasted bread with strangers, and with the common people and the poor he ate his bread. When he would walk to the Emperors' palace, giving alms to the poor before him, he would say to himself, "I am not worthy to walk on God's earth." At the same time, his companion Aglais, a faithful woman, fearing God greatly, all the day would fulfill God's commandments, praying and saying, "Remember me, Lord, your unworthy servant, and grant me fruit from my husband. Let there be to me a son, and let there be to me a guide of my old age for the salvation of my soul." God remembered her for her good deeds, and granted at that time that she should bear a son, and her husband rejoiced in God. They had him baptized and gave him the name Alexis.[3]

When he was a lad six years of age, he was given his first schooling. He learned all his reading and writing and church order so that in a short time he was learned and very wise.[4] When he had reached the age when it was lawful for him to marry, Ephimianos said to his wife, "Let us arrange a marriage for our son." His wife rejoiced at her husband's words, and she ran and fell at his feet, saying, "May God fulfill the words that you spoke. Let us arrange a marriage for our beloved child, and my soul and my spirit shall both see and rejoice, and I shall give even more aid to the wretched and the poor at the command of my God." And they betrothed him to a

33

bride, a maiden of royal birth, and prepared him a wedding. They decorated and beautified the hall of the Church of St. Boniface with icons of the holy saints and led him and the bride into the hall and made merry even until night. Ephimianos said to his son, "Go in, child, and see your bride and come to know your friend." He entered his chamber and found her seated on a golden throne. Taking off his golden ring and wrapping it in crimson silk, he gave it[5] to his betrothed and said, "Take this and keep it and may God be between you and me until God shall look with favor upon our deeds."

He revealed to her certain secrets, said a few words, and left. Having left his chamber, he entered into his storeroom, took some of his wealth, and secretly left Rome by night. He entered into a ship and sailed to Syria, to the city of Laodicia. Getting off the ship, he prayed to God and said, "O God Who made heaven and earth, Who rescued me and my mother's womb, save me now from this vain life, and deem me worthy to stand on Your right hand with all the righteous who have pleased You, for You are a merciful and saving God and unto You we send up glory."

Rising up, at that moment he met some hostlers, and he went with them into the country of Syria, to the city of Edessa where lies the image of our Lord Jesus Christ which our Lord gave to King Avgar during His lifetime. Entering into the city, he sold all that he had and gave it to the poor. He dressed himself in a torn cloak and sat like a poor beggar in the vestibule of the Church of Our Lady the Mother of God, fasting diligently from week to week. Receiving the Holy Mysteries, eating a little bread and drinking a little water, the whole of that time of his life he never slept through a single night, and whatever was given to him he gave to the poor in alms. His father, having searched for him with tears in the city of Rome and not having found him, sent three hundred servants to search for him. When they arrived in the city of Edessa in Mesopotamia, they, his servants, gave him alms without having recognized him. Seeing them and recognizing them, the Man of God praised God and said, "I praise You, O Lord, for You have deemed me worthy to receive alms from my own servants in praise of Your name." The servants returned to their lord and announced that they had not found him.

His mother, from that hour of his wedding when they searched for him and did not find him, entered into her chamber, shuttered up the windows, put on sackcloth, and strewed ashes on her head. She prayed to the Lord, saying, "I will not leave this place until I learn what has become of my son, my only child." His father from that time, on account of his son, no longer came unto his wife but said to her, "Let us pray to God that He spare us this child who was given to us."

After he had served seventeen years on the porch of the Church of the Holy Mother of God, it pleased God that the Holy Mother of God should appear to the sacristan in a dream, saying, "Bring the Man of God into my church, for he is worthy of the kingdom of heaven, for his prayer is like the fragrance of fine myrrh. Like a crown on the head of the Emperor, thus does the Holy Spirit rest upon him. As the sun shines upon the world, thus does his life shine upon all the world, before God and all the angels of God." The sacristan went out and searched for such a man, but did not find him. He prayed to the Holy Mother of God that she reveal to him the Man of God. She appeared again a second time to the sacristan, saying, "The beggar who sits before the doors of the church is the Man of God." The sacristan went out and found him. Taking him by the hand, he led him into the church, and from that time, he began to serve him faithfully.

Word of him spread greatly all throughout that city. The Man of God, seeing that they recognized him there, ran from that city and got into a ship, wishing to sail into Pharsii Catalonia where they would not recognize him. By God's will, the ship was taken off course by a stormy wind and arrived at Rome. Disembarking he said to himself, "As my Lord God lives, I will not be a burden to anyone. I will go to my father's house, for I will not be recognized there." Walking away, he met his father, walking from the Emperors' palace at dinner time. He bowed down before him, saying, "Servant of God, have mercy on me a poor man and a stranger. Take me into your house, and I will be fed with your servants from the crumbs that fall from your table. And your God will bless your years and guide your life upon the earth, and grant you the kingdom of heaven." Hearing this as though from a stranger, his father was pleased and ordered that he be brought into his house. He said to his servants, "Whosoever of you wishes to serve him so as to please him, as my Lord God lives, I shall free him and he shall have a share in my house. So on the porch of my doorway, make him a little room and give him food from my table. Be to him a pleasant servant."

His mother, lamenting and grieving over him, never left her chamber, and her daughter-in-law also said, "I will not leave here until my death but will be like a faithful desert-loving turtle dove until I see what has happened to my husband." Every night, the servants did evil things to him. Some kicked him. Others slapped him. Still others poured their dirty dish water over him. The Man of God, seeing that they were instructed by the Devil, received this joyfully and suffered happily. He lived seventeen years in his father's house, unrecognized by anyone.

When it pleased the Lord that the Man of God should pass away, the Man of God said to his servant, "Bring me parchment, ink, and a reed." When the servant brought them to him, he took them and wrote down all his secrets, both regarding his father and his mother, and the words he had spoken to his betrothed, that he had given her a ring. He wrote down all his life, so that they would recognize him and know that he was their son.

It happened one day, at the end of the holy Liturgy, as the two Emperors, the Archbishop, and all the people were in the church, that they heard a voice coming from the altar which said, "Come unto Me, all you who labor and are heavy laden, and I will give you rest." They marveled and were all awestruck and fell to the ground and cried, "Lord have mercy." Again they heard a second voice saying, "Search for the Man of God, for he prays for the world. Friday at daybreak, his soul will leave the body." On Thursday evening, having gathered in the Church of St. Peter, they prayed to God that he reveal to them the Man of God. A voice said, "His body is in the house of Ephimianos."

Returning from church, the two Emperors said to Ephimianos; "Why did you not tell us that you had such grace within your house?" Ephimianos answered, "As my Lord God lives, I did not know." Calling the eldest of his young servants, he said to him, "Advise us about such a man among your fellow servants." He answered, "As my Lord God lives, I do not know, for they are all worthless."

Then the two Emperors ordered that they go to the house of Ephimianos to search for the Man of God. Ephimianos ordered his servants to prepare tables and thrones with candles and censers to greet them. The Emperors and the Archbishop and all the Emperors' men arrived and sat down, and the silence was great. His mother curtained off her window with a veil, so that no one could see her, and said, "What is this confusion and this uproar, and what is being said?" Their daughter-in-law standing in her chamber saw all of them and thought, "What is taking place and being said?" The servant of the Man of God said to his lord, "Lord, is this not the Man of God, the humble Man of God whom you entrusted to me long ago? I have seen his great and praiseworthy deeds, his glorious wonders. From week to week he partook of the Holy Mysteries, ate two measures of bread and drank two measures of water, and fasted all the rest of the week. All that time, he kept himself from sleep by night. And some of your servants mistreated him. Some kicked him; others beat him; still others threw their dirty dish water over him. He took it with patience and joy."

Ephimianos, having heard these things, ran to him wishing to talk with him, but he was already without voice or hearing. Uncovering his face, he saw his countenance shine like an angel of God, as he had passed away. He held a parchment in his hand. Ephimianos reached for the parchment to take it so as to see what was written on it, but he did not allow him, and he was unable to take it. Ephimianos returned and said to the Emperors, "We have searched for him whom your faith desired, but he is dead." Then he told them all in order, how Alexis had come to him seventeen years before, how he lived in his house, also about the parchment he held in his hand and did not give him. Then the renowned Emperors ordered that a couch be prepared and that the body of the holy one be placed on it. The glorious Emperors and the Archbishop and all the boyars stood up, and all the Emperors' men. The Emperors said to the body of the holy one, "Servant of God, although we are sinners, nevertheless we are Emperors, and He is the father of all the universe. Give us your parchment, that we may see who you are and what is written on that parchment." Immediately, he gave the parchment to the Emperors and the Archbishop. They took it and gave it to the chief archivist of the All Holy Church. The Emperors, the Archbishop, Ephimianos his father, and all the boyars and the people sat, and there was a great silence in the house of Ephimianos. The archivist began to read the parchment, as it was written. When he had read it, Ephimianos leapt from his chair. Tearing his garments out of grief, and pulling his gray hair out by the roots, he ran and fell on the breast of the righteous and honorable body. He lovingly kissed him, saying:

"Woe is me, my son. Why did you do this to me and bring sorrow to my soul? Why have you now caused me this torment? Woe is me, my child, how many years was I in despair, and heard your voice ... and your conversation, and you did not reveal yourself to me, seeing how much your parents cried in their house. Woe is me, master of my old age, where I had a child who is the joy of my heart. From this point it is fitting that I cry bitterly for the wounding of my soul."

His mother, having heard that he was her son, opened her window, and like a lioness from her lair, she ran from her chamber. She tore her garments and loosed her hair, looked strangely into heaven and gazed piteously upon her son, and begged the people, saying, "Take pity on me. Take pity on me. Make room for me that I may reach my hope. Make room for me, men, that mournfully I may see this my beloved child. O my grief, brothers, yes, that I may see this my only son, the lamb of my soul, the fledgling of my nest, fed by my breast." Running in, she threw herself on the breast of the righteous man and lovingly kissed his body, crying and saying, "Take pity on me, my lords, for such as this has taken place and brought grief to our souls, such as has not been experienced for so many years in our house." She placed her hands on his face, sighed painfully, her eyes overflowed unceasingly with tears, and beating her breast, she cried, saying, "Come, cry with me, for he was in my house for seventeen years unrecognized by anyone, and he is my son, my only child. How many years was he in his father's house and did not reveal himself to me, but received beatings and vexation and spitting from his own servants, and bore it meekly. Woe is me, my child, to whom will I look?"

His bride clothed herself in black and ran and threw herself on the breast of the righteous one and cried, "Woe is me, the desert-loving turtle dove.

How many years did I wish to hear your voice or your conversation. Why have you done this, and not revealed yourself to me? How many years was I alone for your sake, appearing by day as a widow, having no one to whom I might look or for whom I might wait? I can endure no more, but from here on will lament my broken heart, and my wounded soul."

The people were all horrified and shed endless tears. The glorious Emperors and the Archbishop ordered that his funeral bed be taken and placed in the middle of the city. They said to the multitudes, "We have searched for this man and found him through your faith." All the inhabitants of the city who heard rushed to see his honorable relics. The sick saw and were freed from every disease. Those who were ill and came to him were all healed. The deaf heard; the blind saw; lepers were cleansed; demons were driven out; and every human ailment was healed. The Emperors saw the miracles and carried the bed along with the Archbishop that they might be free to touch the holy relics of the Man of God. His father held his honorable relics in his arms, trembling and groaning, beating his chest as he walked. His mother also held the body of the holy one in her arms, and her hair spread out over him and she trembled. His bride, in grief and tears, walked behind his bed piteously sobbing and crying. The people crowded round about his bed, and the Emperors and the Archbishop were not able to carry it away from the multitude. The glorious Emperors ordered much gold and silver to be strewn about that the multitude might step back from them and they might carry the body of the Man of God, Alexis, but no one touched the gold, but even more lovingly followed his honorable relics. There was much trouble, and they were barely able to carry his coffin to the Church of St. Boniface.

There for seven days they celebrated a feast over his honorable relics, his father and mother and his bride seated before him. The faithful Emperors ordered a golden tomb decorated with emeralds and glass beads. It was built, and his relics were placed in it in the seventh day of March, on the seventeenth day, in the reign of the glorious Emperors of Rome, Honorius and Arcadius, under the Episcopate of Markianus,[6] in the time of his parents Ephimianos and his mother Aglais. By the grace of God, sweet-smelling myrrh flowed from his tomb, and it being miraculous, all the sick who gathered it and anointed themselves with it, praised and glorified the Father, the Son, and the Holy Spirit, the one true God. Whoever anointed himself with this myrrh, whatever he asked from God was given him, for to Him belongs all glory, honor, and worship, to the Father, the Son, and the Holy Spirit, now and ever and unto the ages of ages. Amen.

Translation by Father Gabriel Nicholas

Notes to the translation begin on page 557.

RESOURCES

Primary Text

"Zhitie sviatogo cheloveka bozhiia Aleksiia." In *Khrestomatiia po drevnei russkoi literature,* ed. N.K. Gudzii. Moscow: Prosveshchenie, 1973, pp. 98–104.

Bezsonov, P. *Kaleki perekhozhie. Sbornik stikhov i issledovaniia. Moskva 1861–1864.* England: Gregg International, 1970. For different variants of "Alexis, Holy Man of God."

Secondary Sources

Literary and Cultural Studies

Fedotov, G.P. *The Russian Religious Mind.* New York: Harper Torchbooks, 1960.

Feuerstein, Georg. *Holy Madness: The Shock Tactics and Radical Teachings of Crazywise Adepts, Holy Fools, Rascal Gurus.* New York: Paragon House, 1990.

Murav, Harriet. *Holy Foolishness: Dostoevsky's Novels and the Poetics of Cultural Critique.* Stanford: Stanford University Press, 1992.

Panchenko, A.M. *Smekhovoi mir drevnei Rusi.* Leningrad: Nauka, 1984.

Saward, John. *Perfect Fools: Folly for Christ's Sake in Catholic and Orthodox Spirituality.* Oxford–New York: Oxford University Press, 1980.

Thompson, Ewa M. *Understanding Russia: The Holy Fool in Russian Culture.* New York–London: University Press of America, 1987.

Ziolkowski, Margaret. *Hagiography and Modern Russian Literature.* Princeton: Princeton University Press, 1988.

Art and Architecture

Alpatov, M.V. *Etiudy po istorii russkogo iskusstva.* Moscow: Iskusstvo, 1967, plate 138.

Vzdornov, G. *Iskusstvo drevnei Vologdy.* Leningrad: Avrora, 1972, p. 31.

Drama and Theater

Kuzmin, Mikhail. "The Comedy of Alexis, Man of God, or The Lost Son Transformed." In *The Russian Symbolist Theatre: An Anthology of Plays and Critical Texts,* ed. and trans. Michael Green. Ann Arbor, MI: Ardis, 1986.

Music

Geistliche Chormusik aus Russland. Don Kosaken Chorus. Conductor, Serge Jaroff. Deutsche Grammophon, n.d.

Ivan Semennich Kozlovsky. Bolshoi Orchestra. Conductor, N. Gusman. Melodiia, 1990.

Svet Khristov prosveshchaet vsekh. Pesnopeniia Russkoi Pravoslavnoi Tserkvi. "Joy of All Afflicted." Choir of the Moscow Church. Conductor, Nikolai Matveev. Moscow Patriarchate, 1984.

~ II ~

The Emerging Self

The centuries following *Igor* and early Orthodox culture saw external continuities in a massive invasion by Mongol tribes and internal ones in the sustenance provided by religious tradition. With the coming of the Mongols, Russia became as firmly linked with Asia as it earlier had been linked with the Byzantium of Asia Minor. Historians usually note major differences between this historical condition and the European experience shaped by the Renaissance. The differences are evident, but they should not be allowed to obstruct similarities, including the strong Renaissance influences amply noted by Dmitry Likhachev and other scholars, as well as the cultural mainsprings of Greek civilization, which continued to nourish both the West and Russia.

On the whole, however, Russian culture under the Mongols retained its vigor thanks to its continued religiosity rather than such secular factors as the humanism that developed in Europe during the Middle Ages. There were many valuable works of art created in this period and many writers of genius, but this culture on its own terms saw the arts and literature to be important in the light of their contribution to religious tradition rather than in their independence or originality as works of aesthetic imagination. Anonymity of the artist in the name of mutual participation in God's harmony saw numerous repetitions over the centuries of the lessons offered by Boris, Gleb, and Alexis, rather than creative breaks with the past.

Humility before God's harmony and a unique talent for finding the gentle colors and symmetries of Orthodoxy were expressed in the icons of Andrei Rublev (c. 1360–1430). In his magnificent artistic achievement under conditions of what the Russians subsequently called the Tatar Yoke, Rublev suggested an aesthetic variant of kenoticism's message of humble spiritual victory over physical aggression. Much later, Andrei Tarkovsky would use the

The actor Anatoly Solonitsin as Rublev in Andrei Tarkovsky's 1966 film *Andrei Rublev*.

possibilities of the icon painter's life and work to film a masterful depiction of creative sensibility in his *Andrei Rublev*. In this later period of Soviet culture, the yoke was as ideological as military, although works of art and literature such as Tarkovsky's film were not unlike the icons of Rublev in their use of an older religious tradition to maintain artistic health.

The Mongol defeat by Dmitry of the Don in 1380, and the subsequent consolidation of a centralized political power in Moscow, provided Russian culture with heroes such as Dmitry himself and morally ambiguous tsars such as Ivan IV ("the Terrible"), who would come to serve as much more interesting aesthetic subjects. Symbols of national identity and unquestioned moral authority continued to be suggested by religious models such as the Trinity Sergius Monastery and its founder, Sergei of Radonezh (d. 1392). One of the monastery's famous acts of patriotism during the early seventeenth century was resistance to yet another invasion, this time from the West in the form of King Sigismund's Polish troops. The historical moment later inspired Mikhail Glinka to create what has been called the first Russian opera, *A Life for the Tsar* (1836). Its hero is yet another humble man, Ivan Susanin, who would eventually give his name to the Soviet version of the work.

The earlier period immediately preceding Susanin's heroic sacrifice on behalf of the new tsar provided even more compelling historical figures for cultural response. Most noticeable among them is Boris Godunov, who would serve Pushkin, Mussorgsky, Aleksei Tolstoy, Ilya Repin, and many others. Godunov's cultural presence depends heavily on the work of nineteenth-century writers, and the historical sources for their literary responses will be noted in the section devoted to that period.

After Godunov and the so-called Time of Troubles that followed him, the seventeenth century saw civil order and the semblance of political conti-nuity come to Russia along with the Romanov dynasty. The Orthodox Church continued to produce basic ideological material for moral debate and judgment; a broad historical hint of the religious establishment's central role in politics and culture is that it provided the first Romanov tsar, Mikhail, who was the son of Patriarch Filaret and the boy saved by Ivan Susanin in Glinka's opera.

Nevertheless, the development of Western contacts—which led to the evolution of aesthetic genres such as theater—as well as a ferment of internal theological issues stimulated a far from placid cultural situation. The con-solidation of political authority supported by the Church during the reigns of Mikhail (1613–45) and his son Aleksei (1645–76) ran parallel to a heightened awareness of ideological dilemmas prodding literary and cul-tural responses.

One of the more prominent literary works of this period was written by

Archpriest Avvakum (1620–1682) in the form of his autobiography. Dmitry Likhachev has good reason to suggest that this minor country cleric became the most important Russian author of the seventeenth century. Writing at a time when vast areas of Siberia were becoming part of Russia, and himself an exiled witness of Siberian tribes, paganism, shamans, and the harsh geography that entered the Russian cultural landscape, Avvakum also opened new aesthetic vistas in his highly personal and forceful use of the Russian vernacular. Literary style, in this case, came out of a particularly forceful reaction to the pressing issues of the day.

On the one hand, Avvakum responded to the echoes of Western and Greek influence heard in the previous century in the works of Maxim the Greek and felt in his own time by way of Simeon Polotsky's writings and Patriarch Nikon's program to revise and retranslate Church books (and thus Church doctrine). On the other, Avvakum, like many of the so-called Old Believers who broke away from the official church, continued theological debates of the past century between the "Possessors" of Joseph of Volokolamsk and the "Nonpossessors" grouped around Nil Sorsky. The first group, ultimately triumphant in Russian history, advocated a strict adherence to ritual, the acquisition of church property, and a theocracy in which all society would become part of the Church. The total merger of church and state occurred with Peter the Great, of course, but on a reverse scale, when the Church became a minor department of government, a historical process that helps to explain the traditional Russian wariness in regard to establishment churchmen. The second group, that of Sorsky's Trans-Volga elders, inspired by Hesychast writings, rejected the material and political concerns of secular society in favor of personal communion with God and a mystical engagement with higher truths.

Avvakum responds to Josephite monasticism in his interest in power and proper ritual and to Nil Sorsky in his rejection of material things. He consciously takes on the kenotic suffering of Russian Orthodoxy and plays out its implications in the story of his own life. His autobiography manipulates traditional literary devices of genre and style, particularly the conventions of hagiography, but it does so in terms of the author himself and by providing a forum for the skills of a writer with a strong independent voice. The "Life" is addressed to another member of the clergy, and its frame is the act of confession, but the standard values of humility and self-measurement before another person endemic to Russian culture in this religious ritual are used to demonstrate Avvakum's own moral superiority. In a similar call on religious tradition, he plays the holy fool to indicate the power of irrational faith, contempt for the ordinary, and the supreme truths of his person and the person of the "fool in Christ," his spiritual son Fedor. His use of the vernacular is an overt manipulation of style in the same kenotic cause, to show the superiority of Russian humility and moral simplicity exemplified by him over the language complexities of Western-educated theologians such as Simeon Polotsky and of the Greek, Latin, and Hebrew nuances evoked by Nikon's retranslation of the holy books. He suggests, thus, both in moral passion and in style, a supreme early example of the individual author's role in society as iconoclast and dissenter.

Avvakum's strategies in regard to divine folly and *iurodstvo*, as holy foolishness was known, can be explained in part by their unusual cultural status in the sixteenth century. Part of the holy fools' effectiveness derived from standard theatrical technique, the capacity to create doubt in the audience in regard to the boundary between play and reality. Sometimes dressed in the typical garb of the homeless and sometimes not dressed at all, the holy fools consciously played at being mad and out of control to shock their audience into an appreciation of matters beyond everyday routine and common sense. Sometimes, of course, the play at madness became self-fulfilling prophecy, but the respect accorded holy fools even in such extreme manifestations continued unabated. Suggestive of the holy fools' central moral positioning are the churches dedicated to them in the sixteenth century; the most famous, the Kazan Cathedral on Red Square constructed by order of Ivan IV, carries the name of one such venerated *iurodivyi* mentioned by Avvakum, Basil the Blessed.

Most of these cultural imperatives are noted in Kenneth Brostrom's rich annotations, which can serve as a sound introduction to Russian ideological concerns, politics, and expanding geography in this period. Avvakum lived on in Russian culture in the passionate convictions of the Old Believer *raskolniki*, or schismatics, who canonized him as a saint. As important, perhaps, for the cultural mainstream, he has come to represent the ideological engagement bordering on fanaticism that Dostoevsky later suggests in the name given Raskolnikov. A similar focus on individual passion confronting society inspired Vasily Surikov in 1887 to create a monumental painting of Avvakum's spiritual ward, the Boyarina Feodosia Prokofievna Morozova. Marfa, the protagonist of Mussorgsky's unfinished *Khovanshchina*, is made of similar stuff; the self-immolation of the Old Believers in the opera's last scene renders in music a moral yearning approaching fanaticism but glorious in its refusal to compromise. In all three cases, such extravagant commitment was familiar and attractive cultural material for Russian men and women of the arts, who continued to view their own roles in society precisely in such terms.

N. R.

4

~Avvakum~

The Life of Avvakum

The Archpriest Avvakum hath been charged to write his *Life* by the monk Epifanij (as this monk is his confessor) so that the works of God shall not pass into oblivion: and to this end hath he been charged by his confessor, to the glory of Christ our God. Amen.[1]

All-holy Trinity, O God and Creator of all the world! Speed and direct my heart to begin with wisdom and to end with the good works about which I, an unworthy man, now desire to speak. Understanding my ignorance and bowing down I pray to Thee; and as I beseech Thee for aid, govern my mind and strengthen my heart to prepare for the fashioning of good works, so that illumined by good works I may have a place at Thy right hand with all Thine Elect on Judgment Day. . . .

And in our Russia there was a sign: the sun was darkened in 7162 [1654], a month or so before the plague. Simeon, the Archbishop of Siberia, was sailing along the river Volga about two weeks before St. Peter's Day, and at midday there was darkness.[2] For about three hours they waited by the shore weeping. The sun grew dim, and from the west a moon approached. According to Dionysios, God was revealing His wrath against men: at that time Nikon the Apostate was defiling the faith and the laws of the Church, and for this God poured forth the vials of His wrathful fury upon the Russian land; a mighty plague it was, there's been no time to forget, we all remember.[3] Afterward, about fourteen years having passed, there was a second darkening of the sun. During the Fast of St. Peter, on Friday during the sixth hour, there was darkness. The sun grew dim and a moon approached from the west, revealing the wrath of God. And at that time in a cathedral church the bishops were shearing the Archpriest Avvakum, that poor, miserable soul, along with some others, and after damning them they cast them into a dungeon at Ugreša.[4] The true believer will understand what is happening in our land because of the turmoil in the Church. Enough talk of it. On Judgment Day it will be understood by everyone. Let us endure to that time. . . .

46

I was born in the Nižnij Novgorod area, beyond the Kudma River, in the village of Grigorovo.[5] My father was the priest Pëtr, my mother Marija, as a nun Marfa. My father was given to hard drink, but my mother fasted and prayed zealously and was ever teaching me the fear of God. Once I saw a dead cow at a neighbor's, and that night I arose and wept much over my soul before the icon, being mindful of death and how I too must die. And from that time I grew accustomed to praying every night. Then my mother was widowed and I, still young, orphaned, and we were driven out, away from our kin. My mother deigned to have me married. And I prayed to the most holy Mother of God that she might give me for a wife a helpmate to salvation. And in the same village there was a girl, also an orphan, who was accustomed to going to church unceasingly; her name was Anastasija. Her father was a blacksmith by the name of Marko, very rich, but when he died everything dwindled away. And she lived in poverty and prayed to God that she might be joined with me in marital union; and so it was, by the will of God. Afterward my mother went to God amid great feats of piety.[6] And being banished I moved to another place. I was ordained a deacon at the age of twenty-one, and after two years I was made a priest. I lived as a priest for eight years and was then raised to archpriest by Orthodox bishops. Since then twenty years have passed, and in all it is thirty years that I have been in holy orders.

And when I was a priest I had many spiritual children; up to now it would be about five or six hundred. Never slumbering, I, a sinner, was diligent in churches and in homes, at crossroads, in towns and villages, even in the capital and in the lands of Siberia, preaching and teaching the Word of God, this for about twenty-five years.

When I was still a priest, there came to me to confess a young woman, burdened with many sins, guilty of fornication and self-abuse of every sort; and weeping she began to acquaint me with it all in detail, standing before the Gospel there in the church. But I, thrice-accursed healer, I was afflicted myself, burning inwardly with a lecherous fire, and it was bitter for me in that hour. I lit three candles and stuck them to the lectern, and raised my right hand into the flame and held it there until the evil conflagration within me was extinguished.[7] After dismissing the young woman, laying away my vestments, and praying awhile, I went to my home deeply grieved. The hour was as midnight, and having come into my house I wept before the icon of the Lord so that my eyes swelled; and I prayed earnestly that God might separate me from my spiritual children, for the burden was heavy and hard to bear. And I fell to the ground on my face; I wept bitterly, and lying there sank into forgetfulness. Nothing could I ken, as I was weeping, but the eyes of my heart beheld the Volga.[8] I saw two golden boats sailing gracefully,

and their oars were of gold, and the masts of gold, and everything was of
gold; each had one helmsman for the crew. And I asked, "Whose boats are
these?" And they answered, "Luka's and Lavrentij's." They had been my
spiritual children; they set me and my house on the path to salvation, and
their passing was pleasing to God. And lo, I then saw a third boat, not
adorned with gold but motley-colored—red, and white, and blue, and black,
and ashen; the mind of man could not take in all its beauty and excellence.
A radiant youth sitting aft was steering. He raced toward me out of the
Volga as if he wanted to swallow me whole. And I shouted, "Whose boat is
this?" And he sitting in it answered, "Your boat. Sail in it with your wife
and children if you're going to pester the Lord." And I was seized by
trembling, and sitting down I pondered: "What is this Vision? And what
sort of voyage will it be?"

And lo, after a little while, as it is written, "The sorrows of death compassed me, and the afflictions of hell gat hold upon me; I found trouble and
sorrow. . . ."[9]

At that same time my son Prokopij was born, who is now locked up,
buried with his mother in the earth. And I took up my staff, and his mother
the unbaptized child, and we wandered whither God might direct, and we
baptized him on the way, just as Phillip baptized the eunuch long ago.
When I had trudged to Moscow, to the Tsar's confessor, Archpriest Stefan,
and to Neronov, Archpriest Ivan, they both announced me to the Tsar, and
the Sovereign came to know me at that time.[10] The fathers sent me again to
my old place with a mandate, and I dragged myself back. And sure enough,
the walls of my dwelling had been torn down. So I set to work there again,
and again the Devil raised up a storm against me. There came to my village
dancing bears with tambourines and domras, and I, sinner that I am, being
zealous in Christ, I drove them out; one against many I smashed their masks
and tambourines in a field and took away two great bears. One of them I
clubbed, he came to life again; the other I set loose in the fields.[11]

Because of all this Vasilij Petrovič Šeremetev, who was sailing along the
Volga to his governorship in Kazan, took me onto his boat, and blistering
me plenty he commanded that his shaven-faced son Matvej be blessed.[12]
But I, seeing that lechery-loving countenance, I did not bless but rebuked
him from Holy Writ. The boyar, being mightily angered, ordered me
thrown into the Volga; and afflicting me much they shoved me overboard.
But later they were good to me. We forgave one another in the antechambers
of the Tsar, and his lady, the Boyarina Vasil'evna, was the spiritual daughter of my younger brother. Thus doth God fashion his people!

Let's get back to my story. Afterward another official raged savagely
against me; coming to my home with others he attacked, shooting with

bows and pistols. But I locked myself in, and with great cry I prayed to
God, "Lord, subdue and reconcile him by the means that Thou knowest!"
And he ran away from my home, driven off by the Holy Spirit. Later that
same night they came running from him and called to me with many tears:
"Father! Master! Evfimej Stefanovič is near death and his shouting is past
bearing; he beats himself and groans, and he says, 'Bring me Father
Avvakum! God is punishing me because of him.' " And I expected they
were tricking me, and my spirit was terrified within me. And lo, I besought
God after this manner: "O Lord, Thou who didst deliver me from my
mother's womb, who broughtest me from nothingness to life! If they strangle
me, number me with Filipp, the Metropolitan of Moscow. If they stab me,
number me with Zacharias the prophet. And if they try to drown me, release
me from them again, as thou didst Stefan of Perm."[13] And praying I rode
over to Evfimej, to his house. When they brought me into the yard, his wife
Nionila ran out and grabbed me by the hand, herself saying, "Please come,
our Lord and Father! Please come, our light and benefactor!" And I said
in answer to this: "Will wonders never cease! Yesterday I was a son of
a whore, and now, Father! It's Christ that has the crueler scourge; your
husband owned up in no time!"

She led me into his room. Evfimej jumped out of the featherbed and fell
at my feet with a howl beyond words to describe: "Forgive me, my lord, I
have sinned before God and before you."[14] And he was shaking all over.
And I answered, "Do you wish to be whole from this time forth?" And
lying there he answered, "Yea, venerable father." And I said: "Arise! God
will forgive you!" But he had been mightily punished and couldn't rise by
himself. And I lifted him and laid him on the bed, and confessed him, and
anointed him with holy oil, and he was well. Christ deigned it so. And in the
morning he sent me home in honor. He and his wife became my spiritual
children, praiseworthy servants of Christ. Thus it is that "God scorneth the
scorners, but he giveth grace unto the lowly."[15]

A little later others again drove me from that place for the second time.
And I dragged myself to Moscow, and by God's will the Sovereign ordered
that I be appointed archpriest in Jur'evec-on-the-Volga.[16] I lived here only a
little, just eight weeks. The Devil instructed the priests and peasants and
their females; they came to the patriarchal chancellery, where I was busy
with church business, and in a crowd they dragged me out of the chancellery
(there were maybe fifteen hundred of them). And in the middle of the street
they beat me with clubs and stomped me, and the females had at me with
stove hooks. Because of my sins, they almost beat me to death, and they
cast me down near the corner of a house. The commandant rushed up with
his artillerymen, and seizing me they raced away on their horses to my poor

home. And the commandant stationed his men about the yard. But people
came up to the yard, and the town was in tumult. Most of all, as I had cut
short their fornicating, the priests and their females were howling, "Kill
the crook, the son of a whore, and we'll pitch his carcass in the ditch for
the dogs!"

After resting, two days later at night I abandoned wife and children and
with two others headed along the Volga toward Moscow. I escaped to
Kostroma—and sure enough there they'd driven out the Archpriest Daniil
too.[17] Ah, what misery! The Devil badgers a man to death! I trudged to
Moscow and presented myself to Stefan, the Tsar's confessor, and he was
troubled with me. "Why did you abandon your cathedral church?" he says.
Again more misery for me! The Tsar came to his confessor that night to be
blessed and saw me there—again more heartache. "And why," he says, "did
you abandon your town?" And my wife and children and the help, some
twenty people, had stayed in Jur'evec, no telling if they were living or dead.
Still more misery.

After this Nikon, our good friend, brought the relics of the Metropolitan
Filipp from the Solovki Monastery. But before arrival the Tsar's confessor
Stefan, along with the brethren (and I there with them), fasted for a week
and besought God concerning the patriarchate, that he might give us a
shepherd for the salvation of our souls. Together with Kornilij the Metropolitan of Kazan, we wrote and signed a petition concerning the Tsar's
confessor Stefan, that he should be patriarch, and we gave it to the Tsar and
Tsarina.[18] But Stefan didn't want it himself and mentioned Metropolitan
Nikon. The Tsar listened to him and sent a message to meet Nikon: "To
Nikon, the most reverend Metropolitan of Novgorod and Velikie Luki and
of all Russia, our greetings," and so on. When he arrived he played the fox
with us—all humble bows and howdy-do's! He knew he was going to be
patriarch and wanted no hitches all the way. Much could be said about his
treachery! When he was made patriarch, he wouldn't even let his friends
into the Chamber of the Cross! And then he belched forth his venom.[19]

During Lent he sent an instruction to St. Basil's, to Ivan Neronov.[20] He
was my confessor; I was with him all the time, living in the cathedral. When
he went anywhere, then I took charge of the cathedral. There had been talk
that I might go to a post at Our Savior's in the palace to replace the late
Sila, but God didn't will it. And little enough zeal there was on my part
anyway. This was just right for me. I stayed at St. Basil's and read the holy
book to the folk. Many people came to listen. In the instruction Nikon
wrote: "Year and date. According to the tradition of the Apostles and the
Holy Fathers it is not your bounden duty to bow down to the knee, but you
are to bow to the waist; in addition, you are to cross yourself with three

fingers."[21] Having come together we fell to thinking; we saw that winter was on the way—hearts froze and legs began to shake. Neronov turned the cathedral over to me and went himself into seclusion at the Čudovskij Monastery; for a week he prayed in a cell.[22] And there a voice from the icon spoke to him during a prayer: "The time of suffering hath begun; it is thy bounden duty to suffer without weakening!" Weeping he told this to me and to Pavel, the Bishop of Kolomna, the same that Nikon afterward burned by fire in the Novgorod region.[23] Next he told Daniil, the Archpriest of Kostroma, and later he told all the brethren. Daniil and I wrote down excerpts from Writ about the conformation of the fingers and obeisances and gave them to the Sovereign; much was written there. But he hid them, I don't know where. It seems he gave them to Nikon. . . .

Later on Boris Neledinskij and his musketeers seized me during a vigil; about sixty people were taken with me.[24] They were led off to a dungeon, but me they put in the Patriarch's Court for the night, in chains. When the sun had risen on the Sabbath, they put me in a cart and stretched out my arms and drove me from the Patriarch's court to Andronikov Monastery, and there they tossed me in chains into a dark cell dug into the earth.[25] I was locked up three days and neither ate nor drank. Locked there in darkness I bowed down in my chains, maybe to the east, maybe to the west.[26] No one came to me, only the mice and the cockroaches; the crickets chirped and there were fleas to spare. It came to pass that on the third day I was voracious, that is, I wanted to eat, and after Vespers there stood before me, whether an angel or whether a man I didn't know and to this day I still don't know, but only that he said a prayer in the darkness, and taking me by the shoulder led me with my chain to a bench and sat me down, and put a spoon in my hands and a little bread, and gave me cabbage soup to sip—my, it was tasty, uncommonly good! And he said unto me, "Enough, that will suffice thee for thy strengthening." And he was gone. The doors didn't open, but he was gone! It's amazing if it was a man, but what about an angel? Then there's nothing to be amazed about, there are no barriers to him anywhere.[27]

In the morning the Archimandrite came with the brethren and led me out; they scolded me: "Why don't you submit to the Patriarch?" But I blasted and barked at him from Holy Writ. They took off the big chain and put on a small one, turned me over to a monk for a guard, and ordered me hauled into the church. By the church they dragged at my hair and drummed on my sides; they jerked at my chain and spit in my eyes. God will forgive them in this age and that to come. It wasn't their doing but cunning Satan's. I was locked up there four weeks. . . .

Later they exiled me to Siberia with my wife and children. And of our many privations on the road there is too much to tell, but maybe a small portion of them should be mentioned. The Archpriestess had a baby, and we carried her sick in a cart to Tobol'sk. For three thousand versts and about thirteen weeks we dragged along in carts, and by water and sledges one-half the way.[28]

The Archbishop in Tobol'sk appointed me to a post. Here in this church great troubles overtook me.[29] In a year and a half I was accused of crimes against the state five times, and one person in particular, the Secretary of the Archbishop's court Ivan Struna, he shook my soul.[30] The Archbishop left for Moscow, and with him gone, because of the Devil's instruction, he attacked me.[31] For no reason at all he took it into his head to afflict Anton, the deacon of my church. But Anton fled him and came running to me in church. That same Ivan Struna, having gotten together with some other people another day, came to me in the church (I was chanting Vespers). He leaped into the church and grabbed Anton by the beard in the choir. At the same time I shut and locked the church doors and didn't let anyone in. All alone Struna whirled about church like a devil. Leaving off Vespers, Anton and I sat him down on the floor in the middle of the church and I lashed him hard with a whip for rioting in church. The others, some twenty people, all fled, driven off by the Holy Spirit. After receiving Struna's repentance, I let him go again.

But Struna's kinswomen, the priests, and the monks, they stirred up the whole town in hopes of doing away with me. At midnight they pulled up to my place in sledges and broke into my house, wanting to take me and drown me. And they were driven away by the fear of God, and again they fled. Nearly a month was I tormented, escaping from them on the sly; sometimes I bedded down in a church, sometimes I went to a commander's house, and sometimes I tried to beg my way into the prison—only they wouldn't let me in. Often Matvej Lomkov went with me, he whose monastic name is Mitrofan. Later on he was steward of church properties in Moscow for the Metropolitan Pavel, and in the Cathedral Church, along with the Deacon Afanasij, he sheared me. He was good before, but now the Devil's swallowed him whole.[32]

Later the Archbishop came back from Moscow, and as just chastisement he put him, Struna, in chains for this reason: a certain man committed incest with his daughter, but after taking fifty kopeks, he, Struna, let the peasant off without punishing him. And his Grace, as well, ordered him fettered remembering my affair. But that one, Struna, he went off to the commanding officers in their chambers and accused me of state crimes.[33] The officers turned him over to Pëtr Beketov, the best son of the boyars, as his guardian. Alas, calamity came to Pëtr's household! And it still brings grief to my soul. The Archbishop thought things over with me, and in accordance with the Canons he started to damn Struna for the sin of incest in the main church on the first Sunday in Lent. This same Pëtr Beketov came into the church, blistering the Archbishop and me.[34] And in that hour, after leaving the church, he fell into a frenzy while going home and died a bitter death. And his Grace and I ordered his body thrown in the middle of the street for the dogs, that the citizens might lament his transgression. For three days we entreated the Deity most diligently that Beketov might be absolved on Judgment Day. Pitying Struna he brought such perdition on himself. And after three days his Grace and I buried his body ourselves with honor. But enough talk of this lamentable affair.

Then a decree arrived. It was ordered that I be taken from Tobol'sk to the Lena River because I was blasting from Holy Writ and blistering the Nikonian heresy. . . .[35]

But when I came to Yenisejsk another decree arrived; it ordered us to carry on into Daurija—this would be more than twenty thousand versts from Moscow.[36] And they handed me over into the troop of Afanasij Paškov; the people there with him numbered six hundred.[37] As a reward for my sins he was a harsh man; he burned and tortured and flogged people all the time. I had often tried to bring him to reason, and here I had fallen into his hands myself. And from Moscow he had orders from Nikon to afflict me.

After we had traveled out of Yenisejsk, when we were on the great Tunguska River, my prame was completely swamped by storm; it filled full of water in the middle of the river, the sail was ripped to shreds, only the decks were above water, everything else had gone under.[38] My wife, bare-headed, just barely dragged the children out of the water onto the decks. But looking to Heaven I shouted, "Lord, save us! Lord, help us!" And by God's will we were washed ashore. Much could be said about this! On another prame two men were swept away and drowned in the water. After putting ourselves to rights on the bank, we traveled on again.

When we came to the Šamanskij Rapids we met some people sailing the other way.[39] With them were two widows, one about sixty and the other older; they were sailing to a convent to take the veil. But Paškov started to turn them around and wanted to give them in marriage. And I said to him, "According to the Canons it is not fitting to give such women in marriage." What would it cost him to listen to me and let the widows go? But no, being enraged he decided to afflict me. On another rapids, the Long Rapids, he started to kick me out of the prame. "Because of you," he says, "the prame don't go right! You're a heretic! Go walk through the mountains, you're not going with Cossacks!" Ah, misery came my way! The mountains were high, the forests dense, the cliffs of stone, standing like a wall—you'd crick your neck looking up! In those mountains are found great snakes; geese and ducklings with red plumage, black ravens, and gray jackdaws also live there. In those mountains are eagles and falcons and gyrfalcons and mountain pheasants and pelicans and swans and other wild fowl, an endless abundance, birds of many kinds. In those mountains wander many wild beasts, goats and deer, Siberian stags and elk, wild boars, wolves, wild sheep—you'll lay your eyes on them but never your hands! Paškov drove me out into those mountains to live with the beasts and the snakes and the birds.[40]

So I wrote him a short little epistle; the beginning went like this: "Man! Fear God, who sitteth above the Cherubim and gazeth into the abyss; before Him the heavenly Powers do tremble and all creation together with mankind. Thou alone dost scorn and exhibit unseemliness"—and so on. A good bit was written there, and I sent it to him. And lo, about fifty men ran up, seized my prame, and rushed off to him (I was camped about three versts away from him). I cooked the Cossacks some porridge, and I fed them. The poor souls, they both ate and trembled, and others watching wept for me and pitied me. A prame was brought up, the executioners seized me and brought me before him. He stood there with a sword, all atremble and started to speak to me. "Are you a frocked or unfrocked priest?" And I answered, "Verily, I am Avvakum the Archpriest. Speak! What is your business with me?" And he bellowed like a savage beast and hit me on one cheek, then on the other, again on top of my head, and knocked me down. Grabbing his commander's axe, he hit me three times on the back as I lay there, and stripping me, he laid seventy-two blows across that same back with a knout.[41] But I was saying, "O Lord, Jesus Christ, Son of God, help me!" And I kept on saying the same thing, the same thing without letup. So it was bitter for him that I was not saying "Have mercy!" Every blow I said a prayer, but in the middle of the beating I cried out to him, "That's enough of this beating!" So he ordered it stopped. And I managed to say, "Why are you beating me? Do you know?" And he again ordered them to beat me, now on the ribs, and then they let me go. I began to tremble and fell down. And he ordered me dragged off to the ammunition prame; they chained my hands and feet and tossed me against the mast bracing. It was autumn, rain was falling on me, and all night long I lay in the downpour. When they were beating, it didn't hurt then, what with the prayers, but lying there a thought strayed into my head: "O Son of God, why did You let him beat me so hard that way? You know I stood up for Your widows! Who will set a judge between me and Thee? You never shamed me this way when I thieved in the night! And this time I don't know how I've sinned!" There's a good man for you!—another shit-faced Pharisee wanting to drag the Lord to court! If Job spoke in this way, he was righteous and pure and moreover had not fathomed Holy Writ; he was outside the Law, in a barbarous land, and knew God from his creation. But I, first, am sinful; second, I find repose in the Law and am supported in all things by Holy Writ, as "we must through tribulation enter into the Kingdom of God"—but I fell into such madness. Alas for me! Why wasn't that prame swamped by the water with me in it? And in those moments my bones started to ache, and my veins went stiff, and my heart gave out, yes, and I started to die. Water splashed in my mouth so I sighed and repented before God. The Lord our Light is merciful; He doth not recall against us our former transgressions, rewarding repentance. And again nothing was hurting.

In the morning they tossed me into a small boat and carried me onward. When we reached the Padun Rapids, the biggest of them all—the river around that place is near a verst in width—they brought me right up to the rapids. Three cascades run across the whole river, fearfully steep; find the gates or your boat will be kindling![42] Down came the rain and snow, and only a poor little caftan had been tossed across my shoulders. The water poured down my belly and back, terrible was my need. They dragged me out of the boat, then dragged me in chains across the rocks and around the rapids. Almighty miserable it was, but sweet for my soul! I wasn't grumbling at God a second time. The words spoken by the Prophet and Apostle came to mind: "My son, despise not thou the chastening of the Lord, nor faint when thou art rebuked of Him. For whom God loveth He chasteneth, and scourgeth every son whom He receiveth. If ye endure chastening, God dealeth with you as with sons. But if ye partake of Him without chastisement, then are ye bastards, and not sons."[43] And with these words I comforted myself.

Afterward they brought me to the Bratskij fortress and tossed me into the dungeon and gave me a little pile of straw. And I was locked up till St. Philip's Fast in a freezing tower.[44] Winter thrives there at that time, but God warmed me even without clothes! Like a little dog I lay on my lump of straw. Sometimes they fed me, sometimes not. The mice were plentiful, and I swatted them with my priest's cap—the silly fools wouldn't even give me a stick. I lay on my belly all the time; my back was rotting. Plentiful too were the fleas and lice. I wanted to shout at Paškov, "Forgive me!" But the power of God did forfend it; it was ordained that I endure. He moved me to a warm hut, and there I lived the winter through in fetters along with hostages and dogs.[45] But my wife and children were sent about twenty versts away from me. Her peasant woman Ksen´ja tormented her that whole winter long, all the time yapping and scolding. After Christmas my son Ivan, still a little boy, trudged over to stay with me awhile, and Paškov ordered him tossed into the freezing dungeon where I had been locked up.

He spent the night, the little love, and almost froze to death. In the morning he ordered him thrown out, back to his mother. I didn't even get to see him. He dragged himself back to his mother—and frostbit his hands and feet.

In the spring we traveled on again. Not much space was given to supplies. One store was looted from top to bottom, books and extra clothes were taken away. But some other things still remained. On Lake Baikal I was swamped again. Along the river Xilok he made me haul on the tow-rope. The going was bitter hard on that river—there wasn't time for eating, much less for sleeping. All summer long we suffered. People keeled over and died from hauling in water, and my legs and belly turned blue. For two summers we tramped around in water, and in the winters we dragged ourselves over portages. . . .[46]

Then we moved to Lake Irgen. A portage is there, and during the winter we started hauling.[47] He took away my workers but wouldn't order others hired in their places. And the children were little—many to eat but no one to work. All alone this poor, miseried old Archpriest made a dogsled, and the winter long he dragged himself over the portage.

In the spring we floated down the Ingoda River on rafts. It was the fourth summer of my voyage from Tobol'sk. We were herding logs for houses and forts. Soon there was nothing to eat; people started dying off from hunger and from tramping about and working in water.[48] The river was shallow, the rafts heavy, the guards merciless, the cudgels big, the clubs knotty, the knots cutting, the torture savage—fire and the rack!—people were starving, they'd only start torturing someone and he'd die! Ah, what a time! I don't know why he went off his head like that! The Archpriestess had an over-dress from Moscow that hadn't rotted. In Russia it'd be worth more than twenty-five rubles, but here, he gave us four sacks of rye for it. And we dragged on for another year or two, living on the Nerča River, all eating grass to keep body and soul together. He was killing everyone with hunger.[49] He wouldn't let anyone leave to get a living, keeping us in a small area. People would roam across the steppes and fields and dig up grasses and roots, and we right there with them. In the winter it was pine bark,[50] and sometimes God gave us horse meat; we found the bones of beasts brought down by wolves, and what the wolf hadn't eaten, we did. And some of those near frozen to death even ate wolves, and foxes, and whatever came their way, all sorts of corruption. A mare would foal and on the sly the starving would eat the foal and the foul afterbirth. And when Paškov found out, he would flog them half to death with a knout. And a mare died. Everything went to waste because the foal had been dragged out of her against nature; he only showed his head and they jerked him out, yes, and even started eating the foul blood. Ah, what a time!

And in these privations two of my little sons died, and with the others we somehow suffered on, roaming naked and barefoot through the mountains and over sharp rocks, keeping body and soul together with grasses and roots.[51] And I myself, sinner that am, I both willingly and unwillingly partook of the flesh of mares and the carrion of beasts and birds. Alas for my sinful soul! "Who will give my head water and a fountain of tears that I might weep for my poor soul," which I wickedly sullied with worldly pleasures?[52] But we were helped in the name of Christ by the Boyarina, the Commander's daughter-in-law Evdokija Kirillovna, yes and by Afanasij's wife Fëkla Simeonovna too. They gave us relief against starvation secretly, without his knowing. Sometimes they sent a little piece of meat, sometimes a small round loaf, sometimes a bit of flour and oats, as much as could be scraped together, a quarter pood and maybe a pound or two more, sometimes she saved a good half pood and sent it over, and sometimes she raked feed out of the chicken trough.[53] My daughter Agrafena, the poor little one, on the sly she would wander over under Boyarina's window. And we didn't know whether to laugh or cry! Sometimes they'd drive the little child away from the window without Boyarina's knowing, but sometimes she'd drag back a good bit. She was a little girl then, but now she's twenty-seven and still unmarried. My poor, dear daughter, now she lives in tears at Mezen with her younger sisters, keeping body and soul together somehow. And her mother and brothers sit locked up, buried in the earth.[54] But what's to be done? Let those broken hearts suffer for the sake of Christ. So be it, with God's help. For it is ordained that we must suffer, we must suffer for the sake of the Christian faith. You loved, Archpriest, of the famed to be friend; love then to endure poor wretch, to the end! It is written: "Blessed is not he that begins, but he that has finished."[55] But enough of this. Let's get back to my story.

We lived in great need in the land of Daurija for about six or seven years, although now and then we found relief. But Afanasij kept blackening my name and sought a death for me without letup. In this time of want he sent me from his household two widows named Mar'ja and Sof'ja (his favorite house servants), who were possessed of an unclean spirit. He had conjured and worked many charms over them, and he "saw that he could prevail nothing but that rather a tumult was made."[56] That devil was uncommonly savage in afflicting them, they'd beat themselves and scream. He summoned me, bowed to me, and said, "Maybe you could take them home and look after them, praying to God: God listens to you." And I answered him, "Master, you ask too much, but after the prayers of our Holy Fathers all things are possible to God." And I took them, the poor things. Forgive me! But it happened during my trials in Russia that three or four lunatics were brought one time or another into my home, and after the prayers of the Holy Fathers the devils departed from them by the command and action of the living God and of our Lord Jesus Christ, the Son of God our Light. I sprinkled them with tears and holy water and anointed them with oil, chanting supplications in Christ's name, and the power of God cast out the devils from these men and they were made whole, not because of my merit—no way in the world!—but because of their faith. . . .

Read the *Life* of Theodore of Edessa, there you will find it, how even a harlot resurrected the dead. In *The Christian's Pilot* it is written: "Not all are ordained of the Holy Spirit, but any man, save a heretic, may be his instrument."[57]

Later the madwomen were brought to me. I myself fasted according to custom and didn't let them eat either, I made supplication, anointed them with oil, and what I know, I did. And in Christ the women became whole in body and in mind. I confessed them and gave them the Sacrament. Afterward they lived in my household and prayed to God; they loved me and didn't go home. He found out they had become my spiritual daughters and again raged against me worse than ever—he wanted to burn me at the stake! "You're rooting out my secrets," he said. Yes, only tell me, good sir, how to give the Sacrament without confession? And without giving a madman the Sacrament there's no way you'll cast out a devil. That devil's no peasant, he's not afraid of a club. He's afraid of the Cross of Christ, and of holy water, and of holy oil, and he plain cuts and runs before the Body of Christ. Except by these Mysteries I am unable to heal. In our Orthodox faith there is no Sacrament without confession; in the Papist faith they do it this way, they are not vigilant about confession. For us who observe the Orthodox rite this is not fitting, but rather that we seek each time after repentance. If because of privations you can't come by a priest, declare your transgressions to a brother tried and true, and God will forgive you, having seen your repentance. And then with a brief little Office partake of the Eucharist. Keep some of the Host with you.[58] If you're on the road or about your work, or however it may be, except in church, having first sighed before the Lord and confessed to your brother in accordance with the above, partake of the precious Mystery with a clear conscience. This way all will be well! After fasting and after your Office, spread out a bit of cloth on a small box before the icon of Christ, and light a little candle, and put a dab of water in a little bowl. Ladle out some with a spoon and with a prayer place a portion of the Body of Christ in the spoonful of water. Cense it all with a censer and having wept say: "I believe, O Lord, and confess that Thou art the Christ, Son of the living God, who came into the world to save sinners of whom I am the first. I believe that this is in truth Thy most

immaculate Body and that this is Thy most virtuous Blood. For its sake I
pray to Thee that Thou wouldst have mercy on me and forgive and diminish
my transgressions for me both voluntary and involuntary, those in word and
in deed, those in knowledge and in ignorance, those in intention and in
thought, and enable me to partake blamelessly of these Thy most immaculate Mysteries for the remission of sins and for life eternal, as Thou art
blessed forever. Amen."[59] Then fall to the ground before the icon and ask
forgiveness, and having arisen kiss the icon and cross yourself, and with a
prayer partake of the Sacrament, sip a little water, and again pray to God.
Well then, glory be to Christ! Though you die right after this, all is well.
But enough talk about this. You yourselves know what's good is good.
Now I'll talk about the two women again.

Paškov took the poor widows away from me and blistered instead of
blessing me. He expected Christ would accomplish this thing simply, but
they began to rave even worse than before. He locked them in an empty hut,
and no one could get in to see them. He summoned the priest of darkness to
them, and they drove him out with logs.[60] So he dragged himself away. I
was at home weeping, but what to do, that I didn't know. I didn't dare go
near his place, he was no end riled at me. Secretly I sent them some holy
water and commanded them to wash and drink abundantly, and they were
somewhat eased, the poor souls. They trudged over secretly to see me
themselves, and I anointed them with oil in Christ's name. So with God's
leave they again became whole, and they went home again. And at night
they came running to me to pray to God. Praiseworthy little ones they
turned out to be, ceased their merrymaking, and observed a goodly rule. In
Moscow they moved into the Voznesenskij Convent with their lady. Glory
be to God in this![61]

Later we turned back from the Nerča River toward Russia; for five
weeks we traveled by dogsled over naked ice. He gave me two miserable
old nags for the little ones and for our pitiful belongings, but the
Archpriestess and myself trudged along on foot, stumbling and hurting
ourselves on the ice. The land was barbarous, the natives hostile. We dared
not leave the horses at length; keeping up with them was outside our
strength—starving and weary people we were. The poor Archpriestess tottered
and trudged along, and then she'd fall in a heap—fearfully slippery it was!
Once she was trudging along and she fell over, and a man just as weary
trudged up into her and right there fell over himself. They were both shouting, but they couldn't get up. The peasant was shouting, "Little mother, my
Lady, forgive me!" But the Archpriestess was shouting, "Why'd you crush
me, father?" I came up, and the poor dear started in on me, saying, "Will
these sufferings go on a long time, Archpriest?" And I said, "Markovna,

right to our very death." And she sighed and answered, "Good enough, Petrovič, then let's be getting on."

We had a little black hen. By God's will she laid two eggs a day for our little ones' food, easing our need. That's how God arranged it. During that time she was crushed while riding on a dogsled because of our sins. And even now I pity that little hen when she comes to mind. Not a hen nor anything short of a miracle she was—the year round she gave us two eggs a day! Next to her a hundred rubles aren't worth spit, pieces of iron! That little bird was inspired, God's creation. She fed us. and there at our side she'd peck the pine-bark porridge right out of the pot, or if some fish came our way, then she'd peck at a little fish. And in return she gave us two eggs a day! Glory be to God, who hath arranged things well! And we came by her in no ordinary way. All Boyarina's hens went blind and started to die, so she gathered them into a basket and sent them to me in hopes that "the good Father might favor us and pray for these hens." Well sir, I thought some on it: To us she'd been a real benefactress, she had little ones and she needed those hens. I chanted prayers of supplication, blessed some water, and sprinkled and censed the hens. Then I tramped around in the forest and built them a trough to eat from. I sprinkled it with the water and sent the whole kit and caboodle back to her. And with a sign from God the hens were cured, made whole, because of her faith. It was from that flock that our little hen came. But enough talk about this. It wasn't today that such became the usual thing with Christ; Cosmas and Damian performed good deeds and healed for both man and beast in Christ's name.[62] All things are needful to God; every little beast and bird lives to the glory of Him, who is our most immaculate Lord, and for the sake of man as well.

Later we dragged ourselves back again to Lake Irgen. The Boyarina showed us her favor: she sent us a frying pan full of wheat, and we filled up on wheat porridge. Evdokija Kirillovna was my benefactress, but the Devil made me squabble even with her, in this way. She had a son Simeon; he was born there, I gave the prayer and baptized him, she sent him to me every day for blessing, and I blessed him with the Cross, sprinkled him with holy water, kissed him, and sent him off again. He was a healthy, good child. Once I wasn't at home and the youngster fell ill. She lost heart and fuming at me sent the baby to a peasant wizard. Hearing about this I flared up at her too, and great strife began between us.[63] The youngster got even sicker, his right arm and leg dried up like little sticks. She brought this shame on herself, she didn't know what to do, and God oppressed her even worse. Her sweet little baby was near death. Nurses came to me weeping, but I said, "If a woman's an evil thorn, let her stick to herself!" But I was expecting her repentance. I saw how the Devil had hardened her heart; I fell down before the Lord that He might bring her to her senses.

And the Lord, our most merciful God, softened the soil of her heart. In the morning she sent her son, the younger Ivan, to me; with tears he begged forgiveness for his mother, all the while moving around my stove and bowing. And I was lying naked under birch bark on top of the stove, and my wife was right in the stove and the children wherever. Rain had set in, our clothes were gone, the shelter leaked—no rest from vexations! To humble her I said, "Command your mother to beg forgiveness from Orefa the sorcerer." Afterward they brought the sick child; she had ordered him laid down before me. And they were all weeping and bowing. Well sir, I got up, pulled my stole out of the mud, and found the holy oil. All the while entreating God and censing, I anointed the youngster with oil and blessed him with the Cross. With God's leave the baby got well again, both the arm and the leg. I gave him aplenty of holy water to drink and sent him back to his mother. You see, my listener, what power was created by the mother's repentance: she doctored her own soul and healed her son! But why not? It's not nowadays only there's a God for penitents! In the morning she sent us some fish and pies, just what we needed, hungry as we were. And from that time we made our peace. After traveling out of Daurija she died in Moscow, the dear soul, and I buried her in the Voznesenskij Convent. Paškov himself found out about the youngster—she told him. Then I went over to see him. And he bowed nice and low to me and himself said, "God save you! You act like a real father, you don't remember our wickedness." And at that time he sent food enough.

But after this he soon wanted to torture me. . . .

Ten years he tormented me, or I him—I don't know. God will sort it out on Judgment Day.[64]

A transfer came for him and a document for me: I was ordered to journey to Russia. He moved on, but he didn't take me—he had a scheme in mind: "Just let him travel alone and the natives will kill him." He was sailing in the prames with both weapons and men, but I heard while traveling that they were trembling and afraid because of the natives.[65] But not I—a month passed after he left, and I gathered together the old and the sick and the wounded, those of no use there, about ten men, and with my wife and children and myself there were seventeen of us in all—we climbed in a boat and, hoping in Christ and placing a Cross in the bow, journeyed wherever God might direct, fearing nothing. I gave *The Christian's Pilot* to the adjutant, and he gave me a peasant pilot in return. And I ransomed my friend Vasilij, who used to fill Paškov's ear with lies about people, who spilled blood and was after my head too. Once after beating me he was about to impale me, but God preserved me still![66] But after Paškov left, some Cossacks wanted to flog him to death. Pleading with them to turn him over for Christ's sake and giving the adjutant a ransom, I carried him to Russia, from death to life. Let him be, poor soul—maybe he will repent his sins.

Yes, and I carried away another loose fish of the same sort. This one they didn't want to give up to me. And he ran into the forest, away from death, waited for me along the way, and weeping flung himself into my boat. But then the hounds were behind him and no place to hide! And I, sir—forgive me—I was a thief in the night: like the harlot Rahab of Jericho who hid the agents Joshua, son of Nun, so I hid him away. I put him on the bottom of the boat and covered him with a sleeping mat, and I ordered the Archpriestess and my daughter to lie on top of him. They searched everywhere, but they didn't budge my wife from her place. They only said: "You go to sleep, little mother, and you too Lady, you've stomached a lot of grief." And I—forgive me for God's sake!—I lied then and said, "He's not here with me"—not wanting to hand him over to death. They searched awhile and then rode off empty-handed, and I carried him back to Russia. Elder and you, servant of Christ! Forgive me for lying then.[67] How does it seem to you? Was my sin a small one? With the harlot Rahab, it seems she did the same thing and the Scriptures praise her for it. . . .[68]

The adjutant gave us about thirty pounds of flour, and a little cow, and five or six little sheep, and a bit of dried meat; we lived the summer on this as we sailed. The adjutant was a good man: he helped baptize my daughter Ksen'ja.[69] She was born when we were with Paškov, but he gave me no myrrh or holy oil, so she went unbaptized a long time; after he left we baptized her. I myself said the prayer for my wife, and with the godfather, the adjutant, I baptized my children; my oldest daughter was godmother, and I was the priest. Likewise I baptized my son Afanasij, and while saying Mass at Mezen I gave him the Sacrament. And I confessed my children and gave them the Sacrament myself, excepting my wife; it's all in the Canons and decreed that it be done so. As for the interdict of the apostates, I trample it in Christ's name, and that anathema—to put it crudely—I wipe my ass with it![70] The Holy Fathers of Moscow bless me, Pëtr and Aleksej and Iona and Filipp.[71] I believe in and serve my God according to their books with clear conscience. But I reject and curse the apostates! They are the enemies of God! I fear them not while I live in Christ! If they pile stones on me, then with the traditions of the Holy Fathers will I lie even under those stones, and not only under that low-down, harebrained Nikonite anathema of theirs! But why go on and on? Just spit on their doings and on that ritual of theirs, yes, and on those new books of theirs too, and all will be well. Let us talk now about pleasing Christ and the most immaculate

Mother of God and enough talk about their thievishness. Dear Nikonians, forgive me please, for blistering you—live as you like. I'm going to talk again about my grief, how you've favored me with your loving kindness. Twenty years have passed already; were God to sustain me in suffering from you again as long, then so be it by me, in the name of the Lord our God and our Savior Jesus Christ! And after that, as long as Christ gives, that long will I live. Enough of this, I've wandered a long way. Let's get back to my story.

We journeyed out of Daurija, and the food ran low. And with the brethren I entreated God, and Christ gave us a Siberian stag, a huge beast. With this we managed to sail to Lake Baikal. Sable hunters, Russians, had gathered in a camp by the lake; they were fishing. The good souls were glad to see us: dear Terentij and his comrades took us and our boat out of the lake and carried us far up the bank. Looking at us they wept, the dear souls, and looking at them we wept too. They heaped us with food, as much as we needed: they carted up about forty fresh sturgeon in front of me, and themselves said, "There you are, Father, God put them in our seines for you; take them all!" Bowing to them and blessing the fish, I commanded that they take them back again: "What need do I have of so many?"

We stayed with them awhile and then, taking a small provision near our need, we fixed the boat, rigged up a sail, and set out across the lake. The wind quit us on the lake, so we rowed with oars—the lake's not so almighty wide there, maybe eighty or a hundred versts. When we put into shore, a squall blew up and it was a hard pull finding a place to land because of the waves. Around it the mountains were high and the cliffs of rock, fearfully high; twenty thousand versts and more I've dragged myself, and I've never seen their like anywhere. Along their summits are halls and turrets, gates and pillars, stone walls and courtyards, all made by God.[72] Onions grow there and garlic, bigger than the Romanov onion and uncommonly sweet. Hemp grows there too in the care of God, and in the courtyards are beautiful flowers, most colorful and good-smelling. There's no end to the birds, to the geese and swans—like snow they swim on the lake. In it are fish, sturgeon and taimen salmon, sterlet and amul salmon, whitefish, and many other kinds. The water is fresh, but huge seals and sea lions live in it; in the great ocean sea I never saw their like when I was living at Mezen.[73] The lake swarms with fish. The sturgeon and taimen salmon are fat as can be; you can't fry them in a pan—there'd be nothing but fat left! And all this has been done for man through Jesus Christ our Light, so that finding peace he might lift up his praise to God. "But man is like to vanity; his days are as a shadow that passeth away." He cavorts like a goat, he puffs himself out like a bubble, he rages like a lynx, he craves food like a snake; gazing at the beauty of his neighbor, he neighs like a colt; he deceives like a devil; when he's gorged himself he sleeps, forgetting his office; he doesn't pray to God, he puts off repentance to his old age and then disappears. I do not know where he goes, whether into the light or into the darkness. Judgment Day will reveal it for each of us. Forgive me, I have sinned worse than all men.[74]

After this I sailed into Russian towns, and I meditated about the Church, that I "could prevail nothing, but that rather a tumult was made." Sitting there feeling heavy at heart, I pondered: "What shall I do? Preach the Word of God or hide out somewhere? For I am bound by my wife and children." And seeing me downcast, the Archpriestess approached in a manner most seemly and said unto me, "Why are you heavy at heart, my lord?" And in detail did I acquaint her with everything: "Wife, what shall I do? The winter of heresy is here. Should I speak out or keep quiet? I am bound by all of you!" And she said to me, "Lord a'mercy! What are you saying, Petrovič? I've heard the words of the Apostle—you were reading them yourself: 'Art thou bound unto a wife? Seek not to be loosed. Art thou loosed from a wife? Seek not a wife.'[75] I bless you together with our children. Now stand up and preach the Word of God like you used to and don't grieve over us. As long as God deigns, we'll live together and when we are separated, don't forget us in your prayers. Christ is strong, and He won't abandon us. Now go on, get to the church, Petrovič, unmask the whoredom of heresy!" Well sir, I bowed low to her for that, and shaking off the blindness of a heavy heart I began as before to preach and teach the Word of God about the towns and everywhere, and yet again did I unmask the Nikonian heresy with boldness.

I wintered in Yenisejsk, and after a summer of sailing, I again wintered in Tobol'sk.[76] And on the way to Moscow, in all the towns and villages, in churches and marketplaces I was ashouting, preaching the Word of God, and teaching, and unmasking the mummery of the godless. Then I arrived in Moscow. Three years I journeyed from Daurija, and going there I dragged along five years against the current.[77] I was carried ever to the east, right into the middle of native tribes and of their camps. There's much could be said about this! Time and again I was even in the natives' hands. On the Ob, that mighty river, they massacred twenty Christians before my eyes, and after thinking over me some, they let me go altogether. Again on the Irtysh River a group of them was lying in ambush for a prameful of our people from Berëzov. Not knowing this I sailed toward them, and drawing near I put in to shore. They leaped around us with their bows. Well sir, I stepped out and hugged them like they were monks, and myself said, "Christ is with me and with you too." And they started acting kindly toward me, and they brought their wives up to my wife. My wife likewise laid it on a bit, as flattery happens in this world, and the women folk warmed up too. We already knew that when the women folk are pleasant, then everything will be pleasant in Christ. The men hid their bows and arrows and started trading with me. I bought a pile of bearskins, yes, and then they let me go. When I came to Tobol'sk I told about this; people were amazed, since the Tatars and Bashkirs were warring all over Siberia then. And I, not choosing my way and hoping in Christ, I had journeyed right through the middle of them. I arrived in Verxoturie, and my friend Ivan Bogdanovič Kamynin was amazed at me: "How did you get through Archpriest?" And I said, "Christ carried me through, and the most immaculate Mother of God led me. I fear no one; only Christ do I fear."[78]

Afterward I came to Moscow; like unto an angel of the Lord was I received by the Sovereign and boyars—everyone was glad to see me. I dropped in on Fëdor Rtiščev; he leaped out of his chamber to greet me, received my blessing, and started talking on and on—three days and nights he wouldn't let me go home, and then he announced me to the Tsar.[79] The Sovereign commanded that I be brought then and there to kiss his hand, and he spoke charitable words: "Are you living in health, Archpriest? So God has ordained that we see one another again." And in answer I kissed and pressed his hand and said myself, "The Lord lives and my soul lives, my Sovereign and Tsar, but what's ahead will be as God deigns." And he sighed, the dear man, and went where he had to. And there were some other things, but why go on and on? That's all past now. He ordered me put in the monastery guest house in the Kremlin, and when his train passed my lodging, often he'd bow nice and low to me, and himself say, "Bless me and pray for me." And another time on horseback he took his cap off to me—a murmanka it was—and he dropped it.[80] He used to lean out of his carriage to see me. Later all the boyars after him started bowing and scraping too: "Archpriest, bless us and pray for us!" How, sir, can I help but feel sorry for that Tsar and those boyars? It's a pity, yes it is! You see how good they were. Yes, and even now they're not wicked to me. The Devil is wicked to me, but men are good to me. They were ready to give me a place wherever I wanted, and they called me to be their confessor, that I might unite with them in the faith. But I counted all this as dung and I gain Christ, being mindful of death, even as all this doth vanish away. . . .[81]

They saw that I was not joining them, so the Sovereign ordered Rodion Strešnev to convince me to keep quiet.[82] I eased his mind: "The Tsar is invested by God, and here he's been good as gold to me"—I expected he might come around little by little. And lo and behold, on St. Simeon's Day they vowed I would be placed in the printing house to correct books.[83] And I was mighty happy; for me this was needful, better even than being a confessor. He showed his favor and sent me ten rubles, the Tsarina likewise sent ten rubles, Luk"jan the Confessor also sent ten rubles, Rodion Strešnev sent ten rubles too, while our great and good old friend Fëdor Rtiščev, he ordered his treasurer to slip sixty rubles into my bonnet.[84] About others there's nothing more to say—everyone pushed and pulled something or other over. I lived all this time in the household of my light, my dear Feodos'ja Prokop'evna Morozova, as she was my spiritual daughter; and her sister Princess Evdokeja Prokop'evna was also my spiritual daughter. My lights, Christ's martyrs! And I was always visiting the home of our dear departed Anna Petrovna Miloslavskaja. And I went to Fëdor Rtiščev's to wrangle with the apostates.[85]

And so I lived this way near half a year, and I saw that these ecclesiastical triflings could prevail nothing but that rather a tumult was made, so I started grumbling again and even wrote a little something to the Tsar, that he should seek after the ancient piety and defend from heresies our common mother, the Holy Church, and that he should invest the patriarchal throne with an Orthodox shepherd instead of that wolf and apostate Nikon, the villainous heretic![86] And when I had prepared the letter, I fell grievously ill, so I sent it to the Tsar in his carriage by my spiritual son Fëdor, the fool in Christ, that Fëdor later strangled by the apostates at Mezen,[87] where they hanged him on the gallows. With boldness he stepped up to the Tsar's carriage with the letter, and the Tsar ordered him locked up in the Red Terrace, still with the letter.[88] He didn't know it was mine. But later, after taking the letter from him, he ordered him released. And Fëdor, our dear departed, after staying with me awhile, he came before the Tsar again in church, and there that blessed fool started in with his silly pranks. And the Tsar, being angered, ordered him sent to the Čudovskij Monastery. There Pavel the Archimandrite put him in irons, but by God's will the chains on his legs fell to pieces, before witnesses. And he, our light, our dear departed, he crawled into the hot oven in the bakery after the bread was taken out and he sat there, his bare backside against its bottom, and gathered the crumbs and ate them. So the monks were in terror, and they told the Archimandrite, who is now the Metropolitan Pavel. And he acquainted the Tsar with this, and the Tsar came to the monastery and ordered him set free in honor. And again he came back to me.

And from that time the Tsar started grieving over me. It wasn't so nice now that I had started to speak again; it had been nice for them when I kept quiet, but that didn't sit right with me. So the bishops started to buck and kick at me like goats, and they schemed to banish me from Moscow again, as many servants of Christ were coming to me, and comprehending the truth they stopped going to their worship with its seductive snares. And there was judgment from the Tsar for me. "The bishops are complaining about you," he said. "You've started to empty the churches. Go into exile again!"[89] The Boyar Pëtr Mixajlovič Saltykov told me this. And so we were taken off to Mezen.[90] Good people started to give us aplenty of this and that in the name of Christ, but it was all left behind. They only took me with my wife and children and the help. But passing through towns I again taught the people of God and those others I exposed for what they are, the motley beasts! And they brought us to Mezen.[91]

After keeping us there a year and a half, they took me to Moscow again alone.[92] My two sons Ivan and Prokopij also journeyed with me, but the Archpriestess and the rest all stayed at Mezen. After bringing me to Moscow, they took me under guard to Pafnut'ev Monastery.[93] And a message came there; over and over they kept saying the same thing: "Must you go on and on tormenting us? Join with us, dear old Avvakum!" I spurned them like devils, but they wouldn't stop plaguing me. I blistered them good in a statement I wrote there and sent along with Koz'ma, the Deacon of Yaroslavl, and a scribe in the Patriarch's Court. But Koz'ma, I don't know of what spirit that man is.[94] In public he tried to win me over, but on the sly he encouraged me, speaking so: "Archpriest! Don't abandon the ancient piety! You'll be a great man in Christ when you endure to the end. Don't pay attention to us, we are perishing!" And I said in answer that he should come again to Christ. And he said, "It's impossible. Nikon's tied me hand and foot!" Putting it simply, he'd renounced Christ before Nikon, and just that fast he couldn't stand on his own two feet, poor man. I wept and blessed him, the miserable soul. More than that there was nothing I could do for him. God knows what will become of him.

After keeping me in Pafnut'ev for ten weeks in chains, they took me again to Moscow, and in the Chamber of the Cross the bishops disputed with me,[95] then led me into the great cathedral, and after the Transposition of the Host they sheared the Deacon Fëdor and me, and then damned us, but I damned them in return.[96] Almighty lively it was during that Mass! And after keeping us awhile in the Patriarch's Court, they carried us away at night to Ugreša, to the Monastery of St. Nikola.[97] And those enemies of God cut off my beard. But what do you expect? They're wolves for a fact, they don't pity the sheep! Like dogs they tore at it, leaving me one tuft on my forehead like a Pole. They didn't take us to the monastery by the road but through marsh and mire so no one would get wind of it. They saw themselves they were acting like fools, but they wouldn't abandon their folly. Befogged by the Devil they were, so why grumble at them? If they hadn't done it someone else would have. . . .

They kept me at St. Nikola's for seventeen weeks in a freezing cell.[98]

There I had a heavenly visitation; read of it in my letter to the Tsar, you'll find it there. And the Tsar came to the monastery. He walked around my dungeon some, groaned, and left the monastery again. It seems from this he was sorry for me, but God willed it so. When they sheared me, there was great turmoil between them and the late Tsarina. She stood up for us then, the dear soul, and later on saved me from execution. Much could be said about this! God will forgive them! I'm not asking that they answer for my suffering now nor in the age to come. It behooves me to pray for them, for the living and for those resting in eternity. The Devil set the breach between us, but they were always good to me. Enough of this!

And Vorotynskij, our poor Prince Ivan, journeyed there without the Tsar to pray, and he asked to come into the dungeon to me, but they wouldn't let the poor soul in. Looking out the little window, I could only weep for him. My dear, sweet friend! He fears God, the little orphan in Christ! And Christ won't abandon him. Come what may, he's our man and Christ's man forever![99] And all those boyars were good to us, only the Devil was wicked. But what can you do if Christ suffered it to be so? They flogged our dear Prince Ivan Xovanskij with canes when Isaiah was burned.[100] They ruined Boyarina Feodos'ja Morozova altogether, killed her son, tortured her. And they flogged her sister Evdokeja with her, separated her from her children, and divorced her from her husband, Prince Pëtr Urusov, whom they married off to another woman. But what's to be done? Leave them be, the dear souls! In suffering they will gain the Heavenly Bridegroom. God will surely lead through this vain age, and the Heavenly Bridegroom will gather them to himself in his mansions, He who is the Sun of justice, our Light and our Hope! Once again, let's get back to my story.

Later they bore me away again to the Pafnut'ev Monastery, where they kept me locked up in a dark cell and in fetters nigh onto a year.[101] Here the cellarer Nikodim was good to me at first. But then, it seems, the poor man used some of that tobacco, sixty poods of which were afterward seized in the house of the Metropolitan of Gaza, along with a domra and other secret monastic doodads used in merrymaking. Forgive me, I have sinned, it's none of my business.[102] And he knows, "to his own master he standeth or falleth." This was said only in passing. . . .[103]

Our dear departed Fëdor, my poor strangled one, journeyed to me there on the sly with my children, and he asked of me, "How do you say I should go about, the old way in a long shirt, or should I don other clothes? The heretics are hunting for me and want to put me to death. I was in Riazan, under guard in the court of the Archbishop," he said, "and he, Ilarion, he tortured me no end—it was a rare day he didn't flog me with whips; he kept me fettered in irons, forcing me toward that new Sacrament of the Antichrist.[104]

I got weak, and at night I'd weep and pray, saying, 'O Lord, thou dost not deliver me, they will defile me and I will perish. What then wilst thou do for me?' " And much did he weep as I talked. "And lo," he said, "Suddenly, Father, all the irons fell from me with a crash, and the door unlocked and opened of itself.[105] So I bowed down to God and got out of there. I came up to the gates, and the gates were open! And I headed along the highroad, straight for Moscow. When it started to get light, here came the hunters on horses! Three men raced past, but they didn't catch sight of me. I was hoping in Christ and kept trudging along. Pretty soon they came riding back toward me barking, 'He took off, the son of a whore! Where can we nab him?' And again they rode past, without seeing me. So now I've trudged over here to ask whether I should go on back there and be tortured or put on other clothes and live in Moscow?" And I, sinner that I am, I directed him to put on the clothes. But I didn't manage to bury him outside the reach of the heretics' hands; they strangled him at Mezen, hanging him on the gallows. Eternal remembrance to him, together with Luka Lavrent′evič. My sweet, good little children! You have suffered for Christ! In them, glory be to God!

Uncommonly stern was the ascetic life of that Fëdor. During the day he played the blessed fool, but all night long he was at prayer with tears. I knew many a good person, but never had I seen such an ascetic! He lived with me about half a year in Moscow—I was still feeble—the two of us stayed in a little back room. Most of the time he'd lie down an hour or two, then get up; he'd toss off a thousand prostrations and then sit on the floor, or sometimes stand, and weep for maybe three hours. But even so I'd be lying down sometimes asleep, but sometimes too feeble to move. When he had wept his fill and even more, he'd come over to me: "How long are you going to lie there like that Archpriest? Get your wits about you. You're a priest, you know! How come you're not ashamed?" And I was very feeble, so he'd lift me up, saying, "Get up, sweet Father of mine, well, come on just drag yourself up somehow!" And he'd manage to stir some life into me. He'd tell me to recite the prayers sitting down, and he'd make the prostrations for me. A friend of my heart for certain! The dear soul was afflicted by this great overstraining. One time seven feet of his innards came out of him and another time twelve feet. Ailing like that and still he kept on measuring those entrails—with him you didn't know whether to laugh or cry! For five years without letup he froze barefoot in the frost in Ustiug, wandering around in just a long shirt.[106] I myself am his witness. There he became my spiritual son as I was coming back from Siberia. In the church vestry, he'd come running in for prayer and say, "When you first come out of that frost into the warm, Father, it's no end burdensome just then." And his feet clattered across the bricks like frozen blocks. But by morning they didn't hurt once again. He had a Psalter from the new printings in his cell then: he still knew only a little bit about the innovations. And I told him about the new books in detail. He grabbed the book and tossed it into the stove then and there, yes, and he damned all innovation. No end fiery was that faith of his in Christ! But why go on and on? As he began, so he ended. He didn't pass his radiant life in storytelling, not like me, accursed man. There's why he passed away in the odor of sanctity.

A fine man too was dear Afanasij, the good soul. My spiritual son he was; as a monk he was called Avraamij.[107] The apostates baked him in their fire in Moscow, and like sweet bread was he yielded up to the Holy Trinity. Before he took the cowl he wandered about both summer and winter barefoot, wearing just a long shirt. Only he was a little gentler than Fëdor, and a wee bit milder in his asceticism. He was a great lover of weeping—he'd walk and he'd weep. And if he was talking with someone, his words were quiet and even, like he was weeping. But Fëdor was most zealous; active no end in the business of God. He endeavored to destroy and expose untruth no matter what. But leave them be! As they lived, so they passed away in our Lord Jesus Christ.

I will chat with you some more about my wanderings. When they brought me from the Pafnut'ev Monastery to Moscow, they put me in a guest house, and after dragging me many a time to the Čudovskij Monastery, they stood me before the Ecumenical Council of Patriarchs.[108] And all of ours were sitting there too, like foxes. Much from Holy Writ did I say to the patriarchs; God opened my sinful lips and Christ put them to shame![109] They said to me at last, "Why are you so stubborn? All ours from Palestine—the Serbs, and Albanians, and Rumanians, and Romans, and Poles—they cross themselves with three fingers, but you stand here all alone in your stubbornness and cross yourself with two fingers.[110] This is not seemly!" But in Christ did I answer them, after this manner: "Teachers of Christendom! Rome fell long ago and lies never to rise. The Poles perished with her; to the end they were enemies of Christians. And Orthodoxy has become motley in color even with you, from violation by Mahomet the Turk. We can't be surprised at you, you are enfeebled. Henceforth, come to us to learn![111] By the Grace of God we have autocracy. In our Russia before Nikon the Apostate, the Orthodox faith of devout princes and tsars was always pure and spotless, and the Church was not mutinous. That wolf Nikon, in league with the Devil, betrayed us through this crossing with three fingers. But our first shepherds, just as they crossed themselves with two fingers, so did they bless others with two fingers according to the tradition of our Holy Fathers, Meletius of Antioch, and Theodoret the

Blessed, Bishop of Cyrrhus, and Peter of Damascus, and Maksim the Greek.[112] What is more, the wise Moscow Council during the reign of Tsar Ivan charged us to cross ourselves and to bless others by conforming our fingers in the manner taught by the Holy Fathers of the past,[113] Meletius and the others. At that council in the time of Tsar Ivan were the Bearers of the Sign Gurij and Varsonofij; the miracle workers of Kazan and Filipp, the Abbot of Solovki—all Russian saints!"[114]

And the patriarchs fell to thinking, but like a bunch of wolf whelps our Russians bounced up howling and began to vomit on their own Holy Fathers, saying, "They were stupid, our Russian saints had no understanding! They weren't learned people—why believe in them? They couldn't even read or write!" O Holy God, how didst Thou bear such great mortification of Thy saints? As for me, poor man, it was bitter, but nothing could be done. I blistered them, I blistered them as much as I could, and at last said unto them: "I am clean, and I shake off the dust clinging to my feet before you; according to that which is written: 'Better one who works the will of God than a multitude of the godless!' " So they started shouting at me even worse: "Seize him! Seize him! He has dishonored us all!"[115] And they started to shove me around and beat me—even the patriarchs threw themselves on me. There were about forty of them there, I expect—a mighty army for the Antichrist had come together! Ivan Uvarov grabbed me and dragged me around some, and I shouted, "Stop it! Don't beat me!" So they all jumped back. And I began to speak to the Archimandrite the interpreter:[116] "Say to the patriarchs: the Apostle Paul writes, 'For such a high priest became us, who is holy, harmless,' and so on:[117] but you after beating a man, how can you perform the liturgy?" So they sat down. And I walked over toward the doors and flopped down on my side. "You can sit, but I'll lie down," I said to them. So they laughed, "This archpriest's a fool! And he doesn't respect the patriarchs!" And I said to them, "We are fools for Christ's sake! Ye are honorable but we are despised! Ye are strong but we weak!"[118] Then the bishops again came over to me and started to speak with me about the Alleluia. Christ gave me the words: I shamed the whore of Rome within them through Dionysios Areopagite, as was said earlier in the beginning. And Evfimej, the cellarer of the Čudovskij Monastery, said, "You're right. There's nothing more for us to talk to you about." And they led me away in chains.[119]

Afterward the Tsar sent an officer with some musketeers, and they carried me off to the Sparrow Hills.[120] There too they brought the priest Lazar and the monk and elder Epifanij.[121] Shorn and abused like peasants from the village they were, the dear souls! Let a man with sense take a look and he'd just weep looking at them. But let them endure it! Why grieve over them?

Christ was better than they are, and He, our Light, He got the same from
their forefathers Annas and Caiaphas.[122] There's no reason to be surprised
at men nowadays—they've got a pattern for acting so! We should grieve a
bit for them, poor souls. Alas! you poor Nikonians! You are perishing from
your wicked, unruly ways!

Then they led us away from the Sparrow Hills to the Andreevskij Monastery and later to the Savvin Settlement.[123] The troop of musketeers
guarded us like brigands, even went with us to shit! Remember it, and you
don't know whether to laugh or cry. How Satan had befogged them! Then
to St. Nikola at Ugreša; there the Sovereign sent Captain Yurij Lutoxin to
me for my blessing, and we talked much about this and that.

Afterward they brought us again to Moscow, to the guest house of St.
Nikola's, and took still more statements from us concerning Orthodoxy.
The gentlemen of the bedchamber Artemon and Dementij were sent to me
many a time, and they spoke to me the Tsar's words: "Archpriest, I know
your pure and spotless and godly life, and I with the Tsarina and our
children beg your blessing. Pray for us!"[124] The messenger said this,
bowing the while. And I always weep for the Tsar; I'm mighty sorry for
him. And again he said, "Please listen to me. Unite with the ecumenical
bishops, only in some little thing." And I said to him, "Even if God
deigns that I die, I will not unite with the apostates! You are my Tsar," I
said, "but what business do they have with you? They lost their own tsar,
and now they come dragging in here to swallow you whole.[125] I will not
lower my arms from the heights of heaven," said I, "till God gives you
over to me!" And there were many such messages. This and that was
said. Finally he said, "Wherever you may be, don't forget us in your
prayers!" Even now, sinner that I am, I entreat God on his behalf as
much as I can.

Later, after mutilating my brethren but not me, they banished us to
Pustozersk.[126] And I sent the Tsar two letters from Pustozersk; the first was
short but the other longer. I talked about this and that. I told him in one
letter about certain signs from God shown me in my dungeons. He who
reads it there will understand.[127] Moreover, a small boon for true believers
was sent to Moscow, the Deacon's gleanings from the brethren and me, a
book, *The Answer of the Orthodox*, with an unmasking of the whoredom of
apostasy.[128] The truth about the dogmas of the Church is written in it. And
then two letters were also sent by the priest Lazar to the Tsar and the
Patriarch. And in return for all this some small boons were sent our way:
they hanged two people in my house at Mezen, my spiritual children—the
above-mentioned fool in Christ Fëdor and Luka Lavrent'evič, both servants
of Christ. This Luka was a Muscovite, his widowed mother's only child, a

tanner by trade, a youth of twenty-five. He journeyed with my children to Mezen, to his death. And when ruin had fallen everywhere upon my house, Pilate questioned him: "How do you cross yourself, peasant?" And he made answer with humble wisdom: "I believe and cross myself, conforming my fingers in the manner of my confessor, the Archpriest Avvakum." Pilate ordered him shut away in a dungeon. Later he placed a noose on his neck and hanged him from a gibbet. So he passed from earthly to heavenly things. What more could they do to him than this? Although he was a youngster he acted like an elder: went straight off to the Lord, he did! If only an old man could figure things out like that!

At that same time it was ordered that my two sons Ivan and Prokopij be hanged. They misreckoned, poor souls, and didn't figure out how to seize the crown of victory. Fearing death they owned their fault. So with their mother for a third they were buried alive in the earth. Now there's a death without death for you! Repent you two locked up there, while the Devil thinks something else! Death is fearsome—that's no surprise! Once denial was made by that close friend Peter too, "and he went out and wept bitterly." And because of his tears he was forgiven.[129] There's no reason to be surprised at these little ones; it's for my sinfulness that Christ suffered them such feebleness. And it's to the good, so be it! Christ is strong enough to have mercy and save us all!

Afterward that same Captain Ivan Elagin was with us at Pustozersk too, having journeyed from Mezen.[130] And he took a statement from us. Thus was it spoken: year and month, and again: "We preserve the ecclesiastical tradition of the Holy Fathers inviolate, and we curse the heretical council of the Palestinian Patriarch Paisij and his comrades." Quite a little else was said then, and a small part of it fell to the lot of Nikon, that breeder of heresies! So they took us to the scaffold, and after an edict was read they led me away to a dungeon without mutilating me. The edict read: "Imprison Avvakum in the earth in a log frame, and give him bread and water." And I spat in answer and wanted to starve myself to death. And I didn't eat for about eight days or more, but the brethren directed me to eat again.

Later they took the priest Lazar and cut his entire tongue from his throat. Just a bit of blood there was, and then it stopped. And he again spoke even without a tongue. Next they put his right hand on the block and chopped it off at the wrist, and lying there on the ground, of itself the severed hand composed its fingers according to tradition, and it lay that way a long time before the people. Poor thing, it confessed even in death the unchanging sign of the Savior. And that, sir, was a miracle that amazed even me: the lifeless convicted the living![131] On the third day after, I felt and stroked inside his mouth with my hand; it was all smooth, no tongue at all. But it didn't hurt. God granted him this speedy healing. They had sliced away at him in Moscow. Some of the tongue remained then but now everything was cut out, nothing left. But he spoke plainly for two years, as if with tongue. When two years had passed there was another miracle: in three days his tongue grew back complete, only a little bit blunt, and again he spoke, praising God and rebuking the apostates.

Later they took the Solovki hermit, the Elder Epifanij, a monk of the angelical image, and they cut out the rest of his tongue.[132] And four of his fingers were chopped off. At first he snuffled his words. Later he entreated the most immaculate Mother of God and both tongues, from Moscow and from here, were shown him on a communion cloth. He took one and put it in his mouth, and from that time he started to speak plainly and clearly. And he had a whole tongue in his mouth. Wonderful are the works of the Lord and inexpressible are the designs of the Most High! He suffers punishment, but He has mercy and heals again. But why go on and on? God's an old hand at miracles, He brings us from nonexistence to life. And surely He will resurrect all human flesh on the last day in the twinkling of an eye. But who can comprehend this? For God is this: He creates the new and renews the old. Glory be to Him in all things!

Later they took the Deacon Fëdor and cut out all the rest of his tongue. But they left a little piece in his mouth, cut slantwise across his throat. It healed then at that size, but afterward it again grew back about like the old one. And when it stuck out of his lips it was a little blunt. They chopped off his hand across the palm. God granted him healing in everything. And he spoke clearly and plainly. . . .[133]

Afterward they covered us up with earth: a log frame was set in the earth [for each of us], and around this another log frame, and again around all of them a common palisade with four bolts. . . .

Later Pilate left us, and after finishing up in Mezen he returned to Moscow.[134] And in Moscow others of ours were roasted and baked. Isaiah was burned, and later Avraamij was burned, and a great multitude of other champions of the Church was destroyed; God will reckon their number. It's a miracle, somehow they just do want to gain true understanding! They want to strengthen the faith by fire, the knout, and the gallows! Now which of the apostles taught that? I don't know. *My* Christ never commanded our apostles to teach this way, that we should bring people to the faith by fire, the knout, and the gallows. Thus was it spoken to apostles by our Lord: "Go ye into all the world and preach Gospel to every creature. He that believeth and is baptized shall be saved; but he that believeth not shall be damned."[135] You see, listener, Christ calls us to come freely; He did not command the apostles to burn the rebellious in the fire or hang them from the gallows. The Tatar god Mahomet wrote in his books after this manner: "It is our charge that the heads of those rebelling against our tradition and law be bowed down by the sword."[136] But our Christ never charged his disciples in this way. And these teachers are brazenfaced like spies of the Antichrist, who in bringing people to the faith destroy and give them over to death. As they believe, so do they act. It is written in the Gospel: "A good tree cannot bring forth evil fruit, neither can a corrupt tree bring forth good fruit; wherefore by its fruit shall each tree be known." [137]

But why go on and on? If there were no champions, there would be no crowns. For him who wants to be crowned, there's no point in going to Persia, Babylon's right here at home.[138] So how about it, you true believers, speak out the name of Christ, stand in the middle of Moscow and cross yourselves with the Sign of our Savior Jesus Christ with two fingers as we have been taught by the Holy Fathers. That's how the Kingdom of Heaven will appear for you right here at home! God will bless; just you suffer for the conformation of the fingers and don't reason overmuch. And I'm ready to die with you for this in Christ. Although I am a man without schooling, still I know that everything in the Church handed down from the Holy Fathers is holy and pure. I will keep the faith to my death just as I received it. I will not move the eternal boundaries established before our time! Let them lie thus forever and ever![139]

After this, I beg forgiveness from every true believer. It seems that, had things been different, there would be no need for me to talk about my life. I have read the Acts of the Apostles and the Epistles of Paul; the apostles reported concerning themselves when God was at work within them: "Not to us, but to our God be the glory!" But I am nothing. I have said, and will say anew:[140] "I am a sinful man, a whoremonger and a plunderer, a thief and a murderer, a friend to publicans and sinners, an accursed hypocrite before every man." Forgive me and pray for me, as I must for you who read and listen to me. I know nothing about living more than this, but what I do, I tell people about; may they pray to God for me! On Judgment Day everyone there will learn of my deeds, whether they be good or evil. But still, I am unschooled in words but not in understanding. I am unschooled in dialectics and rhetoric and philosophy, but I have Christ's understanding with me. As even the Apostle hath said: "Though I be rude in speech but not in understanding. . . ."[141]

Well, Elder, you've listened to more than enough of my gabbling. In the name of the Lord I command you: Write down for the servant of Christ how the Mother of God crumpled that devil in her hands and turned him over to you, and how those ants ate at your private parts, and how that devil set your wood on fire and your cell was burnt but everything in it remained whole, and how you shouted to Heaven, and whatever else you recall, to the glory of Christ and the Mother of God. . . . Tell away, never fear, just keep your conscience clear! Speak, seeking glory not for yourself but for Christ and the Mother of God. Let the servant of Christ rejoice in reading it. When we die, he will read and remember us before God. And we will entreat God on behalf of those who read and listen. They will be our people there at Christ's side, and we theirs, forever and ever. Amen.

Translation by Kenneth Brostrom

Notes to the translation begin on page 558.

RESOURCES

Primary Text

Robinson, A.N., ed. *Zhizneopisaniia Avvakuma i Epifaniia: issledovanie i teksty.* Moscow: Akademiia nauk SSSR, 1963.

Secondary Sources

Literary and Cultural Studies

Benz, Ernst. *The Eastern Orthodox Church: Its Thought and Life.* Garden City, NY: Doubleday Anchor, 1963.

Brostrom, Kenneth, ed. *Archpriest Avvakum. The Life Written by Himself. With the Study of V. V. Vinogradov.* Translations, annotations, commentary, and a historical introduction by Kenneth Brostrom. Ann Arbor: Michigan Slavic Publications, 1979. For the complete translated text and annotations.

Crummey, Robert. *The Old Believers and the World of the Antichrist: The Vyg Community and the Russian State.* Madison: University of Wisconsin Press, 1970.

Hunt, Priscilla, "Avvakúm Petróvich, Protopop (1620–82)." In *Handbook of Russian Literature,* ed. Victor Terras. New Haven: Yale University Press, 1985, pp. 29–31.

Likhachev, D.S. *Chelovek v literature drevnei Rusi.* 2nd ed. Moscow: Nauka, 1970.

———. *Poetika drevnerusskoi literatury.* Leningrad: Akademiia nauk SSSR, 1967.

———. *Velikoe nasledie: klassicheskie proizvedeniia literatury drevnei Rusi.* Moscow: Sovremennik, 1975.

Zenkovskii, Sergei. *Russkoe staroobriadchestvo.* Munich: Wilhelm Frank, 1970.

For additional entries (particularly for holy foolishness), see "Alexis, Holy Man of God."

Art and Architecture

Brumfield, W.C. *A History of Russian Architecture.* New York: Cambridge University Press, 1993, pp. 84–85; 142–44; 145; 164–65; 405, plate 64; 432; 435.

Lazarev, V.N. *Andrei Rublev*. Moscow: Sovetskii khudozhnik, 1960.
Surikov, V.A. *The Boyaryina Morozova* (1887). In *The Tretyakov Gallery Painting*, comp. V. Volodarsky. Leningrad: Aurora, 1981, plate 65.
Voloshin, M.A. *Surikov i Maksimilian Voloshin*. Introduction by V.N. Petrov. Leningrad: Khudozhnik RSFSR, 1985.
Vzdornov, G.I. *Trinity*. By Andrei Rublev. An Anthology. Moscow: Iskusstvo, 1981.

Music

Mussorgsky, Modest. *Khovanshchina*. Opera. Director, Vera Stroyeva. Music editor, Viktor Dombrovsky. Orchestration, D.S. Shostakovich. New York, 1987. One sound disk.

Film

Andrei Rublev. Director, Andrei Tarkovsky. Cinematographer, Vadim Kusov. Mosfilm, 1972.

～ III ～

The Search for Identity

In the eighteenth century Russia turned sharply to the West. The reforms of Peter the Great and of the German princess who became Catherine II reinforced the effects of a delayed Renaissance and of the Enlightenment values then active in Europe. The abruptness of the shift to the West—which became part of Russian culture in the mythology surrounding Peter's rough manners in breaking out a Western "window"—should not be magnified out of proportion. Direct contacts with the West had been quickly established after the Mongol era passed, long before Peter. By the seventeenth century there was already a great deal of economic, political, and cultural intercourse between Russia, neighbors such as Poland, and nations beyond. During the reign of Tsar Alexis (1629–1676), numerous foreigners settled in Moscow and other cities, and it was from them, in fact, that Peter learned some of his early lessons about Europe.

Nevertheless, both Peter and Catherine were extreme in their reforms; their passion for Western models helped create a cultural era in Russia that could be designated the Age of Imitation. Everything from art to zoology responded to Europe; indeed, the shape of the alphabet itself was revised in the light of Western cultural experience. Eventually, of course, through its engagements with the West, Russia became a great European power. Modernization, political aggrandizement, and the emerging contours of empire, however, were accompanied by a profound ambivalence in the cultural response.

On the one hand, the Russians took on, as their own, Renaissance and Enlightenment values emphasizing humankind's central positioning on earth; the manipulation of art, sculpture, and architecture in Neoclassicism to glorify earthly life; and respect for the reasoning and reasonable subject,

Falconet's Bronze Horseman, commissioned by Catherine II to honor Peter I, overlooks the Neva.

common sense, and the emerging empirical sciences. On the other, the limitations of reason, the empirical, the commonsensical, and merely earthly life also troubled men and women of the arts. Toward the end of the eighteenth century, such doubts took full-blown cultural shape in the form of an anti-Enlightenment. The native sources for such aesthetic and ideological ferment continued to be provided by opposing attachments to secularization and the long-standing religious tradition.

The State Russian Museum

Alexandre Benois (1870–1960) dedicated this illustration for Pushkin's "The Bronze Horseman" to his friend Sergei Diaghilev (1872–1929).

As is typical for Pushkin's works, "The Bronze Horseman" (1833) responds to literary and aesthetic tradition—such as the texts of his acquaintance, the Polish poet Adam Mickiewicz—as much as to history. The first part of the poem reflects the early myths of Peter and Petersburg created largely through the panegyrics and odes of Antioch Kantemir, Mikhail Lomonosov, Vasily Trediakovsky, and Aleksandr Sumarokov. In such works, Peter's policies represented the triumph of progress, reason (exemplified, for example, in the neat and logical grid of St. Petersburg streets), human will over nature, the West over Asia, empire over feudal chaos, and enlightened and benevolent monarchy over mob rule or the selfish interests of competing social classes. Étienne Falconet's statue of Peter (cast in 1782), which came to be known as the Bronze Horseman, reflects the same sense of progressive leadership and rational control triumphing over prejudice and ignorance, here in the guise of snakes.

The second part of the poem brings this image of Peter together with a by now familiar set of characteristics evoking humility, poverty, and madness. As counterpoint to the tsar, Pushkin creates the hapless Evgeny, a less than ordinary victim of the historical conditions that impelled the construction of a granite city in swamps and marshes. The new Russian capital's exposure to the elements and periodic flooding from the Neva River are used in Evgeny's story to play out moral and psychological issues concerning the individual's exposure to historical change. By virtue of his madness, a new variant of the holy fool's divine folly, this insignificant clerk glimpses fundamental conflicts between nature, personal life, and the hard and abstract schemes of progress imposed by politicians and their ideologies.

As Russian history moved toward twentieth-century totalitarianism, such conflicts became more acute. Petersburg retained its importance as an organizing and prodding symbol, first in the works of Gogol, Dostoevsky, and other nineteenth-century writers, then in the paintings of twentieth-century artists such as Kuzma Petrov-Vodkin (1878–1939), in literary texts such as Andrei Bely's *Petersburg*, and in poems such as those written by Anna Akhmatova and Osip Mandelstam. The Russians' continued fondness for the historical and moral complexities of Peter's work as a cultural symbol was evident in 1991, when the city discarded communism and regained its name.

Gavrila Derzhavin's (1743–1816) "Felicity," written in 1782, is closer to Enlightenment optimism and is less complex than Pushkin's view of the eighteenth century. Nevertheless, because of the relative rigidity of Neoclassical genre separations of his time, Derzhavin's text can be considered the more daring. The poem celebrates Catherine the Great in terms of allegory, one literary equivalent of the familiar Neoclassical architectural and sculptural imitations constructed in Petersburg and Moscow. In addition to Falconet and Marie Anne Collot's statue of Peter, these include the magnificent palaces and churches designed by Carlo Rossi, Vasily Bazhenov, Bartolomeo Rastrelli, and Charles Cameron.

At times the references to antiquity put an uncomfortable allegorical weight on the subject: two famous examples are Mikhail Kozlovsky's statue of the down-to-earth General Suvorov in the garb and body of a triumphant Mars (Petersburg, 1799–1801), and Ivan Martos's monumental sculpture on Moscow's Red Square of Kuzma Minin and Prince Dmitry Pozharsky (1804–18). The merchant and the prince, who organized the passionate resistance to Polish representatives of Latin civilization in 1612, are depicted as citizens of ancient Rome.

A less problematic example of Neoclassicism is the Academy of Arts building erected by Aleksandr Kokorinov and Jean-Baptiste Michel Vallin de la Mothe in St. Petersburg in the years 1764–88. Values of harmony and Doric order evident in this magnificent structure on the Neva River (as in the Stock Exchange constructed in 1805–10) elegantly honor principles of the Enlightenment in the medium of stone. Kozlovsky's sculpture *Alexander the Great's Vigil* (1780s) and Fedot Shubin's bust of Aleksandr Golitsyn (1775) express a similar respect for proportion and a search for high wisdom in the guise of the enlightened nobleman.

Allegory in all these aesthetic responses is used to suggest that moral order and the good life are linked with reason and a universal and timeless harmony of earthly things. In traditional fashion, Derzhavin sings Catherine's

praise in her Neoclassical guise of Felicity—the voice of virtue and common sense—but combines the high style reserved for such panegyrics with
the low style of satire. The literary result offers a new solution for the old
cultural task of confronting social-political reality with transcendent truths.
The difference is that for Derzhavin, firmly situated in the eighteenth century, it is Enlightenment rather than religious standards that are at issue.

The use of narrative perspective to these ends is well worth noting. In the
self-referential, groveling figure of the *murza*, Derzhavin creates humility
attributes worthy of Avvakum. The *murza* is the sum of the petty and major
immoralities Derzhavin sees in society and particularly in the society of his
fellow aristocrats. By unloading the vices of his class onto his fictional
persona and by contrasting them to the enlightened Felicity, the author
himself, of course, emerges as the unburdened defender of virtue positioned
close to the foot of the throne and ready to receive his just patronage from
it. An underlying message of "Felicity," indeed, is the system of patronage
that provided the economic backbone for all the magnificent examples of
the arts created in the eighteenth century.

War with the French and Napoleon's military offensive in 1812 made
explicit the problematic nature of political and cultural engagements with
Europe. After the Grand Army was driven back and Russian forces occupied
Paris, direct contact with a center of European civilization prodded additional
questions regarding national identity. Not surprisingly, in light of this historical experience, Russian culture at the end of the eighteenth century and
the beginning of the nineteenth was marked by alternating bursts of attrac-
tion and repulsion for the West.

A number of influential Western observers already had provided heady
stimulants for self-reflection and a quest for self-identity evoking Russia's
geographic location between Europe and Asia. Leibniz, Schelling, and
Voltaire, among others, all suggested that Russia had something new to
offer history thanks to its geocultural conditions, and they prodded the Russians
to assert a unique destiny. Two other Western thinkers, one a Frenchman,
Jean-Jacques Rousseau, the other a German inhabitant of Riga, Johann
Gottfried von Herder, exerted a particular cultural influence no less important
in Moscow and St. Petersburg than in Paris and Berlin. Pastor Herder made
the notion of cultural identity respectable and provided material for its
definition and assertion through his vastly influential and frequently translated collections of folk literature. Eventually, thanks in large part to
Herder, the search for a Russian cultural identity was frequently played out
in terms of folklore concerns, such as the song collections of the Slavophile
Ivan Kireevsky (1806–1856) and the fairy tales gathered by Aleksandr
Afanasiev (1826–1871). Rousseau channeled the moral terms in which a

society identifies its goals and culture in the same direction of ordinary and uncorrupted folks. Both appealed strongly to Russian sensibilities, which yearned for new, secular ways of asserting fundamental beliefs and values.

A reassertion of religious principles in secular forms was reflected in a revival of mysticism and rituals through Freemasonry, one of the important social phenomena of this period, and in politics in Alexander I's visionary Holy Alliance (soon to be brought down to earth by the practical Metternich). In literature, given their religious heritage of kenoticism and holy foolishness, it is not surprising that Russians were attracted to Rousseau's definition of a natural order beyond established social forms, or to his arguments for humble protagonists and the simple life. In various works of literature and theater, the somewhat eccentric Russian kenotic protagonist took off his or her hairshirt and put on the clean bucolic garb of a shepherd or a rosy-cheeked country girl. Outside of the external change of costume, the roles of such literary types remained the same: they offered emblems of suffering and meekness to reveal higher moral truths and to indicate the inadequacies of accepted social conditions.

The most important of such literary practices was sentimentalism, and one of its finest Russian achievements is generally recognized to be Nikolai Karamzin's "Poor Liza." Masculine wealth and social rank, in Karamzin's revision of the frequently repeated story, are revealed in all their spiritual inadequacy before a superior morality of feminine humility and meekness. Similar principles in Rousseau's *Émile* and Laurence Sterne's *Sentimental Journey* helped bring to prominence another genre: travel notes. The most famous, Aleksandr Radishchev's *Journey from St. Petersburg to Moscow* (1790), shocked readers with outrageous scenes of injustice and provoked a Siberian prison term for its author. Karamzin's *Letters of a Russian Traveler* (first installments published in 1791) took a different tack by noting Western inadequacies and suggesting the superiority of Peter the Great over Louis XIV. One of the most saccharine examples of sentimental travel literature, V.V. Izmailov's *Journey into Southern Russia* (1800–1802), was promptly parodied in Aleksandr Shakhavskoi's *A New Sterne* (1805) through the absurd love of an overly emotional nobleman for yet another peasant girl.

The quest for national identity often took place in the passionate debates of literary circles, discussion groups, and journals that sprang up and disappeared like Russian mushrooms. The Friendly Literary Society, the Free Society of Amateurs of Letters, the Sciences, and the Arts, and the Free Society of Amateurs of Russian Letters were among some of the four hundred gatherings that provided forums for writers and poets to air the pressing issues of the day. After 1812, a number of writers and poets found in such groups—Pavel Katenin, Konstantin Batiushkov, and Fedor Glinka, among others—were army officers who had returned to Russia from occupied Paris. Notable among them was Denis Davydov (1784–1839). This dashing poet-warrior became a sort of archetypal hussar thanks to Orest Kiprensky's (1782–1836) famous painting of Evgraf Davydov, completed in 1809 and often taken to be a portrait of his relative, and Tolstoy's fictional copy Vasily Denisov in *War and Peace*. The real Davydov created much-imitated poems and wrote on the inadequacy of the present in relation to the glory of the past.

The experience of such men made it difficult to look to the West as the unquestioned arbiter of social and cultural issues. A member of Tsar Alexander's honor guard in Paris, Petr Chaadaev (1784–1856), it is true, was inspired by the quest for identity to decide that Russian civilization had none. More typical were the views of two major literary gatherings, the Beseda circle (full title, Collegium of Amateurs of the Russian Word) and the Arzamas circle. The two groups, the first inspired by the work of Derzhavin and Admiral Aleksandr Shishkov, the second by Karamzin, focused on issues of language to decide Russian cultural directions. Shishkov argued against foreign influences, particularly French, while Karamzin and his followers attempted to demonstrate the advantages of a more open view. Arzamas undoubtedly won the debate, judging by the future evolution of Russian and the literary achievements of Alexander Pushkin, a sympathizer. In any case, the West kept popping up even in the most nationalistic of works, such as Vladislav Ozerov's play *Dmitry Donskoi* (1807). Written in the heyday of patriotic fervor, when Alexander I was eminently comparable to the epic hero Dmitry, the play still managed to portray its protagonist as a typical French romantic lead and one of Rousseau's sentimental literary progeny.

For the Russians, Mikhail Lermontov's (1814–1841) "Borodino" is one of the more familiar poems responding to patriotic tonalities. It was subsequently set to music, and the song became a part of Russian culture remembered with the sort of affection and frequent repetition the British afford "It's a Long Way to Tipperary" or the Americans "The Battle Hymn of the Republic." Lermontov followed Davydov's lead in contrasting the epic glory of the past to the inadequacies of the present. The sacrifice and courage of ordinary soldiers, vividly depicted in colloquial language, suggested the triumph of the common man and native virtues over the foreign emperor's intrusion.

Napoleon, of course, was also an important object of literary scrutiny and metaphor outside of Lermontov's poetry, first in Russian Romanticism influenced by Stendhal and Chateaubriand, then in such works as Tolstoy's *War and Peace*, which contrasts the emperor's superficial ideas about history to the humility of a typical kenotic figure, the peasant Platon Karataev. Tolstoy firmly rejected naive patriotism and maligned its consequences in war. He responded, however, to a period of Russian history when military engagements with the European powers stimulated a new national self-assertion and exerted a broad influence across the arts.

The most obvious cultural consequences were works of sculpture and architecture commemorating 1812, such as the huge Alexander I column erected by Auguste de Montferrand (1786–1858) in Petersburg's Palace Square (1832), Boris Orlovsky's (1793–1838) statues of General Kutuzov and Barclay de Tolly placed in front of St. Petersburg's Kazan Cathedral (itself completed in 1811, Kutuzov's burial place, and widely regarded as a monument to military power), and Fedor Tolstoy's (1783–1873) series of bas relief medallions now found in the Russian Museum of St. Petersburg.

Both architecture and sculpture begun after 1812 tended to assert national spirit by calling upon emigrés, Western classicism, and the Empire style. Typically, one of the more influential architects of this period, Osip (Joseph) Beauvais (frequently transliterated as Bove) (1784–1834), combined Neoclassical patriotism with European origins. Born to a family of Italian immigrants in Petersburg, he died in Moscow after leaving a strong imprint on the architecture of both cities. Reconstruction in Moscow of Theater Square and its principal occupant, the Petrovsky Theater before it became the Bolshoi, was done in grand Neoclassical style under his supervision from 1821 to 1824. Yet another Moscow fire led to further work by Albert Kavos in the 1850s on the building that is identified with the great works of nineteenth- and twentieth-century Russian opera and ballet.

Two other famous examples of architectural patriotism responding to Western models were Carlo Rossi's General Staff Building (1819–29) and Montferrand's St. Isaac's Cathedral (1818–58), both built in St. Petersburg. Just as Kazan Cathedral can be seen to echo St. Peter's in Rome, so St. Isaac's was intended to surpass London's St. Paul's. In music, in addition to Tchaikovsky's *1812* (1880), with its folk melodies, religious hymns, national anthem, and cannon fire, the post-Napoleon patriotic spirit and search for historical and national temperament led Vasily Zhukovsky (1783–1852) to suggest (as late as 1836) that Mikhail Glinka create the opera we have already noted, *A Life for the Tsar*, for which Nicholas I provided the title. In 1942, the year 1812 became the direct subject of opera when Sergei Prokofiev used *War and Peace* to compose yet another musical work that suggested patriotism, but it met with considerable resistance from Soviet bureaucrats.

If army officers and writers earlier traveled to Europe in person or through books, others such as Lermontov, Zhukovsky, Zagoskin, and

Pushkin now found new material—often refracted through European romantic perspectives—in those parts of Asia that had become Russia. Typical for this branch of Russian Orientalism was Pushkin's early poem "The Prisoner of the Caucasus" (1821), which was brought out in a first edition accompanied by a portrait of its author that hardly matched the blond and blue-eyed Russian stereotype. The Caucasus served Russian literature as the Balkans served the English, although, of course, historical and geographical circumstances made for a difference in the acuity of cultural response.

If Derzhavin's *murza* suggests a broad Western cliché for Oriental indolence and cunning standing in contrast to Catherine's European industry and reason, European thinkers such as Herder also encouraged the appreciation of Asian differences. Pechorin, the hero of Lermontov's *A Hero of Our Time* (1840), is defined for us in an Asian setting and in terms of his inability to respond properly to it. "Bela," the first chapter of the novel, in which Pechorin abducts, seduces, and abandons the Circassian young woman of the title, can be read as an allegory of imperialistic treatment of ethnic minorities. "Taman," a chapter that precedes "Bela" chronologically if not structurally, suggests a more complex and rueful explanation for Pechorin's moral-psychological makeup.

Pechorin enters Taman inspired by several stereotypes, including disdain for Asian backwardness and a Romantic appreciation for the physical charms of an Asian girl who he thinks is the reincarnation of Goethe's Mignon. He discovers his stereotypes are naive after she tries to drown him, and his naiveté gives way to the skepticism that marks his future relations with almost everyone, and women in particular. "Taman" suggests the debunkings of a protagonist's flawed perception and ethical vacuity in the presence of exotic ethnic groups that later also mark Tolstoy's *Cossacks* (1863).

As a skillful painter, Lermontov led the way in cross-representational uses of his work. He was followed by Mikhail Vrubel (1856–1910), who left a series of illustrations for *A Hero of Our Time*, and much later by Sergei Paradzhanov, who was inspired by Lermontov in creating the striking imagery of his film *Ashik-Kerib* (1989). Among other Lermontov texts that are not included here but that inspired cross-representational and cross-cultural activity, "Alone I step out on the road," written the year of his death in 1841, is of particular note. The poem became one of the most popular of sung romances, frequently repeated in Russian concert halls. Lermontov was inspired by Heine's "Der Tod, das ist die kühle Nacht," and Rilke returned the favor by translating the Russian verses into German. The text reflects both key elements of Romanticism—in particular, themes of alienation and the reach for extraordinary metaphysical contacts obtained from the religious heritage—and the continued presence of Romanticism in music long after literature moved on to a different way of seeing things.

Lermontov's narrative poem, "The Demon" (1841), in similar fashion, inspired Anton Rubenstein (1830–1894) to write an opera. The opera was given stage design by Vrubel, who also drew illustrations for an edition of the poem and for *A Hero of Our Time*, and who then painted a famous series of separate and increasingly more abstract canvases of Satan. Fedor Chaliapin, inspired by Vrubel, in turn created one of his famous roles in Rubinstein's opera (1904–6).

Among the more prolific cultural genres, which crossed over ethnic boundaries, perceptions of high and popular culture, and written and oral forms of art, was the fairy tale. As Roman Jakobson noted, the fairy tale's survival depended on its continuous and unabashed reflection of widely accepted values, what Jakobson calls a "consensus of the collective body," which inspired oral retelling of the story. As in the case of the closely related genres of epics such as *The Tale of Igor* and the *byliny*, then, fairy tales are useful as ways of noting fundamental cultural attachments.

The fairy tale frequently transcended its popular origins in spectacular ways, as in the poetic language of Alexander Pushkin. Pushkin began his career with the highly stylized folkloric entertainment of "Ruslan and Liudmila" (1820, second version 1828) and continued with "The Tale of the Tsar Sultan" (1831) and "The Tale of the Golden Cockerel" (1834). All were adapted to opera, the last two by Rimsky-Korsakov in 1900 and 1910, respectively, and the first by Mikhail Glinka in 1842.

A mythological creature from a number of Russian folk tales inspired another of the irrepressible Diaghilev's successes with the Ballets Russes in Paris, the ballet *Firebird* (1910). With music by a young Igor Stravinsky, choreography by Mikhail Fokine, and literary suggestions by Aleksei Remizov, the production set a new standard for collaboration among talented representatives of the different arts. The original Russian publication of "The Firebird and Princess Vasilisa" had already incorporated two different art forms. The story was first printed at the end of the eighteenth century in a chap edition, part of Russian *lubok* literature, which stressed woodblock illustrations but frequently included short written narratives.

The folk tale's presence in Russian literature indicates a fundamental cultural engagement with a broad range of ethnic groups in as well as outside of Europe. Versions of the firebird legend exist in the folk tales of Turks, Indians, Bashkirs, Tatars, Kazakhs, Ossetians, and Abkhazians, as well as Europeans from Italy. The oldest printed variants can be found in Straparola's *Le piacevoli notti* and Giambattista Basile's *Pentamerone* of

Hulton-Deutsche Collection

Tamara Karsavina (1885–1978) in the role of the Firebird in Diaghilev's Ballets Russes.

the sixteenth and seventeenth centuries. A closely related version became one of the more popular Russian narratives to cross over between children's literature and the stories read by adults, Petr Ershov's *Little Humpback Horse* (1834). Vasily Zhukovsky, inspired by his friend Pushkin and the time spent with him during the summer of 1831 outside St. Petersburg in Tsarskoe Selo, wrote a version titled "The Tale of Ivan the Tsarevich and the Gray Wolf." There are particular Russian emphases in this and other folk tales—the surprising constructive role played by gray wolves, the positive, even heroic presence of simpletons like Ivan the Fool—but on the whole,

"The Firebird and Princess Vasilisa" suggests a fundamental literary activity of popular culture operating freely across both European and Asian borders.

As is appropriate for a period involving intense border crossings in the arts, two of the texts offered below were translated by Vladimir Nabokov and Sir Charles Johnston, a writer and a poet with unique credentials in language and cultural affinities. Their work, as much as any of the modern responses already noted, demonstrates the rich potential for creative intersections that lies at the heart of Russian cultural identity.

N. R.

5

~Gavrila Derzhavin~

Felicity

Divine Tsarina
Of the Kirgiz and Kazakh dynasty!
Who is clever beyond compare,
Who showed the proper path
To young Prince Khlor[1]
To climb high up that mountain,
Where grows a rose that has no thorns,
Where virtue habitates—
It captivates my mind and spirit,
Please help me to attain its guidance.

Felicity, please show me:
To live well and in truth,
To tame one's passionate emotions
And to be happy on this earth.
Your voice moves me,
Your son is my companion;
But I'm too weak to follow them.
Buffeted by the vanities of life,
Today I might control myself,
Tomorrow I'm a slave of whims.

Unlike your *murzas*,[2]
You often walk on foot,
Your table's graced
By simplest food;
You do not value rest,
Reading and writing by a lectern
Bliss flowing to all mortals
From your pen;

You don't play cards,
As I, from morn to morn.

You don't care much for masquerades,
And you would not set foot into a club;
Preserving traditions, customs,
Quixotic you are not;
And do not saddle the Parnassian steed,[3]
You don't attend assemblies of ghosts,[4]
You don't turn Eastward from your throne;[5]
But following the humble path,
Soul full of worthy charity,
Your days flow by in useful matters.

But after sleeping half the day away,
I smoke tobacco and drink coffee;
Make every day a holiday,
My thoughts in chimeras I whirl away:
Now saving prisoners from Persians,
Now shooting arrows at the Turks;
Now I imagine I'm a Sultan,
Strike universal terror with my glance;
Or smitten suddenly by clothing,
Dash to the tailor for a *caftan.*[6]

Or at luxurious feast,
Holiday given in my honor,
Where tables sparkle silver and gold,
Resplendent with a thousand different courses;
And wonderful Westphalian ham,
And rows of fish from Astrakhan,
Pilaff and *pirogi,*
There with champagne I wash down waffles—
And forget all in the world
Immersed in wines, and sweets, and sweet aromas.

Or in a marvelous orchard,
In arbor, where a fountain murmurs,
While a sweet harp rings out,
Where breeze's breath is scarcely felt,
Where all is luxury,

Leading my thoughts to pleasures,
Tormenting and reviving blood,
On velvet divan I recline,
Stroke tenderly young maiden's feelings,
And fill with love her heart.

Or with a team of glorious horses
In gilded English carriage,
With dog, a jester, or a friend,
Or with some beauty
I amble by the swings;
And stop at taverns to drink mead;
Or if such then begins to bore me,
Since I am prone to change,
With cap askew,
I fly off on a frisky steed.

Then music and then singers,
Or organs all at once and pipes,
Or boxing bouts,
And dances cheer my spirit;
Or all my duties put aside,
I go off hunting
Finding amusement in dogs' barking;
Or on the shores of the Neva
I delight in the sound of evening horns[7]
And in bold oarsmen rowing.

Or sitting home I pass the time in mischief,
Play "fools" together with my wife;
With her I climb to peek at doves,
Or sometimes romp in hide and seek;
Together we enjoy the game of *Svaika*,
Or I use her to explore my hair;[8]
Or dig around in books,
Enlightening my heart and mind,
By reading of Polkan and Bova;[9]
Faced by the Bible, I then yawn and sleep.

That's my debauchery, Felicity!
But everyone resembles me.

Known for whatever wisdom,
Each person's still a lie.[10]
We follow not the paths of light,
We chase dreams of debauchery.
Among the whiner and the idle,[11]
Among all vanity and sin
One only finds, perhaps, by chance
A path direct to virtue.

Once found, can we weak mortals
Forbear from straying off the path,
When even reason stumbles
And is obliged to follow passions;
When learned dolts becloud our sight,
As mist obscuring sight for travelers?
Temptation, flattery surround us,
And luxury oppresses all the pashas.
Where then does virtue live?
Where grows the thornless rose?

To you alone can it be proper,
Tsarina, to create from darkness light;
To shape from chaos structured spheres,[12]
In union strengthen their integrity;
Out of dissension—harmony
Out of brutal desires—happiness
Alone you have the power to create.
The helmsman so, crossing the sea,
A roaring wind traps in the sails,
And can thus guide the ship.

It's you alone who won't treat people badly,
Nor insult anyone,
Abide tomfoolery,
And be intolerant to evil only;
You treat misdeeds with leniency,
Unlike a wolf with sheep, you do not stifle people,
You know their worth.
They're subject to their rulers' will,—
And more to righteous God,
Who lives within their laws.

You judge achievements sensibly,
Honor the well deserved,
You don't include among the prophets,
Who only can weave rhymes,
Although this mind's amusement
Honor and glory of the good Caliphs.[13]
You do indulge as lyric genre;
Poetry pleases you,
Appealing, sweet, and useful,
As summer's tasty lemonade.

It's said about your deeds,
That you are not at all immodest;
Agreeable in business as in fun,
Pleasant and firm in friendship;
Well balanced in misfortune,
But generous enough in glory,
That you refuse the title Wise.[14]
And truthfully it's said,
That it is always possible
To speak to you the truth.

Another matter that's unheard of,
And worthy of just you alone,
It's said that bravely you allow the people
Both in the open and in secret,
To know and think of everything,
And you do not prohibit
Uttering both the truth and rumors about you;
And that the very crocodiles,
Zoiluses of all your kind deeds,[15]
You're always inclined to forgive.

Rivers of tears so pleasant
Well up in my soul.
O! How content with destiny
The folk must be,
Where humble angel, peaceful angel,
Concealed in a purple radiance,
Is heaven sent to take the scepter!
Where conversations may be whispered,

And one does not fear execution after dinner
For toasting not the health of tsars.[16]

There one can smear in accident,
The name Felicity with blotted ink,
Or carelessly to drop
Her portrait to the ground.
There buffoon weddings are not given,
Nor people steamed in an ice bath,[17]
Noblemen's whiskers are not tweeked,
Grand princes, do not cluck as hens,
Nor favorites openly humor them by laughter
Or faces smear with soot.

You know, Felicity! the rights
Of human beings and of tsars;
When you enlighten mores,
You don't befuddle people;
When resting from government matters
You shape morality from tales
And through his alphabet teach Khlor:
"If you will stay away from evil,
The cruelest satirist around
Will prove to be a despised liar."

You are ashamed to be called great,
Lest you elicit fear or hatred;
A savage she-bear should alone
Destroy animals, drink their blood.
Except in the disaster of high fever,
Are lancets wanted if,
They could be done without?
And is it glorious to be a tyrant,
A Tamerlane, in brutality great,[18]
For one whose greatness lies in the benevolence of God?

Felicity—your glory—is God's glory,
You stopped the battles;
Who gave shelter, clothing, food aplenty
To orphans and the poor;
Who grants with eyes of radiance

To fools, cowards, and the ungrateful
As well as righteous men the light;
All mortals equally enlightens,
Comforts the ill, and heals,
Does good alone for goodness' sake.

Who granted freedom
To go to foreign lands,
Who gave permission for the people
To search for silver and for gold;
Who freed the use of waterways
And gave forests to be felled;
Who ordered weaving, spinning, sewing:
Freeing the hands and mind;
Commanded love be given trade and learning
And happiness be found at home.

Whose use of law, as one's right hand
Creates benevolence and justice.
Proclaim, oh wise Felicity!
Where honest men are so distinct from swindlers?
Where in this world wanders not old age?
And merit finds its daily bread?
Where vengeance does no one inspire?
Where conscience, truth are side by side?
Where virtuous human beings shine?—
Only perhaps next to your throne!

But where does your throne shine in this world?
Where blossom you, heavenly branch?
In Baghdad, Smyrna, or Kashmir?
Listen, wherever you reside—
Noting the praises that I give you,
Don't think I hope for jackets, hats
From you to pay for them.
To feel the charm of kindness
Such is real treasure for the soul,
Which Croesus never did acquire.[19]

I ask, let me, great prophet,
Touch dust that's of your feet,

Enjoy your words in their sweet current
And delight in your countenance!
I ask the heavens for their strength,
To spread over you sapphire wings,
Invisibly to thus protect you.
From all the ills, from evil, boredom;
That for posterity your deeds,
Will sound as stars in heavens shine.

1782

Translation by Victoria Gleizer and Nicholas Rzhevsky

Notes to the translation begin on page 573.

Resources

Primary Text

Derzhavin, G.R. "Felitsa." In *Stikhotvoreniia*, ed. V.P. Druzin. Moscow–Leningrad: Sovetskii pisatel', 1963, pp. 82–91.

Secondary Sources

Literary and Cultural Studies

Billington, James H. *The Icon and the Axe: An Interpretive History of Russian Culture.* New York: Vintage, 1966, pp. 208–68.
Eikhenbaum, B.M. "Poetika Derzhavina." *Apollon*, no. 8 (1916).
Hart, Pierre. *G.R. Derzhavin: A Poet's Progress.* Columbus, OH: Slavica, 1978.
Kulakova, L.I. *Ocherki istorii russkoi esteticheskoi mysli XVIII veka.* Leningrad: Prosveshchenie, 1968.
Madariaga, Isabel de. *Russia in the Age of Catherine the Great.* New Haven: Yale University Press, 1981.
Rybakov, B.A., ed. *Ocherki russkoi kul'tury XVIII veka.* Vols. 1–4. Moscow: MGU Press, 1988.
Segel, Harold, ed. and trans. *The Literature of Eighteenth-Century Russia.* Vols. 1–2. New York: Dutton, 1967.
Wren, Melvin. *The Western Impact upon Tsarist Russia.* Chicago: Holt, Rinehart & Winston, 1971.

Art and Architecture

Brumfield, W.C. *A History of Russian Architecture.* Cambridge–New York: Cambridge University Press, 1993, pp. 228–409.
Evsina, N.A. *Russkaia arkhitektura v epokhu Ekateriny II.* Moscow: Nauka, 1994.
Sokolova, Natalya, ed. *Selected Works of Russian Art: Architecture, Sculpture, Painting, Graphic Art: 11th–20th Century.* Leningrad: Aurora, 1976, plates 25–69.

~Anonymous~

The Firebird and Princess Vasilisa

In a certain kingdom, beyond thrice-nine lands in the thrice-tenth, there lived a strong and powerful tsar. This tsar had a fine and valiant archer, and this fine and valiant archer had a magnificent and heroic stallion. One day the valiant archer rode off on his heroic stallion to hunt in the forest; he rode along the path, then rode along the high road, until he suddenly came upon the golden feather of a firebird, sparkling before his eyes as if aflame! His heroic stallion warned him: "Do not take the golden feather; if you take it, great sorrow you will know!" And the valiant archer immersed himself in deep thought—pick it up or not? For to pick up the golden feather and present it to the tsar meant he would be offered a reward; and who does not cherish a tsar's generosity?

The valiant archer did not listen to his stallion. He took the firebird's golden feather and brought it to the tsar as a gift. "Thank you!" said the tsar. "Now since you have found the firebird's feather, why not bring to me the firebird itself? And if you do not, off with your head by my sword!" The valiant archer shed bitter tears and went to his stallion.

"Why do you cry, master?" said the stallion.

"The tsar ordered me to find the firebird," he answered.

"I told you," replied the stallion, "do not take the firebird's feather. If you do, great misfortune you will know! But, do not fear, and do not grieve, this is not real misfortune, real misfortune is still ahead! Go to the tsar and ask that by tomorrow one hundred measures of bright white wheat be spread upon the virgin field."

And the tsar ordered one hundred measures of bright white wheat to be spread on the virgin field. The next day at dawn, the valiant archer rode to that field and let his stallion roam freely while he himself hid behind a tree. Suddenly, the forest stirred and the waves rose upon the sea; it was the firebird in flight; she landed and began to peck the wheat. The magnificent stallion approached the firebird, stepped on her wing, and pressed it hard to the ground. The valiant archer then jumped from behind the tree, ran to the firebird, and tied her with his ropes. He sat on his stallion and rode to the palace. When he brought the firebird to the tsar, the tsar rejoiced, thanked the archer for his services, promoted him to a higher rank, and immediately presented him with another task.

"Since you were able to find the firebird, find me a bride; beyond thrice-nine lands, on the very edge of the world, where the red sun rises, lives Princess Vasilisa—she is the one I desire. If you bring her, I will reward you with gold and silver, and if you do not, off with your head by my sword!"

The valiant archer overflowed with bitter tears and went to his stallion.

"Why do you cry, master?" asked the stallion.

"The tsar ordered me to bring him Princess Vasilisa," said the archer.

"Do not cry, do not worry; this is not real misfortune, real misfortune is still ahead," replied the stallion. "Go to the tsar, ask for a tent with a golden top and various provisions and drinks for the journey."

The tsar gave the archer provisions and drinks and a tent with a golden top. The valiant archer sat on his heroic stallion and left for the thrice-nine faraway land. Whether it was after a long while or after a short while but eventually he came upon the edge of the world where the red sun rises from the blue sea. The valiant archer looked at the blue sea and saw Princess Vasilisa on a silver boat and rowing with golden oars. The valiant archer let his stallion roam the green fields and nibble the fresh grass while he set up the tent with the golden top, spread out the provisions and drinks, sat down in the tent, and treated himself while waiting for the Princess Vasilisa.

Princess Vasilisa saw the golden top, sailed up to the shore, stepped off the boat, and began to admire the tent.

"Good day, Princess Vasilisa!" said the archer. "Welcome. Be my guest, share my bread and salt, and taste these wines from beyond the seas."

Princess Vasilisa entered the tent, they began to eat and drink, and to enjoy themselves. The princess drank a glass of wine from beyond the seas, became tipsy, and fell into a deep sleep. The valiant archer called to his heroic stallion, and the stallion ran up; the archer immediately took down the tent with the golden top, sat on the heroic stallion, picked up the sleeping Princess Vasilisa, and set off on his journey with the speed of an arrow shot out of a bow.

He came to the tsar, who was overjoyed upon seeing the princess. The tsar thanked the archer for his faithful service and rewarded him with a great treasure and appointed him to a great rank. When the princess woke up and realized she was far, far away from the blue sea, she began to cry and to feel melancholy, and her face changed completely. No matter how much the tsar tried to appease her, all was in vain. And so the tsar got the idea of marrying her, but she stated: "Let the one who brought me here go to the blue sea, there in the middle of the water lies a huge stone, under which is hidden my wedding dress. Without that dress I will not marry!"

The tsar immediately sent for the valiant archer: "Go at once to the edge of the world, where the red sun rises, there in the blue sea lies a huge stone, under which is hidden Princess Vasilisa's wedding dress. Get that dress and bring it here; it's time we had the wedding! If you get it you will receive an even bigger reward than before, and if you don't, it will be off with your head by my sword!"

The valiant archer overflowed with bitter tears and went to his heroic stallion. "Now," he thought, "I will not avoid death!"

"What are you crying about, my master?" asked the stallion.

"The tsar ordered me to retrieve Princess Vasilisa's wedding dress from the bottom of the ocean," said the archer.

"I told you not to take the golden feather, that it will bring you sorrow! But do not fear, this is not real misfortune, real misfortune is still ahead. Sit on me and we will ride to the blue sea."

Whether after a long while or after a short while but eventually the valiant archer rode up to the edge of the world and stopped at the blue sea. The heroic stallion saw that a very large sea crab was crawling on the sand and so he stepped on its little neck with his heavy hoof.

The sea crab spoke up: "Don't bring death unto me, give me life! I will do whatever you want."

And the stallion answered: "In the middle of the blue ocean there lies a huge stone, under it is hidden Princess Vasilisa's wedding dress. Get that dress!"

The sea crab shouted in a loud voice to all of the blue sea, the sea immediately stirred and from all over big and small crabs crawled upon the shore—a multitude of them! The elder sea crab gave the order and they all threw themselves into the water and in an hour's time dragged out from the bottom of the sea, from under the huge stone, Princess Vasilisa's wedding dress.

The valiant archer came to the tsar and brought to him the princess's dress, but the princess again replied stubbornly: "I will not marry you until you command your valiant archer to bathe in hot water."

The tsar ordered that a cast-iron cauldron be filled with water and brought to a boil so that the valiant archer could be thrown into the steaming liquid. When everything was ready and the water was boiling, bubbling all over, the poor archer was brought to the cauldron. "Now, this is misfortune," he thought. "Oh, why did I take the firebird's golden feather? Why did I not listen to the stallion?"

He remembered his heroic stallion and said to the tsar: "Oh, mighty sovereign tsar! Please allow me to go and bid farewell to my stallion before I die."

"Very well, go bid him farewell," said the tsar.

The archer came to his heroic stallion and began to weep profusely.

"Why are you weeping, my master?" said the stallion.

"The tsar has ordered me to bathe in boiling water," replied the archer.

"Do not be afraid, do not cry, you will live!" said the stallion and quickly put a spell on the archer so that the boiling water would not harm his white body. The archer returned from the stable and immediately he was grabbed by the servants and was thrown straight into the cauldron. He immersed himself in the water once or twice, jumped out of the cauldron, and turned into such a handsome young lad, that not even a fairy tale or a pen could describe.

When the tsar saw how handsome the archer had become, he himself wanted to take a bath and so like an idiot he jumped into the water and in that same minute was boiled alive. The tsar was buried, and to replace him they chose the valiant archer. He married the Princess Vasilisa, and they lived for many years in love and harmony.

Translation by Tatiana G. Rzhevsky

RESOURCES

Primary Text

Afanas'ev, A.N. "Zhar-ptitsa i Vasilisa-Tsarevna." *Narodnye russkie skazki v trekh tomakh*. Vol. 1. Moscow: Nauka, 1984, pp. 344–46.

Secondary Sources

Literary and Cultural Studies

Abraham, Gerald. *Rimsky-Korsakov*. London: Duckworth, 1945.

Fokin, M. *Protiv techeniia*. Moscow–Leningrad: Iskusstvo, 1962.

Kireevsky, Ivan. "On the Nature of Pushkin's Poetry." In *Literature and National Identity: Nineteenth-Century Russian Critical Essays*, ed. Paul Debreczeny. Lincoln: University of Nebraska Press, 1978, pp. 3–16.

Savchenko, S. *Russkaia narodnaia skazka*. Kiev: Tip. Imp. universiteta sv. Vladimira, 1914.

Sokolov, B. *Russkii fol'klor I–II*. Moscow: Gos. Uchebno-pedagog. izd., 1941.

Spender, Charles. *The World of Serge Diaghilev*. Chicago: Henry Regnery, 1974.

Stravinsky, Igor. *An Autobiography*. New York: Simon & Schuster, 1936.

Literature

Anikin, V.P., D.S. Likhachev, and T.N. Mikhel'son, comp. *Byliny; Russkie narodnye skazki; drevnerusskie povesti.* Moscow: Detskaia literatura, 1979.
Costello, D.P., and I.P. Foote, eds. *Russian Folk Literature: Skazki, Liricheskie Pesni, Byliny, Istoricheskie Pesni, Dukhovnye Stikhi.* Oxford: Clarendon, 1967.
Guterman, Norbert, trans. *Russian Fairy Tales, from the collection of Aleksandr Afanas'ev.* Commentary by Roman Jakobson. New York: Random House, 1973.
Pudova, K., ed. *Alen'kii tsvetochek. Skazki russkikh pisatelei.* Leningrad: Detskaia literatura, 1989.
Reeder, Roberta, ed. *Down Along the Mother Volga.* Philadelphia: University of Pennsylvania Press, 1975.
Serov, S., ed. *Gorodok v tabakerke. Skazki russkikh pisatelei.* Moscow: Pravda, 1989.

Art

Afanas'ev, A.N. *Narodnye russkie skazki v trekh tomakh.* Vol. 1. Moscow: Nauka, 1984, pp. 337–42. For examples of *lubok* illustrations.
Zinov'ev, N.M. *Iskusstvo Palekha.* Leningrad: Khudozhestvo RSFSR, 1968, p. 161.

Drama and Theater Recording

Ershov, Petr. *Konek-Gorbunok.* Read by O. Tabakov. Music, Igor Stravinsky and A. Liadov. Director, V. Khramov. Melodiia, 1989.

Dance

The Firebird. The Royal Ballet. BBC telecast, February 18, 1965. 40 minutes.
Konek-Gorbunok. Director, D. Brantsev. Cast: V. Kirillov, M. Drozdova, V. Sarkisov. Video. Moscow: Stanislavsky Theater, n.d. Distributed by Russian-American Educational Services, Fort Lee, NJ (hereafter RAES).
Krasovskaia, V.M., ed. *Sovetskii baletnyi teatr.* Moscow: Iskusstvo, 1976. Photographs of *Little Humpbacked Horse* in the Kirov Maly Theater and the Bolshoi Theater.

Music

Rimsky-Korsakov, Nikolai A. *Zolotoi petushok.* Opera in 3 acts. Libretto, V. Belyskii. Cast: E. Nesterenko and E. Ustinova. Conductor, Dmitrii Kitaenko. Moscow State Philharmonic Orchestra. Moscow: Melodiia, 1989.
Shchedrin, R. *The Humpbacked Horse.* Ballet in 2 acts. Choreographer, G. Zemchuzhin. Moscow: Stanislavsky Theater, n.d.
Stravinsky, Igor, *The Firebird.* Original 1910 musical score. New York: Dover, 1987.
———. *Zhar-ptitsa.* Musical score. New York: Schott Music, 1933.
———. *Zhar-ptitsa. Skazka-balet v dvukh kartinakh.* Moscow Philharmonic Symphony Orchestra. Conductor, Dmitrii Kitaenko. Melodiia, 1985.

~Nikolai Karamzin~

Poor Liza

Perhaps no one living in Moscow knows the environs of this city as well as I do, because no one spends as much time in the fields as I do, no one wanders around on foot, without a plan, without a goal, wherever his eyes may take him, through meadows and groves, through hills and plains. Every summer I find new pleasant places or fresh beauty in the old ones.

But for me, the most pleasant place of all is the one above which rise the gloomy Gothic towers of the Simonov Monastery.[1] Standing on this hill, you see almost all of Moscow to the right, the terrible mass of houses and churches, which appear before our eyes in the form of a majestic amphitheater: a magnificent picture, especially when the sun is shining on it, when the evening rays burn upon the countless golden cupolas, upon the countless golden crosses rising to the sky! Below, the fertile, dark green, blossoming meadows stretch out, and beyond them, over the yellow sands, the clear river flows, billowing from the light oars of the fishing boats or roaring under the rudders of the massive ships that sail from the fruitful lands of the Russian Empire and provide greedy Moscow with bread. On the other side of the river one can see an oak grove beside which graze numerous herds; there, young shepherds sitting in the shade of the trees sing simple, melancholy songs, thereby shortening the summer days so monotonous for them. A little farther, among the thick, green, ancient elms, shines the golden dome of the Danilov Monastery;[2] and still farther, almost at the edge of the horizon, the Sparrow Hills show blue.[3] On the left side are the vast fields covered with grain, forests, three or four small villages, and, in the distance, the village of Kolomenskoe with its tall palace.[4]

I often come to this spot and almost always welcome the spring here; I also come here in the gloomy days of autumn to grieve along with Nature. The winds howl frightfully in the walls of the deserted monastery,[5] among the graves covered with tall grass, and in the dark passages of its cells. There, leaning on the ruins of the awesome stones, I heed the dull moan of times that have been swallowed up in the abyss of the past, a moan that makes my heart shudder and tremble. Sometimes, I enter the cells and imagine those who used to live there—sad pictures! Here I see a gray-haired old man kneeling before a crucifix and praying for the quick dissolution of his earthly bonds: for all the joy has disappeared from his life, all his feelings have died except those of sickness and weakness. There a young monk with a pale face and languid gaze looks out to the field through the bars on the window; he sees happy birds swimming freely through the sea of air—he sees them and bitter tears pour from his eyes. He languishes, withers, wastes away; and the doleful ringing of the church bell announces his untimely death. Sometimes I look at the depiction on the church gates of miracles that occurred in the monastery—there fish fall from the sky for the nourishment of the inhabitants of the monastery, which had been besieged by numerous enemies; here an icon of the Virgin Mary turns foes to flight. All of this renews in my memory the story of our forefathers—the sad story of those times when the fierce Tatars and Lithuanians laid waste with fire and sword the environs of the Russian capital and when unhappy Moscow, like a defenseless widow, waited for help in the midst of its ferocious calamities solely from God.

But more often, I am attracted to the walls of the Simonov Monastery by the memory of the lamentable fate of Liza, poor Liza. Oh! I love those things that touch my heart and make me shed tears of tender sorrow.

About a hundred and sixty yards from the monastery wall, beside a birch grove in the middle of the green meadow, stands an empty cottage, without doors, windows, or floor; the roof has long since rotted and caved in. In this cottage about thirty years ago lived beautiful, kind Liza and an old woman, her mother.

Liza's father was a rather well-to-do peasant because he loved work, plowed the land well, and always led a sober life. But soon after his death, his wife and daughter became impoverished. The lazy hired hand cultivated the fields poorly, and the grain stopped growing well. They were forced to rent their land and for an extremely small sum. Besides, the poor widow, almost continuously shedding tears over the death of her husband—for even peasant women know how to love!—became weaker by the day and was no longer able to work. Only Liza—who was fifteen when her father died—only Liza worked day and night, sparing neither her gentle youth nor her rare beauty, weaving sackcloth and knitting stockings, picking flowers in the spring, gathering berries in the summer, and selling them in Moscow. The sensitive, kind old woman, seeing the tireless industry of her daughter, often pressed her to her weakly beating heart, calling her God's mercy, her breadwinner, and the joy of her old age, and she prayed that God would reward her for everything she was doing for her mother.

"God gave me hands so I could work," said Liza. "Your breast fed me and took care of me when I was a baby; now it's my turn to take care of you. Just stop grieving, stop crying. Our tears won't bring father back."

But often gentle Liza could not help crying herself. Oh! She remembered that she once had a father and that now he was gone; for her mother's sake, however, she tried to conceal the sadness in her heart and to appear calm and happy.

"In the other world, dear Liza," answered the mournful old woman, "in the other world, I'll stop crying. There, they say, everyone will be happy; I'll probably be happy when I see your father. Only I don't want to die now—what will happen to you without me? Whom can I leave you with? No, first let God find a place for you! Maybe a kind man will appear soon. Then, blessing you my dear children, I will cross myself and lie down calmly in the damp earth."

About two years passed after the death of Liza's father. The meadows filled with flowers, and Liza went to Moscow with lilies of the valley. A young, well-dressed man of pleasant appearance encountered her on the street. She showed him her flowers and blushed.

"Are you selling these, young lady?" he asked with a smile.

"I am," she answered.

"And how much do you want?"

"Five kopeks."

"That's too little. Here's a ruble."

Liza was surprised, dared to glance up at the young man, blushed even more, and lowering her eyes to the ground told him she would not take the ruble.

"Why not?"

"I don't need extra."

"I think that beautiful lilies of the valley picked by a beautiful girl are worth a ruble. But since you won't take it, here are five kopeks. I would always like to buy flowers from you. I'd like it if you would pick the flowers only for me."

Liza gave him the flowers, took the five kopeks, bowed, and wanted to go; but the stranger stopped her by the arm:

"Where are you going, young lady?"

"Home."

"And where is your home?"

Liza told him where she lived; she told him and she left. The young man did not wish to keep her from leaving, perhaps because passersby were beginning to stop, look at them, and smile cunningly.

Arriving home Liza told her mother what had happened.

"You did well not to take the ruble. Maybe he was some kind of bad person . . ."

"Oh no, mother! I don't think so. He had such a kind face, such a voice . . ."

"Still, Liza, it's better to feed yourself by your own labors and not to take anything for free. You still don't know, my dear, how evil people can hurt a poor girl! My heart is never at peace when you go to the city. I always put a candle in front of the icon and pray that the Lord God preserve you from any misfortune and harm!"

Tears welled up in Liza's eyes; she kissed her mother.

The next day, Liza picked the best lilies of the valley and once again went to the city with them. Her eyes quietly searched for something. Many people wanted to buy the flowers from her, but she answered that they weren't for sale and looked from one side to the other. Evening set in, she had to return home, and the flowers were thrown into the Moscow River.

"No one will own you!" said Liza, feeling a sort of sadness in her heart.

The next day toward evening she was sitting by the window, spinning and singing plaintive songs in a soft voice, but suddenly she jumped up and cried out, "Oh! . . ." The young stranger was standing by the window.

"What's happened?" asked her frightened mother, who was sitting beside her.

"It's nothing, mother," Liza answered in a timid voice. "I just saw him."

"Whom?"

"That gentleman who bought the flowers from me."

The old woman looked out the window. The young man bowed to her so courteously, in such a pleasant manner, that she could think nothing but good of him.

"How do you do, kind old woman!" he said. "I am very tired. Do you have some fresh milk?"

The obliging Liza, without waiting for her mother's response—perhaps because she knew it in advance—ran to the cellar, brought a clean milk pot covered with a clean wooden disc, grabbed a glass, washed it, wiped it with a white towel, poured the milk, and offered it through the window, all the while looking at the ground herself. The stranger drank up, and nectar from the hands of Hebe could not have been more delicious.[6] Everyone will guess that afterward he thanked Liza, and he thanked her not so much in words as in looks. In the meantime, the good-hearted old woman told him about her grief and consolation—about the death of her husband and about her daughter's good nature, about her diligence and her gentleness, and so on, and so forth. He listened attentively to her, but his eyes were—well, need one say where? And Liza, shy Liza, occasionally glanced at the young man; but lightning does not flash and disappear into a cloud as quickly as her blue eyes turned toward the ground when they met his glance.

"I would like," he said to the mother, "for your daughter to sell her work to no one but me. Thus, she would not have to go to the city as often, and you would not have to part with her. From time to time, I could stop by."

Liza's eyes sparkled with joy, which she tried in vain to conceal; her cheeks glowed like sunset on a clear summer night; she looked at her left sleeve and plucked at it with her right hand. The old woman accepted this proposal willingly, not suspecting any ill intentions, and assured the stranger that the linens Liza wove and the stockings Liza knitted were exceptionally good and longer wearing than anyone else's. It was getting dark and the young man wanted to leave.

"But what is your name, good sir?" asked the old woman.

"My name is Erast," he answered.

"Erast," said Liza quietly. "Erast!" She repeated this name about five times, as if trying to learn it by heart.

Erast bade them farewell and left. Liza followed him with her eyes while her mother sat pensively; taking her daughter by the hand she told her:

"Oh, Liza! How good and kind he is! If only your betrothed would be like that!"

Liza's heart kept fluttering.

"Mother! Mother! How can that happen? He's a gentleman, but among peasants . . ." Liza did not finish her sentence.

Now the reader should know that this young man, this Erast, was a rather wealthy nobleman with an excellent mind and a good heart, kind by nature, but weak and frivolous. He led a dissipated life, thought only of his own pleasure, searched for it in society's amusements, but often not finding it was bored and complained about his fate. From the first meeting, Liza's beauty made an impression on his heart. He read novels and idylls, had a vivid imagination, and often ruminated about those times (real and unreal) when, if one believes the poets, all people walked around carefree through the meadows, swam in pure springs, kissed like turtle doves, rested under roses and myrtles, and spent their days in happy idleness. It seemed to him that he had found in Liza what his heart had long yearned for. "Nature summons me to its embraces, its pure joys," he thought and decided—at least for a while—to leave high society.

Let's return to Liza. Night had fallen—the mother blessed her daughter and wished her pleasant dreams; but this time her wish was not fulfilled: Liza slept very badly. The new guest of her soul, the image of Erast, was so vivid that she woke up almost every minute, woke up and sighed. Liza rose before sunrise, went down to the bank of the Moscow River, sat down on the grass, and looked despondently at the white mists billowing in the air; floating upward they left shining drops on the green veil of nature. Silence reigned everywhere. But soon the rising sun roused all of creation: the groves and bushes came alive; little birds took flight and started singing; flowers raised their heads so they could drink in the life-giving rays of light. But Liza kept sitting despondently. Oh, Liza, Liza! What has happened to you? Before you awoke with the birds, you were happy like them in the morning, and your pure joyful soul glistened in your eyes like the sun's rays shine in drops of heavenly dew; but now you are pensive and the universal joy of Nature is foreign to your heart. Meanwhile, a young shepherd was driving his herd along the bank of the river, playing his pipes; Liza concentrated her gaze on him and thought:

"If only he who now occupies all of my thoughts had been born a simple peasant, a shepherd, and if he would drive his herd past me now. Oh! I would bow to him with a smile and tell him affably: 'Hello, my dear shepherd! Where are you driving your herd? Green grass grows here for your sheep; and red flowers are here from which you can make a wreath for your hat.' He would look at me affectionately and maybe take my hand . . . It's a dream!"

The shepherd playing his pipes passed by with his colorful herd and disappeared behind a nearby hill.

Suddenly Liza heard the sound of oars, glanced up at the river, and saw a boat, and in the boat was Erast.

Her every fiber began to quiver—and, of course, not from fear. She got up and wanted to walk away, but could not. Erast jumped to the bank, came up to Liza, and her dream was fulfilled for he *looked at her affectionately and took her by the hand* . . . And Liza, Liza stood with a lowered gaze, fiery cheeks, and a trembling heart—she could not take her hand away from him, could not turn away when he came close to her with his pink lips . . . Oh! He kissed her, he kissed her with such passion that the whole universe seemed to her to be a blazing fire. "Dear Liza!" said Erast. "Dear Liza! I love you!"

And those words echoed in the depths of her soul like heavenly enchanting music. She hardly dared to believe her ears and . . . But I throw my brush down. I will only say that at that moment of bliss Liza's shyness disappeared—Erast discovered he was loved, loved passionately, by a fresh, pure, and open heart.

They sat on the grass, and in a way that left very little space between them—they looked into each other's eyes and told each other, "Love me!" and two hours seemed to pass in a moment. Finally, Liza remembered that her mother might be worried about her. They had to part.

"Oh, Erast!" she said. "Will you always love me?"

"Always, dear Liza, always!" he answered.

"And can you give me your pledge?"

"I can, kind Liza, I can!"

"No! I don't need pledges. I believe you, Erast, I believe you. Would you deceive poor Liza? That couldn't be."

"It couldn't, dear Liza, it couldn't."

"I am so happy! And mother will be so happy when she finds out that you love me!"

"Oh no, Liza! She doesn't need to be told anything."

"Why not?"

"Old people are suspicious. She will imagine something bad."

"That cannot happen."

"Just the same, I ask you not to tell her a thing about it."

"Fine. I shall obey you, although I don't want to hide anything from her."

They said farewell, kissed for the last time, and promised to see each other every evening either on the river bank or in the birch grove or someplace near Liza's cottage, but faithfully, and for certain, to see each other. Liza left, but her eyes turned a hundred times toward Erast, who remained standing on the bank watching her.

Liza returned to the cottage in a completely different mood than the one she had left in. On her face and in all of her movements she revealed a heart-felt joy. *"He loves me!"* she thought and rejoiced in this idea.

"Oh, mother!" said Liza to her mother, who had only just awakened. "Oh, mother! What a wonderful morning! Everything is so cheerful in the field! The larks have never sung so well; the sun has never shone so brightly; the flowers have never smelled so pleasant!"

The old woman, leaning on her crutch, went out to the meadow to enjoy the morning, which Liza had described in such charming colors. Indeed, it seemed to her exceptionally pleasant; her kind daughter with her joy had cheered up all of Nature for her.

"Oh, Liza," she said, "everything is so good with the Lord God! It's my sixtieth year on earth, and I do not tire of looking on the works of the Lord; I do not tire of looking at the pure sky, which seems like a high tent, and at the earth, which is covered every year with new grass and new flowers. The Heavenly King must have loved man very much when he decorated this place so well. Oh, Liza! Who would want to die if we never experienced grief? . . . Evidently, it has to be so. Maybe we would forget our souls if tears never trickled from our eyes."

But Liza thought: *"Oh! I would sooner forget my soul than my dear friend!"*

Afterward Erast and Liza, afraid not to keep their word, met every night (after Liza's mother had gone to bed) on the bank of the river, or in the birch grove, but mostly under the shade of the hundred-year-old oaks (about one hundred and ninety yards from the cottage), oaks shading a deep, clear pond that had been dug in ancient times. There, the rays of a tranquil moon shining through the green branches often made silver of Liza's fair hair, with which zephyrs and the hand of her dear friend played; often these rays illuminated a shining tear of love in the tender eyes of Liza, which was always dried by Erast's kiss. They hugged—but chaste, bashful Cynthia did not hide from them behind a cloud;[7] pure and innocent were their embraces.

"When you," Liza said to Erast, "when you tell me, 'I love you, my friend,' when you press me to your heart and look at me with your affectionate eyes—oh!—then I feel so good, so good, that I forget myself, I forget everything but Erast. It's a miracle! It's a miracle, my friend, that I was able to live peacefully and cheerfully without knowing you. Now, I can't understand it; now I think that without you life is not life, but sadness and boredom. Without your eyes the bright moon is dark; without your voice the nightingale's song is dull; without your breath the breeze is unpleasant to me."

Erast was enchanted by his shepherdess—as he called Liza—and, seeing how much she loved him, he even seemed more pleasant to himself. All the shining amusements of high society seemed insignificant to him compared to the pleasure with which the passionate friendship of an innocent soul nourished his heart. He thought with disgust about the contemptuous sensuality he had enjoyed earlier. "I will live with Liza like a brother with a sister," he thought. "I will not use her love for evil and will always be happy!" Unreasonable young man! Do you know your own heart? Can you always answer for your actions? Is reason always the tsar of your senses?

Liza demanded that Erast visit her mother often.

"I love her," she said, "I want good for her, and I think that seeing you is a great happiness for anyone."

The old woman, indeed, was always happy when she saw him. She loved to talk to him about her late husband and to tell him about the days of her youth: about the time she had first met her dear Ivan, how he fell in love with her, and of the love and harmony in which they lived.

"Oh! we could never get enough of each other—up to the very hour when cruel death cut him down. He died in my arms!"

Erast listened to her with genuine pleasure. He always bought Liza's work from her and always wanted to pay ten times more than she asked; but the old woman never took extra.

A few weeks passed in this way. Once toward evening Erast was waiting a long time for his Liza. She finally came, but she was so unhappy that

Erast was frightened; her eyes were red with tears.

"Liza, Liza! What's the matter?"

"Oh, Erast! I was crying!"

"About what? What is it?"

"I must tell you everything. The son of a rich peasant from a neighboring village has been courting me; mother wants me to marry him."

"And do you agree?"

"That's cruel. How can you ask me that? Yes, I feel pity for mother; she cries and says I do not want to see her rest in peace, that she will be tormented at her death if she does not see me married off before she dies. Oh! Mother doesn't know I have such a dear friend!"

Erast kissed Liza and said her happiness was the most important thing in the world to him, that after her mother's death, he would take her and live with her inseparably in the countryside and the dense forest, as if in paradise.

"But you cannot be my husband!" said Liza with a soft sigh.

"But why?"

"I am a peasant."

"You're insulting me. For your friend a sensitive innocent soul is more important than anything—and Liza will always be closest to my heart."

She threw herself into his embrace and at that moment her innocence was destroyed! Erast felt an unusual agitation in his blood. Never had Liza appeared more charming, never had her caresses touched him so strongly, never had her kisses been so ardent; she knew nothing, suspected nothing, feared nothing—the evening darkness nourished her desire—not a single small star glowed in the sky, not a single ray could light up the delusion. Erast felt a quivering inside—Liza too, not knowing why, not knowing what was happening to her ... Oh, Liza, Liza! Where is your guardian angel? Where is your innocence?

The delusion passed in a minute. Liza did not understand her feelings, was amazed and kept asking questions. Erast was silent—he was searching for words and could not find any.

"Oh, I'm afraid," Liza said. "I'm afraid of what has happened to us! It seems to me that I am dying, that my soul ... No, I don't know how to say it! ... You are silent, Erast? Sighing? ... My God! What is it?"

In the meantime, lightning flashed and thunder rolled. Liza kept trembling.

"Erast, Erast!" she said. "I'm terrified! I'm afraid that the thunder will kill me like a criminal!"

The storm was howling fiercely; rain poured down from the black clouds—it seemed as if nature was mourning the loss of Liza's innocence.

Erast tried to calm Liza down and took her back to her cottage. Tears were rolling from her eyes when she said goodbye to him.

"Oh, Erast! Promise me that we will be happy as before!"

"We will, Liza, we will!" he answered.

"God willing! I cannot disbelieve your words: after all, I love you! Only my heart . . . But enough! Goodbye! Tomorrow we will meet, tomorrow."

Their meetings continued, but how everything changed! Erast was no longer satisfied with the innocent caresses of his Liza—with her love-filled glances—with the touches of her hand, her kisses, her pure embraces alone. He wished for more, more, and finally, he did not have to wish for anything—but he who knows his own heart, who can reason about the nature of his most tender pleasures, will agree with me, of course, that the fulfillment of *all* desires is the most dangerous temptation of love. For Erast, Liza was no longer that innocent angel who had in the past inflamed his imagination and delighted his soul. Platonic love had given way to feelings of which he could not be *proud* and that were no longer new to him. As for Liza, she, after having given herself to him completely, she lived and breathed only for him, she obeyed his will in everything like an innocent lamb, and she thought her own happiness was in his pleasure. She had seen a change in him and often said to him:

"You used to be more cheerful; we used to be more peaceful and more happy; and I was never so afraid of losing your love!"

Sometimes, in leaving, he would say to her:

"Tomorrow I cannot see you, Liza. Something important has come up."

And each time she would sigh at these words.

Finally, she had not seen him for five straight days and was greatly worried; on the sixth day he came with a sad face and told her:

"My dear Liza! I must part with you for some time. You know, there is a war going on. I'm in the service; my regiment is going on a campaign."

Liza grew pale and almost fainted.

Erast caressed her. He said he would always love his dear Liza and hoped that upon returning he would never part from her again. She was silent for a long time, then bitter tears began to flow; she grabbed his hand and gazing at him with all the tenderness of her love asked:

"Can't you stay?"

"I can," he answered, "but only in the greatest disgrace, with the greatest stain upon my honor. Everyone will despise me; everyone will abhor me as a coward, as an unworthy son of the fatherland."

"Oh, if that is so," said Liza, "then go, go wherever God commands you! But you could be killed."

"I'm not afraid to die for the fatherland, dear Liza."

"I shall die as soon as you leave this earth."

"But why think of that? I'm hoping to stay alive. I'm hoping to come back to you, to my friend."

"God willing! God willing! Every day, every hour, I will pray it be so. Oh, why can't I read or write! You would inform me of everything that happens to you, and I would write to you—of my tears!"

"No, take good care of yourself, Liza, take care for your friend. I don't want you to cry in my absence."

"Cruel man! You think you can deprive me of this happiness, too! No! After parting from you, I will only stop crying when my heart dries up."

"Think of the pleasant moment when we will see each other again."

"I will, I will think of that! Oh, if it would come quickly! Dear, kind Erast! Remember, remember your poor Liza, who loves you more than herself!"

But I cannot describe everything they talked about then. The next day was to be their last meeting.

Erast wanted to say goodbye to Liza's mother, who could not hold back her tears after hearing that *her tender, good-looking gentleman* had to go off to war. He forced her to take some money, saying:

"I do not want Liza, in my absence, to sell her work, which, by agreement, belongs to me."

The old woman showered him with blessings:

"Lord grant," she said, "that you return to us safely and that I shall see you once again in this lifetime! Perhaps my Liza by then will have found a suitable husband. How I would thank God if you came to our wedding! When Liza has children, you know, sir, that you must be their godfather! Oh! I would very much like to live so long!"

Liza stood beside her mother and didn't dare look at her. The reader can easily imagine how she felt at that moment.

But what did she feel when Erast, after embracing her for the last time, for the last time pressing her to his heart, said: *"Goodbye, Liza! . . ."* What a touching picture! The morning sunrise, like a scarlet sea, was spreading across the eastern sky. Erast stood beneath the branches of a tall oak, holding in his embrace his pale, languishing, grieving friend, who said goodbye to her own soul. All of nature was silent.

Liza sobbed, Erast cried; he left her—she fell, got up on her knees, raised her arms toward the sky, and watched Erast, who was moving farther and farther off and finally disappeared. The sun rose, and Liza, abandoned, poor woman, fainted.

She came to her senses—and the world seemed to her doleful and sad. All of nature's pleasures disappeared for her along with the beloved of her heart. "Oh!" she thought. "Why have I been left in this desert? What is stopping me from rushing after my dear Erast? I am not terrified of war; it is terrifying only where I don't have my friend. I want to live with him, to die with him, or with my death to save his precious life. Wait, wait, my dear! I fly to you!" She had already decided to run after Erast, when the thought *"I have a mother!"* stopped her. Liza sighed and lowering her head tread softly toward her cottage. From this hour her days were days of anguish and grief, which she had to hide from her tender mother: this made her heart suffer even more! It only gained relief when Liza, secluding herself in the depths of the forest, could freely shed tears and grieve about the separation from her dear one. Often a sad turtle dove joined its plaintive voice to her moaning. But sometimes—even though it was quite rare—a golden ray of hope, a ray of consolation illuminated the gloom of her sorrows. *"When he returns to me, how happy I'll be! How everything will change!"* With this thought her eyes became bright, her cheeks rosy, and Liza smiled like a May morning after a stormy night. About two months passed in this way.

One day Liza had to go to Moscow to buy some rose water, with which her mother had been treating her eyes. On one of the main streets she encountered a magnificent carriage and in that carriage—she saw Erast. *"Oh!"* Liza cried out and rushed toward him, but the carriage passed by and turned into a courtyard. Erast got out and was ready to go into the entrance of an enormous house when suddenly he found himself in Liza's embrace. He turned pale, then without answering a word to her exclamations, took her by the hand, led her to his study, shut the door, and said to her:

"Liza! Circumstances have changed; I've announced my engagement. You must leave me in peace and forget me, for your own sake. I did love you and I love you now, that is, I wish all goodness for you. Here are a hundred rubles—take it"—he put the money in her pocket—"let me kiss you for the last time—then go home."

Before Liza could come to her senses he had led her from his study and told his servant:

"Show this girl out."

My heart bleeds at this very moment. I forget the human being in Erast— I am ready to curse him—but my tongue does not move—I look at the sky—and a tear rolls down my face. Oh! Why am I not writing a novel instead of a sad narrative?

Did Erast deceive Liza in telling her that he was going into the army? No, he was, indeed, in the army; but instead of fighting the enemy, he played cards and gambled away almost all of his estate. Soon peace was concluded, and Erast returned burdened by debts. The only way he could improve his situation was to to marry a wealthy, elderly widow who had been in love with him for a long time. So he decided and moved into her house after granting a sincere sigh to his Liza. But can all of this justify him?

When Liza found herself outside, she was in such a state that no pen can describe it. *"He, he drove me out? He loves someone else? I am ruined!"*— these were her thoughts, her feelings! A cruel fainting spell interrupted them for a while. A kind woman who was walking along the street stopped by Liza, who was lying on the ground, and tried to revive her. The unhappy girl opened her eyes, got up with the kind woman's help, thanked her, and walked, not knowing where herself. "I cannot live," Liza thought. "I cannot! . . . Oh, if only the sky would fall down on me! If only the earth would swallow a poor girl! . . . No! the sky does not fall; the earth does not waver! Woe is me!" She left the city and suddenly found herself on the bank of a deep pond beneath the shade of the ancient oaks that, a few weeks earlier, had been silent witnesses to her rapture. This memory jolted her soul; the most terrifying, heart-felt torment was depicted on her face. But after a few minutes she fell into deep thought—then she looked around and saw her neighbor's daughter (a fifteen-year-old girl), walking along the road, called her, took out from her pocket the ten gold coins, and, handing them to her, said:

"Dear Aniuta, dear friend! Take this money to my mother—it's not stolen. Tell her that Liza is guilty before her; that I hid from her my love for a certain cruel man, for E . . . Why say his name? Tell her that he betrayed me; ask her to forgive me—God will help her—kiss her hand the way I am kissing your hand now; tell her poor Liza asked you to kiss her, tell her that I . . ."

Then she threw herself into the water. Aniuta screamed and cried but could not save her. She ran to the village—people gathered and pulled Liza out; but she was already dead.

This is the way a woman beautiful in soul and body ended her life. When we see each other there in the other life, I will recognize you, tender Liza!

They buried her near the pond, underneath a gloomy oak, and placed a wooden cross on her grave. I often sit here, deep in thought, leaning on the receptacle of Liza's remains; the pond flows before my eyes; the leaves rustle above me.

Liza's mother heard about the terrible death of her daughter, her blood turned cold in horror—and her eyes closed forever. The cottage is now deserted. The wind howls inside, and superstitious peasants hearing this noise at night say: *"The dead moan there; poor Liza is moaning there!"*

Erast was unhappy for the rest of his life. After learning of Liza's fate he could not find consolation and considered himself a murderer. I made his acquaintance a year before his death. He told me this story himself and led me to Liza's grave. Now, perhaps they are reconciled!

1792

Translation by Beau Kolodka

Notes to the translation are on page 574.

RESOURCES

Primary Text

Karamzin, N.M. "Bednaia Liza," *Izbrannye sochineniia*. Vol. 1. Leningrad: Khudo-zhestvennaia literatura, 1964, pp. 605–21.

Secondary Sources

Literary and Cultural Studies

Billington, James H. *The Icon and the Axe: An Interpretive History of Russian Culture.* New York: Vintage, 1966, pp. 269–306.

Lotman, Iu.M. *Sotvorenie Karamzina*. Moscow: Kniga, 1987.

Nebel, Henry M., Jr. *N.M. Karamzin: A Russian Sentimentalist*. The Hague: Mouton, 1967, pp. 88–90.

Rogger, Hans. *National Consciousness in Eighteenth-Century Russia*. Cambridge: Harvard University Press, 1960, pp. 120–25.

Segel, Harold, ed. and trans. *The Literature of Eighteenth-Century Russia*. New York: Dutton, 1967.

Art

Sokolova, Natalya, ed. *Selected Works of Russian Art*. Leningrad: Aurora, 1976, plate 52.

8

~Alexander S. Pushkin~

The Bronze Horseman
A Petersburg Tale

Foreword

The event described in this tale is based on fact. The details of the flood are borrowed from newspapers of the time. The curious can consult the account compiled by V.I. Berkh.

Introduction

Upon the brink of the wild stream
He stood, and dreamt a mighty dream.
He gazed far off. Near him the spreading
river poured by; with flood abeam,
alone, a flimsy skiff was treading.
Scattered along those shores of bog
and moss were huts of blackened log,
the wretched fisher's squalid dwelling;
forests, impervious in the fog
to hidden suns, all round were telling
their whispered tale.
         And so thought He:
"From here, proud Sweden will get warning;
just here is where a city'll be
founded to stop our foes from scorning;
here Nature destines us to throw
out over Europe a window;[1]
to stand steadfast beside the waters;
across waves unknown to the West,
all flags will come, to be our guest—
and we shall feast in spacious quarters."

A century went by—a young
city, of Northern lands the glory
and pride, from marsh and overhung
forest arose, story on story:
where, earlier, Finland's fisher sank—
of Nature's brood the most downhearted—
alone on the low-lying bank,
his ropy net in the uncharted
with life and movement, there have come
enormous mansions that are jostling
with graceful towers; and vessels here
from earth's extremities will steer
until the rich quayside is bustling.
Nevá in darkly verdant garden-quarters
her isles have vanished without trace;
old Moscow's paled before this other
metropolis; it's just the same
as when a widowed Empress-Mother
bows to a young Tsaritsa's claim.
     I love you, Peter's own creation;
I love your stern, your stately air,
Nevá's majestical pulsation,
the granite that her quaysides wear,
your railings with their iron shimmer,
your pensive nights in the half-gloom,
translucent twilight, moonless glimmer,
when, sitting lampless in my room,
I write and read; when faintly shining,
the streets in their immense outlining
are empty, given up to dreams;
when Admiralty's needle gleams;
when not admitting shades infernal
into the golden sky, one glow
succeeds another, and nocturnal
tenure has one half-hour to go;
I love your brutal winter, freezing
the air to so much windless space;
by broad Nevá the sledges breezing;
brighter than roses each girl's face;
the ball, its brilliance, din, and malice;
bachelor banquets and the due

hiss of the overflowing chalice,
and punch's radiance burning blue.
I love it when some warlike duty
livens the Field of Mars, and horse
and foot impose on that concourse
their monolithic brand of beauty;
above the smooth-swaying vanguard
victorious, tattered flags are streaming,
on brazen helmets light is gleaming,
helmets that war has pierced and scarred.
I love the martial detonation,
the citadel in smoke and roar,
when the North's Empress to the nation
has given a son for empire, or
when there's some new triumph in war
victorious Russia's celebrating;
or when Nevá breaks the blue ice,
sweeps it to seaward, slice on slice,
and smells that days of spring are waiting.
    Metropolis of Peter, stand,
steadfast as Russia, stand in splendor!
Even the elements by your hand
have been subdued and made surrender;
let Finland's waves forget the band
of hate and bondage down the ages,
nor trouble with their fruitless rages
Peter the Great's eternal sleep!
A fearful time there was: I keep
its memory fresh in retrospection . . .
My friends, let me turn up for you
the dossiers of recollection.
Grievous the tale will be, it's true . . .

(October 29)

Part One

On Petrograd, the darkened city,
November, chill and without pity,
blasted; against its noble brink
Nevá was splashing noisy billows;
its restless mood would make one think

of sufferers on their restless pillows.
The hour was late and dark; the rain
angrily lashed the window-pane,
the wind blew, pitifully shrieking.
From house of friends, about this time.
young Evgeny came home . . .
                                    My rhyme
selects this name to use in speaking
of our young hero. It's a sound
I like; my pen has long been bound
in some way with it; further naming
is not required, though luster flaming
in years gone by might have lit on
his forebears, and perhaps their story
under Karamzin's pen had shone,
resounding to the nation's glory;
but now by all, both high and low,
it's quite forgotten. Our hero
lives in Kolomna, has employment
in some bureau, tastes no enjoyment
of wealth or fashion's world, and no
regret for tales of long ago.

   So Evgeny came home and, shaking
his greatcoat, got undressed for bed—
but lay long hours awake, his head
with various thoughts disturbed and aching.
What did he think about? The fact
that he was penniless; that packed
mountains of work must be surmounted
to earn him freedom, fame, and ease;
that wit and money might be counted
to him from God; and that one sees
fellows on permanent vacation,
dull-witted, idle, in whose station
life runs as smooth as in a dream;
that he'd served two years altogether . . .
And he thought also that the weather
had got no gentler; that the stream
was rising, ever higher lifting;
that soon the bridges might be shifting;

that maybe from Parasha he
would be cut off, two days or three.

   These were his dreams. And a great sadness
came over him that night; he wished
the raindrops with less raging madness
would lash the glass, that the wind swished
less drearily . . .

               At last his failing
eyes closed in sleep. But look, the gloom
of that foul-weather night is paling,
and a weak daylight fills the room . . .
A dreadful day it was!
                  All night
Nevá against the gales to seaward
had battled, but been blown to leeward
by their ungovernable might . . .[2]
That morning, on the quayside, fountains
of spray held an admiring crowd,
that pressed to watch the watery mountains,
the foaming waves that roared so loud.
But now, blocked by the headwinds blowing
in from the Gulf, Nevá turned back,
in sullen, thunderous fury flowing,
and flooded all the islands; black,
still blacker grew the day; still swelling,
Nevá exploded, raging, yelling,
in kettle-like outbursts of steam—
until, mad as a beast, the stream
pounced on the city. From its path
everyone fled, and all around
was sudden desert . . . At a bound
cellars were under inundation,
canals leapt rails, forgot their station—
and Triton-Petropol surfaced
with water lapping round his waist.
Siege and assault! The waves, malicious,
like thieves, burst in through windows; vicious
rowboats, careering, smash the panes;
stalls are engulfed; piteous remains,

debris of cabins, roofing, boarding,
wares that a thrifty trade's been hoarding,
poor household goods, dashed all astray,
bridges the storm has snatched away,
and scooped up coffins, helter-skelter
swim down the streets!
             All sense alike
God's wrath, and wait for doom to strike.
Everything's ruined: bread and shelter!
and where to find them?
             That deathlike,
that frightful year, Tsar Alexander
still ruled in glory. He came out
on the balcony, in grief, in doubt,
and said: "A Tsar is no commander
against God's elements." Deep in thought
he gazed with sorrow and confusion,
gazed at the wreck the floods had wrought.
The city squares gave the illusion
of lakes kept brimming to profusion
by torrent-streets. The palace stood
sad as an island in the ocean.
And then the Tsar spoke out, for good
or evil set in farflung motion
his generals on their dangerous way
along those streets of boisterous waters
to save the people in their quarters,
drowning, unhinged by terror's sway.
And then in Peter's square, where lately
a corner-mansion rose, and stately
from its high porch, on either side,
caught as in life, with paws suspended,
two lions, sentry-like, attended—
perched up on one, as if to ride,
arms folded, motionless, astride,
hatless, and pale with apprehension,
Evgeny sat. His fear's intention
not for himself, he never knew
just how the greedy waters grew,
how at his boots the waves were sucking,
how in his face the raindrops flew;

or how the stormwind, howling, bucking,
had snatched his hat away. His view
was fixed in darkest desperation,
immobile, on a single spot.
Mountainous, from the perturbation
down in the depths, the waves had got
on their high horses, raging, pouncing;
the gale blew up, and, with it, bouncing
wreckage . . . Oh, God, oh God! For there—
close to the seashore—almost where
the Gulf ran in, right on the billow—
a fence, untouched by paint, a willow,
a flimsy cottage; there were they,
a widow and his dream, her daughter,
Parasha . . . or perhaps he may
have dreamt it all? Fickle as water,
our life is as dreamlike as smoke—
at our expense, fate's private joke.
As if by sorcery enchanted,
high on the marble fixed and planted,
he can't dismount! And all about
is only water. Looking out,
with back turned to him, on the retching
waves of Nevá in their wild course
from his fast summit, arm outstretching,
the Giant rides on his bronze horse.

(October 30)

Part Two

But by now, tired of helter-skelter
ruin and sheer rampaging, back
Nevá was flowing, in its track
admiring its own hideous welter;
its booty, as it made for shelter,
it slung away. With his grim crew
so any robber chief will do;
bursting his way into a village,
he'll hack and thrust and snatch and pillage;
rape, havoc, terror, howl, and wail!
Then, loaded down with loot, and weary—

fear of pursuers makes them leery—
the robbers take the homeward trail
and as they flee they scatter plunder.
So, while the waters fell asunder,
the road came up. And fainting, pale,
in hope and yearning, fear and wonder,
Evgeny hurries at full steam
down to the scarcely falling stream.
And yet, still proud, and still exulting,
the waves, still furious and insulting,
boiled as if over flames alight;
they still were lathered, foaming, seething
and deeply the Nevá was breathing
just like a horse flown from a fight.
Evgeny looks: a skiff is waiting—
Godsent—he rushes, invocating
the ferryman, who without a care
for just a few kopeks quite gladly
agrees to take him, though still madly
the floods are boiling everywhere.
The boatman fought the agonizing
billows like an experienced hand;
the cockboat with its enterprising
crew was quite ready for capsizing
at any moment—but dry land
at last it gained.
                           Evgeny, tearful,
rushes along the well-known ways
toward the well-known scene. His gaze
finds nothing it can grasp: too fearful
the sight! before him all is drowned,
or swept away, or tossed around;
cottages are askew, some crumbled
to sheer destruction, others tumbled
off by the waves; and all about,
as on a field of martial rout,
bodies lie weltered. Blankly staring,
Evgeny, uncomprehending, flies,
faint from a torment past all bearing,
runs to where fate will meet his eyes,
fate whose unknown adjudication

still waits as under seal of wax.
And now he's near his destination
and here's the Gulf, here . . . in his tracks
Evgeny halts . . . the house . . . where ever?
he goes back, he returns. He'd never . . .
he looks . . . he walks . . . he looks again:
here's where their cottage stood; and then
here was the willow. Gates were standing
just here—swept off, for sure. But where's
the cottage gone? Not understanding,
he walked round, full of boding cares,
he talked to himself loud and gruffly,
and then he struck his forehead roughly
and laughed and laughed.
                   In deepest night
the city trembled at its plight:
long time that day's events were keeping
the citizenry all unsleeping
as they rehearsed them.
                  Daylight's ray
fell out of tired, pale clouds to play
over a scene of calm—at dawning
yesterday's hell had left no trace.
The purple radiance of the morning
had covered up the dire event.
All in its previous order went.
Upon highways no longer flowing,
people as everyday were going
in cold indifference, and the clerk
left where he'd sheltered in the dark
and went to work. The daring bosses
of commerce, unperturbed, explore
Nevá's inroads upon their store,
and plan to take their heavy losses
out on their neighbor. From backyards
boats are removed.
                That bard of bards,
Count Khvostov, great poetic master,
begins to sing Nevá's disaster
in unforgettable ballads.
But spare, I pray you, spare some pity

for my poor, poor Evgeny, who
by the sad happenings in the city
had wits unhinged. Still the halloo
of tempest and Nevá was shrieking
into his ear; pierced through and through
by frightful thoughts, he roamed unspeaking;
some nightmare held him in its thrall.
A week went by, a month—and all
the time he never once was seeking
his home. That small deserted nook,
its lease expired, his landlord took
for a poor poet. His possessions
Evgeny never went to claim.
Soon to the world and its professions
a stranger, all day long he came
and went on foot, slept by the water;
scraps thrown from windows of the quarter
his only food; always the same,
his clothes wore out to shreds. Malicious
children would stone him; he received
from time to time the coachman's vicious
whiplash, for he no more perceived
which way was which, or what direction
led where; he never seemed to know
where he was going, he was so
plunged in tumult of introspection.
And so his life's unhappy span
he eked out—neither beast nor man—
not this, nor that—not really living
nor yet a ghost . . .
                        He slept one night
by the Nevá. Summer was giving
its place to autumn. Full of spite,
a bad wind blew. In mournful fight
against the embankment, waves were splashing,
their crests on the smooth steps were smashing
for all the world like suppliant poor
at some hard-hearted judge's door.
Evgeny woke. Raindrops were falling
in midnight gloom; the wind was calling
piteously—on it, far off, hark,

the cry of sentries in the dark . . .
Evgeny rose, and recollection
brought up past horrors for inspection;
he stood in haste, walked off from there,
then halted, and began to stare
in silence, with an insensately
wild look of terror on his face.
He was beside the pillared, stately
front of a mansion. In their place,
caught as in life, with paws suspended,
two lions, sentrylike, attended,
and there, above the river's course,
atop his rock, fenced off, defended
on his dark summit, arm extended,
the Idol rode on his bronze horse.[3]

    Evgeny shuddered. Thoughts were hatching
in frightful clarity. He knew
that spot, where floods ran raging through—
where waves had massed, voracious, snatching,
a riot-mob, vindictive, grim—
the lions, and the square, and him
who, motionless and without pity,
lifted his bronze head in the gloom,
whose will, implacable as doom,
had chosen seashore for his city.
Fearful, he looked in that half-light!
Upon his forehead, what a might
of thought, what strength of concentration!
what fire, what passion, and what force
are all compact in that proud horse!
He gallops—to what destination?
On the cliff-edge, O lord of fate,
was it not you, O giant idol,
who, pulling on your iron bridle,
checked Russia, made her rear up straight?

    Around the hero's plinth of granite
wretched Evgeny, in a daze,
wandered, and turned a savage gaze
on the autocrat of half the planet.

A steely pressure gripped his chest.
His brow on the cold railing pressed,
over his eyes a mist was lowering,
and through his heart there ran a flame;
his blood was seething; so he came
to stand before the overpowering
image, with teeth and fists again
clenched as if some dark force possessed him.
"Take care," he whisperingly addressed him,
"you marvel-working builder, when . . ."
He shivered with bitter fury, then
took headlong flight. He had the impression
that the grim Tsar, in sudden race
of blazing anger, turned his face
quietly and without expression . . .
and through the empty square he runs,
but hears behind him, loud as guns
or thunderclap's reverberation,
ponderous hooves in detonation
along the shuddering roadway—
as, lighted by the pale moon-ray,
one arm stretched up, on headlong course,
after him gallops the Bronze Rider,
after him clatters the Bronze Horse.
So all night long, demented strider,
wherever he might turn his head—
everywhere gallops the Bronze Rider
pursuing him with thunderous tread.
And from then on, if he was chancing
at any time to cross that square,
a look of wild distress came glancing
across his features; he would there
press hand to heart, in tearing hurry,
as if to chase away a worry;
take his worn cap off; never raise
up from the ground his distraught gaze,
but sidle off.

         A small isle rises
close to the foreshore. Now and then,
a fisher moors alongside, when

late from his catch, with nets and prizes,
and cooks his poor meal on the sand;
or some official comes to land,
out for a Sunday's pleasure-boating,
on the wild islet. Not a blade
of grass is seen. There, gaily floating,
the floods had washed up as they played
a flimsy cottage. Above water
it showed up like a bush, all black—
last spring they moved it. The small quarter,
empty, was shipped away, all rack
and ruin. Near it, my dim-witted
my mad Evgeny there they found . . .
His cold corpse in that self-same ground
to God's good mercy they committed.

October 31, 1833: Boldino, 5 past 5

Translation by Sir Charles Johnston

Translation of Pushkin's notes begins on page 574.

RESOURCES

Primary Text

Pushkin, A.S. "Mednyi vsadnik. Peterburgskaia povest'." *Sobranie sochinenii v desiati tomakh*, ed. D.D. Blagoi, S.M. Bondi, V.V. Vinogradov, Iu.G. Oksman, and V. Tomashevskii. 3d ed. Moscow: Khudozhestvennaia literatura, 1960–62, pp. 284–302.

Secondary Sources

Literary and Cultural Studies

Billington, James H. *The Icon and the Axe: An Interpretive History of Russian Culture.* New York: Vintage, 1966, pp. 208–68.
Clark, Katerina. *Petersburg, Crucible of Cultural Revolution.* Cambridge: Harvard University Press, 1995.
Kunin, V.V. *Svetloe imia Pushkin. Proza, stikhi, p'esy o poete.* Moscow: Pravda, 1988.
Lednicki, Wacław. *Pushkin's "Bronze Horseman": The Story of a Masterpiece.* Berkeley: University of California Press, 1955.
Mikitich, L.D. *Saint Petersburg, Petrograd: A City of Writers and Poets.* Moscow: Sovetskaia Rossiia, 1991.

Mirsky, D.S. *A History of Russian Literature*. Ed. Francis J. Whitfield. New York: Knopf, 1949, pp. 80–99, 138.
Todd, William Mills. *Fiction and Society in the Age of Pushkin: Ideology, Institution and Narrative*. Cambridge: Harvard University Press, 1986.
———. "Púshkin, Aleksándr Sergéevich (1799–1837). In *Handbook of Russian Literature*, ed. Victor Terras. New Haven: Yale University Press, 1985, pp. 356–60.
———, ed. *Literature and Society in Imperial Russia. 1800–1914*. Stanford: Stanford University Press, 1978.

Literature

Vedeniapin, E.A., ed. *A.S. Pushkin. Mednyi vsadnik*. Moscow: Russkii iazyk, 1980.

Art and Architecture

Brumfield, W.C. *A History of Russian Architecture*. Cambridge–New York: Cambridge University Press, 1993, pp. 201–27, 268–70.
Sokolova, Natalya, ed. *Selected Works of Russian Art*. Leningrad: Aurora, 1976, plate 35.

Music

Gazmanov, Oleg. "Piter." *Moriachka*. Ob. Vostok: Motor Studio, 1994. Audio cassette.
Glière, Rinehold Moritsevich. *Bronze Horseman*. Suites Nos. 1 and 2 from the ballet. Melodiia, n.d.
———. *Mednyi vsadnik*. Suite from the ballet for symphonic orchestra. Conductor's score. Boca Raton, FL: Edwin F. Kalmus, 1992.

Film

Petr I (Peter I). Director, V. Petrov. Screenplay, Aleksei Tolstoi. Cinematographers, Viacheslav Gardanov and Vladimir Iakovlev. Music, Vladimir Shcherbachov. Lenfilm, 1937.

9

~Mikhail Lermontov~

Borodino

"Say, uncle, surely not in vain
Did Moscow burn to ashes
Surrender to the French?
For after all there were great battles?
And it is said amazing battles!
Russians remember for good reason
The day of Borodino!"

"Yes, there were men then in our time,
Not like the present sort:
   The heroes are not you!
Their fate was not a lucky one:
The combat field returned so few . . .
If not for God's almighty will,
   Moscow would not have been surrendered.

For long we silently retreated,
Full of regrets, expecting battle,
   The veterans finding fault:
"What is this! Winter holiday?
Won't the commanders dare
To tear French uniforms
   On Russian bayonets?"

And so we found a sweeping field:
With room to move about at will!
   We built a broad redoubt.
Our ears were ever on alert!
Just as the sun lit up the cannons
And the treetops of the forest—
   The French were promptly there.

I loaded shells tight in the cannon
And thought: I'll treat our friend!
    Just wait, brother *musiu*!
Let's not be clever, come to battle;
A wall of bodies we'll throw up,
And we will stand together strong
    To save our motherland!

Two days we exchanged cannon fire,
What sense in such frivolity?
    We waited for the third.
While everywhere the cry was raised:
"It's time to get down to grapeshot!"
And on the cruel field of battle
    The evening shadow fell.

I dropped to sleep beside my cannon
While all throughout the night we heard,
    The French celebration.
But quiet was our open bivouac:
One soldier cleaned a battered shako,
Another honed his bayonet and growled,
    Biting his long mustache.

And as the sky began to brighten,
All suddenly, loudly stirred,
    And column after column sparkled.
Our colonel was from birth courageous:
Servant to tsar, father to soldiers . . .
Yes, mourn for him, felled by a sword
    He sleeps in the damp earth.

And so he said with his eyes flashing:
"Look men! Is Moscow not behind us?
    Let's die standing next to Moscow,
The way our brothers died!"
And so we vowed
And kept the faithful oath
    In Battle of Borodino.

Oh, what a day! Through flowing smoke
The French moved like storm clouds,

And straight for our redoubt.
Uhlans with bright regalia,
Dragoons and horses' tails,
All flashed before our eyes
    They all, paid us a visit here.

You'll never see such battles! . . .
Banners flickered past like shadows,
    Through smoke the fire glowed,
Swords screeched, the grapeshot whistled,
The soldiers' arms grew tired of stabbing,
And cannonballs were blocked
    By corpses' bloody heap.

That day the enemy discovered,
The meaning of brave Russian combat,
    Our combat hand to hand! . . .
The earth like our hearts trembled,
And piles of steeds and people tangled
The volley of a thousand cannons
    In prolonged howl merged . . .

The darkness came. And all were ready
For a new battle in the morn
    To stand fast till the end . . .
And drums rang out,
The ruffians retreated.
Then we began to count our wounded,
    To count our friends.

Yes, there were men then in our time,
A powerful and daring tribe.
    The heroes are not you!
Their fate was not a lucky one.
The combat field returned so few,
If not for God's almighty will,
    Moscow would not have been surrendered!

1837

Translation by Victoria Gleizer and Nicholas Rzhevsky

RESOURCES

Primary Text

Lermontov, M.Iu. "Borodino." *Sobranie sochinenii v chetyrekh tomakh*. Vol. 1, *Stikhotvoreniia 1828–1841*, ed. B.V. Tomashevskii. Moscow–Leningrad: Akademiia Nauk SSSR, 1961, pp. 408–11.

Secondary Sources

Literary and Cultural Studies

Billington, James H. *The Icon and the Axe: An Interpretive History of Russian Culture*. New York: Vintage, 1966, pp. 296–306.

Brown, Edward W. *A History of Russian Literature of the Romantic Period*. 4 vols. Ann Arbor, MI: Ardis, 1986.

Brown, Malcolm H. "Prokofiev's *War and Peace*: A Chronicle." *Musical Quarterly* 63 (July 1977): 297–326.

Glasse, Antonia. "Lérmontov, Mikhaíl Yúrievich (1814–41)." In *Handbook of Russian Literature*, ed. Victor Terras. New Haven: Yale University Press, 1985, pp. 248–50.

Ivanova, Z.A. *Zhizn' i tvorchestvo M.Iu. Lermontova*. Moscow: Detskaia literatura, 1964.

Manuilov, V. *Letopis' zhizni i tvorchestva M.Iu. Lermontova*. Moscow–Leningrad: Nauka, 1964.

Terras, Victor. *A History of Russian Literature*. New Haven: Yale University Press, 1991, pp. 243–52.

Todd, William Mills, ed. *Literature and Society in Imperial Russia 1800–1914*. Stanford: Stanford University Press, 1978.

Art and Architecture

Brumfield, W.C. *A History of Russian Architecture*. New York: Cambridge University Press, 1993, pp. 348–90.

Los', V., ed. *Kartiny Gosudarstvennoi Tret'iakovskoi Galerei*. Moscow: Izobrazitel'noe iskusstvo, 1974, plate 4.

Sokolova, Natalya, ed. *Selected Works of Russian Art*. Leningrad: Aurora, 1976, plates 55, 58, 60, 64, 66.

Film

Voina i mir (War and Peace). Based on the novel by Leo Tolstoy. Director, Sergei Bondarchuk. Parts 1–4. Mosfilm, 1964.

Music

"Borodino." *On the River Don*. Conductor, Serge Jaroff. Don Cossack Chorus. Decca, n.d.

"Borodino." *Red Army Ensemble*. Artistic Director and Principal Conductor, Colonel Boris Alexandrov. Melodiia, n.d.

"Borodino." *The Yale Russian Chorus*. Conductor, Gregory Burnsite. Yale Russian Chorus. New York: Masterdisc, 1985.

10

~Mikhail Lermontov~

Taman

From A Hero of Our Time

Taman is the worst little town of all the seacoast towns in Russia. I almost died of hunger there and, moreover, an attempt was made to drown me. I arrived late one night with post horses, in a small springless carriage. The driver stopped his tired troika at the gate of the only stone house in Taman, at the town entrance. The sentinel, a Black Sea Cossack,[1] startled in his sleep by the jingle of the harness-bell, yelled out in a wild voice: "Who goes there?" A sergeant and a corporal appeared. I explained to them that I was an officer going on official business to join a detachment on active duty, and demanded governmental quarters. The corporal took me over the town. Every hut we drove up to proved taken. The weather was cold; I had not slept for three nights, I was worn out, and was beginning to get angry. "Take me somewhere, you rascal!" I cried. "Let it be the devil's, but lead me to the place." "There is one more *fatéra* [quarters]," replied the corporal scratching the back of his head, "but your honor won't like it, it's an evil place!" I did not understand the exact sense of that word and ordered the man to go ahead. After wandering for a long time along dirty alleys where, on both sides, I could see nothing but decrepit fences, we drove up to a shanty on the very edge of the sea.

The full moon shone on the rush roof and the whitewashed walls of my new abode; in the yard, within an enclosure of cobbles, there stood, all awry, a second hut, smaller and more ancient than the first. Almost at its very walls, the shore fell abruptly toward the sea, and below, with an incessant murmur, the dark blue waves splashed. The moon mildly surveyed the element, both restless and submissive to her, and by her light, I could distinguish, far from the shore, two ships, whose motionless black rigging was outlined, gossamerlike, against the pale horizon. "There are ships in the harbor," I said to myself. "Tomorrow I'll set out for Gelendzhik."[2]

I had in my service, as orderly, a Cossack from a line regiment. I told him to take out my valise and to dismiss the coachman. Then I began calling the landlord. Silence. I knocked. Silence again. Funny situation. Finally a boy of fourteen or so crept out of the hallway.[3]

"Where is the landlord?" "No landlord." "How's that? None at all?" "None." "And what about a landlady?" "Gone to the settlement." "Then who'll open the door for me?" I asked, and gave it a kick. The door opened of itself, a whiff of dampness came from within. I lit a sulphur match and brought it close to the lad's very nose; it illumined two white eyes. He was blind, totally blind from birth. He stood motionless before me and I began to examine his features.

I confess, I have a strong prejudice against those who are blind, one-eyed, deaf, mute, legless, armless, hunchbacked, and so forth. I have observed that there always exists some strange relationship between the appearance of a man and his soul, as if with the loss of a limb, the soul lost one of its senses.

And so I began to examine the blind lad's face, but what can one read in a face that lacks eyes? For a long time, I kept looking at him with involuntary pity, when all of a sudden a hardly perceptible smile ran over his thin lips, and for some reason it made on me a most unpleasant impression. There was born in my mind the suspicion that this blind lad was not as blind as it seemed; in vain did I try to persuade myself that those white eyes could not be faked—and what would have been the purpose? But I could not help wondering. I am often inclined to prejudice.

"Are you the landlady's son?" I asked him at last. "No." "Who are you then?" "An orphan, a cripple." "And does the landlady have any children?" "No. There was a daughter, but she's run off across the sea with a Tatar." "What Tatar?" "The evil one knows! Some Tatar from the Crimea, a boatman, from Kerch."

I entered the shanty; two benches and a table, plus a huge trunk by the stove, made up all its furniture. Not one ikon hung on the wall—a bad sign! The sea breeze kept blowing through the broken windowpane. I took out of my suitcase a bit of wax candle and, having lit it, began to unpack my things. I placed in one corner of the room my sword and rifle, laid my pistols on the table, spread my felt cloak on one bench, my Cossack spread his on the other: ten minutes later, he began to snore, but I could not fall asleep, the white-eyed lad kept hovering before me in the dark.

About an hour passed in this way. The moon shone in the window and one beam played on the earthen floor of the shanty. Suddenly, upon the bright band that crossed the floor, a shadow flicked by. I raised myself and glanced through the window; once again someone ran past and vanished, God knows where. I could not suppose that this creature had run down the steep slope of the shore; however, there was no other place for it to have gone. I got up, put on my *beshmet*, buckled my dagger on, and as softly as possible stepped out of the shanty: the blind lad appeared before me. I huddled beside the fence, and he went by me with a firm but cautious step. He carried a bundle under his arm; turning toward the harbor, he began to go down the narrow steep path. "On that day the dumb shall cry out and the blind shall see,"[4] I thought, as I followed him at a distance which allowed me not to lose sight of him.

Meanwhile, the moon had begun to clothe herself in clouds and above the sea a mist had risen; through it, a lantern glimmered on the stern of the nearer ship. Close to the beach, there gleamed the foam of the breakers,[5] which threatened to flood it any minute. Descending with difficulty, I groped my way down the precipitous slope, and this is what I saw: the blind lad stopped for a moment, then turned to the right at the bottom of the slope; he walked so close to the water that it looked as if any moment a wave might seize him and carry him away; but evidently this was not the first time he took this walk judging by the assuredness with which he stepped from stone to stone and avoided holes. Finally, he stopped as if listening to something, sat down on the ground, and laid down the bundle beside him. I followed his movements as I stood concealed behind a projecting part of the rocky coast. After a few minutes, a white figure came in sight, from the opposite direction. It advanced toward the blind lad and sat down beside him. From time to time, the wind brought me snatches of their conversation.

"Well, blind one?" said a woman's voice. "The storm is heavy; Yanko will not come." "Yanko does not fear the storm," the other replied. "The mist is getting thicker," the woman's voice retorted with a note of sadness.

"A mist is best for slipping past the patrol ships," was the answer. "And what if he drowns?" "Well, what of it? You'll go to church Sunday without a new ribbon."

There followed a silence; one thing, however, had struck me: to me, the blind lad had spoken in the Ukrainian dialect, now he expressed himself in perfect Russian.

"You see, I was right," spoke the blind lad again, clapping his hands together. "Yanko is not afraid either of the sea or the winds or the mist or the coast guards. Listen! That is not water splashing—one cannot deceive me—it's his long oars!"

The woman jumped up and began to peer into the distance with an air of anxiety.

"You're dreaming, blind one," she said. "I don't see anything."

I confess that no matter how I strained to make out, in the distance, anything resembling a boat, my efforts were in vain. Some ten minutes elapsed; then, amid the mountains of the waves, a black dot appeared; it grew now bigger, now smaller. Slowly rising upon the wave crests, and rapidly coming down them, a boat was nearing the shore. He must be a valiant navigator, indeed, to venture on such a night to cross the straits, a distance of fifteen miles; and it must be an important reason that induced him to do so! These were my thoughts as, with an involuntary throbbing of the heart, I looked at the wretched boat; but she kept diving like a duck and then, with a winglike upsweep of oars, would spring out of the abyss amid a burst of foam; and now, I thought, her impetus will dash her against the shore and she will be smashed to bits; but cleverly she turned sideways and bounded, unharmed, into a cove. A man of medium height, in a Tatar cap of sheepskin, came ashore. He waved his hand, and all three began to drag something out of the boat; the load was so great that, to this day, I cannot understand how she had not sunk. Each having shouldered a bundle, they started to walk away along the coast, and I soon lost sight of them. I had to go back to my lodgings; but, I confess, all these strange things worried me, and I had a hard time awaiting the morning.

My Cossack was much surprised when, upon waking, he saw me all dressed; I did not, however, tell him the reason. After admiring, for a while, from the window, the blue sky strewn with torn cloudlets, and the distant shore of the Crimea, which extended in a lilac line and ended in a rock on the summit of which a lighthouse loomed white, I made my way to Phanagoria[6] Fort to find out from the commandant the hour of my departure for Gelendzhik.

But, alas, the commandant could tell me nothing definite. The ships that lay in the harbor were either patrol ships or merchantmen that had not even begun to load. "Maybe within three or four days the mailboat will come," said the commandant, "and then we shall see." I returned home, gloomy and cross. In the doorway my Cossack met me with a frightened face.

"It's a bad business, sir," he said to me.

"Yes, my friend, the Lord knows when we shall get out of here!" At this he became even more perturbed and, bending toward me, said in a whisper: "It's an evil place![7] Today, I met a Black Sea sergeant; he's a friend of mine who was in our detachment, last year. The moment I told him where we were quartered, he said to me: 'Brother, it's an evil place, those are bad people!' And, true enough, what kind of a blindman is this? Goes alone everywhere, to the market, to get bread, to get water . . . seems all are used to it around here. . . ."

"Well, at least, did the landlady show up?"

"When you were out today, there came an old woman, and her daughter."

"What daughter? She has no daughter."

"The Lord knows who she is then if she is not her daughter. Anyway, the old woman is in her hut now."

I entered the smaller hut. The stove had been thoroughly heated, and in it, a dinner was cooking, fairly luxurious for paupers. To all my questions, the old woman replied that she was deaf, could not hear me. What was I to do with her? I turned to the blind lad who sat before the stove, feeding the fire with brushwood. "Well now, you blind little devil," I said, taking him by the ear, "out with it . . . where did you go prowling last night with that bundle . . . hey?" All at once my blind lad began to weep, to shriek, to moan. "Where did I go? Nowhere at all . . . With a bundle? What bundle?" This time the old woman did hear, and began to grumble: "What things people will make up! And about a poor cripple, too! Why are you after him? What has he done to you?" I got tired of this and left, firmly resolved to obtain the key to this riddle.

I wrapped myself in my felt cloak and, seating myself on a stone beside the fence, fell to looking idly afar. In front of me, there spread the sea, stirred up by last night's storm, and its monotonous sound akin to the murmur of a city settling down to sleep reminded me of past years, and carried my thoughts northward, toward our cold capital. I was troubled by memories and lost myself in them. Thus passed an hour, perhaps even more. Suddenly, something resembling a song struck my hearing. It was, indeed, a song, and the limpid young voice was that of a woman—but where did it come from? I listened; the tune was bizarre, now slow and sad, now fast and lively. I turned—there was no one around; again I listened— the sounds seemed to fall from the sky. I raised my eyes; on the roof of my hut, stood a girl in a striped dress, her hair hanging loose, a regular water nymph. Shading her eyes from the rays of the sun with the palm of her hand, she fixedly peered afar, now laughing and reasoning with herself, now singing her song.

I memorized that song, word for word:

> Over the free franchise
> of the green sea
> good ships keep going,
> white-sailed.

> Among those good ships
> is my own small boat,
> a boat unrigged,
> two-oared.

Let a storm run riot:
the old ships
will lift their wings
and scatter over the sea.

To the sea I shall bow
very low:
"You bad sea, do not touch
my small boat.

My small boat carries
costly things;
it is guided through the dark night
by a bold daredevil."

Involuntarily, the thought struck me that last night I had heard the same voice: I was lost in meditation for a moment, and when I looked again at the roof, the girl was no longer there. All at once, she ran past me, singing some other snatch and then, snapping her fingers, ran into the old woman's hut, upon which a dispute arose between them. The old woman was furious, the girl laughed loudly. Presently, I saw my undine[8] skip out again. On coming up level with me, she stopped and looked fixedly into my eyes as if she were surprised at my presence; then she turned away casually and slowly walked toward the harbor.

This was not the end: all day long she hovered about my dwelling; her singing and skipping did not cease for one minute. What an odd creature she was! Her face showed no signs of insanity; on the contrary, her eyes rested upon me with brisk perspicacity. Those eyes, it seemed, were endowed with some kind of magnetic power, and every time they looked, they seemed to be waiting for a question. But barely did I begin to speak, than she would run away, with a crafty smile.

Really, I had never seen such a woman! She was far from beautiful, but I have my preconceptions in regard to beauty, too. She revealed a good deal of breeding ... breeding in women, as in horses, is a great thing: *les Jeunes-France*[9] are responsible for this discovery. It (that is, breeding, not Young France) is most visible in the gait, in the hands and feet; the nose is especially significant. In Russia, a straight nose is rarer than a small foot. My songstress did not appear to be more than eighteen. The extraordinary suppleness of her figure, a special inclination of the head, peculiar to her alone, her long auburn hair, a kind of golden sheen on the slightly sun-tanned skin of her neck and shoulders, and, especially, her straight nose— all this was enchanting to me. Although I detected in her oblique glances something wild and suspicious, and although there was an odd vagueness about her smile, still such is the force of preconception; her straight nose drove me crazy. I imagined I had discovered Goethe's Mignon,[10] that extravagant product of his German imagination—and indeed, there was a lot in common between them: the same rapid transitions from intense restlessness to complete immobility, the same enigmatic accents, the same capers and strange songs.

Toward nightfall I accosted her by the door and started the following conversation with her:

"Tell me, my pretty girl," I said. "What were you doing today on the roof?"

"Oh, just tried to see whence the wind was blowing."

"What is that to you?"

"Whence the wind comes, happiness comes, too."

"So you were inviting happiness with your song?"

"Where there are songs, there is happiness."

"And what if you chance to sing sorrow in?"

"What of it? Where it will not get better, it will get worse, and then again, it is not far from bad to good."

"And who taught you that song?"

"Nobody taught me, I sing when I feel like singing; he who is meant to hear it, will hear, and he who is not, will not understand."

"And what's your name, my songstress?"

"The one who christened me knows."

"And who christened you?"

"How should I know?"

"What reticence. Yet look, there is something I've found out about you." (Her face did not change, her lips did not move, as if I were not speaking of her.) "I've found out that you went down to the shore last night." At this point I very solemnly related to her all I had seen, expecting she would be taken aback. Not in the least! She burst into roars of laughter. "You've seen much, but you know little," she said. "And whatever you do know, you'd better keep under lock."

"And what if, for instance, I took it into my head to inform the commandant?"

At this point, I assumed a very serious, even severe, expression. Suddenly, off she hopped, broke into song and vanished like some little bird that has been flushed out of the shrubbery. My last words had been entirely out of place: at the time, I did not realize all their importance, but later had a chance to regret them.

It had just got dark; I ordered the Cossack to heat the tea kettle, bivouac-fashion, lit a candle, and sat down at the table, quietly puffing at my traveling pipe. By the time I was finishing my second glass of tea, the door creaked, suddenly, and I heard, behind me, the light rustle of a dress and the sound of steps: I started and turned around—it was she, my undine. Softly, silently, she sat down, facing me across the table, and fixed me with her eyes, and I do not know why, but her look seemed to me wondrously tender;[11] it reminded me of those gazes which, in past years, so despotically toyed with my life. She seemed to be waiting for a question, but I remained silent, filled with an ineffable confusion. A dull pallor, betraying inner agitation, covered her face, her hand strayed over the table aimlessly, and I noticed a slight tremor in it; now her bosom would rise high, and now she would seem to be holding her breath. This comedy was beginning to bore me, and I was prepared to break the silence in a most prosaic way—that is, to offer her a glass of tea—when she suddenly jumped up, twined her arms around my neck and a moist, burning kiss[12] sounded upon my lips. Everything turned dark before my eyes, my head swam, I crushed her in my embrace with all the force of youthful passion, but she, like a snake, glided between my arms, whispering in my ear, "Tonight, when everybody is asleep, come onto the shore," and, like an arrow, sped out of the room. In the hallway, she overturned the kettle and a candle which stood on the floor. "That she-devil!" cried the Cossack, who had made himself comfortable on some straw and had been looking forward to warming himself with the remainder of the tea. Only then did I come to my senses.

Some two hours later, when everything had quieted down in the harbor, I roused my Cossack. "If I fire my pistol," I told him, "come down to the shore, as fast as you can." His eyes bulged and he answered automatically: "At your orders, sir." I stuck a pistol in my belt and went out. She was waiting for me at the edge of the declivity; her garment was more than light, a flimsy kerchief girded her supple figure.[13]

"Follow me!" she said, taking me by the hand, and we started to walk down. I wonder that I did not break my neck: once below, we turned right and went along the same road along which I had tracked the blind lad on the previous night. The moon had not yet risen and only two little stars, like two guiding beacons, sparkled in the dark blue vault. Heavy waves rolled rhythmically and evenly one after the other, hardly raising the lone boat that was moored to the shore. "Let's get into the boat," said my companion. I hesitated—I am no amateur of sentimental promenades on the sea—but this was not the moment to retreat. She jumped into the boat, I followed, and had barely recovered my senses when I noticed that we were adrift. "What does this mean?" I said crossly. "It means," she said, making me sit on a bench, and winding her arms around my waist, "it means that I love you."

Her cheek pressed mine and I felt, on my face, her flaming breath. Suddenly, something fell into the water, with a noisy splash; my hand flew to my belt—my pistol was gone. Ah, what a terrible suspicion stole into my soul. The blood rushed to my head; I looked around—we were a hundred yards from the shore, and I could not swim! I tried to push her away, but she clung to my clothes like a cat, and suddenly a powerful push almost precipitated me overboard. The boat rocked, but I regained my balance, and a desperate struggle started between us; my rage gave me strength, but I soon realized that, in agility, I was inferior to my adversary. "What do you want?" I cried, squeezing her small hands hard. Her fingers crunched, but she did not cry out; her serpent nature withstood this torture.

"You saw," she replied, "you will tell!" And with a superhuman effort she brought me crashing down against the side of the boat; we both hung over from the waist up; her hair touched the water; it was a decisive moment. I braced my knee against the bottom of the boat; with one hand I seized her by the hair, with the other got hold of her throat; she released my clothes, and I instantly shoved her into the waves.

By that time it was rather dark: once or twice, I glimpsed her head amid the foam, and then I saw nothing more . . .

At the bottom of the boat, I found one half of an old oar, after protracted efforts, somehow managed to reach the landing place. As I made my way along the shore toward my hut, I could not help peering in the direction where, on the eve, the blind lad had waited for the nocturnal navigator. The moon was already riding the sky, and it seemed to me that someone in white sat on the shore: egged on by curiosity, I stole close up and lay in the grass on the brink of the steep shore. Sticking out my head a little, I could clearly see from the cliff all that took place below, and was not much surprised, but felt almost glad, to recognize my mermaid. She was wringing the wet foam out of her long hair; her wet shift outlined her supple figure and raised breasts. In the distance, there soon appeared a boat; quickly it approached; out of it, as on the night before, there stepped a man in a Tatar cap, but with his hair cut in the Cossack fashion, and a large knife sticking out of his leather belt. "Yanko," she said, "all is lost!" After this, their conversation continued, but in such low tones that I could not make out a word of it. "And where is the blind one?" Yanko said at last raising his voice. "I sent him on an errand," was the answer. A few minutes later the blind lad appeared hauling, on his back, a sack which they put into the boat.

"Listen, blind one," said Yanko, "you watch that place . . . know what I mean? . . . there are some rich wares there . . . Tell (I did not catch the name) not to count on my services any longer. Things have gone wrong, he will not see me again; it is dangerous now. I'll go to look for work at some other place, but he will never again find such a bold fellow. Also tell him that if he had paid me better for my labors, then Yanko would not have left him: as for me I'll always find an open road wherever the wind blows and the sea sounds!" After a silence, Yanko continued: "She'll go with me, she can't stay here. And tell the old woman that I guess it is time for her to die, she's lived too long, one ought to know when to quit. As to us, she won't see us again."

"And what about me?" said the blind lad in a piteous voice.

"What use are you to me?" was the answer.

Meanwhile, my undine had jumped into the boat and signaled with her hand to her companion; he put something in the blind lad's hand, saying: "Here, get yourself some gingerbread." "Is that all?" said the blind lad. "Well, here's some more,"—and a fallen coin rang against a stone. The blind lad did not pick it up. Yanko got into the boat; the wind blew off-shore; they hoisted a small sail and sped away. For a long time, the white sail glanced in the moonlight amid the dark waves; the blind lad kept sitting on the shore, and presently I heard something resembling a sob, and indeed, the blind little fellow was crying. He cried for a long, long time . . . I felt sad. What business did fate have to land me into the peaceful midst of *honest smugglers*? Like a stone thrown into the smooth water of a spring, I had disturbed their peace, and like a stone, had very nearly gone to the bottom myself! I returned to my lodgings. In the hallway, the burned-down candle spluttered in a wooden plate, and my Cossack, despite my orders, lay sound asleep, holding his rifle in both hands. I left him in peace, took the candle, and went into the interior of the hut. Alas! My traveling box, my sword chased with silver, my Dagestan dagger—a present from a pal—all had disappeared. It was then that I realized the nature of the things that the confounded blind lad had been hauling. Upon rousing the Cossack with a rather uncivil push, I scolded him and vented my anger a little, but there was nothing to be done. Really, would it not be absurd to complain to the authorities that I had been robbed by a blind boy, and had almost been drowned by an eighteen-year-old girl? Fortunately, next morning it proved possible to continue my journey, and I left Taman. What became of the old woman and of the poor blind lad I do not know. And besides, what do I care about human joys and sorrows—I, a military man on the move, and holder, moreover, of a road pass issued to those on official business!

1840

Translation by Vladimir Nabokov in collaboration
with Dmitri Nabokov

Notes to the translation begin on page 574.

RESOURCES

Primary Text

Lermontov, M.Iu. "Taman." *Sobranie sochinenii v chetyrekh tomakh.* Vol. 4, *Proza, pis'ma,* ed. B.M. Eikhenbaum. Moscow–Leningrad: Akademiia nauk SSSR, 1962, pp. 340–55.

Secondary Sources

Literary and Cultural Studies

Eikhenbaum, B.M. *Lermontov: A Study in Literary-Historical Evaluation.* Trans. Ray Parrott and Harry Weber. Ann Arbor, MI: Ardis, 1981.

Glasse, Antonia. "Lérmontov, Mikhaíl Yúrievich (1814–41)." In *Handbook of Russian Literature,* ed. Victor Terras. New Haven: Yale University Press, 1985, pp. 248–50.

Layton, Susan. "Imagining the Caucasian Hero: Tolstoi Is Mordovcev." *Slavic and East European Journal* 30 (Spring 1986): 1–17.

Manuilov, V.A. *Roman M.Iu. Lermontova: "Geroi nashego vremeni." Kommentarii.* Moscow–Leningrad: Prosveshchenie, 1966.

Maryamov, Yuri. "Man's Thinking Is Bold: An Interview with Victor Shklovsky." *Soviet Literature* 9 (1985): 134–39. .

Mersereau, John. *Mikhail Lermontov.* Carbondale: Southern Illinois University Press, 1962.

Scotto, Peter. "Prisoner of the Caucasus: Ideologies of Imperialism in Lermontov's 'Bela.' " *PMLA* (March 1992): 246–60.

Terras, Victor, *A History of Russian Literature.* New Haven: Yale University Press, 1991, pp. 250–52.

Art

Brodsky, Patricia. "The Demons of Lermontov and Vrubel'." *Slavic and East European Arts* 6 (Winter 1990): 16–32.

Iurova, T.V. *Mikhail Aleksandrovich Vrubel'. 1856–1910.* Moscow: Iskusstvo, 1968.

Ivanova, Z.A. *Zhizn' i tvorchestvo M.Iu. Lermontova.* Moscow: Detskaia literatura, 1964.

Film

Ashik-Kerib. Director, Sergei Paradzhanov. Cinematography, Albert Iavurian. Cast. Iurii Migoian, Veronika Metonidze, and Levan Natroshvilli. 9 reels. 1989.

Kniazhna Meri (Princess Mary). Director, V. Barskii. Georgia: Goskinprom, 1926.

Kniazhna Meri (Princess Mary). Director, Isidor Annenskii. Music, Lev Shvarts. Cinematographer, M. Kirillov. Mosfilm, 1955.

~ IV ~

Subversions of Secularization

In the nineteenth century, Russia reached a new stage of political influence and economic development. Formerly a local power, Russia now became a serious competitor for nations like England with their own aspirations to maintain empires. In similar fashion, Russian culture, especially Russian literature, began to exert a strong influence beyond its borders. The reasons for the new strengths in political and economic matters are beyond our scope, but it is appropriate to ask: What contributed to the cultural achievements of the nineteenth century?

One historical process that prodded cultural vitality is perhaps an unexpected source of inspiration for modern secular sensibilities. As we have seen, unlike the eighteenth century, with its strong rejection of religion, the beginnings of the nineteenth saw a religious revival and social and political structures created around religious values and impulses. The religious search for transcendent truths acted as a challenge for writers in new secular conditions. Even those men and women of letters who were not overly diligent in their attendance of church services—although we know that most of the major Russian writers of the nineteenth century did indeed participate in religious rituals and did learn their catechisms in childhood—responded to the long-standing ultimate issues of existence postulated in Russian Orthodoxy. One did not need to have a strong faith in the God of churchmen to attempt to define the nature of God (perhaps a sublimation of human needs, as Feuerbach suggested) or to investigate the psychological and moral implications of love, to question the value of suffering and humility, and to wonder about human directions deprived of a sense of transcendence.

Aesthetic and intellectual creativity stimulated by the challenge of older religious values to secular sensibilities was not unique to Russian culture, of

147

course. The Russians, along with most Western intellectuals, felt the influence of religious-secular transmutations, in philosophy through German idealism and in literature through Romanticism. Most influential teachers of idealism in Russia during the 1820s and 1830s, in fact, had been trained in religious seminaries and academies.

Such training could be felt in an ideological extremism that produced, among the most harmful results, men and women who were willing not only to imagine utopias common to Western social theory but to bring theories into practice no matter what the cost. In the arts, however, extremism stimulated daring, originality, hard work, and commitment to change. In the nineteenth century, Russian fiction, music, and painting played out to extremes some of the vital ideas of Western civilization, before succumbing in the twentieth to the temptations of shaping history according to ideology.

Ideology, of course, suggests communism, and Marx's eventual favored place in Russian history, although ultimately the source of tragedy and totalitarianism, in turn suggests another key element of aesthetic and intellectual vitality. For the reception of Marx in Russia could only have occurred in conditions of an essential openness to the ideas of others. As in most healthy and productive cultures, the nineteenth century in Russia saw an active pluralism invigorate intellectual debate and the arts. This pluralism helps to explain why censorship and authoritarian government under Nicholas I and Alexander III were not dominant or ultimately telling factors in aesthetic results. There was, as noted, an attachment to the long-standing heritage of Orthodoxy and a favored political interpretation of it, but those who wrote novels, composed music, and painted landscapes measured their native religious tradition not so much by politicians as by Schiller, Schelling, Hegel, Feuerbach, Darwin, and Mill, or Goethe, Byron, Stendhal, Dickens, and Dumas. Russian Orthodox theological thought itself interacted freely with Protestant and Catholic views. In result, the key intellectual debates noted in most histories—of the Westernizers, Slavophiles, left Hegelians, utopian socialists, populists—took on universal issues and a passion for synthesis that cut across national and ethnic borders.

Open cultural and economic borders allowed a broad diversity of immigrants, who contributed to the vitality of the arts. We have already noted the architects and painters of the eighteenth and early nineteenth centuries who came out of foreign families or were Russians who had studied abroad. Of the writers included below, Lermontov was the descendant of a Scottish mercenary, Gogol a Ukrainian, and Pushkin, the Russian national poet, the great-grandson of an African slave. All three were the products of a culture that had learned to look not only to the West and East but south as well. Thus, if in politics Russia succumbed to the temptations of imperialism, in the arts its assimilation of the aesthetic and intellectual traditions of others created a rich and fertile ground for creative imagination.

The issues raised by men and women of letters stimulated an unprecedented outburst of interrepresentational activity. The texts included here were all transformed into other art forms and helped shape creative practices outside of literature. The writers responsible for them, however, did not work in cultural hothouses of aesthetic activity removed from outside social and political concerns. Pushkin's *Boris Godunov* is one such central instance of cultural intersections. The text induced major aesthetic transfigurations in music, art, and performance, but Pushkin's work was also a primary example of the Russian literary response to history and, in turn, of the historical sense Russians derived from literature.

Pushkin wrote the play in 1825, largely inspired, as he pointed out, by Nikolai Karamzin and William Shakespeare. The period he chose, the late fifteenth century and the early sixteenth, was a dynamic and unsettled time in Russia, not unlike Elizabethan England. The feudal era and Mongol domination had come to an end after the intelligent rule of Ivan III and the brutal imposition of military power and government terror by his grandson Ivan IV ("the Terrible"), who killed the prospective Ivan V, his oldest son and heir to the throne, an event later made familiar to many Russians through Ilya Repin's striking painting done in 1885. Boris Godunov, a respected member of Ivan's court, began his rule as regent for his brother-in-law, Ivan's other son, Fedor. Another younger son of Ivan IV, Dmitry, died in 1591 under mysterious circumstances but quite definitely from knife wounds. When Fedor in turn passed away in 1598, an Assembly of the Land elected Boris to the throne, a highly democratic process for that time. Votes from representatives of different social classes were taken into account; unfortunately, the political chicanery familiar to elections (and reflected in Pushkin's play) was also evident.

In 1602 a man named Grigory Otrepyev suddenly appeared in Poland claiming to be Dmitry and thus the legitimate heir of Ivan. He invaded Russia with Polish aid; in the course of the invasion in 1605 Boris died. The "False" Dmitry did become tsar for a while but was eventually killed, and his remains were fired back to Poland out of a cannon. The collapse of his reign brought on the so-called Time of Troubles, a chaotic period full of disasters and new invasions by foreign armies. A semblance of political order was brought back to Russian history only with the election, again democratic by seventeenth-century standards, of another tsar, Mikhail (the young boy we have already encountered thanks to Glinka's opera), the first of the Romanovs.

These were the key events related in Karamzin's *History of the Russian State* (12 volumes, 1818–29), Pushkin's primary source. What in them attracted Pushkin to Boris's historical period and what elements of Boris's life made it important for Russian culture? A primary issue, aided considerably in its formulation by Shakespeare, was legitimacy, and legitimacy not merely in the simple monarchist's sense of God's genetic imprimatur but in the larger sense of opposing political and moral claims to determine the course of history. The Russian view that tsars were not just supreme political authorities but "servants" of two masters, God and the people, as well as a traditional distrust of chaotic democratic processes unresponsive to the harmony of transcendent standards, reflected this basic cultural concern. In the play, as in most historical accounts, Boris was recognized to be a wonderfully skilled politician; yet the clever, even wise manipulation of government was not enough and, in fact, was considered to be a prime example of short-sightedness when based on immoral action. Russian preoccupations with Boris's unfortunate life, with Dmitry's death, with the temporary success and eventual failure of the False Dmitry, and with the chaos of the Time of Troubles were part, then, of long-standing convictions that legitimacy in human affairs was related to spiritual legitimacy.

Such views were not confined to Russian culture, of course, and Shakespeare did much to show Pushkin the theatrical ways to explore moral and political illegitimacy in terms of psychological nuances. Western Romanticism's interpretation of Shakespeare and its emphasis on strong personalities in history were also clearly reflected in Boris's central positioning. The Boris story is joined by the Dmitry story in almost all Russian cultural responses, however, and the latter does indeed suggest particular issues inspired by the Byzantine heritage of kenoticism and holy foolishness.

As in the case of St. Dmitry's vita, the Boris and Gleb narratives, and Avvakum's autobiography, prime values incorporated into Pushkin's play included humility, sacrifice, and suspicion of merely earthly well-being. In their light, Dmitry's murder, as retold by Pushkin, indicated once again the moral failure of political expediency and aggrandizement. Both in the play and in Mussorgsky's opera, a *salos,* a holy fool, is used to remind audiences of such long-standing belief in the higher truths.

For Pushkin, as for Karamzin before him and Mussorgsky after, religious values, however, were firmly joined to other, metacultural responsibilities. In play and opera the central role of men and women of culture in interpreting historical events and in judging them by transcendent standards is expressed by the monk Pimen. Pimen's famous monologue, beginning "One more, last narrative," is as finely composed as the best of Pushkin's verse and as memorable as the most engaging of musical motifs. It is as familiar to the Russian intelligentsia as the Pledge of Allegiance is to Americans, and it reflects a firm belief in the power of literature to provide an independent,

honest engagement with vital questions. Although Pimen represents an obvious acknowledgment of the religious imperatives shaping cultural values,
he does not simply offer testimony of God's punishment for a sinful life—
the type of historical evidence naively religious Russians have found in the
Mongol invasion, the Bolshevik revolution, or Stalin's terror. He is, rather,
the archetypal man of letters, aware of the larger patterns, including patterns
of irony and chance that figure prominently in Boris's story and that often
escape short-sighted and self-serving politicians. Pimen, in short, is
Pushkin's and Mussorgsky's pledge to their craft and an affirmation of their
allegiance to the independent governments of drama and music.

The story of Boris Godunov continued to influence Russian culture after
the first production of Mussorgsky's opera in 1870. Nikolai Rimsky-
Korsakov created a redaction of Mussorgsky's score that was to replace
Mussorgsky's own in the repertoire of most opera houses of Russia and the
West. In 1908 the impresario Sergei Diaghilev brought a landmark produc-
tion featuring Fedor Chaliapin to Paris as part of an effort to acquaint
Western audiences with the best of the Russian arts. Chaliapin in the role of
Boris in turn inspired Aleksandr Golovin's famous painting done in 1912.

A relatively successful theatrical version of Pushkin's drama was
produced in 1907 by Vladimir Nemirovich-Danchenko at the Moscow Art
Theater. Vsevolod Meyerhold worked on two unrealized productions, the
last with Sergei Prokofiev in 1936. The post-Stalin era saw directors such
as Anatoly Efros and Sergei Bondarchuk prepare television versions of the
play. Finally, perhaps the most successful theatrical version of *Boris* was
produced in 1982 by Yury Liubimov at the Taganka Theater in Moscow. At
first the play was not admitted into the repertoire; later, during perestroika
and glasnost, the changes in Russian history were sharply reflected in its
fate. Nikolai Gubenko, who played Boris in the first version, came back to
the role in a renewed production while simultaneously performing the
duties of USSR minister of culture under Gorbachev. In both instances, the
continued vitality of the *Boris* text was demonstrated by the equally strong
if completely different cultural resonances of Gubenko's role during the
Brezhnev era and after Gorbachev's reforms. Particularly memorable was
the ending of the performance. Speaking outside of his role, Gubenko delivered Mosalsky's last lines to the audience rather than to the actors and
placed a strong emphasis on the question: Why are you silent?

Boris Godunov has been most prominent, however, in Mussorgsky's
opera version. Out of numerous productions staged throughout the world,
Andrei Tarkovsky's redaction performed at London's Covent Garden
in 1983 and brought to the Kirov Opera in 1990 was one of the most
acclaimed. Tarkovsky used a set racked at a precarious angle and composed

Aleksandr Golovin's portrait of Fedor Chaliapin in the role of Boris Godunov.

of ruins, scaffolding, and debris, a true theatrical deconstruction, one is tempted to say, not so much of Pushkin's text as of the perennial cultural values it involves. The set, along with the more traditional images of holy fool, bell, pendulum, angel, children, and bloody axe, served to bring into stage existence both the moral instability signaled by the political events of Boris's time and the collapse of values and historical insecurity of the Gorbachev era.

Pushkin's "Queen of Spades" (1833), another text become familiar in opera, like *Boris Godunov,* reflected Romanticism. Herman is cast in the mold of a typical Romantic hero, even to the extent of reminding Liza, his prey, of Romanticism's favored historical protagonist, Napoleon. By the 1830s, however, Pushkin was convinced that the only proper fate for truly

Romantic characters was a merciful death, as administered, for example, to the hapless Lensky by his friend Eugene Onegin. Romanticism in the form of willful heroes, political rebels, and demons come to earth now served as a stepping stone, often through parody, to new literary concerns. Herman shows his Romantic genes in his strong and silent personality and his demonic will; his goal, however, is not the heady metaphysical stuff of true Romantic fiction but the quite practical matter of money. On the same pattern of transmutation of earlier cultural motifs, the supernatural is very much present in the story and given a strong Romantic coloring through magical cards, ghosts, and heady passions. Such representations of spiritual forces, however, are now firmly related to mundane psychological and moral causes. Pushkin, thus, firmly moved Russian culture out of the spiritual graveyard taken seriously in the translation of Thomas Grey written by Pushkin's mentor, Vasily Zhukovsky, and in the direction of the explorations of personality and morality undertaken by writers like Nikolai Gogol and Fedor Dostoevsky.

Tchaikovsky's opera, based on Pushkin's text, made Romanticism partially viable again by the force of musical genius. It was, of course, a cultural revitalization repeated over and over again for other Romantic narratives whose existence on the twentieth-century stage was maintained by the musical talents of a Verdi or a Puccini. The most direct prod to Tchaikovsky's imagination, however, was not the Romantic sensibility but a dry commercial request from the Imperial Theater. The libretto was begun by Tchaikovsky's brother Modest together with a now forgotten composer named Klenovsky, who was hired to write the music but who fortunately never completed the work. Tchaikovsky agreed to take on the job in 1889. The opera was finished in a year and premiered at the Mariinsky Theater in 1890.

The libretto, then as now, was received as the weakest part of the opera, particularly when Pushkin's original story was introduced for comparison. Modest Tchaikovsky's talent in opera adaptation was undoubtedly equally far removed from his brother's talent in musical composition and from Pushkin's prose skills. Comparatists of the original and the libretto have been particularly critical of the opera's revised plot. At the conclusion, Herman and Liza both commit suicide in a double dose of melodrama run amok. Nevertheless, Tchaikovsky's melodic discoveries surely transcend the libretto; somehow, magically, the musical result ends in equal company with Pushkin's aesthetic achievement. After a notable 1902 production in Vienna under the baton of Gustav Mahler and the New York premiere of the German version in 1910, *The Queen of Spades* became a familiar presence in the major opera companies of the world.

Pushkin's influence was broader than *Boris Godunov* or "The Queen of Spades" and reflected his central position in Russian culture. While creating models of different literary genres to be used as measures by writers who followed him, he also managed to provide fundamental material for the other arts. The dance master Didelot (1767–1837) turned his "The Prisoner of the Caucasus" into a ballet immediately after its publication and followed that production with a staging of "Ruslan and Liudmila." Mikhail Glinka used the same text to compose his opera in 1842; his musical versions of Pushkin's poems—for example, "Oh, do not sing," "I remember that enchanting moment"—are among the most successful examples of a popular interrepresentational activity undertaken by many Russian composers. Longer musical compositions based on Pushkin's work—including Tchaikovsky's *Eugene Onegin* (1878), Rimsky-Korsakov's fairy tale operas, Rachmaninov's *Aleko* (1892) and *The Fountains of Bakhchisarai*—are now part of the opera canon.

"The Overcoat" (1842), written by Pushkin's acquaintance Nikolai Gogol (1809–1852), exerted an influence equal in importance to the texts noted above. Scholars cannot agree whether a remark attributed to Dostoevsky, "We all came out of Gogol's 'Overcoat,'" is apocryphal, but the sentiment reflects cultural reality. One of the better definitions of Gogol's work is that it represents a form of "Romantic Realism." This designation is very broad indeed and can be taken to mean many things, but it neatly expresses the writer's continued Romantic dissatisfaction with reality. Gogol's misfortune is that his readers have consistently insisted on lowering his sights (along with their own, of course) to dissatisfaction with *social* reality and on depriving his creative vision of its more profound metaphysical *angst*. But this socialized Gogol—from the first praise of him by Vissarion Belinsky (1811–1848) to the last works of scholarship published in the Soviet Union—is the most visible one in Russian culture.

The interpretation of Gogol's work as social criticism resplendent with the much abused combination of "laughter and tears" was wonderfully reflected in a film adaptation directed by Aleksei Batalov and starring Rolan Bykov. The film, within its preferences, demonstrated the best of Russian acting technique and cinematography available in the 1970s. A considerable stimulant to the performing arts was provided earlier by Gogol's *The Inspector General,* viewed as a classic of Russian theater long before Danny Kaye adapted his own brand of inanity to the Hollywood version, and even before the legendary 1926 production of Vsevolod Meyerhold. In 1927 Dmitry Shostakovich composed his version of "The Nose," basing the opera on Gogol's short story, as Modest Mussorgsky had based his *Sorochintsy Fair* (1874–80, unfinished) and Rimsky-Korsakov had based *May's Night* (1880) on texts full of Gogol's humor and play with the supernatural. One of the most popular adaptations of Gogol's work was the 1932 Moscow Art Theater's *Dead Souls*. The play was developed at cross-purposes by two masters—the director Konstantin Stanislavsky and the playwright Mikhail Bulgakov—but it managed to transcend creative differences and to bring tears of laughter to the eyes of numerous audiences. A later opera version was composed by Roman Shchedrin.

The religious and social duality of Gogol's cultural presence was also evident in two major concerns of Russian painters. The first is expressed by the religious themes of his friend Aleksandr Ivanov (1806–1858), who took twenty years to complete his master canvas, *Apparition of Christ to the People,* the works of Nikolai Ge (1831–1894), and Mikhail Nesterov (1862–1942). The second took art to be a form of social indictment and included the paintings of Vasily Perov (1833–1882), Pavel Fedotov (1815–1852), and the Wanderers school of Ivan Kramskoi (1837–1887) and Ilya Repin (1844–1930).

Gogol's dual cultural influence is reflected in two different statues cast in the twentieth century. The first, completed by N.A. Andreev in 1909, represents a hunched-over Gogol, considered to be too pessimistic and self-contained by Soviet authorities. In 1951 it was removed from Gogol Boulevard and eventually placed in the hidden Moscow courtyard of No. 7 Suvorovsky Boulevard, the building in which Gogol died. In 1952 the statue was replaced on the boulevard's more central and accessible site by an upright and ostensibly more optimistic Gogol created by N.V. Tomsky. The Taganka Theater, in a production titled *A Tale of Inspection* (1978), used actors' representations of both statues of Gogol on stage as essential signs of the two political and moral interpretations of the writer. A similar use of a writer's monument to comment on the state of culture was evident in 1988. Journalists pointed out in print that the famous statue of Pushkin on Tverskoi Boulevard (former Gorky Street), object of numerous pilgrimages and companion to innumerable passionate debates of street speakers, was now staring in apparent dejection at the McDonald's Restaurant across the street.

Ivan Turgenev (1818–1883), like Gogol, found inspiration in modes of literary perception known as the natural school in Russia and naturalism in the West. Although sharing intellectual sources, the two literary movements were notably different in several regards; in particular, in Russian literary responses the weight of biological and environmental evidence never overwhelmed the search for a transcendent dimension of humanity, unlike the heavy burden of predetermination carried by Zola's works in France or Dreiser's in the United States. Turgenev, who knew well not only the major

Nikolai Gogol as portrayed by N.A. Andreev (left) and N.V. Tomsky (right).

Russian writers but also Flaubert and Henry James, was trained in German metaphysics at its most pessimistic and bridged the two literary schools. The nature of "Bezhin Meadow" (1851), a central narrative included in Turgenev's *Huntsman's Sketches* (1852), is as majestic as Schelling ever imagined and as all-powerful and indifferent to human hopes as Herbert Spencer, the leading philosopher of naturalism in the West, ever suggested. Much later, in the 1930s, Sergei Eisenstein would use the pessimistic tonalities of Turgenev's story in a film of the same name to show the privileges of the Soviet Future over the reactionary past.

Other expressions of pessimistic detachment in Turgenev's writings led both the right and the left wings of Russian politics to attack him, particularly after the publication of his most influential novel, *Fathers and Children* (1862). That text forever after defined the two generations of the 1840s and 1860s—the first liberal, the second radical—which steered the course of Russian history in its particular pursuit of progress. Dostoevsky could not forgive Turgenev for pretending to hold· himself above the fray (and perhaps for anticipating a cherished theme developed in *The Brothers Karamazov*). The image of Bazarov, the hero of *Fathers and Children* who wants to turn nature into a workshop but whose grave finally becomes part of nature's temple, continued to inspire Russian culture as late as 1982, when the Moscow Art Theater brought out a stage adaptation entitled *Evgeny Bazarov.*

The sense of nature given literary voice by Turgenev was reflected directly in the skillful illustrations of Klavdy V. Lebedev (1852–1916), particularly in his work *Bezhin Meadow* (1884), and in Vladimir E. Makovsky's (1846–1920) *Nighttime* (1879); and in a more general sense in the canvases of two genre painters, Ivan Aivazovsky (1817–1900) and Ivan Shishkin (1832–1898). Aivazovsky's subject (dominant in a rich creative output of approximately six thousand canvases) was the sea, and Shishkin's the forest. Their paintings stimulated the type of affection among the Russian public reserved for works of art reproduced on household objects and carpets. Other painters, such as Vasily Polenov (1844–1927) and Arkhip Kuindzhi (1842–1910), helped make landscapes a central aesthetic form. Chekhov's friend Isaak Levitan (1860–1900) continued the tradition of honoring nature in art; the deceptive simplicity and nuance of his canvases is often reminiscent of Chekhov's and Turgenev's literary styles.

Nikolai Leskov (1831–1895) was influenced by Gogol's humor and moral engagement but defended his own creative and social vision. His fiction—mostly short stories and novels—made famous the technique of *skaz,* a literary style dependent on uses of vernacular idiom and a verbal form of the aesthetic irony familiar to naif painters. Leskov distilled larger cultural patterns in his work by using kenotic types and religious subjects but in fundamental opposition to the church establishment.

Leskov's "Lefty" (1881) depicts one such traditional Russian protagonist caught up in the cross-currents of East and West. The story is laced with sympathetic irony directed at typical generalizations about Russian national character, special ethnic capabilities, and different appreciations of technology evident in Russia and Europe. A memorable adaptation of "Lefty," "one of the greatest hits of the Soviet stage," according to Victor Terras, was done by the Second Moscow Art Theater in 1925 as *The Flea.*[1] Some major aesthetic talents of the day were involved in the production: Evgeny Zamiatin wrote the script, the painter Boris Kustodiev created the stage design, and Aleksei Diky both directed the play and performed the role of Platov.

Another of Leskov's *skaz* tales, "Lady Macbeth of the Mtsensk District" (1865), was adapted by Dmitry Shostakovich to opera in 1932 and viciously attacked by Socialist Realist critics. Shostakovich had every right to be

Evgeny Lebedev (left) as Holstomer and M. Danilov (right) as the groom in a **1976** performance of *The Story of a Horse* directed by Georgy Tovstonogov at the Bolshoi Dramatic Theater.

upset by this reception since his work had changed Leskov's bright moral fable into an often-repeated story of social victimization fully in tune with Soviet ideology. After Stalin, of course, the musical talent of the opera came to be widely recognized even under the new title, "Katerina Izmailova." A theatrical adaptation directed by Andrei Goncharov was more successful in transmitting the irony and play of Leskov's literary style. Subtitled "A Chorus Skaz in Ten Musical Numbers," it featured the irrepressible Natalia Gundareva in the main role and played for a long run in the Moscow Mayakovsky Theater during the late 1970s and 1980s.

The extraordinary influence Fedor Dostoevsky (1821–1881) and Lev Tolstoy (1828–1910) have had on Western culture has frequently brought them together in commentary and appraisals. In spite of obvious differences in ideas and literary methods, there is some justification in the juxtaposition, not only in terms of degree of influence but also in their cultural positioning and the nature of their literary work. Both writers, a broad range of social, political, and aesthetic interactions with Russian culture notwithstanding, used the native religious tradition and the familiar kenotic values of humility and meekness as moral ballast. Exploration of these primary values in terms of complex psychological and social issues is a central inspiration of both literary texts included here but can also be seen to have executive functions in responses throughout the arts to their major novels and other literary works.

Although Dostoevsky never published a play (two he wrote in his youth on historical themes are lost), modern Russian theater is unimaginable without him. Landmark adaptations have included the Moscow Art Theater's *Brothers Karamazov* (1910), *Nikolai Stavrogin* (1913), *The Village of Stepanchikovo* (1917), and *Uncle's Dream* (1929); Georgy Tovstonogov's Bolshoi Dramatic Theater production of *The Idiot* (1957); Anatoly Efros and Victor Rozov's *Brother Alesha* (1972) at the Malaia Bronnaia Theater; and Yury Liubimov's *Crime and Punishment* (1979) at the Taganka Theater. Tolstoy wrote plays such as *The Fruit of Enlightenment* and *The Power of Darkness,* but his novels stimulated an equally vital theatrical response in Prokofiev's opera, the Moscow Art Theater's *Resurrection* (1929) and *Anna Karenina* (1936), and other dramatic and ballet versions.

"The Meek Woman" (1876) and "Holstomer" (1885) each inspired a notable stage version at the Bolshoi Dramatic Theater. The Dostoevsky adaptation was done by Lev Dodin in 1981 and offered the talented actor Oleg Borisov material for a memorable performance; "Holstomer" was staged by Georgy Tovstonogov as *The Story of a Horse* in 1975 and was also the occasion for important work by a well-known actor, Evgeny Lebedev. Both productions were redone in English versions in the West.

Literary appreciations of the two writers suggest some of the reasons for the influence of these texts on theater. A study focusing on feminist issues evaluates "The Meek Woman" as "one of Dostoevsky's greatest stories about women."[2] Robert Belknap interprets the ending of the story to be "the most personal, most emotional, most religious and intertextually most moving passage [Dostoevsky] ever wrote."[3] The text's psychological depth and complexity, in exploring reasons for the young woman's suicide, are of considerable interest to later concerns about the problematic social roles of women, their moral dilemmas, and their relationships with men.

Tolstoy's "Holstomer" engages one of his most sustained uses of *ostra-*

nenie, or the process of "making strange," which literary critics have found to be important. For the Formalists, Tolstoy's manipulation of perspective to reach a strange, unexpected, and above all honest sense of things was one of his primary contributions to moving literature forward. The *ostranenie* impulse canonized by twentieth-century critics can be traced to Tolstoy's appreciation of eighteenth-century dissatisfactions, including Rousseau's dissatisfaction with social and moral hypocrisy. In "Holstomer," frustration with flawed human vision and morality leads to the marginalization of humanity—again strongly appealing in the late twentieth century—and withdrawal to the more natural point of view of the animal kingdom. This unconventional horse perspective unexpectedly inspired a memorable theater transformation at the Bolshoi Dramatic Theater. The production, one of the most popular directed by Tovstonogov, was fully in keeping with Tolstoy's frustrations with human imperfection but demonstrated the theater's very human arts of mimesis and music and a wonderfully strange ostension.

Dostoevsky's and Tolstoy's texts have assumed equally prominent functions in Russian film history. All of their major novels (and a great deal of their short fiction) have been adapted in cinematic versions. The productions show varying degrees of creative success but are equally representative of unflagging interest—both intellectual and commercial—in the two writers. In some instances, Russian, like Western, films have demonstrated the extreme lengths to which producers and directors are willing to go in trivializing the classics. In others, such as Yakov Protazanov's *Father Sergius* (1918), Ivan Pyriev's *The Idiot* (1957), Lev Kulidzhanov's *Crime and Punishment* (1978), as well as Akira Kurosawa's *The Idiot* (1951) and Martin Scorcese's *Taxi Driver* (1976), the literary characters imagined by Tolstoy and Dostoevsky have been profitably extended to deal with issues of the twentieth century. For Russian film, as for the other arts, Dostoevsky's and Tolstoy's texts have served to keep alive cultural memory of complex and profound creative involvements during periods of deadening political repression, but they have also provided cultural beacons during historical moments of unsettling change, disillusionment, and the search for new values and principles.

N. R.

Notes

1. Victor Terras, *A History of Russian Literature,* New Haven: Yale University Press, 1991, p. 599.
2. Nina Pelikan Straus, *Dostoevsky and the Woman Question,* New York: St. Martin's Press, 1994, p. 97.
3. Robert Belknap, *The Genesis of the Brothers Karamazov,* Evanston: Northwestern University Press, 1990, p. 35.

11

~Alexander Pushkin~

Boris Godunov

This work, inspired by his genius and with reverence and gratitude, is dedicated to the memory, dear to Russians, of *Nikolai Mikhailovich Karamzin,*[1] by Alexander Pushkin.

The Kremlin Palace. February 20, 1598

PRINCE SHUISKY *and* PRINCE VOROTYNSKY

VOROTYNSKY
We've made ready to watch over the city,
But now it seems there's no one left to watch.
Moscow's deserted, all the people gone
To the monastery, after the Patriarch.
What do you think will be the end result of the disturbance?

SHUISKY
The end result? It's easy to predict.
The people will continue howling, crying,
Boris will scowl some more,
Like a drunkard sitting over wine,
And, finally, out of his goodness
He will agree to take the crown
And then—and then he'll rule us
As before.

VOROTYNSKY
            But it is now a month
Since, shut up in the monastery with his sister,[2]
He seems to have withdrawn from the world.
Neither the Patriarch, nor boyars of the Duma
Have managed yet to change his mind;

161

He heeds not tearful exhortations,
Nor pleas, nor all of Moscow's groans,
Nor the Great Council's voice.
Appeals to his sister to bless Boris
To take the reign have proven useless.
The sad tsarina-nun
Like him is firm, like him is unappealable.
It seems Boris himself in this encouraged her;
What if the ruler is indeed
Bored with the matters of the reign
And will not powerless ascend the throne?
What would you say?

SHUISKY

                           I'd say for nothing
Was shed the baby prince's blood;
That if it's so, Dmitry could be yet alive.

VOROTYNSKY

A horrible and evil deed! Enough, however, is it true
The Prince was killed by Boris?

SHUISKY

                              And who else?
Who bribed, and all for nothing, Chepchugov?
Who sent both Bitiagovskys there
Together with Kachalov? I was dispatched to Uglich
To look for clues on site
And came upon fresh traces;
All in the town bore witness to the evil deed;
All citizens agreed on what they saw;
When I returned, I could have with one word
Exposed the hidden villain.

VOROTYNSKY

Why did you not destroy him then?

SHUISKY

He, I confess, confused me at that time,
So calm, surprising in his lack of shame.
He looked into my eyes, appearing righteous.

He questioned me in great detail—
And I echoed for him the nonsense,
That he himself whispered to me.

VOROTYNSKY
A dirty business, Prince.

SHUISKY
                          And what was I to do?
Reveal all to Fedor? The Tsar, however, saw
All through the eyes of Godunov.
Heard all with his, Godunov's ears.
If I had even managed to convince him
Boris would have dissuaded him,
And then I would have been imprisoned,
And like my uncle, one fine day,
Quietly strangled in a remote cell.
I am not bragging, but, of course,
No execution frightens me,
I'm not a coward but I'm also not a fool
And won't agree to place a noose around my neck in vain.

VOROTYNSKY
A horrible and evil deed! However listen, it's quite likely
The murderer now is troubled by remorse:
That must be it, the guiless child's blood
Prevents him from ascending to the throne.

SHUISKY
He will step over it! Boris is not so meek!
What honor to us, to all of Russia!
Yesterday's slave, a Tatar, Maliuta's brother-in-law,
An executioner's brother-in-law, at heart,
Himself an executioner,
Will take the wreath and Monomakh's[3] regalia.

VOROTYNSKY
Exactly, his is not a noble family, we are the more distinguished.

SHUISKY
Yes, so it seems.

VOROTYNSKY
                    For, Shuisky, Vorotynsky . . .
Take note, are princes of the blood.

SHUISKY
By blood, and progeny of Rurik.[4]

VOROTYNSKY
But listen, Prince, we'd have the right
To reign following Fedor.

SHUISKY
                    More so
Than Godunov.

VOROTYNSKY
                    And after all!

SHUISKY
                    Why not?
While Boris keeps on being clever,
Let's skillfully stir the people up,
So they abandon Godunov; they have
Their own princes aplenty, they can
Chose any one of them to be their tsar.

VOROTYNSKY
We are not small in number, progeny of Vikings,[5]
But it is hard to battle Godunov:
The people now no longer see us as descendants
Of their ferocious overlords.
For long we've lost our holdings,
For long we've served as vassals to the tsars.
And he has known how, with fear, and love,
And fame, to hypnotize the people.

SHUISKY
                                        (Looking in the window)
He is courageous, that is all, while we . . . enough, look,
The people are returning, one by one.
Let's quickly go, find out, if it is settled.

Red Square

THE PEOPLE

A MAN

He cannot be persuaded! He drove away
Men of the church, boyars, and Patriarch.
They fell low to his feet for nothing;
The throne's aurora frightens him.

SECOND MAN

My God, by whom will we be governed?
Oh, woe is us!

THIRD MAN

　　　　　　Here is the head official
Come out to tell us the Duma's decision.

THE PEOPLE

Be quiet! Quiet! The Duma's official speaks;
Shh—listen now!

SHCHELKALOV

(From the Red Platform)

　　　　　　The council has decreed
To try and to appeal one last time
To our ruler's grief-stricken soul.
At dawn again His Holiness the Patriarch,
Having performed a solemn service in the Kremlin,
Preceded by the saintly banners
With the Vladimir, Don icons,[6]
Will go in a procession; with him the council and boyars,
And groups of nobles, chosen people,
And all the Orthodox inhabitants of Moscow,
We'll all again go beg of the Tsarina,
To pity orphan Moscow,
And bless Boris to take the crown.
And you go to your homes with God,
Pray—so to heavens rises up
Orthodox fervent supplications.

(The people disperse)

Maiden's Field. Novodevichy Monastery[7]

THE PEOPLE

A MAN
They went to the Tsarina's cell,
Boris, the Patriarch,
A crowd of boyars.

ANOTHER MAN
                    What news?

THIRD MAN
                                        He still
Remains stubborn; but there is hope.

A COMMON WOMAN *(with a child)*
Agoo! Don't cry, don't cry; A bogeyman, a bogeyman
Will get you! Agoo, agoo! . . . Don't cry!

A MAN
Can we get past the barrier?

ANOTHER
We can't! Where to! It's even crowded in the field,
Not only over there. You think it's easy? All of Moscow
Is jammed together in this place; just look: the wall, the roofs,
All tiers of the cathedral belfry,
The tops of churches and the very crosses
Are covered totally by people.

FIRST MAN
                            That's true, and what a sight!

A MAN
What is that noise?

ANOTHER MAN
                    Yes, listen! What's that noise?
The folk are howling, falling down in waves,
Row after row . . . another . . . yet another . . .
Well, brother, it's our turn; quick, on your knees!

THE PEOPLE

(On their knees. Moaning and wailing)

Father, be merciful! Reign over us!
Be father to us, tsar!

A MAN

Why are they crying?

ANOTHER MAN

How should we know? The boyars know such things
And not our kind.

A COMMON WOMAN *(with a child)*

And so? When time has come to cry
You've quieted down! I'll give you one! Look there, a bogeyman!
So cry, you spoiled brat!

(Throws child to the ground. Child squeals)
That's better.

A MAN

They're all crying,
Let us cry also, brother.

ANOTHER MAN

Brother, I'm straining
But I can't.

FIRST MAN

Me too. Does anyone have onions?
We'll rub our eyes.

SECOND MAN

No, I will use some spit.
What's happening now?

FIRST MAN

Who knows?

THE PEOPLE

The crown is his! He's tsar! He has agreed!
Our tsar is Boris! Long live Boris!

The Kremlin Palace

BORIS, THE PATRIARCH, BOYARS

BORIS

You, Reverend Patriarch, and all you, boyars,
Before you naked is my soul:
You see, that I accept great power
With trepidation and humility.
What heavy burden is my duty!
For I inherit from the mighty Ivans—[8]
For I inherit from the Angel-Tsar![9]
O righteous one! O Sovereign Father!
Look down from heaven on your faithful servants' tears
And send to one, whom you have loved,
Whom you so marvelously raised up high,
A holy blessing to take power,
So that in glory I will rule my people,
So that I will be good and just, like you.
I expect your cooperation, boyars,
Serve me, as you served him,
When I your labors shared,
Not chosen yet by people's will.

BOYARS

We won't betray the oath we gave.

BORIS

Now let us go pay homage to the graves
Of Russia's rulers in repose,
And then—to call our people all to feast,
They all, from nobles to the beggar blind-man;
They all are free to come, all are our cherished guests.

(He leaves, followed by the BOYARS*)*

VOROTYNSKY

(Stopping SHUISKY*)*

You guessed it.

SHUISKY

What?

VOROTYNSKY

You know, the other day,
Don't you remember?

SHUISKY

No, nothing at all.

VOROTYNSKY

The people, when they went to Maiden's Field,
You said . . .

SHUISKY

Now's not the time to remember,
I recommend forgetfulness now and then.
But by the way, pretending wicked talk
I only wanted then to test you,
Or more exactly, know your secret thoughts;
But there—the people hail the Tsar—
My absence could be noted—
I follow them.

VOROTYNSKY

Sly palace rat!

Night. A Cell in the Chudov Monastery.[10]
The Year 1603

FATHER PIMEN, GRIGORY *asleep*[11]

PIMEN

(Writing before an icon lamp)

One more, last narrative—
And then my chronicle is done,
Fulfilled the duty, God's bequest
To me, a sinner. Not in vain
The Lord made me a witness of so many years
And taught to me the letters' art;
Some day a diligent monk
Will find my dutiful, anonymous work,
He'll light, as I, his lamp—
And, after shaking age's dust from parchment,
Will copy the true narratives,
So progeny of the Orthodox know

Their native land's past fate,
So they commemorate their great tsars
For their labors, for glory, for kind deeds,
And in the case of sins and acts of darkness
The Savior humbly beseech.
In old age I live once again,
Days bygone pass before me,
Has it been long they surged full of events
In tumult, like the ocean-sea?
Now they are without voice and calm,
Not many faces memory for me preserved,
Not many words come back to me,
And all the rest has perished irrevocably . . .
But day is near, the lamp burns down—
One more, last narrative.

(He writes)

GRIGORY

(Awakening)

The very dream! How can it be? Three times!
Cursed dream! . . . And still before the lamp
The old man sits and writes. All night
He did not close his eyes to sleep.
How I love his peaceful demeanor,
When he's immersed completely in the past,
Writing his chronicle; and often
I hoped to guess, what does he write?
Of the Tatars' dark lordship?
Of Ivan's fierce executions?
Of Novgorod's tumultuous Assembly?[12]
Of the fatherland's glory? In vain.
Neither in his high brow, nor in his gaze,
Can one discern his hidden thoughts;
Always the same demeanor, humble and grand.
Just so a government official, grown gray with writs,
Looks calmly down upon the innocent and guilty,
Impartially observing good and evil
And knowing neither pity nor anger.

PIMEN
You're awake, brother.

GRIGORY
                              Bless me,
Holy Father.

PIMEN
                    God bless you
Today, for all time, and eternity.

GRIGORY
You kept on writing without sleep,
While devilish dreams disturbed my rest
The villain muddled me.
I dreamt that a steep ladder
Brought me to a tower; from above
I could see Moscow, as a nest of ants;
The people surged below out on the square
And laughing pointed up at me,
Overcome by embarrassment and fear
I, plunging down, would awaken . . .
Three times I dreamt that very dream
Curious, is it not?

PIMEN
                          Young blood acts up;
Control yourself with fasting and with prayer,
And soon your dreams will fill
With lightsome visions. Now still—if I
Am overcome by unwilled drowsiness,
And do not say a long prayer toward nightfall—
My aged sleep lacks calm, and is not without sin.
I dream of noisy feasts, at times,
At times of army camps, or battle engagements,
The mindless sport of youthful years!

GRIGORY
How gaily passed your youth!
You fought under the towers of Kazan,[13]
Repulsed the Lithuanian army in the time of Shuisky.
You saw the court and grandeur of Ivan!
How fortunate you are! While I from childhood
Wander from cell to cell, poor monk!
Why can't I too find sport in battles,
And feast at table set for tsars?

I would have time, as you, in my old age
With vanities and world to dispense,
To pledge monk's vows
And shut myself away in quiet cloister.

PIMEN

Do not regret, brother, abandoning the sinful world
Early, that little of temptation
Was sent to you by the Almighty. Have faith in me,
We're fascinated at a distance, by fame, opulence,
And woman's cunning love.
I have lived long and much enjoyed;
But bliss I've only known
Since God to monastery brought me.
Think, son, of the great tsars.
Who is above them? Only God. Who dares
Oppose them? No one. And in result? Often
The golden wreath became a heavy burden for them,
And they exchanged it for a cowl.
Tsar Ivan hoped to find some peace
By emulating labor of the monks.
His palace, crowded with proud favorites,
Took on a new monastery's guise:
Hell's own wearing expensive hats and hair shirts
Emerged as obedient monks,
And the stern Tsar as humble abbot.
And here I saw—in this same cell
(Long-suffering Kirill, a righteous man,
Occupied it at that time. By then
God also gave me grace to recognize
The world's vanities), I saw the Tsar right here,
From wrathful thoughts and executions weary.
Among us, pensive, quiet, sat Ivan the Terrible,
We motionless all stood before him,
And quietly he led us in discussion.
He said to the abbot and the monks:
"The cherished day, my fathers, will arrive,
I'll come before you craving for salvation.
You, Nikodim, you, Sergei, you, Kirill,
You all—accept my spiritual pledge:

To you I'll come, cursed criminal,
And take the honest order of a monk,
Falling, O Holy Father, to your feet."
So spoke the sovereign of the state,
And speech flowed sweetly from his lips,
He cried. In tears we prayed,
For love and peace from God
To ease his suffering, tumultuous soul.
And his son Fedor? On the throne
He thirsted for the quiet life
Of monks under a vow of silence. He turned
The Tsar's dwelling into a prayer cell;
There, government's hard disappointments
Did not disturb his holy soul.
God came to love the Tsar's humility,
And Russia under him enjoyed glory
Without strife—and at the hour of his death
A unique miracle took place:
Before his bier, seen only to the Tsar,
Appeared a man of startling brightness,
And with him Fedor spoke
Addressing him as a great patriarch.
And all were struck by fear,
Recognizing Heaven's apparition,
Because the Holy Father then was not
Yet in the palace with the Tsar.
And when he passed away, the chambers
Were filled with holy fragrance,
And his face shone bright as the sun.
We'll see no more this sort of tsar.
Oh horrible, unique sorrow!
We've angered God, we've sinned:
To reign over us, we named
A regicide.

GRIGORY
                For long now, righteous father,
I've wished to ask about the death
Of Prince Dmitry; you were then,
It's said, in Uglich.

PIMEN

Oh, I remember!
God made me witness of an evil deed,
A bloody sin. Then I was sent to distant Uglich
Act of obedience to fulfil;
I came at night. Next morning at the hour of Mass
I suddenly hear ringing, alarm bells struck,
Shouts, noise, and folk running to the Tsarina's home.
I hurry off as well—and all the town is there already.
I look: there lies the slaughtered prince:
His mother the Tsarina unconscious over him,
The wet-nurse weeping in despair,
The people, then, enraged, drag in
The godless traitorous sitter . . .
Suddenly there among them, from malice pale, fierce,
Appears Jude Bitiagovsky.
"Here, here's the villain," rang out a cry from all,
And in an instant he was no more. The crowd
Took up pursuit of three escaping murderers;
In hiding were the villains seized,
And brought before the warm corpse of the infant,
And miracle—the dead boy stirred—
"Repent!"—howled out the people to them:
And horrified under the axe, the villains
Did repent—and named Boris.

GRIGORY

What age was then the murdered prince?

PIMEN

Seven or so; he would be now
(That was ten years ago . . . no, more:
Twelve)—he would be now your age
And reigning; but God judged otherwise.
With this sad tale I will end
My chronicle; since then I've little dealt
In matters of the world. Brother Grigory,
Through literacy you have informed your mind,
I pass my labor on to you. In hours,
Free from spiritual endeavors,
Describe, without recourse to cunning cerebration,
All you will witness in your life:

Both war and peace, the goverance of tsars,
The miracles of holy saints,
The prophecies and signs of heaven—
And as for me, it's time to rest
And douse the icon lamp . . . But they now ring
For Matins . . . Bless, God,
Your servants! . . . Give me the crutch, Grigory.

(Exits)

GRIGORY

Oh, Boris! Boris! All shake in fear before you,
And no one dares remind you of
The hapless infant's fate.
But all the while, in a dark cell
A hermit writes a terrible denunciation;
And you will not escape the world's judgment,
As you will not escape the judgment of God.

The Patriarch's Chambers

THE PATRIARCH, THE ABBOT *of Chudov Monastery* [14]

PATRIARCH
And he ran away, Father Abbot?

ABBOT
He ran away, Holy Father. It's been three days now.

PATRIARCH
The damn rogue! What family is he?

ABBOT
He's one of the Otrepyevs, children of Galician boyars. He was tonsured as
a youth, not known where, lived in Suzdal, in the Efimev Monastery,
left it, passed through a number of cloisters, finally arrived at my
Chudov brotherhood, and I, seeing that he was still young and
unformed, first turned him over to Father Pimen, a modest and
unassuming elder; and he was well versed in letters; he read our
chronicles, wrote canons for the saints; but it is evident his literacy
did not come from the Lord God.

PATRIARCH

Oh, those men of letters! What he managed to dream up! "I'll be Tsar in
Moscow!" Him, the Devil's vessel! However, there's no reason to report
this to the Tsar. Why worry the Tsar? It will suffice to report his flight to
the official Smirnov or to the official Efimev. What heresy! "I'll be Tsar
in Moscow! . . ." Catch him, catch him, the evildoer, and send him to the
Solovetsky Monastery, for eternal repentance. After all, this is heresy,
Father Abbot.

ABBOT

It is heresy, Holy Father, sheer heresy.

The Tsar's Chambers

TWO COURT SERVANTS

THE FIRST
Where is the Tsar?

THE SECOND
                    In his bed chambers
He's shut himself away with some sorcerer.

THE FIRST
That is his favorite subject:
Wizards, seersayers, sorcerers.
Always fortunetelling, just as a blushing bride.
I'd like to know, what does he want to conjure up?

THE FIRST
And here he comes. Would you like to ask him?

THE SECOND
How grim he looks!

THE TSAR
                    I have attained ultimate power;
I've reigned in peace now for six years,
But do not feel contentment in my soul. Is it not so
When young we fall in love and yearn
For love's solace, but only satisfying
The heart's hunger with quick possession,
Cooling, become restless and bored?
For naught the sorcerers predict

Long years of power without strife.
Neither power, nor life bring joy;
Ahead I sense the heavens' thunder, woe.
There is no happiness for me. I thought to calm
My people with prosperity, glory,
By generosity to win their love,
But hollow acts of charity rejected.
The masses hate the power of the living.
They only know love for the dead.
Such imbeciles are we, when the applause of people
Or raging howls touch our hearts!
God sent down upon us a famine,
The people wailed, died in torment;
I opened for them grain bins; gold
I spilled for them, I found them work—
And they, possessed, cursed me!
When fires destroyed their homes,
I built for them new shelters.
And they accused me of the flames!
There's common people's judgment; try then to find their love.
My family I hoped would bring some comfort,
I thought to give my daughter happiness in wedlock—
And as a storm, death carries off the groom . . . [15]
And here as well the gossip places slyly
Blame for my daughter's widowhood
On me, on me, the hapless father!
Whoever dies, I am the secret murderer:
I hastened Fedor's end,
I poisoned my own sister, the Tsarina,
A nun so meek . . . All I!
Ah! Nothing can, I feel,
Bring peace to us in this sad life;
There's nothing, nothing . . . only conscience, perhaps.
If sound, it will defeat
Dark calumny and malice.
But if there is a single spot,
A single spot that happens to appear,
Then—woe! As if a deadly ulcer
The soul will burn, the heart will fill with poison.
Reproach will hammer in the ears,
And constant nausea, the head spinning

And boys in blood before one's eyes.
Eager to flee, nowhere to go . . . How horrible!
Yes, pitiful is he, whose conscience is unclean.

An Inn on the Lithuanian Border

MISAIL *and* VARLAAM, *beggar monk*s,
GRIGORY OTREPYEV *in street clothes*, LANDLADY

LANDLADY
How can I help you, honest elders?

VARLAAM
Whatever God provides, mistress. Is wine available?

LANDLADY
Of course it is, my fathers. I'll bring it right away.

(Exits)

MISAIL
Why so preoccupied, comrade? Here's the Lithuanian border you were so
  eager to reach.

GRIGORY
I'll rest easy when I'm in Lithuania.

VARLAAM
Why are you so in love with Lithuania? Now Father Misail and I, sinners
  that we are, since we skipped out of the monastery, worry about nothing.
  Lithuania or Russia, here or there: it's all dandy if drink is handy . . . and
  here's the brandy!

MISAIL
Well said, Father Varlaam.

LANDLADY

(Entering)

Here, my fathers. Drink and be welcome.

MISAIL
Thank you, my dear, God bless you.

(The monks drink; VARLAAM begins to sing,
"In the city of Kazan . . . ")

VARLAAM

(To GRIGORY*)*

Why don't you join us, in song or in drink?

GRIGORY
I don't want to.

MISAIL
To each his own.

VARLAAM
And paradise to drunks, Father Misail! Let's drink a glass to the mistress, a
    fair lass . . .
However, Father Misail, when I drink, sober people do not appeal to me;
    inebriation's one thing, conceit another; If you like our ways, be
    welcome—if you don't, be off, begone. A clown is not fit company for
    clerics.

GRIGORY
Drink and think, but to yourself, Father Varlaam! See, I too, at times, can be
    witty.

VARLAAM
And what am I to think to myself?

MISAIL
Leave him alone, Father Varlaam.

VARLAAM
What manner of teetotaler is he? He has imposed his friendship on us. One
    knows not who he is, or where he's from, yet he takes on airs; perhaps
    he's had a whiff of the whipping post . . .

(Drinks and sings,
"The young novice tonsured was . . .")

GRIGORY

(To LANDLADY*)*

Where does this road lead?

LANDLADY
To Lithuania, benefactor, to Luyov Hills.

GRIGORY
Is it far to Luyov Hills?

LANDLADY

Not far at all, one could get there by evening, if it were not for the Tsar's
  border posts and the watchmen.

GRIGORY

What, border posts! What do you mean?

LANDLADY

Someone ran off from Moscow, and orders have gone out to stop everyone
  and to search them.

GRIGORY

(To himself)

Well, Granny, that's George's day for you![16]

VARLAAM

Hey, comrade! I see you've cozied up to the landlady. So you prefer young
  women to vodka! That's more like it, brother, more like it! To each his
  own; Father Misail and I only worry about one thing: bottoms up, drink,
  and have another cup.

MISAIL

Sweetly said, Father Varlaam.

GRIGORY

For whom are they looking? Who ran away from Moscow?

LANDLADY

God knows, thief or robber—only now even decent people can't get
  through—and what's the good of it? None at all, they won't catch
  anyone: as if there wasn't another route, a highway practically, to get to
  Lithuania! From here you go left, follow the woods along the path to the
  chapel, the one on Chekhan Brook, from there straight through the bog to
  Khlopino, then to Zakharyevo, and from there any boy can guide you to
  Luyov Hills. All these watchmen do is persecute travelers and fleece us
  poor folk. *(Noise)* What's that? Ah, speaking of the devil, here they are
  on patrol.

GRIGORY

Mistress, is there some other nook in the hut?

LANDLADY

No, dear, there isn't. I'd be happy to hide myself. They patrol all right, but you've also got to serve them wine, and bread, and God knows what else—may they croak, damn them! May they . . .

(WATCHMEN enter)

WATCHMEN
Greetings, mistress!

LANDLADY
Welcome, dear guests, make yourselves at home!

A WATCHMAN

(To another)

Well, well, they're drinking here. Looks like we'll make out well.

(To the monks)

Who are you?

VARLAAM
We are God's elders, humble prelates, who wander from village to village gathering donations from Christians for the monastery.

WATCHMAN

(To GRIGORY)

And you?

MISAIL
He's our friend . . .

GRIGORY
I'm a citizen from the town outskirts, accompanying the elders to the border. From here I'm going home.

MISAIL
So you've changed your . . .

GRIGORY

(Softly)

Be quiet.

WATCHMAN
Mistress, how about some more wine? We'll sit, have a drink and chat with the fathers.

ANOTHER WATCHMAN
The fellow seems cleaned out. There's nothing to be had from him; on the other hand, the monks . . .

FIRST WATCHMAN
Shut up, we'll get to them right away. So, good fathers, how are things?

VARLAAM
Not good, my son, not good at all. Christian folk nowadays are stingy, they
like their money and they hide it away. They give little to God. Great sin
has come down upon people of the world. All are engaged in buying and
selling, all are afflicted, thinking of earthly riches and not of saving their
souls. We walk and walk, beg and beg for contributions, and sometimes
we don't get three half-pennies in three days. It's such a sin! A week will
pass, then another, we look in our purse and there's so little there that it's
embarrassing to show our faces in the monastery. What's to be done?
From grief one ends up drinking the rest away. Trouble and more
trouble. Oh, things are bad, it seems the end of time has come . . .

LANDLADY

(Crying)

God have mercy and preserve us!

(During VARLAAM'S *monologue*
the FIRST WATCHMAN *closely observes* MISAIL *)*

FIRST WATCHMAN
Alex, my boy! Do you have the Tsar's warrant with you?

SECOND WATCHMAN
I do.

FIRST WATCHMAN
Come over here.

MISAIL
Why are you staring at me like that?

FIRST WATCHMAN
Here's why: a certain vicious heretic, Grishka Otrepyev, ran away from
Moscow. Have you heard that?

MISAIL
No, I haven't.

WATCHMAN

(To VARLAAM*)*

Can you read?

VARLAAM
I knew how in childhood, but I've forgotten.

WATCHMAN

(To MISAIL*)*

And you?

MISAIL
God hasn't given me the brains.

WATCHMAN
I have the Tsar's warrant for you.

MISAIL
What do I need it for?

WATCHMAN
It seems to me the escaped heretic, thief, swindler—is you.

MISAIL
Me! Be reasonable! Come on!

WATCHMAN
Hold on! Watch the door! Now we'll see.

LANDLADY
Oh, the damned oppressors! They won't even leave an elder alone!

WATCHMAN
Who's literate here?

GRIGORY

(Stepping forward)

I'm literate.

WATCHMEN
Here take it! Who taught you?

GRIGORY
Our sexton.

WATCHMEN

(Handing him the warrant)

Read it aloud.

GRIGORY

(Reads)

"An unworthy monk from Chudov Monastery, Grigory, of the Otrepyev family, fell into heresy and possessed by the Devil dared to disturb the holy brothers with all sorts of temptations and illegalities. Investigations determined that he, accursed Grishka, has run off to the Lithuanian border . . ."

WATCHMAN

(To MISAIL*)*

And you say that's not you?

GRIGORY

"And the Tsar has ordered that he is to be caught . . ."

WATCHMAN

And hung.

GRIGORY

It doesn't say "to be hung" here.

WATCHMAN

You're lying. Not every word is always written out. Read: "To be caught and to be hung."

GRIGORY

"And to be hung. He, the thief Grishka, is approximately

(Looking at VARLAAM*)*

fifty years old. Medium height, his forehead is spotted, his beard is gray, his stomach is fat . . ."

(All look at VARLAAM*)*

FIRST WATCHMAN

Fellows! It's Grishka! Grab him, tie him up! And I would have never thought, never guessed . . .

VARLAAM

(Grabbing the paper)

Leave me alone, sons of bitches! What sort of Grishka am I? How's that! Fifty years old, gray beard, fat stomach! No, brother! You're too young to make fun of me. I haven't read anything in a long time, and can't make things out too well, but make them out I will, since it's come down to the noose.

(Reading by syllables)

"He is ap-pro-xi-mate-ly twenty years old." Well, brother, where does it say
   fifty here? Do you see? Twenty.

SECOND WATCHMAN
Yes, I remember, twenty. That's what we were told.

FIRST WATCHMAN

(To GRIGORY*)*

Well, brother, it seems you're a jokester.

(During the reading GRIGORY *stands*
looking down, his hand in his jacket)

VARLAAM

(Continuing)

"He is short of height, broad-chested, one arm is shorter than the other, his
   eyes are blue, hair red, there is a wart on his cheek, and another on his
   forehead." Why, friend, can this be you?

*(*GRIGORY *suddenly pulls out a knife; all step*
back before him, he jumps out of the window)

WATCHMEN
Grab him! Grab him!

(All run about in confusion)

Moscow. Shuisky's House

SHUISKY *and numerous guests at supper*

SHUISKY
More wine.

(Gets up, followed by everyone)

Well, my dear guests,
The final cup! Boy, read the prayer.

BOY
Father in Heaven, in all and ever present,
Heed now the prayers of your slaves:
Let us pray for our Ruler,
Chosen by you, the pious Tsar
And Autocrat of all the Christians.
Protect him in the home, the battlefield,

In travel, and on his couch of sleep.
Grant victory to him over his foes,
May his glory resound from sea to sea.
And his own family in health blossom,
Its precious branches cover
The entire world. To us, his slaves,
May he be generous as before,
And gracious and forever patient,
And may the spring of his infinite,
Wisdom, flow down on us;
And raising the Tsar's cup to that,
We pray to you, Oh Father of the Heavens.

SHUISKY

(Drinks)

The health of the Great Sovereign!
Excuse me, my dear guests;
Thank you for not refusing to partake
My table's bread and salt. Excuse me and have pleasant dreams.

(The guests exit, he sees them to the door)

PUSHKIN[17]
They finally took themselves off. I thought, Prince Vasily Ivanovich, that
we would not manage to have a talk.

SHUISKY

(To the servants)
Why are you standing around with your mouths hanging open? You are
always eavesdropping around your betters. Clear the table and get out.
What's the matter, Afanasy Mikhailovich?

PUSHKIN

All wondrous things and nothing else.
Gavrila Pushkin, who's my nephew, sent
A messenger to me today from Kraków.

SHUISKY
And.

PUSHKIN

Strange news, my nephew writes.
The son of Ivan the Terrible . . . wait.

(Goes to the door and looks)
The rightful heir,
Killed thanks to Boris's obsession . . .

SHUISKY
That's nothing new.

PUSHKIN
                    But wait:
Dmitry lives.

SHUISKY
            I see! That's news indeed!
The prince's alive! How truly wondrous.
And only that?

PUSHKIN
                Just listen to the end.
Whoever he may be, a rescued prince,
Some spirit in his image,
Or a brave rogue, shameless imposter,
Dmitry now has appeared there.

SHUISKY
It cannot be.

PUSHKIN
            With his own eyes Pushkin saw him,
When he arrived first at the palace
And through the ranks of Lithuanian nobility
Went straight to the King's private rooms.

SHUISKY
And who is he? Where is he from?

PUSHKIN
                        That I don't know.
It's known earlier he was the servant
Of Vishnevetsky, and while on his sick bed
Confessed to his spiritual father,
And the proud man, discovering his secret,
Took care of him, raised him from bed
And afterward took him to Sigismund.[18]

SHUISKY
And what is said about this dexterous fellow?

PUSHKIN
It's rumored he is smart, gregarious, quick,
Pleasing to all. He's charmed
The Moscow runaways. The Latin priests
Are for him one and all. The King is kind to him
And promises, it's said, to give him aid.

SHUISKY
All this is such a muddle, brother,
That one's head spins, like it or not.
There is no doubt, he's an imposter,
But, I confess, the danger is not small.
The news is critical! And if it is known by
The people, a great storm will arise.

PUSHKIN
A storm of such proportion that one doubts
Tsar Boris will preserve the crown on his wise head.
And such will be his just desserts! He rules us,
As did Tsar Ivan (not to be mentioned in the dark).
What good, that we no longer have public executions,
That on the bloody stake, in unison we don't
Intone canons to Christ, that we're
Not burned out on the square, and that the Tsar
Does not prod coals with his own staff?
Are we secure in our poor lives?
Each day we can expect disfavor,
Prison, Siberia, the cowl, or chains,
And there—in desolate place the noose or hungry death.
Where are the noblest of our families?
Where are the Princes Sitsky, Shestunovy,
The Romanovs—our nation's hope?
Imprisoned, tortured, or exiled.
Give it some time: you'll share their fate.
How can one bear it, tell me! At home,
Disloyal slaves, as Lithuanians lay siege to us,
The thieves bought by the government
Are always prompt to sell their tongues.
Our fate depends on the first serf,

Whom we may choose to punish.
And now—he's planned to set aside St. George's Day.
We have no power on our estates.
We cannot drive away the indolent!
Like it or not, feed him; dare not to lure
The worker!—Or suffer bondsmen orders.
Was ever it in Ivan's reign
So bad? And are the people better off?
Just ask them. If the imposter tried
Promising them the old St. George's Day,
Then we would have a merry time.

SHUISKY

                                   Pushkin, you're right.

But do you know? About all this
Let us for now keep silent.

PUSHKIN

                         Of course,
Keep to yourself your thoughts. You are a man of sense
I'm always glad to have our chats,
And when I'm troubled over something
I can't resist sharing it all with you.
Moreover, now your mead and velvet beer
Loosed so my tongue . . .
Farewell, then, Prince.

SHUISKY

                    Farewell, brother, good-bye.

                                        (Sees PUSHKIN *out)*

The Tsar's Chambers

THE HEIR *sketching a map.* THE PRINCESS

KSENIA

                                        (Kissing a portrait)
My dear bridegroom, handsome prince, It wasn't I, your bride, but a dark
    grave in foreign lands that received you. I will never find consolation, I
    will always weep over you.

NANNY

Now, Princess! A young maiden cries as the dew falls; the sun will come out and the dew will dry. You'll have another bridegroom who will be both handsome and pleasant. Once you fall in love with him, sweet child, you'll forget your prince.

KSENIA

No, nanny, I will be faithful to him even in death.

(BORIS *enters*)

THE TSAR

Well, Ksenia? Well, my dear?
A bride and also a sad widow!
Still crying over the dead groom,
My child! Fate did not allow
For me to bring you joy.
Perhaps, I angered heaven,
And I could not bring happiness to you.
You're innocent, so why then do you suffer?—
And you, my son, what are you doing? What is this?

FEDOR

A sketch of Moscow; of our realm
From end to end. Here, see, here's Moscow,
Here's Novgorod, here's Astrakhan. Here is the sea,
Here's the dense forests found in Perm,
And here's Siberia.

THE TSAR

                    And what is this
Weaving a pattern?

FEDOR

                    That is the Volga.

THE TSAR

Well done! Sweet fruit of education!
As from a cloud, it's possible to see
The kingdom all at once: the borders, cities, rivers.
Study, my son: for knowledge mitigates
The trials of a swiftly flowing life.
A time will come, and soon, perhaps,
When all the regions you now put

So cleverly on paper,
All will come under your own rule.
Study, my son, and easier and clearer
The art of governance will seem to you.

(SEMYON GODUNOV enters)

Here's Godunov, come to report to me.

(To KSENIA)

My darling, go now to your quarters;
Forgive me, dear. May God bring you some peace.

(KSENIA exits with NANNY)

What do you have to say, Semyon Nikitich?

SEMYON GODUNOV

Just now

To me at dawn, came Prince Vasily's man
And Pushkin's servant with reports.

THE TSAR
And.

SEMYON GODUNOV

Pushkin's servant brought information
That in the morning, yesterday, came to their house
A messenger from Kraków—and in an hour
Was sent, without a message, back.

THE TSAR
The messenger is to be seized.

SEMYON GODUNOV

They've gone after him now.

THE TSAR
What about Shuisky?

SEMYON GODUNOV

In the evening he received
His friends, both Miloslavskys
Buturlins, Mikhail Saltykov,
And Pushkin—several others;
They parted late. Pushkin alone
Stayed with his host
And had a long discussion with him.

THE TSAR
Send after Shuisky now.

SEMYON GODUNOV
                          Your Highness,
He is already here.

THE TSAR
                     Then send him in.

                                                    (GODUNOV *exits*)

With Lithuania contacts! What can this be?
The Pushkin family, prone to rebellion, annoys me,
And Shuisky is not to be trusted:
He is evasive, although brave and sly . . .

                                              (SHUISKY *enters*)

I must, Prince, speak to you.
But then, it seems, you've come yourself
On business; I would like to hear you first.

SHUISKY
Yes, Highness, it is my duty to tell you
Of some important news.

THE TSAR
                          I'm listening.

SHUISKY

                          (*In a low voice, indicating* FEDOR)
However, Highness . . .

THE TSAR
                          The Heir may know,
Anything known to Prince Shuisky. Speak.

SHUISKY
From Lithuania, Your Highness, I've received news . . .

THE TSAR

                                           Not news, perhaps,
The messenger last night brought to Pushkin?

SHUISKY
He knows it all!—I thought, Your Highness,
You had not ascertained this secret yet.

THE TSAR
There is no need for that. I want to understand
The information; or we will never learn
The truth.

SHUISKY
              I only know that
A pretender has appeared in Kraków
And that the King and nobles support him.

THE TSAR
So what is said? Who's this pretender?

SHUISKY
I do not know.

THE TSAR
                   But . . . how is he a threat?

SHUISKY
There is no question, Highness, that your reign is strong,
With generosity, great zeal, munificence
You've won your subjects' hearts.
But as you know yourself, the masses have no sense:
Traitorous, prone to rebellion, superstitious,
Easily lured by empty hopes,
Obedient to instant suggestions,
Deaf to the truth, indifferent
Fables provide their sustenance.
They favor acts of blatant courage.
So if this yet unknown rogue
Crosses the Lithuanian border,
A frenzied mob he will attract
Thanks to Dmitry's resurrected name.

THE TSAR
Dmitry's! . . . How? That infant's name!
Dmitry's! . . . Prince, please leave us.

SHUISKY
His face has reddened so; a storm is brewing!

FEDOR
                             Tsar,
Allow me to . . .

TSAR
              It cannot be, my son, do go.

                                              (FEDOR *exits*)

Dmitry's name!

SHUISKY
              He did not know a thing.

THE TSAR
Now listen, Prince. Measures are to be taken;
To block off Lithuania from Russia
With pickets that a single soul
This border may not cross; a hare
Is not to skip to us from Poland; a crow
Is not to fly to us from Kraków. Go.

SHUISKY
I'm off.

THE TSAR
              No, wait. Is it not true, this news
Is curious? When have you ever heard,
The dead to rise from coffins
In order to interrogate the tsars; the tsars lawfully
Appointed, chosen by the nation as whole,
Crowned by the August Patriarch?
Laughable, no? So why are you not laughing?

SHUISKY
Me, Majesty? . . .

THE TSAR
              Now listen, Prince Vasily:
When I found out that this boy was . . .
That this boy somehow lost his life
You were sent to investigate; and now
With cross and God I you entreat,
In clear conscience, declare the truth:
Did you identify the murdered infant,
Was there perhaps a substitute? Answer.

SHUISKY
I swear to you . . .

THE TSAR
                     No, Shuisky, do not swear,
But say: was that the Heir?

SHUISKY
                        Yes, it was he.

THE TSAR
Think, Prince. I'll be forgiving,
Past lies, I will not punish by
Useless disgrace. But if you now
Are being sly with me; by my son's head
I swear—you will experience an evil execution;
The sort of execution that Tsar Ivan
Will spin in horror in his grave.

SHUISKY
I fear not execution, but only your disfavor;
Would I dare lie before you?
And could I be so blind as to
Not recognize Dmitry? Three days
I visited his corpse in the cathedral,
Accompanied by all of Uglich.
Around him lay the thirteen bodies
The people tore apart, and over him
Corruption noticeably spread,
The heir's childish face was clear, however,
And fresh, at peace, as fallen into sleep;
The deep ulcer was not smoothed over,
The features of his face remained the same.
No, Majesty, there is no doubt: Dmitry
Sleeps in the coffin.

THE TSAR

                                                              (Calmly)

                Enough. And you may go.

                                                    (SHUISKY *exits*)

How hard it is! . . . I'll catch my breath . . .
I felt the blood flow to my face—
And drain away so slowly . . .
So that is why for thirteen years

I saw the murdered child in my dreams!
Yes, yes—indeed! I understand.
But who is he? My terrible opponent?
Who lays a siege to me? An empty name, a shadow,
A shadow, can it be, will snatch the purple from me,
A sound deprive my children of inheritance?
I'm mad! Of what am I afraid?
Blow on this apparition—and it's gone.
So it's decided: I'll not show fear—
But should neglect nothing.
How heavy is the crown of Monomakh!

Kraków. Vishnevetsky's House

THE PRETENDER *and* FATHER CHERNIKOVSKY

PRETENDER
No, Father, there will be no problem;
I know the temper of my people;
In them godliness is without passion.
For them their Tsar's example is sacred.
And tolerance most often is indifferent.
I'll guarantee, before two years are up
All of my people, all the Northern Church,
Will recognize the rule of Peter's heir.

THE PRIEST
May St. Ignatius help you
When the new age dawns.
Meanwhile, Prince, preserve
Within your soul the seeds of Heaven's grace.
Duplicity before a senseless world
At times our spiritual duty does oblige;
Men judge your words and actions,
Intentions God alone knows.

PRETENDER
Amen. Who's there?

(A servant enters)

Say we'll grant audience now.

*(The door opens and a large crowd of
Russians and Poles enters)*

Comrades! We leave tomorrow
From Kraków. I will stop, Mnishek,
With you in Sambor for three days.
I know: your hospitable castle
Is radiant with noble opulence
And is renowned for its young mistress.
I hope to see the fair Marina there.
And you, my friends,
Lithuanians, Russians. We raise
Fraternal banners up against a common foe,
Against my cunning villain.
The progeny of Slavs, I soon will lead
Your terrifying regiments into the long-awaited battle.
But there's new faces in your midst.

GAVRILA PUSHKIN
They've come to ask Your Grace
For sword and service.

THE PRETENDER
                                    I'm glad to have you, lads.
Be with me, friends. But who, do tell me, Pushkin,
Is this personable man?

PUSHKIN
                                    Prince Kurbsky.[19]

THE PRETENDER
                                                        The name says much!
                                                        (To KURBSKY*)*

Are you related to the hero of Kazan?

KURBSKY
I am his son.

THE PRETENDER
                    Does he still live?

KURBSKY
                                    He passed away.

THE PRETENDER

A brilliant mind! A man for battle and advice!
But since the time when he appeared
To take bitter revenge for insults caused him
With Lithuanians in front of Olga's ancient city,[20]
No more's been heard of him.

KURBSKY

                    My father

Lived out his days in Volynia,
On the estates Bathory[21]
Gave to him. Alone, at rest,
In sciences he looked for happiness;
But peaceful labor failed to console him:
His youth's native land he remembered,
And till the last, he grieved for it.

PRETENDER

Unhappy lord! How bright was the ascent
Of his so clamorous and stormy life.
I'm glad, noble-born knight, to see
His blood make peace with fatherland.
One should forget a father's faults;
Peace to his resting place! Approach, Kurbsky, your hand!
Is it not strange? The son of Kurbsky guides
Toward the throne, and whom? The son of Ivan.
All stand for me, people and fate.
And who are you?

A POLE

                    I am Sobansky, a free noble.

THE PRETENDER

Praise, honor to you, freedom's child!
Advance a third of his wages to him.—
But who is this? I recognize on them
The clothing of my native land. They are our kind.

KHRUSHCHEV

                                                        (Genuflecting)

Just so, Your Majesty, our lord. We are
Your diligent and persecuted serfs.

We, in disfavor, ran away from Moscow
To you, our tsar—and we are ready to
Lay down our heads for you, our corpses may they be
Your steps to the tsar's throne.

PRETENDER
Be brave, innocent sufferers—
Just wait until I get to Moscow,
And there Boris will pay for all.
You are?

KARELA
                Sent from the Don, a Cossack.
Come to you from free armies, and their brave chiefs,
From Cossacks of the Upper and the Lower Don
To gaze upon the Tsar's clear eyes,
To pledge their heads to you.

PRETENDER
I knew the people of the Don. I had no doubt
Of seeing in our ranks Cossack horse-tail emblems.
We thank our army of the Don.
We know, that Cossacks now
Unjustly are oppressed and persecuted;
But if God should help us to mount
Our forefathers' throne, then as in days of old
We will be generous to our true, free Don.

POET
                                        (Approaches, bowing low, and grabbing
                                              at the hem of GRISHKA'S *coat)*
Great Prince, most luminous Heir.

PRETENDER
What do you want?

POET
                                        (Hands him a sheet of paper)
                Accept with condescension
This humble fruit of unrelenting toil.

PRETENDER
What do I see? Verses in Latin!
A hundredfold is holy the union of a lyre and sword!
A common laurel them entwines in friendship.
I was born under Northern skies,
Familiar is to me, however, the Latin muse's voice,
And I do love the flowers of Parnassus.
I have faith in the prophecy of poets.
No, not for nothing in their fiery breast
Seethes ecstasy: a deed is blessed
If it they glorify beforehand!
Approach, my friend. To honor me
Accept this gift.

(Gives him a ring)

When fate's behest
Comes true, when the ancestral crown
I put upon my head, I hope again to hear
Your voice so sweet, your hymn inspired.
Musa gloriam coronat, gloriaque musam.[22]
And so, my friends, until tomorrow, until we meet again.

ALL
To arms, to arms! Hail Dmitry!
Hail, the Great Muscovite Prince!

The Castle of Commander Mnishek in Sambor.
A Number of Illuminated Rooms. Music

VISHNEVETSKY, MNISHEK

MNISHEK
He only spoke to my Marina,
Marina she alone interests him . . .
The matter smacks greatly of marriage;
Well, did you think, confess then, Vishnevetsky,
My daughter would become Tsarina. Well?

VISHNEVETSKY
Yes, miracles . . . And Mnishek, did you think,
My servant would ascend the Moscow throne?

MNISHEK
And what say you of my Marina?
I simply told her: Do be careful!
Don't let Dmitry get away! . . . And now
It's done. He is already in her nets.

(Polish music. THE PRETENDER *and* MARINA
are the first dancing couple)

MARINA

(Softly to DMITRY*)*

Yes, then tomorrow in the evening, at eleven,
The fountain in the linden grove.

(They separate. Another couple)

CAVALIER
What does Dmitry see in her?

LADY

What do you mean! She is

A beauty.

CAVALIER
Yes, a marble nymph:
The eyes, such lifeless lips, without a smile . . .

(Another couple)

LADY
When's the campaign?

CAVALIER

When the Tsarevich orders.
We all are ready; but it seems
Miss Mnishek keeps us prisoner with Dmitry.

LADY
A nice imprisonment.

CAVALIER

Of course, if you . . .

(They leave. The room empties)

MNISHEK
We old folks dance no longer,
The din of music lures us not,
Enchanting hands no longer do we squeeze or kiss—

Oh, I have not forgotten the old pranks!
Now it is not, it's not, the same:
The young, tut-tut—are not as brave,
And beauty's not so blithe.
Admit, my friend, all's somehow so depressing.
Let us leave them; my comrade, come
A bottle of Hungarian wine, covered with grass,
We'll order they dig up,
Together in some nook we'll sip
The fragrant flow, the stream, as thick as fat,
We'll ponder also over certain matters.
So let us go.

VISHNEVETSKY

          Quite right, my friend, let's go.

Night. Garden. The Fountain

THE PRETENDER, MARINA

THE PRETENDER

(Enters)

And so the fountain. She will come here.
It seems that I am not a coward;
Right next to me I've seen death,
And faced with death I did not tremble,
Eternal bondage menaced me,
Pursued—I did not fall in spirit,
Avoided capture by being bold.
What at this moment, then, constricts my breathing?
What means this trembling beyond control?
Is this the shuddering of taunt desire?
No—this is fear. I've waited now all day
To meet in secret with Marina,
I've pondered all I will tell her,
How I'll seduce her haughty mind,
How I will name her Moscow's Queen,—
But come the hour, and everything's forgotten.
The speeches I have memorized are gone;

Love muddles my imagination . . .
But something flickered suddenly . . . a rustling . . . quiet . . .
No, it's just light from the deceptive moon,
And noise made by a breeze.

(MARINA enters)

It's she! All of my blood has stilled.

MARINA
Dmitry! You?

PRETENDER
           Oh magical, sweet voice!

(Approaches her)

It's you, at last? It's really you, alone with me,
Under the cover of the quiet night?
How slowly passed the boring day!
How slowly evening's glow died down!
How long I waited in the gloom of night!

MARINA
The hours fly, and time is dear to me—
I did not ask to meet you here
To listen to a lover's tender speeches.
Words are not needed. I believe
You are in love; but listen, I've decided
Together with your destiny, both stormy and uncertain,
To link my own; I have the right
Then to demand one thing, Dmitry:
And I demand, that you reveal to me
Your soul's secret desires,
Intentions, even fears;
So hand in hand I boldly can
Live with you, not as a blind child,
Not as a slave to husband's frothy wants,
Your silent concubine,
But, as a spouse worthy of you,
The helpmate of the Moscow tsar.

PRETENDER
Oh, for an hour at least allow me to forget
The cares and dangers of my fate!
Forget that you now see

Heir to the Tsar, Marina! Take me
To be a lover, chosen by you,
Made happy by your single glance.
Oh, listen to the pleas of love,
Allow me to express all in my heart.

MARINA

Now's not the time. You dally, Prince,
While cools the loyal ardor of your minions.
The dangers, difficulties hour by hour
Become more dangerous and difficult,
Already dubious rumors fly about,
One novelty replaces yet another;
And Godunov his measures takes . . .

PRETENDER

What about Godunov? Has Boris any power
Over your love, my one delight?
No, no. I now look with indifference
Upon his throne, the government of tsars.
Your love . . . what's life to me without it,
Fame's glitter, or the Russian state?
In desolate steppes, in poor earth hut—
You will replace for me the crown of tsars,
Your love . . .

MARINA

                For shame; do not forget
Your great and sacred destiny;
More precious should your title be
Than all life's happiness, seductions,
There's nothing you can find that's as important.
And be aware. Not to a seething youth,
Madly infatuated by my charm,
In solemn pledge I give my hand
But to the Heir of Moscow's throne,
To the Tsar's son, who was by fate delivered.

PRETENDER

Don't torment me, oh beautiful Marina,
Don't say you chose my title
Over me, Marina! You do not know,

How painfully you wound my heart—
What! Then if . . . oh, horrible the doubt!
So speak: if a blind fate had not
Me chosen to be born a tsar,
If I was not the son of Ivan,
This boy so long forgotten by the world—
And then . . . and then would you love me? . . .

MARINA
Dmitry, you could not be any other;
I cannot love anyone else.

PRETENDER
                    No! That's enough:
I do not want to share with a dead man
A mistress, who belongs to him.
An end to my pretenses! So listen to
The entire truth; and know, that your Dmitry
Has perished long ago, is buried—and will not be resurrected;
And do you want to learn, who might I be?
Have it your way: I'm a poor monk;
Bored by monastery's confinement,
Under the cowl, I thought about my daring plan,
Prepared a miracle for all the world—
And finally escaped the cell.
To the Ukrainians I went, to their wild troops.
I learned to master horse and saber;
And came to you; I named myself Dmitry
And tricked the brainless Poles.
What say you now, haughty Marina?
Are you content that I confessed?
Why don't you speak?

MARINA
                    What misery! What shame!

                                              (Silence)

PRETENDER
                                              (Softly)

How far astray vexation took me!
The happiness hard to arrange
I now, perhaps, destroyed forever.
What have I, madman, done?

(Aloud)

I see, I see:

You are embarrassed by love that is not princely.
So say the fateful word to me;
My fate is in your hands,
Decide, I wait.

(Falls on his knees)

MARINA

Get up, you low pretender,

By kneeling do you really hope,
As with a girl weak and trusting
To touch the conceit of my heart?
You are mistaken, friend: for at my feet I've seen
Noble-born counts and knights;
But I did not coldly reject their pleas
In order for a monk that's run away . . .

PRETENDER

(Gets up)

Don't scorn the young Pretender;
He may, perhaps, have hidden gifts
Well-suited to the Moscow throne,
And worthy of your priceless hand . . .

MARINA
More worthy of a shameful noose, arrogant man!

PRETENDER
I'm guilty; seized by pride,
I deceived God and tsars,
To world I lied; but you, Marina, can't
Condemn me; before you I am in the right.
No, I could not deceive you.
You were my only sacred thing,
I did not dare dissimulate before it.
Love, love, jealous and blind,
Love, it alone, compelled me
To declare all.

MARINA

What are you proud of, madman!

Who asked that you confess?

If you, a vagabond who's nameless,
Could wondrously two nations lead astray
At least, then you ought to be worthy
Of your success
Secure your bold deception
By stubborn, deep, eternal secrecy.
How can I give myself to you, tell me,
How can I bind, forgetting my high birth
And maiden's modesty, my destiny to yours,
When you, with such charming simplicity,
So heedlessly reveal your shame?
Because of love he blabbed out everything!
I am surprised that to my father
From friendship you did not reveal yourself,
Or out of happiness to our king
Or yet again to Pan Vishnevetsky
Because of servant's loyal zeal.

PRETENDER

I swear to you, my heart's confession
You solely could extort.
I swear to you, that never, nowhere,
Neither in feast before the addling cup,
Neither in friendly, intimate conversation,
Under the knife, or agonizing torture
Will I reveal these deep secrets.

MARINA

You swear! And so, I must believe—
Oh, I believe!—By what, pray tell, however,
Do you swear? Not in the name of God,
As godly ward of Jesuits?
Or in the name of honor, noble knight,
Or, then perhaps, by virtue of the word of Tsar,
As a tsar's son? Is that not so? Tell me.

PRETENDER

                                                         (Proudly)

Ivan the Terrible's shade adopted me,
Named me Dmitry from the grave,
Around me agitated countries
And for my victim Boris ordained.

I am the Heir. Enough, I am ashamed
To stoop to a vain Polish woman.—
Good-bye, for good. The play of bloody war,
The broad concerns allotted by my fate
Will still, I hope, love's yearning.
Oh, how I will begin to hate you when
My passion's shameful fever passes by!
I go—whether the crown or death
Awaits my head in Russia,
Whether I die, warrior, in honest battle,
Or criminal on execution block in public square,
You will not be my one companion,
You will not share my fate;
Perhaps, however, you'll regret
The destiny renounced by you.

MARINA
And if your arrogant deception
Before all else I will reveal to all?

PRETENDER
Do you then really think I fear you?
A Polish girl will be believed,
More readily than Russia's Heir?—Consider,
Neither the King, nor Pope, nor noblemen
Care for the truth behind my words.
Dmitry I may be or not—what does it matter to them?
But I provide excuse for strife and war.
That's all they need, and you,
Rebellious one! Believe me, they'll force to hold your tongue.
Farewell.

MARINA
               Wait, Prince. At last
I hear the words not of a boy, but of a man.
They reconcile me to you, Prince.
Your senseless outburst I forget
And see before me once again Dmitry. But—listen:
It's time, it's time! Wake up, delay no longer;
To Moscow quickly lead your troops.
Clean out the Kremlin, take the Moscow throne,
Then after me send wedding envoys;

But—God's my witness—before your foot
Is firmly placed on steps up to the throne,
Before Godunov is overthrown by you,
I will not listen to speeches of love.

(Exits)

PRETENDER

No—easier it is for me to battle Godunov
Or play at intrigue with court Jesuit,
Than with a woman—the hell with them; I have no strength,
She slithers, weaves, confuses,
Slips out of hand, hisses, threatens, and stings.
A snake! A snake!—No wonder I was trembling.
She almost ruined me.
But it's decided: in the morning I will put the army on the move.

Lithuanian Border. October 16, 1604

PRINCE KURBSKY *and* PRETENDER, *both mounted.*
The army approaches the border.

KURBSKY

(Gallops up first)

Here, here it is! The Russian border!
Fatherland! Holy Russia, I'm yours!
I brush away contemptuously the dust
Of foreign soil—with greed drink in new air:
It is my own!—Your spirit now,
Father, will be consoled, and in the grave
The disgraced bones will now rejoice!
Our family sword again flashes,
Sword glorious, the thunderbolt of dark Kazan,[23]
That solid sword, servant of Moscow tsars!
It will enjoy its own feast now
On the behalf of its own hope and Tsar!

PRETENDER

(Riding quietly, head lowered)

How glad he is! How his pure soul
Responds to happiness and glory!

My knight! I envy you.
The son of Kurbsky, raised in exile,
Forgetting wrongs borne by his father,
Having redeemed his guilt beyond the grave,
You now prepare to shed your blood
For Ivan's son; returning lawful Tsar
To fatherland . . . You're right,
Your soul must glow with happiness.

KURBSKY

Can you not be content in spirit?
Here is our Russia; it is yours, Prince.
There wait for you your people's hearts:
Your Moscow, Kremlin, and your state.

PRETENDER

Oh Kurbsky, Russian blood will flow!
You've all raised up swords for the Tsar; you're innocent.
I, on the other hand, lead you against your brothers; Lithuania
I've summoned against Russia; to fair Moscow
I have shown enemies a cherished road!
But let my sin lay heavy not on me
But on you Boris, on you tsar-murderer!
Forward!

KURBSKY

                Yes, forward! Woe to Godunov!
                        (They gallop. The regiments cross the border)

The Tsar's Duma

THE TSAR, THE PATRIARCH, *and* BOYARS

TSAR

How can it be? A defrocked monk, a runaway monk
Leads vicious regiments against us,
Dares threaten us! That is enough,
It's time to calm the madman!—Ride
Trubetskoy, and you Basmanov;
My diligent commanders need your help.

The rebel has besieged Chernigov.
Go save city and citizens.

BASMANOV
                              Your Majesty,
Three months won't pass, and we
Will hear no more of the pretender;
To Moscow him we'll bring, like animal
From foreign lands, in a steel cage. By God
I swear to you.

                                        (Exits with TRUBETSKOY*)*

TSAR
                              The Swedish king
Had his envoys offer alliance;
But we do not need foreign help;
We have enough of our own fighting men,
To turn back traitors and the Poles.
I refused him.
                              Shchelkalov! Send
Decrees to all commanders everywhere,
That they mount horses, take on men
In service as in days of old;
In monasteries also choose
Recruits from lower ranks. In prior years,
When fatherland was threatened by disaster,
The monks themselves would come to battle.
Nowadays we do not want to trouble them;
We'll let them pray for us. Such is
The Tsar's decree and the boyars' decision.
Now to resolve a vital question:
You know, the insolent pretender
Put cunning rumors out;
Letters he sent everywhere
Have spread unrest and doubt;
The whispers of revolt pass through the public squares,
Ideas boil up . . . They must be cooled;
I would like to forestall executions,
But by what means and how? Let's now decide.
You first, Most Holy Father, tell us your thoughts.

PATRIARCH

Be blessed He on high, having instilled
Spirit of charity and humble patience
In your soul, great Tsar;
You do not want destruction for the sinner,
You quietly await—him gone astray to find his way:
Indeed he shall, the sun of truth eternal
Shall light up all.
                    Your loyal supplicant of God,
Unwise in matters of the world,
Today dares to give you advice.
The cursed, unfrocked, son of the Devil
Managed to pass himself off as Dmitry;
Shamelessly he arrayed himself, as in a cloak
That's stolen from a priest,
Using the name of the Tsar's son:
But it is only to be torn away—and he
Will be in shame from his own nakedness.
To that end God himself sent us the means:
Know, Majesty, six years ago—
That very year, when you were blessed
By God to govern as the tsar,—
At night once came to me
A simple shepherd, already very old,
And told me of a wondrous mystery.
"When I was young," he said, "I lost my sight
And from then I could not tell day from night
Till my old age; all my attempts to heal
With herbs or secret incantations failed;
And useless were the pilgrimages I made
To places of the great miracle workers;
With no effect I sprinkled healing water
From saints' wells on my beclouded eyes;
God would not send healing to me.
And finally, I lost all hope,
Became accustomed to the dark, and even dreams
Did not reveal to me visible things,
I would dream only sounds. Then once,
During deep sleep, I heard a child's voice;
It said to me: 'Rise, grandfather, go
To Uglich-town, to the Cathedral of Transfiguration;

There pray over my little grave,
God's merciful—and I will then release you.'
'But who are you?' I asked the child's voice.
'I am the Prince Dmitry. The Lord
Accepted me among his angels,
And now I am a great worker of miracles!
Thus go, old man.' I woke and thought:
And so? Perhaps God will indeed
Grant me a late healing.
I'll go. And I set off on a long journey.
When I arrived at Uglich, I went
To the holy cathedral, I listened to the Mass,
And, deeply touched in my aspiring soul, I cried
So sweetly, that my blindness seemed
To seep with tears out of my eyes.
When people there began to leave, I said
To my grandson: 'Ivan, take me
To Prince Dmitry's tomb.' The boy
Led me—and after I offered
A quiet prayer before the tomb,
My eyes completely cleared, I saw
God's earth, and my grandson, and the small grave."
That, Majesty, is what the elder said to me.

(General confusion. During the monologue BORIS
wipes his face several times with a handkerchief)

I sent especially then to Uglich,
And did confirm that many sufferers
Obtained a similar dispensation
At the gravestone of the Tsar's son.
Here's my advice: To the Kremlin transpose
The holy relics, place them in the Cathedral
Of Archangel; the people then will clearly see
The trickery of the godless villain,
And like the dust the Devil's power will be gone.

(Silence)

PRINCE SHUISKY
Holy Father, who understands the ways
Of the Almighty? It's not for me to judge.
Repose without decay and miracle worker's power
He can give to a youth's remains,

But one should analyze with care
Without undue emotion what the people say;
In times so violent with unrest
Should we take on such an important matter?
Won't it be said that we arrogantly used
The sacred to serve secular ends?
The people, as it is, are wavering irrationally,
There are more than enough loud rumors;
It's not the time to worry people's minds
With this so unexpected and important novelty.
I see myself; the rumor spread
By this defrocked monastic must be quenched;
But there are other, simpler means.
So, Majesty—when you allow,
I will myself go to the public square,
Exhort, prod conscience in the midst of madness,
And there expose the vagabond's malicious fraud.

TSAR
Let it be so! Lord Patriarch
Please join me in the chambers,
Today I need to talk with you.

(Exits followed by all the BOYARS*)*

A BOYAR
(Softly to another)

Did you see how the Tsar turned pale,
How ample sweat poured from his face?

ANOTHER BOYAR
I—to confess—dared not raise up my eyes,
Dared not to breathe, not even move.

FIRST BOYAR
Prince Shuisky came to the rescue. What a fine man!

A Field near Novgorod-Seversk.
Battle. December 21, 1604

SOLDIERS   *(Running in disorder)*
Disaster! Disaster! The Prince! The Poles! They're here! They're here!

(CAPTAIN MARGERET *and* CAPTAIN WALTER ROSEN *enter*)

MARGERET

Where are you going, where? *Allons*[24] . . . Go back!

ONE OF THE DESERTERS

You can go yourself, to . . . if you like, damn foreigner.

MARGERET

Quoi? Quoi?[25]

ANOTHER DESERTER

Quack! Quack! A foreign frog like you can quack all he wants at a Russian prince; us now, we're Orthodox folk.

MARGERET

Qu'est-ce à dire orthodox? . . . Sacrés gueux, maudite canailles! Mordieu, mein herr, j'enrage: on dirait que ça n'a pas des bras pour frapper, ça n'a que des jambes pour foutre le camp.[26]

W. ROSEN

Es is Schande.[27]

MARGERET

Ventre-saint-gris! Je ne bouge plus d'un pas—puisque le vin est tiré, il faut le boire. Qu'en dites-vous, mein herr?[28]

W. ROSEN

Sie haben Recht.[29]

MARGERET

Tudieu, il y fait chaud! Ce diable de Pretender, comme ils l'appellent, est un bougre, qui a du poil au cul. Qu'en pensez-vous, mein herr?[30]

W. ROSEN

Oh, ja![31]

MARGERET

Hé! Voyez donc, voyez donc! L'action s'engage sur les derrières de l'ennemi. Ce doit être le brave Basmanoff, qui aurait fait une sortie.[32]

W. ROSEN

Ich glaube das.[33]

(GERMAN SOLDIERS *enter*)

MARGERET
Ha, ha! voici nos Allemands. Messieurs! . . . Mein herr, dites leur donc de se rallier et, sacre bleu, chargeons![34]

W. ROSEN
Sehr gut. Halt!   (THE GERMANS *form ranks.*)
Marsch![35]

GERMANS

                                                                   (On the march)
Hilf Gott![36]

                                        (Battle. The Russians again run away)

POLES
Victory! Victory! Hail Tsar Dmitry.

DMITRY

                                                                (On horseback)
Sound the call to cease fire! We've won. Enough: spare Russian blood. Cease fire!

                                                (Trumpets and drums sound)

Moscow. Square in Front of the Cathedral

THE PEOPLE

A MAN
Will the Tsar come out soon from the cathedral?

ANOTHER MAN
Mass is over; they're holding a special service.

FIRST MAN
What? Has *he* already been anathematized?

ANOTHER MAN
I stood at the barrier and heard the deacon bellow: Grishka Otrepyev—anathema!

FIRST MAN
Let them ban him; the Tsar's son's got nothing to do with Otrepyev.

ANOTHER MAN
They're commemorating the Tsar's son.

FIRST MAN
Commemorating a live man! They'll get their just rewards, godless
    people.

THIRD MAN
Sh! That noise! Can it be the Tsar?

FOURTH MAN
No, it's a holy fool.

(HOLY FOOL *enters wearing an iron cap and
chains and surrounded by* BOYS)

BOYS
Nick, Nick—iron cap! . . . trrrrr . . .

OLD WOMAN
Get away from the blessed man, you young devils.—Pray for me Nick,
    sinner that I am.

HOLY FOOL
Give me, give me, give me a kopek.

OLD WOMAN
Here's a kopek for you; remember me in your prayers.

HOLY FOOL

(Sits on the ground and sings)

Moon shines,
Kitten cries,
Fool, arise
Pray to God!

(The BOYS *again surround him)*

ONE OF THEM
Greetings, Nick; Why don't you take off your hat?

(Strikes it with his finger)

Oh, it rings!

HOLY FOOL
I have a kopek.

BOYS
That's not true! Let's see it.

(They grab the kopek and run away)

HOLY FOOL

(Weeping)

They took my kopek; they've hurt Nick!

THE PEOPLE
The Tsar, the Tsar is coming.

(The TSAR *comes out of the cathedral.*
A BOYAR *hands out alms.* BOYARS*)*

HOLY FOOL
Boris, Boris! The children hurt Nick.

TSAR
Give him alms. Why is he crying?

HOLY FOOL
Little children hurt Nick . . . Order them to be butchered, like you butchered
the little prince.

BOYARS
Get away . . . fool! Grab him!

BORIS
Leave him alone. Pray for me, poor Nick.

(Exits)

HOLY FOOL

(Calling after him)

No, no! One can't pray for Tsar Herod—the Virgin Mary won't allow it.

Sevsk

THE PRETENDER, *surrounded by his people*

PRETENDER
Where is the prisoner?

POLE

He's here.

PRETENDER

Bring him to me.

(A RUSSIAN PRISONER *enters)*

And who are you?

PRISONER
                    Rozhnov, a Moscow nobleman.

PRETENDER
Are you long in service?

PRISONER
                         It's now a month.

PRETENDER
Do you not feel shame, Rozhnov,
For raising sword against me?

PRISONER
                              It was not up to me.

PRETENDER
Were you in battle next to Seversk?

PRISONER
                              I came
Two weeks after the battle—from Moscow.

PRETENDER
How's Godunov?

PRISONER
                    He was much worried
By the defeat in battle and the wounds
Mstislavsky suffered, he sent Shuisky
The army to command.

PRETENDER
                    And why did he
Basmanov call back to Moscow?

PRISONER
The Tsar rewarded his accomplishments with honor
And gold. Basmanov sits now in
The Tsar's Duma.

PRETENDER
                    He is more needed in the army.
And how is Moscow?

PRISONER

All, thank God, is quiet.

PRETENDER
Oh? Do they wait for me?

PRISONER

God knows;
About you now no one dares say very much.
Some will have tongues cut off, others
Their heads—such is, in truth, the current situation!
Each day, another execution. The prisons are stuffed full.
Whenever, on the square, three persons come
Together, in a wink, a spy slinks by.
The Tsar in idle moments
Himself questions informers.
In evil times it's better to keep silent.

PRETENDER
So enviable is the life of Boris's subjects!
How is the army?

PRISONER

What about it? It's clothed, fed,
Content with all.

PRETENDER

How many are there?

PRISONER
God knows.

PRETENDER

Would there be thirty thousand?

PRISONER
One could even count fifty or so.

> (*The* PRETENDER *is lost in thought.*
> *The others look at each other*)

PRETENDER
Well! What's said about me in your ranks?

PRISONER
They speak of your benevolence,
That you are, so to say (and not to make you angry),
A thief, but a fine fellow.

PRETENDER
                                                        (Laughing)
                    So I will prove to them
In practice. Friends, let us not wait
For Shuisky; I congratulate you;
The battle is tomorrow.
                                                        (Exits)

ALL
                    Hail Dmitry!

A POLE
The battle is tomorrow! They are fifty thousand,
While we scarcely manage fifteen.
He has gone mad.

ANOTHER
                    That's nothing, friend. One Pole
Alone can challenge fifty Russians.

PRISONER
Challenge perhaps. But when it comes to fighting
You'll run away from even one, you braggart.

POLE
If you were armed, insolent prisoner,
Then I would calm   *(Showing his saber)*
                    you down with this.

PRISONER
Our Russian sort can manage without sabers:
How would you like a bit of this instead,
                                                        (Shows him his fist)
                    Dimwit!
                    (THE POLE *proudly looks at him and walks
                    away without speaking. General laughter)*

Forest

PRETENDER
Poor horse! His gallop was so brisk
Today, to final battle
And wounded he so swiftly carried me.
Poor horse!

PUSHKIN

(To himself)

       That's really something to regret!
A horse! When our entire army
Is smashed to bits!

PRETENDER
          Just look, perhaps,
He's only tired from his wound
And will recover.

PUSHKIN
         No chance of that! He's dying.

PRETENDER

(Approaching his horse)
Poor steed of mine! . . . What's to be done? Take off the bridle,
Loosen the girth and let him die
In freedom.

      *(Takes off bridle and saddle from the horse.
      Several* POLES *enter)*

      Gentlemen, good day!
Why don't I see Kurbsky among you?
I saw him penetrate the thick of battle.
The brave man was encircled by
A host of sabers rippling like ears of wheat;
His sword was raised above all others,
And his stern cry drowned out them all.
Where is my knight?

POLE
                    He fell on the field of death.
PRETENDER
Honor his courage, peace to his soul!
How few of us survived the battle.
Traitors! The villains Zaporozhian Cossacks—
Damn lot! You, you caused our defeat!
Not to withstand three minutes even of resistance!
I'll see to them! One out of ten I'll hang,
The crooks!

PUSHKIN
                Whoever is to blame,
We're still thoroughly beaten,
Destroyed.

PRETENDER
                And victory was ours;
I almost crushed the forward ranks—
The Germans cleanly fought us off;
What fine fellows! I swear to God, they're fine,
It's such I like—and without fail
Will form from them an honorary guard.

PUSHKIN
And where are we to sleep tonight?

PRETENDER
Why in the forest, here. How is this not a place to sleep?
At break of dawn, we're off; by lunch we'll be in Rylsk.
Good night.
                    (Lies down, places his head on a saddle, and falls asleep)

PUSHKIN
                Sweet dreams, my Prince!
Beaten completely, saving himself in flight,
He is unworried, like a stupid child;
Protected he's, of course, by providence;
We, friends, will not despair.

Moscow. The Tsar's Chambers

BORIS, BASMANOV

TSAR

He is defeated, what good is that?
We have achieved a solid victory.
He once again gathers the dispersed troops
And threatens us from the Putivl walls.
What are our heroes doing in the meantime?
They are in Krom, where a small thong of Cossacks
Laughs at them from behind a rotting barricade.
Here's glory for you! No, I am dissatisfied with them,
I will send you to take command;
Not lineage but brains I'll place to lead the army.
Let them regret their arrogance about their rank;
It's time for me to scorn the mutterings of well-born rabble
And do away with deadly precedent.

BASMANOV

Oh, Tsar, a hundred times be blessed
That day when books of genealogy
Full of dissension and the pride of birth
Will be consumed by fire.

TSAR

                              That day is not far off;
First only let me calm unrest
Among the people.

BASMANOV

                              Why worry about them;
They're always prone, in secret, to unrest:
So a swift steed gnaws at its reins;
A youth so is indignant at his father's power;
And, in result? The rider calmly guides the steed,
And father gives injunctions to the youth.

TSAR

Steeds have been known to unhorse the rider,
The son is not always under his father's full control.

Only by vigilence and strictness
Can people be controlled. So Ivan thought,
And he calmed, wise autocrat,
So thought also his fierce grandson.
No, people don't respond to kindness:
Do good—they won't thank you;
Indulge in pillage, executions—And you'll be no worse off.

(A BOYAR *enters)*

Yes, what?

BOYAR
            We've brought guests from abroad.

TSAR
I'll go receive them; Basmanov, wait.
Stay here: I still have need to talk
With you.

(Exits)

BASMANOV
            A lofty autocratic sensibility.
May God help him manage that damned
Otrepyev, and he'll accomplish much,
Much that is good, in Russia yet.
His mind gave birth to an important thought.
It should not be allowed to cool. For what
Great things will open to me, when
He breaks the back of titled boyars!
I have no peers equal to me in battle;
I will be first at the Tsar's throne . . .
And then perhaps . . . What's that strange noise?

(Panic. BOYARS *and* PALACE SERVANTS *run
about in confusion, stop and whisper to each other)*

A MAN
Get a physician!

ANOTHER
            Quick, to the Patriarch.

THIRD MAN
The Prince, he wants the Prince!

FOURTH MAN
A priest!

BASMANOV
    What is the matter?

FIFTH MAN
The Tsar is ill.

SIXTH MAN
    The Tsar is dying.

BASMANOV
        My God!

FIFTH MAN
On throne he sat and suddenly fell—
Blood poured out of his mouth and ears.

        (The TSAR *is carried in on a chair;*
        the entire royal family and BOYARS *enter)*

TSAR
All leave—leave me alone
Except the Heir.   *(All exit)*
        I'm dying;
Let us embrace, farewell, my son, it's now
You will begin to reign . . . Oh God, oh God!
I will appear before you now—and there's
No time to cleanse my soul by repentance.
But—son, I feel to me you are more dear
Than my own soul's salvation . . . And so be it!
By birth I was of service rank and I
Should die in dark obscurity serving;
But I attained the highest power . . . How?
Don't question me. Enough that you are innocent,
That you will now reign in the right.
I, I alone, for all, will answer before God . . .
Dear son, don't let falsehood seduce you,
Don't blind yourself by choice.
You will take reign in an unsettled time:
He's dangerous; this wondrous imposter,

He is armed with a terrifying name . . .
In governance long practiced, I
Could have controlled rebellion and unrest;
Before me, they trembled in fear;
Betrayal dared not raise its voice.
But you, a young, unpracticed ruler,
How will you govern under threat,
Douse out revolt, confuse betrayal?
But God is great! For youth He provides wisdom,
Weakness endows with strength . . . Hear me:
Choose, first of all, for your advisor
One trustworthy, mature and cool in years,
Loved by the people—and respected
Among boyars for family or fame—
Shuisky perhaps. The army needs at present
Skillful command: appoint Basmanov,
Firmly withstand boyars complaints.
From childhood you sat with me in Duma,
You know the process of the government;
Don't change the course of things. For habit is—
The soul of governments. Recently I
Had to restore exiles, executions—
You may stop them; you will be blessed,
As blessed was your uncle, when he
Ascended to Ivan the Terrible's throne.
With time little by little
Tighten the reins of government.
Then loosen them, without releasing from your hands . . .
Be gracious and accessible to foreigners,
With trust their service take.
Preserve strictly the doctrines of the Church;
Be prone to being silent; for tsar's voice
Should not be lost in empty air;
Like holy ringing of the bells, it should only
Announce great sorrow or great holiday.
Oh my dear son, you're entering the age
Our blood is stirred by woman's image.
Cherish, cherish the holy purity,
Of innocence and pride in modesty:
He who, in youth, acquired the habit of
Indulging feelings of the sinful pleasures

Is, as a man, blood-thirsty and morose,
His mind darkening prematurely.
Always be suzerein within your family;
Your mother show respect but govern on your own.
You are a man and Tsar; love your sister,
You are the one protector that she has.

FEDOR

(On his knees)

No, no—live on and reign for ages more:
The people, we are lost without you.

TSAR

The end is here—my eyes grow dark,
I feel the graveyard's chill . . .

(THE PATRIARCH, PRIESTS, *after them* BOYARS *enter.*
The TSARINA *is led in supported on both sides;*
the PRINCESS *is crying)*

Who's there?
Aha! Monk's robes for taking vows . . . So, holy tonsuring . . .
The hour has struck, Tsar passes into monkhood—
And the dark grave will be my monastery cell . . .
Give me a moment, Holy Father,
I am still Tsar: heed me, boyars:
This is to whom I leave the realm;
So kiss the cross in loyalty to Fedor . . . Basmanov,
My friends . . . I beg, in presence of the coffin,
You serve him with hard work and truth!
He is so young and sinless yet . . .
Do you so swear?

BOYARS

We swear.

TSAR

I am content.
Forgive me my temptations and my sins
And slights intended or covert.
Holy Father, approach, I am prepared.

(The ritual of tonsuring begins. The women
are carried out unconscious)

Headquarters

BASMANOV *shows in* PUSHKIN

BASMANOV
Enter and speak without constraint.
And so, he sends you to see me?

PUSHKIN
He offers you his friendship
And to be first with him in Moscow's government.

BASMANOV
But Fedor has already raised
Me high. The army I command,
On my behalf he's spurned established rank,
And boyars' wrath—I took an oath to him.

PUSHKIN
You took an oath to the throne's lawful heir;
But what if there's alive another,
More lawful yet? . . .

BASMANOV
                    Hear me, Pushkin, enough,
Don't repeat nonsense to me; I know,
Exactly who he is.

PUSHKIN
                    Russia and Lithuania
Have long recognized him as Dmitry,
But, by the way, I don't insist on it.
Perhaps he is the true Dmitry,
Perhaps imposter he may be. Only
I know, whether sooner or later,
Boris's son will give Moscow to him.

BASMANOV
For now I stand for the young Tsar,
Until he leaves the throne;
We have enough of troops, God knows!
With victory I will inspire them,

And whom will you against me send?
Karela the Cossack? Or perhaps Mnishek?
And you are few, only eight thousand.

PUSHKIN
You're wrong: We don't have even that—
I'll be the first to say, our army is sheer rubbish,
The Cossacks know only to pillage villages,
The Poles only to boast and drink,
And the Russians . . . what's there to say . . .
I'll not attempt to mislead you;
But do you know what is our strength, Basmanov?
No, not in army or in Polish aid,
But in opinion; yes! Public opinion.
The triumphs of Dmitry you remember
And his peaceful conquests,
When everywhere, without a shot,
Cities would willingly to him surrender
And stubborn people in command would be tied up by mobs?
You saw yourself, did your men willingly
Take arms against him? When? When under Boris!
And now! . . . Basmanov, no, it's late to argue
And stir the cold embers of war:
With all your astute mind and will
You won't be able to resist; would it not be
Better for you to set a wise example first,
Proclaim Dmitry as the tsar
And thus make friend of him forever?
What do you think?

BASMANOV
                    Tomorrow you'll find out.

PUSHKIN
Decide.

BASMANOV
        Farewell.

PUSHKIN
                Give it some thought, Basmanov.   *(Exits)*

BASMANOV

He's right, he's right; treason is ripe everywhere—
What can I do? Should I then wait,
Until rebels also place me in ironsl
And hand me over to Otrepyev? Is it not better to
Forestall the surge of the tumultuous flood
And to oneself . . . But to betray one's oath!
To bring dishonor down on future generations!
The trust of the crown's youthful bearer
Repay with horrible betrayal . . .
It is not hard for a disgraced exile
To contemplate insurgency and plots,
For me, for me, the Tsar's favorite, however . . .
But death . . . power . . . the nation's plight . . .

(He is lost in thought)

Come here! Who's that?   *(Whistles)*

A horse! Muster the men.

The Scaffold of Proclamations and Executions

PUSHKIN *enters surrounded by people*

THE PEOPLE

The Heir sent a boyar to us.
Let's listen what he has to say.
Here! Over here!

PUSHKIN

(From the scaffold)

Citizens of Moscow,
The Heir bid me pay you homage.

(Bows)

You know how thanks to Heaven's providence
The Heir was saved from murderers' hands;
He marched to execute his villain,
But God's judgment struck Boris down.
Russia has been conquered by Dmitry;
Basmanov on his own and with sincere repentance
Has brought his regiments to take their oath to him.
Dmitry comes to you with love, with peace.

Will you, to please the Godunovs,
Raise up your hand against the lawful Tsar,
Against grandson of Monomakh?

THE PEOPLE
Of course, we won't.

PUSHKIN
                        Citizens of Moscow!
The world has seen your suffering
Under the cruel intruder's rule:
The persecution, executions, the dishonor, taxes,
Hard work, hunger—you have experienced all of these.
Dmitry, on the other hand, wants to be generous to you,
To boyars, courtiers, those in service, army,
Our guests, merchants—to all the honest folk.
Will you unreasonably be so stubborn
As to reject his favors in conceit?
He mounts the throne of tsars, of his
Forefathers, attended by a terrifying force.
Don't anger, then, the Tsar, fear God. Swear on
The cross your loyalty to lawful lord;
Humble yourselves and send immediately
Into Dmitry's camp the Metropolitan,
Boyars, officials, and your representatives,
To pledge their loyalty to Father and to Tsar.
                              (Steps down. The people clamor)

THE PEOPLE
What's there to argue then? He speaks the truth.
Long live Dmitry, he's our lord!

A MUZHIK ON THE SCAFFOLD
People! People! Go the Kremlin! To chambers of the Tsar!
Be off! Shackle Boris's pup!

THE PEOPLE
                              (Moving en masse)

Shackle! Drown them! Long live Dmitry!
Destroy the clan of Boris Godunov!

Kremlin. The House of Boris.

GUARDS *on the steps.* FEDOR *next to a window*

A BEGGAR
Alms, for the sake of Christ!

GUARDS
Get away, it's not permitted to speak with prisoners.

FEDOR
Old man, go, I am more destitute than you, you have freedom.
                              (Ksenia, wearing a shawl, also approaches the window)

ONE OF THE PEOPLE
Brother and sister. Poor children, like small birds in a cage.

ANOTHER MAN
Found someone for whom to feel sorry! Cursed family!

THE FIRST MAN
The father was a villain, but the children are innocent.

ANOTHER MAN
No apple falls far from the tree . . .

KSENIA
Brother, brother, I think the boyars come to us.

FEDOR
It is Golitsyn, Mosalsky. I don't know the others.

KSENIA
Oh, brother, I grow cold with fear.
                    *(*GOLITSYN, MOSALSKY, MOLCHANOV, *and* SHEREFEDINOV *enter.*
                              They are followed by three guardsmen)

THE PEOPLE
Give way, give way. The boyars come.

                                        (They enter the house)

ONE OF THE PEOPLE
Why are they here?

ANOTHER MAN

Probably to have Fedor Godunov pledge his allegiance.

THIRD MAN

Really? Listen, what's the noise, inside the house. What bedlam, they're fighting . . .

THE PEOPLE

Did you hear? A cry!—That's a woman's voice—Let's go in!—The doors are locked.—The shouts have stopped.

(The doors open. MOSALSKY *appears on the porch)*

MOSALSKY

People! Maria Godunova and her son Fedor have taken poison. We have seen their dead bodies.

*(*THE PEOPLE *are silent in horror)*

Why are you silent! Shout: Long live Tsar Dmitry, son of Ivan!

*(*THE PEOPLE *are speechless)*

Translation by Nicholas Rzhevsky

Notes to the translation begin on page 575.

RESOURCES

Primary Text

Pushkin, A.S. *Boris Godunov. Sobranie sochinenii v desiati tomakh,* ed. D.D. Blagoi, S.M. Bondi, V.V. Vinogradov, Iu.G. Oksman, and V. Tomashevskii. Vol. 4. Moscow: Khudozhestvennaia literatura, 1960, pp. 201–98.

Secondary Sources

Literary and Cultural Studies

Aranovskaia, O.P. "O vine Borisa Godunova v tragedii Pushkina." *Vestnik Russkogo khristianskogo dvizheniia* 143 (1984): 128–56.
Besançon, Alain. *Le Tsarevitch immolé.* Paris: Plon, 1967.
Durylin, S.N. *Pushkin na stsene.* Moscow: Akademiia nauk SSSR, 1951, pp. 75–79.
Emerson, Caryl. *Boris Godunov: Transpositions of a Russian Theme.* Bloomington: Indiana University Press, 1986.
———. "Pretenders to History: Four Plays for Undoing Pushkin's *Boris Godunov*." *Slavic Review* 44 (Summer 1985): 257–79.

————, and Robert Oldani. *Modest Musorgsky and Boris Godunov: Myths, Realities, Reconsiderations.* New York: Cambridge University Press, 1994.

Gorodetskii, B.P. *Tragediia A.S. Pushkina "Boris Godunov."* Leningrad: Prosveshchenie, 1969, pp. 69–71.

Karamzin, N.M. *Istoriia gosudarstva rossiiskogo.* Moscow: Nauka, 1989.

Rzhevsky, Nicholas. "Adapting Drama to the Stage: Liubimov's *Boris Godunov.*" *Slavic and East European Arts* 3 (Winter–Spring 1985): 171–76.

Slonimskii, A.L. "'Boris Godunov' i dramaturgiia 20-kh godov." In *Boris Godunov A.S. Pushkina,* ed. K.N. Derzhavin. Leningrad: Gosudarstvennyi Akademicheskii teatr dramy, 1936, pp. 67–68.

See additional entries under "The Bronze Horseman."

Literature

Kunin, V.V., ed. *Svetloe imia Pushkin. Proza, stikhi, p'esy o poete.* Moscow: Pravda, 1988.

Tolstoi, A.K. "Tsar Boris." In *Dramaticheskaia trilogiia.* Leningrad: Sovetskii pisatel', 1939.

Art

Favorskii, V.A. Illustration in *A.S. Pushkin. Boris Godunov.* Leningrad: Detgiz, 1960.

Golovin, A.I. "F.I. Shaliapin v role Borisa Godunova." In *Gosudarstvennyi Russkii Muzei.* Moscow–Leningrad: Izobrazitel'noe iskusstvo, 1959, plate 81.

Grigorev, M. *A.S. Pushkin. Boris Godunov. Al'bom illiustratsii.* Leningrad, 1947.

Kibrik, E.A. In *A.S. Pushkin. Boris Godunov.* Moscow: Detskaia literatura, 1965.

Music

Mussorgsky, Modest. *Boris Godunov.* Cast: E. Obraztseva, E. Nesterenko, V. Atlantov. Conductor, M. Ermlev. Chorus and Orchestra of the USSR Bolshoi Theatre. Melodiia, 1985. 4 records.

————. *Boris Godunov.* With Giorgio Tozzi. Conductor, Dmitry Mitropoulos. Metropolitan Opera and Chorus and Orchestra. New York, 1956.

————. *Boris Godunov.* With Nikolai Ghiaurov and Galina Vishnevskaya. Conductor, Herbert von Karajan. Vienna Philarmonic. London: Decca, 1970.

————. *Boris Godunov.* With George London and Irina Arkhipova. Conductor, Aleksandr Melnik-Pashaev. Chorus and Orchestra of the Bolshoi Theater. CBS, 1975.

————. *Boris Godunov.* With Ivan Petrov. Conductor, Aleksandr Melnik-Pashaev. Chorus and Orchestra of the Bolshoi Theater. Melodiia, 1980.

Film

Boris Godunov. Producer, Irina Morozova. Music, Modest P. Mussorgsky and Nikolai A. Rimsky-Korsakov. Cast: Tamara Siniavskaia, Vladimir Piavko, and Evgenii Nesterenko. Conductor, Aleksandr Lazarev. Chorus and Orchestra of the Bolshoi Theater. National Video Corporation and Gosteleradio, 1987. Videocassette recording of opera.

Musorgskii. Director, G. Roshal'. Cast: A. Borisov, N. Cherkasov. Lenfilm, 1950. Late Stalinist film biography.

Pushkin, A.S. *Boris Godunov.* Director, Sergei Bondarchuk. Cast: Irina Skobtseva, Natalia Bondarchuk, Sergei Bondarchuk. Mosfilm, 1989. Adaptation of play.

12

~Alexander Pushkin~

The Queen of Spades

"The queen of spades represents secret ill-will."
The Latest Book of Fortune-Telling

1

On days of foul weather
They would get together
Often;
They would double bets—God forgive them—
From fifty,
To a hundred,
And they would win,
And write it off, with
Chalk.
So on days of foul weather,
They would occupy themselves with
Work.

Once a card game was in progress at the residence of Narumov, an officer of the cavalry guards. The long winter night imperceptibly came to an end; supper was served shortly before five in the morning. The winners ate with great appetite; the others sat absent-minded before their empty plates. But champagne appeared, the conversation became more animated, and everyone joined in.

"How did you do, Surin?" asked the host.

"I lost, as usual. You must admit I am unlucky; I play for small stakes, I never get emotional, nothing ever distracts me, and I still lose all the time!"

"And you never have been tempted? You never played a hunch?... Your resolve astonishes me."

"And how about Herman?" said one of the guests, indicating a young officer of the Engineers. "Herman has never picked up a deck of cards in his life, he has never wagered a single bet, and he still sits with us till five in the morning and studies our game!"

"The game interests me very much," said Herman, "but I cannot sacrifice what is indispensable in hope of obtaining what is superfluous."

"Herman is German; he is a calculating sort, and that's all there is to it!" noted Tomsky. "Whom I really do not understand is my grandmother, Countess Anna Fedotovna."

"Why?" the guests exclaimed.

"I cannot fathom," Tomsky continued, "why my grandmother does not wager on cards!"

"Why is it so surprising," said Narumov, "that an old woman of eighty doesn't gamble?"

"So you know nothing about her?"

"No, really, nothing!"

"Well, then listen. Some sixty years ago my grandmother went to Paris and became very popular there. People ran after her to see *la Vénus moscovite*. Richelieu followed her around and grandmother assures me he almost shot himself because she was so standoffish.

"In those days women played faro. Once at court she lost a very large sum to the Duke of Orleans. Upon arriving home, while taking off her beauty spots and untying her hoop-skirts, she announced her losses to grandfather and ordered him to take care of them.

"Grandfather, now deceased, was, as far as I remember, a sort of servant for grandmother. He feared her like fire; however, upon hearing of such a terrible loss of money, he became completely beside himself, brought out bills, showed her that they had gone through half a million in half a year, noted they did not have their suburban Moscow or their suburban Saratov villages to fall back on adjacent to Paris, and refused point-blank to pay up. Grandmother slapped his face and went to sleep alone as a token of her displeasure.

"The next day she sent for her husband, hoping the domestic punishment had taken effect, but discovered him to be unwavering. For the first time in her life she found herself trying to be reasonable and persuasive with him. She thought of appealing to his conscience by proving that debts must be honored and that there is a difference between a prince and a coachmaker. Nothing doing! Grandfather was in a state of revolt. No, and that's it! Grandmother did not know what to do.

"She had recently become acquainted with a truly remarkable person. You've heard of Count Saint-Germain, of whom so many curious things have been said.[1] You know he claimed to be the Wandering Jew, the inventor of a life-giving elixir and of the philosopher's stone, and so on. People made fun of him as a charlatan, while Casanova in his *Memoirs* says he was a spy. But Saint-Germain, in spite of his mysterious aura, was very presentable in appearance and very pleasant in social gatherings. Grandmother is still extremely fond of him and becomes angry if he is mentioned with disrespect. Grandmother knew Saint-Germain had access to a lot of money. She decided to make use of him. She wrote a note and asked that he immediately come to see her.

"The old eccentric came right away and found her in the throes of terrible sorrow. She described her husband's barbaric behavior in the bleakest colors and ended by placing all her hopes on Saint-Germain's friendship and congeniality.

"Saint-Germain fell into deep thought. 'I can readily give you that amount,' he said, 'but I know you will not be happy until you pay me back, and I would not like to be the cause of fresh distress. There is another way: you can recoup your losses.'

" 'But, my dear Count,' answered grandmother, 'I'm telling you, we have absolutely no money.'

" 'No money is necessary in this instance,' rejoined Saint-Germain. 'Please listen to what I have to say.' And then he revealed a secret for which any of us would pay dearly."

The young gamblers redoubled their attention. Tomsky lit a pipe, puffed on it, and continued.

"That same evening grandmother arrived at Versailles, *au jeu de la reine.*[2] The Duke of Orleans held the bank; grandmother apologized briefly for not bringing the money she owed, made up a small tale to justify herself, and began to bet against him. She chose three cards and placed them down one after the other. All three cards won, and grandmother totally recouped her losses."

"Chance!" said one of the guests.

"A fairy tale," noted Herman.

"Perhaps it was a marked deck?" a third man joined in.

"I don't think so," solemnly answered Tomsky.

"How's that now!" said Narumov. "You have a grandmother who can guess three cards in a row, and you haven't yet made use of her cabalistic talents?"

"Not a chance in hell!" answered Tomsky. "She has four sons, one of whom is my father. All four are passionate gamblers, and she has not revealed her secret to any of them, although it would have done them some good, and even done me some good. But here is what my uncle, Count Ivan Ilyich, said, swearing on his word of honor. The late Chaplitsky, the very one who died in poverty after squandering millions, once in his youth lost—to Zorich if memory serves me—approximately three hundred thousand.[3] He was in total despair. Grandmother, who always frowned upon the misbehavior of the young, for some reason took pity on Chaplitsky. She told him of the three cards, on condition that he bet on them one after the other, and beforehand obtained his promise never to gamble again. Chaplitsky went back to his opponent; they sat down to play. Chaplitsky bet fifty thousand on the first card and won; he doubled, doubled again, won everything back and even a bit extra. . .

"But it's time for bed: it is already quarter to six."

Indeed, dawn was already breaking; the young men finished their drinks and went their separate ways.

2

"Il parait que monsieur est décidément pour les suivantes."
"Que voulez-vous, madame? Elles sont plus fraiches."[4]

A conversation in society

The old Countess X was sitting in her boudoir before a mirror. Three young women surrounded her. One held a jar of rouge, another a box with hairpins, a third a tall bonnet with ribbons of a fiery color. The Countess did not have the slightest pretensions to beauty, which had long since faded away, but she maintained all the habits of her youth, paid close attention to the fashion of the seventies, and took as much time and as much care in dressing as sixty years ago. At a small window, a young woman, her ward, sat in front of an embroidery frame.

"Hello, *Grand'maman,*" said a young officer entering. *"Bon jour, Mademoiselle Lise. Grand'maman,* I have a favor to ask."

"What is it, Paul?"

"Allow me to introduce one of my friends and to bring him to meet you at the ball on Friday."

"Take him straight to the ball and present him to me there. Did you go to the _____s yesterday?"

"I should say so! It was very lively; the dancing went on till five. Eletskaya was beautiful!"

"But, my dear, what's so beautiful about her? Was her grandmother Princess Daria Petrovna at all like her? By the way, I should think she has aged considerably, the Princess Daria Petrovna?"

"What do you mean aged?" answered Tomsky in confusion. "She died seven years ago."

The young woman raised her head and made a sign to the young man.

He remembered that deaths of women her age were kept secret from the old Countess and bit his lip. But the Countess reacted to the news with great indifference.

"She died!" she said. "And I did not even know! We became maids of honor at the same time, and when we were presented, Her Majesty . . . "

And the Countess for the hundredth time told her grandson her story.

"Well, Paul," she said afterward, "now help me to get up. Lizzie, where is my snuffbox?"

And the Countess accompanied by her girls went behind the screen to complete dressing. Tomsky remained with the young woman.

"Whom do you want to introduce?" softly asked Lizaveta Ivanovna.

"Narumov. Do you know him?"

"No. Is he in the army or a civilian?"

"In the army."

"A military engineer?"

"No. He's cavalry. Why did you think he was an engineer?"

The young woman laughed and did not say a word.

"Paul!" the Countess shouted from behind the screen. "Send me some new novel, only please, nothing written recently."

"How's that, *Grand'maman*?"

"That is, a novel in which the hero does not strangle either his father or his mother, and in which there are no drowned corpses. I am very afraid of drowned people."

"There are no such novels today. Would you like something written in Russian?"

"Are there indeed Russian novels? Send me one, my boy, please, do send one!"

"My excuses, *Grand'maman:* I am in a hurry . . . Good-bye, Lizaveta Ivanovna! Why did you think Narumov was a military engineer?"

And Tomsky left the boudoir.

Lizaveta Ivanovna remained alone: she put down her work and looked out the window. Soon a young officer appeared from behind a corner house on the other side of the street. A blush spread over her cheeks; she began to work again and lowered her head to the canvas. At that moment the Countess came in fully dressed.

"Order the carriage, Lizzie," she said, "and let's go for a ride."

Lizzie got up from the embroidery frame and began to put away her work.

"What are you, girl, deaf or something!" shouted the Countess. "Order the carriage quickly."

"Right away!" the young woman quietly answered and ran off to the foyer.

A servant came in and handed the Countess books from Prince Pavel Aleksandrovich.

"Good! Thank him," said the Countess. "Lizzie, Lizzie! Where are you running?"

"To get dressed."

"You have plenty of time for that, girl. Sit over here. Open the first volume; read aloud . . . "

The young woman picked up the book and read several lines.

"Louder!" said the Countess. "What is the matter with you? Have you lost your voice? Wait: move the bench to me, closer . . . well! . . . "

Lizaveta Ivanovna read two more lines. The Countess yawned.

"Put down that book," she said. "What nonsense! Send it back to Prince Paul with our thanks. . . . Where is the carriage?"

"The carriage is ready," said Lizaveta Ivanovna, glancing out on the street.

"And why aren't you dressed?" said the Countess. "You always make people wait for you! That's unbearable, my dear."

Liza ran off to her room. Two minutes had not gone by before the Countess began to ring with all her strength. Three girls ran in through one door and the head butler through another.

"Why is it so hard to call you?" the Countess said to them. "Tell Lizaveta Ivanovna I am waiting for her."

Lizaveta Ivanovna came in wearing a coat and hat.

"Finally, my girl!" said the Countess. "What sort of get-up is that! What's it for, who is there to seduce? And how's the weather, it appears to be windy."

"Not at all, madam! It's very calm outside," said the head butler.

"You're always saying things off the top of your head! Open the little window. There it is, wind! And cold as can be! Cancel the carriage! Lizzie, we are not going; you got all dressed up for nothing."

"And that's my life!" thought Lizaveta Ivanovna.

In truth, Lizaveta Ivanovna was a most unhappy being. Bitter to the taste is another's bread, says Dante, and steep are the steps of someone else's porch. And who can better know the bitterness of dependence than the poor ward of an old noblewoman? The Countess, of course, was not mean-spirited; but being a woman spoiled by society she was willful, miserly, and coldly egotistic, not unlike all old people who expend their capacity for love early in life and who are out of touch with the present. She participated in all the hustle and bustle of grand society and dragged herself to all the balls, where she sat in a corner rouged and dressed up in the ancient fashion, a freakish and indispensable decoration of the ballroom. Arriving guests would greet her with low bows, as in an established ritual, and no one would pay any further attention to her. At home she would receive the entire city, following a strict code of etiquette and not recognizing anyone. Her multitude of servants, grown fat and gray in her foyer and the women's quarters, did whatever they wanted and vied with each other in stealing from the dying old woman. Lizaveta Ivanovna was the house martyr. She poured tea and was reprimanded for using too much sugar; she read novels aloud and was guilty of all the author's mistakes; she accompanied the Countess on her excursions and answered for the weather and the road conditions. She was assigned an allowance, which was never paid in full, although she was expected to dress as everyone, that is, as very few could afford to dress. In society she played the most pitiful of roles. Everyone knew her and no one took notice of her. At balls she only danced when there were not enough *vis-à-vis,* and women would take her by the arm each time they needed to go to the ladies' room to fix something in their apparel.[5] She was vain, acutely felt her situation, and looked about impatiently awaiting someone to come to her rescue; but the young men, calculating in their frivolous vanity, did not deign to pay her attention, although Lizaveta Ivanovna was much more pleasant than the arrogant and cold brides among whom they hovered. How many times, after quietly exiting the boring and opulent living room, she would go to cry in her poor chamber, where stood screens pasted over with wallpaper, a bureau, a small mirror, and a painted bed frame, and where a tallow candle burned darkly in a copper candlestick.

Once—two days after the evening described at the beginning of this story and a week before the last episode we noted—once, Lizaveta Ivanovna, sitting next to a window at the embroidery frame, accidentally glanced out on the street and saw a young military engineer standing motionless and staring at her window. She lowered her head and occupied herself with work; five minutes later she glanced up again—the young officer stood in the same position. Not being in the habit of flirting with passing officers on the street, she stopped looking and sewed for approximately two hours without raising her head. Dinner was served. She got up, began to put away the frame, and by chance glanced out again and saw the officer. She took this to be rather strange. After dinner she went to the window with some feeling of disquiet, but by then the officer was gone— and she forgot about him. . . .

Two days later, leaving with the Countess to get into the carriage, she saw him again. He stood right next to the driveway, his face hidden in a beaver collar, his black eyes flashing out from under the hat. Lizaveta Ivanovna was frightened, herself not knowing why, and got into the carriage quivering unexplainably.

After returning home she ran up to the window—the officer was standing in the same place directing his eyes at her. She moved away, tortured by curiosity and agitated by feelings entirely new to her.

From then on not a day passed without the young man's appearing at a certain hour under the windows of their house. An unpremeditated form of contact was established between them. Sitting at work in her place she would feel his presence nearby—she would raise her head and look at him longer and longer each day. The young man, it seemed, was grateful for her condescension. She saw, with the sharp sight of youth, how a quick flush would cover his pale cheeks each time their glances met. In a week she smiled at him. . . .

When Tomsky asked permission to introduce his friend to the Countess, the poor girl's heart began to race. But, finding out that Narumov was not an engineer but a cavalry guardsman, she regretted the careless question that gave away her secret to the flighty Tomsky.

Herman was the son of a Russified German, who had left him a small inheritance. Eager to be self-sufficient, Herman did not touch even the interest earned on his capital, lived on his salary alone, and did not allow himself the slightest indulgence. Because he was secretive and ambitious, his friends had little opportunity to make fun of his extreme thrift. He was moved by strong emotions and had a fiery imagination, but a firm resolve saved him from the usual errors of youth. Thus, for instance, being at heart a gambler, he never picked up a deck of cards, for he calculated that his financial condition did not allow him (as he would say) *to sacrifice what was indispensable in hope of obtaining what was superfluous;* and in the meantime, he would spend entire nights at the card table, following the game in feverish agitation.

The story of the three cards had a strong influence on his imagination and troubled him the entire night. "What if," thought he, wandering in Petersburg the next evening, "what if the old Countess reveals her secret to me! Or tells me the three winning cards! Why shouldn't one try one's luck? Introduce oneself to her, curry her favor—perhaps become her lover—but all that needs time and she is eighty-seven years old—she can die in a week—in two days! And the story itself? Can it be believed? No! Calculation, moderation, and diligence: those are my three sure cards, that is what will create my fortune, increase my capital sevenfold, and bring me peace and self-sufficiency!"

Lost in such thoughts, he found himself on one of Petersburg's main streets in front of a house constructed in an old architectural style. The street was full of carriages, one after another they drove up to the lit entrance. Each minute either the shapely leg of a young beauty, or a squeaking military boot, or a striped sock and diplomatic shoe would be lowered from a carriage. Furs and coats flashed by the grandiose majordomo. Herman stopped.

"Whose house is this?" he asked a policeman on the corner.

"Countess X's," answered the policeman.

Herman quivered in excitement. He again remembered the astonishing story. He began to pace next to the house and to think of its proprietor and of her wondrous gift. He returned late to his quiet room; he stayed awake for a long time, and when he finally fell asleep, his dreams were full of cards, a green table, a stack of money, and a mountain of gold coins. He bet card after card, doubled without hesitation, won endlessly, scooped up the gold, and placed the money in his pocket. Awaking when it was already late, he sighed that his fantastic wealth had vanished and went to wander up and down the city. He again found himself in front of the house of Countess X. An unknown force, it seemed, drew him to it. He stopped and began to look at the windows. In one of them, he saw a petite dark-haired head, bent in all likelihood over a book or work. The petite head looked up. Herman saw a wholesome face and black eyes. That minute decided his fate.

3

Vous m'écrives, mon ange, des lettres de quatre pages plus vite que je ne puis les lire.[6]

A correspondence

The moment Lizaveta Ivanovna took off her coat and hat, the Countess sent for her and ordered the carriage. They went out. At the moment when two lackeys were lifting the old woman and shoving her through the carriage doors, Lizaveta Ivanovna saw her engineer standing next to the wheel. He grabbed her hand, she was overcome with fright; the young man disappeared—a letter remained in her hand. She hid it in her glove and did not see or hear anything for the entire journey. The Countess liked to ask questions one after the other in the carriage: Whom did we just meet? What is the name of that bridge? What's written on the sign over there? On this occasion, Lizaveta Ivanovna, answering whatever came into her head and without reference to the questions, angered the Countess.

"What has happened to you, girl! Have you been struck deaf and dumb? Can't you hear or don't you understand me? . . . God knows, I don't slur my words and I still have my wits!"

Lizaveta Ivanovna did not listen. Upon returning home she ran to her room and took the letter out of her glove. It was unsealed. Lizaveta Ivanovna read it. The letter included a declaration of love: it was tender, respectful, and taken word for word out of a German novel. But Lizaveta Ivanovna did not know German and was very content with it.

However, she was very worried about accepting the correspondence. For the first time she was entering into a secret, intimate relationship with a young man. His impudence terrified her. She blamed herself for careless behavior and did not know what to do: to stop sitting in front of the window and by not paying attention to him dampen the young officer's inclination for further pursuit? To send back the letter? To answer coldly and decisively? She had no one to consult; she had neither friends nor advisors. Lizaveta Ivanovna decided to answer.

She sat down at the small desk, picked up pen, paper—and fell into thought. Several times she began a letter—and tore it up: the phrases appeared to be too gracious, or too cruel. Finally, she managed to write several lines to her satisfaction. "I am convinced," she wrote, "that you have honorable intentions and that you do not want to insult me with careless acts; but our acquaintance should not begin in this fashion. I am returning your letter, and I hope I will not have cause to complain of an unjustified lack of respect in the future."

The next day, seeing Herman walking on the street, Lizaveta Ivanovna got up from the embroidery frame, went out to the hall, opened a small window, and, placing her hopes on the agility of the young officer, threw the letter out on the street. Herman ran to it, picked it up, and entered a shop for sweets. Tearing off the seal he found his letter and Lizaveta Ivanovna's answer. It was exactly what he expected, and he returned home engrossed in his scheme.

Three days later a young mademoiselle, with darting eyes, brought Lizaveta Ivanovna a note from a fashionable shop. Lizaveta Ivanovna nervously opened it, expecting a bill, and abruptly recognized Herman's handwriting.

"You have made a mistake, my dear," she said. "This note is not for me."

"No, it very definitely is for you!" answered the bold young woman not bothering to hide a sly smile. "Please be so kind as to read it."

Lizaveta Ivanovna skimmed through the note. Herman demanded a rendezvous.

"It can't be!" said Lizaveta Ivanovna, frightened by the haste of the demand and the means of delivery. "This letter really is not for me!" And she tore it up into little pieces.

"If the letter isn't for you why did you tear it up?" asked the mademoiselle. "I would have returned it to him who sent it."

"Please, dearest!" said Lizaveta Ivanovna flaring up from her remark. "In the future do not bring me notes. As for who sent you, tell him he should be ashamed. . . ."

But Herman did not abate his efforts. Each day Lizaveta Ivanovna received a letter from him delivered in one way or another. They were no longer translated from the German. Herman wrote inspired by passion and in his own language. The letters expressed both the unconditional nature of his hopes and the chaos of an uncontrolled imagination. Lizaveta Ivanovna no longer thought of sending them back; she reveled in them, began in turn to answer—and each of her notes grew in length and tenderness. Finally, she threw the following letter out of the window:

"Today Ambassador X is giving a ball. The Countess will be there. We will stay till about two. This is your chance to see me alone. As soon as the Countess leaves, her servants are likely to disperse. The majordomo will stay in the hallway, but he too usually goes to his room. Come at eleven-thirty. Go straight up the stairs. If you meet anyone in the foyer, ask if the Countess is home. You'll be told she is not and that will be that. You will have to leave. But in all likelihood you will not meet anyone. The girls all sit together in their room. From the foyer turn left, then keep going straight till the Countess's bedroom. In the bedroom, behind the screens, you'll see two small doors, the one on the right is to the study; the Countess never enters it. The one on the left is to the corridor. It leads directly to a narrow, winding staircase and my room."

Waiting for the appointed time, Herman was as agitated as a tiger. By ten in the evening he was already in front of the Countess's house. The weather was dreadful: the wind howled; wet snow fell in huge flakes; the street lamps provided a dim light; the pavements were empty. Infrequently a coachman on his lean horse would pass by looking for a late fare. Herman stood wearing nothing more than a frock coat and feeling neither the wind nor the snow. Finally, the Countess's carriage was driven out. Herman saw lackeys carry the bent-over old woman enveloped in a mink fur, and following in her footsteps, her ward, wearing a coat that did not provide warmth, head adorned by fresh flowers. The doors slammed shut. The carriage laboriously rolled off on the crumbling snow. The majordomo locked the door. The windows grew dark. Herman began to pace next to the empty house. He went up to a lamppost, glanced at his watch—it was twenty after eleven. He remained under the lamppost, fixed his gaze on the clock hand, and waited for the remaining minutes to pass. Exactly at eleven-thirty, Herman went up the Countess's porch and entered the brightly lit entrance. The majordomo was not there. Herman ran up the stairs, opened the doors to the foyer, and saw a servant sleeping in an old soiled armchair under a lamp.

Walking softly and without hesitation, Herman went past him. The halls and living room were in shadows, lit dimly by a lamp in the foyer. Herman entered the bedroom. A golden lamp glowed in front of a small icon table, covered with ancient holy images. Faded damask chairs and sofas with feather pillows and worn gold embroidery stood in sad symmetry near the walls covered by Chinese wallpaper. Two portraits, painted in Paris by Madame Lebrun, hung on the wall.[7] One of them depicted a pink, stout man of forty in a light green uniform and wearing a star; the other, a young beautiful woman with an eagle's nose, hair combed back on the forehead, and a rose in her powdered hair. Porcelain shepherds protruded from all sides, as well as boxes, a desk clock made by the genial Leroy, knick-knacks, fans, and various ladies' toys created at the end of the past century in the time of Montgolfier's balloon and Mesmer's magnetism. Herman went behind the screens. In back of them stood a small iron bed; to the right was the door to the study, to the left, another to the corridor. Herman opened it and saw the narrow, winding staircase leading to the poor ward's room . . . But he turned back and entered the dark study.

Time passed slowly. All was silent. The clock struck twelve in the living room; throughout the house clocks could be heard ringing twelve one after another. Then again all was silent. Herman stood leaning against a cold stove. He was calm; his heartbeat was steady, as of a man who had decided to do something dangerous but necessary. The clocks struck one, then two o'clock, and he heard the distant rumble of a carriage. He was seized by an involuntary nervousness. The carriage drove up and stopped. He heard the sound of lowered steps. The household awoke. People began to run about, voices rang out, and the lights were turned on. Three old housemaids ran into the bedroom; the Countess, barely alive, entered and sank into a Voltaire armchair. Herman looked through a crack: Lizaveta Ivanovna passed next to him. Herman heard her hurried steps up the staircase. He felt something like guilt pangs, which then went away. He froze in place.

The Countess began to undress in front of a mirror. Her bonnet, decorated by roses, was unpinned; the powdered wig was taken off her gray and closely cropped head. Pins, like rain, cascaded around her. The yellow dress with silver trim fell at her swollen feet. Herman was witness to the repulsive secrets of her toilette. Finally, the Countess was attired in a bed jacket and nightcap. In this outfit, more appropriate to her age, she appeared to be less horrible and freakish.

Like all old people in general, the Countess suffered from insomnia. After undressing she sat down next to the window in a Voltaire armchair and sent away the housemaids. The candles were carried out, the room again was lit only by the icon lamp. The Countess sat, all yellow, swaying from right to left, barely moving her pendulous lips. Her clouded eyes showed a total absence of thought; looking at her one could think the frightening old woman's swaying was caused not by her will but by an act of hidden galvanism.

Suddenly, the dead face inexplicably changed. The lips stopped moving, the eyes came to life. An unknown man stood in front of the Countess.

"Don't be frightened, for God's sake, don't be frightened!" he said in a clear and quiet voice. "I don't intend to harm you, I've come to ask a favor."

The Countess silently looked at him and appeared not to have heard. Herman, thinking she was deaf, bent close over her ear and repeated the same words. The old woman remained silent as before. "You can," continued Herman, "make me happy for life, and it will cost you nothing. I know you can guess three cards one after the other . . . "

Herman stopped. The Countess appeared to understand what was wanted of her. She seemed to be searching for words to answer.

"It was a joke," she said finally. "I swear to you! It was a joke!"

"This is no joking matter," Herman rejoined angrily. "Remember Chaplitsky, whom you helped win back his money."

The Countess seemed confounded. Her facial features expressed strong emotional stirrings, but she quickly returned to her former insentient state.

"Will you," continued Herman, "name me those three winning cards?"

The Countess was silent; Herman continued.

"For whom are you keeping your secret? For your grandsons? They are rich as it is; moreover, they don't know the value of money. Spendthrifts won't be helped by your three cards. Someone incapable of preserving his father's legacy will die poor anyway, despite the most demonic attempts. I am not a spendthrift; I know the value of money. Your three cards won't be lost on me. So! . . . "

He stopped and nervously awaited her answer. The Countess remained silent. Herman got on his knees.

"If at some time," he said, "you knew the feeling of love, if you remember its ecstasy, if you smiled even once at the cry of a newborn son, if something human ever stirred in your heart, then I implore you in the name of the feelings of spouse, mistress, mother—all that is holy in life—do not refuse my request! Reveal your secret to me! What's it to you? Perhaps some horrible sin is involved that makes all hope of eternal bliss impossible, a devil's pact . . . Think, you are old; you don't have long to live—I am ready to take your sin on my head. Only reveal your secret to me. Remember, the happiness of a human being is in your hands, and not only I, but my children, my grandchildren, and great-grandchildren will bless your memory and honor it as holy. . . "

The old woman did not answer a word.

Herman got up.

"You old witch!" he said, grinding his teeth. "I'll make you answer."

With those words he took a pistol out of his pocket.

At the sight of the pistol the Countess expressed strong emotions for a second time. She began to toss her head and raised her hand as if to ward off a shot . . . Then she rolled onto her back . . . and remained still.

"Stop being childish," said Herman, taking her hand. "I am asking you for the last time: Do you want to tell me your three cards or not? Yes or no?"

The Countess did not answer. Herman saw that she had died.

4

May 7, 18—
Homme sans moeurs et sans religion! [8]

A correspondence

Lizaveta Ivanovna, still in her formal attire and lost in deep thought, sat in her room. After arriving home, she said that she would undress herself, quickly dismissed a half-asleep maid who unwillingly offered her services, and nervously entered her room anxious to find Herman yet hoping he would not be there. From the first glance she convinced herself of his absence and thanked fate for the obstacle that had interfered with their rendezvous. She sat down without undressing and started to remember all the events that had occurred in such a short time and that had brought her to such an extreme situation. Three weeks had not yet passed since she had first seen the young man outside the window, and she was already corresponding with him, and he had already managed to get her to agree to a night tryst! She knew his name only because some of his letters had been signed. She had never spoken to him, had never heard the sound of his voice, and, strangely enough, up till this very evening had never heard of him. How odd! This very evening at the ball Tomsky, sulking because the young Princess Pauline was for once flirting with someone else, and wishing to obtain revenge through indifference, invited Lizaveta Ivanovna to dance an endless mazurka. Throughout he made fun of her preferences for officers of the Engineers and assured her that he knew much more than she could surmise. Some of his jokes were so well directed that Lizaveta Ivanovna several times had occasion to think her secret was known to him.

"Who has told you all this?" she asked, laughing.

"A friend of the special person known to you," answered Tomsky. "A wonderful human being indeed!"

"And who is this wonderful human being?"

"His name is Herman."

Lizaveta Ivanovna did not answer, but her arms and legs grew cold.

"Herman," continued Tomsky, "is a truly romantic figure: he has the profile of Napoleon, and the soul of Mephistopheles. I think he must be guilty of at least three evil deeds. How pale you've become! . . . "

"I have a headache . . . So what did this Herman, or whatever his name is, say?"

"Herman is very unhappy with his friend: he states he would act entirely differently in his place . . . I even think Herman himself has designs on you; in any case he is not at all indifferent when he hears his friend's declarations of love."

"But where could he have possibly seen me?"

"In church, perhaps, or on a stroll. God knows! Maybe in your room, while you were asleep: he is capable of . . . "

The approach of three women with the question: *"Oubli ou regret?"*[9] interrupted the conversation, which had become so painfully fascinating for Lizaveta Ivanovna.

The woman Tomsky chose for a partner was the Princess herself. She had time to clear up matters with him, after dancing an extra circle and taking an extra turn around her chair. Tomsky, upon returning to his place, was no longer thinking either of Herman or of Lizaveta Ivanovna. She wanted to resume the interrupted conversation without fail; but the mazurka ended and soon afterward the Countess took her leave.

Tomsky's words were nothing more than mazurka chatter, but they left a deep impression on the young dreamer. The portrait, sketched by Tomsky, coincided with the image she herself had put together. Thanks to the latest novels, this already banal figure frightened and captivated her imagination. She sat, bare arms crossed, head still decorated with flowers, bent over her open breasts. Suddenly the door opened and Herman entered. She quivered.

"Where have you been?" she asked in a frightened whisper.

"In the old Countess's bedroom," answered Herman. "I came from there. The Countess is dead."

"My God, what are you saying?"

"And, it appears," continued Herman, "that I am the cause of her death."

Lizaveta Ivanovna stared at him, and Tomsky's words came back to her:

"He must be guilty of at least three evil deeds!" Herman sat down on the window next to her and told her everything.

Lizaveta Ivanovna heard him out in horror. And so, those passionate letters, the red hot demands, the arrogant, stubborn pursuit, all that was not love! Money—was his passion! It was not up to her to satisfy his desire and to make him happy! The poor ward was nothing but the blind accomplice of a thief, who had murdered her benefactress! She began to cry bitterly in belated, painful repentance. Herman silently looked at her. He also was in anguish, but neither the poor girl's tears nor the surprising charm of her sorrow troubled his stern soul. He did not feel pangs of guilt at the thought of the dead old woman. Only one matter horrified him: the irredeemable loss of a secret he had thought would make him wealthy.

"You are a monster!" said Lizaveta Ivanovna finally.

"I did not want her to die," said Herman. "My pistol is not loaded."

They fell silent.

Morning came. Lizaveta Ivanovna put out the burnt-down candle; a pale light illuminated her room. She wiped her tear-filled eyes and raised them to look at Herman; he sat on the windowsill, arms crossed and sternly frowning. In this pose he bore a striking resemblance to Napoleon's portrait. Their similarity amazed even Lizaveta Ivanovna.

"How are you going to get out of the house?" she said finally. "I thought of taking you down a hidden staircase, but it goes past the bedroom and I am scared."

"Tell me how to find this hidden staircase and I'll get out."

Lizaveta Ivanovna got up, took a key out of her bureau drawer, handed it to Herman, and gave him detailed instructions. Herman shook her cold, unresponsive hand, kissed her inclined forehead, and left.

He went down the twisting stairs and again entered the Countess's bedroom. The dead old woman sat still as stone; her face expressed a profound calm. Herman stopped in front of her, looked at her for a long time, as if wishing to convince himself of the horrible truth. Finally, he entered the study, felt a door behind the wall covering, and troubled by strange feelings began to go down a dark staircase. On this very staircase, he thought, perhaps sixty years or so ago, to this very bedroom, at this very hour, in an embroidered coat, hair combed *a l'oiseau royal*,[10] three-cornered hat pressed to his heart, crept a lucky young man, now long decayed in the grave, while the heart of his aged mistress today ceased to beat . . .

Under the staircase Herman found a door. He opened it with the same key and found himself in a drafty corridor leading out to the street.

5

That night the deceased Baroness Von-B* came to me. She was all in white and she said: "Hello, Mister Councilor."

Swedenborg

Three days after the fateful night, at nine in the morning, Herman set off to the monastery where a funeral service for the late Countess was to take place. He did not feel any pangs of repentance, but he could not block out entirely the voice of his conscience, which repeated over and over: you are the murderer of an old woman! Having little true faith, he had many superstitions. He believed the departed Countess could have an evil effect on his life, and he decided to make an appearance at the funeral to ask her forgiveness.

The church was full. Herman could hardly get through the crowd of people. The coffin stood on a richly decorated catafalque under a velvet canopy. The deceased woman, wearing a lace bonnet and a white velvet dress, lay in it, arms crossed on her chest. Her household staff stood around her: servants, in black coats and ribbons with the family coat of arms draped on their shoulders, holding candles in their hands, relatives wearing deep mourning, children, grandchildren, and great-grandchildren. No one cried; tears would have been—*une affectation.* The Countess was so old that her death could not have surprised anyone; her relatives looked upon her as someone who had long outlived her years. A young archpriest gave the funeral oration. In simple and touching words he described the peaceful departure of the righteous woman whose long years were spent in quiet, tender preparation for a Christian death. "The Angel of Death found her," he said, "in meditation of the goodly and awaiting the Midnight Groom." The service ended with the sad proprieties. The relatives went first to bid the deceased farewell. Next were the many guests, who had come to pay their respects to a participant of such long standing in their vain entertainments. After them came the household servants. Finally, an old gentry housekeeper, the same age as the deceased woman, approached. Two young girls held her by the arms. She did not have the strength to bow to the ground and was the only one to shed some tears, after kissing the cold hand of her mistress. Herman decided to go up to the coffin after her. He bowed to the ground kneeling for several minutes on the cold floor strewn with fir boughs. Finally, he got up, as pale as the deceased, walked up the steps of the catafalque and bent down . . . At that moment he thought the dead woman laughed and looked up at him squinting one eye. Herman hurriedly moved away, misstepped, and crashed down on his back. He was picked up. At the same time Lizaveta Ivanovna was carried to the church entrance in a faint. This incident momentarily upset the pomposity of the gloomy ritual.

A slight murmur arose among the visitors, and a very thin chamberlain, a close relative of the deceased, whispered into the ear of an Englishman standing next to him that Herman was the Countess's illegitimate son. To which the Englishman coldly answered: "Oh?"

Herman was extremely upset the entire day. Dining in a remote tavern, contrary to usual habit he drank very much, hoping to drown out an internal perturbation. But wine stimulated his imagination even more. When he returned home he threw himself on the bed without getting undressed and fell sound asleep.

He woke when it was already night; the moon illuminated his room. He glanced at the clock: it was a quarter to three. He was no longer sleepy; he sat up on the bed and began to think of the old Countess's funeral.

At that moment someone on the street looked into his window and immediately walked away. In a minute he heard the door being unlocked in the front room. Herman thought his orderly, drunk as usual, had returned from a night jaunt. But he heard an unfamiliar step; someone was walking, softly shuffling his feet. The door opened and a woman in a white dress entered. Herman took her to be his old nursemaid and was surprised she had come at such an hour. But the woman in white, gliding, was suddenly next to him—and Herman recognized the Countess!

"I come to you against my will," she said in a firm voice, "but I was ordered to satisfy your request. A three, seven, and ace will win for you in that order, but only if you do not bet more than one card in twenty-four hours and then never gamble again. I forgive you my death, if you will marry my ward Lizaveta Ivanovna . . . ."

With those words she turned quietly, went to the door, and disappeared, shuffling her feet. Herman heard the outer door slam and again saw someone glance through the window into his room.

For a long time Herman felt disoriented. He went into the next room. His orderly was sleeping on the floor; Herman barely managed to wake him. The orderly was drunk as usual. It was impossible to get anything sensible out of him. The door to the entrance was locked. Herman returned to his room, lit a candle, and wrote down what he had seen.

6

"*Attendez!*"
"How dare you say '*attendez*' to me?"
"Your Excellency, I said '*attendez*, sir!' "[11]

Two fixed ideas cannot exist simultaneously in the spiritual world, just as two bodies cannot occupy the same place in the physical one. The three, seven, ace soon blocked out the dead old woman in Herman's imagination. Upon seeing a young girl he would exclaim: "How well-proportioned she is! . . . Exactly like a three of hearts." He would be asked, "What time it is?" and he would answer: "Five minutes to a seven." Every man with a round belly would remind him of an ace. The three, seven, ace haunted his dreams, taking on all possible shapes: the three would blossom before him in the image of an opulent large flower; the seven would appear as a gothic gate; the ace as a huge spider. All his thoughts merged into one—to make use of the secret that had cost him dearly. He began to think of resigning his commission and of traveling. He wanted to steal a treasure out from under the nose of mystified fortune in the public gaming houses of Paris. Chance spared him the inconvenience.

In Moscow a group of rich gamblers began meeting under the leadership of the affable Chekalinsky. Chekalinsky had spent a lifetime at cards and had been known to have gathered in millions, winning chits and losing real money. His long experience earned him the trust of his friends; an open house, an excellent cook, affability, and good humor brought him public respect. He came to Petersburg. The young set flocked to his home, forgetting balls in favor of cards and preferring the lure of faro to the seduction of women. Narumov brought Herman to him.

They walked through several magnificent rooms filled with attentive waiters. A number of generals and councilors were playing whist; young people sprawled on damask sofas and ate ice cream or smoked pipes. In the living room, at a !ong table surrounded by a crowd of approximately twenty gamblers, sat the host administering the bank and dealing cards. He was about sixty and most respectable in appearance. His head was covered by silver gray hair; his full and vivacious face expressed good humor; his eyes sparkled, made lively by an ever-present smile. Narumov introduced Herman. Chekalinsky shook his hand in a friendly fashion, asked him not to stand on ceremony, and continued to deal the cards.

The game was long. There were more than thirty cards on the table. Chekalinsky stopped after every deal to give players time to make a decision; he wrote down losses, respectfully listened to demands, and even more respectfully straightened card corners players had absent-mindedly bent back. Finally, the game ended. Chekalinsky shuffled the cards and prepared to deal another round.

"Allow me to bet on a card," said Herman, stretching out his hand from behind a fat gentleman who was also placing wagers. Chekalinsky smiled and without saying anything bowed in sign of assent. Narumov, laughing, congratulated Herman for finally abandoning his long standing fast and wished him a happy beginning.

"You're on!" said Herman, having written his bet in chalk on the card.

"How much is it?" asked the dealer. "Forgive me, I cannot make it out."

"Forty-seven thousand," answered Herman.

At those words all heads turned instantly and all eyes were directed at Herman. "He's gone mad!" thought Narumov.

"Allow me," said Chekalinsky with his unchanging smile, "to note for your benefit that your stakes are very high. No one till now has placed more than two hundred seventy-five on any one hand."

"And so?" rejoined Herman. "Do you accept my wager or not?"

Chekalinsky bowed, demonstrating the same quiet acquiescence.

"I only have to tell you," he said, "that in light of the trust my friends have placed in me, I cannot wager against anything but currency. On my part I am, of course, convinced your word is enough, but in the interests of the rules of the game and of proper accounts I ask you to place your money on the card."

Herman took out a banknote and handed it to Chekalinsky, who after glancing at it placed the note on Herman's card.

He began to deal. A nine came up on the right, a three on the left.

"I've won!" said Herman showing his card.

A murmur arose among the players. Chekalinsky frowned but a smile immediately returned to his face.

"Would you like to be paid now?" he asked Herman.

"Be so kind."

Chekalinsky took several banknotes out of his pocket and immediately settled accounts. Herman took his money and moved away from the table. Narumov was flabbergasted. Herman drank a glass of lemonade and went home.

Next day in the evening he again appeared in Chekalinsky's house. The host was dealing. Herman went up to the table; the players immediately made room for him. Chekalinsky gave him a gentle bow.

Herman waited for a new game, put down a card, and bet his forty-seven thousand and yesterday's winnings.

Chekalinsky began to deal. A jack came up to the right, a seven to the left.

Herman showed his seven.

There was a general commotion. Chekalinsky appeared to be nonplused. He counted out ninety-four thousand rubles and handed them to Herman. Herman calmly accepted the money and left immediately.

The next night Herman again appeared at the table. Everyone awaited him. The generals and councilors left their whist to observe such an extraordinary game. The young officers jumped up from the sofas, all the waiters gathered in the living room. All surrounded Herman. Other players did not put down their cards impatiently awaiting for Herman to finish. Herman stood at the table preparing to bet alone against the pale but still smiling Chekalinsky. Each unsealed a deck of cards. Chekalinsky shuffled. Herman took a card and placed his wager, a heap of banknotes, on it. The game had the appearance of a duel. Dead silence prevailed all around.

"The ace won!" said Herman and revealed his card.

"Your queen has been beaten," Chekalinsky said tenderly.

A shudder ran through Herman. Indeed, instead of an ace he had the queen of spades. He could not believe his eyes, could not comprehend how he could have made such a mistake.

At that moment the queen of spades seemed to wink and smile. The unusual resemblance staggered him. . .

"The old woman!" he cried in horror.

Chekalinsky drew in the lost banknotes. Herman stood without moving. When he walked away from the table a noisy chatter rose up. "Well bet!" said the players. Chekalinsky again shuffled the cards; the game continued as usual.

Conclusion

Herman went mad. He sits in Room 17 of the Obukhovsky Hospital not answering any questions and mumbling rapidly: "Three, seven, ace! Three, seven, queen! . . . "[12]

Lizaveta Ivanovna married a very pleasant young man. He has a job somewhere and decent assets. He is the son of a steward once employed by the old Countess. Lizaveta Ivanovna is bringing up a girl, a poor relative.

Tomsky has been promoted to captain and will marry Princess Pauline.

1833

Translation by Nicholas Rzhevsky

Notes to the translation are on page 577.

Resources

Primary Text

Pushkin, Aleksandr S. "Pikovaia dama." *Sobranie sochinenii v desiati tomakh,* ed. D.D. Blagoi, S.M. Bondi, V.V. Vinogradov, and Iu.G. Oksman. Vol. 5. Moscow: Khudozhestvennaia literatura, 1960, pp. 233–62.

Secondary Sources

Literary and Cultural Studies

Bayley, John. *Pushkin: A Comparative Commentary.* Cambridge: Cambridge University Press, 1971.

Brown, David. "Pyotr Il'yich Tchaikovsky." *Russian Masters: Glinka, Borodin, Balakirev, Musorgsky, Tchaikovsky.* New York: Norton, 1986, pp. 145–250.

Brown, W.E. *A History of Russian Literature of the Romantic Period.* 4 vols. Ann Arbor, MI: Ardis, 1986.

Chizhevskii, Dmitrii. *History of Nineteenth-Century Russian Literature. Vol. 1—The Romantic Period, Vol. 2—The Realistic Period,* ed. Serge Zenkovsky. Trans. R.N. Parker. Nashville, TN: Vanderbilt University Press, 1974.

Cornwell, Neil. *Pushkin's "Queen of Spades."* London: Bristol Classical Press, 1993.

Debreczeny, Paul. "Poetry and Prose in 'The Queen of Spades.'" *Canadian American Slavic Studies* 11 (1977): 91–113.

Emerson, Caryl. "'The Queen of Spades' and the Open End." In *Pushkin Today,* ed. David Bethea. Bloomington: Indiana University Press, 1993, pp. 31–37.

Garden, Edward. *Tchaikovsky.* London and Melbourne: Dent, 1984.

Iarustovskii, B.M. *"Rabota nad opernym libretto."* In *Dramaturgiia russkoi opernoi klassiki.* Moscow: GosMuzIzdatel'stvo, 1953, p. 181.

Mersereau, John, Jr. "Pushkin's Concept of Romanticism." *Studies in Romanticism* 3 (1963): 24–41.

Poznansky, Alexander. *Tchaikovsky: The Quest for the Inner Man.* New York: Schirmer, 1991.

Ridenour, Robert. *Nationalism, Modernism, and Personal Rivalry in Nineteenth-Century Russian Music.* Ann Arbor, MI: UMI Research Press, 1981.

Roberts, Carolyn. "Pushkin's 'Pikovaja dama' and the Opera Libretto." *Canadian Review of Comparative Literature* 6 (1979): 9–26.

Schmidgall, Gary. *Literature as Opera.* New York: Oxford University Press, 1977.

Terras, Victor, ed. *A History of Russian Literature.* New Haven: Yale University Press, 1991, pp. 204–16.

Todd, William Mills. *Fiction and Society in the Age of Pushkin: Ideology, Institution and Narrative.* Cambridge: Harvard University Press, 1986.

———. "Púshkin, Aleksándr Sergéevich (1799–1837)." In *Handbook of Russian Literature,* ed. Victor Terras. New Haven: Yale University Press, 1985, pp. 356–60.

See additional entries under "The Bronze Horseman" and *Boris Godunov.*

Theater

The Queen of Spades. Director, Peter Fomenko. Distributed by RAES, n.d. Video recording of stage adaptation.

Music

Alexander Pushkin's "The Queen of Spades." International Instructional Television Co-operative, Inc. Indiana University Audio-Visual Center, 1978.

Tchaikovsky, Peter I. *Pikovaia dama* (The Queen of Spades). Cast: Vladimir Atlantov, Tamara Milashkina, Valentina Levko, and Andrei Fedoseyev. Conductor, Mark Ermler. Chorus and Orchestra of the Bolshoi Theater. Netherlands: Program International, 1985.

————. *Pikovaia dama*. Conductor, Vladimir Fedoseyev. Cast: Dmitri Hvorostovsky, Irina Arkhipova, and Alexander Vedernikov. Yurlov State Academic Russian Chorus, Gosteleradio Bolshoi Symphony Orchestra. MCA Classics, 1990.

————. *Pique-Dame* (The Queen of Spades). Opera in 3 acts. Libretto by Modest Tchaikovsky. English version, Boris Goldovsky. New York: Schirmer, 1951.

————. *The Queen of Spades*. Conductor, Seiji Ozawa. Cast: Vladimir Atlantov, Mirella Freni, Katherine Ciesinski, and Dmitri Hvorostovsky. Tanglewood Festival Chorus. Boston Symphony Orchestra. BMG Music, 1992.

————. *Pikovaia dama*. Conductor, Iurii Simonov. Cast: Vladimir Atlantov, Tamara Milashkina, Elena Obraztsova. Gosteleradio, n.d. Film of opera on stage.

Film

Evgenii Onegin. New York: Corinth Video, 1984. 1960 film of Bolshoi Opera Production.

Malenkie tragedii (Little Tragedies). Director M. Shveitser. Cast: Vladimir Vysotskii, Valerii Zolotukhin, Sergei Iurskii, Innokentii Smoktunovskii. Fort Lee: RAES Video, 1994, 1979.

Pikovaia dama (The Queen of Spades). Director, Roman Tikhomirov. Conductor, Evgenii Svetlanov. Cast: O. Strizhenov, O. Krasina, E. Polevitskaia, V. Kulik, V. Medvedev. Chorus and Orchestra of the Bolshoi Theater. West Long Branch, NJ: Kultur, 1985.

Stantsionnyi smotritel' (The Station Master). Director, S. Soloviev. Mosfilm, 1973.

13

~Nikolai Gogol~

The Overcoat

In the department of . . . but better not to name the department.[1] There's
nothing touchier than departments, regiments, offices—in a word, any kind
of official body. Nowadays each individual considers an insult to himself to
be an insult to all of society. There's the story of the petition received
recently from a certain police captain—I don't recall what town he was
from—in which he clearly explained that state directives were doomed and
that the state's sacred name was definitely being uttered in vain. As proof,
he enclosed an oversized volume of some romantic composition in which a
police captain appeared every ten pages, in some passages quite drunk even.
Therefore, to avoid any unpleasantness, better to call the department in
question *a certain department.*

And so, in *a certain department* there worked *a certain clerk,* a clerk
who could not be said to be very remarkable: rather short, face somewhat
pockmarked, hair somewhat red, eyes somewhat myopic-looking, balding
slightly at the forehead, with wrinkles down both sides of his cheeks, and
his face hemorrhoidal in color, one would say. . . . It can't be helped! Blame
it on the Petersburg climate. In regard to his rank (for among us we must
declare our rank before all else) he was what they call a perpetual civil
servant,[2] fully ridiculed and mocked, as is well known, by various writers
who have the commendable habit of pouncing upon those who cannot bite
back. The clerk's last name was Bashmachkin. It is obvious from the very
name that it at one time evolved from a shoe; yet nothing is known about
when, in what era, or how it evolved from a shoe. His father and his
grandfather and even his brother-in-law, absolutely all the Bashmachkins,
wore boots, replacing soles only a few times a year. His name was Akaky
Akakievich.[3] Perhaps the name will strike the reader as somewhat strange
and contrived, but be assured it was not in any way a matter of choice, for
circumstances in themselves were such that it was totally impossible to give
him a different name, and this is exactly how it happened. Akaky
Akakievich, if my memory does not fail me, was born on the night of the

twenty-third of March. His late mother, the wife of a clerk and a very fine woman, made up her mind, as is proper, to christen the baby. The mother was still lying in a bed facing the doors, while to her right stood the godfather, Ivan Ivanovich Yeroshkin, a most excellent man, who worked as head clerk in the Senate, and the godmother, Arina Semyonovna Belobriushkova, the wife of a police officer and a woman of rare virtue. The mother was given three names to choose from, whichever one she wished: Mokia, Sosia, or she could name the child after the martyr Hozdazat. "No," thought the deceased, "the names are all so . . . " To please her, they turned the calendar to a different place and another three names came up: Trifily, Dula, and Varakhasy. "Now this is a punishment," said the old woman. "What names! I really have never heard of the like.[4] If it were at least Varadat or Varukh, maybe, but Trifily and Varakhasy!" They turned the page again—Pavsikakhy and Vakhtisy came up. "Well, I can see," said the old woman, "it's obvious, such is his fate. If that's how it is, then better he be named like his father. His father was Akaky, so let the son be Akaky too." In this way Akaky Akakievich came into being. The baby was christened, at which time he began to cry and made such a face, as if he had a premonition he would be a titular councillor.

So, that's how it all happened. We have brought this matter up so the reader might see for himself it was absolutely inevitable and in no way could another name be given. When and at what time he joined the department, and who assigned him, no one could recall. No matter how many times the director and various superiors were changed, he could always be seen in the same place, in the same position, at the same post, the same copying clerk, so that people later were convinced that he obviously had been born into the world completely ready, in uniform, a bald patch on his head. No respect whatsoever was shown him in the department. Not only did the watchmen not bother to stand up whenever he passed, they did not even look at him, as if a common housefly had flown across the reception area. His superiors treated him somehow coldly, despotically. Some assistant to the head clerk would thrust papers directly under his nose without even saying, "Copy this," or, "Here's something interesting, a nice little job," or something pleasant, as is usually done in well-mannered offices. And he would take the work, looking only at the paper and not glancing to see who put it there or if they had the right to do so. He would take it and at once set to copying. The young clerks made fun of him and cracked jokes, to the full extent of office humor. Right in front of him they told various made-up stories about him, and about his landlady, an old woman of seventy, saying that she beat him, asking when their wedding would be, sprinkling scraps of paper on his head and calling it snow. But Akaky Akakievich said not a word to any of this, as if there were no one in front of him. It did not even affect his work. Amid all the bother he never made one mistake in his copying. But only if the joke was simply too unbearable, when they nudged his hand preventing him from his occupation, he would say, "Leave me alone, why do you torment me?" And there would be something strange in his words and the voice in which he pronounced them. In it could be heard something that so moved one to pity that a young man recently appointed to his job, who, following the example set by others, had allowed himself to make fun of him, suddenly stopped as if transfixed; and from that time everything seemed to change before his eyes and to appear in a different light. Some unnatural force repelled him from the friends he had made, assuming them to be decent, refined people. And long after, during the most cheerful of moments, the small clerk with the bald patch on his forehead would appear before him with the piercing words, "Leave me alone, why do you torment me?" And in these heart-rendering words rang other words: "I am your brother." And the poor young man would cover his face with his hands and many times thereafter in his life he would shudder, seeing how much inhumanity there is in man, how much savage coarseness lurks beneath refined, worldly manners, and, oh God! even in that person whom the world deems to be noble and honorable . . .

It is doubtful one could find a person anywhere who lived so much for his work. It is not enough to say he served with zeal; no, he served with love. There, in that copying work, he glimpsed his own multicolored and enchanting world. The delight he felt was evident from his expression; Certain letters were his favorites, and whenever he came across them, he was simply beside himself. He chuckled and winked and helped by moving his lips, so it seemed one could read in his face every letter his pen was forming. If he had been rewarded commensurate with his zeal, he might have actually become a counsellor of state, to his amazement.[5] But, as those witty fellows, his co-workers, expressed it, all his service got him was a buckle in his buttonhole and hemorrhoids in his backside. It cannot really be said, however, that he was totally neglected. A certain director, being a good person and wishing to reward him for his long service, ordered he be given something more significant to do than the usual copying; to wit, he was instructed to write some kind of memorandum to another office from a prepared file. The job only consisted of altering the heading and changing verbs here and there from the first person to the third. This proved to be such a project for him that he broke out in a complete sweat, kept wiping his brow, and said at last, "No, better let me copy something." After that he was left to do his copying forever.

Outside of such copying work, nothing appeared to exist for him. He did not pay any attention to his clothing; his uniform was not green but a sort of muddy rust color. His collar was narrow and low, so that his neck, although it was not long, seemed unusually so standing out from the collar, like those plaster kittens with their bobbing heads that Russian foreigners carry on their heads by the dozens. And there was always something stuck to his uniform: either a small piece of hay or some bit of thread. What is more, he had this special talent for arriving beneath a window at precisely the moment when someone was throwing various trash from it, and for that reason he was perpetually carrying off melon rinds and other such bits of nonsense on his hat. Not once in his life did he pay attention to what was going on and happening daily in the street, to all those things that, as everybody knows, his young fellow clerk would see instantly, with a bold stare so acute, that he could even note who on the other side of the sidewalk had a rip in his pants' stirrup, something that always evoked a sly grin on his face.

But even if Akaky Akakievich looked at something, he only saw his neat, evenly handwritten lines, and only when a horse's head would come up out of nowhere on his shoulder and the nostrils would let loose an entire gust of wind onto his cheek would he realize he was not in the middle of a line but rather in the middle of the street. Upon arriving home, he would sit down immediately, quickly gulp down his cabbage soup, and partake of a piece of beef with onions, without noticing the taste at all, and eating it complete with flies and anything else which God then might have happened to send along. When he noticed that his stomach was beginning to feel bloated, he would get up from the table, take out a small jar of ink, and copy the documents he had brought home with him. If there was no copying to be done, he would make a copy for his own pleasure, especially if the document was remarkable—not for the beauty of its style, but for its address to some new or important person.

Even during those hours when the gray Petersburg sky becomes completely overcast and the whole of bureaucratic society has eaten its fill and finished a dinner in keeping with each person's salary and personal taste, when everyone has already rested after the pen-pushing, the running around, one's own and others' indispensable occupations, and everything the industrious man makes himself do voluntarily, more even than necessary when the clerks hasten to devote whatever free time they have to pleasure—the bolder sort rushing off to the theater, another using the time to step outside and survey some hats; another to waste his evening at a party paying compliments to some pretty girl, the star of a small circle of clerks; another, and this is what happens most frequently, simply going to visit his fellow man on the third or fourth floor, to a two-room apartment with an entryway, or with a kitchen and pretensions to style, a lamp or some other little thing that, bought at great sacrifice, meant going without dinner or amusement—in a word, even when all the government workers scattered among their friends' small apartments to play some whist while sipping tea out of glasses and eating kopek biscuits, puffing on their long pipes, relaying, as the cards were being dealt, bits of gossip that had reached their ears from high society, something no Russian could ever and under any circumstances pass up, and even retelling the old anecdote about the commandant who was informed the tail of the horse on the Falconet Monument[6] had been cut off—in a word, even when everybody was anxious to enjoy themselves, Akaky Akakievich never indulged in any entertainment. No one can say he has ever seen him at any evening gathering. Having written to his heart's content, he would go to sleep, smiling in anticipation and thinking of the next day: What will God send me to copy tomorrow? Thus continued the peaceful life of a human being who, making a salary of four hundred rubles, knew how to be happy with his lot, who perhaps would have arrived at old age had it not been for the various calamities strewn along life's highway, not only for titular councillors, but even for privy, actual, court,[7] and all sorts of other councillors, including those who don't counsel anyone or receive any themselves.

There is in Petersburg a powerful enemy of all who receive a yearly salary of four hundred rubles or so. This enemy is none other than our northern frost, although, by the way, it is said to be very good for the health. At nine in the morning, exactly when the streets are crowded with people walking to their offices, it begins dealing out such powerful and biting stings to all noses without discrimination that the poor clerks have absolutely no idea where to put them. And when even higher officials feel the powerful frost sting their foreheads and their eyes begin to tear, the poor clerks are occasionally defenseless. The only salvation lies in running as quickly as possible in a skimpy overcoat for five or six blocks, and then giving the feet a good stomping in the lobby, until all one's capacity and talent for administrative functions, frozen on the way, thus thaw out. Some time ago Akaky Akakievich had begun to feel the cold penetrate his back and shoulders with particular force, although he tried to run the prescribed distance as quickly as possible. He finally began to wonder whether there was some defect in his overcoat. Having closely inspected it at home, he discovered that in two or three places, at the back and shoulders to be exact, the overcoat had become a real sieve. The material was so worn that it allowed drafts through, and the lining had fallen apart.

It should be known that Akaky Akakievich's overcoat served as another object of the clerks' jokes; they even took away its noble name of overcoat and called it a dressing gown. It did, in fact, have a rather strange form: the collar shrank more and more each year, since it was being used as material to patch up the other areas. Such patchwork was not representative of the tailor's skills, and in fact looked quite awkward and unsightly. Seeing what the trouble was, Akaky Akakievich decided the overcoat would have to be taken to Petrovich the tailor, who lived somewhere on the fourth floor up the back stairs, and who, despite being one-eyed and pockmarked, was fairly successful at mending the pants and frock coats of clerks and others—that is, when he was in a sober state and not contemplating some other endeavor. Of course, one really should not say too much about this tailor, but since it has become the custom in stories to depict fully every single character, we have no choice, so let's have Petrovich here as well. In the beginning he was called simply Grigory and was the serf of some landowner. He began to be called Petrovich when he was granted his freedom and started drinking rather heavily on every holiday, at first the major ones, and then without distinction on every church holiday, just so the day was marked on the calendar with a cross. In this respect he was true to the customs of his forefathers, and, when bickering with his wife, would call her a woman of the world and a German. Since we have already mentioned his wife, it will be necessary to say a word or two about her as well; but, regrettably, not much was known about her, except perhaps that Petrovich had a wife who even wore a bonnet rather than a kerchief. But beauty, it seems, was not her forte; at least, upon meeting her, only Guards' soldiers would peep under her bonnet, after twitching their mustaches and emitting some odd sound.

Climbing the staircase leading to Petrovich's rooms, a staircase that, to do it justice, was all covered with water and refuse and permeated with the alcoholic stench that stings the eyes and, as everyone knows, exists as a matter of course on all the back stairs of Petersburg buildings—climbing the staircase, Akaky Akakievich was already wondering how much Petrovich would charge and deciding not to pay more than two rubles. The door was open because the missus, while preparing some kind of fish, had filled the kitchen with so much smoke you couldn't even see the cockroaches. Akaky Akakievich walked through the kitchen without her even noticing him, and at last entered the room, where he saw Petrovich sitting on a wide, plain wooden table, his legs tucked under him like a Turkish pasha. His feet, as is customary among tailors who sit while working, were bare. An immediate focus of attention was provided by Petrovich's big toe, well known to Akaky Akakievich, which had some sort of deformed nail, thick and strong like a turtle shell. Around Petrovich's neck hung a skein of silk and thread, and on his lap was some sort of rag. For about three minutes he had been trying to thread a needle, had kept missing, and therefore was very angry at the darkness and even at the needle itself, grumbling under his

breath: "It won't go through, the damn thing. It's driving me crazy, the
no-good!" Akaky Akakievich felt uncomfortable that he had arrived at the
very minute Petrovich was angry. He liked to ask Petrovich to do something
when he was already a bit under the influence or, as his wife would say,
"drowning in raw vodka, the one-eyed devil." In that state, Petrovich was
generally agreeable and made concessions willingly, even bowing and saying thank you on each occasion. Afterward, it is true, his wife would come
crying that her husband had been drunk and that was why he had charged so
little, but then adding another ten kopeks would conclude the matter. Now,
apparently, Petrovich was in a sober state, and therefore curt, intractable,
and likely to charge the devil knew what prices. Akaky Akakievich was
aware of this and would have liked to hightail it out, as they say, but it was
too late. Petrovich very intently fixed his only eye on him and Akaky
Akakievich blurted out:

"Good day, Petrovich!"

"Good day to you, sir," said Petrovich, and slanted his eye toward Akaky
Akakievich's hands, hoping to catch a glimpse of what kind of money the
other had with him.

"I've come to see you, Petrovich, to uh . . . "

Akaky Akakievich, it should be known, usually had the habit of expressing
himself in prepositions, adverbs, and, finally, in such parts of speech that
have no meaning whatsoever. If the matter at hand was very involved, he
even had the habit of not finishing sentences at all, so that quite often beginning
to speak with the words: "This, really, is completely so . . . " with nothing
following—he would forget and think he had already said everything.

"Well, what is it?" said Petrovich, inspecting Akaky Akakievich's whole
uniform with his one eye, starting from the collar, then down to the sleeves,
back, tails, and buttonholes, all of which were very familiar, because it was
his own work.

That's just the way tailors are: it's the first thing they do upon meeting
someone.

"I just, well, Petrovich . . . the overcoat, um . . . the cloth . . . you see, it's
really strong in all the other places, it's a bit dusty and it looks old, but it's
new, just in this one place it's a bit so . . . on the back, and here in one
shoulder it's a little worn through, and also in this shoulder it's a bit—you
see? That's all. Just a little work . . . "

Petrovich took the cloak, spread it out on the table, examined it at length,
then shook his head and groped around on the window sill for a round
snuffbox with the portrait of some general on it, exactly which general is
not known, for the spot where the face once was had been punctured by a
finger and then glued over with a square scrap of paper. After taking some

snuff, Petrovich spread out the cloak in his hands, held it up to the light, and again shook his head. He then turned it so the lining faced upward, shook his head once more, again removed the lid with the general glued over with paper, and after inhaling a large pinch of snuff into his nose, closed the box, put it away, and said at last:

"No, it can't be mended—the garment is no good!"

At these words Akaky Akakievich's heart skipped a beat.

"But why not, Petrovich?" he asked, sounding almost like a pleading child. "I mean, it's only worn through at the shoulders. You must have some scraps of cloth or something . . . "

"Sure, I could find some scraps, scraps are easy to find," said Petrovich, "but I can't sew them on. The whole thing is rotted through. Touch a needle to it, and it will crumble."

"Let it, let it, and you'll patch it up right away."

"But there isn't anywhere to put a patch, there's nothing for it to hold on to. The material is too worn. It can barely be called cloth. One gust of wind and the whole thing'll fly apart."

"Well, then, just reinforce it. How can it be, really, that! . . . "

"No," said Petrovich firmly. "There's nothing I can do. It's a disaster. You'd be better off making it into foot coverings when the cold weather comes, since stockings don't keep you warm. The Germans came up with that to rake in more money for themselves." (Petrovich loved to slur the Germans whenever he had the chance.) "And as for the overcoat, obviously you'll just have to make yourself a new one."

At the word "new," Akaky Akakievich's eyes clouded over and everything in the room began to dance before his eyes. The only thing he saw clearly was the general with the pasted-over paper face on the lid of Petrovich's snuffbox.

"What do you mean a new one?" he said, as if still in a dream. "But I don't have any money for that."

"Yes, a new one," said Petrovich, with barbaric calm.

"Well, and if I did have to have a new one, what might it, um . . . "

"You mean what would it cost?"

"Yes."

"You'd have to come up with three fifties plus," said Petrovich, and he pressed his lips together meaningfully. He loved to have a strong effect, loved to take someone completely aback and then to glance sideways to see the face his victim made after hearing such words.

"A hundred and fifty rubles for an overcoat!" cried out poor Akaky Akakievich, cried out for perhaps the first time in his life, since he was always noted for his quiet voice.

"Yessir," said Petrovich, "and that depends on the type of coat. Put marten on the collar and add a silk-lined hood, and we're talking two hundred."

"Petrovich, please," said Akaky Akakievich imploringly, without hearing or even attempting to hear what Petrovich said, with all his effects, "mend it somehow, so it can serve its purpose at least a while longer."

"Oh no, that would just be a waste of work and money," said Petrovich, and following these words Akaky Akakievich left, completely devastated.

After his departure, Petrovich remained standing a long time without returning to work, his lips pressed together meaningfully, proud that he had neither discredited himself nor betrayed the art of the tailoring profession.

Out on the street, Akaky Akakievich felt as if he were dreaming. "So that's it, it's like that," he repeated to himself. "I really had no idea it would end so ... " and then, after a short silence, he added: "So that's it! Look how it ended up, and I never really would have guessed it would be like this." A long silence followed, after which he exclaimed: "So that's it! How's that for a completely unexpected, this ... in no way could it ... what a state of affairs!" Having said this, instead of going home, he headed in completely the opposite direction, without realizing it himself. On the way, a chimney sweep brushed against him with his entire dirty side and blackened his whole shoulder; a full container of whitewash poured on him from the top of a house under construction. He noticed none of this, and only later, when he bumped against a policeman who had placed his club down and was shaking tobacco out of a horn into his callused fist, only then did he come to his senses a bit, and only because the policeman said to him, "Watch who you're pushing. Don't you have enough sidewalk?" This made him look around and turn for home. Only then did he begin to collect his thoughts. He saw his situation in a clear and true light. He began talking to himself, no longer in fragments, but reasonably and frankly, as with a sensible friend with whom one can talk about the most heartfelt and intimate matters.

"Well, no," said Akaky Akakievich, "now's not the time to talk to Petrovich. Now he's, um ... his wife must have given him a beating. Better I'll go see him Sunday morning. After Saturday night he'll squint and be half-asleep, so he'll need to take care of his hangover, and his wife won't give him any money—and that's when I'll slip him ten kopeks, so he'll be more open to persuasion, and that overcoat then ... "

So Akaky Akakievich reasoned with himself, strengthened his resolve, and waited for the next Sunday, when seeing at a distance that Petrovich's wife was going out of the house somewhere, he went straight to him. After Saturday, Petrovich was indeed squinting hard, hanging his head, and was totally half-asleep. But in spite of all that when he realized what was up, it was as if the Devil had prompted him. "It can't be done," he said. "You must order a new one." At this point Akaky Akakievich slipped him the ten kopeks.

"Thank you, sir, I will refresh myself with a little drink to your health," said Petrovich, "and please don't worry about the overcoat; it simply ain't good for nothing. I'll sew you a wonderful new one, I guarantee it."

Akaky Akakievich began saying something else about mending the old coat, but Petrovich didn't listen and said, "I'll make you a new one, without fail, you can count on it, I'll do my best. We can even make it like the latest fashion—put buttons with silver-plated clasps on the collar."

Right then Akaky Akakievich realized he could not manage without a new overcoat, and he lost heart completely. How, after all, with what money was he to pay for it? Of course, he could fall back in part on his upcoming holiday bonus, but that money had been distributed and allocated long beforehand. He needed to get new pants, had to pay the shoemaker an old debt for attaching new tops to old shoes, and he had to order three shirts from the seamstress and two pieces of the type of clothing too indecent to mention in print—in a word, all the money was to be completely spent, and even if the director were kind enough to give a bonus of forty-five or fifty rubles instead of forty, only a little bit would be left over anyway, a drop in the bucket for the capital necessary to pay for an overcoat. Although Akaky Akakievich was aware, of course, that Petrovich was prone to ask suddenly, on a whim, the Devil knows what exorbitant price, so that even his wife couldn't keep from crying out, "Are you crazy, you idiot? Either he works for nothing, or the Evil One's got him asking such a price that he himself isn't worth it." Although he knew, of course, that Petrovich would do it for eighty rubles, where were those eighty rubles to come from? Half the sum perhaps could be found, half would turn up, maybe even a little more, but where would the other half come from? First, however, the reader should know the source of the first half. Akaky Akakievich had the habit of putting away half a kopek of every ruble he spent into a little locked box, which had a slot cut out on top for dropping in money. At the end of every six months he would inspect the accumulated copper and would exchange it for a little bit of silver. So he continued doing for a long time, and in this way over several years the accumulated amount reached over forty rubles. Therefore, half was at hand. But where was the other half to come from? What about the other forty rubles?

Akaky Akakievich thought and thought some more, and decided that he would have to cut his daily expenses for one year at least: to stop taking tea in the evenings, not to light candles at night, and if something needed to be done, to go to the landlady's room and work by her light, to walk on the street stepping as lightly and carefully as possible over the pebbles and stones, almost on tip-toe, so as not to wear out shoe soles too soon; to do laundry as infrequently as possible, and in order not to wear out the clothes, to change at home into a thin cotton bathrobe, very ancient and spared even by time itself.

To tell the truth, in the beginning he had trouble getting used to such privations, but later he grew used to them and all started to go smoothly. He had even learned to go completely hungry in the evenings; but on the other hand, he was nourished spiritually by the eternal idea of his future overcoat. From this time on it was as if his very existence had become somehow fuller, as if he had married, as if some other person had joined him, as if he were not alone, but some pleasant companion had agreed to walk down the path of life with him; and this companion was none other than that very overcoat, with its thick quilting and strong, durable lining. He somehow became more alive, more stable of character even, like someone who has defined and set himself a goal. All doubt and indecision—in a word, all hints of hesitation and uncertainty—disappeared from his face and manner. At times a gleam appeared in his eyes. The most daring and courageous thoughts even went through his mind: Perhaps, marten indeed should be put around the collar? Such reflections nearly drove him to distraction. Once, while copying a paper, he even came close to making a mistake, so that he almost cried out loud: "Ooh!" and crossed himself. During the course of each month he went to see Petrovich at least once to talk about the overcoat, where it would be best to buy the cloth, and which color, and at what price, and, although somewhat anxious, he would always return home satisfied, contemplating the thought that the time would come finally when everything would be bought and the overcoat would be made.

Things went even more quickly than he expected. Contrary to all expectation, the director bestowed on Akaky Akakievich not forty or forty-five rubles but a whole sixty rubles. Whether he foresaw that Akaky Akakievich needed a new overcoat, or whether it just happened, Akaky Akakievich thus found himself with twenty extra rubles. This circumstance accelerated the course of events. Some two to three months more of a little starvation, and Akaky Akakievich had indeed accumulated around eighty rubles. His heart rate, usually very calm, increased dramatically.

On the very first day he set out for the shops with Petrovich. They bought some very good-quality cloth, and no wonder, since they had been thinking about it for six months, and hardly a month went by without them going into a shop to compare prices. In this case Petrovich himself said there was no better cloth. For the lining they chose calico, of such good, solid quality that according to Petrovich it was even better than silk and even more showy and lustrous to the eye. They didn't buy marten because it was as expensive as predicted; instead they chose cat, the best the shop had to offer, cat, which from afar could easily be taken for marten. Petrovich spent two entire weeks on the overcoat, due to all the quilting that had to be done; otherwise, it would have been ready earlier. For the work Petrovich took twelve rubles—there was no way it could be done for less; it was all sewn using silk thread with a fine double stitch. Petrovich went over every stitch with his own teeth, pressing out various patterns with them.

On ... it's hard to say exactly what day it was, but it was probably the most solemn day in Akaky Akakievich's life when Petrovich finally brought him the overcoat. He brought it in the morning, right before it was time to go to the office. The overcoat could not have come at a better time, since quite severe frosts were beginning and were apparently threatening to grow even worse. Petrovich appeared with the overcoat in a way befitting a good tailor. On his face was a meaningful expression Akaky Akakievich had never before seen. Apparently, he was convinced he had performed a considerable feat and that he had demonstrated suddenly the vast expanse that separates those tailors who just sew in linings and mend from those who create anew. He took the overcoat out of the kerchief in which he had brought it (the kerchief had just come back from the laundress) and then folded it up for future use and put it in his pocket. After taking out the coat, he proudly looked it over and using both hands threw it quite deftly over Akaky Akakievich's shoulders. He then pulled it down, making it smooth in back with his hands, then draped it, unbuttoned, over Akaky Akakievich. Akaky Akakievich, like a man getting on in years, wanted to check how the sleeves fit. Petrovich helped him put through his arms. It turned out the sleeves fit well too. In a word, it turned out that the coat was perfect and fit just right.

Petrovich did not miss this opportunity to mention that it was only because he lived without a signboard on a small street and because he had known Akaky Akakievich for a long time that he charged so little. On Nevsky Prospect,[8] he said, they'd take seventy-five rubles for the labor alone. Akaky Akakievich did not want to discuss the point with Petrovich, fearing those enormous sums with which Petrovich liked to cloud the issue. He paid the money, thanked Petrovich, and set off at once for the office. Petrovich walked out behind him and, standing on the street, gazed for a long time at the overcoat from a distance, and then expressly walked off to the side, so that, by cutting around a twisting lane, he could come out into the street again and look at his coat one more time from a different angle, that is, directly from the front.

Meanwhile, Akaky Akakievich walked on in a most festive disposition of all his senses. Every second of every minute he was aware that he had a new coat on his back, and he even chuckled a few times from inward pleasure. Indeed, there were two pluses: one was that it was warm, and the other that it felt good. He did not notice the journey at all and suddenly found himself at the office. He took off the overcoat in the foyer, looked it over, and entrusted it to the doorman's special care. Magically, everybody in the department suddenly learned that Akaky Akakievich had a new overcoat and that the robe no longer existed. Everybody immediately ran out into the foyer to see Akaky Akakievich's new overcoat. They began to greet and congratulate him, so that at first he only smiled, but then he actually became embarrassed. When they surrounded him and began saying the new overcoat must be baptized, and that the least he could do was to throw them all a party, Akaky Akakievich became completely flustered, not knowing how to react, what to answer, or how to get himself out of it. A few minutes later, red with embarrassment, he even attempted to assure them, quite artlessly, that it was not at all a new overcoat, that it was just an ordinary one, an old one. Finally, one of the office workers, some assistant to the head clerk no less—to show probably that he was not in the least bit proud, and associated even with those beneath him—said, "So be it, I'm giving the party instead of Akaky Akakievich, and invite everyone to my home for tea. Today coincidentally, happens to be my name day." The clerks, naturally, congratulated the assistant to the head clerk and gladly accepted his invitation. Akaky Akakievich started making excuses, but everyone began saying that it would be impolite, that it would just be a crying shame, and that he simply could not refuse. But then he was pleased when he remembered he would have the chance to stroll about at night in his new overcoat.

The entire day seemed to Akaky Akakievich like the most festive holiday. He returned home in the best of moods, took off the overcoat, and hung it carefully on the wall, admiring once more the cloth and lining, and then he purposely pulled out his old robe, now entirely frayed, for comparison. He looked at it and he even had to laugh; such was the enormous difference! And at dinner for a long time long afterward, whenever he thought about the state of his old robe, he kept on chuckling. He ate cheerfully and after dinner did not copy any documents but stretched out luxuriously on the bed, until it became dark. Then, without dragging the matter out, he dressed, put on the overcoat, and went outside.

Unfortunately, we cannot say where exactly the clerk having the party lived. Our memory is beginning to fail us, and everything in Petersburg, all the streets and houses, are so mixed up in our head that it is very difficult to get anything proper out of it. Nevertheless, it is at least likely the clerk lived in a better part of town; consequently, quite a long way from Akaky Akakievich. First, Akaky Akakievich had to pass some deserted, dimly lit streets, but they became livelier, busier, and brighter the closer he came to the clerk's apartment. Pedestrians appeared more frequently; beautifully dressed ladies began to materialize and men wearing beaver collars. Coach drivers in wood-trellised sledges studded with gilded nails were less frequently seen. On the contrary, one could see daredevils wearing crimson velvet caps, in lacquered sledges with bear rugs, and carriages with decorated boxes dashing along, their wheels screeching in the snow.

Akaky Akakievich looked at all this as a novelty. It had been a few years since he had gone out in the evening. Out of curiosity he stopped before a lighted store window to look at a picture in which a beautiful woman was taking off her shoe and exposing her entire leg, which was far from unsightly, while in back of her, peeking out from the next room, was a man with sideburns and a handsome beard on his chin. Akaky Akakievich shook his head and smiled and continued on his way. Why did he smile? Was it because he had encountered something entirely unfamiliar to him but about which every person retains some sixth sense? Or perhaps, not unlike many other clerks, he was thinking: "Oh those Frenchmen! You can't deny it, if they want anything, they certainly . . . " But perhaps this was not at all what he thought. For one just cannot pop into a man's soul and find out everything he's thinking.

Finally, he arrived at the home of the assistant to the head clerk. The assistant to the head clerk lived in grand style: a lamp lit the stairway, and his apartment was on the third floor. Upon entering the hall, Akaky Akakievich saw an entire row of galoshes. A samovar puffed noisily among them in the center of the room. Along the wall hung coats and cloaks, and some actually had beaver collars or velvet lapels. Behind the wall could be heard noise and chatter, which suddenly became clear and sonorous when the door opened and a footman came out holding a tray piled with empty glasses, a cream pitcher, and a basket of biscuits. It was evident the clerks had arrived long before and had already finished their first round of tea.

Akaky Akakievich hung up his coat himself, went into the room, and was immersed all at once in candles, clerks, pipes, and card tables, while his ears were struck by the blurred sounds of rapid conversation rising around him and the noise of scraping chairs. He stopped rather awkwardly in the middle of the room, looked about, and tried to figure out what to do. But he had already been noticed and greeted with a shout; everyone immediately went out into the entrance hall to inspect his overcoat once again. Although embarrassed at first, Akaky Akakievich was too open-hearted not to be happy to see everyone admiring the coat. Then, of course, everyone forgot about him and his coat and turned their attention as usual to the card tables.

The noise, the chatter, the crowd of people were all strange to Akaky Akakievich. He simply did not know how to act, where to put his hands, his feet, his entire body. Finally, he joined the players, looked at the cards, stared at one face then another, and after a while started to yawn, to feel bored, all the more so since this was the time he usually went to bed. He wanted to say goodnight to the host but they would not let him, saying he absolutely must have a drink of champagne in honor of his new acquisition. An hour later dinner was served, consisting of salad, cold veal, pâté, pastries, and champagne. Akaky Akakievich was made to drink two glasses, after which he felt the room become a livelier place, although he was unable to forget it was already midnight and long since time for him to go home. So that the host would not detain him, he stole out of the room, looked for his coat, which he found not without regret on the hallway floor, shook it, brushed off any lint, put it on, and went downstairs to the street.

It was still bright outside. Some small shops, those irreplaceable meeting places for servants and all sorts of people, were open; others that were closed, however, still showed a long stream of light through an opening in the door, which meant they were not yet empty of humanity—probably maids or servants finishing their chatting and conversations, leaving their masters utterly bewildered as to their whereabouts. Akaky Akakievich walked along cheerfully and for some reason even decided suddenly to run after a woman who had passed by like a flash of lightning and whose every body part was full of unusual motion. But he stopped at once and returned to walking quietly, himself wondering at this sudden sprint that came out of nowhere. Soon deserted streets stretched before him, streets that were not very cheerful in daytime, and thus even less so in the evening. Now they had become even more dead and desolate; fewer and fewer street lamps flickered as he went by—evidently less oil was being allocated to them; wooden houses and fences came into view; not a soul was in sight; only the snow glittered on the streets, and the sleepy low hovels with closed shutters had turned a somber black. He neared a place where the street was cut off by an unending square seeming to loom ahead like a frightening desert, its houses barely visible on the other side.

In the distance, God knows where, a small light flickered in a booth appearing to stand on the edge of the world. At this point Akaky Akakievich somehow lost much of his cheerful disposition. He stepped into the square not without some feeling of uncontrollable trepidation, as if his heart foresaw something ill-boding. He looked behind him and to each side; it was just like the sea around him. "No, better not look," he thought, and continued walking, his eyes shut, and when he opened them to see whether he was nearing the end of the square, he suddenly saw standing before him, practically under his nose, some kind of people with mustaches, but what kind they were exactly, he could not make out. His eyes clouded over and his heart began to palpitate.

"Hey, that's my overcoat!" said one of them in a thunderous voice, grabbing him by the collar.

Akaky Akakievich was already about to yell "Help!" when another man put a fist the size of a clerk's head up to his mouth, adding, "Just you try yelling." Akaky Akakievich only felt them removing his overcoat, then a blow with a knee, and he fell backward onto the snow and felt nothing more.

After a few minutes he came to and stood up, but there was no longer anyone there. He felt cold in the open space, and that his overcoat was gone; he began yelling, but his voice, it seemed, had no intention of reaching the ends of the square. In despair and still yelling, he started running across the square straight to a booth, beside which stood a policeman, who, leaning on his halberd, was looking with what appeared to be curiosity to see why in damnation someone was yelling and running toward him from the distance. Akaky Akakievich ran up to him and began yelling breathlessly that he was asleep on the job and not looking after things, and that he hadn't even seen a man being robbed. The policeman replied that he saw nothing, that he saw two men stop him in the middle of the square, and that he thought they were acquaintances, and that instead of cursing in vain he should go tomorrow to the police chief and the police chief would find out who had taken the overcoat.

Akaky Akakievich ran home in complete disorder: the little hair he still had on his temples and the back of his head was completely disheveled. His side and chest and pants were covered with snow. His old landlady, hearing a frightening knocking at the door, hurriedly jumped out of bed and with only one shoe on ran to open the door, modestly clutching her night dress to her bosom; but on opening the door she fell back, seeing Akaky Akakievich's condition. When he told her what had happened, she clasped her hands and said he should go straight to the police commissioner because the district chief would only dupe him, make promises, and give him the runaround; that it would be best to go straight to the commissioner, that she was even acquainted with him because Anna, the Finnish woman who had formerly been her cook, was now working for the commissioner as a nurse; that she often saw him when he passed by their house and he would be in church every Sunday, praying and at the same time cheerily looking around at everybody, and that, therefore, on all accounts he must be a good man.

Having listened to all this advice, Akaky Akakievich sadly plodded along to
his room. How he spent the night will be left to the imagination of those
who can in some way place themselves in another person's shoes.

Early in the morning he set out to see the police commissioner but was
told he was sleeping. He came at ten o'clock and was told the same thing:
sleeping. He came at eleven and was told that the commissioner was out. At
lunch time he came back, but the clerks in the lobby would not let him pass
and demanded to know his reason for coming and what brought him there
and what had happened. Finally, and for the first time in his life, Akaky
Akakievich decided to show some firmness of character and said brusquely
that he must see the commissioner himself, in person, that they did not dare
to interfere, that he had come from the office on a government matter, and
that if he were to register a complaint about them then they would see. The
clerks did not dare say anything in response, and one of them went to call
the commissioner. The commissioner reacted to the story of the robbery in a
very strange way. Instead of turning his attention to the heart of the matter,
he began interrogating Akaky Akakievich: Just why had he been coming
home so late? Perhaps he had dropped by or had been in some house of ill
repute? In result, Akaky Akakievich was completely flustered, and he left
unsure whether the proper steps would be taken concerning his overcoat.

All that day he was absent from the office (the only time in his life). The
next day he appeared, all pale and wearing his old dressing gown, which
was in an even sorrier state than before. Although some clerks did not miss
the opportunity even then to poke fun at Akaky Akakievich, his account of
the theft, nevertheless, touched many of them. They made up their minds on
the spot to pool some money for him, but the sum they collected was most
trifling, because the clerks had already spent a large amount for a portrait of
the director and for some book suggested by the head of the department,
who was a friend of the author. And so, the sum was quite insignificant. A
certain somebody, prompted by compassion, decided at least to help Akaky
Akakievich with some words of wisdom and advised him not to go to the
district chief, for although it was possible that the officer, wishing to gain
the approval of his superiors, might somehow track down the overcoat, it
would nevertheless remain in the hands of the police unless he furnished
legal proof that the coat belonged to him. The best action to take would be
to go see a certain *important person*. This *important person* could hurry
matters along by writing to and communicating with the right people. Without
any other recourse, Akaky Akakievich decided to go see the *important person*.

The exact nature of the *important person's* duties is unknown to this day.
It should be noted that this *certain important person* had only recently
become an important person, and that until then he had been an unimportant

person. Even now, by the way, his post was not considered important in comparison to other even more important ones. But there will always be those people for whom a person unimportant in the eyes of others is an important person. Nevertheless, this important person attempted to increase his importance by various means, to wit: by insisting that his subordinates meet him on the stairway when he arrived at work, that no one dare report to him directly, and that everything follow the strictest of procedures—the collegiate registrar would report to the governmental secretary, the governmental secretary to the titular one, or to whomever necessary, and that only then, in this manner, the matter would come to him.[9] That's the way it is in Holy Russia; everyone is infected with imitation, everyone apes and mimics his superior. They even say that when a certain titular councillor was made manager of a small separate office, he immediately partitioned off a special room for himself, calling it "the reception room," and placed ushers in red collars and ribbons by the doors to open them for every visitor, although "the reception room" was barely large enough for an ordinary writing desk.

The manners and ways of the *important person* were solid and majestic but not at all complex. The chief foundation of his system was strictness. "Strictness, strictness, and more strictness," he would say, and usually follow the last word with a meaningful look into the face of the person to whom he was speaking. There was, however, no reason for this, because the ten clerks or so who constituted the office's entire administrative mechanism already trembled appropriately in fear. When they caught sight of him from afar, they would stop their activity and stand erect, waiting for the chief to pass through the room. A typical conversation with his subordinates resounded with strictness and consisted almost entirely of three sentences: "How dare you? Do you know with whom you are speaking? Do you realize who is standing before you?" Nevertheless, he was a good man at heart, kind to his friends, obliging; but the rank of general had completely gone to his head. After obtaining the promotion, he somehow became disoriented, went astray, and did not have the faintest idea of how to act. If he happened to be among people of equal rank, he was a decent human being, very proper, and in many respects not at all a stupid person, but as soon as he found himself in the company of people even one rank lower than his own, he simply became impossible: he spoke not at all, became silent, and his situation evoked pity, especially since he himself knew that he could be spending his time in a much more pleasant fashion. Every so often one could detect in his eyes a strong desire to join some interesting conversation and group, but he would be stopped by the thought: Would it not be too much on his part? Would it not be too undignified, and would he not thus damage his self-importance? In result of such reasoning he always remained in the same silent condition, only grunting monosyllabic sounds from time to time, and thus earning himself a reputation as a very dull person.

Our Akaky Akakievich appeared before this *important person,* and indeed he appeared at a most inauspicious time, inopportune for him it is true, but quite opportune for the important person. The important person was in his office, conversing quite animatedly with an old acquaintance and childhood friend who had arrived just recently and whom he had not seen for many years. At this moment it was announced that a Bashmachkin had arrived. "Who is he?" he asked curtly. "Some clerk," came the answer. "Ah! He can wait. Now is not the time," said the important person. It must be noted here that the important person had uttered a complete lie. He did have time. He and his friend had long since finished saying everything there was to say and had long since been interrupting their conversation with protracted silences, merely poking each other in the thigh and exclaiming: "So that's how it is, Ivan Abramovich!" "That's the way it is, Stepan Var-lamovich!" Yet for all that he ordered the clerk to wait, in order to show his friend, who had long been out of the civil service and who was living at home in the countryside, how long clerks had to wait for him in the front room.

When they finally had their fill of talk, and even more of silence, and having sat in very comfortable reclining armchairs and smoked their cigars to the end, he at last appeared suddenly to recollect, and said to the secretary, who had stopped at the door with documents for a report: "Oh yes, that clerk, I think, must be standing there. Tell him he may come in." Upon seeing Akaky Akakievich's humble appearance and his old uniform, he turned to him brusquely and said: "What is it you want?" in a curt and firm voice, which he had deliberately rehearsed alone in his room in front of the mirror a week before being appointed to his present post and rank. Akaky Akakievich had been overcome by the proper timidity well beforehand, and now, somewhat confused and as much as his tongue could manage, explained with even more "that's" than ever before that the overcoat was entirely new, and that he had now been robbed in a most inhuman fashion, and that he was appealing to him to intercede and write to his honor the chief of police or to someone else and find the overcoat. The general, for some reason, found this approach too familiar.

"What is the matter with you, my dear man?" he continued in the same brusque manner. "Don't you know the proper procedure? Do you know where you are? Don't you know how things are done? For this matter you should have submitted a petition to the office; it would then reach the head clerk, then the department clerk, then it would be given to the secretary, and only then would the secretary give it to me . . . "

"But, Your Excellency," said Akaky Akakievich, trying to maintain whatever presence of mind he might have had, and feeling at the same time that he had broken out in a terrible sweat, "I took the liberty of troubling you, Your Excellency, because the secretaries, uh . . . they're an unreliable lot . . ."

"What, what, what?" said the important person. "Where did you pick up such an attitude? Where did you pick up such ideas? What sort of unruly behavior to directors and superiors has spread among young people?"

Apparently, the important person had not noticed that Akaky Akakievich was over fifty. Consequently, even if he was to be called a young man, then it could only be said relatively; that is, relative to someone who was already seventy.

"Do you know to whom you are saying this? Do you realize who is standing before you? Do you? Do you, I ask you?"

At this point he stamped his foot, raising his voice to a pitch so powerful it would have frightened someone other than Akaky Akakievich. Akaky Akakievich froze in place, staggered, began shaking throughout his entire body, and was completely unable to stand. Had the doormen not come over immediately to support him, he would have plopped to the floor. He was taken out almost completely immobilized. And the important person, pleased that the effect had even surpassed expectations and absolutely thrilled at the thought that his words could deprive a man of his senses, took a sidelong glance at his friend to see how he was taking all this in and saw not without pleasure that his friend was in a most bewildered state and was himself beginning to feel frightened.

How he walked down the stairs, how he walked out on the street, Akaky Akakievich could not remember at all. He had no sensation in either his arms or his legs. Never in his life had he been reprimanded so strongly by a high official, and a high official from a department that was not his own at that. Stumbling off the sidewalk, gaping, he walked through a snowstorm that whistled in the streets. The wind, as is usual for Petersburg, blew at him from all four sides, from every alley. In an instant he had a sore throat, and he arrived home without the strength to utter a word. He took to his bed, his body completely swollen. That's how potent a proper reprimand can sometimes be! The following day found him with a high fever. Thanks to the generous assistance of the Petersburg climate, the illness progressed beyond all expectation, and when the doctor arrived, he felt his pulse and could do nothing but prescribe a poultice, if only so that the patient would not be left without benefit of medicine. At the same time he announced that Akaky Akakievich would certainly be kaput in a day and a half. Turning to the landlady he added, "And you, my dear, don't waste time. Order a pine casket now—oak would be too expensive for him."

Whether or not Akaky Akakievich heard these fateful words, whether or not they had a profound effect on him if he did indeed hear them, and whether he regretted his miserable life is unknown, for he was in a constant state of fever and delirium. Apparitions kept appearing before him, one stranger than the next. Now he saw Petrovich and gave him an order for an overcoat with some kind of traps for thieves he thought were under his bed, and he was constantly calling his landlady to pull out the one hiding under his blanket; then he would ask why his old robe was hanging in front of him since he had a new overcoat; then he imagined he was standing before the general receiving a proper dressing-down and repeating, "Guilty, Your Excellency!" Then, finally, he began to curse, uttering such terrible words that the old lady actually crossed herself, having in all her days heard nothing of the sort from him, especially immediately following the words "Your Excellency." After that he spoke utter gibberish and became completely incomprehensible, although his mixed up words and thoughts obviously revolved around the same overcoat.

Finally, poor Akaky Akakievich gave up the ghost. Neither his room nor his belongings were sealed because, in the first place, there were no heirs, and, second, what remained to be inherited was not much at all: a bunch of goose quills, a packet of white legal paper, three pairs of socks, two or three buttons that had come off a pair of pants, and the robe with which the reader is already familiar. God only knows who got all this; I admit even the narrator of this story was not interested in the fate of his possessions.

They took Akaky Akakievich away and buried him. And Petersburg was left without Akaky Akakievich, as if he had never existed there. So disappeared and vanished a being protected by no one, dear to no one, of no interest to anyone, who did not even attract the attention of a naturalist eager for the chance to stick an ordinary fly on a pin and examine it under a microscope, a being who humbly endured the office jokes about him and who went to his grave without any extraordinary fuss, but for whom in any case, at least before the very end of his life, there briefly appeared a radiant visitor in the form of an overcoat, enlivening for a moment a wretched life, and upon whom unbearable misfortune came crashing down, as it does upon the tsars and rulers of this world . . .

A few days after his death, a janitor from the office was sent to his apartment with an order for him to appear at once because the head of the department demanded it, but the janitor had to return empty-handed and to report that he could no longer come, and to the question "Why?" reply:

"Well, the thing is, he's dead. They buried him four days ago." In this way the department found out about Akaky Akakievich's death, and by the next day a new clerk was already sitting in his place, a much taller clerk who produced letters not in his upright handwriting but in a much more sloping and slanted fashion.

But who could have imagined that this was not the last of Akaky Akakievich, that he was fated to live on noisily for a few days more after his death, as if in reward for a life that had gone by unnoticed by anyone? Yet that is indeed what happened, and our humble narrative unexpectedly takes on a fantastic ending. Rumors suddenly began to circulate in Petersburg that a corpse had begun appearing by the Kalinkin Bridge10 and far beyond, a corpse in the form of a clerk looking for some sort of stolen overcoat and who, using this overcoat as an excuse, would tear all kinds of overcoats off the shoulders of everyone, regardless of rank or title—overcoats made from cat fur, beaver, cotton wool, raccoon, fox, bear—in a word, every type of fur or hide people have thought up for their own covering. One of the clerks from the department saw the corpse with his own eyes and recognized him immediately as Akaky Akakievich; however, this instilled such fear in him that he ran off as fast as his legs would go and therefore he did not make out the details very well and saw only that the corpse shook his finger at him in a threatening manner from afar.

There were constant complaints from all sides that the backs and shoulders not only of titular councillors but even of privy councillors had become susceptible to chills due to the nocturnal swiping of overcoats. Orders were given to the police to apprehend the corpse at any cost, dead or alive, and to punish him most severely as a lesson to others, and this they indeed almost succeeded in doing. To be precise, a policeman from some block on Kiriushkin Lane had firmly grabbed the corpse by the collar at the very scene of the crime, as he attempted to pull a frieze overcoat off a retired musician who in his day had whistled on the flute. After nabbing him by the collar, the policeman yelled for two of his fellow officers, whom he entrusted with holding the corpse while he reached quickly into his boot to pull out a snuffbox, to revive his nose, which had been frostbitten six times in his life. The snuff, however, was probably of such a quality that even a corpse couldn't stand it. The policeman, closing his right nostril with his finger, had hardly inhaled half a handful up his left when the corpse sneezed so violently that he completely bespattered all three in the eyes. By the time they had raised their fists to wipe them off, the corpse had vanished without a trace, so that they were not even sure he had ever been in their hands. From that time on the police grew so afraid of the dead that they also became leery of arresting the living and would merely shout from afar:

"Hey you! Get moving!" In result the dead clerk began appearing even beyond Kalinkin Bridge, instilling much fear in all timid people.

But it seems we have completely neglected *a certain important person,* who, in reality, could be said to be the reason for the fantastic turn taken by what is, by the way, a completely true story. Above all, it is only fair to say that the *certain important person,* shortly after poor Akaky Akakievich left with his tail between his legs, felt something akin to pity. Compassion was not unfamiliar to him; his heart was open to many kindly feelings, despite the fact that rank very frequently prevented them from coming to the surface. As soon as his visiting friend had left his office, he actually became lost in thought over poor Akaky Akakievich. And from that time on nearly every day he imagined the pale Akaky Akakievich, who had not withstood his official dressing-down. Thinking about Akaky Akakievich disturbed him to such a degree that after a week had passed he even decided to send over a clerk to see how he was and whether he could not indeed be helpful in some way. And when he was informed that Akaky Akakievich had died suddenly in a fever, he was actually stunned, suffered pangs of conscience, and was out of sorts the entire day.

Anxious to find some diversion and to get over the unpleasant impression left on him, he went that evening to a friend's house, where he found quite decent company, and what's more, everyone present was nearly of the same rank, so he could be completely uninhibited. This had a wonderful effect on his emotional disposition. He relaxed, became pleasant in conversation and amiable—in a word, he spent a very agreeable evening. At dinner he drank a couple of glasses of champagne, not a bad way, as we know, to promote good cheer. The champagne put him in the mood for some extracurricular activities; that is, he decided not to go home but to drop by a woman he knew, Karolina Ivanovna, a woman, apparently, of German extraction, for whom he had feelings of great friendship. It should be noted that the important person was no longer a young man, that he was a good husband and the respected father of a family. Two sons, one of whom was already serving in an office, and a pleasant-looking daughter of sixteen who had a slightly turned up but nice little nose and came to him every day and kissed his hand, saying: "Bonjour, papa." His wife, still exuding freshness and actually not at all bad-looking, would first give him her hand to kiss and, turning hers over, would then kiss his. The important person, although, by the way, quite satisfied with these displays of family affection, nevertheless found it fitting for the sake of friendship to have a lady friend on the other side of town. This lady friend was in no way better or younger than his wife, but such are the puzzling things that exist in this world, and it is not our place to pass judgment upon them.

And so, the important person went down the stairs, sat in his sleigh, and said to the coachman, "To Karolina Ivanovna's," while he enveloped himself quite luxuriously in a warm overcoat, remaining in that pleasant state of mind of which you'll find none better for a Russian—that is, when you are thinking about nothing and thoughts simply pop into your head, one more pleasant than the other, without putting you through the trouble of chasing them down or searching them out. Utterly content, he recalled all the cheerful moments of the evening he had spent, all the words that had had the intimate circle of people roaring with laughter; he even repeated a number of them softly to himself and found that they were as funny as before, so it's no wonder that he chuckled heartily. From time to time, however, he was bothered by the gusty wind, which, coming from God knows where and heaven knows for what reason, bit at his face, pelted him with clumps of snow, puffed out the collar of his coat like a sail, or suddenly blew it over his head with unnatural force and caused endless bother in untangling it.

Suddenly the important person felt someone grab him quite forcefully by the collar. Turning around, he noted a short man wearing a shabby uniform and not without horror recognized him to be Akaky Akakievich. The clerk's face was as pale as the snow and looked utterly corpselike. But the horror that had seized the important person surpassed all expectations when he saw the corpse's mouth twist open and, directing at him the terrible odor of the grave, heard it utter the following words: "Aha! Here you are at last! At last I've done it, got you by the collar! It's your overcoat I want! You didn't trouble yourself over mine, even reprimanded me. Now give me yours!"

The poor *important person* nearly died. No matter how much character he had at the office and in front of his subordinates, and no matter that anyone looking at his manly appearance and build would say, "Oh, what character he has!"—at this moment he, like many others who possess a heroic appearance, was consumed by such terror that he even began, and with good reason, to fear a bout of illness. He even promptly and without anyone's help threw off the overcoat from his shoulders and yelled to the coachman in a strange voice: "Home as fast as you can!" The coachman, hearing his voice, which he ordinarily heard in critical moments even accompanied by something more effective, ducked his head to be on the safe side, raised the whip, and took off like a shot. In a little more than six minutes the important person was already in front of the doorway to his house.

Pale, frightened, and minus his overcoat, he arrived home instead of going to Karolina Ivanovna's, just barely dragged himself to his room, and spent the night quite shaken up, so that the next day, while having his morning tea, his daughter told him frankly: "You look very pale, Papa." But papa said nothing and told no one what had happened to him, where he had been, or where he had intended going. This incident made a deep impression on him. From then on he would say, "How dare you, do you realize who is before you?" much less frequently to his subordinates; and if he did happen to say it, then it was not until he had first heard them out. But what is even more remarkable is that from then on the appearance of the clerk-corpse ceased completely. Evidently, the general's overcoat fit him perfectly, at least, there were no more accounts of anyone's overcoat being yanked off.

Nevertheless, many active and concerned people simply refused to calm down and said the clerk's corpse could still be seen in the more remote parts of town. And, in fact, a certain policeman from Kolomna[11] with his own eyes saw a ghost appear from behind a house; but being by nature somewhat frail—so that once an ordinary, adult piglet, darting out of someone's house, knocked him off his feet, to the great amusement of the cabmen standing around, from whom he demanded a half kopek each for the sneers to buy some snuff for himself—and so, being by nature somewhat frail, the policeman did not dare arrest the ghost and simply followed behind it in the darkness, until at last the ghost looked around, stopped, and asked him, "What do you want?" while showing him a fist that could not be found even among the living. "Nothing," the policeman said, and at once turned back. The ghost, however, was now much taller and sported a huge mustache and, directing its steps apparently toward the Obukhov Bridge,[12] vanished completely into the darkness of the night.

Translation by Sara Grossman

Notes to the translation begin on page 577.

RESOURCES

Primary Text

Gogol, Nikolai V. "Shinel'." *Polnoe sobranie sochinenii.* Vol. 3. Moscow: Akademiia nauk SSSR, 1938, pp. 39–174.

Secondary Sources

Literary and Cultural Studies

Chizhevskii, Dmitrii. "Gogol: Artist and Thinker." *Annals of the Ukranian Academy of Arts and Sciences in the United States* 4 (1952).

Eikhenbaum, Boris. "Kak sdelana 'Shinel'' Gogolia." *Voprosy poetiki* 4 (1924): 172, 182–83.

Erlich, Victor. *Gogol and Kafka: A Note on "Realism" and "Surrealism."* The Hague: Mouton, 1956.

Fanger, Donald. "Gógol, Nikolái Vasílievich." In *Handbook of Russian Literature*, ed. Victor Terras. New Haven: Yale University Press, 1985, pp. 174–77.

Maguire, Robert. *Exploring Gogol.* Stanford: Stanford University Press, 1994.

———, ed. *Gogol from the Twentieth Century.* Princeton: Princeton University Press, 1976.

Mashinskii, S. *N.V. Gogol' v russkoi kritike i vospominaniiakh sovremennikov.* Moscow–Leningrad: Detskaia literatura, 1951.

Terras, Victor. *A History of Russian Literature.* New Haven: Yale University Press, 1991, pp. 254–63.

Art and Architecture

Gay, Nikolai. *Calvary.* In *Selected Works of Russian Art,* ed. Natalya Sokolova. Leningrad: Aurora, 1976, plate 88.

Ivanov, Alexander. *Apparition of Christ to the People.* In *Selected Works of Russian Art,* ed. Natalya Sokolova. Leningrad: Aurora, 1976, plates 77, 78.

Ivanov, Alexander. *Birth of Isaac Announced to Abraham.* In *Selected Works of Russian Art,* ed. Natalya Sokolova. Leningrad: Aurora, plate 79.

Kozhevnikov, R. *Skul'pturnye pamiatniki Moskvy.* Moscow: Moskovskii rabochii, 1983, pp. 227–29.

Music

Schnittke, Alfred. *Gogol-Suite.* Chester, NY: Schirmer, 1980. Score for orchestra.

Shchedrin, R. *Mertvye dushi* (The Dead Souls). Bolshoi Theatre Chorus and Orchestra. Conductor, Iu. Temirkanov. Moscow: Melodiia. 1982. 3 records. Opera scenes based on Gogol's poem.

Shostakovich, D. *Nos* (The Nose). Opera in 3 acts. Moscow Chamber Music Theatre. Conductor, G. Rozhdestvenskii. Moscow: Melodiia, 1976, 2 records.

Film

Mirgorod. Director, M. Ilyenko. Mosfilm, 1983.

Shinel' (The Overcoat). Director, Grigorii Kozintsev. Cinematographers, Andrei Moskvin, Evgenii Mikhailov. Leningrad: Leningradkino, 1926.

———. Director, Aleksei Batalov. With R. Bykov. Lenfilm, 1960.

The String Sounds Through the Fog. Director, A. Chikris. Based on "The Diary of a Mad Man" by Nikolai Gogol, 1989. Distributed by RAES.

Audio recording

Shinel' (The Overcoat). Read by Sergei Balshchov. A musical-literary composition. N.d. Distributed by RAES.

14

~Ivan Turgenev~

Bezhin Meadow

It was a beautiful July day, one of those days that come only when the weather has been settled for some time. The sky is clear from earliest morning; the sunrise does not blaze like a fire but spreads a gentle blush. The sun is not ignescent or scorching hot as it is during a sultry drought, nor is it a murky crimson as before a storm, but it is bright and affably radiant—peacefully arising beneath a long narrow cloud, freshly gleaming through it and submerged in its lilac mist. The delicate upper border of the long line of clouds gleams like a serpent; the gleam is like the gleam of forged silver . . . But then again the playful beams pour forth—cheerfully and majestically, as if flying up, radiating a more powerful light. Toward midday a mass of round high clouds usually appears, golden-gray, with delicate white borders. They are almost motionless, like islands washed by an endlessly flowing river that spills over them in deeply transparent streams of flat blue; further toward the horizon, they begin to merge and cluster and the blue between them can no longer be seen, while they are themselves just like the azure of the sky: they are all imbued through and through with light and warmth. The color of the horizon is light, a pale lilac; in a whole day it does not change and is the same all around; it does not darken anywhere, there is no thickening thunderstorm; perhaps here and there a barely noticeable rain drizzles from pale blue columns that stretch downward. Toward evening these clouds disappear; the last of them, blackish and vague like smoke, settle in pinkish puffs before the setting sun; in the place where it has descended just as peacefully as it arose in the sky, the crimson glow lingers for a short time above the darkening earth and twinkling softly, like a cautiously carried candle, the evening star glows. On such days the tints are all subdued, bright but not dazzling; everything somehow bears the stamp of a touching humility. On such days the heat is sometimes very strong, sometimes even "steams" across the sloping fields; but the wind blows away and disperses the accumulated heat and swirling dust—a sure sign of constant weather—moves high white columns along the road through the plowed fields. The scent of absinthe, cut rye, and buckwheat is in the pure, dry air; even an hour before nightfall you can feel no dampness. It is this kind of weather the farmer wants for harvesting his grain . . .

Once, on just such a day, I went hunting for black grouse in the Chernsk District in the province of Tula. I found and bagged quite a few birds; my full hunting bag cut unmercifully into my shoulder; but the evening glow was already dying away, still bright but no longer lit by the rays of the setting sun, and cold shadows had begun to thicken and spread in the air when I finally decided to return home. With swift steps I crossed a long "square" of bushes, ascended a hill, and instead of the usual familiar plains with a little oak wood on the right and a humble white church in the distance, I saw a completely different place unknown to me. A narrow valley stretched out at my feet; ahead of me, a dense aspen grove towered like a steep wall. I stopped in bewilderment and looked around . . . "Really!" I thought, "but I haven't been here before at all. I must have turned too far to the right." And amazed at my own mistake, I swiftly descended the hill. I was immediately enveloped by an unpleasant motionless dampness, as if I had walked into a cellar; the thick tall grass at the bottom of the valley, soaking wet, shone white as a smooth tablecloth; to walk through it was somehow terrifying. I quickly scrambled across to the other side and keeping to the left walked parallel to the aspen wood. In the air above its sleeping treetops the bats were already flitting, circling mysteriously and quivering in the dimly pale sky; a small hawk out late flew by swiftly and directly in the distant heights, rushing to its nest. "Now as soon as I get to that corner," I thought to myself, "the road will be right there and I'll have made a detour of about three-quarters of a mile!"

I finally reached the corner of the woods, but there was no road there at all: some sort of unkempt low bushes stretched out broadly before me and beyond them, far, far off, an empty field was visible. I stopped again. "What is this? . . . And where am I?" I began to recall how and where I had walked during the course of the day . . . "Aha! This must be the Parakhin Brush!" I exclaimed at last. "Precisely! Over there must be the Sindeev Grove . . . But how did I get all the way over here? How did I go so far? . . . It's strange! Now I'll have to go to the right again."

I went to the right, through the bushes. Meanwhile, night was closing in and thickening like a thundercloud; it seemed that along with the evening mist, darkness was rising up all around and even pouring down from the heights. I found some kind of uneven, overgrown path and started out along it, looking ahead attentively. It had quickly become black and quiet all around—only some quail cried out occasionally. A small night bird, rushing along inaudibly and low on its soft wings, almost collided with me and fearfully dove to the side. I came out to the edge of the bushes and plodded along the boundary of a field. It was already difficult to make out distant objects; all around the field glimmered vaguely; beyond it, coming closer with every minute, a gloomy darkness loomed in huge puffs. My steps reverberated hollowly in the thickening air. The whitening sky began to turn blue again—but it was already the blue of night. In it the small stars began to twinkle and stir.

What I had taken for a grove turned out to be a dark, round knoll. "But where on earth am I?" I repeated again aloud, stopping for the third time and looking inquiringly at my yellow English skewbald dog Dianka, absolutely the most intelligent of all four-legged creatures. But the most intelligent of all four-legged creatures only wagged her little tail, blinked her dejected, tired small eyes and did not offer me any useful advice. She made me feel ashamed and, in despair, I pushed forward as if I had suddenly guessed where I had to go, went around the knoll, and found myself in a shallow hollow that had been plowed all around. A strange feeling immediately came over me. This hollow had the appearance of an almost perfect caldron with gently sloping sides; on its bottom several large white rocks were sticking up—it appeared as if they had crept down for a mysterious conference—and it was so silent and deserted there, and the sky hung so flat and cheerlessly up above, that my heart sank. Some sort of small animal squeaked weakly and plaintively among the rocks. I rushed to get back on to the knoll. Up to now I had not lost hope of finding the way home; but finally I was convinced I was completely lost, and I no longer in the least tried to recognize my surroundings, which were almost totally submerged in the gloom. I walked straight, by the stars—recklessly . . . I walked nearly a half hour so that putting one foot in front of the other was difficult. It seemed I had never in my life been in such empty spaces: nowhere did a flame flicker, not a single sound was heard. One gently sloping hill merged into another; fields stretched endlessly past fields; bushes arose suddenly from the earth under my very nose. I kept walking and was already preparing to lie down somewhere until morning when suddenly I found myself above a terrible abyss.

I quickly drew back my outstretched leg and through the barely transparent dusk of night I saw an enormous plain far below me. A wide river skirted around it, curving away from me in a half-circle; steely reflections of water occasionally flickered dimly and marked its course. The hill on which I was standing descended suddenly into an almost vertical precipice; its huge outline could be distinguished from the bluish airy void by its blackness, and directly under me, in the angle formed by the precipice and the plain, beside the river, which in this place stood like a motionless, dark mirror under the steep slope of the hill itself, two fires burned red and smoked, one beside the other. Around them people were swarming, shadows were swaying to and fro, sometimes brightly revealing the front half of a small curly head . . .

I realized at last where I was. This meadow is known in our region as the Bezhin Meadow . . . Now there was no possibility of returning home, especially at night; my legs were collapsing under me with fatigue. I decided to head toward the fires and wait for daybreak in the company of those people, whom I took to be herdsmen. I safely went down but had not yet managed to let go of the last branch I had grasped when suddenly two large white shaggy dogs rushed at me barking furiously. The sound of children's voices rang out around the fires; two or three little boys quickly got up from the ground. I answered their inquiring cries. They ran up to me, immediately calling off the dogs, who had been particularly startled by the appearance of my Dianka, and I walked toward them.

I had made a mistake in taking the people sitting around the fires for herdsmen. They were simply peasant boys from a neighboring village who were watching over horses. In the hot summertime, they drive the horses out at night to graze in the field: during the day flies and gadflies give them no peace. To drive the herd out before evening and to drive it back at dawn is a big treat for the peasant boys. Sitting without hats in old sheepskin coats, riding the most lively nags, they race along with cheerful whooping and shouting, dangling their arms and legs, bobbing high up and down, laughing loudly. Delicate yellow clouds of dust rise up and swirl along the road; far off the steady beat of hooves is heard as the horses prick up their ears and start running; in front of them all, pulling up his tail and changing pace incessantly, gallops a kind of shaggy chestnut with burdock in its loose mane.

I told the boys I was lost and took a seat near them. They asked me where I was from and were silent for a bit and avoided me. We talked for a while. I lay down under a bush and began looking around. It was a beautiful picture: a round reddish reflection quivered around the fires and seemed to die out as it came up against the darkness; flaring up, the flame occasionally cast fast sparks beyond the line of that circle; a delicate tongue of light licked the naked twigs of the willow and at once disappeared; sharp, long shadows, breaking in for a moment, in their turn reached out to the very fires: darkness was warring with light. Sometimes when the flames were burning weakly and the circle of light was narrowing, the head of a horse would emerge suddenly from the approaching dark, a bay, with sinuous markings or entirely white, would look at us attentively and vacantly, adeptly chew the long grass and again lowering would immediately vanish. One could only hear it continue to chew and snort. From the illuminated

place, it was difficult to see what was going on in the darkness and therefore nearly everything seemed to be covered by an almost black curtain; but
in the distance toward the horizon, hills and woods were vaguely visible in
long patches. The dark pure sky stood solemnly and immensely high above
us in all of its mysterious splendor. My chest sweetly tightened inhaling that
special languorous and fresh scent—the scent of a Russian summer night.
Almost no sound could be heard around us. . . . Occasionally in the nearby
river a large fish would splash with a sudden sound, and reeds on the bank
would make a gentle noise, barely stirring in waves that rippled up . . . Only
the fires crackled quietly.

The boys were sitting around them; and those two dogs that would have
liked to devour me were sitting in the same place. For a long time now they
had not been able to reconcile themselves to my presence and narrowing
their eyes sleepily, squinting at the fire, occasionally they growled out of a
special feeling of their own worth; first they growled and then they yelped
gently as if complaining about the impossibility of fulfilling their desire.
There were five boys in all: Fedya, Pavlusha, Ilyusha, Kostya, and Vanya.
(I found out their names from their conversation, and now I intend to
acquaint the readers with them.)

The first of them, the oldest, Fedya, seemed to be about fourteen. He was
a well-built boy with handsome, delicate, somewhat shallow features, curly
blond hair, light eyes, and a constant half-cheerful, half-distracted smile. By
all indications, he belonged to a well-off family and had somehow ridden
out to the field not out of necessity but just for fun. He wore a multicolored
cotton shirt with a small yellow border; a small new peasant's coat thrown
over his shoulders was scarcely supported by his narrow frame; on his pale
blue belt hung a small comb. His boots with narrow tops were precisely
that—his boots, not his father's. The second boy, Pavlusha, had tousled
black hair, gray eyes, broad cheekbones, a pale, pockmarked face, a large,
straight mouth, and an enormous head—as they say, big as a beer barrel; his
body was stocky and clumsy. It cannot be denied!—the boy was not much
to look at—-but just the same I liked him: his gaze was very intelligent and
direct and what's more his voice sounded strong. He could not boast of his
clothes: in their entirety they consisted of a simple shirt and patched trousers. The face of the third boy, Ilyusha, was quite ordinary: long, hook-
nosed, weak-sighted, it expressed a kind of dull, sickly thoughtfulness; his
compressed lips did not move and his knit brows never relaxed, as if he
were always squinting from the fire. His yellow, almost white hair stuck out
in sharp angles from underneath a narrow felt cap he kept pulling down
around his ears with both hands. He was wearing new sandals and socks; a
thick rope wound carefully three times around his waist held his neat black

cloth coat closed. Both he and Pavlusha appeared to be no more than twelve years old. The fourth, Kostya, a boy of about ten, piqued my curiosity with his pensive and mournful look. His whole face was small, thick, freckled, and pointed downward like a squirrel's; his lips could barely be discerned, but a strange impression was made by his large, black shining eyes, which glittered moistly: it seemed they wanted to say something for which there were no words in language—at least his language. He was short, of frail build, and dressed quite poorly. The last boy, Vanya, I had not even noticed at first: he was lying on the ground, having curled up very quietly under some bent matting and only occasionally poking out his curly brown head from under it. This boy was about seven.

So I lay under a bush to the side and looked over the boys. A small pot hung above one of the fires; in it some taters were being cooked. Pavlusha was looking after them and kneeling down he poked the boiling water with some kindling. Fedya was lying propped on his elbow with his coat spread around him. Ilyusha was sitting next to Kostya and all the while still squinting tensely. Kostya hung his head a little and gazed off somewhere into the distance. Vanya did not stir from under his matting. I pretended to be asleep. Little by little the boys started talking again.

At first they chatted about this and that, about tomorrow's work, about the horses; but suddenly Fedya turned to Ilyusha and, as if resuming a previous conversation, asked him:

"Well now, did you really see the house spirit?"

"No, I didn't see him and it's not even possible to see him," answered Ilyusha in a hoarse, weak voice, the sound of which matched the expression on his face exactly, "but I heard him . . . And it wasn't only me."

"Where did you see him?" asked Pavlusha.

"In the old rollin'-room."[1]

"D'ya really work in the factory?"

"Sure we do. My brother Avdyushka and me are pressers."[2]

"No kiddin'—so you're factory workers! . . . "

"Well, so how'd ya hear him?" asked Fedya.

"Here's how. My brother Avdyushka and me and Fyodor Mikheevsky and Ivashka Kosoy and another Ivashka from Red Hills, and another Ivashka Sikhorukov and still more kids were there; so there was about ten of us kids—the whole shift, see, and we had to spend the night in the rollin'-room, that is, not exactly had to, but Nazarov, our boss, wouldn't let us go; he said, 'What d'you kids,' he said, 'gotta hang around at home for; tomorrow there's lots of work, so don't you kids go home.' So we stayed, we did, and lay down all together and Avdyushka starts to speakin': 'Guys, what if,' he said, 'well, what if that house spirit comes? . . . ' And he,

Avdey, hardly finished speakin' when all of a sudden someone comes in over our heads; but we're lyin' down below and he's walkin' upstairs by the wheel. We listen: He walks, the planks underneath him are really bendin' and really creakin'; then he passes by right over our heads; suddenly the water starts to rushin' and rushin' against the wheel; the wheel starts to knockin' and knockin' and turnin' around; but the gates of the keep[3] were down. We're surprised: who could've raised'm that the water was runnin' through; but the wheel turned and turned, see, and then it stopped. Again he walks to the door upstairs and starts comin' down the stairs and so he comes like he wasn't in no hurry; the steps under him was even groanin' . . . Well, so he comes up to our door, waits and waits—the door all of a sudden gets throw'd wide open. We're scared to death, we look—nothin's there . . . All of a sudden, lo and behold, near one of the vats, the form[4] began to stir, got up, dipped itself, walked and walked like through the air, like someone rinsed it, and then went back to its place again. Then near another vat a hook came off its peg and then back again; then it was like someone came to the door and started coughin' like anything, clearin' his throat, like a sort of sheep and shrill like . . . We all jumped into a heap trying to hide one under the other . . . Boy! were we scared that time!"

"No kiddin'!" said Pavel. "Why did he have that fit of coughin'?"

"I don't know; mighta been from the dampness."

They all became silent for a while.

"How about the taters, are they done?" asked Fedya.

Pavlusha felt them.

"Nope, still raw . . . Listen, a splash," he added, turning his face in the direction of the river. "Must be a pike . . . And over there a little star's fallin'."

"I'll tell you something guys," Kostya said in a soft voice. "Listen to what I heard my dad saying the other day."

"Okay, we're listening," said Fedya in a patronizing way.

"Y'know Gavrila, the village carpenter?"

"Sure we know him."

"But d'ya know why he's always so unhappy and always quiet, do you? Here's why he's so unhappy: Once he went, Dad told me he went out into the forest for nuts, you see. So he went into the forest for nuts and he got lost. So he sat down under a tree; 'I'll wait' he said, 'til mornin' '—he sat down and began to doze off. He dozed off and all of a sudden he hears someone calling him. He looks—there's no one there. He dozes off again—again someone calls. Again he looks and looks: and before him a mermaid's sittin' on a branch, swingin' and callin' to him, but dyin' of laughter herself, she is . . . and the moon is shinin' strong, so strong, the moon is shinin' clear—everything was clear, guys. So she calls him and like she herself was

all light and white sittin' on the branch like a kind of minnow or gudgeon—
or another carp like that, whitish, silver . . . Gavrila the carpenter jus' about
fainted, guys, but she was laughin' away and kept beckoning to him, see,
with her hand. So Gavrila was about to get up and would've obeyed the
mermaid, guys, but you know, the Lord give him an idea: to cross himself . . .
But it really was hard for him to cross hisself, guys; he said his hand was
simply like a rock, wouldn't budge, it wouldn't . . . So when he crossed
himself, guys, the mermaid stops laughin' and suddenly starts cryin' . . .
She cried, guys, wipin' her eyes with her hair and her hair was green, like
your hemp it was. Then Gavrila looked and looked at her and starts to
askin' her: 'Why're you crying, you sly forest thing?' And the mermaid
said to him, 'If you hadn't crossed yourself, little man,' she said, 'you could
have lived with me in joy to your dyin' day; and I'm cryin' and grievin'
because you crossed yourself; and now not only will I grieve by myself:
you, too, may you grieve to the end of your days.' Then, guys, she vanished
and Gavrila right away understood how to get out, out of the forest, that is . . .
And jus' since that time he's always been unhappy."

"Gosh!" said Fedya after a short silence. "But how is it such an evil
forest spirit can ruin a Christian soul—he didn't obey her, after all, did he?"

"Yes, it's true!" said Kostya. "And Gavrila said that her voice, he said,
was so thin and mournful like a toad."

"Your dad himself said all this?" Fedya went on.

"Himself. I was lyin' down in the tent and heard the whole thing."

"What an amazin' thing! Why would he be unhappy? . . . And you know
that she liked him 'cause she called to him."

"Sure she liked him!" Ilyusha chimed in.

"Why not! She wanted to start ticklin' him; that's what she wanted.
That's their thing, these mermaids."

"And right here and now there's probably mermaids around," observed
Fedya.

"No," Kostya answered, "this here's a clean place, it's in the open.
Only—the river is close by."

They all fell silent. Suddenly somewhere in the distance a prolonged
ringing, an almost groaning sound was heard, one of those mysterious night
sounds that rise up sometimes out of the deep silence; they rise, linger in the
air, and at last they slowly disperse as if dying away. You listen intently to
the sound and it's as if nothing were there, but it goes on ringing. It seemed
as though someone had cried out next to the very horizon for a long, long
time and someone else had answered from the forest with reedy, shrill
laughter and a weak, hissing whistle that swept over the river. The boys
looked at each other and shuddered . . .

"The power of the cross be with us!" whispered Ilya.

"Aw, you chickens!" Pavel cried. "What're you scared of? Look, the taters are done." (They all moved up to the little pot and began eating the steaming potatoes; only Vanya didn't stir.) "What's the matter with you?" asked Pavel.

But he didn't crawl out from under his matting. The little pot was soon emptied.

"Did you hear, guys," began Ilyusha, "what happened not long ago near here in Varnavitsy?"

"At the dam?" asked Fedya.

"Yeah, that's it, at the dam, where it's burst. Now that's an unclean place, so haunted it is, and so deserted. There's gullies and ravines around everything and in the ravines there's lots of snakes."

"Well, what happened? Tell us . . . "

"Here's what happened. Fedya, maybe you don't know it, but we have a drowned man's buried there; and he drowned a long time ago when the pond was still deep; you can still see his grave, but only jus' barely: like a little mound . . . The other day the steward calls the dog keeper Yermil; he says: 'Yermil,' he says, 'to the post office!' Our Yermil always rode after the mail; he did in all his dogs, for some reason his dogs never survive, that is they never survive anyways, and he's a good dog keeper who did everything. So Yermil rides to the post office but he hangs around in town and he's already tipsy on the ride back. And the night's a bright one: the moon's shinin' . . . So Yermil rides across the dam 'cause that's where the road took him. He rides that way, the dog keeper Yermil, and sees a lamb, kind of white, curly haired and pretty walkin' around near the drowned man's grave. And so Yermil thinks: 'I'll take him—why should he go to waste.' He climbs down and takes it in his arms . . . And the lamb doesn't flinch. So Yermil walks to his horse, but the horse backs away from him, snorts and shakes its head; but he calms it down, climbs up on it with the lamb and rides off again, holdin' the lamb in front of him. He looks at it and the lamb stares straight into his eyes. Yermil the dog keeper gets terrified: 'I don't remember,' he said, 'that a lamb ever looked someone in the eye like that,' but so be it. So he starts strokin' its fur and says: 'Baa, baa!' And the ram all of a sudden bares its teeth and says right back to him: 'Baa, baa . . . ' "

The narrator had barely gotten out this last word when suddenly both dogs got up at once and barking convulsively darted back from the fire and disappeared into the darkness. All the boys were frightened. Vanya jumped out from under his mat. Pavlusha ran after the dogs with a shout. Their barking quickly moved away . . . The restless running of the disturbed horses could be heard. Pavlusha cried loudly: "Gray! Zhuchka! . . . " After a

few moments the barking ceased; Pavel's voice already sounded far away . . .
A little more time passed; the boys looked around in bewilderment as if
waiting to see what would happen . . . Suddenly a horse's hoofbeats rang
out; the horse stopped abruptly right near the edge of the campfire, and
clutching at the mane, Pavlusha jumped from it. Both dogs also leapt up to
the circle of light and immediately sat down, their red tongues sticking out.

"What's there? What is it?" the boys asked.

"Nothin'," replied Pavel, waving the horse off, "jus' somethin' the dogs
smelled. I thought it was a wolf," he added in an indifferent voice, his chest
heaving rapidly.

My instinctive response was to admire Pavlusha. He was very appealing
at that moment. His unattractive face, animated from the fast ride, burned
with bold daring and strong determination. Without a switch in his hand and
at night he had not hesitated at all and had galloped off alone after a wolf . . .
"What a splendid boy!" I thought, gazing at him.

"And did you see 'em, those wolves, did you?" asked the little coward
Kostya.

"There's always lots of 'em here," answered Pavel, "but they're only
restless in winter." Again he settled himself in front of the fire. Sitting on
the ground he let his hand fall on the shaggy head of one of the dogs and for
a long time the happy animal didn't turn his head but only looked to the
side at Pavlusha with grateful pride.

Vanya again took refuge under his mat.

"But what scary things you been tellin' us Ilyushka," said Fedya, who as
the son of a rich peasant had to be the leader; just the same he spoke very
little himself, as if he were afraid of losing face. "That could be why the
dogs was twitchin' uneasily and barkin' . . . And it's true, I heard that place
of yours is unclean."

"Varnavitsy? . . . Course! It's real unclean! They say, people used to see
an old landowner there, a dead landowner. He walks around, they say, in a
long caftan and he's always sorta moanin', searchin' for somethin' on the
ground. Grandfather Trofimych met him once. 'What are you searchin' for
on the ground, Ivan Ivanych, sir?' he said."

"Did he ask him?" interrupted the amazed Fedya.

"Yeah, he asked."

"Well, good for Trofimych after that . . . Well, so what'd he say?"

" 'Split-grass,'[5] he said. 'That's what I'm searchin' for.' And in such a
hollow voice, so hollow: 'split-grass.' 'And what do you want the split-
grass for, Ivan Ivanych, sir?' 'The grave,' he said, 'the grave is crushing
me, Trofimych; I want to get out, to get out . . . ' "

"So that's it!" Fedya said. "It means he didn't live enough."

"Well, I'll be!" said Kostya. "I thought you could only see dead people on Parents' Saturday."[6]

"Dead people can be seen any time," confidently put in Ilyusha, who as far as I could tell knew all the village superstitions better than the others . . . "But on Parents' Saturday you can also see the livin', that is, the ones who'll be dyin' in that year. You only have to sit at night on the church porch and you'll see everything on the road. They'll go past you on the road, the ones, that is, who'll die that year. Last year our Granny Yuliana went to the church porch."

"Well, and did she see anyone?" asked Kostya with curiosity.

"Why, 'course she did. First of all, she sat a long, long time and didn't see or hear no one . . . only all the while it was like as if a dog was barkin' and barkin' somewhere . . . All of a sudden she sees: a boy wearing nothing but a tattered shirt is walkin' along the road. She peers close and its Ivashka Fedoseev walkin' . . . "

"The one who died in the spring?" interrupted Fedya.

"The very one. He walks along and he doesn't raise his little head . . . But Yuliana recognized him . . . But then she looks: a woman's walkin' along. She looks and looks—oh my gosh!—she herself's walkin' along the road, Yuliana herself."

"Not really her?" asked Fedya.

"You bet it was."

"Well, after all, she ain't dead yet, right?"

"No, a year ain't passed yet. But look at her: what her soul is holding on to."

Again they all became quiet. Pavel threw a handful of dried out twigs into the fire. They turned black abruptly in the suddenly sputtering flames, crackled, smoked, and buckled, their burnt ends curling slightly. The reflection of light burst out on all sides quivering fitfully, especially upward. Suddenly, out of the blue, a white pigeon flew directly into the reflected light, fluttered around fearfully in one place entirely surrounded by hot sparks, and disappeared beating its wings.

"He probably strayed from home," noted Pavel.

"Now it'll fly, come across something in a while, and wherever it lands it'll spend the night 'til dawn."

"What do you think, Pavel?" said Kostya. "Maybe that's a righteous soul flyin' to heaven, eh?"

Pavel threw another handful of twigs into the fire.

"Maybe," he said at last.

"But please tell us, Pavlusha," began Fedya, "did you see the heavenly apparition[7] in Shalamov, too?"

"That time you couldn't see the sun? Yeah, sure we did."

"I bet you got scared as well?"

"Yeah, but not only us. Our master, even though he told us beforehand, he said, 'You'll have an apparition and it'll get dark,' and when it got dark he himself was such a coward that you wouldn't believe it. But listen, in the yard hut granny cook, as soon as it got dark, went and smashed all the pots in the oven:

" 'There's no eatin' for anyone now,' she said, 'it's the end of the world.' The cabbage soup spilled all over the place. In our village there was such rumors goin' around, brother, that white wolves would be running around all over, eatin' people, that birds of prey'll take wing, and Trishka[8] himself would show up."

"Who's this Trishka?" asked Kostya.

"Don'tcha know?" put in Ilyusha fervently. "Well, brother, how's it possible you don't know Trishka? It's dimwits you have in your village, real dimwits! Trishka will be an amazing person who'll come; and he'll be such an amazin' person that it'll be impossible to catch a hold of him and it'll be impossible to do nothin' to him: that's how amazin' he'll be. Say the peasants, for example, go and try to catch him, they'll go at him with cudgels and surround him, but he'll distract them—he'll distract them so they'll beat each other. They'll put him in the stockade and, say, he'll ask for a little water to drink in a bucket; they'll bring him the ladle and he'll dive in and totally vanish, every trace of him. If they put chains on him, he'll just clap his hands and they'll fall off. Well, and this Trishka will walk through the villages and towns; and this Trishka, the Sly One, he'll seduce the Christian folk . . . well, and it'll be impossible to do anything to him . . . That's how amazin' he'll be, the Sly One."

"Well, sure," Pavel went on in his unhurried voice, "that's who he is. He's the one we've been waitin' for. The old people used to say that when the heavenly apparition starts, 'Trishka will come,' they'd say. And then the apparition began. All the people spilled out into the streets, into the field, and waited to see what'd happen. We have a big, open space there, you know. They look—suddenly from the settlement on the hill they see some sort of man comin', so strange lookin', with such an amazin' head . . . They all start to shoutin': 'Ooh! Trishka's comin'! Ooh! Trishka's comin'!' And everyone hides where they can! Our elder crawled into a ditch; his wife got stuck under the gate and began shouting at the top of her lungs and frightened her own dog so much that it broke loose from its chain, jumped through the fence, and ran into the forest; and Kuzka's father, Dorofeich, jumped into the grain field, squatted down, and started making quail sounds: 'Maybe,' he said, 'the villain, the murderer'll spare birds at least.'

That's how scared they all got! . . . But the man who was comin' was our cooper, Vavila; he'd bought himself a new wooden bowl and had put the empty bowl on his head."

All the boys started laughing and again grew silent for a moment, as often happens with people who are having a conversation in the open air. I glanced around: the night was solemn and regal; the damp freshness of late evening had turned into the dry mildness of midnight, and it would lie like a cover on the sleeping fields for a while yet; there was still much time remaining until the first faint noises, until the first rustles and stirrings of morning, and the first dewdrops of dawn. There was no moon in the sky; it was that season of the year when it rose late. Countless golden stars seemed to flow quietly, all vying with one another, twinkling, in the direction of the Milky Way, and truly, in gazing at them, you could vaguely feel the headlong, nonstop movement of the earth yourself . . .

A strange, shrill, sickly cry suddenly rang out twice over the river, and after a few moments it was repeated even further away . . .

Kostya shuddered. "What is it?"

"A heron's cry," answered Pavel calmly.

"A heron," Kostya repeated . . . "Then what was it I heard last night, Pavlusha?" he added after a brief pause. "Maybe you know . . . "

"What'd you hear?"

"Here's what: I was goin' from the Stone Ridge to Shashkino; and first I went 'cross our whole hazel grove and then I went 'cross the meadow— y'know the place where it comes out like a narrow bend—the place where there's a deep hole with water; y'know, it's the one that's all overgrown with reeds; so I went past this hole, guys, and suddenly out of that hole someone starts groanin', and pitiful, so pitiful it was; 'oooh-oooh . . . ooh-oooh . . . oooh-oooh!' I got so scared, guys: it was late and that voice was so sickly. So that I thought I'd start to cryin' myself . . . What could that have been? Eh?"

"Last summer thieves drowned Akima the forester in that hole," Pavlusha said, "so maybe it was his soul complainin'."

"But, guys," Kostya said, opening his already enormous eyes even wider . . . "I didn't know Akima was drowned in that hole: I would have been scared even more."

"They also say there's these small frogs," Pavel went on, "that'll cry so mournful."

"Frogs? Well, no, this wasn't frogs . . . What frogs . . . " The heron cried again over the river. "Darn it!" Kostya said involuntarily. "It cries like a wood-goblin."

"The wood-goblin don't cry, it's mute," put in Ilyusha. "It only claps its hands and crackles . . . "

"So you've seen the wood-goblin, have you?" Fedya interrupted him sarcastically.

"No, I ain't seen him and hope to God I don't; but others have. Why, not long ago one lured a muzhik from our village: he led him and led him through the forest and all around one meadow . . . He barely made it home by dawn."

"Well, did he see him?"

"Yeah. He said he was big, really big, dark, all covered up, since he was behind a tree you couldn't make him out too good, like he was hidin' from the moon, and he looked and looked, blinkin' and blinkin' his eyes . . . "

"Oh you!" exclaimed Fedya, trembling slightly and shrugging his shoulders. "Phooey! . . . "

"And why's this filth roamin' the world?" Pavel asked. "I don't understand, really!"

"Don't curse. Watch out, he'll hear," said Ilya.

Silence again ensued.

"Look, guys," the childlike voice of Vanya suddenly rang out. "Look at God's little stars—like bees swarmin'!"

He poked his fresh face out from under the mat, slowly raising his big quiet eyes upward and leaning on his little fist. The eyes of all the boys looked up to the sky and did not lower for a long time.

"Tell me, Vanya," Fedya started tenderly. "Tell me, how's your sister Anyutka, okay?"

"She's fine," replied Vanya, burring slightly.

"Tell her—she should come see us . . . Why doesn't she?"

"I dunno."

"Tell her she should come."

"I'll tell her."

"Tell her I'll give her a present."

"But will you give me one?"

"I'll give you one, too."

Vanya sighed:

"Well, no, I don't need one. It's better if you give her one: she's so kind."

And Vanya put his head on the ground again. Pavel got up and took the empty pot in his hands.

"Where are you going?" Fedya asked him.

"To the river, to ladle some water. I want some water to drink."

The dogs got up and followed him.

"Watch out, don't fall into the river," Ilyusha shouted after him.

"Why would he fall?" said Fedya. "He's careful."

"Yes, he's careful. But anything can happen. He might be bendin' down startin' to ladle the water, and the water ghost'll grab him by the hand and pull him down below. Then they'd say: 'He fell, he did, the little one fell into the water . . . ' But what kind of fall is that? Over there, he's climbed into the reeds," he added, listening.

The reeds were, indeed, moving, "swooshing," as they say here.

"But is it true," asked Kostya, "that the fool Akulina went off her head after she went into the water?"

"Yes, after that . . . And now look at her! They say she used to be a real beauty. The water ghost ruined her. Probably he didn't expect that she'd be dragged out so quickly. So right there in his place at the bottom he ruined her."

(I had met this Akulina myself a number of times. Covered in rags, terribly thin, with a face black as coal, a tormented look, and forever baring her teeth, she stomped for hours on end in one place somewhere on the road, rigidly pressing her bony hands to her chest and slowly shifting from one leg to the other like a wild animal in a cage. She did not understand anything said to her and only occasionally laughed convulsively.)

"But they say," Kostya went on, "Akulina jumped into the river 'cause her lover deceived her."

"That's exactly it."

"D'you remember Vasya?" Kostya added sadly.

"What Vasya?" asked Fedya.

"The one who drowned," replied Kostya, "in this very river here. What a lad he was! My, what a lad he was! His mother, Feklista, how she loved her Vasya! And it was like she sensed it, Feklista, that he would die from water. Vasya used to come with us kids in the summer to swim in the river—she was always so afraid. The other women didn't worry goin' past with their wash tubs, back and forth, but Feklista would put the wash tub down on the ground and start callin' him: 'Come back,' she'd say, 'come back, darling! Ay, come back my little falcon!' And how he drowned, Lord alone knows. He was playin' there on the bank and his mother was there, too, rakin' up the hay. All of a sudden she hears a sound like somebody blowin' bubbles in the water—she looks and sees only Vasya's little cap's floatin' in the water. And ever since then Feklista too has been out of her mind: she comes and lies in that place where he drowned, she lies there, guys, and strikes up a song—remember, Vasya was always singin' some song—so now she sings it, too, and cries and cries, complainin' bitterly to God . . . "

"Here comes Pavlusha," said Fedya.

Pavel came up to the fire with a full pot in his hand.

"So, guys," he began, after a pause, "it's a bad business."

"What?" Kostya asked in a hurry.

"I heard Vasya's voice."

Everyone shuddered.

"What d'you mean, what d'you mean?" babbled Kostya.

"Swear to God. I was just startin' to bend down to the water and all of a sudden I hear a voice like Vasya's callin' to me like it's comin' from under the water: 'Pavlusha, hey Pavlusha!' I listen: and it calls again: 'Pavlusha, come here!' I moved away. But I got some water."

"Oh, Lord! Oh, Lord!" said the boys crossing themselves.

"Why, it was that water ghost callin' to you Pavel," added Fedya. "And we was only jus' talkin' about him, about Vasya."

"Oh, this is a bad omen," Ilyusha said slowly.

"Well, it's nothin', never mind!" declared Pavel resolutely and sat down again. "You can't change your fate."

The boys fell silent. It was obvious that Pavel's words had made a deep impression on them. They began settling down in front of the fire as if they were getting ready to go to sleep.

"What's that?" Kostya asked suddenly, raising his head up.

Pavel listened:

"It's sandpipers flyin', they're whistlin'."

"Where they flyin' to?"

"To a place where they say there's no winter."

"Is there really such a place?"

"There is."

"Far away?"

"Far, far away, beyond the warm seas."

Kostya sighed and closed his eyes.

More than three hours had passed since I had sat down near the boys. The moon had risen at last; I did not notice it right away: it was so small and thin. This moonless night, it seemed, was just as magnificent as before . . . But many stars, which not long before had been high in the sky, were already descending to the dark edge of the earth; as usually happens only toward morning, it was perfectly quiet everywhere: everything was in a solid, motionless, predawn sleep. The air no longer carried such a strong scent—and again it seemed as if dampness were pouring out of it . . . These short summer nights! . . . The boys' conversations died out with the fires . . . The dogs dozed off as well; the horses, as far as I could make out by the light streaming weakly down from the stars, were also lying down with their heads bowed . . . A slight drowsiness came over me and passed over into sleep.

A fresh current blew against my face. I opened my eyes: morning had broken. The dawn was not glowing pink yet but it was already beginning to turn light in the east. Everything came into view, although in vague outline. The pale gray sky shone bright, turned cold and blue; the stars either twinkled with a weak glow or disappeared; the earth was damp, the leaves were dew covered, here and there sounds of life began to emerge, voices could be heard, and a faint early breeze already wandered and fluttered above the earth. My body responded with a slight, cheerful shiver. I got up quickly and walked over to the boys. They were all dead asleep around the smoldering campfire; only Pavel raised himself up halfway and gazed at me intently.

I nodded my head to him and went home along the river, which was enveloped in a smoky mist. I had not gone a mile and a half when sunlight began to flow around me—over the wide wet meadow, and ahead along the hills, which were starting to turn green from forest to forest, and behind along the far dusty road over the sparkling crimson bushes, and across the river turning a bashful blue under the thinning mist—golden streams of young, hot sunlight, first flowing white, then red ... Everything began to stir, to wake up, to sing, to resound, to speak. Everywhere large drops of dew glowed like radiant diamonds. The pure and clear sounds of bells rushed toward me as if they too were washed in the morning coolness, and suddenly, driven by my young friends, the refreshed herd raced past me ...

Unfortunately, I have to add, Pavel died that same year. He did not drown: he was killed when he fell from his horse. What a shame, he was a splendid lad!

Translation by Therese M. Malhame

Notes to the translation are on page 578.

RESOURCES

Primary Text

Turgenev, Ivan. "Bezhin lug." *Sobranie sochinenii v dvenadtsati tomakh.* Moscow: Khudozhestvennaia literatura, 1958, pp. 136–67.

Secondary Sources

Literary and Cultural Studies

Allen, Elizabeth Cheresh. *Beyond Realism: Turgenev's Poetics of Secular Salvation.* Stanford: Stanford University Press, 1992.

Ehre, Milton. "Turgénev, Iván Sergéevich (1818–1883)." In *Handbook of Russian Literature,* ed. Victor Terras. New Haven: Yale University Press, 1985, pp. 488–89.

Freeborn, Richard. *Turgenev: The Novelist's Novelist.* London: Oxford University Press, 1960.
Leyda, Jay. "Eisenstein's *Bezhin Meadow.*" *Sight and Sound* 28 (Spring 1959): 74.
Pahomov, George. *In Earthbound Flight: Romanticism in Turgenev.* Rockville, MD: Kamkin, 1983.
Pischulin, Iu.P. *Ivan Sergeevich Turgenev. Zhizn', iskusstvo, vremia.* Moscow: Sovetskaia Rossiia, 1988.
Pritchett, V.S. *The Gentle Barbarian: The Life and Work of Turgenev.* New York: Random House, 1977.
Robinson, David. "The Two Bezhin Meadows." *Sight and Sound* 37 (Winter 1967–68): 33.
Terras, Victor. *A History of Russian Literature.* New Haven: Yale University Press, 1991, pp. 272–73.
Valkenier, Elizabeth. *Russian Realist Art. The State and Society: The Peredvizhniki and Their Tradition.* Ann Arbor, MI: Ardis, 1977.

Art and Architecture

Isaac Levitan. Trans. Vladimir Maximov, intro. Alexei Fedorov-Davydov. Leningrad: Aurora, 1981.
Sokolova, Natalya, ed. *Selected Works of Russian Art.* Leningrad: Aurora, 1976, plates 77–79, 96–100.
Turgenev, Ivan S. *Zapiski okhotnika.* Moscow: Nauka, 1991. Includes reproduction of Lebedev's *Bezhin lug.*

Film

Bezhin lug (Bezhin Meadow). Director, Sergei Eisenstein. Mosfilm, 1935–37, 1967.

15

~Fedor Dostoevsky~

The Meek Woman
A Fantastic Story

From the Author

I ask forgiveness of my readers for providing only a tale on this occasion instead of the *Diary* in its usual form. But I really was occupied by this tale for most of the month. In any case I ask the reader's indulgence.

Now about the story itself. I titled it "fantastic" although I myself consider it to be realistic to the highest degree. But the fantastic is present here and specifically in the narrative's form, which to my mind should be explained beforehand.

In fact, this is neither a story nor a sketch. Imagine a husband whose wife, a suicide, is laid out on a table, having thrown herself out of a window some hours ago. He is disoriented and has not yet managed to focus his thoughts. He walks about his rooms and attempts to understand what has happened, to "gather his thoughts." Moreover, he is a total hypochondriac, the kind who talks to himself. And this is what he does, talks to himself, relates the matter, *clarifies* it for himself. In spite of the narrative's apparent coherence he contradicts himself several times both in logic and in feelings. He both justifies himself and accuses her, and he goes off on tangential explanations: coarseness of mind and heart is evident, as is profound feeling. Little by little he indeed *clarifies* the matter for himself and "gathers his thoughts." The series of reminiscences he elicits inevitably brings him, finally, to the *truth*; the truth inevitably ennobles his mind and heart. Toward the end even the story's tone changes in contrast to its disorderly beginning. The truth is revealed to the unhappy man rather clearly and definitely, at least for him.

Such is the theme. Of course, the narrative process lasts for several hours, in spurts, with sudden reversals, and in a confused form; at times he speaks to himself, at times he seems to address an unseen listener, some sort of magistrate. And that's how it always is in reality. If a stenographer could listen to him and take everything down the result would be somewhat rougher, less polished than what I am offering, but I rather think the psychological order, perhaps, would remain the same. This presupposition of a stenographer taking everything down (after which I polish up the notes) is precisely what I call the fantastic in this story. But it is not the first time something analogous has been permitted in art; Victor Hugo, for instance, in his masterpiece "The Last Day of a Man Condemned to Execution" used an almost equivalent device, although he did not introduce a stenographer and, moreover, allowed a gross implausibility in assuming the condemned could take notes (and have time for them) not only during his last day but during his last hour and literally his last minute. But without allowing this fantasy the work itself could not exist—a work that is the most realistic and truthful of all he has written.

CHAPTER ONE

1

Who I Was and Who She Was

While she is still here—everything is fine; I go up and look every minute. But tomorrow they will take her away and . . . is it possible, I will be left alone? She is now in the hall on the table—two card tables placed together—and the coffin will be available tomorrow, a white, white shroud, but that's not it . . . I keep pacing back and forth wanting to clarify matters for myself. For six hours now I have wanted to clarify matters and still cannot gather my thoughts. The point is I keep walking, walking, walking . . . This is what happened. I will narrate everything in order (order!) Gentlemen, I am far from a literary person, as you can see, and so what, I will tell it as I myself understand matters. That's what is horrible, that I understand everything!

If you want to know, if one is to begin at the beginning, she simply came to me then to pawn things, to pay for an advertisement in *The Voice* stating that such and such a tutor was willing to travel, to give lessons at home, and so on, and so forth. That was at the very beginning, and I, of course, did not single her out from the others; she would come like the others, and so on. And then I began to single her out. She was so thin, with white hands, medium height. With me she was always hesitant, as if she were embarrassed

(I think such was her manner with all strangers, and I, of course, was like everyone else, that is, taken as a man and not as a pawnbroker). The moment she received the money she would turn and leave. And always in silence. Others would argue, ask, bargain for more, but she, no, whatever was given . . . I can't seem to get things straight . . . Yes, I was first struck by her things: silver gilded earrings, an awful medallion worth twenty kopeks. She herself knew they were worth kopeks but in her face I saw they were precious to her, and indeed that was all that remained from her father and mother, I later discovered. Only once I allowed myself to make fun of her things. For, you see, I never permit myself to behave that way, my tone with the public is that of a gentlemen: a few words, politely and sternly. "Sternly, sternly, sternly." But she unexpectedly had the nerve to bring in the remnants (that is literally) of an old rabbit jacket, and I could not restrain myself and abruptly said something to her in the nature of a witticism. My God, how she flared up! She has big blue thoughtful eyes—and how they blazed! But she did not utter a word, took her "remnants" and left. That's when I first *especially* noticed her and began to think of her in that way, that is, precisely in a special way. Yes, I also remember, if you like, it was the main impression, a synthesis of everything, that she was terribly young, young enough to be fourteen. Although she was then already three months shy of sixteen. But that's not what I wanted to say, the synthesis was not in that at all. She came again the next day. I found out later she had gone to Dobronravov and Mozer with that jacket, but they accept only gold and wouldn't even talk to her. I, on the other hand, accepted a cameo from her (a miserable object), surprising myself after realizing what I had done. I also do not accept anything except gold and silver, and I permitted her a cameo. This was my second impression of her, that I remember.

This time, that is, after Mozer, she brought an amber cigar holder, a so-so object for nonprofessionals, but again not worth anything to us because—we only take gold. Since she came after yesterday's *revolt*, I met her sternly. My sternness is a dry manner. Nevertheless, in giving her two rubles I could not refrain from saying as if with some irritation, "I'm only doing this *for you*; Mozer would not accept such an object." The words *for you* I particularly stressed, specifically giving them *a certain shade of meaning*. I was angry. She flared up again, heard out the *for you*, but did not say anything, did not throw down the money, took it. That's poverty! And how she flared up! I understood I had struck a nerve. And after she had gone I suddenly asked myself whether this triumph over her was really worth two rubles? Hee, hee, hee! I remember suddenly asking myself that question twice: "Is it worth it? Is it worth it?" And laughing, I answered myself in the affirmative. I became extremely cheerful then. But it was not a bad emotion: I deliberately, intentionally wanted to test her, because I suddenly began to think of her in a certain way. This was my third *particular* idea of her.

. . . So that's when it all began. Naturally, I immediately attempted elsewhere to find out all the circumstances and I awaited her visit with special impatience. For I sensed she would soon come. When she came I began a pleasant conversation in an unusually polite manner. I have a decent upbringing and know my manners. Hmm. At this point I understood she was good-hearted and meek. The good-hearted and meek do not resist for long, and although they do not open up very much at all they don't know how to get out of a conversation; they provide brief answers but they do answer, and the further you go the more they answer, only be persistent if you're after something. Of course, at that time she herself did not explain anything to me. I only found out about *The Voice* and all the rest later. She then was desperately advertising, at first, of course, arrogantly, "governess, ready to travel, inform of conditions," and then, "willing to do anything, to teach, personal care, household aid, to look after the sick, and knows how to sew," and so on, and so forth, all the familiar stuff! Naturally, all this was put in her ad in each subsequent issue, and toward the end, when it came down to despair, then even, "without pay, for meals." No, she did not find a job! I decided then to test her one last time. I abruptly picked up today's edition of *The Voice* and showed her an advertisement: "Young woman, total orphan, seeks tutoring position for young children, preferably with an elderly widower. Can help with household."

"You see, this woman advertised in the morning and she probably found a position by evening. That's how one should advertise!"

She flared up again, again her eyes glowed, she turned and left immediately. I was very pleased. But, of course, by then I was sure of everything and was not afraid; no one would accept a cigar holder. And she was even out of cigar holders. And that's what happened, three days later she came in, so pale, agitated—I understood something had happened at home, and indeed it had. I'll explain presently what happened, but now I just want to remember how I impressed her then and gained stature in her eyes. My intentions came to me abruptly. For she brought in this icon (made up her mind to bring it in) . . . Ah, listen! Listen! Now is when it began, I was mixing things up . . . The point of the matter is I want to remember all this now, every triviality, every dot and dash. I keep wanting to gather my thoughts, and—I can't, while those dots and dashes . . .

An icon of the Mother of God. The Mother of God with infant, a household icon, a family icon, ancient, in a silver gold-gilded cover worth—well, worth six rubles or so. I could see it meant a lot to her, she wanted to pawn the whole icon without removing the cover. I told her it would be better to remove the cover and keep the icon, for to pawn the holy image, after all, is somewhat questionable.

"Aren't you permitted?"

"No, it is not that, but perhaps, you yourself . . . "

"Well, remove it."

"You know what, I won't take off the cover, but I will put it over there in the cabinet," I said, after thinking a bit, "next to the other icons under the lamp (since opening the shop I always kept an icon lamp burning), and you simply take ten rubles."

"I don't need ten, give me five, I will certainly redeem it."

"You do not want ten rubles? The icon is worth it." I added, noting her eyes flare up again. She remained silent. I brought out the five rubles. "Don't scorn anyone, I myself was in such straits and even worse, and if you now see me engaged in such matters . . . it is only after everything I have had to go through . . . "

"You want to take revenge on society? Yes?" She interrupted me suddenly with a rather caustic smile, in which, however, there was much innocence (that is, of a general sort, because she then decidedly did not distinguish between me and others and said it almost without malice). "Aha," I thought, "that's what you're like, there's some character showing, a new side."

"You see," I added immediately, half-jokingly, half-mysteriously, "I—I am part of that part of the whole that would do evil but doeth good . . . "[1]

She looked at me quickly and with great curiosity, in which, by the way, there was much of the child.

"Wait . . . what is that idea? Where is it from? I've heard it somewhere . . . "

"Don't rack your brains. Mephistopheles recommends himself to Faust in those words. Have you read *Faust*?"

"No . . . not carefully."

"That is you have not read it at all. You should. But I see again a mocking curl to your lips. Please, don't assume I have so little sense of decorum as to wish to embellish my pawnbroker's role by recommending myself to you through Mephistopheles. Once a pawnbroker, always a pawnbroker. We all know that."

"You're strange somehow . . . I did not mean to say anything of the sort . . . "

She intended to say: I did not expect you to be an educated person, but she did not, although I knew she thought it. I made a big impression on her.

"You see," I noted, "one can do good in any walk of life. I am not speaking of myself, of course; I suppose I only do bad things, but . . . "

"Of course one can do good in any occupation," she said glancing at me quickly and intensely. "Certainly in any occupation," she added abruptly.

Oh, I remember, I remember all those moments! And I also want to add, when these young people, these nice young people want to say something intelligent and insightful, you can suddenly read too much sincerity and naiveté in their faces expressing, "Now I am telling you something brilliant and insightful." And it's not out of vanity, as with our sort, but you can see she herself thinks it very important, and believes it, and respects it, and thinks you too respect it all exactly as she does. Oh, sincerity! That's how they overcome. And how splendid it was in her!

I remember, I have not forgotten anything! After she left I immediately made up my mind. That same day I went to make my last inquiries and I found out all the rest about her, the current secrets. I already knew all the past secrets from Lukerya, who then worked for them and whom I had already bribed several days earlier. These secrets were so horrible that I do not understand how one could still laugh as she did then and be curious about Mephistopheles' words while in such a horrible situation. But—youth! I thought with pride and joy of her then precisely in those terms, because this also shows magnanimity of soul: although on the verge of doom, so to speak, and Goethe's great words still create an impression. Youth is always magnanimous, although a little bit off the mark. That is, I only have her, her alone, in mind. And most of all, by then I already considered her to be *mine* and did not doubt my power. You know that's an exceedingly voluptuous thought, when one no longer doubts.

But what's the matter with me? If I go on this way when will I ever focus my thoughts? Quickly, quickly—that's not it at all, oh God!

2

The Marriage Proposal

The "secrets" I found out about her I will explain in a nutshell: the mother and father died a long time ago, three years before, and she was left to live with her unsuitable aunts. That is, more than unsuitable. One aunt was a widow with a large family of six children, one smaller than the other, the second an old maid, old and vile. They were both vile. Her father was a bureaucrat, but of the clerical sort and merely a nonhereditary member of the nobility—in other words everything was just right for me. I appeared as if from a higher world, a retired captain, after all, from a dazzling regiment, a nobleman by birth, independent, and so on, and as for the pawnshop the aunts could only think of it with respect. Three years she was enslaved by her aunts, but still she passed an exam somewhere—managed to pass it, broke away from the daily merciless drudgery to pass it—and that showed a yearning for something better and nobler on her part! Why, after all, did I want to get married? But, forget about me, that's for later . . . And what does that have to do with anything! She taught the aunt's children, sewed linen, and finally not only sewed linen but—in spite of her chest—she washed floors. They simply beat her even, reproached her for eating. They ended up intending to sell her. Ugh! I leave out the ugly details. Afterward she told me everything in full. All this was observed for an entire year by a neighboring, fat shopkeeper, not a mere shopkeeper but one with two grocery shops. By then he had already done away with two wives and was looking for a third, and so he spotted her, "so to say quiet, grew up poor, and I will marry for the orphans' sake." He indeed had orphans. He began courting, began making plans with the aunts, and he's fifty years old; she was horrified. That's when she came to me in order to advertise in *The Voice*. Finally, she began asking the aunts to give her just a little bit of time, to think. They gave her a little bit, but no more, and laid siege to her: "We ourselves don't know where to get food even without an extra mouth to feed." I already knew all this and made my decision that same day after the morning's events. In the evening the merchant came and brought a pound of candies worth fifty kopeks from the shop; she was with him and I summoned Lukerya from the kitchen and told her to go whisper that I was at the gate and wished to tell her something in the most urgent fashion. I felt pleased with myself. And in general that entire day I felt very pleased.

Right there at the gate, next to Lukerya, I explained to her, astonished as she was at my summons, that I would consider it an honor and the greatest happiness . . . Second, she should not be surprised by my behavior and by my being at the gate because "I was, so to say, a straightforward person and had studied the situation." And I was not lying in saying I was a straightforward person. Oh, forget it. But I was not only well-mannered in speech, that is, demonstrating I was a person of upbringing, but I was also original, and that's the main thing. Is it a sin to confess that? I want to put myself on trial, and I am doing so. I must speak pro and contra, and so I speak. Even afterward I remembered that with satisfaction, stupid as it is: I declared then without any embarrassment that, first, I was not very talented, not very intelligent, perhaps not even very kind, a rather cheap egoist (I remember the expression, I thought of it on the way and was happy with it), and that I had in me, perhaps, a great deal, a great deal of other unpleasant failings. It was all said with a special sort of pride, that manner of speech is well known. Of course, I had enough sense of decorum not to start on my positive attributes after nobly pointing out my faults but instead noted, "On the other hand I have such and such, such and such, and so on." I saw she was still horribly frightened, but without softening anything, seeing moreover her fright, deliberately continued in even stronger terms: I said directly she would not go hungry, but there would be no fancy clothes, theater tickets, balls, only perhaps later after I had attained my goals. This stern tone decidedly appealed to me. I added, again as offhandedly as possible, that although I had taken up such an occupation, that is the pawnshop, I only had one goal in mind, that there was one set of circumstances . . . But I had every right indeed to speak in such a manner, I really had such a goal and there was such a set of circumstances. Wait now, gentlemen, my entire life I more than anyone despised the pawnshop, but in fact, although it's comical to talk to oneself in mysterious phrases, I did want "to take revenge on society," really, really, really! Thus her witticism in the morning about my "taking revenge" was unjust. That is, you see, if I had said directly, "Yes, I am taking revenge on society," she would have burst out laughing, as then in the morning, and it would have indeed been comical. On the other hand, by hinting indirectly, uttering a mysterious phrase, it turned out, one could arouse the imagination. Moreover, by then I was afraid of nothing; I knew that, after all, to her the fat shopkeeper was at least more vile than I and that I, standing at the gate, appeared as a liberator. I understood it, after all. Oh, human beings understand base things particularly well! But was it base? How is one to judge a person here? Did I not already love her then?

Wait. Of course I did not say anything to her about charity, but rather the opposite, oh the opposite: "It is I, so to say, who is the beneficiary and not *you.*" So I even put it in words, I could not help it, and perhaps it came out stupid, because I noted a brief frown on her face. But, on the whole, I decidedly came out on top. Wait, if one is remembering all the vile stuff, then I will note the last odious detail. I stood and thoughts ran through my head, you are tall, trim, well educated, and, and—finally, without boasting, you are not bad looking. That's what I thought. Of course, right there at the gate she said *yes.* But . . . but, I must add: she thought for a long time there at the gate before she said *yes.* She was so immersed in thought, so immersed, that I asked: "Well, what about it?" And I even could not restrain myself and with a certain flourish, asked "Well, what about it, madam?"

"Wait. I am thinking."

And her face was so serious, so serious I could have understood it even then. But I took offense. "Is it possible she is choosing between me and the shopkeeper?" Oh, I did not yet understand! I did not understand anything, anything! Until today I did not understand! I remember Lukerya ran after me, stopped me in the street, and said quickly, "God will reward you, sir, for taking our dear young lady. Just don't say anything to her, she's proud."

Well, proud! I myself like the proud ones. The proud are especially good when . . . well, when you no longer doubt your power over them, right? Oh, base, clumsy man! Oh, how pleased I was! You know, she, when she stood there at the gate lost in thought over saying yes to me, and I was surprised, you know, she even could have been thinking, "If it's misery either way, then wouldn't it be better to choose the worst straight out, that is, the fat shopkeeper, so that he'll kill me when he's drunk!" Ah? What do you think, could she have been thinking that?

Even now I do not understand—even now I do not understand anything! I just said she might have had this idea: to pick the worse of two unhappy choices, that is the shopkeeper? And who was worse for her then—I or the shopkeeper? A shopkeeper or a pawnbroker citing Goethe? It remains a question! What question? You don't understand that either. The answer is lying on the table, and you ask a question! And forget about me! The issue is not me at all . . . By the way, what's it to me—whether the issue is about me or not? Now that is something I certainly cannot resolve. Better go lie down. My head hurts . . .

3

The Most Noble Human Being, But I Myself Don't Believe It

I could not go to sleep. And how could I? There is some kind of pulse beating in my head. One wants to understand it all, all this filth. Oh, filth! Oh, out of what filth I dragged her! She must have understood, must have appreciated my good deed! I also liked entertaining different thoughts, for instance, that I was forty-one and she only sixteen. I was fascinated by it, this sense of inequality. It's very sweet, very sweet.

I, for example, wanted a wedding *à l'anglaise,* that is, strictly the two of us and only two witnesses, one of whom would be Lukerya, then immediately off to the train, perhaps to Moscow (where coincidentally I had a business matter) to a hotel for a couple of weeks. She protested, she would not allow it, and I was forced to pay my respects to the aunts as if they were relatives from whom I was taking her. I relented and the aunts received their due. I even presented those creatures with a hundred rubles apiece and promised more, not telling her anything, of course, so as not to bring her any distress over the squalid matter. The aunts immediately became smooth as silk. There was also an argument over the dowry; she had nothing, almost literally, but she did not want anything. I, however, managed to persuade her absolutely nothing wouldn't do, and so I put together the dowry, for who else could have? But forget me. Several of my ideas, however, I managed to convey to her, so she knew of them at least. I was in too much of a hurry, perhaps. Most important, from the very beginning, no matter how much she steeled herself, she threw herself at me with love, she would meet me joyfully when I came home in the evening and prattle (the charming prattle of innocence!) all about her youth, childhood, her family home, her father and mother. But I immediately threw cold water upon all this rapture. That was precisely my idea. I would answer rapture with silence, benevolent, of course ... but nevertheless she quickly understood we were different, and that I was—an enigma. And I, most important, depended on the enigma! In order to create an enigma I, perhaps, started this whole stupid thing! First, strictness, so with strictness I brought her into my home. In a word, I then made up an entire system, although I was content. Oh, it took shape all by itself without any difficulty. And it could not be otherwise, I had to devise this system because of an unavoidable circumstance—why am I, after all, slandering myself! The system was a true one. No, listen, if one is to put a person on trial then do so knowing the evidence ... Listen!

How is one to begin, for it is very difficult. When you begin justifying yourself—that's what's difficult. You see, for instance, young people despise money; I immediately concentrated on money, I stressed money. And I stressed it so much that she grew more and more silent. She would open her big eyes wide, listen, look, and grow silent. You see, young people are magnanimous, that is, good young people are magnanimous and prone to outbursts, but they have little patience, once something is not right immediately there's—disdain. And I wanted breadth, I wanted to graft breadth straight onto her heart, to infuse her heartfelt convictions, is that it? Let's take a banal example: How was I to explain my pawnshop to such a person? Of course I did not speak straight out, for it would have seemed I was asking forgiveness for the pawnshop, rather I used dignity, so to say, spoke almost silently. For I am a master at speaking silently, I have spent my entire life speaking silently and lived through entire tragedies in solitary silence. Oh, after all, I too was unhappy! I was discarded by all, discarded and forgotten, and no one, no one knows it! And suddenly, after the fact, this sixteen year old picked up these details about me from vile people and thought she knew everything, while the most precious thing remained deep in the heart of that person! I remained silent. I always remained silent, and especially, especially with her, right up to yesterday. Why did I remain silent? As a proud person, I wanted her to find out for herself, without me but not from the tales of villains so that *she herself solved* the enigma of this person and got to know him! Taking her into my home I wanted full respect. I wanted her to stand before me in prayer for my suffering—and I was worth it. Oh, I was always proud, I always wanted all or nothing!

Precisely because I am not ready for half-baked happiness and wanted everything, that is why I had to take the actions I did: "In other words, solve the enigma yourself, woman, and appreciate its value." Because, you must agree, if I myself provided explanations and hints, began to squirm and ask for respect, it would be equal to asking for charity ... But, on the other hand, on the other hand, why am I speaking of this!

It's stupid, stupid, stupid, and stupid! In a straightforward fashion, ruthlessly (and I stress that it was ruthless), I explained to her in terse words that youthful magnanimity is wonderful but not worth a kopek. Why not? Because it is acquired cheaply, not formed by life, all that, so to say, is "the first impressions of existence," but I'd like to see you at work! Cheap magnanimity is always easy, even sacrificing one's life is cheap, because that's only blood at a boil and an excess of vitality, a passionate yearning for beauty! No, let's see a hard deed of magnanimity, quiet, unheard, without glitter, combined with slander, in which there is a great deal of sacrifice and not a drop of glory—when you, a person of glowing attributes, are presented to everyone as a scoundrel, although you are more honest than anyone on earth—try accomplishing that deed, will you. No sir, you'll refuse! And I, my entire life, all I did was carry the weight of that deed on my shoulders. At first she argued, and how, and then she grew silent, even completely silent, only she would open her eyes very wide, listening, such large, large attentive eyes. And ... and suddenly I would notice a smile, a wicked, mistrustful, mute smile. And it was this smile she wore when I brought her into my home. It is also true that by then there was nowhere else for her to go ...

4

Plans and More Plans

Who started it?

No one. It started all by itself from the outset. I said I brought her into my home under strict conditions, but right away I made them less demanding. When she was still a bride it was explained to her she would be taking in pawned objects and handing out money, and she, after all, did not say anything then (please note). Moreover, she even took up the work zealously. Well, of course, the apartment, furniture, all remained the same. The apartment—two rooms, one a large living room with the pawnshop behind a partition and the second, also large, our room, shared, the bedroom here as well. My furniture is sparse, even the aunts' was better. My icon stand and a lamp are in the pawnshop area; in my room there is a cabinet with several books and the deposit box; I have the keys. Then a bed, tables, chairs. During our engagement I had already told her one ruble a day and no more was to be allocated for our upkeep, that is for food for me, her, and Lukerya, whom I lured into our employ. "For I need three thousand in three years and one cannot otherwise save money." She was not opposed, and I myself raised the upkeep by thirty kopeks. The theater also. During our engagement I told her there would be no theaters, and nevertheless I allowed the theater once a month, and in proper fashion in the better seats. We went together, three times, saw *The Pursuit of Happiness* and *La Perichole,* I think.[2] (Oh, forget it, forget it!) We would go in silence and return in silence. Why, why did we take to not speaking from the very beginning? There was, after all, no quarrel at the beginning, but there was silence. She, I remember, kept glancing at me surreptitiously; when I noticed, I intensified the silence. It is true I was the one who emphasized silence, not she. There were outbursts on her part once or twice, she would fling herself on me with an embrace, but since the outbursts were unsettled, hysterical, and I needed firm happiness together with her respect, I received her coldly. And I was right; each time after an outburst, the next day, there would be a quarrel.

That is, again, not quarrels, but silence, and—and more and more arrogance in her demeanor. "Revolt and independence"—that's what it was, only she did not know how to go about it. Yes, her meek face became more and more insolent. Believe it or not, I was becoming vile to her; I studied this, after all. And she would lose control of herself totally in outbursts, of that there was no doubt. For instance, coming out of such squalor and indigence, after washing floors, how could she turn up her nose over our poverty! You see, this wasn't poverty but economy, and when necessary even luxury, in regard to linen, for example, or cleanliness. Even earlier I had always imagined a husband's cleanliness would be attractive to a wife. But she really didn't complain about poverty but about my supposed miserly economics: "He has goals, so to say, to show off his strength of character." She herself suddenly refused the theater. And the scornful lines in her mouth began appearing more and more ... while I grew even more silent, grew even more silent.

One could not start off on self-justifications, after all. The main point was the pawnshop. Permit me, I knew that a woman and moreover a sixteen year old could not but be totally obedient to a man. There is no originality in women, for me that's—that's an axiom, even now it is an axiom! So what if she's lying there in the hall? What's true is true! Even Mill himself cannot do anything about it![3] While a loving woman, oh, a loving woman will worship even the vices, even the wickedness of her beloved one. He himself will never come up with the rationalizations for his evil acts, she will. This is magnanimous but unoriginal. The one thing that has ruined women is their lack of originality. And why, I repeat, why do you show me the table? Is that original, what's on the table? O-oh!

Listen: I was certain then of her love. Even then she would throw her arms around my neck. That meant she was in love, or more accurately—she wanted to be in love. Yes, that's how it was: She wanted to be in love, she searched for love. And the main point is there was really no villainy that she would have had to rationalize away. You say: a pawnbroker, and everyone says it. And so what? That means there was a reason for the most magnanimous of human beings to become a pawnbroker. You see, ladies and gentlemen, there are ideas ... that is, you see, if a certain idea is expressed, put into words, it becomes horribly stupid. It embarrasses you. And why? For no reason. Because we are all vile and cannot stand the truth, or I don't know. I just said, "the most magnanimous of human beings." That is comical, and nevertheless that's exactly how it was. For such is the truth, the most truthful truth! Yes, I *had the right* to want to be well off and to open up that pawnshop. "You rejected me, you, you people, that is, you drove me off with disdainful silence. You answered the passionate way in which I reached out to you with an irreparable insult. Now, therefore, I am right in putting up a wall to separate myself from you, to collect those thirty thousand rubles, and to live out my existence somewhere in the Crimea, on the Southern shore, among the mountains and vineyards, on one's own estate bought for that thirty thousand, and the main point, far away from all of you, but without feeling any malice toward you, with ideals, with a beloved woman, a family if God allows, and helping the local inhabitants." Of course, it's a good thing I am now saying this to myself, for what could have been more foolish than if I had described it aloud to her? That's the reason for the proud silence, that's why we did not speak to each other. Because what could she have understood? Sixteen years old, the first stages of youth. What could she have understood of my self-justifications, my suffering? What one had here was the straight and narrow, lack of knowledge about life, cheap youthful convictions, the nearsightedness of a chicken ("of marvelous hearts of gold"), and the main point was the pawnshop—and basta! (And was I a villain in the pawnshop? Did she not see my actions, and whether I overcharged?) Oh, how horrible is truth on earth! This delightful woman, this meek woman, this heaven on high was a tyrant, the unbearable tyrant of my soul and a torturer! I would be slandering myself if I did not say so! You think I did not love her? Who can say I did not love her? You see it was ironic, it turned out to be the irony of fate and nature! We are cursed, on the whole, human life has a curse on it! (Mine, in part!) I now understand, after all, that I made some kind of a mistake! Something went wrong. Everything was clear, my plan was as clear as the sky: "Strict, proud, and does not need moral condolences from anyone, suffers silently." And so it was, I did not lie, did not! "Later she herself will see there was magnanimity, only she did not manage to note it, and when at some time she does guess the truth, she will value it ten times over and will be crushed, clasping her hands beseechingly." That was the plan. But I forgot something, or failed to take it into account. I failed to do something here. But enough, enough. And of whom can one ask forgiveness now? If it's over, it's over. More courage, man, and show some pride! You are not to blame!

All right, I will speak the truth, I will not be afraid to face the truth directly: *She* is to blame, *she*!

5

The Meek Woman Revolts

The quarrels began because she suddenly decided to hand out money in her own way, to price objects above their value, and twice even managed to argue with me on the subject. I was not persuaded. But at this point the captain's widow turned up.

An old woman, the widow of a captain, came in with a medallion—the gift of her deceased husband, obviously, a keepsake. I turned over thirty rubles. She began whining sadly, asked that the object be treated with care—of course, we would take care of it. Well, to make it short, suddenly five days later she came in to exchange it for a bracelet not worth eight rubles; I, of course, turned her down. She must have read something in my wife's eyes, and whatever the reason came back when I was out and my wife exchanged the medallion for her.

Having found out about it the same day, I spoke up, quietly, but firmly and reasonably. She sat on the bed, looking down on the floor, tapping the toe of her right foot on the carpet (her mannerism); an unpleasant smile was on her lips. Without raising my voice at all, I declared the money was *mine,* that I have the right to look at life through *my* eyes, and that when I invited her into my home, after all, I did not hide anything from her.

She suddenly jumped up, suddenly began shaking all over, and—what do you think—suddenly stamped her feet at me. This was a beast, this was a fit, this was a beast having a fit. I froze in amazement; I never expected such shenanigans. But I did not lose control, I did not even move, and again in the same calm voice I declared that from now on I was depriving her of participation in my activities. She laughed in my face and left the apartment.

The point of the matter is she was not supposed to leave the apartment. Nowhere without me—such was the agreement even during the engagement. By evening she returned; I did not say a word.

The following day she left again, and the day after. I locked up the office and set off to see the aunts. I had broken off relations with them from the time of the wedding, did not receive them or visit them. Now it turned out she had not been at their place. Having heard me out with curiosity, they laughed in my face: "That's what you deserve." But I had anticipated their mockery. I bribed the youngest aunt right there and then with a hundred rubles, twenty-five rubles down. Two days later she came to me: "There is an officer involved, Efimovich, a lieutenant, your former friend in the regiment." I was very surprised. This Efimovich had done me the most harm in the regiment, and once or twice a month ago, being shameless, had come to the pawnshop under the pretext of pawning something and, I remember, began joking with my wife. I then immediately had gone up to him and had told him not to dare come back, in light of our former relationship, but I had not even thought of anything else, just simply that he was an oaf. Now the aunt suddenly announces he has a rendezvous already planned with my wife and that everything is in the hands of the aunts' former acquaintance, Yulia Samsonovna, a widow and moreover a colonel's widow: "Your spouse now visits her."

I'll make it short. The whole matter cost me about three hundred rubles, but in two days it was arranged that I would be standing in an adjacent room, behind a slightly opened door, and I would be listening to the first rendezvous of my wife alone with Efimovich. While we waited, the night before, we had a brief scene that was all too important to me.

She returned before nightfall, sat down on the bed, and smiling and tapping her little foot on the carpet, stared at me. Looking at her I suddenly had the thought that during this entire last month, or better the last two weeks up till the present, she had not been herself, one could even say she was totally opposite to her usual self: a boisterous, aggressive being had appeared. I would not say it was shameless, but it was disorderly and itself seeking disorder. Asking for disorder. Meekness, however, interfered. When such a woman rebels, then, even if she goes too far, it is obvious she is forcing herself, pushing herself, and that she herself is first in being unable to overcome her own innate wisdom and sense of shame. That's why such women sometimes go way too far, so that one cannot trust one's reasoned observations. A soul used to depravity, on the contrary, will always make things less extreme and more vile, but under the guise of order and decency, even taking the superior stance over you.

"Is it true you were dismissed from the regiment because you were scared of fighting a duel?" she suddenly asked, her eyes flashing.

"It's true. I was asked to leave the regiment by an officer's court, although, by the way, I had already turned in my commission earlier."

"Expelled you as a coward?"

"Yes. According to their verdict I was a coward. But I refused the duel not as a coward but because I did not want to submit to their tyrannical verdict and to provoke a duel when I myself did not feel insulted. You know"—I could not hold back at this point—"to actively oppose such tyranny and to accept all the consequences was to express much more courage than any sort of duel."

I could not hold back and seemed to be justifying myself in that phrase, and that was all she needed to add to my humiliation. She laughed in a mean-spirited way.

"And is it true you then wandered the streets of Petersburg for three years as a beggar and begged for kopeks and slept under billiard tables?"

"I slept in the Vyazemsky House on Sennaya Square.[4] Yes, it is true, after I left the regiment there was much shame and degradation in my life, but not moral degradation, because I was the first to despise my actions, even then. It was only degradation of my mind and will and was elicited by my desperate circumstances. But that has passed . . . "

"Oh, now you're a personality—a financier!"

That is, a hint about the pawnshop. But by then I had already managed to bring myself under control. I saw she longed for explanations to humiliate me—and I did not provide them. At that moment a customer rang and I went out to him into the office. Afterward, an hour later, when she was already dressed to go, she came up to me and said:

"You, however, did not tell me any of this before the wedding?"

I did not answer, and she left.

So the following day I stood in this room behind the door and listened as my fate was being decided, and in my pocket I had a revolver. She was dressed up, sat at the table, and Efimovich put on a show for her benefit. And so: what happened (I say this to my credit) was exactly what I had imagined and sensed beforehand, although I did not understand I was imagining or feeling it. I do not know whether I explain myself clearly.

This is what happened. I listened for an entire hour and for an entire hour I was present at a confrontation between the noblest and most elevated of women and a worldly, debauched, stupid creature with the soul of a reptile. And how, I thought amazed, how did this naive, meek, taciturn woman know all this? The wittiest author of high society comedies could not have created such a scene of ridicule, naive hearty laughter, and holy disdain that goodness felt for vice. How her words and remarks sparkled; how pointed were her swift rejoinders, how true her judgments! At the same time, how much of it represented an almost girlish simplicity. She laughed in his face in reply to his declarations of love, over his gestures, his propositions. Intending a crudely direct course of action and not expecting resistance, he was brought to a standstill. At first I might have thought she was simply flirting—"the flirtation of a depraved but witty creature wishing to show herself in the best light." But no, the truth shone like the sun, and it was impossible to doubt. Out of an affected and erratic hatred of me, she, inexperienced as she was, could have decided on this tryst, but when it came down to brass tacks, she immediately grasped what was what. She was just a person desperately searching to humiliate me in any way possible, but, she was having decided on the vile step unable to bear the impropriety. And Efimovich, or anyone you like of those high society types, could hardly seduce someone of her sort, sinless and pure, idealistic. On the contrary, he could only provoke her laughter. The whole truth rose up from her soul, and indignation elicited sarcasm from the depths of her being. I repeat, in the end this buffoon was completely dumbfounded and sat frowning, hardly answering, so that I actually became concerned he would risk insulting her out of a base desire for revenge. And I again repeat, to my credit, that I heard out the entire scene without any surprise. It is as if I had only encountered the familiar. And that I had gone there expressly to encounter it. I went there not believing anything, any of the accusations, although I did take the revolver in my pocket—such is the truth! And could I have imagined her otherwise? Why then did I love her? Why did I esteem her? Why did I marry her? Oh, of course, I became all too certain how much she despised me then, but I also became certain of how pure she was. I put an end to the scene suddenly by opening the door. Efimovich jumped up, and I took her by the arm and invited her to leave with me. Efimovich gathered his wits and suddenly rang out in prolonged laughter.

"Oh, I have nothing against the holy bonds of matrimony, take her away, take her away! And you know," he shouted after me, "although a decent person really shouldn't duel with you, I am at your service, out of respect for your lady . . . If you yourself, that is, are willing to take the risk . . ."

"Do you hear that!" I stopped her for a second on the threshold.

Then not a word all the way home. I led her by the arm and she did not resist. On the contrary, she was completely overwhelmed, but only up to the house. Arriving home she sat down in a chair and fixed her gaze on me. She was extremely pale; although her lips immediately curled into a mocking smile, she now had a solemn and stern challenge in her glance, and she seemed seriously convinced in the first moments that I was going to kill her with the revolver. But without saying anything I took out the revolver and put it on the table. She looked at me and at the revolver. (Note, the revolver was familiar to her. I had had it and kept it loaded from the very opening of the pawnshop. When I opened the pawnshop I had decided against maintaining huge dogs, or a strong servant, as Mozer did, for instance. My customers are received by the cook. But those in our profession cannot neglect their self-defense just in case, so I elected to keep the revolver. During her first days in my home she had been very interested in the revolver and asked me about it; moreover, I explained to her how it worked and even persuaded her once to fire at a target. Note all that.) Without paying attention to her frightened expression, I lay down half-dressed on the bed. I was totally exhausted; it was about eleven o'clock. She remained sitting without moving in the same spot for an hour or so, then she doused the candle and lay down, also dressed, on the sofa next to the wall. For the first time she did not lie down next to me. Note that too . . .

6

A Terrible Recollection

Now this terrible recollection . . .

I woke up in the morning, I think at eight, and the room was almost entirely light. I awoke immediately to full consciousness and suddenly opened my eyes. She was standing at the table and holding the revolver in her hands. She did not see I was awake and that I was looking. Suddenly I saw her begin moving toward me with the revolver in her hands. I quickly closed my eyes and pretended to be soundly asleep.

She came up to the bed and stood over me. I heard everything; although the silence was deadly, I heard this silence. Then there was a convulsive movement, and unable to stop myself I suddenly, unwillingly, opened my eyes. She was looking at me straight in the eye, and the revolver was already at my temple. Our eyes met. But we looked at each other for not more than a split-second. I forced myself to close my eyes and decided that instant with all the strength I had not to stir again and not to open my eyes, no matter what awaited me.

It really happens that a person in deep sleep will suddenly open his eyes, even raise his head for a second and look around, then immediately without regaining consciousness put his head down on the pillow and fall asleep without remembering anything.

When I met her glance and felt the revolver next to my temple and then without moving suddenly closed my eyes as if in deep sleep, she definitely could have assumed I was in fact asleep and did not see anything, particularly since it is highly unlikely that seeing what I saw one would close one's eyes at *such* a moment.

Yes, it is unlikely. But she still could have guessed the truth—that is what suddenly flashed through my mind, all in the same moment. Oh, what a swirl of thoughts and feelings passed in less than an instant through my mind, and hail the electricity of human thought! In the case (I felt) that she had guessed the truth and knew I was not asleep, then I had already crushed her with my readiness to die and her hand might tremble. An initial resolve could be smashed by a new extreme impression. It's said those standing at an extreme height are themselves seemingly drawn to the edge, into the abyss. I think many suicides and murders are committed only because the revolver was already picked up. This is also the abyss, an incline of forty-five degrees down which one must slide, and something beyond resistance calls out for you to pull the trigger. But the awareness that I saw everything, knew everything, and waited silently for death by her hand could have stopped her on the edge.

The silence continued and suddenly I felt the cold touch of iron at my temple, next to my hair. You ask, did I have firm hopes of surviving? I will tell you as if before God: I had no hope whatsoever, except perhaps one chance out of a hundred. So why was I ready to die? And I will ask in turn: What did I have to live for after I had a revolver pointed at me by the person I worshiped? Moreover, I knew with all the power of my being that at that very moment the two of us were engaged in a battle, a terrible duel of life and death, a duel by that same coward of yesterday thrown out for cowardice by his friends. I knew, and she knew, if she had indeed guessed the truth that I was not asleep.

Perhaps nothing of the sort happened, perhaps I did not have those thoughts then, but it certainly must have happened, even without thought, because all I have done since, each and every hour of my life, has been to think about it.

But you will ask yet another question: Why did I not save her from committing an evil act? Oh, afterward I asked myself that question a thousand times—each time feeling a cold shiver run down my spine when I remembered that moment. But my soul then was in dark despair: I was perishing, I myself was perishing, so how could I save anyone else? And how do you know whether I wanted to save anyone then? How can one tell what I may have felt then?

My mind, however, worked at a feverish pitch; the seconds passed in dead silence, she still stood over me, and suddenly I quivered with hope. I quickly opened my eyes. She was no longer in the room. I got up from the bed; I had won—and she was beaten for life!

I went out to the samovar. In our home the samovar was always served in the first room, and she always poured the tea. I sat down at the table and silently accepted a cup of tea from her. After five minutes or so I glanced at her. She was extremely pale, even paler than yesterday, and she was look-ing at me. And suddenly—suddenly, seeing I was looking at her she smiled in a pale way, with pale lips, with a timid question in her eyes. "So she still doubts and is asking herself: Does he know or doesn't he? Did he see or didn't he?" With indifference I looked away. After tea I locked up the cashbox, went to the market, and bought an iron bed and a screen. After returning home I ordered the bed to be placed in the living room and to be partitioned off with the screen. The bed was for her, but I did not say a word. And without a word being said she understood, thanks to the bed, that I "saw everything and knew everything" and that there no longer could be any doubt. I left the revolver on the table overnight as usual. In the evening she silently went to her new bed; the marriage was dissolved: "She was beaten but not forgiven." During the night she be-came delirious, and in the morning she had a fever. She stayed in bed for six weeks.

CHAPTER TWO

1

A Dream of Pride

Lukerya has just announced she will not live with me and will leave as soon as the mistress is buried. I prayed on my knees for five minutes, although I intended to pray for an hour, but I kept on thinking, thinking, and the thoughts were all painful, and my head ached. What prayer could there be? Only sin! It's strange also I do not want to sleep; during intense grief, after the first powerful moments of trauma, one always wants to sleep. Those condemned to execution, it's said, fall into an exceptionally deep sleep the last night. And that's how it should be, nature takes its course, otherwise we could not bear it . . . I lay down on the sofa but did not fall asleep . . .

. . . For the six weeks of her illness we looked after her day and night—myself, Lukerya, and a trained nurse I hired from the hospital. I did not begrudge the money, I actually wanted to spend it on her. I called a doctor, Shreder, and paid him ten rubles a visit. When she regained consciousness I began to stay out of sight more. But what am I describing, after all? When she was on her feet again, she quietly and silently sat down in my room at a special table that I had also bought for her then . . . Yes, it is true, we were absolutely silent; that is, we began to speak afterward, but only the usual. I was reserved on purpose, of course, but I clearly noted she seemed glad also not to utter an extra word. This seemed to me entirely natural on her part. "She is too shaken and too beaten," I thought, "and of course she should be allowed to forget and to get used to it." So we kept silent, but every minute I was preparing myself inwardly for the future. I thought she was, too, and I found it quite engrossing to guess what exactly she was now thinking to herself.

I will say also: Oh, of course, no one can grasp what I went through moaning over her sickbed. But I moaned inwardly, and I stifled my moans in my chest, hidden even from Lukerya. I could not imagine, even suppose, she would die and not find out everything. When she was out of danger and began to recover her health, I remember, I quickly stopped worrying altogether. Moreover, I decided to *postpone our future* as long as possible and to leave everything in its present form. Yes, something strange and exceptional happened to me then, there is no other way to describe it: I had triumphed and the awareness of that alone satisfied me completely. And that is how the entire winter passed. Oh, I was content as never before, and for the entire winter.

You see, in my life there was one horrible external circumstance, which up until then, that is, right up until the catastrophe with my wife, was a burden I carried every day and every hour, namely, the loss of my reputation and that separation from the regiment. In brief, I was subjected to a tyrannical injustice. It is true my friends did not like me for my difficult character, and perhaps for my comical character, although does it not often happen that what is exalted for you, what you respect and consider to be sacred, for some reason at the same time is comical to a horde of your friends? Oh, I was never liked even in school. I was never liked anywhere. Even Lukerya cannot like me. The incident in the regiment, however, although it was elicited by dislike for me, undoubtedly happened by chance. I'm saying this because there is nothing more galling and unbearable than to perish from a chance incident that did not have to happen, from an unfortunate set of circumstances that could have passed by like clouds. For an intelligent being it is humiliating. The incident happened as follows.

During an intermission in the theater I went out to the buffet. Hussar A-v came in abruptly and in front of all the officers and spectators present loudly began telling two of his fellow hussars that a captain of our regiment, Bezumtsev, had just caused a scandal "and was, apparently, drunk." The conversation did not proceed any further, and there was a mistake, moreover, since Captain Bezumtsev was not drunk, and the scandal was not really a scandal. The hussars began speaking about something else and that ended it, but the following day the story reached our regiment and immediately people began saying I was the only one present in the buffet from our regiment and that when Hussar A-v had made insulting remarks about Captain Bezumtsev I did not go up to A-v and stop him. But what possible reason was there to do so? If he had something against Bezumtsev then it was their personal matter and why should I have interfered? The officers, on the other hand, concluded that the matter was not personal but concerned the regiment and that since I was the only officer present from our regiment it thus showed to all the officers and members of the public in the buffet that there were officers of our regiment who were not very concerned about their honor or the regiment's honor. I could not agree with such a conclusion. I was told I could still put matters right even at this late date if I would see fit to seek formal satisfaction from A-v. I did not see fit, and since I was irritated proudly refused. Then I immediately resigned my commission—and that is the entire story. I left proud but spiritually shattered. My will and mind collapsed. Right at that time my sister's husband in Moscow squandered our small fortune, including my share of it, a very small share, but I was left on the street without a kopek. I could have taken a job but I did not; after a glittering uniform I could not go to work somewhere on the railroad. So if it was to be shame, then shame, if disgrace then disgrace, if degradation then degradation, and the worse the better—that is what I chose. Then three years of grim recollections and even Vyazemsky House. A year and a half ago a rich old woman, my godmother, died and unexpectedly left me, among others, three thousand in her will. I thought about it and right then decided my destiny. I decided on the pawnshop, without apologies: money, then my own small place, and a new life far from former memories—that was the plan. Nevertheless, the dismal past and my reputation, ruined forever, tormented me every hour, every minute of the day. But then I got married. Whether it was by chance or not, I do not know. But in bringing her into my home I thought I was bringing a friend, my need for a friend was so great. But I clearly saw the friend had to be prepared, supplemented, and even conquered. And could I explain anything immediately to this sixteen-year-old girl with preconceptions? For instance, if the terrible catastrophe with the revolver had not accidentally come to my aid, how could I have convinced her I was not a coward and that I had been unjustly accused of being a coward in the regiment? But the catastrophe came at a good time. By enduring the revolver I took revenge on my entire dismal past. And although no one knew, *she* knew, and that meant everything to me, because she herself was everything, the one hope of my dreams for the future! She was the one person I was preparing for myself, and I needed no other—and then she found out everything; she found out, at least, that she was unjustly hasty in siding with my enemies. I was enraptured by that idea. In her eyes I could no longer be a scoundrel, only a strange person, but now, after everything that had happened, that idea did not displease me either. Being strange is not a sin; on the contrary, it sometimes is attractive to the feminine character. In a word, I deliberately put off the dénouement; what had happened was more than adequate for my piece of mind, and it provided more than enough images and subjects for my daydreams. That's the beastly thing, that I am a daydreamer; for me there were ample subjects for daydreaming and about her I thought: *She can wait.*

The entire winter passed in that way, in expectation of something. I loved to watch her surreptitiously when she sat at her table. She occupied herself with work, the linen, and sometimes in the evening read books, which she took from my cabinet. The book collection in the cabinet must have also been in my favor. She scarcely went out anywhere. Before nightfall, after dinner, I would take her out for a stroll, and we would have our exercise, but not in silence as before. I specifically attempted to pretend we were not silent and were compatible in our conversations, but as I have already said, we both avoided speaking at length. I did it deliberately, and she, I thought, "needed time." Of course, it is strange I did not once until winter's end notice that here I was enjoying looking at her surreptitiously and that I did not once during the entire winter catch her return glance directed at me! I thought it was her timidity. Moreover, she seemed so timidly meek, so helpless after her illness. No, better wait, and "she suddenly will come to you herself."

I was completely enthralled by that thought. I will only add, at times I seemed to incite myself deliberately, and I would actually provoke my mind and spirit to the extent of feeling an apparent offense from her. And so it would continue for some time. But my malice could never mature and take hold in my soul. And I myself felt that it was only something of a game. And even then, although I dissolved the marriage by buying the bed and screen, I could never, never think of her as a woman who transgressed. And this was not because I thought her transgression to be unimportant but because I had intended to forgive her completely from the very first day, even before I bought the bed. In short, for me this was strange, for I am morally strict. On the contrary, in my eyes she was so beaten, so humiliated, so crushed, that I felt agonizing pity for her, although there's no question in spite of all this that I sometimes liked the thought of her humiliation. I liked the thought of our inequality . . .

By chance I had the occasion that winter deliberately to perform several good deeds. I forgave two debts, and I gave money to a poor woman without any security. I did not tell my wife about it, and I did not do it at all in order for her to find out, but as it so happened the woman herself came to express her gratitude almost on her knees. So it became known; it seemed to me she was indeed pleased when she found out about the woman.

But spring was on the way, it was already the middle of April, the double windows were taken out, and the sun began lighting up our silent rooms with bright rays. A veil covered my eyes, however, and blinded my thinking. A fatal, terrible veil! How did it happen that everything suddenly cleared from my eyes and I suddenly saw and understood everything? Was it by chance? Had the right day come, or did the sun's rays bring to light ideas and answers in my dulled mind? No, this was neither ideas nor answers, but a tiny nerve that burst into action, a once dead nerve that quivered, came to life, and lit up the whole of my torpid soul and my hellish pride. I then seemed to jump suddenly. And it happened suddenly and unexpectedly. It happened before evening, at about five, after dinner.

2

The Veil Suddenly Falls

First two words. During the previous month I had already noticed a strange state of meditation in her, not really silence, but actually meditation. I also noticed that all of a sudden. She then was sitting at her work, head bent over her sewing, and she did not see me looking at her. And I was abruptly struck by how slim, how thin, she had become, how pale her face was and how white her lips—the overall impression of her combined with her pensiveness was abrupt and very strong. Earlier I had heard a small dry cough, at night especially. I got up immediately and went to call Shreder, without saying anything to her. Shreder came the next day. She was very surprised and stared at Shreder and me in turn.

"But I am not sick," she said, vaguely smiling.

Shreder did not give her a thorough examination (these medical people are sometimes aloof and careless) and only told me in the other room that this was an after-effect of the illness and that it would not be a bad idea once spring came to take a trip to the sea, or if that was impossible then simply to move to a summer cottage. In other words, he did not say anything except that she was weak or something or other. When Shreder left she suddenly said again, looking at me very seriously:

"I am completely, completely healthy."

But having said it she suddenly blushed, apparently out of embarrassment.

It seemed to be embarrassment. Oh, now I understand: She was embarrassed that I was still *her husband,* that I was worrying about her, as if I were still her real husband. But I did not understand then and attributed her blushes to humility (the veil!).

And so, a month later at five o'clock, in April, on a bright sunny day, I was sitting at the cashbox and tallying accounts. Suddenly, I heard her, working in our room at her table, softly, softly . . . begin singing. This novel occurrence exceedingly amazed me, and I still do not understand it. Up until then I had never heard her sing, only perhaps during the very first days when I brought her home and when we could still play around shooting the revolver at the target. At that time her voice was still rather strong and resonant, although not accurately pitched, but awfully pleasant and healthy. Now her song was so weak—oh, not to say melancholy (it was some romance), but it was as if there were something cracked in her voice, broken, as if her little voice could not manage, as if the song itself were sickly. She sang at half-voice, and suddenly rising up the voice broke—such a poor little voice, it broke so pathetically. She coughed and again, softly, softly, and little by little began singing . . .

My agitation might seem comical, but no one will ever understand the reason for my agitation! No, I was not sorry for her still, but it was something totally different. At first, at least in the first minutes, I felt perplexed and horribly surprised, horribly and strangely, in an unhealthy and almost spiteful way: "She's singing, and in my presence! *Has she forgotten about me? Is that it?*"

Shaken to the core, I remained in place then suddenly got up, took my hat, and went out, apparently without thinking. At the very least I do not know why or where. Lukeriya started to hand me my coat.

"She sings?" I involuntarily asked Lukerya. She did not understand me and continued looking at me without comprehension; I was, it's true, really incomprehensible.

"Is that the first time she's been singing?"

"No. When you're not here she sometimes sings," answered Lukerya.

I remember everything. I went down the stairs, went out on the street, and walked off aimlessly. I walked to the corner and began looking at something. Pedestrians passed me, I was shoved and did not feel anything. I hailed a cabby and asked to be taken to the Police Bridge, I do not know why.[5] Then I suddenly got out and gave him twenty kopeks.

"That's for the bother," I said laughing senselessly, but in my heart I began to feel some kind of rapture.

I turned for home, quickening my steps. The cracked, pitiful, broken note suddenly resounded in my soul again. I could hardly breathe. The veil was coming down, it was coming down! Since she began singing when I was there that meant she had forgotten about me—that was clear and frightening. I felt this in my soul. But rapture was strong in my heart, and it was overcoming the fear.

Oh, the irony of fate! There was nothing and there could not have been anything in my heart all winter, after all, except for this very rapture, but where was I myself the entire winter? Was I with my heart? I ran up the stairs in a great hurry. I do not know whether I went in timidly. I only remember that the entire floor seemed to stir and I seemed to flow on a river. I went into the room. She was sitting in her former place, sewing, head bent but no longer singing. She threw me a glance without any curiosity, but it was not a glance but more like a habitual and indifferent gesture when someone enters the room.

I went up directly and sat down next to her in a chair, close, like a madman. She quickly looked at me, as if in fright. I took her by the hand and I do not remember what I said to her, or rather what I wanted to say to her, because I could not say anything properly. My voice broke and I could not control it. And I really did not know what to say and could only catch my breath.

"Let's talk . . . you know . . . tell me something!" I suddenly blurted out some nonsense. Oh, but was it a time for being reasonable? She again trembled and moved back in fright, looking at my face, but suddenly—a *stern wonderment* was expressed in her eyes. Yes, wonderment, and *stern*. She looked at me with large eyes. This sternness, this stern wonderment totally shattered me: "So you also want love? Love?" she seemed to ask in this wonderment, although she was silent. But I understood everything, everything. I was totally overcome and right there I fell to her feet. Yes, I dropped to her feet. She quickly jumped up, but with extraordinary strength I held her back by both hands. And I totally understand my despair, oh, I understand! But believe it or not, the rapture overflowed in my heart to such an extent I thought I would die. I kissed her feet in ecstasy and happiness. Yes, happiness beyond measure and infinite, and this in full awareness of my inescapable despair! I cried, said something, but could not say anything. Her fright and surprise suddenly changed to some worrisome thought, some urgent question, and she looked at me strangely, wildly even, she wanted to understand something quickly, and smiled. She was very embarrassed I was kissing her feet and she snatched them away, but I immediately kissed the floor where her foot had stood. She saw this and abruptly began laughing out of embarrassment (you know when people laugh out of embarrassment). Then she became hysterical, I saw it, her arms quivered—I paid no attention and continued mumbling to her that I loved her, that I would not

get up. "Let me kiss your dress . . . let me worship you like this all my life . . . "
I don't know, I don't remember—and suddenly she burst into tears and
began shaking all over; she had a terrible fit of hysterics. I frightened her.

I carried her to the bed. Sitting up in the bed and looking very downcast
when the seizure passed, she grabbed my hands and asked me to calm
down. "That's enough. Do not torture yourself. Calm down!" And again she
began to cry. That whole evening I stayed at her side. I kept on telling her I
would take her to Boulogne to bathe in the sea, now, immediately, in two
weeks, that she had such a cracked little voice, I just heard it; that I would
close the pawnshop, sell it to Dobronravov; that a new life would begin, and
that especially to Boulogne, to Boulogne! She listened and continued to be
frightened. She became more and more frightened. But what mattered most
to me was not that, but my desire, more and more uncontrollable, to lie at
her feet again, and again to kiss, kiss the ground on which her feet stood,
and to pray to her, and I kept repeating over and over, "I will not ask
anything, anything else of you, do not answer me at all, do not take any
notice of me, only let me look at you from the side, turn me into your thing,
your dog . . . " She cried.

"And I thought you would leave me that way," suddenly she blurted out
involuntarily, so involuntarily that she perhaps did not notice at all how she
said it, although—oh, these were the most important, the most fateful and to
me the clearest words she spoke that entire night, and it was as if they drove
a knife into my heart! She explained everything to me, everything, but
while she was next to me, before my eyes, I had irresistible hopes and was
immensely happy. Oh, I completely tired her out that evening, and I understood it, but I kept on thinking I would now change everything! Finally,
toward night, she grew very weak, I persuaded her to sleep, and immediately she fell into a deep sleep. I expected delirium, there was delirium
but only very slight. During the night almost every minute I got up and
softly in slippers came to look at her. Looking at this pale being I wrung my
hands over her as she lay on the poor cot, the little iron bed I had bought for
her then for three rubles. I kneeled, but since she was sleeping I did not dare
kiss her feet (against her will!). I would begin praying to God, but would
jump up again. Lukerya kept looking in from the kitchen. I went out to her
and told her to lie down and that tomorrow "would be totally different."

And blindly, mindlessly, completely I believed it. Oh, rapture, rapture
overwhelmed me! I only waited for tomorrow. Most of all, I did not believe
anything could go wrong, in spite of all the signs. Sense had not yet
returned entirely, in spite of the fallen veil, and would not for a long, long
time—oh, until today, until this very day! And how could it then: she was,
after all, still alive then, she was right in front of me, and I in front of her.

"She will wake up tomorrow, and I will tell her all this, and she will understand everything." That is what I thought then, clear and simple, and that was the reason for my rapture! The main point was that trip to Boulogne. For some reason I thought Boulogne was everything, that in Boulogne something definite would be resolved. "To Boulogne, to Boulogne! ... " I waited feverishly for morning.

3

I Understand Too Much

And that, after all, was only a few days ago, five days, only five days, last Tuesday! No, no, if only there were a little more time, if only she had waited for a little while, and—and I would have cleared away the darkness! And did she not calm down? The very next day she listened to me and smiled, in spite of her confusion ... The main point is, all that time, the entire five days, she was confused or embarrassed. She was also frightened, very frightened. I won't argue the point, I will not contradict myself like a lunatic. There was fear, but how could she not be afraid? We had been estranged for so long, after all, had become such strangers to each other, and suddenly all this ... But I did not consider her fear, there was a new dawn! ... It is true, undoubtedly true, that I made a mistake. Perhaps many mistakes. When I got up the next morning (that was Wednesday), even then I suddenly made a mistake: I suddenly made her my friend. I was in too much of a hurry, too much, too much, but a confession was necessary, unavoidable—much more than a confession! I did not even hide what I had hidden from myself all my life. I said directly I had been convinced of her love the entire winter. I explained to her that the pawnshop was only the collapse of my will and mind, my personal idea of self-castigation and self-glorification. I explained to her I really had been cowardly then in the buffet, because of my personality, because of my trepidation; I was overwhelmed by the situation, overwhelmed by the buffet; I was overwhelmed by the idea: How could I suddenly step forward, and would it not look foolish? I was afraid not of the duel but of looking foolish ... And afterward I did not want to admit it and tormented everyone, and tormented her because of it, and married her to torment her for it. In general, I spoke for the most part as if in a fever. She herself took me by the hand and asked me to stop: "You are exaggerating ... you are tormenting yourself." And again the tears would begin, and again new seizures! She kept asking me not to talk about it and not to think back.

I paid no attention to her requests or very little attention: spring,

Boulogne! The sun there, our new sun, that's all I talked about! I closed the pawnshop and turned over the business to Dobronravov. I suddenly suggested to her that everything be given to the poor, except for the original three thousand received from my godmother, which we would use to go to Boulogne and then return and begin a new life of work.[6] So we decided, because she did not say anything ... she only smiled. I think she smiled mostly out of sensitivity, in order not to disappoint me. I did see, after all, that I was a burden for her. Do not think I was so stupid or such an egoist as not to see. I saw everything, everything to the last detail. I saw and understood better than anyone. All my despair was plain to see!

I kept on talking to her about me and about her. And about Lukerya. I told her that I cried ... Oh, but I also changed the subject, I also did all I could to avoid reminders of certain things. And she even came to life, once or twice, I remember, indeed I remember! Why do you say I looked and saw nothing? And only if *this* had not happened, then everything would have been resurrected. She was, after all, telling me three days ago—when we began talking about reading, and about her reading that winter—she was after all telling me and laughing when she remembered that scene between Gil Blas and the Archbishop of Grenada.[7] And with what childlike laughter, delightful, exactly as during her engagement (a moment! a moment!); how happy I was! That part about the Archbishop amazed me a great deal, by the way, for that meant she had found enough peace in her soul and happiness to be able to laugh over a masterpiece when she was sitting that winter. Thus, she was beginning to calm down completely, beginning to believe completely I would leave her *that way*. "I thought you would leave me *that way*," is what she said then on Tuesday! Oh, an adolescent's notion! And after all she believed, she believed everything would indeed remain *that way*: she sitting at her table, I at mine, and both of us like that until sixty. And suddenly—I approached her, a husband, and a husband needs to be loved! Oh, what a misunderstanding, oh, my blindness!

It was also a mistake for me to look at her with such rapture. I should have restrained myself, for the rapture was frightening. But I did restrain myself; I did not kiss her feet again. I did not indicate even once that ... well, that I was a husband. Oh, I did not even think of such a thing, I only prayed! But one could not keep entirely silent, after all, not say anything at all! I suddenly told her I took delight in her conversation and considered her to be incomparably, incomparably more educated and refined than I. She grew very red and in confusion said I was exaggerating. At this point, idiotically, I was unable to restrain myself and told her how delighted I was then standing behind the door, listening to her duel, a duel of innocence with that creature, and how I delighted in her intelligence, her flash of wit, and childlike ingenuousness. She seemed to shudder, murmured again I was exaggerating, and then abruptly her face darkened completely. She covered it with her hands and burst into sobs ... At this point I too broke down: I again threw myself down before her, again I began to kiss her feet, and again it ended in a hysterical fit, as on Tuesday. This was yesterday in the evening, and in the morning ...

In the morning?! Madman! But that morning was today, only a little while ago, a little while!

Listen and try to understand. After all, when we sat down together at the samovar a little while ago (after yesterday's seizure), she herself even struck me by her calm, that's what it was! I, on the other hand, shuddered all night from worry about yesterday's events. But she suddenly came up to me, herself stood in front of me, and crossing her arms (just a little while ago, a little while!) began to tell me that she was a criminal, that she knew this, that her transgression had tortured her all winter, it tortured her now ... that she valued my magnanimity too much ... "I will be your faithful wife, I will respect you ... " At this point I jumped up and like a madman embraced her! I kissed her, kissed her face, on the lips, like a husband, for the first time after a long separation. And why did I go out just a little while ago, only for two hours ... our foreign passports ... Oh, God! If only to return five minutes, five minutes earlier? ... And then that crowd of people at our gate, those stares at me ... Oh, God!

Lukerya says (oh, I'll never let her go now, she knows everything, she was here all winter, she will tell me everything), she says that when I left the house and only some twenty minutes before my return, she suddenly went in to her mistress, into our room to ask something, I do not remember, and saw that her icon (that same icon of the Mother of God) was out standing in front of her on the table, and she seemed to have just been praying in front of it.

"What's the matter, mistress?"

"It's nothing Lukerya, go ... Wait, Lukerya." She walked up to her and kissed her.

"Are you happy, mistress?" Lukerya said.

"Yes, Lukerya."

"The master should have asked your forgiveness long before ... Thank God, you've made up."

"All right, Lukerya," she said. "Go now." And she smiled so, so strangely. So strangely that ten minutes later Lukerya abruptly returned to have a look at her.

"She was standing next to the wall, right next to the window, her arm on the wall and her head pressed to her arm, standing and thinking. And she was in such deep thought standing there that she did not notice me looking at her from the other room. I saw that she seemed to be smiling, standing there thinking and smiling. I looked at her, turned quietly away, and went out thinking to myself, only I suddenly heard her open the window. I immediately went back to say, 'It's cool out, mistress, don't catch a cold,' and suddenly I saw her standing on the windowsill and she was already standing at her full height in the open window, her back to me, holding the icon in her hands. My heart sank right there and I shouted, 'Mistress, mistress!' She heard, made a move as if to turn to me, but didn't and instead took a step forward. She pressed the icon to her chest and threw herself out the window."

I only remember that when I went in through the gate she was still warm. The main point is, they were all staring at me. At first they were shouting and then suddenly they fell silent and everyone stepped back to let me pass and ... and there she was, lying with the icon. I remember, as in total darkness, I silently went up and looked for a long time, and everyone crowded around saying something to me. Lukerya was there, but I did not see her. She says she spoke to me. I only remember that tradesman: he kept yelling to me, "Only a handful of blood came out her mouth, a handful, a handful!" and pointed to the blood there on the stone. I think I touched the blood with my finger, stained it, looked at the finger (that I remember), and he kept on at me: "A handful, a handful!"

"What about a handful?" I howled, they say, with all my might, raised my hands and lunged at him ...

Oh, how strange, how strange! A misunderstanding! How implausible! Impossible!

4

Only Five Minutes Late

Isn't that so? Is this plausible? Can one say it is possible? For what reason, why did this woman die?

Oh, believe me, I understand, but the reason for her death is still an open question. She became frightened of my love, seriously asked herself whether she should accept it or not, and could not endure the question, and died instead. I know, I know, there is no reason to rack one's brains: She made too many promises, she became frightened she could not keep them—that's clear. There are several quite horrible circumstances here.

Because the question is still open: Why did she die? The question is hammering, hammering in my brain. I would have left her *that way,* if she had wanted me to leave her *that way*. She did not believe it, that's what it is! No—no, I'm lying, that's not it at all. It was simply because one had to be honest with me: to love, then love completely, and not how she would have loved the merchant. And since she was too chaste, too pure, to agree to the kind of love necessary for the merchant, she did not want to deceive me. She did not want to deceive with a half-love in the guise of love, or a fourth of love. They are too honest, that's what, ladies and gentlemen! I wanted to infuse breadth of heart then, remember? A strange thought.

It's very curious: Did she respect me? I do not know, did she despise me or not? I do not think she despised me. It's very strange: Why during the entire winter did I never think even once she despised me? I was completely convinced of the opposite, up to that very minute when she looked at me with *stern surprise*. Precisely, *stern*. That's when all at once I understood she despised me. Understood it irrevocably, forever! Ah, she could have, could have despised me for the rest of her life even, but—if only she were alive, alive! Just a short while ago she was still walking, speaking. I cannot understand how she threw herself out of the window! And how could I have known even five minutes before it happened? I called Lukerya. I won't let Lukerya go now for anything in the world, for anything!

Oh, we yet could have come to an understanding. We only became horribly estranged during the winter, but why couldn't we once again grow accustomed to each other? Why, why couldn't we have joined together and begun a new life again? I am generous at heart, she was also—and there's the point of conjunction! Only a few more words, two days, not more, and she would have understood everything.

Most of all, it is such a shame it was all by chance—simple, barbaric, torpid chance. That's such a shame! Just five minutes, I was late by just five minutes! If I had come five minutes earlier, the moment would have passed like a cloud, and it would have never afterward come into her head. It would have ended with her understanding everything. And now again empty rooms, I am again alone. There's the pendulum ticking, it's not involved, it's not sorry for anything. There's no one—that's what's wrong!

I walk up and down, I keep on walking up and down. I know, I know, don't tell me. You think it's funny I complain about chance and the five minutes? But it's self-evident. Only consider: she did not even leave a note as everyone does indicating, so to say, "Do not blame anyone for my death." Could she really not even consider that Lukerya could get into trouble: "You were alone with her and so it was you who pushed her"? At the very least she would have been harassed without any fault of her own if four people outside in the yard and from the windows of the adjacent building had not seen that she stood with the icon in her hands and jumped herself. But that's also by chance, that people were standing there and saw it. No, it was all a split second, only one heedless moment. Suddenness and fantasy! And what if she did pray before the icon? That did not have to mean she was about to die. The entire moment, perhaps, lasted only some ten minutes, the whole decision—exactly when she stood at the wall leaning her head on her arm, smiling. The idea popped into her head, set her mind spinning, and—and she could not resist it.

There is a clear misunderstanding involved, whatever you say. She could still have lived with me. And what if it was anemia? Simply from anemia, from the wasting away of life's energy? She had become tired in the winter, that's what . . .

I was too late!!!

How thin she is in the coffin, how gaunt her small nose! Her eyelashes lie like small arrows. And how she fell—she did not shatter anything, did not break anything! Only that one "handful of blood." A teaspoon, that is. Internal contusions. A strange idea: What if she did not have to be buried? Because if she is taken away, then . . . oh, no, it's almost impossible for her to be taken away! Oh, I know she must be taken away, I am not mad and I am not at all delirious; on the contrary, my mind has never been more lucid. But how can there again be no one in the house, two rooms again, and me alone again with the pawned objects? Delirium, delirium, that's delirium!! I tormented her to the extreme. That's what!

What are your laws to me now! Why do I need your customs, your mores, your life, your government, your faith? Let your judge try me, let them take me to court, to your public court, and I will say I admit to nothing.[8] The judge will cry out, "Be silent, sir!" And I will shout at him, "What power do you think you have now to make me obey? Why did dark ignorance destroy everything most precious? What need now do I have of your laws? I withdrew." Oh, I do not care!

She's blind, blind! She's dead, she does not hear! You don't know what a paradise I would have created for you. Paradise was in my heart. I would have brought it to life around you! So, you would not have loved me—and so, so what? You would have walked down the street with him and laughed and I would have watched from the other side . . . Oh, anything, if only she would once open her eyes! For a moment, for just one moment! She would glance at me just as a while ago when she stood there and swore to be a faithful wife! Oh, she would understand everything in one glance!

Torpidity! Oh, nature! People are alone on earth—that's what's disastrous! "Is there a human being alive in the field?" cries out the Russian knight. I, not a knight, cry out too, and no one answers. They say the sun brings life to the universe. The sun goes up and—look at it, is it not a corpse? Everything is dead, and the dead are everywhere. There are only people, and they are surrounded by silence. That is the world! "People, love one another,"—who said that? Whose commandment is that? The pendulum coldly ticks away, it's horrible. Two in the morning. Her small shoes are next to the bed, as if waiting for her ... No, seriously, when she is taken away tomorrow, what am I to do?

Translation by Nicholas Rzhevsky

Notes to the translation are on page 578.

RESOURCES

Primary Text

Dostoevskii, Fedor M. "Krotkaia. Fantasticheskii rasskaz." *Sobranie sochinenii v desiati tomakh. Proizvedeniia 1873–1880 gg.* Vol. 10. Ed. L.P. Grossman and A.S. Dolinin. Moscow: Khudozhestvennaia literatura, 1958, pp. 378–419.

Dostoevskii, Fedor M. *Polnoe sobranie sochinenii v tridatsati tomakh.* Vol. 24. Ed. G.M. Fridlender et al. Leningrad: Nauka, 1982, pp. 5–35.

Secondary Sources

Literary and Cultural Studies

Belknap, Robert. "Dostoévsky, Fyódor Mikháilovich (1821–1881)." In *Handbook of Russian Literature,* ed. Victor Terras. New Haven: Yale University Press, 1985, pp. 102–8.

———. *The Genesis of the Brothers Karamazov.* Evanston: Northwestern University Press, 1990.

Frank, Joseph. *Dostoevsky: The Miraculous Years. 1865–1871.* Princeton: Princeton University Press, 1995.

Ninov, A.A., ed. *Dostoevskii i teatr. Sbornik statei.* Leningrad: Iskusstvo, 1983.

Novitskaia, E.L., ed. *O Dostoevskom. Tvorchestvo Dostoevskogo v russkoi mysli 1881–1931 godov.* Moscow: Kniga, 1990.

Seduro, Vladimir. *Dostoevsky in Russian and World Theatre.* North Quincy, MA: Christopher, 1977.

Smelianskii, A. *Nashi sobesedniki.* Moscow: Iskusstvo, 1981.

Terras, Victor. *A History of Russian Literature.* New Haven: Yale University Press, 1991, pp. 270–74.

Art

For book illustrations and stage design, see "Dostoevsky and Today's World." *Soviet Literature* 12 (1981): 34–35, 78–79, 112–13, 188–89.

Drama and Theater

Idiot. A. Vasil'ev Theater. Moscow, n.d. Video recording. Distributed by RAES.

Rudnitsky, K.L. *Russian and Soviet Theater: Tradition and the Avant-Garde.* London: Thames and Hudson, 1988, pp. 296–97. Photos of Moscow Art Theater production of *Uncle's Dream.*

————. *Russkoe rezhisserskoe iskusstvo 1908–1917.* Moscow: Nauka, 1990, pp. 296–97.

Music

Prokofiev, Sergei. *Igrok* (The Gambler). Opera in 4 acts. Conductor, G. Rozhdestvenskii. Moscow Radio Choir and Orchestra. Moscow: Melodiia, n.d.

Film

Brat'ia Karamazovy (The Brothers Karamazov). Director, Ivan Pyriev. Cast: Mikhail Ulianov, Kirill Lavrov, Andrei Miagkov. Mosfilm, 1969.
Idiot (The Idiot). Director, Ivan Pyriev. Mosfilm, 1957.
Igrok (The Gambler). Director, Aleksei Batalov. Mosfilm, 1972.
Krotkaia (The Meek Woman). Director, Aleksandr Borisov. Lenfilm, 1961.
Lary, N.M. *Dostoevsky and Soviet Film.* Ithaca: Cornell University Press, 1986.
Nikolai Stavrogin. Director, Iakov Protazanov. Cinematographer, Evgenii Slavinskii. Design, Nikolai Suvorov. 1915.
Prestuplenie i nakazanie (Crime and Punishment). Director, Lev Kulidzhanov. Cinematographer, Viacheslav Shumskii; Music, Mikhail Ziv. Mosfilm, 1970.
Zapikski iz mertvogo doma (The House of the Dead). Director, V. Feodorov. Cinematographer, Vasilii Pronin. Music, V. Kriukov. Mezhrabpromfilm, 1932.

∽Nikolai Leskov∾

Lefty

A *Skaz* about Cross-eyed Lefty from Tula and a Steel Flea[1]

1

When the Emperor Alexander Pavlovich[2] finished attending the Council of Vienna, he decided to take a tour of Europe and to look at the wonders different nations had to show him. He traveled through all the countries, and everywhere, and because of his gentle manner, he always had the most heart-to-heart chats with all sorts of people, everyone had something amazing to show him, and they all wanted to get on his good side. But the Emperor had a Don Cossack with him—Platov[3] his name was—who did not like his taking sides in that fashion, and, being homesick, he kept trying to convince the Emperor to go back to Russia. Whenever Platov noticed the Sovereign getting really interested in something foreign, the rest of the entourage would be silent, but he would say right away, "That's how it is, but things back home are no worse," and somehow he'd divert the Emperor's attention.

The Englishmen knew this, and for the Sovereign's arrival they thought up all kinds of cunning ways of fascinating him with strange-foreign things and of getting his mind off the Russians. In many cases they succeeded, especially at large assemblies where Platov couldn't completely speak in French. But then, he had little interest in such anyway, for he was a married man and thought all French talk to be trifling and not worth the imagination. When the Englishmen started inviting the Sovereign to all their warehouses, arsenals, and soapworks, so as to show their superiority in everything over us and thus to make a name for themselves, Platov said to himself:

"Well, I've had it. I've been patient until now, but no further. Whether I can speak or not, I won't let our people down."

No sooner had he said those words to himself than the Sovereign said to him:

"Here's how it is: Tomorrow you and I are going to look at their arms museum. They've got such examples of natural perfection there," he said, "that once you've seen them you'll stop arguing with the fact that we Russians are good for nothing."

Platov didn't answer the Sovereign, he just lowered his humped nose down into his shaggy cloak. When he got back to his rooms he told his orderly to get him a flask of Caucasian grape vodka from his trunk, swallowed a full glass of it, said his prayers in front of his travel icon, covered himself with his cloak, and started snoring so loud that none of the Englishmen in the whole house could get any sleep.

He thought, "The morning is wiser than the night."

2

The next day the Sovereign and Platov went to the museums. The Sovereign took no other Russians with him because the carriage he had been given was a two-seater.

They came to a huge building with an entrance beyond description, endless corridors, and rooms one after another, and finally, in the middle of the very main hall filled with all sorts of tremendous busts, there was a statue of Apollo Belvedere under a canopy.

The Sovereign kept looking back at Platov to see whether he was amazed and to find out what he was looking at, but Platov walked with his eyes fixed on the floor, as if he didn't see anything; he just kept twisting the end of his mustache into a ring.

The Englishmen immediately started showing them all sorts of marvels and explaining how and what they had adapted for military circumstances. They had naval barometers, camel's hair coats for the infantry, and waterproof cloaks for the cavalry. The Sovereign was glad to see all of this, everything seemed very good to him, while Platov controlled his agitation and pretended that none of it meant anything to him.

The Sovereign said:

"How's it possible? Why are you so indifferent? Isn't there anything here that impresses you?"

And Platov replied:

"I am only impressed that my Cossack boys fought without all this and drove off twelve nations."

The Sovereign said:

"That's unreasonable."

Platov answered:

"Well, I don't know what to attribute it to, but I don't dare argue and I must keep quiet."

The Englishmen, noticing the Sovereign quarreling, right away brought him to the statue of Apollo Belvedere and took a Mortimer rifle out of one of his hands and a pistol from the other.

"This," they said, "is the kind of production we have," and they handed him the rifle.

The Sovereign looked calmly at the Mortimer rifle, because he had similar rifles at Tsarskoye Selo, and then they handed him the pistol and said:

"This is a pistol of an unknown and unsurpassed craftsman. Our admiral pulled it from the belt of a bandit chief in Kandelabria."[4]

The Sovereign took one look and couldn't take his eyes off the pistol. He ooh-ed and ahh-ed at length.

"Ah, ah, ah," he said, "how's it possible? . . . how can one make it so fine!" And he turned to Platov and said to him in Russian:

"Now if I only had one such craftsman in Russia I would be very happy and proud, and I would make that craftsman a nobleman on the spot."

Hearing this, right away Platov put his right hand in the pocket of his wide trousers and pulled out a gunsmith's screwdriver. The Englishmen said: "That doesn't open," but Platov, paying no attention to them, began to pick at the lock. He turned it once, twice—and the gun opened up. Platov showed the Sovereign the trigger, and right on the curve was the Russian inscription: "Ivan Moskvin, Tula-City."

The Englishmen were surprised and said nudging each other:

"Uh oh! That was a mistake!"

And the Sovereign sadly said to Platov:

"Why did you have to embarrass them so much? Now I feel sorry for them. Let's go."

They got back into their two-seater carriage and left. The Sovereign went to a ball that day, and Platov put away an even bigger glass of grape vodka and slept the sound sleep of a Cossack.

He was glad that he had embarrassed the Englishmen and that he had brought attention to the Tula craftsman, but he was annoyed too: Why did the Sovereign have to feel sorry for the Englishmen at such a moment?

"Why did the Sovereign feel so bad?" thought Platov. "I can't understand it at all." Worried by these thoughts, he got up twice, crossed himself, and drank so much vodka he forced himself to fall sound asleep.

At the same time, the Englishmen couldn't sleep either, for they were wound up as well. While the Sovereign was enjoying himself at the ball, they cooked up such a new marvel for him that they completely took away all of Platov's breath.

3

The next day, when Platov came to bid the Emperor good morning, the latter said to him:

"Tell them to get the two-seater ready, and let's go look at their other museums."

Platov even dared to repeat that maybe they'd looked at enough foreign products, and that maybe it would be better to head back home to Russia, but the Sovereign said:

"No, I still want to see some other novelties here. They've been boasting about the first-class sugar they make."

So off they went.

The Englishmen showed everything to the Sovereign, all the different first-class brands they had, and Platov looked and looked and then he suddenly said:

"Can you show us some Molvo Sugar from your factories?"[5]

But the Englishmen didn't know what Molvo was. They whispered and winked at each other and kept repeating: "Molvo, Molvo," but they couldn't understand that it's the kind of sugar we make in Russia, and they had to admit that they had all sorts of sugar, but no "Molvo."

Platov said:

"Well, then, you haven't got anything to brag about. Come visit us and we'll serve you tea with real 'Molvo' from Bobrinsky's Factory."[6]

But the Sovereign tugged at his sleeve and said quietly:

"Please, don't spoil the politics for me."

Then the Englishmen invited the Sovereign to look at their very latest museum, where they had a collection of minerals and Infusoria from all over the world, from the biggest Egyptian pyramid to the skin-infesting flea, which cannot be seen with the naked eye and can bite you between skin and body.

So the Sovereign went there.

They looked at the pyramids and mummies, and when they were on their way out, Platov thought to himself: "Well, thank God everything went all right: there was nothing to impress the Sovereign."

But as soon as they walked into the very last room, they saw English workers standing around, in waistcoats and aprons, holding a tray that had nothing on it.

The Sovereign was very surprised to be given an empty tray.

"What does this mean?" he asked, and the English craftsmen replied:

"This is our humble gift to Your Majesty."

"But what is it?"

"Well," they said, "would you be so kind as to see this little speck?"

The Sovereign looked and saw that there was the tiniest speck of dust lying on the silver tray.

And the workers said:

"If you would, Your Majesty, wet your finger and put it on your palm."

"What am I to do with this speck of dust?"

"It isn't a speck of dust," they answered. "It's a flea."

"Is it alive?"

"No, Sir," they said, "it's not alive. We made it out of pure English steel in the form of a flea, and inside it has a spring and a winding mechanism. Be so kind as to wind it with the key, and it will dance a little right away."

The Sovereign became very curious and asked:

"But where's the key?"

And the Englishmen said:

"The key is here too, right before your eyes."

"Then why can't I see it?" asked the Sovereign.

"Because," they said, "you need a microscope."

They brought a microscope, and the Sovereign saw that there really was a key lying next to the flea on the tray.

"Be so kind as to take it in your hand," they said. "It has a hole for winding in its belly, and the key will take seven turns. Then it will dance . . . "

With great difficulty, the Sovereign grabbed hold of the key and could barely hold it in his fingers. With his other hand he picked up the flea and as soon as he put in the key, he felt it move its whiskers. Then it started to shuffle its feet, and at last it jumped suddenly and flying around danced two variations to one side, then to the other, and altogether, in three variations, it danced a whole quadrille.

The Sovereign immediately ordered that a million be given to the Englishmen in any kind of money they themselves liked—in silver or small bills, whatever they wished.

The Englishmen asked to be paid in silver because they didn't trust paper money, and then they pulled another one of their tricks: they made a present of the flea, but they didn't bring a case for it. Without a case, you couldn't hold onto either the flea or its key, because they would get lost and be thrown out with the garbage. The case was made out of a solid diamond nut with a place for the flea carved out in the middle. They would not bring the case, however, because they said it belonged to the government, and in matters of government property, they said, they were very strict, and they couldn't give it away, even to the Emperor.

Platov was about to lose his temper, and he said:

"Why all this swindling! They made a present and got a million for it, and it still isn't enough?! The case," he said, "always comes with everything."

But the Sovereign said:

"Leave it alone, please; it's not your business and don't spoil the politics for me. They have their own customs." And he asked, "How much does that nut for the flea cost?"

So, the Englishmen asked another five thousand for it.

The Sovereign Alexander Pavlovich said, "Pay them," and put the flea in the nut himself, and the little key along with it, and so as not to lose the nut he put it into his gold snuffbox, and he ordered that the snuffbox be put in his small traveling jewel box, all inlaid with mother-of-pearl and whalebone. The Sovereign dismissed the English craftsmen with honor and said to them, "You are the best craftsmen in the whole world, and my people cannot do anything comparable to your work."

They were very pleased with this, and Platov could say nothing to contradict the Sovereign's words. Only he took the microscope and, without saying a word, put it in his pocket, because "it belongs with this stuff," he said, "and you've taken a lot of money from us anyway."

The Sovereign knew nothing about this until he returned to Russia. They left soon because military affairs had made the Sovereign very melancholy and he decided to go to Father Fedot in Taganrog to have a spiritual confession.[7] There was little pleasant conversation between them during the trip because the thoughts that occupied them were too opposite: the Sovereign thought that nobody could equal the English in their craftsmanship, and Platov insisted that our people too could make anything they laid their eyes on, except they didn't have a useful education. He pointed out to the Sovereign that English craftsmen have completely different rules for life, science, and the food rations, and each person among them has all the absolute conditions available to himself, and for that reason the sense in him is totally different.

The Sovereign did not want to listen to that for long, and Platov, realizing it, did not press him. So they rode in silence, only Platov would get out at every station and in frustration would drink a cider glass of vodka, chase it down with a salty bagel, light up his briar pipe, which held a whole pound of Zhukov tobacco, and then get back in the carriage and sit there beside the Tsar in silence. The Sovereign would look in one direction and Platov would stick his pipe out the opposite window and puff into the wind. In this way,

they reached St. Petersburg, and when the Sovereign went to see Father
Fedot, he did not take Platov at all.

"You," he said, "are too intemperate for spiritual conversation, and you
smoke so much that my head is full of soot from your pipe."

Platov stayed home on his couch, offended, and so he lay smoking
Zhukov tobacco without stop.

4

The amazing flea of English blue steel remained in Alexander Pavlovich's
whalebone jewel box until he passed away in Taganrog, after giving it to
Father Fedot to pass on to the Empress when she had sufficiently calmed
down. The Empress Elizaveta Alekseevna looked at the flea's variations
and smiled, but she didn't spend any time with it.

"My affairs now," she said, "are those of a widow, and no amusement
can tempt me." When she returned to St. Petersburg she handed over this
curiosity with all the other valuables to be included in the new sovereign's
inheritance.

The Emperor Nikolai Pavlovich at first paid no attention to the flea
either, for when he took the throne there was an uprising,[8] but later one day
he began looking through the little jewel box he inherited from his brother,
and he pulled out the snuffbox, and out of the snuffbox came the diamond
nut, and in it he found the steel flea, which had not been wound up for a
long time and therefore was not moving but lay there at attention, as still as
if it were numb.

The Sovereign took a look and was very surprised.

"What is this trifle, and why did my brother put it in such safekeeping!"

The courtiers wanted to throw it out, but the Sovereign said:

"No, it must mean something."

They called a chemist from the pharmacy opposite Anichkin Bridge,
who weighed poisons on the most precise scales, and they showed him the
flea, and he immediately took the flea and put it on his tongue and said, "I
feel something cold, like hard metal." Then he squished it lightly with his
teeth and announced:

"Whatever you please, but this is not a real flea, it's an Infusoria, and it's
made of metal, and the work is not ours, not Russian."

The Sovereign ordered immediately that inquiries be made where it came
from and what it meant.

They rushed to look through files and records, but there was no mention
of it there. They began asking one person after another, but nobody knew

anything about it. Fortunately, the Don Cossack Platov was still alive and, as a matter of fact, was still sulking on his couch and smoking his pipe. As soon as he heard about the commotion in the palace, he rose from his couch, threw down his pipe, and in all his decorations appeared before the Sovereign.

The Sovereign said:

"What do you want of me, courageous old man?"

And Platov replied:

"I don't want anything for myself, Your Majesty, for I eat and drink all I want and I'm happy with everything. But I've come here," he said, "to report about that Infusoria that's been found. This is the way it was," he said, "and this is how it happened right before my eyes in England. There's a little key next to it, and I have their own microscope, which can help you see it, and with that little key you can wind it up through its little belly, and then it will jump around in any space you like and do variations to all sides."

So they wound it up and it began to jump, and Platov said:

"It's true," he said, "Your Majesty, that the work is very fine and interesting, but we shouldn't only marvel over it with delight. It should undergo Russian inspection in Tula or Sesterbek (Sestroretsk was still called Sesterbek back then), to see whether our craftsmen couldn't do better, so that the English wouldn't be superior to the Russians."

The Sovereign Nikolai Pavlovich had great confidence in his Russian people and didn't like to yield to any foreigner, so he replied to Platov:

"You've said it well, courageous old man, and I entrust the proof of the matter to you. I don't need this box now anyway with all I have to do, and I want you to take it with you and forget about sulking on your couch. Instead, go down to the quiet Don and have a heart-to-heart talk with my Cossack boys about their life and loyalty and what they prefer. And when you pass through Tula, show this Infusoria to my Tula craftsmen and let them ponder it. Tell them from me that my brother marveled at this thing and highly praised the foreign craftsmen who made this Infusoria, but that I have faith in my own people and believe that they are no worse than anybody. They won't disregard my words and they'll do something about it."

5

Platov took the steel flea, and as he passed through Tula on his way to the Don he showed it to the Tula gunsmiths, passed the Sovereign's words on to them, and then asked:

"Now what are we going to do about it, Orthodox kinsmen?"

The gunsmiths replied:

"We are honored by the gracious words of our Sovereign, and we'll never forget him because he has confidence in his own people, but we can't tell you right this minute what we should do in the present instance because the English nation isn't stupid either; they're even pretty clever, and their craft makes a lot of sense. To compete with it," they said, "one must think a great deal and ask for God's blessing. And you, sir, if Your Grace trusts us like our Sovereign does, go home to your quiet Don and leave us this little flea as it is, in its case, and in the Tsar's golden snuffbox. Have a good time on the Don, heal the wounds you have suffered for the fatherland, and when you're passing through Tula on your way back, stop here and send for us; by that time, God willing, we'll have thought of something."

Platov wasn't very pleased that the Tulakians wanted so much time and, moreover, that they would not say clearly what exactly they had in mind. He asked them this way and that, and he spoke to them in all sorts of cunning Don Cossack ways, but the Tulakians were no less cunning than he, for they had already thought up such a plan that they did not expect even Platov to believe them, and they wanted to carry out their bold idea right away and only then hand over the flea.

They said:

"We don't yet know ourselves what we're going to do, only we'll put our trust in the Lord and perhaps the Tsar's words won't be put to shame through our doing."

So Platov tried some cunning wriggling, but so did the Tulakians.

Platov wriggled and wriggled until he realized that he could not out-wriggle the people from Tula, and then he gave them the snuffbox with the Infusoria and said:

"Well, there is nothing to be done," he said. "Have it your way. I know the type of people you are, but what can I do? I believe you; but watch out, you'd better not swap diamonds on me, and don't spoil the fine English work, and don't fiddle around too long, because I travel swiftly—in two weeks I'll be on my way back from the quiet Don to St. Petersburg, so make sure I have something to show the Sovereign."

The gunsmiths reassured him completely:

"We won't spoil the fine work," they said, "and we won't swap the diamonds, and two weeks is time enough for us. When you return, there'll be *something* for you to show the Sovereign that will be worthy of His Majesty's greatness."

But *exactly* what that *something* was they still did not say.

6

Platov left Tula, and the gunsmiths' three most talented men—including a cross-eyed lefty with a birthmark on his cheek and hair on his temples that had been pulled during his apprentice years—bade farewell to their friends and families, and without saying anything to anybody took their bags, put what food they needed into them, and disappeared from town.

People only noticed that they didn't leave through the Moscow gate but through the opposite one, in the direction of Kiev, and it was thought that they had gone to Kiev to pray at the tombs of the saints or to seek advice from the holy men still alive there, of whom there was always a great abundance in Kiev.

Although this was close to the truth it was not the whole truth. Neither time nor distance allowed the Tula craftsmen to walk three weeks to Kiev and then have time to make something that would put the English nation to shame. They would have been better off going to pray in Moscow, which was only "twice ninety versts" away and also had not a few saints resting in peace. In the other direction it was "twice ninety versts" to Orel, and from Orel to Kiev was a good five hundred versts more. You could not make a trip like that in a hurry, and if you did, it would take you a while to rest, for your legs would be numb and your hands would shake for a long time.

Some people even thought the craftsmen had gotten carried away bragging to Platov but after thinking it over had lost their nerve and run away, taking with them the Tsar's golden snuffbox, the diamond, and the English steel flea that had caused all the trouble.

However, this assumption was also completely groundless and unworthy of the talented people on whom the hopes of the nation now rested.

7

The Tulakians, who are clever and knowledgeable in the art of metal work, are also well known as primary experts in religion. Their fame in this respect has reached all corners of their native land, and even Holy Mount Athos: not only are they masters at church singing, but they are also expert painters of the picture *Evening Bells,* and if any of them dedicates himself to greater service and joins a monastery, he becomes known as the manager of his cloister, and the most talented collectors of funds come out of their ranks. On Holy Mount Athos, everybody knows Tulakians are the most useful people, and if it were not for them, the dark corners of Russia would probably never have seen many sacred relics from the distant East, and Mount Athos would have been deprived of many useful donations produced by Russian piety and generosity. Today, the "Mount Athos Tulakians" carry holy objects all over our motherland and skillfully collect funds even where there is nothing to collect. The Tula native is full of religious piety and is very practiced in religious matters, and that is why the three craftsmen who took it upon themselves to come to the defense of Platov, and with him all of Russia, made no mistake by going south and not toward Moscow. They were not going toward Kiev at all but toward Mtsensk, the district town of Orel Province, where stands the ancient "stone graven" icon of St. Nikolai, which had come floating down the Zusha River on a huge cross also of stone, in the most ancient times. This "grim and terrifying" icon is a life-size depiction of the Myro-Lycian saint in silver-gilt robes, with a dark face, holding a temple in one hand and the sword "Victory of War" in the other. Victory was the key: St. Nikolai, in general, and "Nikolai of Mtsensk" in particular, is the patron saint of commerce and warfare, so it was to him that the Tulakians had gone to pray. They held a service before the icon itself, then before the stone cross, and finally they returned home at night, and without saying a word to anyone, they began their task in terrible secrecy. All three of them gathered together in Lefty's small house, locked the doors, closed the shutters, lit a lamp before the icon of St. Nikolai, and started to work.

One day, two days, three days they stayed there without going out; they just kept tapping away with their little hammers. They were forging something, but what it was they were forging was completely unknown.

Everybody was curious, but nobody could find out anything, for the workers said nothing and did not show themselves outside the house. Many people came up to the small house and knocked on the door with all sorts of excuses, asking for a light or a pinch of salt, but the three crafty men would not answer under any pretext, and nobody even knew what they had to eat. An attempt was made to scare them by shouting that the house next door was burning; it was hoped they would run out in fright and reveal what they had done, but nothing would trick those crafty craftsmen. Only once Lefty stuck his head out and shouted:

"You can burn all you want, we don't have time!" And he hid his plucked head inside again, closed the shutters, and returned to his work.

Only through small cracks people could see a flickering light and hear small hammers ringing on the anvils.

In other words, the whole business was conducted in such secrecy that it was impossible to find out anything until the return of the Cossack Platov on his way to the Sovereign, and all that time the craftsmen did not see or talk to anyone.

8

Platov traveled in a great hurry and with ceremony. He himself sat in the carriage, and on either side of the coachman sat a Cossack with a whip in his hand, and they pounded the coachman mercilessly so that he would keep driving fast. If either of the Cossacks dozed off, Platov himself would give him a kick from inside the carriage, and the carriage would race forward even more fiercely. Such methods of motivation worked so well that it was impossible to rein in the horses at any station, and they always overshot the hitching post by a hundred paces. Then the Cossacks would work the coachman in the opposite direction, and they would go back to the entrance.

In this way they came rolling into Tula. Here again they first flew a hundred paces past the Moscow stop, and then the Cossacks worked the coachman over with their whips in the other direction, and they came up to the entrance to change horses. Platov did not leave the carriage, but he ordered the Cossacks to bring him, as quickly as possible, the craftsmen with whom he had left the flea.

One of the Cossacks ran off to tell the craftsmen to hurry and deliver the work that was supposed to put the Englishmen to shame, but before he had gone far, Platov sent more Cossacks after him to speed things up.

He sent off all the guardsmen and then started sending simple folks from the curious crowd, and then he himself even put his legs out of the carriage to run there, so impatient was he and gritting his teeth with rage for it seemed to him that they all were taking too long.

That's how quickly and efficiently everything had to be done in those days, so as not to lose a minute that might be useful to Russia.

9

The Tula craftsmen who were making that marvelous piece of work were then just finishing. The Cossacks got to them out of breath, and the simple folks from the curious crowd did not get there at all, for they were not accustomed to such running and their legs gave out, they collapsed on the way, and later on, out of fear of facing Platov, they ran home and hid wherever they could.

As soon as the Cossacks reached the house they gave a shout, and when they saw that no one was opening the door they unceremoniously jerked at the bolts on the shutters, but the bolts were so strong that they would not give at all; then they tried to open the doors, but the doors were fastened from the inside with big oak bars. Then the Cossacks picked up a big log from the street, put it under the eaves of the roof the way firemen do, and in a second pulled the whole roof right off the small house. But as soon as they took off the roof, they themselves collapsed, because the cramped room where the gunsmiths were ceaselessly working was full of such a foul sweaty smell that a man used to fresh air couldn't stand one whiff of it.

The messengers yelled:

"What are you doing, you so-and-so's, you swine! And how dare you knock us over with such a stink! Isn't there any fear of God left in you?"

And the craftsmen replied:

"We're just hammering in the last nail, and as soon as it's in, we'll bring our work out."

And the messengers said:

"He'll eat us alive by then and leave nothing to remember us by."

But the craftsmen replied:

"He won't have time to swallow you because while you were talking we knocked in the last nail. Run and tell him we'll bring it right over."

The Cossacks ran off, but without conviction; they thought the craftsmen might trick them, so they kept looking back as they ran. But the craftsmen were behind them and they were in such a hurry that the clothes they threw on were not quite appropriate for a meeting with an important person, and while they went they hooked up their coats. Two of them were empty-handed, but the third one, Lefty, held the Tsar's jewel box wrapped in a green cover with the English steel flea inside.

10

The Cossacks ran up to Platov and said:

"Here they are themselves!"

Platov turned immediately to the gunsmiths:

"Is it ready?"

"Everything," they replied, "is ready."

"Hand it over."

They handed it over.

The carriage was ready, and the coachman and the postilion were in their places. The Cossacks had taken their seats on either side of the coachman and had raised their whips in readiness over him.

Platov ripped off the green cover, opened the jewel box, took the golden snuffbox out of its cotton padding, and the diamond nut out of the snuffbox. The English flea was lying there as before, but apart from that there was nothing else.

Platov said:

"What is the meaning of this? Where's the work with which you were going to please the Sovereign?"

And the gunsmiths answered:

"Our work is there too."

Platov asked:

"Well, then, would you explain what kind of work it is?"

And the gunsmiths replied:

"What's to explain? It's all there in front of your eyes, take a good look at it."

Platov raised up his shoulders and yelled:

"Where's the key to the flea?"

"Why, it's right here," they answered. "The key's where the flea is, in the same nut."

Platov wanted to take hold of the key, but his fingers were too short and stubby. He tried and tried, but he couldn't grasp either the flea or the key for its stomach mechanics, and he suddenly lost his temper and started cursing in the Cossack manner.

He shouted:

"You villains, you haven't done a thing, and you've probably ruined it to boot! I'll have your heads for this!"

And the Tula craftsmen answered him:

"You shouldn't insult us like that; we have to put up with your insults because you're the Sovereign's messenger, but since you doubted us and thought we were capable of cheating our Sovereign, we won't tell you the secret of our work now; just be so kind as to take it to the Sovereign—he'll see what kind of people he has and whether there is any reason for him to be ashamed of us."

But Platov shouted:

"In case you're lying, you villains, I won't let you off so easy! One of you is coming with me to Petersburg and I'll find out from him there what sort of tricks you've been up to!"

With that, he reached out, grabbed the cross-eyed Lefty by the collar with his short, stubby fingers, so that all the hooks flew off Lefty's coat, and threw him down in the carriage at his feet.

"Sit here like a poodle," he said, "until we get to Petersburg. You'll answer for all of them. And you," he said to the Cossacks, "get a move on!

Don't gawk, I want to be in Petersburg, at the Emperor's, the day after tomorrow."

All the craftsmen dared to do for their comrade was ask Platov why he was taking him away from them without a "doctumint" because he wouldn't be able to get back without one! But Platov showed them his fist instead of an answer—a frightening red fist, all scarred and haphazardly healed—and shaking it at them, he said: "Here's your doctumint!"

And to his Cossacks, he said:

"Let's move it, boys!"

The Cossacks, the coachman, and the horses all started working at once, and they whisked Lefty away without a doctumint, and in a day, as Platov had ordered, they drove up to the Sovereign's palace, and having driven up at a gallop, they actually flew right past the columns.

Platov got out, pinned on his decorations, and went to the Sovereign, telling the Cossacks to watch over Lefty at the palace entrance.

11

Platov was afraid to show his face to the Sovereign, for Nikolai Pavlovich always noticed and remembered and never forgot a thing. Platov knew that he most certainly would ask him about the flea. And although he never feared an enemy in his life, he was so frightened then that after he entered the palace with the jewel box, he quietly placed it behind a stove in one of the rooms. Having hidden the jewel box, Platov appeared before the Sovereign in his study and quickly began his account of what the Cossacks were debating among themselves on the quiet Don. He thought he would thus engage the Sovereign's attention, and then, if the Sovereign himself remembered and started talking about the flea, he would have to give him the jewel box and answer for it, but if the Sovereign didn't mention it, he would keep quiet. He then would tell the valet to hide the jewel box and he'd put Lefty from Tula in a fortress cell indefinitely where he would remain until he might be needed.

But the Sovereign Nikolai Pavlovich did not forget anything, and as soon as Platov had finished reporting on the Cossack debates, he asked him:

"Well, how did my Tula craftsmen prove their worth in regard to the English Infusoria?"

Platov answered the way he saw the matter.

"The Infusoria, Your Majesty," he said, "is the same as it was and I brought it back, and the Tula craftsmen couldn't do anything more wonderful."

The Sovereign replied:

"You are a courageous old man, but what you're telling me cannot be true."

Platov began convincing him and told him how everything had happened, and when he got to the part where the Tula craftsmen asked him to show the flea to the Emperor, Nikolai Pavlovich slapped him on the shoulder and said:

"Bring it. I know that my people wouldn't let me down. There's something incomprehensible here."

12

They brought the jewel box from behind the stove, took off the cloth cover, opened the gold snuffbox and the diamond nut, and there was the flea, lying there just as it had been lying there before.

The Sovereign looked at it and said:

"What the devil?" But his faith in his Russian craftsmen wasn't shaken, and he sent for his favorite daughter, Alexandra Nikolaevna, and commanded her:

"You have slender fingers. Take the little key and quickly wind up the stomach mechanism in the Infusoria."

The princess began to turn the key and the flea immediately started wiggling its whiskers, but its feet didn't move. Alexandra Nikolaevna wound it up as far as it would go, but the Infusoria didn't do its dance or toss off a single variation as before.

Platov turned completely green and roared:

"Oh, those dirty dogs! Now I understand why they didn't want to tell me anything there. It's a good thing I brought one of their fools with me."

With those words he ran out to the entrance, caught Lefty by the hair, and began to yank him back and forth so violently that clumps of his hair started flying all over the place. And when Platov had stopped beating him, Lefty fixed himself up and said:

"My hair was all pulled out during my apprenticeship anyway, but I don't see why I deserve it again."

"I'll tell you why!" said Platov. "It's because I counted on you and I vouched for you, but you ruined a rare object."

Lefty replied:

"We are very grateful that you vouched for us, but as for ruining we didn't ruin anything. Take a look through your most powerful microscope."

Platov ran back to tell them about the microscope, but first threatened Lefty:

"You so-and-so-and-so," he said, "I'll give it to you yet."

He ordered the Cossacks to keep Lefty's arms even tighter behind his back, and he himself went up the steps out of breath and muttering a prayer: "Holy Father's Holy Mother, immaculate and pure," and so on as is proper. The palace inhabitants who were standing on the steps all turned away from him, for they all thought he was in real trouble now and that he'd be thrown out of the palace. They couldn't stand him because he was brave.

13

As soon as Platov conveyed Lefty's words to the Sovereign, the Tsar joyfully said:

"I knew my Russian people wouldn't let me down." And he ordered a microscope to be brought in on a cushion.

The microscope was brought in that very minute, and the Sovereign took the flea and put it under the glass, first on its little belly, then on its little side, then on its little back—in other words, he turned it every way possible, but there was nothing to be seen. Even then, however, the Sovereign did not lose faith but only said:

"Bring me at once that gunsmith that's downstairs."

Platov said:

"He ought to be properly dressed. He's wearing the same clothes he was caught in, and now he looks in an evil state."

But the Sovereign replied:

"That's all right, bring him as he is."

Platov said:

"Now, you so-and-so, go answer before the Sovereign yourself."

And Lefty said:

"So what, then? I'll go and I'll answer."

He went as he was: in his torn boots, with one trouser leg tucked in and the other dangling, wearing an old coat that would not fasten because the hooks were all torn off and with a collar all in shreds, but he was not in the least embarrassed.

"What of it?" he thought. "If the Sovereign wants to see me, I must go, and if I ain't got a doctumint it's not my fault, and I'll tell him how it happened."

As soon as Lefty came in and bowed, the Sovereign said to him:

"What does this mean, brother? We've looked at it this way and that way and put it under the microscope, but we can't find anything remarkable about it."

And Lefty replied:

"Did Your Majesty look at it the right way?"

The noblemen signaled to him to let him know he wasn't talking the right way, but he didn't understand how to talk like a courtier using flattery or cunning, and he continued to talk simply.

The Sovereign said:

"Stop being clever with him. Let him answer the way he knows how."

And then he explained to Lefty:

"We put it this way," he said, and placed the flea under the microscope. "Look for yourself," he said, "you can't see a thing."

Lefty answered:

"That way, Your Majesty, you can't see anything indeed, because our work is much more confidental than that size."

The Sovereign asked:

"Then which way should it go?"

"You have to put only one of its feet in full detail under the microscope," Lefty said, "and look separately at each of the heels it steps on."

"Have mercy," said the Sovereign, "that's really too small!"

"Well, it can't be helped," answered Lefty. "That's the only way to see our work, but then you can see the whole wonder."

So they put it down as Lefty had told them, and as soon as the Sovereign took one look at it through the glass, his face beamed with joy. He grabbed Lefty just as he was, unwashed, unkempt, and dusty, embraced him and kissed him, and then turned to all the courtiers and said:

"You see, I knew better than any of you that my Russians wouldn't let me down. Take a look, if you please: why, the rascals have shod the English flea's feet!"

14

Everybody came up one by one and had a look at the flea: each of the flea's feet had indeed been shod with real shoes, but Lefty said that wasn't the only marvel.

"If you had a better microscope," he said, "one that would blow it up five million times," he said, "you'd see a craftsman's name on each shoe. They carved it there so as to show which Russian craftsman made which shoe."

"Is your name there too?" asked the Sovereign.

"No sir," answered Lefty, "mine's the only one that isn't."

"Why isn't it?"

"Well," he said, "because my work was smaller than those flea shoes. I made the nails to hammer in the shoes. You can't see them with any microscope."

The Sovereign asked:

"But where's your microscope, the one you used to make this marvel?"

And Lefty replied:

"We're poor people and we can't afford a microscope, but our eyes are sharp because they're used to it."

And at that point, seeing that Lefty's affairs had turned out well, the courtiers started to kiss him too, while Platov gave him a hundred rubles and said:

"Forgive me brother, for yanking your hair out."

Lefty replied:

"God will forgive you, it's not the first time that sort of thing has happened to me."

And he said no more, in fact, he did not have time to talk to anyone, for the Sovereign immediately ordered the shod Infusoria to be packed and sent back to England, as sort of a present, to show the Englishmen that it did not impress us. And the Sovereign ordered the flea to be carried by a special courier who knew all languages, and that Lefty should go with him so that he himself could show the Englishmen his work and what kind of craftsmen we have in Tula.

Platov made the sign of the cross over him.

"May God's blessing be with you," he said, "and I'll send you my own grape vodka for the road. Don't drink too little, don't drink too much, drink within reason."

And he did indeed send the vodka.

Count Kiselvrode[9] gave orders to wash Lefty in the Tula Public Baths, cut his hair in a barbershop, and dress him in the full-dress coat of a court chorister, so that it would seem that he had some sort of respectable rank, too.

So they processed him in this fashion, filled him up for the road with tea spiked with Platov's grape vodka, pulled in his belt as tight as possible to keep his intestines from shaking, and sent him off to London. That marked the beginning of Lefty's foreign adventures.

15

The courier and Lefty were traveling very fast, so they didn't stop to rest anywhere between St. Petersburg and London, they just pulled their belts one notch tighter at every station to keep their intestines from getting tangled up with their lungs. But since after his presentation to the Sovereign Lefty, on Platov's orders, was allowed to drink as much vodka as he wanted at the expense of the government, he kept himself going on vodka alone, without any food, and all the way through Europe he sang Russian songs, only adding a foreign refrain:

"*Ai, luli, luli, c'est très joli.*"

As soon as the courier brought him to London, he reported to the proper people to hand over the jewel box, leaving Lefty in a hotel room, but Lefty soon got bored there, and besides, he was hungry. He knocked on the door and pointed to his mouth when the servant came, and the servant at once took him to the room for eating.

Here Lefty sat at the table, but he didn't know how to ask for anything in English. But then he figured it out: he simply would knock his knuckle on the table and point to his mouth, and the Englishmen would guess and bring him food, only not always what was wanted; but he wouldn't eat anything that did not suit him. They brought him their concoction of hot pudding in flames, and he said: "I don't know if this can be eaten," and he wouldn't touch it; so they took it away and brought him something else instead. He wouldn't drink their vodka either, because it was green, as if they had mixed it with copper sulfate, so he chose what was most natural and then waited, cooling off with his flask, for the courier.

Meanwhile, the people to whom the courier handed over the Infusoria immediately looked at it through their most powerful microscope and sent a description right off to the newspapers so that it could be published for everybody's information in the morning papers.

"And we want to see the craftsman himself right away," they said.

The courier took them to the hotel room and from there to the room for eating, where our Lefty had already managed to become quite flushed, and said: "There he is!"

The Englishmen patted Lefty on the shoulder and shook hands with him as an equal. "Comrade," they said, "comrade, you're a good craftsman. We'll talk business with you a little later, but first we want to drink to your well-being."

They ordered a lot of wine and gave Lefty the first glass, but he politely refused to be the first one to drink. "Maybe you want to poison me in your vexation," he thought.

"No," he said, "that's not proper, and there's no proper order in Poland either, so you go first."

The Englishmen tasted each of the different wines before him and then began to fill his glass. He stood up, crossed himself with his left hand, and drank to their health.

They noticed that he crossed himself with his left hand and asked the courier:

"What is he? A Lutheran or a Protestant?"

"No, he's neither a Lutheran nor a Protestant," answered the courier. "He's of the Russian faith."

"Then why does he cross himself with his left hand?"

"He's a lefty and does everything with his left hand."

The Englishmen were even more amazed and began filling Lefty and the courier up with wine, and for three whole days they entertained them this way, and then they said: "Now that's enough." They each drank a bottle of seltzer and, completely refreshed, began to question Lefty. Where and what he had studied, and how far had he gone in arithmetic?

Lefty replied:

"Our studies are simple. We read the Book of Psalms and the Book of Half-Dreams, but we don't know even a little arithmetic."

The Englishmen looked at each other and said:

"That's amazing."

And Lefty answered:

"That's how it is in our country."

"And what is the Russian Book of Half-Dreams?" they asked.

"That," he said, "is the book where you can find some extra explanations to the reading of dreams that King David left unclear in his Book of Psalms."

They said:

"That's a pity. It would've been much better if you knew at least the four rules of addition in arithmetic, that would've been more useful to you than the whole Book of Half-Dreams. Then you would've been able to figure out that every mechanism is calculated to a certain power, for even though you're very skillful with your hands, you didn't figure out that such a small mechanism as the one inside the Infusoria was calculated very precisely and that it can't carry the flea shoes. That's why the Infusoria doesn't jump anymore and does not do its dance."

Lefty agreed.

"There's no argument about that," he said. "We didn't get far in book learning, but we're very loyal to our fatherland."

And the Englishmen said to him:

"Stay here with us. We'll give you a good education, and you'll become a wondrous craftsman."

But to this Lefty would not agree.

"I have parents back home," he said.

The Englishmen offered to send money to his parents, but Lefty would not take it.

"We are devoted to our country," he said, "and my dad is an old man already, and my mother's an old lady, and they're used to going to church in their own parish, and anyway, I'd get bored being here all alone because I'm still of the bachelor calling."

"You'll get used to it," they said. "You'll accept our ways and we'll marry you off."

"That," answered Lefty, "can never be."

"Why not?"

"Because," he said, "our Russian faith is the most righteous one, and as our forefathers believed in it so must their descendants."

"You don't know our faith," said the Englishmen. "We have the same Christian ways and uphold the same Gospel."

"It's true," said Lefty, "that everyone has the same Gospel, but our books are thicker than yours and our faith has more in it."

"What makes you say that?"

"We've got all the obvious proof of it," he answered.

"What sort of proof?"

"Well," he said, "we have icons created by God, and relics of saints, and you ain't got nothing, and except for Sunday alone, you don't even have any extra holidays; and the second reason is that even if I were lawfully wedded to an English girl it would be confusing to live with her."

"Why is that?" they asked. "Don't look down on our girls. Our women, too, dress very neatly and they're good housewives."

And Lefty said:

"I don't know them."

The Englishmen answered:

"That doesn't matter, you'll get to know them: we'll fix up a grandezvous for you."

Lefty started blushing.

"Why bother the girls for nothing?" he said and turned them down. "A grandezvous is for gentlemen and wouldn't suit us, and if they ever found out about it back home in Tula, they'd make me a laughing-stock."

The Englishmen asked, full of curiosity:

"If you don't have grandezvous, then how do you arrange such matters at home to be sure you make a pleasant choice?"

So Lefty explained our way to them.

"In our country," he said, "when a man wants to make his serious intentions about a girl known, he sends a talkative woman, and after she's made a proposal, they politely go together to the girl's house and see her publicly, in front of all her relatives, not in secret."

They understood but replied that they had no talkative women and no such customs, and Lefty said:

"That's all the better then, because if I was to start this sort of business, I'd have to have serious intentions, and since I don't feel that way about a foreign nation, then why bother the girls for nothing?"

The Englishmen were pleased with his reasoning, and they patted him on the shoulders and on the knees again in a friendly manner and asked:

"Just out of curiosity," they said, "we'd like to know one thing. What flaws have you noticed in our girls that make you so anxious to avoid them?"

Here, Lefty was very frank with them and said:

"I don't mean to put them down. I just don't like the way their clothing billows around them somehow, and you can't tell what they've got on and what for. Here she has one thing, and down below she has something else pinned on, and on her hands she has some sort of stockings. And with those velveteen cloaks on they just look like sapajou monkeys."

The Englishmen laughed and said:

"Why is that such an obstacle for you?"

"It's no obstacle," he replied. "I'm just afraid I'd be ashamed watching her and waiting for her to get out of all that stuff."

"Are your fashions really any better?" they said.

"Our fashions in Tula are simple," he replied. "Each girl wears her own lace, and even fine ladies wear our lace."

They introduced him to their own ladies, and there they served him tea and asked him:

"Why are you puckering your face?"

He answered, "We're not used to drinking it so sweet."

Then they served it to him the Russian way, with lumps of sugar on the side.

They thought that would be worse, but he said:

"To our taste, this way is tastier."

The Englishmen could not do anything to make him like their way of life. They could only convince him to stay for a short while as their guest and said they would take him to all kinds of factories during that time and show him all their craftsmanship.

"And then," they said, "we'll take him in one of our own ships and bring him safe and sound to Petersburg."

He agreed to that.

16

The Englishmen took Lefty under their own protection and sent the Russian courier back to Russia. Although the courier was a man of rank and knew various languages, they were not interested in him, but they were interested in Lefty, and they took him around and showed him everything. He saw all their factories: the metal ones, and the soap ones, and the sawmills; he liked the way they managed things, and he especially liked how they took care of their workers. Each one of their workers had enough to eat, and he was not dressed in rags but had a decent jacket on and thick boots with iron tips, so as not to stub his foot anywhere; and he did not work from fear of beatings but because of education and proper understanding. Each one had the multiplication table hung where he could see it in front of him and an erasable slate handy. Whatever any craftsman did, he would look at the table and check it over knowledgeably, and then he'd write one thing down on the slate and erase something else, and then put it together neatly: and whatever was written down in numbers really came out that way in the work. During a holiday, they'd get together in couples, take a walking stick in their hands, and go out for a stroll in a noble and proper way.

Lefty had a good look at their life and their work, but he paid the most attention to something that considerably surprised the Englishmen. He was less concerned with the way they made new rifles than with the condition of the old ones. He'd walk around and look at everything, and he'd praise it and say:

"We can do that as well."

But whenever he came across an old rifle, he'd stick his finger in the barrel, move it around inside, and sigh:

"That way's better than ours beyond compare."

The Englishmen could not figure out what Lefty noticed, and he asked them:

"Could you tell me, please, if our generals ever looked at this?"

They answered:

"Those who have been here must've seen it."

"But when they were here," he asked, "did they have gloves on or not?"

"Your generals are always on parade," they said. "They always wear gloves, so they must've had them on when they were here."

Lefty said nothing, but he suddenly became restless and homesick. He longed for his home more and more, and he said to the Englishmen:

"I thank you humbly for all your hospitality. I was very pleased with everything here, but I've already seen everything I wanted to see, and now I'd like to get home as quickly as possible."

They could not convince him to stay any longer. They could not let him go by land because he didn't know all the languages, and it was dangerous to send him by sea because it was autumn and the weather was stormy, but he kept insisting: "Let me go."

"We've looked at the barometer," they said. "There's going to be a storm, you could drown. This isn't your Gulf of Finland, this is the real Hardterranean Sea."

"It doesn't matter where a man dies," he said. "It all depends on God's will. I just want to get back home quickly, because otherwise I might get some variety of madness."

They didn't keep him against his will. They fed him, rewarded him with money, presented him with a gold watch as a farewell gift, and gave him a woolen overcoat with a hood for the cold weather at sea on the late autumn trip. They dressed him up very warmly and took him aboard a ship that was going to Russia. They gave him the best cabin, like a real nobleman, but he felt embarrassed and didn't like to stay inside with the other gentlemen, so he would go out on the deck, sit under the tarpaulin, and ask: "Which way is our Russia?"

The Englishman he would ask would point with his hand or nod with his head in the direction and Lefty would face that way and look impatiently toward his motherland.

As soon as they sailed into the Hardterranean Sea, his longing for Russia grew so strong that it was impossible to comfort him. The pitching of the ship became quite awful, but Lefty wouldn't go down to his cabin. He continued to sit under the tarpaulin with his hood on and his eyes fixed in the direction of the fatherland.

Many times the Englishmen came up to ask him to go down below where it was warm, and he actually began to lie so they would not bother him.

"No," he would say, "I feel better out here. If I went inside, I'd get seasick."

So he stayed out all the time except when he had to go for a special reason, and because of this a certain first mate got to like him. To the misfortune of our Lefty, this first mate could speak Russian, and he could not get over his amazement that a Russian landlubber could put up with all the rough weather.

"You're a fine lad, Russ!" he said. "Let's have a drink!"

So Lefty had a drink.

And the first mate said:

"Another one!"

So they had another one, and they got drunk.

And the first mate asked him:

"What's the secret you're taking to Russia from our country?"

Lefty replied:

"That's my business."

"Well, if that's the way it is," said the mate, "then let's make an English bet."

Lefty asked:

"What kind?"

"We'll bet that we'll never drink alone, but together and always the same amount, and whoever outdrinks the other wins the bet."

Lefty thought: "The sky's full of clouds, my belly's full, too. I'm bored to death, and it's still a long way home—it'll be fun to make a bet."

"All right," he said. "It's a bet!"

"But play fair!"

"About that," he said, "you don't have to worry."

They agreed and shook hands on it.

17

Their bet began in the Hardterranean Sea, and they drank all the way to Riga Dunamunde, and they were neck and neck, neither one giving way to the other. They were so even with each other that when one of them looked out at the sea and saw the Devil creeping out of the water, the other one immediately saw the same thing. Only the mate saw a redheaded devil and Lefty said it was black as tar.

Lefty said:

"Cross yourself and turn away: It's the Devil from the deep."

But the Englishman argued that it was a "deep sea diver."

"If you want," he said, "I'll toss you overboard. Don't be afraid, he'll hand you back to me at once."

And Lefty replied:

"If that's true, toss me over."

The mate took him on his shoulders and carried him to the rail.

The sailors saw this, stopped him, and reported it to the captain, who ordered them to be locked up below and to be given rum, wine, and cold food so that they could drink and eat and keep their bet, but he ordered the flaming pudding kept away from them, fearing it might set the alcohol inside on fire.

So they traveled locked up the rest of the way to Petersburg, and neither one of them won the bet. There they were put in different carriages. The Englishman was taken to the English embassy on the English Quay and Lefty to the police station.

From then on their fates differed greatly.

18

As soon as the Englishman was brought to the embassy, a doctor and a pharmacist were called. The doctor ordered him to be put in a warm bath in his presence, and the pharmacist rolled up a gutta-percha pill right away and put it in his mouth himself. Then both of them took and laid him on a feather bed, covered him with a fur coat, and left him to sweat, and so that he'd not be bothered, they gave orders in the embassy not to sneeze. The doctor and the pharmacist waited until the mate fell asleep, and then they prepared another gutta-percha pill for him, put it on a little table near the head of his bed, and left.

Meanwhile, Lefty was brought to the police station, thrown on the floor, and asked:

"Who are you and where do you come from? Have you got a passport or any other doctumint?"

But from sickness and drunkenness and the tossing about at sea, he was so weak that he couldn't say a word and just groaned.

Then they immediately searched him, took off his good clothes, took away his gold watch and his money, and the police captain ordered him sent to a hospital in the first passing sleigh for free.

A policeman took Lefty out to have him put in a sleigh, but for a long time he could not catch a single one, for sleigh drivers avoid the police. And all that time Lefty was lying on the cold pavement. Then the policeman caught a cabbie at last, but one without a fur rug, because in such cases sleigh drivers hide the fur rug under them so that the policemen's feet freeze faster. So they drove Lefty uncovered, and whenever they transferred him from one sleigh to another, they kept dropping him, and they yanked his ears every time they picked him up so that he'd come to. They brought him to one hospital, but the hospital would not admit him without a doctumint, they brought him to another—it was the same story, and the same in a third, and in the fourth they went on until morning, dragging him through all the distant, twisting alleys and transferring him from one sleigh to another, so that he was all banged up. Then, one doctor's assistant told the policeman to take Lefty to the Obukhvin Public Hospital, where everyone of unknown origin was taken to die.

There they gave orders to write out a receipt and to leave Lefty on the floor in the corridor until they straightened matters out.

At the very same time, the next day the English first mate got up, took the second gutta-percha pill, had a light breakfast of chicken and rice, washed it down with seltzer, and said:

"Where's my Russian comrade? I'm going to look for him."

He got dressed and went out.

19

In a somewhat amazing manner, the first mate very soon found Lefty, only they had not yet put him on a bed; he was still lying in the hall on the floor, and he complained to the Englishman.

"I've got to have a couple of words with the Sovereign."

The Englishman ran to see Count Kleinmikhel[10] and raised a ruckus:

"How can this be allowed! He may be wearing only a sheepskin coat, but he still has a human soul underneath."

For that brilliant reasoning the Englishman was immediately kicked out of there, so that he would not dare mention the human soul again. Then someone told him: "You should go see the Cossack Platov. He's down-to-earth."

The Englishman found Platov, who was back on his couch. Platov listened to him and remembered Lefty.

"Why, brother," he said, "I know him very well. I even yanked his hair. Only I don't know how to help him in this sort of trouble because I have finished the service and have retired altogether. Now I don't get any more respect. Why don't you go quickly to Commandant Skobelev.[11] He's got power and he's experienced in this sort of business; he'll do something."

So the first mate went to Skobelev and told him everything: what sort of illness Lefty had and how it all happened.

Skobelev said:

"I know that illness, only the Germans can't treat it. What you need is a doctor from the spiritual profession because they've grown up with cases like that and can help. I'll send the Russian doctor Martyn-Solsky[12] over there right away."

But when Martyn-Solsky got there, Lefty was already dying, for the back of his head had been cracked open on the pavement, and he could only say one thing clearly:

"Tell the Sovereign that the English don't clean rifle barrels with brick dust: we shouldn't clean them that way either because God forbid there should be a war, they won't be no good for shooting."

And with that expression of his devotion, Lefty crossed himself and died.

Martyn-Solsky immediately went and reported this to Count Chernyshev[13] so that he could bring it to the Sovereign's attention, but Count Chernyshev shouted at him:

"Stick to your laxatives and purgatives," he said, "and keep your nose out of other people's business. There are generals in Russia for that."

So the Sovereign was not told and the rifles continued to be cleaned that way right up to the Crimean War. When they started loading the rifles, the bullets just rattled in them because the barrels had been cleaned out with brick dust.

Then Martyn-Solsky reminded Count Chernyshev about Lefty, but Count Chernyshev said:

"Go to hell, you stupid pipette, and mind your own business, because I'll deny I heard anything from you and then you'll be the one to get in trouble."

Martyn-Solsky thought: "He really will deny everything." So he kept quiet.

And if they had reported Lefty's words to the Sovereign in time, the war in Crimea would have turned out quite differently.

20

But all this now is "a matter of bygone days" and "a tale of ancient times," although not too ancient, and we need not be in a hurry to forget such a tale despite its fable qualities and the epic nature of its hero. Lefty's real name, like the names of many of the greatest geniuses, has been lost to posterity forever, but he is interesting as the personification of a myth created by the folk imagination, and his adventures can serve for the remembrance of an epoch whose general spirit has been faithfully and accurately rendered.

Naturally, such fabulous craftsmen as the legendary Lefty can no longer be found in Tula. Machines have evened out inequality in endowment and talent, and genius no longer yearns to compete with diligence and accuracy. Although they encourage an increase in earnings, machines do not encourage artistic daring, which, at times, had gone far beyond all calculation and had inspired the folk imagination of people to create such fabulous legends as this one.

The workers, no doubt, appreciate the advantages they derive from the practical applications of mechanical science, but they remember the old days with pride and affection. This is their epic tale, and one with a lot of "human soul" at that.

Translation by Bella Ginzbursky-Blum

Notes to the translation begin on page 578.

RESOURCES

Primary Text

Leskov, Nikolai. "Levsha (Skaz o tul'skom kosom levshe i o stal'noi blokhe)." *Sobranie sochinenii v odinnadtsati tomakh.* Vol. 7. Moscow: Khudozhestvennaia literatura, 1958, pp. 26–59.

Secondary Sources

Literary and Cultural Studies

Emerson, Caryl. "Lady Macbeth of Leningrad." *Stagebill* (November 1994): 8–32.
McLean, Hugh. "Leskóv, Nikolái Semyónovich (1831–1895)." In *Handbook of Russian Literature.*, ed. Victor Terras. New Haven: Yale University Press, 1985, pp. 250–54.
———. *Nikolai Leskov: The Man and His Art.* Cambridge: Harvard University Press, 1977.
Taruskin, Richard. "A Martyred Opera Reflects Its Abominable Time." *The New York Times,* November 6, 1994, pp. 25, 34–35.
Terras, Victor. *A History of Russian Literature.* New Haven: Yale University Press, 1991, pp. 362–64.

Drama and Theater

Rudnitsky, Konstantin. *Russian and Soviet Theatre: Tradition and the Avant Garde.* Trans. Roxane Permar, ed. Lesley Milne. London: Thames and Hudson, 1988, pp. 232–33.
Zamiatin, Evgenii. "Blokha: igra v chetyrekh deistviiakh." In *Blokha.* Leningrad: Mysl', 1926.

Art

Dangulov, Savva. "With Tula Craftsmanship: Leskov's Great Fable." Illustrated by Kukrynitsky. *Soviet Literature* 12 (1975): 174–82.
Leskov, Nikolai. *Levsha. Skaz o tul'skom kosom levshe i o stal'noi blokhe.* Illustrated by Arkadii Turin. Moscow: Gosnak, 1973.

Music

Shostakovich, Dmitrii. *Katerina Izmailova.* Opera in 4 acts. Shevchenko Opera Choir and Orchestra. Conductor, S. Turchak. N.d. 5 records.

Film

Ledi Makbet Mtsenskogo uezda (Lady Macbeth of the Mtsensk District). Director, K. Balaian. Mosfilm, 1990.
Levsha (Lefty). Director, Sergei Ovcharov. Mosfilm, 1987.
Ocharovannyi strannik (The Enchanted Wanderer). Director, N. Poplavskaia. Cast: A. Rostotskii, A. Mikhailova. Mosfilm, 1990.

~Leo Tolstoy~

Holstomer

The Story of a Horse

Dedicated to the memory of M.A. Stakhovich[1]

1

Ever higher rose the sky, wider spread the dawn, the dull silver of the dew became whiter, the sickle moon became more lifeless, the woods more alive with sounds, people began to get up, and at the owner's stable yard one could hear more and more snorting, a racket in the straw, and the angry, shrill neighing of horses crowded together and quarreling over something.

"No-o-o! What's the rush! Hungry, are you!" said an old herdsman, opening a squeaking gate. "Where you off to?" he shouted, swinging at a filly who had lunged for the gate.

The herdsman, Nester, was dressed in a short Cossack coat belted by a strap of inlaid leather. His whip was lashed over his shoulder and a loaf of bread wrapped in cloth was stuck in his belt. In his arms he carried a saddle and a bridle.

The horses were not in the least frightened or offended by the mocking tone of the herdsman; they pretended to be indifferent and without hurrying moved away from the gate. Only one old dark bay with a long mane laid back her ear and quickly turned her rear. With that a younger filly, standing in the back and not at all involved, squealed and knocked her rump against the first available horse.

"No-o-o!" the herdsman shouted in an even sterner and louder voice and turned to go to the corner of the yard.

Of all the horses in the paddock (there were about a hundred), a skewbald gelding showed the least impatience; he was standing alone in a corner under an overhang, screwing up his eyes and licking an oak post in the shed. It's impossible to say how the post tasted to the skewbald, but his expression was serious and thoughtful as he licked it.

"Steady now!" the herdsman addressed him again in the same tone and, walking up, put a saddle and a worn saddle cloth next to him on a pile of muck.

The skewbald gelding stopped licking and stood still, looking for a long time at Nester. He did not laugh, did not become angry, did not grow sullen, but only heaved his whole belly, sighed very heavily, and turned away. The herdsman placed his arm on the gelding's neck and put a bridle on him.

"Why are you sighing?" asked Nester.

The gelding flicked his tail, as if to say, "It's nothing, Nester." Nester put the saddle cloth and the saddle on him. The gelding pulled back his ears, probably intending to convey his displeasure, but he was only called a scoundrel for this and the saddle girth was tightened. The gelding then swelled himself up, but a finger was shoved into his mouth and he was kicked in the stomach with a knee so that he had to let out the air. Nevertheless, when Nester tightened the saddle strap with a tooth, once again he laid back his ears and even looked around. Although he knew this would not help, he considered it necessary to show that it was unpleasant and that he would always make his feelings known. When he was saddled, he thrust out a swollen right foot and began to champ at the bit, again for some special reason of his own, because by now he ought to have realized that bits have no taste.

Using a shortened stirrup Nester climbed onto the gelding, unwound the whip, freed the coat from under his knees, established himself on the saddle in a special way typical for coachmen, hunters, and herdsmen, and jerked the reins. The gelding lifted his head, indicating his readiness to go wherever he was ordered, but he did not move from the spot. He knew that before leaving much shouting still had to be done sitting there, that orders had to be given to the other herdsman, Vaska, and to the horses. And indeed Nester began to shout, "Vaska! Hey, Vaska! Did you let the brood mares out or didn't you? Where are you going, you idiot? No-o-o? Are you sleeping? Open the gate! Let the brood mares go first," and so on.

The gate creaked. Vaska, angry and sleepy, holding a horse by the halter, stood by the gateposts and let the horses through. The horses started to file out, carefully stepping through the straw and sniffing at it: young mares, yearlings, nursing foals, and heavy brood mares with their heavy bellies carefully passed through the gates one by one. The young horses crowded sometimes by twos or threes, putting their heads over each other's backs and churning their legs in the passage, for which they received a few curses from the grooms every time. The nursing foals sometimes threw themselves at the feet of mares they did not belong to and loudly neighed in reply to their sharp cackling.

One young mischievous filly, as soon as she had run out of the gates, bent her head down and to the side, bucked her hind quarters, and squealed; but just the same she did not dare to run ahead of the old, gray dappled Zhuldyba, who with quiet, heavy steps, her belly shifting from side to side, gravely, as usual, walked ahead of all the horses.

In a few minutes the paddock, which had been so animated and full of life, was sadly deserted; the posts beneath the empty overhang stuck up sadly, and all that could be seen was matted, manure-strewn straw. No matter how accustomed the skewbald gelding was to this desolate picture, it affected him sorrowfully just the same. Slowly, as if he were bowing, he lowered and raised his head, sighed as deeply as the tight cinches would allow, and hobbling on his bent, stiff legs, carrying old Nester on his bony back, plodded off after the herd.

"I know, when we ride out onto the road, he'll start striking a light and smoking his wooden pipe with its bronze inlay and small chain," thought the gelding. "I'm glad because early in the morning, with the dew, this smell is pleasant and reminds me of many pleasant things; the only annoyance is that with the pipe between his teeth the old man always puts on airs, imagining himself to be someone, and sits sideways, without fail sideways; and that's the side that hurts me. However, God bless him, it's nothing new for me to suffer for the pleasure of others. Already, I've even begun to find a sort of horse pleasure in it. Let him preen himself, the poor fellow. After all, he only makes a show of bravery when no one sees him, let him sit sideways," the gelding reasoned and stepping carefully with hobbled legs walked in the middle of the road.

2

Having driven the herd to the river near which the horses were to graze, Nester dismounted and unsaddled the gelding. The herd, meanwhile, had already begun to scatter slowly over the yet ungrazed dew-covered meadow, and a mist rose from both the field and the river curving around it.

After removing the bit from the skewbald gelding, Nester scratched under his neck, in reply to which the gelding closed his eyes as a sign of gratitude and pleasure. "He loves it, the old dog!" remarked Nester. The gelding in no way loved this scratching and only pretended to find it pleasant out of decorum, but he tossed his head in a sign of agreement. Suddenly, completely unexpectedly, and for no reason, Nester, assuming perhaps that too much familiarity could give the skewbald gelding a false sense of importance, with no warning pushed his head away, raised the bridle threateningly, hit the gelding very hard with the buckle across his bony leg, and without a word went up onto the knoll to a stump near which he usually sat.

But although these acts had hurt the skewbald gelding, he made no sign of it, and slowly swishing his molting tail and sniffing at something, nibbling now and then at the grass only for diversion, he went to the river. Not paying the least attention to the goings-on around him of the young fillies, yearlings, or foals, who were rejoicing about the morning, and knowing that the healthiest thing of all, especially at his age, was first to drink his fill on an empty stomach and then to eat, he chose a place on the bank that was the least steep and the most spacious, and wetting his hoofs and fetlocks, he thrust his muzzle into the water and began to suck it through his torn lips, moving his swelling sides and swishing in pleasure his sparse, skewbald tail with the exposed bone.

A chestnut filly, a troublemaker who was always teasing the old fellow and playing all kinds of unpleasant tricks, came up to him in the water now as well as if she had some reason of her own, but only, in fact, to muddy the water in front of his nose. But the skewbald had already drunk his fill, and as if he had not noticed the chestnut filly's intention, he calmly dragged out his bogged down legs one after the other, shook his head, and moving away from the younger horses, began to graze. Shifting his legs in various ways without stepping unnecessarily on any grass, he grazed for exactly three hours practically without lifting his head. Having eaten so much that his belly hung like a sack from his thin, steep ribs, he settled evenly on all four of his aching legs so as to minimize the pain, especially in his right foreleg, which was the weakest, and dozed off.

There is old age that is majestic, there is old age that is odious, and there is old age that is pitiful. There is old age that is both odious and majestic at the same time. The old age of the skewbald gelding was exactly this type.

The gelding was of a great height, no less than fifteen hands. His color was once black and white skewbald; that's what he had been, but now the black patches had become a dirty chestnut color. His skewbaldness consisted of three patches: one on the head with an irregular bald spot on the side of his nose that reached halfway down his neck. His long mane, full of burrs, was white in some places and chestnut in others. Another spot went down his right side and halfway to his belly; the third was on his croup, taking in the upper part of the tail and going halfway down his flanks. The rest of his tail was whitish and streaked. His big bony head, with deep hollows above the eyes and a drooping black lip that had been torn at some time, hung heavily and low from a neck bent from thinness so that it appeared to be made of wood. Because of the drooping lip, a blackish tongue was visible off to one side, as well as the yellow stumps of his ground-down lower teeth. The ears, one of which was slit, drooped low at the sides and only occasionally twitched lazily to scare off clinging flies. One tuft from the still long forelock hung behind his ear; his broad forehead was sunken and rough; his skin hung down in bags at his broad jowls. On his neck and head the veins were knotted and quivered and trembled with each touch of a fly. The expression of his face was austerely patient, deeply thoughtful, and long-suffering. His forelegs were bent at the knees like a bow; there were sores on both hooves, and on the one that had markings that stretched halfway down his leg, near the knee, was a large lump as big as a fist. The hind legs were fresher but had been rubbed bare at the flanks, apparently long ago, and hair no longer grew back in these places. All of his legs seemed disproportionately long for his thin body. His ribs, although steep, were so bare and tautly covered that the skin seemed to be stuck to the spaces between them. The withers and back were covered with marks from old beatings, and toward the rear a still fresh sore swelled and oozed; the long, almost bare black stump of his tail stuck out with its vertebrae exposed. On his chestnut-colored croup, near the tail, was an old palm-sized wound something like a bite, overgrown with white hair; and on his front shoulder there was visible yet another scar from a wound. The hind quarters and tail were soiled from a chronic stomach disturbance. The hair all over his body, although it was short, stood on end. But despite the disgusting old age of this horse, one involuntarily fell into thought after looking at it, and an expert would say immediately that in its day it had been a remarkably good horse.

An expert would even say that there had been only one stock in Russia with such a broad frame, such enormous bones, such hooves, such slender leg bones, such a set of the neck, and in particular, such a skull, such large eyes, black and bright, and such thoroughbred veins knotted around the head and neck, and such fine skin and hair. There was truly something magnificent in the figure of this horse and in its awful conjunction of the repulsive signs of decrepitude, accentuated by colorful skin, and the manners and expressions of self-assurance and serenity due to consciousness of beauty and strength.

Like a living ruin, he stood alone in the middle of the dew-filled meadow, while not far from him rang out the hoofbeats, whinnying, and youthful neighing and snorting of the dispersed herd.

3

The sun had already climbed above the forest and shone brilliantly on the grass and the bends of the river. The dew was evaporating, forming drops here and there around the marsh; above the forest the last of the morning mist was dissipating like smoke. The small clouds were curling, but there was no wind yet. Beyond the river, prickly green shoots of rye stood furled into tubes, and there was a scent of fresh verdure and flowers. The cuckoo called out hoarsely from the forest, and Nester, lounging on his back, contemplated how many years he had left to live. The larks rose over the rye and the meadow. A late rabbit got in among the herd and after escaping sat down listening next to a bush. Vaska had dozed off, his head down in the grass; the fillies, wandering ever wider, skirted him and scattered down the hill. The older horses, snorting, made a light trail through the dew eversearching for a place where no one would disturb them, but they were not grazing anymore, only munching on the tasty grass. The whole herd moved imperceptibly in one direction. And again old Zhuldyba staidly strutted ahead, leading the way for the other horses. Mushka, a young black mare who had just foaled for the first time, neighed continually and lifting her tail snorted at her lilac-colored suckling colt, stumbling near her on trembling knees. The dark bay filly Lastochka, as smooth as satin with shining hair, lowered her head so that black silky forelocks covered her forehead and eyes; playing, she would nibble the grass, throw it, and tap her foot with its fluffy fetlock wet with dew. One of the older colts, apparently imagining some sort of game, raised his short curly tail like a plume of feathers and galloped twenty-six times around his mother, who, already accustomed to her son's personality, nibbled on the grass calmly and only occasionally took a sidelong glance at him with her large, black eye. One of the smallest foals, black, with a big head, a forelock protruding up between his ears in astonishment, and a tail still twisted to the side on which it had been turned in his mother's belly, with ears cocked and vacant eyes, unmoving, intently watched the colt galloping and backing up; it's unclear whether he watched with envy or disapproval. Some of the foals were nursing, nudging with their noses, others for no known reason, despite the calls of their mothers, were running in a small, awkward trot straight to the far side, as if looking for something, and then stopping and neighing in a despairing, piercing voice; others were lying every which way next to each other; others were learning to graze; others were scratching behind their ears with their hind legs. Two mares, still in foal, walked separately, and slowly shifting their feet, continued grazing. Evidently their condition was respected by the others, and none of the young horses dared to approach and bother them. But even if some mischievous colt had the notion to go closer, one twitch of the ear and tail was enough to show him all the impropriety of such behavior.

The yearlings and the year-old fillies, pretending that they were already grown-up and dignified, seldom jumped and gathered into cheerful companies.

They grazed sedately, bending their clipped necks like swans and, as if they too had tails, waved their docked stumps. Just like adult horses, several of them were lying down, rolling about, or scratching each other. The most cheerful company of all consisted of the two and three year olds and the unmated mares. Almost all of them wandered together in a separate group of maidens. Among them one heard tramping, squealing, neighing, and snorting. They would bunch up, put their heads on one another's shoulders, sniff at one another, jump, and sometimes snort, and raising their tails like trumpets would prance proudly and coquettishly half at a trot and half at a canter before their friends. The leading beauty and instigator among all these youngsters was a mischievous chestnut filly. Anything she would dream up, the others would do; wherever she would go, the whole herd of beauties would follow. The mischievous filly was in an especially playful mood this morning. The cheerful mood had come upon her just as it comes upon people. At the watering place, after playing the trick on the old horse, she had run through the water pretending she had been frightened by something, snorted, and then bolted into the field at top speed so that Vaska had to gallop after her and the others who had followed. Then, after grazing a little, she began to roll around, then to tease the old mares by walking ahead of them, then to separate one of the foals and to begin to run after him as if she wanted to bite him. The mother became frightened and stopped grazing; the foal cried out in a pathetic voice, but the mischievous filly did not even touch him and merely scared him a bit, putting on a performance for her friends, who watched her antics with empathy. Next she ventured to turn the head of an unobtrusive roan pulling a plow for a muzhik far beyond the rye. She halted proudly, standing a little to one side, lifted her head, shook herself, and began to neigh sweetly, tenderly, and long. And mischief, feeling, and a certain sadness were in that neighing. It also expressed desire, the promise of love, and a longing for it.

Here, a landrail in the thick reeds, rushing from place to place, passionately calls to his mate; there, a cuckoo and a quail sing of love, and flowers send their aromatic pollen to each other through the wind.

"And I, too, am young, and good-looking, and strong," said the neighing of the mischievous filly, "but up to now I haven't had the opportunity to experience the sweetness of that feeling, not only haven't I had the opportunity, but no lover—not a single one, has looked upon me yet."

And the neighing, so full of meaning, echoed sadly and youthfully from the valley and field and was heard from afar by the roan. He pricked up his ears and stopped. The muzhik kicked him with his sandal, but the roan was enthralled by the silvery sound of the distant neighing, and he neighed in response. The muzhik became angry, pulled on the reins, and kicked the roan again, this time in the belly, so that he was not able to finish his neighing and continued pulling the plow. But the roan was filled with feelings of sweetness and sadness, and from the distant rye fields for a long time the sounds of the passionate neigh begun by the roan and the angry voice of the peasant carried to the herd.

If the roan was so befuddled by the sound of this voice alone that he forgot his duties, what would have happened if he could have seen the beautiful mischievous filly in her entirety, as she, ears cocked and nostrils flaring, gulped in air and, yearning and trembling with all of the youth and beauty of her body, called to him.

But the mischievous filly did not think about her feelings for long. When the voice of the roan died out, she neighed again mockingly, lowered her head, began pawing the ground with her hoof, and then went to awaken and tease the skewbald gelding. The skewbald gelding was accustomed to suffering and to the teasing of the carefree youngsters. In fact, he suffered more from these youngsters than from people. He did no evil to either group. People needed to use him, but why did the young horses torture him so?

4

He was old, they were young; he was gaunt, they were well fed; he was boring, they were cheerful. Therefore, he was quite alien and strange, quite another being, and it was impossible to feel pity for him. Horses pity only themselves and occasionally only those in whose skin they can easily imagine themselves. But after all, was the skewbald gelding to blame for being old, skinny, and disfigured? ... It would seem not. In the horses' opinion, however, he was to blame, and it was always only those who were strong, young, and happy who were in the right, those who had everything before them, those whose every muscle quivered and whose tails rose up like stakes with unnecessary exertions. Perhaps the skewbald gelding himself understood this and in calm moments agreed that he was to blame to have already lived out his life and that he had to pay for that life; but just the same he was a horse, and often, looking at all these youngsters who were punishing him for something they would all be subject to at the end of their lives, he could not help but feel insulted, sad, and indignant. The reason for this lack of compassion on the part of the horses was also an aristocratic sentiment. Every one of them could trace his lineage by father or mother to the famous Smetanka, but no one knew the skewbald's lineage; the skewbald was a newcomer, bought at a fair three years ago for eighty paper rubles.[2]

The chestnut filly, as though she were casually strolling around, walked up to the skewbald gelding's very nose and pushed him. He already knew what was happening and without opening his eyes laid back his ears and bared his teeth. The filly turned her back and made believe she wanted to hit him. He opened his eyes and walked off in the other direction. He did not feel like sleeping anymore and he began to graze. Again, the mischievous filly, in the company of her friends, approached the gelding. A blazed two-year-old filly, very stupid, always imitating and always following the chestnut, came up with her and, as is common for imitators, began overdoing the instigator's actions. The chestnut filly usually walked up as if minding her own business and went past the gelding's very nose, not so much as glancing at him, so that he could not at all decide whether or not to get angry, and this was actually funny. She also did this now, but the blazed filly, who was following her and who was in an especially cheerful mood, struck the gelding with her chest. Again he bared his teeth, squealed, and with an alacrity that no one could have expected of him raced after her and bit her on the thigh. The blazed filly turned her back and struck the old horse hard in his thin bare ribs. The old horse wheezed and wanted to rush at her again, but then he changed his mind and sighing heavily walked off to the side. The youngsters in the herd must have taken the impertinence the skewbald gelding had permitted himself in regard to the blazed filly as a personal insult; the entire rest of the day they resolutely prevented him from grazing and would not give him a moment of peace, so that the herdsman had to calm them several times and could not understand what had happened to them. The gelding was so hurt that he himself went to Nester when the old man was preparing to drive the herd home, and he felt happier and calmer after he had been saddled and mounted.

God knows what the old gelding was thinking carrying away old Nester on his back. Whether he was reflecting bitterly about the persistent and cruel youngsters or whether he was forgiving his persecutors with the disdainful and silent pride peculiar to the old, he did not reveal his thoughts all the way home.

That night some friends came to visit Nester, and driving his herd past the peasant huts he noticed a cart and a horse tied to his porch. After driving in the herd, he rushed so much that he led the gelding into the yard without removing the saddle, shouted to Vaska to take care of the herd horse, locked the gates, and went to see his friends. Whether as a result of the insult to the blazed filly, a great granddaughter of Smetanka, inflicted by a "scabby good-for-nothing" bought at a horse fair who knew neither his father nor mother, and who was, therefore, an insult to the aristocratic feelings of the whole paddock, or whether as a result of the gelding's remaining in a high saddle without a rider and therefore presenting a strange and fantastic spectacle for the horses, the fact of the matter is something unusual happened that night in the paddock. All the horses, young and old, chased after the gelding with bared teeth, running after him around the yard, and the noises of hooves kicking against his gaunt sides and heavy groaning resounded. The gelding could not bear it anymore, could no longer avoid the blows. He stopped in the middle of the yard, on his face was an expression of the repulsive, weak bitterness of impotent old age, and then of despair; he laid back his ears and suddenly he did something that made all the horses quiet down instantly. Vyazopurikha, the oldest mare, approached the gelding, sniffed at him and sighed. The gelding also sighed.

5

In the middle of the moonlit yard stood the tall, gaunt figure of the gelding with a high saddle and its upright, knobbed pommel. The horses stood around him motionless and in deep silence, as if they had learned something new and unusual from him. And they did, indeed, learn something new and unexpected from him.

Here is what they learned:

The First Night

Yes, I am the son of Lyubezny I and Baba. My name by pedigree is Muzhik I. I am Muzhik I by pedigree, but my street name, Holstomer, was given to me because of my long and sweeping stride, for which there was no equal in Russia. There's no horse on earth who has blood lines better than mine. I would never have told you this. What for? You never would have recognized me, just as Vyazopurikha, who was with me in Khrenovo, didn't and has only now guessed who I am. Even now you would not have believed me if not for the testimony of Vyazopurikha. I never would have told you. I don't need the pity of other horses. But you asked for it. Yes, I am that very Holstomer for whom sportsmen search but do not find, that very Holstomer who was known by the Count himself and who was sold from the stud farm because I outran his favorite Lebed.

When I was born I did not know the meaning of *skewbald,* I thought I was a horse. The first disapproving comment about my markings, I remember, made a deep impression on me and my mother. I must have been born at night; toward morning, having already been licked clean by my mother, I stood up on my legs. I remember that I always wanted something and that everything seemed to me exceedingly amazing and at the same time exceedingly simple. Our stalls were in a long warm corridor with latticed doors through which everything could be seen. My mother offered me her teats—but I was still so new to the world that I poked my nose first underneath her forward legs and then underneath her rear. Suddenly my mother glanced at the latticed door and, stepping across my legs, stood to the side. The day groom was looking at us in the stall through the lattice.

"How do you like that, Baba foaled," he said and opened the latch. He walked across the fresh straw and put his arms around me.

"Look, Taras," he shouted. "What a skewbald, just like a magpie."

I jerked free from him and stumbled onto my knees.

"How do you like that, the little devil," he remarked.

My mother was agitated but did not try to defend me, only sighed very heavily and stepped aside a little. The grooms came in and they too began to examine me. One ran to inform the head groom. Looking at my markings everybody laughed, and they gave me all sorts of strange names. Neither my mother nor I could understand the meaning of these words. Until my birth there had never been even one skewbald in my family. We did not think there was anything bad in this. But even then, everyone praised my build and my strength.

"See how frisky he is," said the groom. "You can't hold him."

After a while, the head groom came and began to express his wonder at my color; he even seemed chagrined by it.

"What a freak," he said. "The General will never let him stay on the farm. Oh, Baba, you really did it to me." He turned to my mother. "If you'd foaled a blazed one at least—but a total skewbald!"

My mother did not give any answer and, as she always did in similar circumstances, sighed again.

"What the hell does he look like? Just like a peasant, he is," the groom continued. "He can't stay on the farm, too embarrassing, but he's a good horse, mighty good," he said. And everybody else looking at me said the same. In a few days the General himself came to have a look at me, and again everybody was somehow horrified, and they rebuked me and my mother for the color of my skin. "But he's a good horse, very good," everybody repeated as soon as they saw me.

Until the spring we foals lived in the mares' quarters, each with his own mother, only now and then, when the snow on the roofs of the paddocks had begun to melt from the sun, did they begin to let us out with our mothers into a broad yard covered with fresh straw. Here for the first time I met all my kin both close and distant. Here I saw all the famous mares of the time as they came out from different gates with their nursing foals. Here was old Golanka, Mushka, the daughter of Smetanka, Krasnukha, the saddle horse Dobrokhotikha, all the famous horses of the past. They all assembled with their new foals, strolled around in the sunshine, rolled in the fresh straw, and sniffed each other just like ordinary horses. To this very day I have not been able to forget the way the paddock looked filled with the beauties of that time. It must seem strange to you to think and believe that I was once young and spirited, but so it was. Here was this very Vyazopurikha, then still a year-old filly, a darling, a gay and spirited horse; but no offense to her, although she is considered a rarity among you because of her blood lines, at that time she was among the worst horses of that issue. She herself will confirm this.

My colorful markings, which humans don't care for, appealed very much to horses; they all circled around me, admired me, and played with me. I began to forget the things that humans said about my color and felt happy. But soon I experienced the first sorrow of my life, and the cause of this was my mother. As soon as the thaw had begun, when sparrows were chirping under the overhang and there was a strong feeling of spring in the air, my mother began to treat me differently. Her entire disposition changed; at one moment, for no discernible reason, she would suddenly begin to play, running through the yard in a way that was absolutely inappropriate for her age; next she'd become lost in thought and start to neigh; or she'd bite and kick her sister mares; or she'd start to sniff at me and snort in a displeased manner; or going out into the sun, she would put her head over the shoulder of her cousin Kupchikha and pensively scratch her back for a long time while pushing me away from her teats. Once the head groom came, gave an order for her halter to be put on, and she was led out of the stable. She started to neigh, I answered her and raced after her, but she did not even glance back at me. Taras, the groom, grabbed me in his arms just as they shut the door behind my mother. I broke free, knocking the groom down in the straw, but the door was shut and I could only hear the ever-receding neigh of my mother. And in this neighing I no longer heard a beckoning call for me but something else expressed. In response to her voice another powerful voice answered from the distance, which I later found out was Dobry I, who was being taken between two grooms for a rendezvous with my mother. I don't remember Taras leaving my stall: I was too sad. I felt I had lost my mother's love forever. And all because I was a skewbald, I thought, remembering the humans' words about my coat, and such a wave of anger seized me that I began to beat against the stable walls with my head and knees, and I kept on beating until I worked up a good sweat and had to stop from exhaustion.

After some time my mother returned to me. I heard her trot along the corridor to our stall in an unusual stride. They opened the door for her, but I didn't recognize her; she had become younger and better looking. She sniffed at me, snorted, and began to cackle. From her whole expression I could see that she did not love me. She described to me how handsome Dobry was and her love for him. These dates with him continued while relations between mother and me became colder and colder.

Soon they let us out into the grass. From this time on I came to know new joys, which replaced the loss of my mother's love. I now had playmates, colts and fillies, and together we learned how to graze, to neigh, to neigh just like the adults, and lifting our tails, to prance around our mothers. This was a happy time. Everything was forgiven me, everybody loved me, admired me, and looked indulgently upon everything I did. But it did not last long. Soon something terrible happened to me. The gelding sighed very heavily and walked away from the other horses.

Dawn had already begun. The gate creaked and Nester entered. The horses dispersed. The herdsman fixed the saddle on the gelding and drove the herd out.

6

The Second Night

As soon as the horses were driven home, they crowded around the skewbald again and he continued his story:

In the month of August they separated us from our mothers, but I did not experience any particular sorrow. I saw that my mother was already carrying my younger brother, the famous Usan, and I was no longer what I had once been. I wasn't jealous, but I felt that I was becoming colder toward her. Besides, I knew that in leaving my mother I would join the general herd of foals stabled by twos and threes and that every day this entire group of youngsters went outdoors. I shared a stall with Mily. Mily was a saddle horse, and subsequently the Emperor rode him and he was depicted in paintings and statues. But at the time he was still a simple nursing foal with a lustrous tender coat, a swanlike neck, and even, thin legs like strings. He was always cheerful, even-tempered, and amiable; he was always ready to play, to give you a kick, and to play a joke on a horse or a person. Living together as we did, we couldn't help but become friends, and this friendship continued throughout our youth. He was lively and carefree. Even then he was already beginning to fall in love, to flirt with the young mares, and to laugh at my innocence. And to my misfortune, out of vanity, I began to imitate him; and very quickly I grew interested in love. And this precocious disposition of mine was responsible for the greatest change in my fate. I became infatuated.

Vyazopurikha was one year older than I; we were particularly good friends, but toward the end of autumn, I noticed that she had begun avoiding me . . . But I am not going to start telling you the entire sad story of my first love. She herself remembers my mad infatuation, which ended for me with the most important change of my life. The grooms chased after her and they beat me. In the evening they drove me into a special stall; I neighed the whole night as though I had a foreboding of the events of the coming day.

The next morning the General, the head groom, the grooms, and the herdsmen came to the corridor of my stall and a terrible uproar began. The General shouted at the head groom, the head groom defended himself saying he had not ordered that I be turned loose but that the grooms had done so on their own. The General said that he'd whip all of them but that it wasn't possible to keep young stallions. The head groom promised he'd do everything necessary. They quieted down and left. I didn't understand at all, but I saw that something had been planned for me.

The next day after this I stopped neighing forever; I became what I am now. The whole world changed in my eyes. Nothing appealed to me; I retreated into myself and began to meditate. At first everything was repellent to me. I even stopped drinking, eating, and walking about, not to mention playing. Sometimes I imagined jumping, prancing a little, neighing; but immediately the terrible question would occur to me: Why? For what purpose? And my last bits of strength would fade away.

Once in the evening I was being led home as the herd was being driven back from the fields. From the distance I could still see a cloud of dust from the vague but familiar outlines of all our brood mares. I heard cheerful whinnying and the clatter of hooves. I stopped, although the halter-rope by which the groom was leading me cut into the back of my head, and I began to look at the approaching herd just as one looks at a lost and irretrievable happiness. As they came closer I was able to make them out, one by one, all the familiar, beautiful, majestic, healthy, and well-fed figures. A few of them also looked around at me. I did not feel the pain caused by the groom pulling on my halter. Involuntarily, as of old, I began to neigh and broke into a trot, but my neighing echoed sorrowfully in a funny and absurd manner. None of those in the herd laughed, but I noticed that many of them turned away from me out of decency. Apparently they found it odious, pitiful, and shameful, and above all—they thought me comical. They found something funny in my thin, unexpressive neck, my large head (I had lost weight at this time), my long clumsy legs, and the stupid trotting gait with which I ran around the groom out of old habit. None of them responded to my neighing, and they all turned away from me. I suddenly understood everything, understood how I would always remain far removed from all of them, and I don't recall how I came home behind the groom.

Even earlier I had shown an inclination to seriousness and deep thought, but now a decisive change occurred in me. My skewbaldness, which aroused such a strange disdain in people, my strange unexpected sorrow, and also some kind of special role I assumed on the farm, which I felt but in no way was able to explain to myself, forced me to withdraw inwardly. I thought about the unfairness of people who had judged me because of my skewbaldness; I thought about the inconstancy of motherly love, and female love in general, with its dependence on physical causes; and above all, I pondered the qualities of that strange breed of animals with which we are so closely connected and which we call people, those qualities that shaped my special role on the farm, which I felt but could not understand. The significance of this special role and the human qualities on which it was based were revealed to me in the following event.

It was during the winter holidays. The whole day I was left without hay and nobody watered me. As I found out later, this was because the groom had gotten drunk. The same day the head groom came in to see me, saw that there was no hay, began shouting the most horrible words about the absent groom, and then left. The next day the groom came into our stable with a friend to give us our hay. I noticed that he was especially pale and sad; in the expression of his long back there was something especially significant and evoking compassion. He angrily threw the hay from the grating; I was about to poke my head across his shoulder, but he punched me so hard on the snout with his fist that I jumped aside. He kicked me again in the stomach with his boot.

"If it weren't for this mangy critter, nothin' would've happened," he said.

"Why?" asked another groom.

"He don't go to check on the Count's horses, but he visits *his own* little stallion twice a day, he does."

"So, did they give him that skewbald?" asked the other.

"Sold it, maybe gave it, who the hell knows. You could starve all the Count's horses to death and nothin'd happen; but just you dare 'n not feed hay to *his* foal. 'Lie down,' he says. An' did he give me a wallopin'. Ain't no Christian mercy in him. A beast is pitied more'n a man. No cross on him for sure; kept count himself, the brute. The General never whipped me like that; covered my whole back with welts, he did; plain to see he ain't got no Christian soul in him."

I understood what they said about whipping and about Christianity quite well. But I had no idea what they meant by the words *his own, his* stallion. I saw that in these words the people proposed some kind of link between me and the head groom. But at the same time I was totally unable to understand what the nature of that link was. It was only much later, after they separated me from the other horses, that I understood what it meant. At that time, I could not understand what it meant when they called *me* the property of a person. The words "my horse," used with reference to me, a living horse, seemed as strange as the words "my land," "my air," "my water."

But these words had an enormous influence on me. I thought about them continually, and only long after the most diverse interactions with people did I come to understand at last the meaning they ascribe to these strange words. Their meaning is this: The lives of human beings are guided not by deeds but by words. They love not so much the possibility of doing or not doing something as the possibility of talking about various things in words agreed upon among themselves. Such are the words considered to be very important among them, such is the essence of the word *mine,* which they use for different things, creatures and objects, even for land, people, and horses. They agree that only one person can say *mine* about the same thing. And according to this game agreed upon by them, whoever can say *mine* about the greatest number of things is considered to be the happiest. Why this is so I don't know, but it is so. For a long time I tried to explain it to myself in terms of some sort of direct benefit, but this turned out to be an injustice.

Many of the people who, for example, called me their horse, never rode me, and it was entirely different people who did so. It was not they who fed me, but again it was someone else. And those who did me good were not the ones who called me their horse, but coachmen, horse doctors, and generally people who were strangers. Subsequently, having expanded the range of my observations, I became convinced it was not only in regard to us horses that the concept *my* has no basis except for a low and bestial human instinct that they call the sense or the right of property. A person says *my house* and never lives in it but only worries about its construction and maintenance. A merchant says *my shop, my fabric shop,* for example, and doesn't have any clothes made from the better cloth he has in the shop. There are people who call land theirs but have never seen or set foot on this land. There are people who call other people theirs but have never laid eyes on these people; and their entire relationship with them consists of doing them evil. There are people who call certain women their women or wives, but these women live with other men. And people strive in life not to do what is considered good but to call as many things as possible *theirs.* I am certain now that the essential difference between people and us lies in this notion. And that is why, without even mentioning our other advantages over human beings, we can say with confidence based on this alone that we stand higher in the hierarchy of living creatures than people: their actions—at least those with whom I have had dealings—are guided by words; ours, however, by deeds. And so, the head groom received the right to say about me, *my horse,* and because of it he beat the groom. This discovery struck me strongly, and combined with those thoughts and opinions that my skewbald skin aroused in people and with the pensiveness provoked in me by my mother's betrayal, it forced me to become the serious and contemplative gelding I am.

I was thrice unfortunate: I was a skewbald, I was a gelding, and people imagined I belonged not to God and to myself, as is natural for all living things, but to the head groom.

There were many consequences of their assumptions about me. The first was that I was kept separate, fed better, exercised more frequently, and put into harness earlier than other horses. I was harnessed initially when I was three. I recall the first time the head groom himself—who imagined that I belonged to him—began to put the harness on me with a throng of stable hands, expecting violence or resistance from me. They twisted my lips. They wound ropes around me, backing me between the shafts; they put a wide strap on my back in the form of a cross and tied it to the shafts so that I would not strike out with my hind quarters; and I was only waiting for the opportunity to demonstrate my desire and love for work.

They marveled that my pace was that of an experienced carriage horse. They began to train me, and I began to practice trotting. Everyday I had more and more success, so that after three months the General himself and many others praised my gait. But there was one strange thing, namely, that because they imagined I was not theirs but the head groom's, my gait had for them quite another meaning.

The young stallions, my brothers, were raced on the track; their gaits were measured; people came out to look at them, they were driven in gilded droshkies, and they were dressed in expensive regalia. I drove an ordinary droshky that belonged to the head groom and took him on business at Chesmenka and other farms. All this stemmed partly from my having been born a skewbald but mainly because in their view I was not the Count's, I was the property of the head groom.

Tomorrow, if we are still alive, I'll tell you about the main consequence for me of this right of property that the head groom imagined he had.

All day the horses treated Holstomer respectfully. But Nester's treatment was rude as always. The muzhik's roan stallion, who was working close to the herd, neighed, and the chestnut filly once again began flirting with him.

7

The Third Night

A new moon was born, and its rather narrow sickle illuminated the figure of Holstomer in the middle of the yard. The horses crowded around him, and the skewbald continued:

The most astonishing consequence for me of not belonging to the Count or to God but to the head groom was that what constitutes our main accomplishment, a spirited stride, became the cause of my banishment. Lebed was being paced around the course, and the head groom from Chesmenka rode up on me and stood near the track. Lebed passed by us. He moved well, but nevertheless he acted like a dandy, didn't have that efficiency which I had perfected in myself so that the instant one leg touched down, the other came up and I did not waste a drop of strength in idleness but used all my effort to propel myself forward. Lebed went past us. I pulled toward the track, the head groom did not restrain me. "So, want to pace, my little skewbald?" he shouted, and when Lebed got even with us again, he let me loose. The other had already picked up speed, and therefore I fell behind in the first lap, but in the second I began to gain on him, approached his droshky, began to draw even, began to pass, and passed him. We tried a second time—the same thing happened. I was the more nimble. And this caused terror in everyone. They decided that I should be sold quickly and far away so that there would not be any rumors "or else the Count will find out and watch out!" They sold me to a dealer as a center horse for troikas. I didn't stay long at the dealer's. A hussar who had come to buy fresh horses took me. All this was so unjust, so cruel, that I was glad when they led me out of Khrenovo and separated me permanently from everything that was familiar and dear to me. It was too painful among them. They had the prospect of love, honor, and freedom; for me there was work and humiliation and humiliation and work until the end of my life! For what? Because I was a skewbald and for that reason I had to become someone's horse.

Holstomer could not continue his story further that evening. There was an event in the paddock that made a great commotion among all the horses. Kupchikha, a mare in foal who was overdue and who had been listening from the beginning, suddenly turned and slowly walked under the shed. There she began to groan so loudly that all the horses turned their attention to her; then she lay down, then she got up again and lay down again. The old brood mares understood what was happening to her, but the youngsters became agitated and, leaving the gelding, surrounded the sick horse. Toward morning there was a new colt swaying on its little legs. Nester shouted at the head groom, and the colt with its mare was led into the stable while the horses were driven out without them.

8

The Fourth Night

In the evening, when the gates were closed and everything had become quiet, the skewbald continued:

I managed to make many observations about people and horses during my travels from hand to hand. I spent the longest amount of time with two owners: a prince who was an officer in the hussars, and then an old woman who lived near the Church of Nikola's Apparition.

I passed the best times of my life with the hussar officer.

Although he was the cause of my ruin, although he never loved anything or anybody, I loved him and I love him just for this. I admired him precisely because he was handsome, happy, and rich, and because he was handsome, happy, and rich he did not love anybody. You understand this lofty feeling, which is unique to us horses. His coldness and cruelty and my dependence on him all gave a special force to my love for him. "Kill me! Drive me to death!" I would think during our good times, "and I'll be happy for it."

He bought me from the horse dealer to whom the head groom had sold me for eight hundred rubles. He bought me because nobody had a skewbald horse. This was the best of times for me. He had a mistress. I know this because every day I carried him to her and sometimes I carried them both together. His mistress was a beauty and he was handsome, and even his coachman was handsome. And because of this I loved them all. And I was delighted to be alive. My life went like this: In the morning the groom came to brush me down, not the coachman himself, but a groom. The groom was a young fellow fresh from the country. He would open the door, air out the stable, let out the horse smells that had accumulated during the night, clean out the manure, take off the horse cloths, begin to run a brush over my body, and with a horse-comb drop whitish rows of fluff on the hoof-scarred floor. I would bite playfully at his sleeves and paw with my leg. Then we would be brought, one by one, to a tub of cold water, and the boy would admire the smooth results of his labors on my coat, my leg, straight as an arrow with a broad hoof, and my croup and back, broad enough to sleep on. Hay was piled into high racks and oats were poured into an oak trough. Then Feofan, the head coachman, would come in.

The master and coachman were alike. Neither one was afraid of anything, neither one loved anybody except himself, and everybody loved them for this. Feofan went around in a red shirt, velveteen trousers, and a fitted coat. I loved it when on a holiday he, pomaded and wearing his coat, would walk into the stable and call out, "Well, you beast, you forgot yourself!" and he would push me in the haunches with the handle of a pitchfork, but never painfully—just as a joke. I understood at once that it was a joke and pricking up my ears would click my teeth.

We had a black stallion, one of a pair. In the evenings they used to harness me with him. Polkan didn't understand a joke and was simply mean as the devil. I stood in the stall next to his, and we bit each other often. Feofan was not afraid of him. He would approach straight on, yell, appear as though he was ready to kill—but no, he would go past and put the harness on. Once we went off together in a gallop along Kuznetsky. Neither the master nor the coachman was afraid. Both were laughing, shouting at the people, pulling back on the reins, and turning so that finally we did not run anyone over.

In their service I lost my best attributes and spent half of my life. It was here they gave me too much water and ruined my legs. But despite this, it was the best time of my life. At noon they would come, harness us, smear our hooves with grease, dampen forelocks and mane, and put us between the shafts.

The sleigh was made of wicker with velvet upholstery. The harness had little silver buckles and silken reins, which were also ornamented with drawn thread work. The harness was such that when the reins and thongs were adjusted and buckled up it was impossible to distinguish where it ended and the horse began. We were harnessed in the barn. Feofan would enter, his backside broader than his shoulders, wearing a red sash under his armpits. He would examine the harness, sit down, fix his caftan, thrust his foot in the stirrup, always make a joke about something, attach his whip, which almost never flicked me and was only for show, and say, "Let's go!" And playing with each step, I would move out of the gates, and the cook, leaving the house to pour out the slops, would stop on the threshold, and the muzhiks bringing firewood into the yard would stare at me. We would ride out, go a short distance, and stop. Lackeys would come out, coachmen would drive up, and conversation would begin. Everyone would wait. Sometimes we'd stand as much as three hours by the entrance; occasionally we'd drive a little, turn around, and then stop again.

Finally, there would be a noise at the door, and gray-haired, pot-bellied Tikhon would run out in his dress coat to command: "Drive up!" In those days they didn't have the stupid custom of saying "Forward!" as if I didn't know that one goes forward and not backward. Feofan would make a smacking noise. We would drive up, and hurriedly and carelessly, acting as if there were nothing wondrous—about the sleigh, about the horses, or about Feofan who bowed his back and extended his hands in such a way that it seemed impossible to hold them for long—the prince would come out wearing a military cap and an overcoat with a gray beaver collar hiding his rosy, dark-browed handsome face, which should never have been hidden; he'd come out with his sword and spurs, and with the bronze-tipped heels of his boots rattling, and he'd step on the carpet as though hurrying and without paying attention to me or to Feofan, whom everyone was looking at and admiring except him. Feofan would make the smacking noise, I'd lean into my harness, and we'd drive up honestly, at a walk, and stop; I'd glance sideways at the prince, toss my thoroughbred head and fine forelocks. When the prince was in a good mood he would joke with Feofan; Feofan would answer, hardly turning his handsome head, and without lowering his hands, he would make a barely noticeable movement of the reins understandable to me, and one-two, one-two, ever wider, wider, with each muscle quivering and throwing snow and dirt under the front of the sleigh, I would be off. Then, too, they did not have today's stupid custom of crying out "Ho-o-o!" as though the coachman had some kind of incomprehensible pain. "Careful now! Careful now!" Feofan would shout out, and people would move to the side and stop, twisting their necks, looking at the handsome gelding, handsome coachman, and handsome master.

I loved to overtake a trotter. When from afar Feofan and I would see one worthy of our exertion flying like a whirlwind, we would slowly begin to draw closer and closer. By then I'd be throwing dirt against the back of the sleigh, drawing even with the driver, snorting over his head, drawing even with the harness, even with the bow-shaft, and I would no longer see him but only hear from behind me ever-receding sounds. And the prince, Feofan, and I would all remain silent and act as if we were simply going about our business and that we didn't even notice whom we encountered on our route with their inferior horses. I loved to overtake, but I also loved to meet a good trotter: a moment, a sound, a glance, and we would again be flying alone each to his own side.

The gate creaked and the voices of Nester and Vaska were heard.

The Fifth Night

The weather began to change. It was cloudy in the morning and there was no dew, but it was warm and the gnats stuck like glue. As soon as the herd was driven in, the horses gathered around the skewbald and he finished his story:

My happy life soon ended. I lived that way for only two years. At the end of
the second winter I experienced joy and, after it, my greatest misfortune. This
was at Shrovetide. I took the prince to the racetrack. Atlasny and Bychok were
racing. I don't know what he did in the clubhouse, but I know that he came out
and ordered Feofan to drive onto the track. I remember being led onto the track
and being positioned, and Atlasny was positioned, too. He pulled a racing rig
and I, just as I was, pulled a city sleigh. At the turn I raced by him and laughter
and roars of delight greeted me.

When I was led away a crowd followed me. And about five men offered
the prince thousands of rubles. He only laughed, showing his white teeth.

"No," he said. "This is not a horse, but a friend. I wouldn't take a
mountain of gold for him. Goodbye, gentlemen." He unhooked the sleigh
curtain and sat down.

"To Stozhinka!" That was the apartment of his mistress. And we flew
off. This was our last happy day.

We arrived at her place. He called her his own. But she loved somebody
else and had left with him. He found this out at her apartment. It was five
o'clock, and without unharnessing me he went after her. Never before was I
whipped and allowed to gallop. For the first time I broke my gait; I became
ashamed and wanted to correct myself, but suddenly I heard the prince cry
out in a voice that was not his own, "Go ahead!" And the whip whistled and
cut me and I galloped off hitting my legs against the metal of the sleigh
front. We overtook her after sixteen miles. I had managed to bring him
there, but I was trembling the whole night and unable to eat anything. The
next morning they gave me water. I drank and forever stopped being the
horse that I was. I became ill, they tortured me and made me lame—"curing"
me, as people call it. My hooves deteriorated and swelled and my legs
became bowed. My chest caved in and my whole body became flabby. I
was sold to a horse dealer. He fed me carrots and something else and made
of me something quite unlike what I was, but such that it could deceive one
who did not know me. I no longer had any strength or speed in me. Moreover, the horse dealer tortured me whenever customers came, he would
come into the stable, whip me savagely and frighten me, in order to drive
me into a rage. Then he would rub down the welts from the whip and lead
me out. An old woman bought me from the horse dealer. She used to drive
me to the Church of Nikola's Apparition and she whipped her coachman.
The coachman cried in my stall. And here I found out that tears have a
pleasant, salty taste. Then the old woman died. Her bailiff took me to the
country and sold me to a dry goods dealer. Then I ate too much wheat and
became even sicker. They sold me to a muzhik. There I was set to work
plowing, almost never ate, and my leg was cut on a plowshare. Again I

became ill. The muzhik traded me to a gypsy who tortured me terribly and finally sold me to the present bailiff. And here I am.

Everyone was silent. It began to drizzle.

9

Returning home the next evening, the herd met the owner and a guest. Zhuldyba, approaching the stable, saw two male figures out of the corner of her eye: one was the young master in a straw hat; the other, a tall, bloated, paunchy officer. The old mare squinted at the men and pressed past him. The others, the youngsters, became alarmed and did not know what to do, especially when the master and his guest deliberately walked into the midst of the horses, pointing something out to each other and talking.

"Here's the one I bought from Voikov, that dappled gray," said the master.

"And whose is this young black filly with the white legs?" asked the guest. "It's a nice one." They looked over many of the horses, going to the sides and stopping them. They noticed the chestnut filly, too.

"This is one of the mounts left over from the Khrenovo breed," said the owner.

They could not look at all the horses on the move. The owner called out for Nester, and the old man, hurriedly digging his heels into the side of the skewbald, came up at a trot. The skewbald hobbled, slightly lame in one leg, but in the way he ran it was obvious that in no way would he grumble even if he were ordered to run as far as his strength would last, to the end of the world. He was even ready to run at a full gallop and, indeed, attempted this with his right leg.

"There is, I dare say, no horse in Russia better than this mare," said the master, pointing at one of the horses. His guest praised her. The owner bustled about, running here and there, showing the horses, and telling the history and breed of each one. The guest was apparently bored listening to the owner, and he thought up questions in order to appear interested.

"Yes, yes," he said absent-mindedly.

"Take a look," said the owner without answering. "Look at the legs. She was expensive, but I've already gotten three from her; and she's in harness."

"Is she running well?" asked the guest.

In this manner they looked over almost all of the horses until there was nothing more to show. And they fell silent.

"Well, shall we go?"

"Let's." They went out through the gates. The guest was glad that the exhibition was over and that they were going to the house, where one could eat, drink, and smoke; he cheered up visibly.

In passing Nester, who was sitting on the skewbald awaiting further orders, the guest slapped the horse's croup with his big, plump hand.

"Look how colorful he is," he said. "I once had a skewbald just like this. You remember, I told you about him."

The master realized that the conversation was not about his horses and did not bother to listen further, but glancing back, he continued looking at his herd.

Suddenly, right next to his ear, a stupid, weak, and senile neighing was heard. It was the skewbald who had neighed; he did not finish and, as though embarrassed, cut it short. Neither the guest nor the owner paid any attention to this neighing, and they went on home. In the dropsical old man Holstomer had recognized his beloved owner, the former brilliant, rich, and handsome Serpukhovskoy.

10

It continued to drizzle. It was gloomy in the paddock, but the manor house was quite different. The mistress had laid out a sumptuous evening tea in the sumptuous drawing room. The tea was for the benefit of the host, the hostess, and their newly arrived guest.

The hostess, who was pregnant, a fact quite apparent from her protruding stomach, her erect but curved posture, her plumpness, and especially her eyes, large eyes, which looked meekly and solemnly inward, sat behind the samovar.

The master held a box of special ten-year-old cigars, which, according to him, no one else had and about which he was about to brag to his guest. The master was a handsome twenty-five year old, fresh, well groomed, and with nicely styled hair. At home he dressed in a new, roomy, thick cloth suit made in London. On his watch chain were large expensive seals. The massive cufflinks of his shirt were also large, gold with turquoise. His beard was à la Napoleon III, and his pomaded mouse-tail tips protruded in such a way that the style could have originated only in Paris. The mistress was wearing a dress of silk and muslin in a pattern of large bouquets of mixed flowers. She had some sort of special large golden pins in her thick light brown hair, which though it was not quite all her own was beautiful nevertheless. On her hands were many bracelets and rings, all expensive. The samovar was silver, the service of fine china. The lackey, magnificent in his swallowtail coat and white vest and tie, stood near the door like a statue, awaiting orders. The furniture was of bent-wood, winding and colorful; the wallpaper was dark with large flowers. Near the table an unusually slender .

Italian greyhound tinkled a silver collar; it had an unusually difficult English name, badly pronounced by both owners, who did not know English. In the corner stood a piano with inlaid work and surrounded by flowers. Newness, luxury, and rarity emanated from everything. Everything was very fine, but it all bore a particular stamp of excess, wealth, and the absence of any intellectual interests.

The host was a trotting enthusiast, a robust, sanguine fellow, one of those who are never in short supply, who go about in sable coats, throw expensive bouquets to actresses, drink the most expensive wines of the latest brands in the most expensive hotels, give prizes in their own names, and keep the most expensive women.

The visitor, Nikita Serpukhovskoy, was a man past forty, tall, heavy, balding, with a large mustache and side whiskers. He must have been very handsome. Now he had apparently fallen into decline—physically, morally, and financially.

He had so many debts that he had to work to keep from being put into jail. He was now traveling to a provincial town in the capacity of a stud farm administrator. He had obtained this position through influential relatives. He was dressed in a military jacket and blue trousers. The jacket and trousers were such that only a wealthy person would think of making for himself, and his underwear was of the same sort, as was his English watch. His boots had some type of miraculous soles as thick as a finger.

In his lifetime Nikita Serpukhovskoy had squandered away a fortune of two million rubles, and he still owed another hundred and twenty thousand. From such a lump sum there always remains a life style that provides credit and the possibility of living almost luxuriously another ten years or so. The ten years or so were ending along with the life style, and Nikita's life had become a sorrowful one. He had already begun to drink—that is, to get drunk on wine—something that had never happened to him before, although in truth he had never really begun and had never ended drinking. His deterioration was most noticeable in the anxiety of his gaze (his eyes were always shifting) and in the lack of firmness in his intonation and movements. This anxiety was striking because it seemed to be of recent origin; one could see he had been accustomed all his life not to fear anybody or anything and that now only recently he had, through intense suffering, arrived at fear so alien to his nature. The host and hostess noticed this, and exchanging glances in mutual understanding and evidently postponing a detailed discussion of the subject until bedtime, they put up with poor Nikita and even waited on him. The young host's appearance of happiness humiliated Nikita and, remembering his own irretrievable past, forced him to feel a painful envy.

"Do cigars bother you, Mary?" he asked, turning to the woman with that particular tone, elusive and acquired only by experience—polite, friendly, but not totally respectful, which men with knowledge of the world use when they speak to their mistresses as distinct from their own wives. Not that he wanted to be offensive; on the contrary, he now wanted to ingratiate himself with her and her master as quickly as possible, although he would never think of admitting this to himself. But he had been long accustomed to speaking in such a way with such women. He knew she would have wondered herself, even would have been offended, if he treated her as a lady. Moreover, it was necessary to hold in reserve a certain hint of a respectable tone for the actual wife of his equal. He always treated such women respectfully, not because he shared the so-called convictions promulgated in magazines (he never read that rubbish) about respect for each person's personality, about the irrelevance of marriage, and so on, but because all decent people behaved so, and he was a decent person although he had come down in the world.

He took a cigar. But the host awkwardly picked up an entire handful and offered it to the guest.

"No, you'll see how good they are. Take them."

Nikita declined the cigars with his hand, and his eyes flickered with barely noticeable offense and shame.

"Thank you." He took out his cigar case. "Try mine."

The hostess was sensitive. She noticed what had transpired and hastened to strike up a conversation with Nikita.

"I really love cigars. I would smoke myself if everyone around me wouldn't."

And she smiled her pretty, kind smile. He smiled in reply to her, but without conviction. He was missing two teeth.

"No, try this one," the insensitive host continued. "The others are a weaker sort. *Fritz, bringen sie noch eine Kasten,*" he said, "*dort zwei.*"[3]

The German lackey brought the other box.

"Which ones do you prefer? Strong ones? These are very good. Take them all." He went on pushing them forward. He was evidently happy to have someone to whom he could show off his rare possessions, and he did not notice anything. Serpukhovskoy lit up and hurried to resume the interrupted conversation.

"So, how much did you pay for Atlasny?" he asked.

"I had to pay a lot, no less than five thousand, but at the very least I've already broken even. What offspring! I'm telling you!"

"Are they racing?" asked Serpukhovskoy.

"They're racing well. His colt recently took three prizes: in Tula, in

Moscow, and in Petersburg, where he ran with Voeykov's Vorony. That scoundrel of a jockey threw him off his gait four times or he would have left the others behind at the flag."

"He's a little too fleshy. Too much Dutch blood, is what I say," said Serpukhovskoy.

"Well, what are brood mares for? I'll show you tomorrow. I gave three thousand for Dobrynya. Two thousand for Laskovaya."

And again the host began to enumerate his riches. The hostess saw that this was unpleasant to Serpukhovskoy and that he was pretending to listen.

"Will you have some more tea?" she inquired.

"I won't," said the host and went on talking.

She got up, the host stopped her and embraced and kissed her. Looking at them Serpukhovskoy smiled an unnatural smile for their benefit, but when the host got up, put his arm around her, and walked out to the portière, Nikita's expression suddenly changed. He sighed heavily and his bloated face assumed an expression of despair. Even malice could be seen on it.

11

The host returned smiling and sat down opposite Nikita. They were silent for a while.

"Yes, you were saying, you bought him from Voeykov," said Serpukhovskoy in an offhand way.

"Yes, I was speaking of Atlasny. I've always wanted to buy some mares from Dubovitsky. But he only had rubbish left."

"He's broke," said Serpukhovskoy and suddenly stopped and looked around. He recalled that he owed twenty thousand to the very person who was broke. And if it could be said someone was "broke" then indeed it was probably being said about him. He fell silent.

They did not speak for a long time. The host was mentally conducting a search for something to brag about to his guest. Serpukhovskoy was trying to think of a way to show that he did not consider himself broke. But the minds of both were in a state of lethargy, despite their attempt to enliven themselves with cigars. "Well, when do we have a drink?" thought Serpukhovskoy. "We must have a drink without fail or I'll die of boredom with him," the host thought.

"So, how long will you be staying here?" asked Serpukhovskoy.

"Why, about another month. What do you say, shall we eat supper? Fritz, is it ready?"

They went into the dining room. Under a lamp in the dining room stood a table set with candles and the most extraordinary things: siphons with little figures on the corks, extraordinary wines in carafes, extraordinary appetizers and vodka. They drank, ate, drank some more, ate some more, and the conversation picked up. Serpukhovskoy grew flushed and began to speak without hesitation.

They spoke about women. Who had what kind: a gypsy, a dancer, a Frenchwoman.

"Well, have you left Mattie?" asked the host. She was the mistress who had bankrupted Serpukhovskoy.

"No, she was the one who left. Ah, brother, when you think what I've squandered in my life! Now I'm glad when a thousand rubles come my way and I'm glad, really, to get away from everyone. I can't stand Moscow anymore. Ah, what can I say!"

The host was bored listening to Serpukhovskoy. He wanted to talk about himself—to boast. And Serpukhovskoy wanted to talk about himself—about his brilliant past. The host poured him some wine and was waiting for him to finish so he could talk of himself, of how his farm was arranged as none had ever been before. And of how his Mary loved him not only for his money but sincerely, from the heart.

"I wanted to tell you that at my farm . . ." he started to say. But Serpukhovskoy interrupted him.

"There was a time, no doubt," he began, "when I liked living well and knew how to live well. You're talking about racing—well, tell me, which is your liveliest horse?"

The host was happy for the opportunity to talk some more about his stud farm and began doing so, but Serpukhovskoy again interrupted him.

"Yes, yes," he said. "But you breeders only do it out of vanity, not for pleasure and for life. For me, however, that's not how it was. I told you earlier I had a harness horse, a skewbald—with spots just like the one your groom was riding. Oh, what a horse it was! You couldn't have known it; it was back in '42, I had only just arrived in Moscow. I went to the dealer— and I saw a skewbald gelding. It had good lines. I liked him. The price? A thousand rubles. I liked him, took him, and began driving around with him. I never before had such a horse, and you never had one like that and never will. I've never seen a better horse—for riding, for strength, or for beauty. You were still a boy, you couldn't have known, but I think you probably heard of him. All of Moscow knew of him."

"Yes, I heard," said the host reluctantly, "but I wanted to tell you about my . . ."

"So you did hear. I bought him just like that without a pedigree, without a certificate; it was only later I found out. Voeykov and I tracked it down. He was the son of Lyubezny I, Holstomer, they called him. You could measure cloth with his stride.[4] Because of his skewbaldness, he was taken out of the Khrenovo farm and given to the head groom, who gelded him and sold him to a dealer. There aren't any such horses left, my boy! Oh! What a time it was. Oh, youth!" he sang from a gypsy song. He began to get tipsy. "Yes, those were the days. I was twenty-five. I had eighty thousand in silver rubles a year then, not one gray hair, all my teeth, and they were like pearls. No matter what I tackled everything succeeded, but that's all over."

"Well, the horses weren't as spirited then," said the host, taking advantage of the interruption. "I tell you, my first horses started walking without . . . "

"Your horses! Horses used to be more spirited."

"How's that?"

"More spirited. I remember as though it were today. Once I drove him to the races in Moscow. My horses were not running. I didn't like trotters, I had thoroughbreds—General, Shole, Mohammed. I used the skewbald to get around. My coachman was a fine fellow. I was fond of him. He also became a drunk. So, I drive up. 'Serpukhovskoy,' I was asked, 'when will you start keeping trotters?' 'Your muzhiks—the devil take them—my skewbald can outrun them all.' 'No, he can't.' 'A thousand rubles' wager.' We agreed. We raced. He was faster by five seconds. I won a thousand rubles. But that's nothing. On a troika of thoroughbreds I went sixty-six miles in three hours. All of Moscow knows."

And Serpukhovskoy began to lie so glibly and unceasingly that the host could not get in a word and sat opposite him with a doleful look on his face, only adding wine to their glasses as a way of entertaining himself.

Dawn began to break. But they kept sitting there. The host was horribly bored. He got up.

"When it's time to sleep, it's time to sleep," said Serpukhovskoy getting up, and swaying and puffing he walked to the room given him.

The host and his mistress were in bed.

"No, he's impossible. He got drunk, and he lies without stopping."

"And he was making advances to me."

"I'm afraid he's going to ask for money."

Serpukhovskoy, breathing heavily, was lying on the bed without undressing. "It seems I did a lot of lying," he thought. "Well, so what. The wine was good, but he's a dreadful swine. There's something mercantile about him. And I'm a dreadful swine too," he said to himself and burst out laughing. "Once I used to keep women, and now I'm being kept. Yes, the Winkler woman is keeping me—I take money from her. Serves him right, it does. But it's time to undress; I can't get my boots off."

"Hey! Hey!" he called out, but the servant assigned to him had long since gone to bed.

He sat up, took off his jacket and vest, and somehow managed to pull off his trousers, but for a long time he could not pull off his boots, his soft belly got in the way. Somehow he finally got off one boot, struggled and struggled with the other, huffing and puffing until he became tired. And so, with one foot stuck in the top of the boot, he slumped over and started to snore, filling the entire room with the odor of tobacco, wine, and filthy old age.

12

If Holstomer had more reminiscences that night, then Vaska distracted him from them. He threw a horse cloth on him, galloped off, and until morning kept him standing at the door of a tavern next to a muzhik's horse. They licked each other. In the morning when he returned to the herd he kept scratching.

"Somehow I'm itching badly," he thought.

Five days passed. They sent for the veterinarian. He said joyfully:

"Scabs. Sell him to the gypsies."

"What for? Cut his throat, only get rid of him today."

The morning was quiet and clear. The herd went out into the field. Holstomer stayed behind. A strange man came, thin, black, and dirty in a caftan splattered with something black. He was a slaughterman. Without looking at him, he took Holstomer's rope halter and led him away. Holstomer went calmly without looking back, as always dragging his legs and catching his hind legs in the straw. Going out the gates, he tried to pull toward the well, but the slaughterman jerked the halter and said, "There's no need."

The slaughterman, followed by Vaska in the rear, arrived at a glen behind the brick barn, and they stopped, as if this most ordinary place were something special. After handing over the bridle to Vaska, the slaughterman took off his caftan, rolled up his sleeves, took a knife and a whetstone out of the top of his boot, and began to sharpen the knife. The gelding stretched himself toward the bridle and, from boredom, wanted to chew on it, but it was too far. He sighed and closed his eyes. His lip drooped down, showing his worn yellow teeth, and he started to doze to the sound of the knife being sharpened. Only his sick and oozing foreleg trembled intermittently. Suddenly he felt that he had been taken under the jowls and that his head was lifted up. He opened his eyes. Two dogs were in front of him. One sniffed in the direction of the slaughterman, the other sat looking at the gelding as if expecting something, something from him. The gelding glanced at them and began to rub his head against the hand holding him.

"They want to cure me," he thought. "Let them."

And in fact, he felt that something had been done to his throat. It hurt, he shuddered and kicked out a leg, but he controlled himself and began to wait for what might come next. What came next was that some kind of liquid poured out in a big stream onto his neck and chest. He sighed with his entire body. And he began to feel much better. He felt relieved of all the burdens of his life. He closed his eyes and began to droop his head—nobody was holding it. Then his neck began to droop, then his legs began to tremble, and his whole body swayed. He was not so much frightened as astonished. Everything had become so new. He was astonished and jerked forward, upward. But instead, his legs moved out of place and became entangled, he began to keel to one side, and meaning to shift his feet, he pitched forward, onto his left side. The slaughterman waited until the spasms stopped, chased away the dogs who had pressed in closer, and taking the gelding by his leg and turning him over onto his back, he told Vaska to hold the leg while he began to skin him.

"This was some horse once," said Vaska.

"If he'd been fed better it would have been a good hide," said the slaughterman.

In the evening the herd passed over the hill, and those horses passing on the left could see something red below, near which dogs were bustling nervously and above which ravens and kites were flying. One dog, pushing with paws against the carcass and shaking its head, tore off with a crackling sound the meat she had sunk teeth into. The chestnut filly stopped, stretched out her head and neck, and for a long time drew in deep breaths. Only with difficulty were they able to drive her away.

At dawn in the ravine of an old forest, in the low-lying thicket of a small meadow, big-headed wolf cubs were joyfully howling. There were five of them: four were about the same size, but one was small, with a head bigger than his body. A skinny she-wolf with shedding fur, dragging a full belly with sagging teats along the ground, came out of the bushes and sat across from the cubs. The cubs stood in a semicircle opposite her. She approached the smallest and dropping down on one knee and leaning her snout downward, she made a few convulsive movements, opened her large-toothed jaws, and straining, hawked up a large piece of horse meat. The larger cubs pushed toward her, but she threatened them and gave everything to the little one. The cub growled as though he were angry, stashed the horse meat under him, and began to guzzle it down. In the same way the she-wolf hawked up meat for the second cub, and the third, and for all five, and then she lay down opposite them to rest.

After a week, only a large skull and two shoulder bones lay next to the brick shed, the rest had all been dragged off. In the summer, a muzhik gathering bones carried off both the shoulder bones and the skull and put them to use.

The dead body of Serpukhovskoy, which had been walking about in the world eating and drinking, was put into the earth much later. Neither the skin, nor the flesh, nor the bones from his body were of any use. And just as his dead body walking about in the world for twenty years had been a great burden to everyone, so also its disposal in the earth only caused people additional bother. For a long time he had been of no use to anyone, for a long time too he had been a burden to all, but just the same, the dead burying the dead found it necessary to clothe his already decaying, puffy body in a good military uniform and good boots, to place him in a good new coffin with new tassels in its four corners, then to place this new coffin in another leaden one, and to bring it to Moscow, and there to unearth ancient human bones and precisely there to hide this decaying, worm-infested body in its new uniform and polished boots and to cover it all with earth.

Translation by Howard Blue

Notes to the translation are on page 579.

RESOURCES

Primary Text

Tolstoi, L.N. "Kholstomer. Istoriia loshadi." *Polnoe sobranie sochinenii.* Vol. 26. Moscow: Khudozhestvennia literatura. Ed. V. Chertkov et al. 1928–58, pp. 3–37.

Secondary Sources

Literary and Cultural Studies

Christian, R.F. *Tolstoy: A Critical Introduction.* New York: Cambridge University Press, 1969.

Erlich, Victor. *Russian Formalism: History–Doctrine.* 3d ed. The Hague: Mouton, 1981.

Gustafson, Richard F. *Leo Tolstoy, Resident and Stranger: A Study in Fiction and Theology.* Princeton: Princeton University Press, 1986.

Schefski, H.K. "The Changing Focus of Eikhenbaum's Tolstoi Criticism." *Russian Review* 37 (1978): 298–307.

Shklovskii, Viktor. *Sobranie sochinenii.* Moscow: Khudozhestvennaia literatura, 1973–74.

Smelianskii, Anatolii. *Nashi sobesedniki.* Moscow: Iskusstvo, 1981, pp. 183–219.

Drama and Theater

Poliakova, E. *Teatr L'va Tolstogo.* Moscow: Iskusstvo, 1978. For criticism, photos of and commentary on Tovstonogov's production, as well as other theater adaptations of Tolstoy's works.

Rudnitsky, Konstantin. *Russian and Soviet Theater: Tradition and the Avant Garde.* Trans. Roxane Permar, ed. Lesley Milne. London: Thames and Hudson, 1988, pp. 298–99. Photos of Moscow Art Theater production of *Resurrection.*

Strider. Play with music by Mark Rozovsky. English stage version by Robert Kalfin and Steve Brown. New York: Samuel French, 1981.

Music

Prokofiev, Sergei. *Voina i mir* (War and Peace). Opera in 13 scenes. Conductor, Melik-Pashaev. Bolshoi Theatre Chorus and Orchestra. Melodiia, n.d. 4-record set.

Shchedrin, R. *Anna Karenina.* Ballet in 3 acts. Choreographer, Iu. Simonov. Bolshoi Theatre Orchestra. Melodiia, n.d. 2-record set.

Film

Anna Karenina. Director, Aleksandr Zarkhi. Cinematographer, Leonid Kalashnikov. Design, A. Borisov. Music, Rodion Shchedrin. Cast: Tat'iana Samoilova, Nikolai Tritsenko, Anastasiia Vertinskaia. Mosfilm, 1968.

Dva gusara (Two Hussars). Director, V. Khrishtofovich. Cast: Oleg Iankovskii and Aleksandr Abdulov. 1986.

Kreitserova sonata (Kreutzer Sonata). Director, Mikhail Shveitzer. Cast: Oleg Iankovskii, Alla Demidova. Mosfilm, 1986.

Tolstoi: From Rags to Riches. Producer, Jonathan Stedall. Editor, Jonathan Gili. Narrator, Richard Hurndall with Malcolm Muggeridge and Theodore Roszak. BBC Film, n.d.

Voina i mir (War and Peace). Director, Sergei Bondarchuk. Cinematographers, Aleksandr Shelenkov, Anatolii Petritskii. Music, Viacheslav Tikhonov. Mosfilm, 1966.

Voskresenie (Resurrection). Director, Mikhail Shveitzer. Cinematographer, Eva Saveleva. Design, D. Vinitskii. Music, G. Sviridov. Cast: Tamara Semina, Evgenii Matveev. Mosfilm, 1962.

~ V ~

New Aesthetic Languages

The end of the nineteenth century saw vast social and economic changes in Russia. Freedom for the peasants, the dream of the intelligentsia and the cornerstone of all Russian progressive political programs, was now established social reality. Along with emancipation of the lower classes came massive industrialization, agricultural reform, and a free-enterprise system supported by government officials like Sergei Witte and Petr Stolypin. The Russian economy measured by the traditional statistical yardsticks was now in competition with the leading industrial powers. The literate members of society doubled in fourteen years after the turn of the century (to 45 percent of the population), creating a huge new audience for the arts.

Anton Chekhov's (1860–1904) *The Cherry Orchard* (1903) responded to such changes and to Chekhov's own social evolution from grandson of a peasant to leading writer of his day. A host of other talented artists, writers, and patrons, such as Aleksei Peshkov (Maxim Gorky, 1868–1936), Fedor Chaliapin, and Savva Mamontov, testified to the beneficial cultural effects of upward mobility. As Chekhov suggests in his play, however, such social dislocations also provided a rich source of problematic issues for writers. Unlike Tolstoy (whom he knew and debated) or Dostoevsky, Chekhov worked more at indicating the dilemmas he saw around him than at providing solutions to them. His most famous social act is typical: it was not, like Tolstoy's, the creation of a school for peasant children or, like Dostoevsky's, the mobilization of Russian self-identity in a speech on Pushkin but a census he undertook of convicts on the island of Sakhalin.

"The Lady with the Lapdog" (1899) follows the same Chekhovian pattern of refusing to suggest ready answers. Written in the course of transition to the sustained theater work of his major plays, its pathos of hope and

401

Aleksei Batalov as Gurov and Iya Savvina as Anna in the 1960 film *Lady with the Lapdog* directed by Josif Heifetz.

late-blooming love before the impossibility of resolution suggests Chekhov's familiar dramatic themes. Gurov and Anna's anguish and talk of the future are mirrored in the anguish of characters such as Masha and Vershinin of Chekhov's *Three Sisters* and the monologues of Trofimov in *The Cherry Orchard*. In one of the better examples of Soviet film adaptation (Lenfilm, 1959), Josif Heifitz realized many of these dramatic possibilities through the acting of Aleksei Batalov and the cinematography of Andrei Moskvin. The film was particularly successful in using nature symbolism suggesting regal indifference before the triviality of human affairs and reminiscent of the humble power of Levitan's landscapes.

In refusing to argue loudly for transcendent truths, Chekhov reflected a dominant mode of Russian cultural secularization and a turn to professional methodology reflected in a broad array of creative and theoretical works by writers, composers, and painters such as Valery Briusov, Nikolai Rimsky-

Korsakov, and Vasily Kandinsky. The concern for analytical exploration of cultural tools—words, paints, notes—rather than their messages stimulated a tremendous outburst of experimentation and creativity. The technical refinements of the early twentieth century eventually produced seminal new works by Kandinsky in art, Fokine and Balanchine in ballet, Chaliapin in vocal performance, Rimsky-Korsakov, Stravinsky, Prokofiev, and Shostakovich in musical composition, and Stanislavsky and Meyerhold in theater.

Yet Russian culture, in exploring aesthetic signs and in creating new ones, did not avoid moral, social, or political issues. The early part of the century saw not only an outburst of artistic experimentation—in Diaghilev's World of Art, Stanislavsky's and Nemirovich-Danchenko's Moscow Art Theater, and Mikhail Fokine's Mariinsky and Paris productions—but also a religious renaissance that once again invigorated aesthetic endeavors with the eternal questions. A bridge between philosophy, theology, and the arts was provided by Vladimir Soloviev (1853–1900), whose philosophical writings and poetry inspired the primary texts of Russian Symbolism created by Alexander Blok (1880–1921), Dmitry Merezhkovsky (1865–1941), Viacheslav Ivanov (1866–1949), and Andrei Bely (1880–1934), just as they inspired the religious-philosophical works of Nikolai Berdyaev (1874–1948), Leo Shestov (1866–1938), the Trubetskoi brothers, Sergei and Evgeny, Pavel Florensky (1882–1943), and Sergei Bulgakov (1871–1944). The transcendent patterns Soloviev saw, particularly in his central concept of a feminine principle in history he named Sophia or the Divine Wisdom, were accompanied by a pervasive irony and skepticism about the transcendent meanings of signs. Irony and skepticism, in fact, were as much Soloviev's legacy to the writers, philosophers, and poets who followed as were the philosophical insights and magnificent synthesis of social, metaphysical, and aesthetic concepts in his thought.

Blok's *The Puppet Show*, a play that originated in the poem included below, was staged by Vsevolod Meyerhold on December 30, 1906. In the production, Meyerhold built on Soloviev's and Blok's skepticism about transcendent meanings to make the theatrical manipulation of signs itself a subject of performance. The "cardboard helmet" and the "cranberry juice" that replaced blood became part of Meyerhold's "Theater of Conditionality," in which signs were detached from stable referents in reality and became conditional parts of the aesthetic world created for them by stage practice. In this world the Devil could be brought down to earth to express evil's banality, as in Fedor Sologub's (1863–1927) *Petty Demon* (1907) or in the stage adaptation that followed in 1909. But even the Devil's reality was a conditional function of his aesthetic uses according to the Symbolists, and poets could only hope to grasp a "tenth part," as Valery Briusov (1873–1924) put it in his poem, of the

Listen! The Taganka Theater, Moscow.

real world that appeared through the senses and symbols. Much later Briusov's text was transposed to song in V. Panin's 1990 film adaptation *I Will Love if I Want to Love,* based on "Last Pages of a Lady's Diary."

Generally judged to be the most talented of Symbolist novels, Andrei Bely's *Petersburg* (1916) combined familiar issues of East and West with a vivid cross-representational sensibility. Bely brought together the favored symbols of European presence in Russian culture—such as the capital itself and the Bronze Horseman—with Symbolist concerns for the Asian influence on Russia. In the novel, as in other of his prose works and poems, he explored the interrelationships of literature and music. A correlative of the characteristic Symbolist desire to fuse the arts was provided in Mikhail Chekhov's 1925 theater adaptation of *Petersburg.* Typically, as in his responses to history, Bely reacted with a sense of lost control: he complained to Meyerhold that his text had become a new "shared child" of the theater's creative process.

Although they frequently reacted against Symbolist metaphysics, numerous other aesthetic programs sprang up in Russia inspired by the freedom Symbolists gave signs to break through aesthetic conventions and long-honored boundaries of signification. The subjective confidence of Russian Modernism developed in these conditions, and young iconoclasts such as Vladimir Mayakovsky (1893–1930) began to argue that the meaning of stars was a function of the poet's personal creativity and needs. "Listen!" demands that attention be paid to the importance of poets and the new languages they create; after a 1967 adaptation of Mayakovsky's verse, the poem title became part of Moscow's theater landscape as a permanent signboard on the Taganka Theater's facade.

Views that poetic symbols and words should be judged for their technical efficacy and that language could be manipulated without reference to higher realities beyond the poetic "I" were expressed in shocking fashion by Mayakovsky's colleagues among the Futurists. Their famous manifesto, "A Slap in the Face of Public Taste" (1912), mocked the pretensions of literary tradition. Mayakovsky combined with the newly liberated Meyerhold to offer both ideological and representational forms of transition in *Mystery-Bouffe* immediately after the 1917 revolution. By adapting the Bible to stage farce, they intended commentary on current political events and a secularization of fundamental beliefs. The Futurist performance of *Victory Over the Sun* in 1913 had already brought poetry, music, and art together in an exuberant play with interrepresentational signification. Cubo-Futurism, in similar fashion, combined art and literature, while Imagism, founded by the former Futurist Vadim Shershenevich, argued for the pictorial element in language. Acmeists such as Osip Mandelstam (1891–1938) and Nikolai Gumilev (1886–1921) deemphasized the transcendent by singing poetic praises of physical and concrete matters such as works of architecture.

The early years of the twentieth century saw the recognition of women in culture. If Catherine II was an exception to the secondary roles to which women were limited in salon discourse, minor literature, and the performing arts as objects of desire, artists such as Rozanova, Exter, Serebriakova, Goncharova, and Gurko now joined Anna Pavlova in dance and Yermolova in acting to become leading masters of painting, sculpture, and design. In literature, Zinaida Hippius (1869–1945), Anna Akhmatova (1889–1966), and Marina Tsvetaeva (1892–1941) began to demonstrate a similar aesthetic power and influence, formerly reserved for men. With them a new feminine sensibility entered Russian culture to illuminate women–men relationships and other perennial issues.

Although she thought it to be an inferior poem and disliked its musical interpretation, Akhmatova's "The Gray-Eyed King" became one of the favored songs of Aleksandr Vertinsky's repertoire both in emigration and when he returned to the Soviet Union. Sergei Prokofiev later turned to the same work in his *Cinq poésies d'Anna Akhmatova,* Op. 27, and Scriabin provided yet another musical dimension to Akhmatova's verse. Tsvetaeva's poignant and sometimes barbed appraisal of men and the moments of private life, together with her finely tuned sense of language and capacity to create a seldom rivaled poetic intensity, are evident in "I ask the mirror for a glimpse . . . " and "Verses about Moscow." Like Akhmatova's texts, Tsvetaeva's verses were later widely adapted to musical performance, most notably in one of the most popular Russian films of the 1970s, E. Rezanov's and L. Gaidai's *The Irony of Fate*. The two poets, however, were not naive advocates of lyrical language, feminism, and intimate subjects; they considered themselves part of a highly skilled poetic tradition that cut across gender lines and was dependent on critical acumen and verse mastery. Much of their poetry is about poetry and is complemented by their analytical studies of peers such as Pushkin, Briusov, and Blok.

The refinement of technique and craft in all the arts occurred against a historical background of vast changes involving two wars, two revolutions, the collapse of the monarchy, and the victory of Bolshevik ideology. The religious renaissance did not have time to evolve into new belief structures independent of politics or to balance prevalent dissatisfactions and skepticism. Once the Bolsheviks came to power, they quickly exiled or killed the philosophers, theologians, and priests, who they realized would be major rivals in defining new directions and primary values.

Russian culture in the first decades of the twentieth century could be seen to express many of the typical concerns and discontents of Modernism, but it took particular shape, as did Weimar culture in Germany or Futurism in Italy, under the influence of local political and ideological history. Russian writers and artists shared the post-Kantian skepticism for representations of ultimate essences but continued to feel nostalgia, in Lyotard's apt formulation, for the unpresentable.[1] A yearning for the lost sublime inspired their technical innovations and the dissatisfaction they felt over conventional forms of representation.

Eventually, the emphasis placed on technique and professional manipulation of aesthetic signs allowed former Futurists and avant-garde writers such as Mayakovsky's friend Osip Brik (1888–1945) to fall into line with totalitarianism; literary language in their view was only a tool to be used by craftsmen of the word responding to "social orders." Before political demands overwhelmed Russian culture, however, the early part of the twentieth century saw the development of some of its most brilliant technical achievements in the arts and a new rich legacy of analytical and creative advances available to the future.

N. R.

Note

1. Jean-François Lyotard, "Answering the Question: What is Postmodernism," ed. Thomas Docherty. In *Postmodernism: A Reader*. New York: Columbia University Press, 1993, pp. 481–82.

18

~Anton Chekhov~

The Lady with the Lapdog

1

They said someone new had appeared on the wharf, a lady with a lapdog. Dmitry Dmitrych Gurov, after living in Yalta for two weeks and accustomed to the local ways, was one of those who took an interest in new faces. Sitting in Vernet's cafe, he watched as a young woman strolled along the wharf—a slight blonde in a beret, a white Pomeranian scurrying behind her.

Later, he would run into her several times a day in the town garden and in the park. She walked alone, always wearing the same beret, with the white Pomeranian; nobody knew who she was, and she was simply referred to in that way: the lady with the lapdog.

"If she's here without a husband or friends," thought Gurov, "then it might not be amiss to get to know her."

He was not yet forty, but he already had a twelve-year-old daughter and two sons in secondary school. He had married early, while still a second-year student, and now his wife seemed to be twice as old as he was. She was a tall woman with dark eyebrows: straightforward, pompous, solid, and, as she always described herself, intellectual. She read a great deal, did not use the hard sign in her correspondence,[1] addressed her husband not as Dmitry, but *Dimitry,*[2] and secretly he thought her to be stupid, narrow-minded, and clumsy, feared her, and disliked spending time at home. He had begun cheating on her long ago; he cheated often, which is probably why he did not think much of women, and when they were discussed in his presence he would refer to them as "the lower species."

He felt that he had enough bitter experience to refer to them in any way he pleased. Nevertheless, without this "lower species" he would not have survived two days. In public, he found the company of other men boring; with them he felt out of place and was cold, aloof. In the presence of women, however, he felt free and knew exactly what to say and how to behave—with them it was easy for him even to remain silent. In his appearance, his character, his entire personality there was something attractive, elusive in some way that predisposed women to him and enticed them, and he himself was drawn also by some sort of force to them.

Frequent, truly bitter experience had taught him long ago that all these relationships, which at first brought so much pleasant variety to life and which decent people, especially Muscovites, who are hard to prod into action and irresolute, thought to be charming and light adventures, invariably grew into large problems, became increasingly complicated and finally an encumbrance. But at each new encounter with an interesting woman this lesson somehow slipped his memory, and one wanted to live, and everything seemed simple and amusing.

And so one day, toward evening, as he was dining in the garden, the lady in the beret casually walked up to seat herself at the next table. Her expression, walk, dress, and coiffure told him she was from decent society, married, in Yalta for the first time and alone, and that she was bored here . . . Many of the rumors of Yalta's immorality were inaccurate; he scorned them, knowing they were mostly contrived by people who would themselves like to sin, if they only knew how. But when the lady sat at the next table, not three steps from him, he remembered those tales of easy victories, of trips to the mountains, and the seductive thought of a quick, fleeting relationship, of a romantic affair with an unfamiliar woman whose name one did not know, suddenly overwhelmed him.

He gently beckoned to the Pomeranian and when it approached shook his finger at it. The Pomeranian growled. Gurov shook his finger again.

The lady glanced at him, then immediately lowered her eyes.

"He doesn't bite," she said, and blushed.

"May I give him a bone?" When she nodded, he asked affably, "Have you been in Yalta long?"

"About five days."

"And I've already survived my second week here."

They were quiet for a while.

"Time goes fast, and yet it's so boring here!" she said, not looking at him.

"It's just the fashion to say it's boring here. Your ordinary fellow lives somewhere at home in Belyov or Zhizdra and isn't bored, but when he comes here it's: 'Oh, how boring! Oh, the dust!' You'd think he had come from Granada."

She laughed. Then both continued eating in silence, like strangers; but after dinner they left together and began the light, playful conversation of free and contented people to whom nothing mattered, neither where they went nor what they discussed. They strolled and talked about the strangely luminous sea; the water was a soft and warm lilac color, shot through with a streak of gold from the moon. They spoke of how stuffy it was after a hot day. Gurov related that he was a resident of Moscow educated in philology but working in a bank; at one time he had studied to sing in a private opera company but gave it up; he owned two Moscow houses ... And from her he learned that she had grown up in Petersburg but had married in S., where she now had lived for two years, that she would be in Yalta for about another month, and that her husband also would like a vacation and might join her. She could not for the life of her explain where her husband worked—was it the provincial executive office or the local assembly?—and she herself thought this to be funny. And Gurov also learned her name was Anna Sergeevna.

Later in his hotel room he thought about her, about meeting her in all likelihood, tomorrow. It had to be. Lying down to sleep, it occurred to him that she was a high school student not too long ago, just as his daughter was now; he recalled how much timidity and awkwardness was still in her laugh, in her conversation with a stranger—this must have been the first time in her life that she was alone, in a situation in which she was followed and looked at and spoken with only thanks to one secret intention she could not help guessing. He remembered her slender, weak neck, her beautiful gray eyes.

"There is, after all, something vaguely pathetic about her," he thought and began falling asleep.

2

A week passed after their initial acquaintanceship. It was a holiday. In the rooms it was stifling, while outdoors whorls of dust swept through the streets, spiriting hats away. One felt thirsty the whole day, and Gurov often went inside the cafe to offer Anna Sergeevna a soft drink or an ice cream. There was nowhere to go.

In the evening, when the wind had abated a little, they went to the pier to watch the steamer dock. On the pier were many strollers; they had gathered to meet someone and were holding bouquets. And here two peculiarities of the elegant Yalta crowd distinctly caught one's attention: the older women were dressed like young ones, and there were lots of generals.

Because of rough seas, the steamer was delayed, arrived after sunset, and maneuvered for quite some time before coming alongside the pier. Through her lorgnette, Anna Sergeevna peered at the steamer and the passengers as though looking for acquaintances, and when she turned to Gurov her eyes were sparkling. She spoke a great deal, her questions were abrupt, she immediately forgot what she had asked; then she lost her lorgnette in the crowd.

The elegant crowd dispersed, one could no longer see faces, the wind had totally subsided, but Gurov and Anna Sergeevna stood there as though they were expecting someone else to get off the boat. Anna Sergeevna by now was silent and sniffed the flowers without looking at Gurov.

"The evening weather has gotten better," he said. "Where shall we go now? Shall we take a drive?"

She did not reply.

Then he looked at her intently and suddenly embraced her and kissed her on the lips, inhaling the moist perfume of the flowers, and immediately he looked around fearfully: What if someone had seen?

"Let's go to your place," he said quietly.

And they both hurried off.

Her room was stuffy and filled with the scent of perfume she had bought in a Japanese shop. Gurov, looking at her now, thought: "What strange encounters one has in life!" From past experiences he remembered carefree, kind women, full of joy from love and grateful to him for happiness, however brief; there were those such as his wife who loved insincerely, with excessive chattering and posturing, with a touch of hysteria, with an expression that said it was not love or passion but something more significant; others, two or three, were very beautiful and cold as ice, on whose faces suddenly flickered a predatory expression, a stubborn desire to take, to grab from life more than it could give, and they were past youth, capricious, shallow, domineering, unintelligent women, and when Gurov would cool toward them, their beauty aroused nothing but hatred, and the lace on their lingerie then would seem to him like scales.

But here there was only the same timidity, awkwardness of inexperienced youth, and uncomfortable feelings; and there was an impression of confusion as if someone had suddenly knocked at the door. Anna Sergeevna, this "lady with the lapdog," regarded what had happened in some particular way, very seriously, as though she had done something immoral—so it seemed, and it was strange and inopportune. Her features grew pale and hollow, and her long hair hung miserably down either side of her face; she fell into thought in a melancholy pose, like a fallen woman in an old painting.

"This is bad," she said. "Now you'll be the first not to respect me."

On a table in the hotel room was a watermelon. Gurov cut himself a slice and began eating it slowly. At least half an hour passed in silence.

Anna Sergeevna was touching; she radiated the purity of a proper, naive woman who had seen very little of the real world. The one candle burning on the table barely revealed her face, but she was obviously tormented.

"Why would I stop respecting you?" asked Gurov. "You have no idea what you are saying."[3]

"God forgive me!" she exclaimed, her eyes brimming with tears. "This is horrible!"

"It's as if you're trying to excuse yourself!"

"How can I make excuses? I am a vile, base woman. I despise myself and am not thinking of excuses. It isn't my husband I've deceived but myself. And not only at present, but for a long time now. My husband may be an honest, good person, but he's a flunkey! I don't know what he does at that office, but I know only that he's a flunkey. I was twenty when I married him, I was aching with curiosity, I wanted something better. 'After all,' I told myself, 'there must be another sort of life.' I wanted to live! To live and live . . . Curiosity was burning me up . . . you don't understand this, but I swear to God I just couldn't control myself any longer, something had happened to me, I couldn't be held back. I told my husband I was sick, and I came here . . . And here I've been wandering around in a daze, like a madwoman . . . and now I've become a vulgar, worthless woman for everyone to despise."

Gurov was already growing bored listening. He was annoyed by the naive tone, by this confession, so unexpected and unwarranted; if not for the tears in her eyes, one could have thought she was joking or playing a role.

"I don't understand," he said quietly. "What do you want?"

She buried her face on his chest and pressed close to him.

"Believe me, oh, please believe me," she said. "I love a decent, pure life, and sin disgusts me. I don't know myself what I am doing. The common people say: 'The Devil confounded me.' And now I can say about myself that the Devil confounded me."

"Enough, enough . . . " he murmured.

He looked into her still, frightened eyes, kissed her, spoke quietly and tenderly, and before long she calmed down and her cheerfulness returned. They both began laughing.

Later, when they walked out, the boardwalk was deserted, the town with its cypresses seemed quite dead, but the sea still roared and crashed against the shore; a solitary boat bobbed on the waves, its small lantern glinted drowsily.

They hailed a cab and rode to Oreanda.

"I just saw your last name written on the board downstairs: 'von Diederitz,'" said Gurov. "Is your husband German?"

"No. It seems he had a grandfather who was German, but he is Russian Orthodox."

In Oreanda they sat on a bench near the church, looking down at the sea silently. Yalta was barely visible through the morning mist; white clouds hung motionless over the mountaintops.

Not a leaf moved on the trees; cicadas chirruped, and the monotonous, dull roar of the sea, coming up from below, spoke of tranquility, of the everlasting slumber that awaits us. So it roared before there ever was a Yalta or an Oreanda; it roars now and will go on roaring indifferently and dully after we're gone. And in this constancy, in total indifference to the life and death of each of us, is perhaps hidden the pledge of our eternal salvation, the never-ending movement of life on earth, never-ending perfection. Seated beside the young woman who appeared so lovely in the dawn, soothed and charmed by such magical surroundings—of the sea, the mountains, the clouds, the vast sky—Gurov reflected how, in essence, if you thought it over, everything in this world was beautiful, everything except our own thoughts and actions, when we forget about the loftier goals of existence and our own human worth.

Somebody approached, most likely a watchman, looked at them, and went away. And this detail seemed very mysterious and also beautiful. They could see the Feodosia steamer arrive, lit by the sunrise, its lights already extinguished.

"There's dew on the grass," said Anna Sergeevna after a period of silence.

"Yes. Time to go home."

They returned to town.

Then they met each noon on the promenade, had lunch and dinner together, went for walks, and admired the sea. She complained that she was sleeping poorly and that her heart was beating nervously and asked him the same questions over and over, worrying, now jealous, now fearful that he did not respect her enough. And often, in the square or in the park, when no one was close by, he would suddenly draw her to himself and kiss her passionately. The complete idleness, these kisses in broad daylight with glances over the shoulder to make sure no one had seen, the heat, the smell of the sea, the constant fleeting glimpses of idle, elegant, satisfied people seemed to rejuvenate him; he told Anna Sergeevna how lovely she was, how seductive; he was impatiently passionate, never once leaving her side, but she was often lost in thought and kept asking him to admit that he did not respect her or love her in the least and that he only saw in her a vulgar woman. Almost every evening, at a fairly late hour, they would go somewhere out of town, to Oreanda or to a waterfall; and the excursions were successful; on each occasion they were left with beautiful and grand impressions.

They waited for her husband's arrival. But a letter came from him in which he explained that he was having a problem with his eyes and begged her to return home quickly. Anna Sergeevna made haste.

"It's good that I'm leaving," she told Gurov. "It's fate itself."

She took a carriage, and he accompanied her. They rode all day. After she had taken a seat on the express train and after the second bell, she said:

"Let me look at you again . . . just once. There."

She did not cry, but she was sad, as if she were ill, and her face was quivering.

"I'll be thinking of you . . . remembering you," she said. "God bless you. Stay, don't think badly of me; we'll never see one another ever again. That's the way it should be because we never should have met. God bless you."

The train left quickly, its lights soon disappeared, and after a minute its sound could no longer be heard, as though it had all been prearranged to cut off that sweet reverie, that madness. And standing alone on the platform, staring off into the darkness, Gurov listened to the cry of the grasshoppers and the hum of the telegraph wires, feeling as if he'd just awakened. And he thought how this had been one more affair or adventure in his life, and it too was already over, and now the memory remained . . . He was touched, sad, and felt somewhat guilty; after all, this young woman whom he would never see again had not been happy with him; he had been warm and affectionate to her, but just the same, in his behavior, in his tone and caresses, there was a hint of light mockery, the coarse arrogance of a satisfied male who was, moreover, nearly twice her age. Throughout, she had called him kind, exceptional, lofty; apparently he had appeared to her different from what he actually was, so he had inadvertently deceived her . . .

At the station autumn was already in the air; the evening was chilly.

"It's time for me also to go back north," thought Gurov as he stepped off the platform. "High time!"

3

At home, in Moscow, everything was already in a state of winter. The stoves were warmed up, and it was still dark when the children had their morning tea and prepared for school, so the nurse had to light the lamp briefly. Frost was already appearing. When the first snow falls, on the first day for sleigh rides, it's pleasant to see the white ground, the white rooftops, to inhale the soft, marvelous air; and this time of year brings back childhood memories. The old limes and birches, white with rime, have a genial look and are dearer to the heart than cypresses and palms; near them one no longer wants to think about the mountains and the sea.

Gurov was a Muscovite who returned to Moscow on a good crisp day; when he donned his fur coat and warm gloves and took a walk down Petrovka, and when on Saturday night he heard the bells ringing, his recent trip and the places he had been lost all of their charm for him. Gradually he immersed himself in Moscow life, devouring three newspapers a day while proclaiming that he did not read Moscow newspapers out of principle. He was already drawn to the restaurants, the clubs, the formal dinners and anniversaries, and he was flattered to entertain distinguished attorneys and artists and to play cards with a professor at the Physicians' Club. He was already able to eat an entire portion of *selyanka* in a frying pan . . . [4]

A month or so would pass, it seemed to him, and Anna Sergeevna would fade into a dim memory, to visit only occasionally in his dreams, smiling her tender smile, like all the others. But more than a month passed, deepest winter had arrived, and his memory remained vivid, as though he and Anna Sergeevna had parted only yesterday. And the memories became even more persistent. Whether in the quiet of the evening, with the voices of his children preparing their lessons floating into his study, or when he heard a love song or an organ playing in a restaurant, or when the winter wind would begin howling in the chimney, suddenly everything would come to life in his memory; the business on the pier, the early morning mist in the mountains, the steamer from Feodosia, the kisses. He would pace around his room for hours, and remember, and smile, and the memories would turn into daydreams, and in his imagination the past mingled with the future. He did not dream of Anna Sergeevna, but she was everywhere with him, like a shadow, observing him. Closing his eyes he saw her, as in life, and she appeared lovelier, younger, and more tender than she had been, and he himself seemed better than he had been in Yalta. In the evenings, she would gaze at him from the bookshelf, the fireplace, or the corner; he heard her breathing, the tender rustling of her clothing. His eyes would follow women on the street, seeking out someone who resembled her . . .

And then he was overcome with the desire to share his memories with someone. He could not bring up the subject at home, and outside his home there was nobody. He could not speak with the tenants after all, or anyone at the bank. And what would he say? Had he loved her then? Was there anything beautiful, poetic, enlightening, or even interesting about his relationship with Anna Sergeevna? And so he had to talk in generalities about love and women, and nobody guessed what his point was; only his wife would raise her dark eyebrows and say:

"You, *Dimitry,* were not cut out to be pretentious."

One night as he was emerging from the Physicians' Club with his card partner, a civil servant, he could not help saying:

"If you only knew what a fascinating woman I met in Yalta!"

The civil servant had seated himself in his sledge and was driving off when he suddenly turned and shouted:

"Dmitry Dmitrich!"

"Yes!"

"You were absolutely right! The sturgeon was a bit off."

These words, so ordinary, seized Gurov with outrage; they seemed degrading and obscene. What vile manners, what people! What ridiculous nights and boring, pointless days! Compulsive card playing, gluttony, drunkenness, endless conversations about the same topics. Inconsequential matters and conversations about the same topics would eat up the best part of one's time and energy, and what remained in the end was a sort of abbreviated, uninspired life, a sort of trivia, and it was impossible to go away or to escape, as if one were in a madhouse or on a chain gang!

Gurov was up all night, boiling with indignation, and all of the next day he had a splitting headache. The following nights he again slept badly; he sat up in his bed and thought, or paced back and forth in his room. He was sick of his children, sick of the bank, and he lost all desire to go anywhere or talk about anything.

When the December holidays arrived, he packed his things and told his wife he was off to Petersburg to help a young man—and he departed for S. Why? He himself did not understand it very well. He wanted to see Anna Sergeevna and to speak with her, to arrange a meeting, if possible.

He arrived in S. in the morning and obtained the hotel's best room, which was carpeted with gray army cloth and contained a gray dusty ink stand on a table, topped by a headless horseman waving a hat. The porter gave him the necessary information: von Diederitz lived on Staro-Goncharnaya Street in his own home—it was not far from the hotel—lived well, was wealthy, kept his own horses, and everyone knew him. The porter pronounced the name "Dridiritz."

Without hurrying, Gurov made his way to Staro-Goncharnaya and located the house. Directly opposite it was a long gray fence studded with nails.

"A fence like that could indeed make one run away," thought Gurov, glancing at the windows and back at the fence.

He considered: today was a holiday, so the husband was probably home. It did not matter anyway, because it would be tactless to embarrass her by going into the house. If he sent a note, it might fall into her husband's hands and then everything might be ruined. It would be better to rely on chance. He kept walking back and forth on the street and along the fence, waiting for this chance. He saw a beggar go in the gate and the dogs attacked him;

then, an hour later, he heard a piano, and the sounds were faint and indistinct. That must have been Anna Sergeevna playing. Suddenly, the front door opened and an old lady emerged, followed by the familiar white Pomeranian. Gurov was on the verge of calling to the dog, but his heart suddenly began to pound and from nervousness he could not remember the Pomeranian's name.

He strode on, regarding the gray fence with a mounting hatred, and he already thought with irritation that Anna Sergeevna had forgotten about him and, perhaps, had already found someone else to divert her, which was only natural for a woman who had to sit looking at this damned fence day in day out. He went back to his hotel room and sat for a long time on his sofa, not knowing what to do; then he ate dinner, and then he slept for a long time.

"How stupid and upsetting all of this is," he thought as he woke and looked at the dark windows. It was already evening. "Now that I've slept so much, what will I do tonight?"

He sat on the bed, which was covered with a cheap gray blanket, like those in a hospital, and mocked himself in vexation:

"So much for a lady with a lapdog. So much for your adventure! So keep on sitting here."

That morning at the station he had noticed a poster announcing, in very large lettering, the local theatrical premiere of *The Geisha*.[5] He remembered it and left for the theater.

"It's quite possible that she attends opening nights," he thought.

The theater was packed. As in most provincial theaters, there was a mist above the chandelier, and the gallery crowd carried on noisily. Before the performance began the local dandies stood around in the first row with their hands behind their backs. In the front seat of the Governor's box sat the Governor's daughter, wearing a boa, while the Governor himself occupied a more humble position behind the partition, so that only his hands were visible. The curtain stirred and the orchestra took its time tuning up. While the audience came in and took their seats, Gurov hungrily searched with his eyes.

Anna Sergeevna came in, too. She took a seat in the third row, and when Gurov glanced at her his heart constricted and he realized with exact clarity that there was not a person now in the world closer, dearer, or more important to him; this little woman with nothing significant about her, with a vulgar lorgnette in her hands, was now his entire life; she was his joy and agony, the only happiness he desired; and to the sounds of the bad orchestra, the wretched playing of the second-rate violins, he thought how lovely she was. He thought and daydreamed.

A very tall, round-shouldered young man with small whiskers came in with Anna Sergeevna and sat beside her; with each step he nodded his head so it seemed as if he were continually bowing. This was undoubtedly the husband whom, in a fit of bitterness in Yalta, she had called a flunkey. Actually, in his lanky figure, his whiskers, and his small bald spot, there was indeed something servile and humble; he smiled sweetly, and the alumnus button of some educational establishment gleamed in his buttonhole like the number on a lackey's coat.

At the first intermission, the husband went out to smoke while she remained in her seat. Gurov, who was also seated in the orchestra, went up to her and said in a trembling voice, with a forced smile:

"Hello."

She looked up at him and blanched, and looked up again in horror, not believing her eyes, clutching the fan and lorgnette in her hands, apparently struggling with herself not to fall into a faint. Both were silent. She sat, he stood, frightened by her distress, unable to decide whether to sit down next to her. Violins and flutes sang out as they were being tuned, and suddenly Gurov and Anna became horrified, it seemed that they were being watched from all the surrounding boxes. But then she rose and quickly went to the exit; he followed her, and they both wandered aimlessly through corridors, up and down staircases; all sorts of people flashed by them, in the uniforms of legal officials, schoolteachers, and civil servants, all wearing pins; ladies flashed by them, and fur coats on hooks, and they could feel a draft bearing the odor of cigarette butts. Gurov, his heart thudding in his chest, thought: "Oh Lord! What are all these people doing here, and why this orchestra . . . "

At that moment, he suddenly recalled the evening at the station when he had bid Anna Sergeevna farewell and when he had told himself that it was all over and they would never meet again. But how far it was yet from being over!

On a narrow, dark stairway with a sign that said "To the Amphitheater" she stopped.

"How you frightened me!" she said, breathing heavily, and still pale and stunned. "Oh, how you frightened me! I'm barely alive! Why did you come? Why?"

"But Anna, try to understand . . . " he murmured hurriedly. "I beg you, try to understand . . . "

She gazed at him with shock, with entreaty, with love; she gazed intently, in order to fix his features firmly in her memory.

"I'm so miserable!" she went on without listening to him. "All I've thought about is you. Thoughts of you have kept me alive. And I've been trying so hard to forget. To forget. But why did you come? Why?"

On the landing above two schoolboys were smoking and looking down at them, but Gurov did not care; he drew Anna Sergeevna toward him and began kissing her face, her cheeks, her hands.

"What are you doing? What are you doing?" she said in horror, pushing him away from her. "We've gone mad! Leave today, right now . . . I beg you by all that is sacred, I implore you . . . Someone's coming!"

Someone was climbing the stairs.

"You've got to leave," Anna Sergeevna went on, whispering. "Do you hear me, Dmitry Dmitrich? I'll come to you in Moscow. I never was happy, I'm unhappy now, and I never, ever will be happy, never! Don't make me suffer still more! I will come to Moscow, I swear! But we have to part now! My dear, kind, darling, we have to part!"

She pressed his hand and ran downstairs quickly, looking back up at him all the way, and in her eyes it was obvious she was indeed unhappy . . . Gurov stood there for a while, listening, and when all was quiet, he found his coat and left the theater.

4

And Anna Sergeevna began coming to see him in Moscow. Every two or three months she left the town of S., telling her husband she was consulting a specialist about a feminine problem—and her husband believed her and did not believe her. When she arrived in Moscow, she would always register at the Slavyansky Bazaar and immediately send a bellboy for Gurov. Gurov would come to her room, and nobody in Moscow knew a thing about it.

One day he was going to see her, as usual; it was a winter morning (the messenger had called on him the night before, but he had been out). With him was his daughter, whom he had wanted to take to school; it was on the way. The snow fell in thick, wet flakes.

"It's three degrees above zero, but it's snowing!" Gurov said to his daughter. "This is because it's only warm near the ground, you see. In the upper layers of the atmosphere, the temperature's completely different!"

"Papa, why isn't there any thunder in the winter?"

He explained this, too. As he spoke he thought of going to a rendezvous that not one living soul knew about, nor was ever likely to know. He had two lives: one in the open, which everyone who wanted to saw and knew, full of relative truths and conventional lies, just like all his friends and acquaintances; and another that went on secretly. By some strange turn of circumstances, perhaps purely by accident, everything important to him, interesting, necessary, about which he was sincere and did not delude himself, that constituted the core of his life, proceeded in secret; everything that was false for him, the shell in which he hid to conceal the truth, as, for example, his job at the bank, his conversations at the club, the "lower species," attending anniversaries with his wife—that was in the open. And he judged others by himself, and did not believe in what he saw, and always supposed that every person's real and most interesting life was lived in secret, as if under cover of night. Each individual life depends on its secret core, and perhaps this, in part, was why cultured people were so nervously concerned about personal secrets being respected.

Having dropped his daughter at school, Gurov proceeded to the Slavyansky Bazaar. He left his coat downstairs, went up, and knocked softly at the door. Anna Sergeevna, wearing his favorite gray dress, exhausted by the trip and by anticipation, had been expecting him since the previous evening; she was pale and looked at him, unsmiling, and he had barely walked through the door when she threw herself on his chest. Their kiss was long and lingering, as if they had not seen one another in two years.

"Well, how are you doing there," he asked. "What's new?"

"Wait, I'll tell you in a minute . . . I can't."

She could not speak, because she was crying. She turned away from him and pressed a handkerchief to her eyes.

"Well, let her cry it out, and I'll sit in the meantime," he thought, moving to an armchair.

He rang for tea, and as he drank it she stood the whole time turned toward the window . . . She wept out of emotion, out of the mournful realization that their life had turned out so sadly; they saw each other only in secret, hiding from people, like thieves! Was not their life shattered?

"Now, stop it!" he said.

It was obvious to him that their love would not end soon; no one knew when. Anna Sergeevna became more strongly attached to him, she worshiped him, and it was unthinkable to tell her it would have to come to an end sometime; and besides, she would not have believed it.

He went up and put his hands on her shoulders to comfort her, to cheer her up, and at that moment caught sight of himself in the mirror.

His hair was already beginning to turn gray. And it seemed strange to him that he had become so old in the past years, had lost so much of his looks. The warm shoulders under his hands were shivering. He felt compassion for this living being, still so warm and beautiful, but probably already approaching the point of withering and aging, like his life. Why did she love him so much? He always appeared to women as something other than what he was; they loved him not for himself but as a man fashioned out of their own imagination, someone they had sought with yearning all their lives. Then, after they had noticed their mistake, they went on loving him anyway. And not one of them had been happy with him. Time passed; he met new women, had affairs with them, and left them, but he had never once been in love; everything had happened but love.

And only now, when his hair was turning gray, was he truly, properly in love—for the first time in his life.

Anna Sergeevna and he loved one another like people who are very close and intimate, as husband and wife, as dear friends; they thought fate had destined them for one another, and they could not understand how he could have a wife and she a husband; they were like two passing birds, male and female, who had been caught and forced to live in two separate cages. They forgave one another everything that they had been ashamed of in their past, they forgave everything in the present, and they felt that this love of theirs had changed them both.

Before, in moments of sadness, he had consoled himself with all sorts of rationalizations that would cross his mind; now he was beyond such reasoning, he felt deep compassion, and wanted to be sincere, gentle . . .

"Stop, darling," he said, "you've had your cry, that's enough. Now, let's talk it over, let's think of something."

Then they talked for a long time, discussing how to rid themselves of the need to hide, to deceive, to live in separate towns not seeing each other for so long. How could they overcome these intolerable conditions?

"How? How?" he asked, holding his head. "How?"

And it seemed as though a solution was just within reach, and then they would begin a new, wonderful life; and it was clear to both of them that the end was still far, far away and that the most complicated and difficult part was only just beginning.

1899

Translation by Basil Muir and Nicholas Rzhevsky

Notes to the translation are on page 579.

RESOURCES

Primary Text

Chekhov, Anton P. "Dama s sobachkoi." *Sobranie sochinenii.* Vol. 8. Moscow: Khudozhestvennaia literatura, 1963, pp. 389–405.

Secondary Sources

Literary and Cultural Studies

Debreczeny, Paul. "Chekhov's Use of Impressionism in 'The House with the Mansard.'" In *Russian Narrative and Visual Art,* ed. Roger Anderson. Gainsville: University of Florida Press, 1994, pp. 101–23.
Kataev, V.B. *Proza Chekhova: Problemy interpretatsii.* Moscow: Izd-vo Moskovskogo universiteta, 1979.

McLean, Hugh. "Chékhov, Antón Pávlovich (1860–1904)." In *Handbook of Russian Literature*, ed. Victor Terras. New Haven: Yale University Press, 1985, pp. 79–81.

Schmid, Herta. *On the Theory of Descriptive Poetics: Anton P. Chekhov as Story-Teller and Playwright*. Lisse: Peter de Ritter Press, 1978.

Terras, Victor. *A History of Russian Literature*. New Haven: Yale University Press, 1991, pp. 467–70.

Film

Anton Chekhov: A Writer's Life. Producer, Harold Mantell. Harold Mantell Inc. Films for the Humanities. Trans. Anthony Sheehan. Princeton, NJ, n.d.

Chelovek v Futliare (The Man in a Case). Director, Isidor Annenskii: Design, L. Putievskaia. Music, A. Golubentsov. Sovetskaia Belarus, 1939.

Dama s sobachkoi (The Lady with the Lapdog). Director, Josef Heifitz. Cinematographer, Andrei Moskvin. Music, N. Simonian. Cast: Iya Savvina, Aleksei Batalov. Lenfilm, 1960.

Dom s mezoninom (The House with the Mezzanine). Director, Iakov Bazelian. Cast: Ninel Myshkova, Larisa Gorteichik, Sergei Iakovlev. Yalta Studio, 1960.

Duel' (The Duel). Directors, T. Berezantseva, L. Rudnik. Cast: Liudmila Shagalova, Oleg Strizhenov. Mosfilm, 1957.

Nevesta (The Bride). Director, G. Nikulin, V. Shretel'. Lenfilm, 1956.

Poprygun'ia (The Grasshopper). Director, Samson Samsonov. Cinematographer, F. Dobronravov. Music, Nikolai Kriukov. Cast: Sergei Bondarchuk, Ludmila Tselikovskaia. Mosfilm, 1955.

Step' (The Steppe). Director, Sergei Bondarchuk. Mosfilm, 1978.

19

~Anton Chekhov~

The Cherry Orchard

ACT I

A room that to this day is called the nursery. One of the doors leads into ANYA'S *room. Dawn, the sun will soon be rising. It is already May, the cherry trees are in bloom; but in the orchard it's cold, a morning frost. The windows in the room are closed.*

DUNYASHA *with a candle, and* LOPAHIN *with a book in his hand.*

LOPAHIN: The train is in, thank God. What time is it?

DUNYASHA: Nearly two. *(Blows out the candle)* It's already daylight.

LOPAHIN: Just how late was the train? At least two hours. *(Yawns and stretches)* I'm priceless—I really am—look at the stupid thing I did! I drove here on purpose just to meet her at the station, and then all of a sudden I oversleep! Fell asleep sitting up. Stupid . . . You could've at least woke me up.

DUNYASHA: I thought you'd gone. *(Listens)* Listen. I think they're coming.

LOPAHIN: *(Listening)* No . . . what with the luggage and everything. *(Pause)* Lyuboff Andreyevna's lived abroad five years. I don't know what she's like now—she's a good person. An easygoing, simple person. I remember when I was a boy, about fifteen years old, my father, who's at rest now—he ran a shop here in the village then—slugged me in the face with his fist; blood ran from my nose. We'd come to the yard together for something, and he was a little gassed. Lyuboff Andreyevna, I still remember, so very young, so slim, took me to the washbasin here in this very room, the nursery. "Don't cry," she says. "My little peasant, it'll heal before your wedding." *(Pause)* Little peasant . . . My father, it's true, was a peasant, and here I am in a white vest and yellow shoes. Like a pig feasting in a bakery . . . Only I'm rich, lots of money, but if you really stop and think about it, I'm

422

nothing but a peasant. *(Thumbs through a book)* Here I was reading a book and didn't understand a thing. I was reading and fell asleep. *(Pause)*

DUNYASHA: And all night long the dogs didn't get a wink of sleep; they know their owners are coming.

LOPAHIN: What's wrong, Dunyasha, you're so . . .

DUNYASHA: My hands are trembling. I'm going to pass out.

LOPAHIN: You're just too delicate, Dunyasha. And dressed up like a countess and a hairdo to match. Better not: remember who you are.

EPIHODOFF *enters with a bouquet: he wears a jacket and highly polished boots that squeak loudly. As he enters, he drops the bouquet.*

EPIHODOFF: *(Picks up the bouquet)* Here, the gardener sent these; he says they're for the dining room. *(Gives the bouquet to DUNYASHA)*

LOPAHIN: And bring me some kvass.

DUNYASHA: Yes, sir. *(Exits)*

EPIHODOFF: There's a morning frost now, three degrees; and all the cherry trees are in bloom. I don't approve of our climate. *(Sighs)* I don't. Our climate can never quite make up its mind. Listen, Yermolay Alexeyevich, allow me to elaborate. I bought myself boots the day before yesterday, and they, I want you to know, squeak so much that it's impossible. What could I grease them with?

LOPAHIN: Stop it. I'm fed up with you.

EPIHODOFF: Every day bad luck haunts me. But I don't complain; I'm used to it and even smile. (DUNYASHA *enters; serves* LOPAHIN *the kvass)* I'm going. *(Stumbles across a chair, which falls over)* There . . . *(As if triumphing)* there, you see, pardon the expression, a thing like that, among others . . . It's downright remarkable. *(Exits)*

DUNYASHA: And I have to confess, Yermolay Alexeyevich, Epihodoff has proposed to me.

LOPAHIN: Ah!

DUNYASHA: I don't really know what to do. He is a quiet man, but sometimes when he starts talking, you can't understand a thing he says. It's all very nice, and full of feeling, only it doesn't make much sense. I sort of like him. He's crazy about me. He's an unhappy man; everyday there's something or other. They've nicknamed him around here: Mister Twenty-Two Disasters . . .

LOPAHIN: *(Cocks his ears)* Listen, I think they're coming . . .

DUNYASHA: They are! But what's wrong with me . . . I'm cold all over.

LOPAHIN: They're really coming. Let's go meet them. Will she recognize me? It's been five years since we've seen each other.

DUNYASHA: *(Excitedly)* I'm going to pass right out. Ah, I'm going to!

Two carriages are heard driving up to the house. LOPAHIN *and* DUNYASHA *quickly exit. The stage is empty. In the adjoining rooms a noise begins.* FIERS *hurries across the stage, leaning on a cane; having gone to meet* LYUBOFF ANDREYEVNA, *he wears old-fashioned livery and a high hat; he mutters something to himself, but not a word can be understood. The noise offstage gets louder and louder. A voice: "Look! Let's go through here . . . "* LYUBOFF ANDREYEVNA, ANYA, *and* CHARLOTTA IVANOVNA, *with a little dog on a leash, all dressed for traveling;* VARYA, *in a coat and kerchief;* GAYEFF, SEMYONOFF-PISHCHIK, LOPAHIN, DUNYASHA, *with a bundle and umbrella; servants with things—all pass through the room.*

ANYA: Let's go through here. Mama, do you remember what room this is?

LYUBOFF ANDREYEVNA: *(Happily, through tears)* The nursery!

VARYA: How cold it is; my hands are stiff. *(To* LYUBOFF ANDREYEVNA*)* Your rooms, the white and the violet ones, are just as you left them, Mama.

LYUBOFF ANDREYEVNA: The nursery, my dear beautiful room . . . I slept here when I was little . . . *(Crying)* And now I'm just like a child— *(Kisses her brother and* VARYA, *then her brother again)* And Varya is just the same as ever; she looks like a nun. And I knew Dunyasha *(Kisses* DUNYASHA*)*

GAYEFF: The train was two hours late. How do you like that? What kind of orderly system is that?

CHARLOTTA: *(To* PISHCHIK*)* My dog—he eats nuts.

PISHCHIK: *(Astonished)* What do you know! *(Everyone exits except* ANYA *and* DUNYASHA*)*

DUNYASHA: We waited so long . . . *(Takes off* ANYA'S *coat and hat)*

ANYA: I didn't sleep a wink any of the four nights of our trip. And now I feel so chilly.

DUNYASHA: You left during Lent; it was snowing then; there was frost, and now? My dearest, *(Laughing, kissing her)* I waited so long for you, my joy, my life . . . I'm telling you now, I can't stand it another minute.

ANYA: *(Wearily)* There we go again . . .

DUNYASHA: The clerk Epihodoff proposed to me after Holy Week.

ANYA: You're always talking about the same thing . . . *(Fixing her hair)* I've lost all my hairpins . . . *(She is tired to the point of exhaustion)*

DUNYASHA: I just don't know what to think anymore. He loves me; he loves me so!

ANYA: *(Looks through the door tenderly)* My room, my windows, it's just as if I had never gone away. I'm home! Tomorrow morning I'll get up, run into the orchard ... Oh, if only I could go to sleep! I didn't sleep all the way, I was terribly nervous.

DUNYASHA: The day before yesterday, Pyotr Sergeyevich arrived.

ANYA: *(Joyfully)* Petya!

DUNYASHA: He's asleep in the bathhouse; he lives there, too. I'm afraid, he says, of being in the way. *(Looking at her pocket watch)* Someone ought to wake him up, but Varvara Mikhailovna wouldn't allow it. Don't wake him up, she said.

VARYA: (VARYA *enters, a bunch of keys on her belt)* Dunyasha, coffee, quick. Mama is asking for coffee.

DUNYASHA: Right away. *(Exits)*

VARYA: Well, thank God, you've come back. You're home again. *(Caressingly)* My darling's back! My beauty's back!

ANYA: I've had a difficult time.

VARYA: I can imagine!

ANYA: I left during Holy Week; it was cold then. Charlotta talked all the way and did her tricks. Why did you load me down with Charlotta!!!

VARYA: But you couldn't have traveled alone, sweetheart, at seventeen!

ANYA: We arrived in Paris! It was cold there, snow. I speak terrible French. Mama lived on the fifth floor; I went to see her; there were some French people at her place, ladies, an old priest with a prayer book, full of smoke, uncomfortable. Suddenly I felt pity for Mama, such pity, I put my arms around her head, held her close, and couldn't let her go. Then Mama began hugging me, crying ...

VARYA: *(Tearfully)* Don't, don't ...

ANYA: She had already sold her villa near Menton; she has nothing left, nothing. And I didn't have a kopek left. We almost didn't make it here. And Mama doesn't understand! We sit down to dinner at a station and she orders, insists on ordering the most expensive things and gives the waiters a ruble tip apiece. Charlotta's the same. Yasha also demands his share; it's simply awful. You know Mama has a butler, Yasha; we've brought him here ...

VARYA: I saw the conniver.

ANYA: Well, how are things? Has the interest on the mortgage been paid?

VARYA: How could it be?

ANYA: My God, my God . . . .

VARYA: In August the place will be sold . . .

ANYA: My God . . .

LOPAHIN: *(Looking in through the door, bleats)* Me-e-e. *(Exits)*

VARYA: *(Tearfully)* I'd like to give him one . . . *(Threatening with her fist)*

ANYA: *(Embraces* VARYA *quietly)* Varya, has he proposed? *(*VARYA *shakes her head)* But he loves you . . . Why don't you have it out with him? What are you two waiting for?

VARYA: It'll never work out for us. He's got so much to do; he doesn't have time for me . . . And he doesn't pay any attention to me. I wash my hands of him; it's painful for me to see him. Everyone talks about our marriage; everyone congratulates us; but the point is it's nothing. It's all like a dream . . . *(In a different mood)* You have a brooch in the shape of a bee.

ANYA: *(Sadly)* Mama bought it. *(Going toward her room, speaking gaily, like a child)* And in Paris I flew in a balloon!

VARYA: My darling is back! My beauty is back! *(*DUNYASHA *has returned with the coffee pot and is making coffee.* VARYA *stands by the door)* Darling, I'm busy all day around the house and I go around dreaming. If only you could be married to a rich man, then I'd be more at peace too; I'd go all by myself to a cloister, then to Kiev, to Moscow, and I'd keep going like that from one holy place to another . . . I'd go on and on. Wonderful!

ANYA: The birds are singing in the orchard. What time is it now?

VARYA: Must be around three. It's time you were in bed, darling. *(Going into* ANYA's *room)* Wonderful!

YASHA: *(*YASHA *enters with a shawl and a traveling bag. Crosses the stage on tiptoe)* May I go through here?

DUNYASHA: We hardly recognize you, Yasha. How you've changed abroad!

YASHA: Hm . . . And who are you?

DUNYASHA: When you left here, I was like that . . . *(Lowers her hand to the floor)* I'm Dunyasha, Fyodor Kozoyedoff's daughter. Don't you remember!

YASHA: Hm . . . A little cucumber! *(Looks around before embracing her; she shrieks and breaks a saucer;* YASHA *quickly exits)*

VARYA: *(At the door, in a vexed tone)* What's going on here?

DUNYASHA: *(Tearfully)* I broke a saucer . . .

VARYA: That's good luck.

ANYA: *(Comes from her room)* We ought to warn Mama: Petya's here.

VARYA: I told them not to wake him up.

ANYA: *(Pensively)* Six years ago Papa died; a month later our brother Grisha drowned in the river; a beautiful seven-year-old boy. Mama couldn't take it; she went away, went away without ever looking back ... *(Shudders)* How perfectly I understand her; if she only knew how I did. *(Pause)* And Petya Trofimoff was Grisha's tutor; he might bring back memories ...

FIERS *enters; he is in a jacket and white waistcoat.*

FIERS: *(Goes to the coffee urn; busies himself with it)* The mistress will have her breakfast here ... *(Puts on white gloves)* Is the coffee ready? *(Sternly to* DUNYASHA*)* You! What about the cream?

DUNYASHA: Ah, my God ... *(Exits quickly)*

FIERS: *(Busily at the coffee pot)* Ah, you loggerhead ... *(Mutters to himself)* Come back from Paris ... And the master used to go to Paris too ... by coach ... *(Laughs)*

VARYA: Fiers, what are you doing?

FIERS: At your service. *(Joyfully)* My mistress came back! It's what I've waited for! Now I can die ... *(Cries out of joy)*

LYUBOFF ANDREYEVNA, GAYEFF, *and* SEMYONOFF-PISHCHIK *enter.* PISHCHIK *is wearing a long, finely-pleated Russian coat and loose Turkish trousers, tight at the ankles.* GAYEFF *is gesturing with his hands and body, as if playing billiards.*

LYUBOFF ANDREYEVNA: How is it now! Let me remember ... Yellow in the corner pocket and off the cushion into the middle pocket!

GAYEFF: Straight into the corner pocket! Sister, you and I once slept here in this very room, and now I am fifty-one years old, strange as it may seem ...

LOPAHIN: Yes, time passes.

GAYEFF: Whose?

LOPAHIN: Time, I say, passes.

GAYEFF: And it smells like patchouli here.

ANYA: I'm going to bed. Good night, Mama. *(Kisses her mother)*

LYUBOFF ANDREYEVNA: My sweet little child. *(Kisses her hands)* Are you glad to be home? I still can't pull myself together.

ANYA: Goodbye, Uncle.

GAYEFF: *(Kisses her face and hands)* God be with you. How like your mother you are! *(To his sister)* Lyuba, at her age you were exactly like her. (ANYA *offers her hand to* LOPAHIN *and* PISHCHIK; *exits, closing the door behind her)*

LYUBOFF ANDREYEVNA: She's very tired.

PISHCHIK: I'm afraid it was a long trip.

VARYA: *(To* LOPAHIN *and* PISHCHIK*)* Well then, gentlemen? It's almost three o'clock; time to be going.

LYUBOFF ANDREYEVNA: *(Laughs)* Just like you, Varya. *(Draws her to her and kisses her)* There, I'll drink my coffee; then we'll all go. (FIERS *puts a small cushion under her feet)* Thank you, my dear. I'm used to coffee. I drink it day and night. Thank you, my dear old soul. *(Kisses* FIERS*)*

VARYA: I'll go see if they brought all the luggage . . . *(Exits)*

LYUBOFF ANDREYEVNA: Is it really me sitting here? *(Laughs)* I'd like to jump around and wave my arms. *(Covers her face with her hands)* But I may be dreaming! God knows I love my country, love it dearly; I couldn't look out of the car window; I just kept crying. *(Tearfully)* However, I must drink my coffee. Thank you, Fiers, thank you, my dear old soul. I'm so glad you're still alive.

FIERS: The day before yesterday.

GAYEFF: He doesn't hear well.

LOPAHIN: I'm off for Kharkov at about five o'clock in the morning. What a bother! I wanted to look at you . . . You're beautiful as you ever were.

PISHCHIK: *(Breathes heavily)* Even more so . . . Dressed in the Paris style. I'll be darned, thrice over!

LOPAHIN: Your brother, Leonid Andreyevich here, says I'm a boor. A peasant money grubber, but that's all the same to me. Absolutely. Let him talk. All I want is for you to trust me as you used to and for your marvelous, tender eyes to look at me as they did before. Merciful God! My father was your father's and your grandfather's serf, but you, you personally, you did so much for me once that I've forgotten all that and love you like my own blood . . . more than my own blood.

LYUBOFF ANDREYEVNA: I can't sit still—I simply can't. *(Jumps up and walks about in great excitement)* I won't survive this joy. You're laughing at me, I'm foolish . . . My very own little bookcase! *(Kisses the bookcase)* My little table!

GAYEFF: And when you were gone, the nurse here died.

LYUBOFF ANDREYEVNA: *(Sits down and drinks coffee)* Yes, may she rest in peace. They wrote to me.

GAYEFF: And Anastasy died. Cross-eyed Petrushka left me and lives in town now at the police officer's. *(Takes a small box of hard candy out of his pocket and sucks on a piece)*

PISHCHIK: My daughter, Dashenka . . . sends her regards . . .

LOPAHIN: I want to say something very pleasant, cheerful to you. *(Glances at his watch)* I'm off now; no time to talk . . . Well, a word or two. You already know, your cherry orchard is to be sold for debts; the auction is set for the twenty-second of August, but don't you worry, my dear one. You just sleep in peace; there's a way out. Here's my plan. Please pay attention! Your estate is only twelve miles from town. The railroad runs by it, and if the cherry orchard and the land along the river were divided into building lots and then leased for summer cottages, you'd have at the very least twenty-five thousand rubles a year out of it.

GAYEFF: Excuse me, what nonsense!

LYUBOFF ANDREYEVNA: I don't quite understand you, Yermolay Alexeyevich.

LOPAHIN: You'll get at least twenty-five rubles a year for the summer cottages, on a two and a half acre lot, and if you advertise now, I'll bet you anything that by autumn you won't have a single piece of land left; they'll buy up everything. In a word, congratulations; you're saved. The location is wonderful; the river's deep. Only, of course it's got to be set up, cleared . . . For example, let's say, raze all the old buildings and this house, which isn't of use anymore, and cut down the old cherry orchard . . .

LYUBOFF ANDREYEVNA: Cut it down? My dear, forgive me. You don't understand anything. If there's one thing in the whole province that's interesting—even remarkable—it's our cherry orchard.

LOPAHIN: The only thing remarkable about this cherry orchard is that it's very big. There's a crop of cherries once every two years, and even then they're hard to get rid of. Nobody buys them.

GAYEFF: This orchard is even mentioned in the *Encyclopedia.*

LOPAHIN: *(Glances at his watch)* If we don't think up something and don't arrive at a decision, the cherry orchard and the entire estate will be sold at auction on the twenty-second of August. You have to decide! I swear to you, there's no other way out. No and no . . .

FIERS: There was a time, forty, even fifty years ago, when the cherries were dried, soaked, pickled, made into jam, and, it used to be . . .

GAYEFF: Be quiet, Fiers.

FIERS: And the dried cherries used to be shipped by the wagonload to Moscow and Kharkov. And there was plenty of money! And the dried cherries were soft then, juicy, sweet, fragrant . . . They knew a method then . . .

LYUBOFF ANDREYEVNA: And what happened to this method?

FIERS: They've forgotten it. Nobody remembers.

PISHCHIK: *(To* LYUBOFF ANDREYEVNA*)* What's happening in Paris? How are things? Did you eat frogs?

LYUBOFF ANDREYEVNA: Crocodiles.

PISHCHIK: Think of that . . .

LOPAHIN: Up to now in the rural areas there were only the gentry and the peasants, but now summer folk have appeared. All the towns, even the smallest ones, are surrounded with summer cottages. In about twenty years the summer resident will probably multiply tremendously. Now he only drinks tea on the balcony, but it could very well happen that on his two hand a half acre lot he'll go in for farming, and then your cherry orchard will be happy, rich, magnificent . . .

GAYEFF: What nonsense! *(*VARYA *and* YASHA *enter)*

VARYA: Here, Mama, two telegrams for you. *(Selects a key and opens the old bookcase noisily)* Here they are.

LYUBOFF ANDREYEVNA: From Paris. *(Tears up the telegrams without reading them)* Paris is over and done with . . .

GAYEFF: And do you know how old this bookcase is, Lyuba? A week ago I pulled out the bottom drawer, looked, and there was the date burned in. The bookcase was made exactly a hundred years ago. How about that? Ah? We could celebrate its anniversary. It's an inanimate object, but all the same, be that as it may, it's a bookcase.

PISHCHIK: *(In astonishment)* A hundred years! Think of that!

GAYEFF: Yes . . . That's something . . . *(Touches the bookcase)* Dear, respected bookcase! I congratulate your existence, which for more than a hundred years has been directed toward the shining ideals of goodness and justice; your silent call to fruitful labor has not weakened during the course of a hundred years, sustaining *(Tearfully)* throughout generations of our family the belief in a better future and nurturing in us ideals of goodness and social consciousness. *(Pause)*

LOPAHIN: Yes . . .

LYUBOFF ANDREYEVNA: You're the same as ever, Lyonya.

GAYEFF: *(Slightly embarrassed)* Carom to the right into the corner pocket. Cut into the side pocket!

LOPAHIN: *(Glances at his watch)* Well, time to go.

YASHA: *(Gives some medicine to* LYUBOFF ANDREYEVNA*)* Perhaps you'll take the pills now.

PISHCHIK: You should never take medicines, my dearest . . . They don't help or hurt. Give them here . . . my dear. *(Takes the pills, pours them into his palm, blows on them, puts them into his mouth, and washes them down with kvass)* There!

LYUBOFF ANDREYEVNA: *(Startled)* You've really gone mad!

PISHCHIK: I swallowed all the pills.

LOPAHIN: What a glutton! *(Everyone laughs)*

FIERS: He stayed with us during Holy Week and ate a half bucket of pickles. *(Mutters)*

LYUBOFF ANDREYEVNA: What's he muttering about?

VARYA: He's been muttering like that for three years. We're used to it.

YASHA: Old age. (CHARLOTTA IVANOVNA *in a white dress—very thin, tightly laced, with a lorgnette at her belt—crosses the stage)*

LOPAHIN: Excuse me, Charlotta Ivanovna, I haven't had a chance yet to welcome you. *(Attempts to kiss her hand)*

CHARLOTTA: *(Draws her hand away)* If I let you kiss my hand, next will be my elbow, then my shoulder . . .

LOPAHIN: It's not my day *(Everyone laughs)* Charlotta Ivanovna, do a trick!

LYUBOFF ANDREYEVNA: Charlotta, do a trick!

CHARLOTTA: Don't! I want to go to sleep. *(Exits)*

LOPAHIN: We'll see each other in three weeks. *(Kisses* LYUBOFF ANDREYEVNA'S *hand)* Till then, goodbye. It's time. *(To* GAYEFF*)* See you soon. *(Kisses* PISHCHIK*)* Goodbye. *(Shakes* VARYA'S *hand, then* FIERS'S *and* YASHA'S*)* I don't feel like going. *(To* LYUBOFF ANDREYEVNA*)* If you think it over about the summer cottages and decide, let me know. I'll get a loan of fifty thousand rubles. Think about it seriously.

VARYA: *(Angrily)* Go already!

LOPAHIN: I'm going, I'm going . . . *(Exits)*

GAYEFF: Boor. Incidentally, pardon . . . Varya is going to marry him; that's Varya's little fiancé.

VARYA: Don't talk too much, Uncle.

LYUBOFF ANDREYEVNA: Well, Varya, I shall be happy. He's a good man.

PISHCHIK: A man, to tell the truth . . . who is most worthy . . . And my Dashenka . . . also says that . . . all kinds of things. *(Snores but immediately wakes up)* Still, dearest one, give me a loan of two hundred and forty rubles . . . Tomorrow the interest on my mortgage has got to be paid . . .

VARYA: *(Frightened)* There isn't any, not any!

LYUBOFF ANDREYEVNA: Really, I haven't got anything.

PISHCHIK: Something will come up. *(Laughs)* I never give up hope. There, I think, all is lost, ruined, and lo and behold—a railroad cut across my land and . . . they paid me. And then, just wait, something else will happen . . . if not today, tomorrow . . . Dashenka will win two hundred thousand. She has a lottery ticket.

LYUBOFF ANDREYEVNA: The coffee's gone. Now we can go to bed.

FIERS: *(Cleans* GAYEFF'S *clothes with a brush)* You've got on the wrong trousers again. What am I going to do with you!

VARYA: *(Softly)* Anya is asleep. *(Opens the window softly)* The sun has risen already—it's not cold. Look, Mama, what wonderful trees. My God, what air! The starlings are singing!

GAYEFF: *(Opens another window)* The orchard's all white. You haven't forgotten, Lyuba? That long lane runs straight across—like an extended belt; it gleams on moonlit nights. Do you remember? You haven't forgotten?

LYUBOFF ANDREYEVNA: *(Looks out the window at the orchard)* Oh, my childhood, my innocence! I slept in this nursery! I looked out on the orchard from here; happiness awoke with me every morning; and it was just as it is now; nothing has changed. *(Laughs with joy)* All, all white! Oh, my orchard! After a dark, rainy autumn and cold winter, again you're young, full of happiness; the heavenly angels have not deserted you . . . If only the weight were lifted from my breast, from my shoulders; if only I could forget my past!

GAYEFF: Yes, and the orchard will be sold for debts, strange as that may seem.

LYUBOFF ANDREYEVNA: Look, Mother is walking through the orchard . . . in a white dress! *(Laughs with joy)* It's she.

GAYEFF: Where?

VARYA: God be with you, dear Mama!

LYUBOFF ANDREYEVNA: There's no one, I only imagined it. To the right, as you turn to the summer house, a little white tree is leaning there just like a woman . . . *(TROFIMOFF, in a well worn student's uniform and glasses, enters)*

LYUBOFF ANDREYEVNA: What an amazing orchard! White masses of blossoms, the blue sky . . .

TROFIMOFF: Lyuboff Andreyevna! *(She looks around at him)* I'll just pay my respects and I'll be off immediately. *(Kisses her hand warmly)* I was told to wait until morning, but I didn't have the patience . . . couldn't hold out . . . (LYUBOFF ANDREYEVNA *looks at him with perplexity)*

VARYA: *(Tearfully)* This is Petya Trofimoff.

TROFIMOFF: Petya Trofimoff, the former tutor of your Grisha . . . Have I really changed so much? *(LYUBOFF ANDREYEVNA embraces him and cries quietly)*

GAYEFF: *(Embarrassed)* Enough. Enough, Lyuba.

VARYA: I told you, Petya, to wait till tomorrow.

LYUBOFF ANDREYEVNA: My Grisha . . . My little boy . . . Grisha . . . Son . . .

VARYA: What can we do, Mama? It's God's will.

TROFIMOFF: *(Softly through his tears)* That will do, that will do.

LYUBOFF ANDREYEVNA: *(Weeps softly)* My boy perished, drowned . . . Why? Why, my friend? *(More quietly)* Anya is asleep there, and I'm talking so loud. Making so much noise . . . But why, Petya? Why did you lose your looks? Why did you grow so old?

TROFIMOFF: An old woman on the train called me a shabby-looking gentleman.

LYUBOFF ANDREYEVNA: You were only a boy then, a sweet young student, and now your hair has thinned, glasses. Are you really still a student? *(Goes to the door)*

TROFIMOFF: It's so ordained. I'll be a perennial student.

LYUBOFF ANDREYEVNA: *(Kisses her brother, then* VARYA*)* Well, go to bed. You've grown older, too, Leonid.

PISHCHIK: *(Follows her)* So that's it, we are going to bed now. Oh, my arthritis! I'll stay here . . . I'd like, Lyuboff Andreyevna my soul, early tomorrow morning . . . two hundred and forty rubles.

GAYEFF: There he goes again.

PISHCHIK: Two hundred and forty rubles—to pay the interest on the mortgage.

LYUBOFF ANDREYEVNA: I haven't any money, dear man.

PISHCHIK: I'll give it back, my precious. A trifling sum . . .

LYUBOFF ANDREYEVNA: Well, fine, Leonid can do it . . . You give it to him, Leonid.

GAYEFF: I'll give it to him, all right. Open up your pockets.

LYUBOFF ANDREYEVNA: What can we do? Give it to him, he needs it. He'll give it back *(LYUBOFF ANDREYEVNA, TROFIMOFF, PISHCHIK, and FIERS exit. GAYEFF, VARYA, and YASHA remain)*

GAYEFF: My sister hasn't lost the habit yet of throwing money away. *(To YASHA)* Get away, my boy, you smell like a chicken coop.

YASHA: *(With a grin)* And you, Leonid Andreyevich, haven't changed a bit.

GAYEFF: What? *(To VARYA)* What did he say?

VARYA: *(To YASHA)* Your mother's here from the village. She's been sitting in the servants' quarters since yesterday. She wants to see you.

YASHA: God bless her, once and for all!

VARYA: Ah, you're shameless!

YASHA: She's all I need! She could have come tomorrow. *(Exits)*

VARYA: Mama's the same as ever: she hasn't changed a bit. If she had anything to do with it, she'd give away everything she had.

GAYEFF: Yes . . . *(Pauses)* If too much medicine is being prescribed, you know for sure the sickness is incurable. I keep thinking. I wrack my brains, I have many remedies, a great many, which means, really, I haven't any at all. It would be nice to inherit a fortune from someone; it would be nice to marry off our Anya to a very rich man, it would be nice to go to Yaroslavl and try our luck with our aunt, the Countess. Auntie, you know, is very, very rich.

VARYA: *(Crying)* If only God would help us!

GAYEFF: Don't bawl! Auntie is very rich, but she doesn't like us. To begin with, my sister married a lawyer, not a nobleman. *(ANYA appears at the door)* She did not marry a nobleman, and one cannot say she behaved very virtuously. She's good, kind, a fine person. I love her very much, but no matter how much you allow for extenuating circumstances, one must admit she is immoral. You feel it in her slightest movement.

VARYA: *(Whispers)* Anya is standing in the doorway.

GAYEFF: What? *(Pauses)* It's amazing; something's in my right eye. I've begun to see poorly. And on Thursday, when I was in the District Court . . .

(ANYA enters)

VARYA: But why aren't you sleeping, Anya?

ANYA: I don't feel like sleeping. I can't.

GAYEFF: My tidbit. *(Kisses ANYA's face and hands)* My child. *(Tearfully)* You're not my niece; you are my angel; you're everything to me. Believe me; believe . . .

ANYA: I believe you, Uncle. Everyone loves, respects you . . . But dearest Uncle, you must keep quiet, just keep quiet. What were you saying, just now, about my mother, about your own sister? What did you say that for?

GAYEFF: Yes, yes . . . *(Puts her hand over his face)* Really, it's terrible! My God, God save me! And today I made a speech to the bookcase . . . How stupid! And only when I finished did I understand that it was stupid.

VARYA: It's true, Uncle, you ought to keep quiet. Just keep quiet, that's all.

ANYA: If you keep quiet, you'd really be more at peace with yourself.

GAYEFF: I'll keep quiet. *(Kisses* ANYA'S *and* VARYA'S *hands)* I'll keep quiet. Only about business: On Thursday I was in the District Court; well, a few of us gathered together and a conversation began about this and that; and it seems that it will be possible to arrange a loan on a promissory note to pay the bank the interest due on the mortgage.

VARYA: If the Lord would only help!

GAYEFF: Tuesday I'll go and talk it over again. *(To* VARYA*)* Don't bawl! *(To* ANYA*)* Your mother will talk to Lopahin; of course, he won't turn her down . . . And you as soon as you rest up, you'll go to Yaroslavl to the Countess, your great-aunt. And that's how we'll make our moves from three directions—and it's in the bag. We'll pay the interest; I'm convinced of that . . . *(Puts candy in his mouth)* On my honor I'll swear, by anything you like, that the estate won't be sold! *(Excitedly)* I swear by my happiness! Here's my hand. Call me a worthless dishonorable man if I let it come up for auction! I swear it with all my being!

ANYA: *(A quieter mood returns to her; she is happy)* How good you are, Uncle; how clever! *(Embraces her uncle)* I feel at peace now! I feel at peace! I'm happy!

FIERS *enters.*

FIERS: *(Reproachfully)* Leonid Andreyevich, have you no fear of God! When are you going to sleep?

GAYEFF: Right away, right away. Go on, Fiers. It's all right. I'll undress myself. Well, children, off to bed! The details tomorrow, but now go to sleep. *(Kisses* ANYA *and* VARYA*)* I am a man of the eighties. They don't call it the best of times, but all the same I can say I've suffered quite a lot for my convictions in my life. There's good reason why peasants love me. One must know the peasant! One must know from what . . .

ANYA: At it again, Uncle!

VARYA: Uncle dear, keep quiet.

FIERS: *(Angrily)* Leonid Andreyevich!

GAYEFF: Coming. Coming ... Go to bed. A double bank into the side pocket! I sink the white ... *(Exits;* FIERS *hobbles after him)*

ANYA: I feel at peace now. I don't feel like going to Yaroslavl; I don't like Great-aunt, but still I feel at peace. Thanks to Uncle. *(Sits down)*

VARYA: I must get to sleep. I'm going. And it was unpleasant here without you. In the old servants' quarters, as you know, only the old servants live there—Yefimyushka, Polya, Yevstigney, well, and Karp. They began to let every good-for-nothing spend the night with them—I didn't say anything. But then I hear they've spread rumors I'd given orders to feed them nothing but beans. Out of stinginess, you see. And all that from Yevstigney. Fine, I think to myself. If that's the way it is, I think to myself, then just you wait. I call in Yevstigney—*(Yawns)* He comes. How is it, I say, that you, Yevstigney, you're such a fool ... *(Glances at* ANYA*)* Anechka! *(Pause)* Asleep! *(Takes* ANYA *by the arm)* Let's go to bed. Come on! *(Leading her)* My little darling fell asleep! Come on. *(They exit. Far away, beyond the orchard, a shepherd is playing on a reed pipe.* TROFIMOFF *walks across the stage and, seeing* VARYA *and* ANYA, *stops)* Shh—She's asleep ... asleep ... Let's go, my dearest.

ANYA: *(Quietly, half-dreaming)* I'm so tired. The bells on and on ... Uncle dear ... And Mama and Uncle ...

VARYA: Let's go, my dearest, let's go. *(They go into* ANYA'S *room)*

TROFIMOFF: *(Tenderly)* My little sun! My spring!

Curtain. End Act I

1903

Translation by Edward J. Czerwinski

RESOURCES

Primary Text

Chekhov, Anton P. "Vishnevyi sad." *Sobranie sochinenii.* Vol. 9. Moscow: Khudo-zhestvennaia literatura, 1963, pp. 607–25.

Secondary Sources

Literary and Cultural Studies

Amiard-Chevrei, C. *Le Théâtre artistique de Moscou 1898–1917.* Paris: Centre national de la recherche scientifique, 1979.

Barricelli, Jean-Pierre, ed. *Chekhov's Great Plays: A Critical Anthology*. New York: New York University Press, 1981.

Benedetti, Jean. *Stanislavski: An Introduction*. New York: Theatre Art Books, 1982.

Bowlt, John E. *Russian Stage Design: Scenic Innovation 1900–30*. Exhibition catalogue, Jackson, Mississippi Museum of Art, and other cities. 1982.

Czerwinski, E.J., ed. and trans. *Chekhov Reconstructed. Slavic and East European Arts*. 4, no. 3 (1986): 143–81. For the full translated text and introduction.

Kleberg, Lars, and Åke Nilsson, eds. *Theater and Literature in Russia 1900–1930*. Stockholm: Alinqvist and Wiksell, 1984.

McLean, Hugh. "Chékhov, Antón Pávlovich (1860–1904)." In *Handbook of Russian Literature*, ed. Victor Terras. New Haven: Yale University Press, 1985, pp. 79–81.

Peace, Richard. *Chekhov: A Study of the Four Major Plays*. New Haven: Yale University Press, 1983.

Slonim, Mark. *Russian Theatre from the Empire to the Soviets*. Cleveland: World Publishing, 1961.

Smelianskii, Anatolii. *Nashi sobesedniki*. Moscow: Iskusstvo, 1981, pp. 267–305.

Stanislavsky, Konstantin. *Selected Works*. Comp. Oksana Korneva. Moscow: Raduga, 1984.

Stanislavsky on the Art of the Stage. Trans. David Magarshack. London–Boston: Faber and Faber, 1967.

Terras, Victor. *A History of Russian Literature*. New Haven: Yale University Press, 1991, pp. 491–94.

Valency, Maurice. *The Breaking String: The Plays of Anton Chekhov*. New York: Schocken, 1983.

Drama and Theater

Chekhov, A. *Sobranie sochinenii*. Moscow: Khudozhestvennaia literatura, 1963. Vol. 9. Photo of 1915 Moscow Art Theater production, p. 624.

Marshall, Herbert. *The Pictorial History of the Russian Theatre*. New York: Crown, 1977.

Film

Chaika (The Seagull). Director, Iulii Karasik. Mosfilm, 1971.

Diadia Vania (Uncle Vanya). Director, Andrei Mikhalkov-Konchalovskii. Cinematographer, Georgii Rerberg. Design, N. Dvigubskii. Music, Alfred Schnittke. Cast: Sergei Bondarchuk, Irina Kupchenko. Mosfilm, 1971.

Iubilei (The Anniversary). Director, Vladimir Petrov. Mosfilm, 1944.

Medved' (The Bear). Director, Isidor Annenskii. Cast: Mikhail Zharov. Belgoskino, 1938.

Neokonchennaia p'esa dlia mekhanicheskogo pianino (Unfinished Piece for a Player Piano). Director, N. Mikhalkov. Mosfilm, 1977.

Tri sestry (Three Sisters). Director, Samson Samsonov. Mosfilm, 1969.

Vishnevyi sad (The Cherry Orchard). Director, Josif Heifitz. Cinematographer, Andrei Moskvin. Cast: Aleksei Batalov. Lenfilm, 1959.

20

~Alexander Blok~

A Puppet Show

Look, a puppet show opened
For good, happy kids who behave.
A boy and a girl are hoping
To see kings with their ladies, and devils.
And this music from hell can be heard:
A doleful bow howls.
The devil who caught that little roly-poly is horrid.
And cranberry juice trickles down.

THE BOY

He will be saved from the rage of the black one.
With a wave or the sleight
Of a white hand. Look: little lights
Approach from the left.
Do you see smoke? Can you see the torchlights?
Certainly, it is the queen herself.

GIRL

Oh no, why do you tease me?
That is the devil's retinue . . .
The queen, she comes out in daylight,
Laced all around with garlands of roses.
Swords clanking, a retinue of sighing
Knights carry her train.

All of a sudden, a fool leans across the footlights.
And shouts: Help!
I'm hemorrhaging cranberry juice!

> I'm bandaged with rags!
> On my head, there's a helmet of cardboard,
> And in my hand, a sword made of wood.
>
> The girl and boy burst into tears,
> And the curtain is drawn on the fun puppet show.

1905

Translation by Timothy Westphalen

RESOURCES

Primary Text

Blok, Alexander. "Balaganchik." *Sobranie sochinenii v shesti tomakh. 1898–1906.* Vol. 1. Leningrad: Khudozhestvennaia literatura, 1980, pp. 358–59.

Secondary Sources

Literary and Cultural Studies

Braun, Edward. *The Theatre of Meyerhold: Revolution on the Modern Stage.* New York: Drama Book Specialists, 1979.

———, ed. and trans. *Meyerhold on Theatre.* London: Methuen, 1990, pp. 49–64, 119–45. The best possible introduction to the stage version of Blok's verse from a participant in the creative process.

Briusov, Valery. "Nenuzhnaia pravda." In *The Russian Symbolist Theatre: An Anthology of Plays and Critical Texts,* ed. and trans. Michael Green. Ann Arbor, MI: Ardis, 1986, pp. 25–30.

Elik, M., ed. *Blok i muzyka: sbornik statei.* Leningrad, Moscow: Izd-vo Sovetskii kompozitor, 1972.

Fedorov, A. *Teatr A. Bloka i dramaturgiia ego vremeni.* Leningrad: Izd-vo Leningradskogo universiteta, 1972.

Gromov, P. *A. Blok, ego predshestvenniki i sovremenniki.* 2d ed. Leningrad: Sovetskii pisatel', 1986.

Mochulski, K. *Aleksandr Blok.* Trans. Doris V. Johnson. Detroit: Wayne State University Press, 1983.

Peterson, R.E. "A History of Russian Symbolism." *Linguistic and Literary Studies in Eastern Europe* 29 (1993).

Poggioli, Renato. *The Poets of Russia, 1890–1930.* Cambridge: Harvard University Press, 1960.

Pyman, Avril. *A History of Russian Symbolism.* Cambridge: Cambridge University Press, 1994.

———. *The Life of Aleksandr Blok.* New York: Oxford University Press, 1979.

Rodina, T. *Aleksandr Blok i russkii teatr nachala XX veka.* Moscow: Nauka, 1972.

Rubtsov, A.B. *Dramaturgiia Aleksandra Bloka.* Minsk: Vyssheishaia shkola, 1968.

Rudnitsky, K.L. *Meyerhold the Director.* Ed. S. Schultze. Ann Arbor, MI: Ardis, 1981.

———. *Russkoe rezhisserskoe iskusstvo.* Moscow: Nauka, 1990.

Schmidt, Paul, ed. *Meyerhold at Work.* Austin: University of Texas Press, 1980.

Venclova, Tomas. "Blók, Aleksándr Aleksándrovich (1880–1921)." In *Handbook of Russian Literature,* ed. Victor Terras. New Haven: Yale University Press, 1985, pp. 54–57.

Vogel, Lucy. "Illusions Unmasked in Blok's Puppet Motifs." *Canadian American Slavic Studies* 24 (Summer 1990): 169–98.

West, James. *Russian Symbolism: A Study of Vyacheslav Ivanov and the Russian Symbolist Aesthetic.* London: Methuen, 1970.

Westphalen, Timothy. "The Carnival Grotesque and Blok's 'The Puppet Show.'" *Slavic Review* 52 (Spring 1993): 49–66.

———. *Lyric Incarnate: The Dramas of Alexander Blok.* London: Harwood Academic Press (forthcoming, 1996).

Literature

Proffer, Carl and Ellendea, eds. *The Silver Age of Russian Culture: An Anthology.* Ann Arbor, MI: Ardis, 1975.

Drama and Theater

Green, Michael, ed. and trans. *The Russian Symbolist Theatre: An Anthology of Plays and Critical Texts.* Ann Arbor, MI: Ardis, 1986, pp. 45–57.

21

~Anna Akhmatova~

The Gray-Eyed King

Hail to you, oh, inconsolable pain;
Death brings an end to the gray-eyed king's reign.

That evening in autumn was sultry and red,
My husband came home and to me calmly said:

"From the hunt he was brought, so they say
Near an old tree of poplar, he lifelessly lay.

Oh, his poor queen. So young, it's not right! . . .
Her hair turned to gray, in the course of one night."

He picked up his pipe, from the fireplace shelf
And went off to work for the night by himself.

And my daughter I'll now go to awake
In her gray eyes briefly a glance I will take.

And murmuring poplars outside can be heard:
"Your king is no longer here on this earth."

December 11, 1910
Tsarskoe Selo

Translation by Rachel Winokur

RESOURCES

Primary Text

Akhmatova, Anna. "Seroglazyi korol'." *Stikhotvoreniia i poemy.* Ed. F.Ia. Priima. Leningrad: Sovetskii pisatel', 1977, p. 44.

Secondary Sources

Literary and Cultural Studies

Bristol, Evelyn. *A History of Russian Poetry.* New York: Oxford University Press, 1991, pp. 206–16.

Driver, Sam Norman. *Anna Akhmatova.* New York: Twayne, 1972.

Kelly, Catriona. *A History of Russian Women's Writing 1820–1992.* Oxford: Clarendon Press, 1994.

———, ed. *An Anthology of Russian Women's Writing 1777–1992.* New York: Oxford University Press, 1994.

Ketchian, Sonia. "Akhmátova, Ánna Andréevna." In *Handbook of Russian Literature,* ed. Victor Terras. New Haven: Yale University Press, 1985, pp. 14–16.

Vinogradov, V.V. *Anna Akhmatova: o simvolike—o poezii.* Leningrad: Mysl', 1922.

Music

Ironiia sud'by (Irony of Fate). Director, E. Riazanov. Mosfilm, 1975. For music based on poetry by Akhmatova.

Prokofiev, Sergei. *Cinq poésies d'Anna Akhmatova.* Opus 27. Voice and piano. England: Boosey & Hawkes, 1947. Score.

Vertinskii, A. *Cherneet doroga Pritorskogo sada.* No. 15. Moscow: Melodiia, 1989. 2 records.

22

∼Vladimir Mayakovsky∼

Listen!

Listen!
If, stars are lit—
then—someone needs it?
Then—someone wants them to exist?
Then—someone calls these bits of spit
pearls?
And, straining
in the storms of midday dust
bursts in on god,
afraid, of being late,
cries,
kisses his veined hand,
asks—
For a star indeed to exist!
swears—
he will not bear this starless suffering!
And after
walks about worried,
but calm on the exterior.
Says to someone:
"Now nothing
Frightens you?
Yes?"
Listen!
If stars are lit—
then—someone needs it?
Then—it's absolutely necessary,
that every night
above the roofs
at least one star burst into light?!

1914

Translation by Nicholas Rzhevsky

RESOURCES

Primary Text

Maiakovskii, V.V. "Poslushaite!" *Sobranie sochinenii v vos'mi tomakh.* Vol. 1. Moscow: Pravda, 1968, pp. 58–59.

Secondary Sources

Literary and Cultural Studies

Brown, E.J. *Mayakovsky: A Poet in the Revolution.* Princeton: Princeton University Press, 1975.

Paperno, Irina, and Joan Delaney Grossman, eds. *Creating Life: The Aesthetic Utopia of Russian Modernism.* Stanford: Stanford University Press, 1994.

Janecek, Gerald. *The Look of Russian Literature: Avant-Garde, Visual Experiments 1900–1930.* Princeton: Princeton University Press, 1984.

Markov, Vladimir. *Russian Futurism: A History.* Berkeley: University of California Press, 1968.

Shklovsky, Victor. *Mayakovsky and His Circle.* Trans. Lily Feiler. New York: Dodd & Mead, 1972.

Terras, Victor. *Vladimir Mayakovsky.* Twayne's World Authors Series. New York: Twayne, 1983.

Woroszylski, W. *The Life of Mayakovsky.* Trans. Boleslaw Taborski. New York: Orion, 1970.

Drama and Theater

Poslushaite! Adaptation by Iu. Liubimov and V. Smekhov. Stage design, E. Stenberg. Music, Edvard Denisov. Taganka Theater. Video recording in *Russian Literary Theatre: Ten Plays at the Taganka Theatre.* NJR Video, 1984.

23

~Marina Tsvetaeva~

I ask the mirror for a glimpse . . .

I ask the mirror for a glimpse
Into a dream obscured
I need to know—where your path leads
Your final destiny.

Then I see: the mast of a ship,
And you—are on the deck . . .
You—in train-engine mist . . . meadows
In evening lament . . .

The evening meadows draped in dew,
Above them—crows in flight . . .
I bless you, go, wherever
You may like!

May 3, 1915

Translation by Rachel Winokur

RESOURCES

Primary Text

Tsvetaeva, Marina. "Khochu u zerkala, Gde mut'." *Izbrannye proizvedeniia.* Ed. A. Efron and A. Saak´iants. Moscow–Leningrad: Sovetskii pisatel', 1984, p. 68.

Secondary Sources

Literary and Cultural Studies

Karlinsky, Simon. *Marina Tsvetaeva: The Woman, Her World and Her Poetry.* Cambridge: Cambridge University Press, 1985.

Kelly, Catriona. *A History of Russian Women's Writing, 1820–1992.* Oxford: Clarendon Press, 1994.

Losskaia, V. *Marina Tsvetaeva v zhizni: neizdannye vospominaniia sovremennikov.* Tenafly, NJ: Hermitage, 1989.

Makin, Michael. *Marina Tsvetaeva: Poetry of Appropriation.* Oxford: Clarendon Press, 1993.

Tsvetayeva: A Pictorial Biography. Intro. Carl Proffer. Ann Arbor, MI: Ardis, 1980.

Music

Ironiia sud'by ili s legkim parom. Director, E.R. Riazanov. Mosfilm, 1975. For music based on "I ask the mirror for a glimpse . . ."

Pugacheva, Alla, i grupa Retsital. "Kogda ia budu babushkoi." In *Kak trevozhen etot put'.* Moscow: Melodiia, 1983.

Schnittke, Alfred. *Three Poems of Marina Tsvetaeva.* Chester, NY: G. Schirmer, 1978. Score.

Shostakovich, D. *Six Poems of Marina Tsvetaeva.* Opus 143. Conductor, R. Barshai. Moscow Chamber Orchestra. Moscow, n.d.

Audio Recording

Marina Tsvetaeva: Fifty Years Past. Based on the poetry and correspondence of Marina Tsvetaeva. N.d. Distributed by RAES.

Tsvetaeva and Ehrenburg. 25 min. N.d. Distributed by RAES.

24

~Marina Tsvetaeva~

Verses About Moscow

There are clouds—above,
Moscow domes—above,
Biggest of embraces
Isn't big enough!
I'm singing praise to you,
Lighter burden of mine,
Little weightless seedling of mine!

My Metropolis,
Peaceful, marvelous!
Even when I'm dead
It will bring me joy!
It will see you reign,
It will see you grieve,
And receive my crown
First-born to the throne!

You should fast in Lent,
Blacken not your brows,
Honor the countless domes—
All "sorok sorokoff."[1]
The unbounded space of the Seven Hills [2]
Striding youthfully
You should measure off!

Once your turn has come,
You will hand this town
To a daughter of yours
With tender bitterness.
As for me—the deep, everlasting sleep,

And the bell that tolls,
And the early dawns
At the cemetery,
At Vagankovo.

March 31, 1916

Translation by Yelena Posina

Notes to the translation are on page 579.

RESOURCES

Primary Text

Tsvetaeva, Marina. "Stikhi o Moskve." *Izbrannye proizvedeniia.* Ed. A. Efron and A. Saak´iants. Moscow–Leningrad: Sovetskii pisatel', 1984, pp. 78–79.
For additional resources, see listings on pp. 445–46, above.

25

~Valery Briusov~

Barely a Tenth

Boundless, oh rapture! Abysmal, oh torment!
Passion, your depths know no limits it seems!
Revealed in the course of a lifetime—barely a
Tenth, barely a tenth!

If sorrow and happiness somehow have touched us
The moments are gone, they have faded away
And memory only preserves—barely a
Tenth, barely a tenth!

We've lived, and we've loved, we've searched and encountered
To weep, to believe, to applaud and to scorn
But joyous occasions have left us—barely a
Tenth, barely a tenth!

Our moments of love, just as swings, they have rocked us
We soared to the sky and then miserably fell . . .
But life's flash of triumph comprises—barely a
Tenth, barely a tenth!

So why are we struggling, as in the beginning
To craft of our moments a tapestry weave
The thread that we long for will bring together—barely a
Tenth, barely a tenth!

And though we, the singers, have sung of ourselves!
What sort of power does song really hold?
The anguish a song can preserve—barely a
Tenth, barely a tenth!

1916

Translation by Rachel Winokur

RESOURCES

Primary Text

Briusov, Valerii. "Desiataia chast'." *Sobranie sochinenii. Stikhotvoreniia. 1909–1917.*
   Vol. 2. Moscow: Khudozhestvennaia literatura, 1973, p. 210.

Secondary Sources

Literary and Cultural Studies

Bristol, Evelyn. *A History of Russian Poetry.* New York: Oxford University Press, 1991,
   pp. 168–78.
Rice, Martin P. *Valery Briusov and the Rise of Russian Symbolism.* Ann Arbor, MI:
   Ardis, 1975.
West, James. *Russian Symbolism: A Study of Vyacheslav Ivanov and the Russian
   Symbolist Aesthetic.* London: Methuen, 1970.

Film

Zakhochu–Poliubliu (I'll Love If I Want To). Director, V. Panin. Skify, 1990. Includes
   song version of "A Tenth Part" and adaptation of Briusov's "Last Pages of a Lady's
   Diary."
Zhazhda strasti (Thirst for Passion). Director, A. Kharitonov. Cast: Anastasiia Vertinskaia,
   Igor Kostolevskii. Distributed by RAES, 1990.

26

~Andrei Bely~

Petersburg

From Chapter 2
"The Escape"

Alexander Ivanovich was returning home along empty avenues next to the
Neva; the light of a court carriage flew by; the Neva opened up before him
under the arch of the Winter Canal; there, on a curved little bridge, he
noticed the nightly shadow.

Alexander Ivanovich was returning to his humble domicile, to sit alone
among brown spots and to observe the life of lice in the damp cracks of the
walls. After nighttime his morning outing more than anything else seemed to
be an escape from crawling lice; Alexander Ivanovich's many observations
had long brought him to the idea that the peace and quiet of his night
depended directly on the peace and quiet of his day; of late he had brought
home with him only what he had experienced on the streets, in the restaurants, in the tea rooms.

So what was he bringing home today?

What he had experienced dragged after him in a tail flying behind strong
and invisible to the eye. Alexander Ivanovich experienced the experiences he
experienced in reverse order, consciousness running away to the tail (that is,
behind the back): at those moments it always seemed to him that his back
opened and from it, as from a door, some kind of a giant's body prepared to
jump into the abyss: this giant's body was in fact the experiences of the past
twenty-four hours; they puffed out in a tail.

Alexander Ivanovich thought: when he returns, the events of the past
twenty-four hours would try to break in; he would still attempt to squeeze
them out with the attic door, severing tail from back; and the tail would still
break in.

Alexander Ivanovich left the bridge shining in diamonds behind him.

Further, beyond the bridge, on the background of nighttime St. Isaac's,
the same cliff rose up out of the green haze; stretching out a heavy and

green-covered hand, the same enigmatic Horseman raised up his bronze laurel wreath over the Neva; the perplexed horse threw out two front hoofs over a sleeping grenadier's shaggy fur hat; and below, under the hoofs, the drowsing old man's shaggy hat swayed slowly. A medallion falling from the hat struck the bayonet.

A rippling half-shadow covered the Horseman's face; and the face metal was split by two expressions; his palm cut into the turquoise air.

From that momentous time when the metallic Horseman had dashed up to the Neva shore, from that time's momentous days when he propelled a steed onto the gray Finnish granite, Russia had split in two, the very destinies of the fatherland had also split in two; Russia, split in two, suffering and wailing till the last.

You, Russia, are like a steed, with two front hoofs hovering over the darkness, the void, and two back ones firmly planted in the granite soil.

Would you like to break away from the stone that holds you, as some of your wild progeny have broken away, would you like to break away from the stone that holds you and hang in the air, unbridled, later to plunge into the water's chaos? Or, perhaps, would you like to plunge through the fog, through the air, to disappear along with your progeny in the clouds? Or is it that you, Russia, rearing up, for many years, are contemplating the harsh destiny that has brought you here—in the midst of this desolate North, where the very dawn lasts for hours, where time itself alternates in bursts of freezing night, and—of blazing day? Or, fearing the leap, will you again, snorting, lower your hoofs in order to carry the great Horseman off into the depths of the plains away from deceptive lands?

It will not be! . . .

Once it has reared up and measured the air with its eyes, the bronze steed will not lower its hoofs: there will be—a leap over history; there will be great tumult; the earth will split asunder; the very hills will collapse from a great shuddering; the native plains will erupt in humps. On the humps will be Nizhnii, Vladimir, and Uglich.

Petersburg will sink.[1]

Then all the earth's peoples will rise up from their places; there will be great combat—combat unlike anything the world has seen; yellow regiments of Asiatics, moving from their settlements, will redden European fields with oceans of blood; there will be—Tsushima! There will be—a new Kalka![2]

Kulikovo Field, I await you![3]

Then the last Sun will shine on my native land. If, Sun, you do not rise up, then, oh Sun, European shores will sink under the heavy Mongolian heel, and a foam will curl over these shores; earthborn creatures will again

sink to the ocean's bottom—to primeval, long-forgotten chaos . . .
Arise, oh Sun!

. . . .

A turquoise fissure broke in the sky; and toward it flew a spot of burning phosphorous, which unexpectedly turned into a brightly shining moon; for a moment everything lit up: the waters; chimneys, granite, silver gutter pipes, two goddesses over an arch, the roof of a four-storied building; St. Isaac's cupola seemed translucent; the Horseman's forehead, bronze laurel wreath —flared up; the island lights died down; and the ambiguous boat in the middle of the Neva turned into a simple fishing schooner; a bright dot flashed spark-fast on the captain's bridge, perhaps the pipe light of the blue-nosed boatswain's mate in a Dutch cap with earmuffs, or the bright small lamp of a sailor keeping watch. A light half-shadow flew from the Bronze Horseman as if it were light ash; and the shaggy grenadier with the Horseman was sketched out in dark silhouette on the concrete slabs.

For a moment human destiny was distinctly illuminated for Alexander Ivanovich; one could see what would be, one could know what would never be: everything became so clear; fate, it seemed, had been revealed; but he was afraid to peer into his fate; he stood before it, shaken to the core, agitated, melancholy.

And—the moon cut into a cloud.

Again ragged arms-clouds flew madly into motion; into motion flew fog strands of some kind of witches' braids; and the spot of burning phosphorous gleamed ambiguously in the distance among them . . .

Then a deafening, inhuman howl rang out; flashing a huge light, an automobile moving from under the arch and in the direction of the river sped by unbearably close, sputtering kerosene. Alexander Ivanovich could see yellow Mongolian mugs cutting across the square; he fell down from the suddenness of it; his wet hat fell in front of him. Then in back a mumbling noise rose up, sounding like an incantation.

"My God, Jesus Christ! Save us and spare us!"

Alexander Ivanovich turned and grasped that the old Nicholas grenadier was whispering next to him.

"My God, what is it?"

"An automobile; distinguished Japanese guests . . . "

There was no trace of the automobile.

1916

Translation by Nicholas Rzhevsky

Notes to the translation are on page 579 .

454   *Andrei Bely*

RESOURCES

Primary Text

Belyi, Andrei. *Peterburg. Roman v vos'mi glavakh s prologom i epilogom.* Introduction by Georgette Donchin. Chicago: Bradda Books, 1967 (reprint of 1916 ed.), pp. 105–8.

Belyi, Andrei. *Peterburg.* Moscow: Khudozhestvennaia literatura, 1978 (reprint of 1928 ed.).

Secondary Sources

Literary and Cultural Studies

Bely, Andrei. *The Dramatic Symphony: The Forms of Art.* Edinburgh: Polygon, 1986.

———. *Petersburg.* Trans. and ed. Robert A. Maguire and John E. Malmstad. Bloomington: Indiana University Press, 1978.

Bristol, Evelyn. *A History of Russian Poetry.* New York: Oxford University Press, 1991.

Brostrom, Kenneth N. "Bély, Andréi." In *Handbook of Russian Literature,* ed. Victor Terras. New Haven: Yale University Press, 1985, pp. 45–47.

Clark, Katerina. *Petersburg, Crucible of Cultural Revolution.* Cambridge: Harvard University Press, 1995.

Dolgopolov, L.K. *Andrei Belyi i ego roman "Peterburg."* Leningrad: Sovetskii pisatel', 1988.

———. *Na rubezhe vekov.* Moscow: Sovetskii pisatel', 1985.

Janecek, Gerald. *The Look of Russian Literature: Avant-Garde, Visual Experiments 1900–1930.* Princeton: Princeton University Press, 1975.

Steinberg, Ada. *Word and Music in the Novels of Andrey Bely.* Cambridge: Cambridge University Press, 1982.

West, James. *Russian Symbolism: A Study of Vyacheslav Ivanov and the Russian Symbolist Aesthetic.* London: Methuen, 1970.

Drama and Theater

Bely, Andrei. *Gibel' senatora. (Peterburg): istoricheskaia drama* (Death of the Senator [Petersburg]: A Historical Drama). Ed. John Malmstad. Berkeley: Berkeley Slavic Specialities, 1986.

Rudnitsky, K.L. *Russian and Soviet Theater: Tradition and the Avant-Garde.* London: Thames and Hudson, 1988, p. 227. For photographs of the 1925 production with Mikhail Chekhov.

~ VI ~

Thresholds:
Soviet Culture and Beyond

The tragic course of Russian history as it discovered communism was marked by opposite cultural extremes: poets and artists who died in prison camps, and superb aesthetic achievements and magnificent acts of talent and courage. Both extremes came out of the past. One plausible explanation for the success of Soviet communism in winning over the Russians even under devastating conditions of massive repression and social genocide is that it provided new ideological language for the old values of poverty, self-sacrifice, and humility. Hatred for the prosperous peasant known as the *kulak* and for the capitalist was nurtured by the long-standing disrespect for material accumulation and self-aggrandizement we have seen develop in Russian culture from the early days of Boris and Gleb. When Lenin and the Georgian seminary student who succeeded him displaced the monarchy, they also replaced values of the old religious legacy with standards of self-abnegation to larger political goals, the saints with the party, and Christian hope and faith in transcendent verities with belief in materialism and the self-sacrificing Leaders of the People (some ultimately mummified to give a grotesque physical presence to moral symbols). The moral corruptions of the Soviet era, when one could feel self-righteous in denouncing neighbors to the secret police because of their well-appointed apartment, or could undertake the execution of a lover because he stood on the opposite side of the political fence, as in the classic Soviet film *The Forty-First* (1928, 1956), were consciously and cleverly manipulated by the government in the interests of political control.

Literature as the prime carrier of fundamental values and beliefs bore

A 1964 production of *Virgin Soil Upturned*, directed by Georgy Tovstonogov at the Bolshoi Dramatic Theater, featured T. Doronina as Lushka and P. Luspekaev as Nagulnov.

primary responsibility for the realization of Soviet ideology in Russian history, but it also enconcouraged both concern for that history's moral dilemmas and the eventual abandonment of communism under glasnost, the new cultural condition of openness, of saying and writing thoughts previously hidden.

The works of fiction that led the Russians to accept the party and totalitarianism were anticipated and often guided by Chernyshevsky's *What Is to Be Done?*, a nineteenth-century novel that inspired Lenin's primary political text of the same name. In the Soviet era, these works included government-endorsed models of literature, such as Aleksandr Fadeyev's (1901–1956) *The Rout* (1927), Mikhail Sholokhov's (1905–1984) *Virgin Soil Upturned* (1932–60), and Dmitry Furmanov's (1891–1926) *Chapayev* (1923). *The Rout* imitated Tolstoy's prose technique and the kenotic ethos we encountered as early as *Boris and Gleb* to represent the ritual sacrifice of a Red Army detachment in the name of future victories. *Virgin Soil Upturned,* Sholokhov's major work after his magnificent *Quiet Don* (1928–40), is one of the better and more typical novels representing Socialist Realism, the Soviet government program that controlled literature and the arts from the 1930s to the era of Gorbachev.

Virgin Soil Upturned provided moral justification for the genocide of the peasantry, but it also made talented use of folk idiom and nature sensibility. Davydov, Makar Nagulnov, and Andrei Razmetov, the positive heroes of the work, come to understand in typical fashion the importance of learning from the people of the Cossack village they introduce to collectivization. Their ideological epiphany occurs thanks to firm political guidance from above in the person of the local party secretary, Comrade Nesterenko. Davydov learns that his personal life, made vigorous by Lushka, a Cossack woman of enormous sexual potential, is secondary to his public obligations. The exuberant Lushka also undergoes a spiritual transformation and becomes an excellent worker thanks to the gentle influence of the OGPU, the predecessor of the KGB.

Among similar justifications of the secret police and its tactics of terror, particularly noticeable was *The Aristocrats* (1935), a play by Nikolai Pogodin (Nikolai Stukalov, 1900–1962). In the initial 1934 production, staged at the Realistic Theater with a skillful use of nonrealistic stage devices by Nikolai Okhlopkov (1900–1967), forced labor in the construction of the Baltic–White Sea Canal was shown to produce a miraculous moral meta-morphosis in the most despicable of convicts and political prisoners.

The more believable moral transformations that began in Soviet culture after Stalin's death were, in turn, heralded by literature about labor camps and the secret police, but now written from the antigovernment perspectives of Aleksandr Solzhenitsyn (1918–), Varlam Shalamov (1907–1982), and Evgenia Ginzburg (1896–1980). Solzhenitsyn led the way with *One Day in the Life of Ivan Denisovich* (1962), *First Circle* (1955–1958), and the massive *Gulag Archipelago* (1973–75). The latter work inspired one of glasnost's strongest and most typical genres, independent journalism.

Dmitry Furmanov's *Chapayev* (1923) also claimed the style of factual reporting but, like Sholokhov's *Virgin Soil Upturned*, typified the earlier period of ideological mimicry. Widely considered to be a primary early stimulant to Socialist Realism, the novel combined the sacrifice of a mythologized positive hero with a broad hint that the party should be heeded even by Red Army *bogatyri*. In 1934, *Chapayev* was adapted to cinema by Georgy and Sergei Vasiliev. The film became one of the most popular Socialist Realist contributions to the Soviet equivalent of the cowboys and Indians genre (the cowboys were typically Red Army soldiers and the Indians their White counterparts from the Civil War).

As is common in popular culture, Chapayev's image attained an extreme of heroism that eventually prodded ridicule in the form of numerous jokes regarding the brave commander and his sidekicks, Petka and Anka. In spite of government sponsorship, Furmanov's text was boring and largely unreadable; the anecdotes based on it, however, expressed a lively tradition of popular creativity as suggestive of carnival impulses in Russian culture and fundamental literary processes as were the folk tales we noted earlier.

The manipulation of official fiction, such as the original *Chapayev,* was made easier by treatment of aesthetic texts as totally relative objects with ever changing meanings. The fictionality of literature became part of the cynical understanding by government functionaries that words could mean everything and be used to argue for anything. Texts in the arts—such as *Virgin Soil Upturned*—were continuously adjusted and sometimes drastically changed to reflect the shifting political concerns of the day. Religion, of course, with its emphasis on unchanging commandments and transcendent values, was understood to be a major obstacle to local political demands; atheism became one of the first major objectives of Soviet propaganda. The uses of atheism were quickly followed by other concerns in literature dictated by changes in prevalent ideological demands. Socialist Realist texts contributed to Soviet history by paying close attention and reacting quickly to government programs arguing for collectivization, loyalty to the state, mobilization for war, and the search for "enemies of the people."

In such a historical context, poetry offered one of the more appealing art forms, providing a haven for the self's exploration in the midst of unprecedented social-political encroachments and an opportunity to turn inward and preserve aesthetic and moral integrity. Like so much other honest Russian literature in the Soviet period, many poems were written "for the desk drawer," that is, for the author, to be hidden away from society. But desks could be opened, as poets were well aware, and poetry, like all language, could not, in any case, exist in a void or at the bottom of desk drawers. In result, the intrusions of the social-political context, the basic dilemmas of public and private imperatives in art, and the clash between social codes and individual commitments were constant concerns reflected in verse. None of the poets included here led even a minimally settled life. All—even Vladimir Mayakovsky, poet laureate of the early Soviet state—suffered history as an imposition and challenge to be dealt with in their work.

Art could only save so much. Mayakovsky committed suicide, as did Sergei Esenin (1895–1925) before him after opening a vein to write in blood "Farewell, my friend, farewell." In a notorious incident of Soviet cultural history, Mayakovsky composed an answer to the dead Esenin, attacking him for his sentimentalism and lack of gumption. The sentiment of poets, however, exerted its revenge in Mayakovsky's own suicide. Marina Tsvetaeva returned from emigration and also took her own life. Mandelstam died in a concentration camp, never fully reconciled with his age and unable to fight it off with his only weapon—poems such as "January 1, 1924," and

"We live without feeling . . . ," the devastating epigram on Stalin that led to his arrest. Pasternak lived through the worst of the terror years, but when he wrote about the pressures of history on the artist in "Hamlet" (*Dr. Zhivago*, 1957), he was promptly brought to the limits of endurance by his government. Like Pasternak, Akhmatova survived to raise a bitter poetic toast to her age. Victim of Zhdanov's notorious reaffirmation of Socialist Realist doctrine after the war, she became an object of passionate worship and emulation by young poets such as Joseph Brodsky (1940–1996) and Dmitrii Bobyshev (1936–) after Stalin's death.

In one of the ironies of Soviet culture, poetry, precisely because of its withdrawal from the moral corruptions of society into a private aesthetic realm of integrity, itself became a major public event. Beginning with the 1950s, Russians in the thousands came to hear writers such as Andrei Voznesensky (1933–) and Yevgeny Yevtushenko (1933–) read their verse; the poet took on the moral authority earlier enjoyed by church elders. Eventually, with the development of technology and the cassette recorder, poets were joined as objects of public worship by bards like Vladimir Vysotsky (1938–1980) and Bulat Okudzhava (1924–). In 1971, Vysotsky, the most popular singer-poet in the post-Stalin era, created an unforgettable example of representational and literary-historical conjunctions by reciting Pasternak's "Hamlet" before appearing in Shakespeare's play at the Taganka Theater. His own composition "Morning Exercise" (1968) shaped a wonderful mockery of the in-step aerobics of Soviet mores during the so-called Brezhnev era of stagnation.

Vysotsky and the Taganka had a rich tradition of Soviet humor to call upon, a tradition the theater honored in a 1981 adaptation of Isaak Babel's works titled *Five Stories by Babel*. In his life and work, Babel (1894–1941) had played out cultural dilemmas of separation and belonging. On the one hand, he was an important participant in the prolific new contributions of Russian Jews to the arts and a writer whose education in the Judaic tradition suggested the creative possibilities that religions outside of Russian Orthodoxy could offer Russian culture. His Odessa stories signaled the diversity of Soviet culture and the later contributions to it by such writers as Chingiz Aitmatov (1928–) and Anatoly Kim (1939–). On the other hand, like his Odessa rogue Benya Krik, Babel was attracted to the margins, to the curiosity and disengagement of the writer looking in from the outside of his fiction. Eventually, Soviet culture refused such curiosity and Babel paid for the dilemmas of marginality with his life. The postcommunist period saw a strong revival of interest in Babel and a number of film adaptations of the play *Sunset* (1928), itself an adaptation from the prose world of Benya Krik.

The problematic role of humor in Soviet culture was evident in the works of Yury Olesha (1899–1960), Valentin Kataev (1897–1986), Ilya Ilf (1897–1937) and Evgeny Petrov (1903–1942) (pseudonyms of I. Fainzilberg and Evgeny Kataev), and Mikhail Zoshchenko (1895–1958). Ilf and Petrov's *The Twelve Chairs* (1928), and its sequel, *The Golden Calf* (1931), created one of the most popular of Soviet literary protagonists, the irrepressible Ostap Bender. Unlike Chapayev, who elicited folk laughter through a juxtaposition of high seriousness and epic qualities with the ridiculous person of an illiterate Red Army commander, Ostap came out of the tradition of the *plut, picaro,* or rogue that went back to the adventures of Lazarillo de Tormes, Tom Jones, and Chichikov. In the picaresque's customary fashion, Ostap's travels offer a perspective from below on the moral failings and hypocrisies of society. His quest is inspired by greed, which is reflected, along with other basic deficiencies, in the various social types he encounters.

In *The Twelve Chairs,* "The Union of the Sword and the Plow," despite its ironic visual reference to the hammer and sickle, managed to stay within permitted boundaries by targeting humor at ostensibly un-Soviet traits—such as the urge to possess wealth hidden in one of the twelve chairs—left over from past capitalist mores. The laughter of Mikhail Zoshchenko's play *Crime and Punishment* (1933), adapted to film in Leonid Gaidai's popular *It Can't Be* (1975), served a similar function as literary safety-valve, allowing writers to vent outrage and frustration over the common social problems of housing, loose morals, and alcoholism but in strictly delimited channels and infused with the hot air of propaganda. The play was based on Zoshchenko's story "A Hurried Matter" (1926). Published in *Red Virgin Soil,* one of the livelier journals of early Soviet culture, it was performed in the Leningrad Music Hall the same year and is representative of Soviet vaudeville.

Zoshchenko, like Sholokhov, was a convinced communist; their works, it could be argued, maintained an ideological integrity that sometimes ended in awkward moral dilemmas and elicited vicious government attacks on the notion that writers could hold independent ideological convictions. Daniil Kharms (1905–1942), a member of the Oberiu group (Association for Real Art), and Mikhail Bulgakov (1891–1940), on the other hand, were among the few writers whose uses of humor in the problematic Soviet context suggested a literary integrity totally hostile to Soviet ideology. Kharms did so by using the absurd as a counterpoint to predominant ideological sense. "Makarov and Peterson" unleashes the chilling humor of the irrational at a loss of human identity that is universal but is here characterized by specific Soviet tonalities. Bulgakov took a different approach to similar issues by reasserting the laughter of Gogol and other artistic and intellectual principles of prerevolutionary Russia.

Thanks, in large part, to his talent in keeping alive the older Russian cultural tradition, Bulgakov became somewhat of an idol during the post-

Soviet period when authoritative literary models were desperately needed. During his lifetime, however, he was subject to a particular Soviet form of representational discrimination. He was more influential in theater than in literature for one simple reason: it was dangerous to print his works. Once Stalin—in one of those frequent moments of Soviet black magic—intervened on Bulgakov's behalf, theater allowed the writer a livelihood. His imagination gave birth to adaptations of his own *White Guard,* which under the new title of *Days of the Turbins* (1926) became one of the most popular post-Chekhov Moscow Art Theater productions, and other reworkings, such as of Gogol's *Dead Souls* (1932).

Exactly in keeping with this cultural situation, Bulgakov wrote *The Master and Margarita* (1940), one of the great texts of Russian literature, without much hope of publishing it. His act of faith was reflected in the novel, which celebrates the magical survival of values such as courage, honesty, and love along with the creative imagination itself—a major theme of the carnival chapter "Black Magic and Its Exposure"—in the face of brutal social and political pressures. Politicians and bureaucrats such as Pontius Pilate and the administrative staff of the Variety Theater are shown to be lacking both the imagination to recognize the importance of ultimate truths and the courage to act on them rather than on immediate self-serving realities.

The novel was not published until 1966, and it was another seven years before a relatively complete and uncensored text was made available to Russian readers. In the era of glasnost, Bulgakov's work simultaneously attained both the popularity of a best seller, with printings in the hundreds of thousands, and the reputation of a classic to be placed next to Gogol and Pushkin. In 1977 Yury Liubimov produced an adaptation of *The Master and Margarita* at the Taganka Theater, which inspired other versions throughout the world. In the last decade of the century, Russian composers, painters, and writers joined authors such as Salman Rushdie in recognizing the importance of Bulgakov's texts.[1]

During the heyday of Soviet culture, Bulgakov and his fellow writers and artists maintained a precarious perch on aesthetic thresholds. They looked back for inspiration and courage, glanced warily around, and waited for the appropriate moment when their art could jump forward off the stoop. One large step out of the past, over the sterile ground of Socialist Realism, and into the future was taken by post-Stalin writers such as Vladimir Soloukhin (1924–), Valentin Rasputin (1937–), Vasily Belov (1932–), Sergei Zalygin (1913–), Vasily Shukshin (1929–1974), Boris Mozhaev (1923–), and Fedor Abramov (1923–1980), whose "Wooden Horses" (1969) is representative of their literary movement, known as village prose.

When Western critics first became aware of his work in the 1960s, Abramov was hailed as a major literary talent. In later years he was over-

A performance of *The Master and Margarita* at the Taganka Theater.

shadowed by Solzhenitsyn, Rasputin, and others. "Wooden Horses," how-ever, remains a minor masterpiece of the village prose tradition. It looks back to Sholokhov's sense of folk idiom and nature—not surprisingly, since Abramov, literary scholar as well as writer, had produced a dissertation on *Virgin Soil Upturned*—and it is resonant with the ecological sensibility and moral-psychological exploration typical for the genre. The protagonist, Vas-ilisa Milentyevna, is close kin to our folklore heroine Vasilisa the Beautiful, to perennial kenotic types such as Turgenev's Lukerya in "A Living Relic," and to Solzhenitsyn's Matryona. Her qualities of beauty, gentleness, pa-tience, will, sense of duty, work, and closeness to nature suggest a touch-stone of humble feminine redemption before the hard, bleak life of the Soviet era. Abramov's text offers a modern reaffirmation of kenoticism's literary role.

Such traditional values affected social and ideological trends outside of literature when—in typical fashion for the late twentieth century—Rasputin and other writers and performers took on government functions. Prodded by their moral authority and a more general dissatisfaction with communism and capitalism alike, attempts to find solutions to the puzzles of Russian national identity after the breakup of the Soviet Union strongly responded to the issues raised in village prose.

In the arts, the texts of Abramov and his literary colleagues exerted an equally vigorous interrepresentational influence, particularly in film and

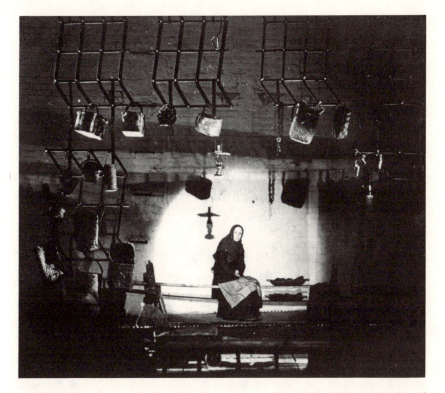

Alla Demidova played Vasilisa Milentyevna in the Taganka's 1974 production of *Wooden Horses*.

theater. Among the most talented transpositions were provided by Vasily Shukshin, who wrote, directed, and acted in such films as *Red Snowball Tree* (1974). Abramov's prose (*Brothers and Sisters, The House*) elicited numerous theater adaptations by Lev Dodin and others. *Wooden Horses* was staged in 1974 by Yury Liubimov's Taganka company in collaboration with the author. The audience entered the theater through the stage and in direct contact with the wooden implements, pestles, looms, and birch boxes described in the text. The basic material of Russian culture, as in the central metaphor of wooden horses, was given a performance correlative for the fundamental cultural space occupied by Milentyevna.

The uses of wood in text and performance contrasted strongly to the granite and cement typical of Soviet architecture and sculpture during the heyday of Socialist Realism. The shapes and forms to which the respective materials were put, of course, suggested a clash of cultural values. If sculptures such as Vera Mukhina's famous *Worker and Collective Farm Woman* (1937) and the innumerable high-rise construction projects were marked by Western Neoclassical reference, Abramov's text indicated a

Vera Mukhina's *Worker and Collective Farm Woman* (1937).

renewed yearning for older traditions in which wood served as the soft, pliable, and ever-yielding material of icons and churches.

After Mikhail Gorbachev's government collapsed and the attempt to preserve communist principles in the political and economic forms of perestroika failed, Russian culture was left a problematic legacy and an uncertain future. The past political intrusions into all spheres of life had aggregated deep-seated dilemmas of cultural patronage. On the one hand, the governments of Lenin, Stalin, Khrushchev, and Brezhnev, recognizing the political importance of the arts, had provided massive financial subsidies that were no longer available; on the other, the price of government patronage had been artists' subjugation to the demands of politicians—including, as in the notorious case of the Bolshoi ballet corps, sexual demands. The films of Eisenstein, the music of Shostakovich and Prokofiev, and the dancing of Ulanova were created in this cultural condition of government economic nurturing combined with heavy doses of hypocrisy and moral debasement. With the demise of the Soviet Union, the solid economic base of the arts was gone, but so was the necessity to compromise and observe Soviet ideology.

What was left was a magnificent technical tradition carried on by numerous talented artists and master teachers. The surviving craftsmanship was now free to derive inspiration from without through new access to other cultures and from within through a rich store of neglected or hidden literary texts from the past. The possibilities for cross-references between literature and intellectual history, long blocked by government ideology, were manifest in the simultaneous cultural return from the past of a philosopher who wrote on literature, Mikhail Bakhtin, and Mikhail Bulgakov, who responded in fiction to the perennial issues explored by Russian thinkers.

One of the more accurate indications of postcommunist culture, in fact, would be provided by a rereading of the works we have already read, a fundamental form of cultural activity undertaken with a liberated enthusiasm and new energy by Russian writers, painters, composers, and performers as the twentieth century drew to a close. If the end of the twentieth century was reminiscent of its beginnings in the return to issues and values that figured in the pre-Soviet cultural tradition, the postcommunist period and the dissolution of the Soviet empire was also reminiscent of earlier instabilities rich in aesthetic opportunity.

For the collapse of the old order before the revolution, as we have seen, was accompanied by an outburst of activity in literature, ballet, music, painting, and theater. The collapse of the Soviet political order and the ideology on which it rested created similar possibilities for debate and engagement with vital questions. The questions themselves—touching on the individual's roles in history and society, ethical possibilities whether deprived of or informed by a transcendent order of things, and the nature of human identity—were hardly likely to change; thus the appeal of the older literary and religious tradition. But the loss of authority and answers provided by government and society presented a fresh challenge to the Russian creative spirit.

As the century drew to a close, such challenges to the arts were not in some abstract and separate realm of aesthetic practice but, typically for Russian culture, were part of fundamental social and ideological debate, whether dealing with national identity, the roles of women, the ethnic and moral dilemmas raised anew in Grozny, devastated capital of the Chechens, the persistent appeal of communist principles for capitalist societies, or the attempt to find new values to live by in a postmodern age of deprivilegization of values. Russian literature and the art forms related to it have thrived precisely by responding to challenges of this sort in the past, and given the close attention accorded such writers as Akhmatova, Mandelstam, Bulgakov, and Solzhenitsyn, the future could be seen to offer new hope for cultural vision and achievement inspired by literature.

N.R.

Note

1. Noted by Lesley Milne in *Mikhail Bulgakov: A Critical Biography,* Cambridge: Cambridge University Press, 1990, p. 262.

27

~Isaak Babel~

The King

The wedding ended, and the Rabbi sank down into an armchair. Then he left the room and saw tables set up all along the length of the courtyard. There were so many of them that they stretched their tail past the gate and out onto Hospital Street. Covered with velvet, the tables wound through the courtyard like snakes, to whose bellies patches of all colors had been applied, and they sang in deep voices, these patches of orange and red velvet.

Apartments had been turned into kitchens. Cloudy smoke, drunken and puffy, pounded through the soot-covered doors. In its smoldering rays, old women's faces, their jiggling double chins and soiled breasts, roasted. Sweat, pink like blood, pink like the foam of a mad dog, streamed around those masses of sweetly stinking, overgrown human flesh. Three cooks, not counting the dishwashers, were preparing the wedding dinner. Over them reigned eighty-year-old Reysel, tiny and hunched, traditional as a scroll of the Torah.

Before dinner, a young man unknown to the guests slipped into the courtyard. He asked for Benya Krik.[1] He took Benya Krik aside.

"Listen, King," said the young man. "I have a couple of words I've got to tell you. I was sent by Aunt Hannah from Kostetsky Street . . . "

"Okay," answered Benya Krik, who was nicknamed the King. "What are those couple of words?"

"A new chief came into the precinct yesterday. Aunt Hannah ordered me to tell you."

"I knew about that the day before yesterday," answered Benya Krik. "Go on."

"The chief gathered the whole precinct and gave them a talk . . . "

"A new broom sweeps clean," answered Benya Krik. "He wants to round us up? Go on."

"And when's the roundup going to happen? Do you know, King?"

"It'll be tomorrow."

"It'll be today, King."

"Who told you that, kid?"

"Aunt Hannah told me that. You know Aunt Hannah?"

"I know Aunt Hannah. Go on."

"The chief gathered the whole precinct and gave them a talk. 'We have to smother Benya Krik,' he said, 'because where there is a Sovereign Emperor, there is no King. Today, when Krik gives away his sister and everybody is there, the roundup has to happen today.' "

"Go on."

"Then the pigs started to get scared. They said, if we carry out the roundup today, in the middle of a celebration, Benya will get pissed and a lot of blood will flow!

"So then the Chief said, 'My pride is dearer to me . . . ' "

"Okay go," said the King.

"What should I tell Aunt Hannah about the roundup?"

"Tell her Benya knows all about it."

So he left, this young man. Maybe a few of Benya's friends followed him. They said they'd come back in half an hour. And they did come back in half an hour. And that's that.

They were not seated around the table by seniority. Foolish old age is just as pathetic as cowardly youth. Or by wealth either. The lining of a heavy purse is sewn from tears. The bride and the groom sat at the head of the table. It was their day. Sender Eikhbaum, the King's father-in-law, sat next to them. It was his right. The story of Sender Eikhbaum must be told, because it is no ordinary story. How did Benya Krik, a bandit, the King of the bandits, become Eikhbaum's son-in-law? How did he become the son-in-law of a man who had, give or take, sixty milk cows? The answer is in a holdup. Less than a year before Benya had written to Eikhbaum:

"Monsieur Eikhbaum," he wrote. "Put twenty thousand rubles, I beg you, under the gate of No. 17 Sofievsky Street tomorrow morning. If you don't do this, something unheard of awaits you, and you will be the talk of all Odessa. Respectfully yours, Benya the King."

Three letters, each clearer than the one before, were left unanswered. Then Benya took certain measures. They came in the middle of the night: nine men with long poles in hand. The tops of the poles were wrapped with tarred rags. Nine flaming stars blazed over Eikhbaum's barnyard. Benya broke the locks off the barn and began leading the cows out one by one. A young guy with a knife was waiting for them. In a single blow he would fell the cow and plunge his knife into the cow's heart. On the ground, which was flooded with blood, torches bloomed like fire roses. Shots rang out. With the shots Benya chased away the women who were running toward the cow shed. After him the other members of Benya's gang began to shoot into the air, because if you don't shoot into the air you could kill someone. And so, when the sixth cow, with a mortal sigh, fell to the King's feet, Eikhbaum ran out into the courtyard in just his pajamas and asked:

"What is going to come of this, Benya?"

"If I don't get my money, you won't get your cows, Monsieur Eikhbaum. It's as simple as two times two."

"Come into the house, Benya."

Inside the house they came to an agreement. The slaughtered cows were divided up equally. Eikhbaum's safety was guaranteed. To that end a certificate with a stamp was issued. But the miracle came later.

In the course of the holdup on that terrible night, when the stabbed cows were bellowing and the calves were sprawling in their mothers' blood, when the torches were dancing like black maidens and the women were screaming and running out under the shots of the friendly Brownings—on that terrible night Selia, old Eikhbaum's daughter, ran into the courtyard wearing nothing but a low-cut nightgown. And the King's victory became his downfall.

Two days later, without warning, Benya returned all the money to Eikhbaum and after this showed up for a visit that evening. He was dressed in an orange suit, and from under his cuff shone a diamond bracelet. He walked into the room, said hello, and asked Eikhbaum for the hand of his daughter Selia. The old man suffered a mild shock but then came to. The old man still had another twenty years or so of life in him.

"Listen, Eikhbaum," the King said to him. "When you die, I will bury you in the first Jewish cemetery, right at the gate itself. I will build you a monument of pink marble. I will make you an elder of the Brodsky Synagogue. I will quit my line of work, Eikhbaum, and become your business partner. We will have two hundred cows, Eikhbaum. I will kill all the dairy farmers besides you. No thief will ever walk down the street where you live. I'll build you a summer house out by Big Fountain.[2] And remember, Eikhbaum, you weren't exactly a rabbi yourself in your younger days. Who was the one that fixed the will, not to talk about it out loud. And your son-in-law won't be some young snot nose but me, the King, Eikhbaum."

And he got his way, Benya Krik, because he was passionate, and passion governs the universe. The newlyweds spent three months in Bessarabia, among grapevines, abundant food, and lovers' sweat. Then, Benya came back to Odessa to marry off his forty-year-old sister Dvoira, who suffered from a goiter. Now, having told the story of Sender Eikhbaum, we can return to the wedding of Dvoira Krik, the King's sister.

Turkey, roast chicken, goose, gefilte fish, and fish soup, in which lemon lakes shone like mother of pearl, were served for dinner at the wedding. Flowers, like luxuriant plumage, swayed over the dead goose heads. But do the foamy waves of the Odessa Sea really wash roast chicken to shore?

On that starry and navy blue night, all that was noblest among our contraband, all that the land is famous for from end to end, did its destructive, its seductive work. A foreign wine warmed the stomachs, sweetly weakened the knees, fogged brains, and caused resonant belching like a call to arms. The black cook from the *Plutarch,* which had arrived two days before from Port Said, carried past customs round-bellied bottles of Jamaican rum, buttery Madeira, cigars from the plantations of Pierpont Morgan, and oranges from the outskirts of Jerusalem. This is what the foamy waves of the Odessa Sea wash to shore. This is what is sometimes bestowed upon Odessa beggars at Jewish weddings. At Dvoira Krik's wedding they got Jamaican rum. And as a result, the Jewish beggars, snorting like pigs, started to bang their crutches together deafeningly. Having loosened his vest, Eikhbaum, with one eye squinting, looked around at the rowdy gathering and hiccupped tenderly. The orchestra played a flourish. It was like a battalion review. A flourish—nothing but a flourish. The gangsters, who were sitting in closed formation, were initially uncomfortable in the presence of the outsiders, but later on they let loose. Lyova Katsap smashed a bottle of vodka on the head of his beloved, Monya the Gunner fired into the air.[3] But their ecstasy reached its peak when, according to tradition, the guests began to shower the newlyweds with gifts. Jumping up on tables, the shamases from the synagogue sang out the amount of rubles and silver spoons given under the din of the cacophonic flourish. And here the King's friends showed what blue blood is worth and that Moldovanka chivalry had not yet died out. Carelessly they flung gold coins, rings, and long strands of coral onto silver trays. Moldovanka aristocrats, they were corseted into raspberry-colored vests, rust-colored blazers were wrapped around their shoulders, and azure-colored hide threatened to burst on their fleshy legs. Drawing themselves up to their full height and puffing out their bellies, the gangsters clapped in time to the music, shouting "Bitter!"[4] The bride was showered with flowers, and she, the forty-year-old Dvoira, the sister of Benya Krik, the sister of the King, disfigured by illness, with an overgrown neck and with eyes that were popping out of their sockets, sat on a mountain of pillows next to a puny boy who had been bought with Eikhbaum's money and who was dumb with sadness.

The gift ceremony was coming to an end. The shamases had grown hoarse, and the bass was out of tune with the violin. Suddenly a faint smell of something burning wafted over the courtyard.

"Benya," said old man Krik, the old ruffian known among the ruffians as a rude bastard. "Benya, you know what it seems to me? It seems to me that we have some soot burning."

"Old man," Benya answered his drunken father, "please just eat and drink, don't worry about these stupid things . . . "

And old man Krik took his son's advice. He ate and drank. But the cloud of smoke was becoming more and more poisonous. Here and there the edges of the sky had already started turning pink. And already a tongue of flame, narrow as a sword, shot upward. The guests, having gotten up part way, began sniffing the air, and their women screeched. The gangsters glanced around at each other. And only Benya, who noticed nothing, was inconsolable.

"They are ruining my celebration," he screamed, full of despair. "My dear guests, I beg you, keep eating and drinking . . . "

But at this time the same young man who had come at the beginning of the evening appeared in the courtyard.

"King," he said, "I have a couple of words I've got to tell you . . . "

"Well, talk," answered the King. "You always have a couple of words in store."

"King, it's really funny, the precinct is burning like a candle," pronounced the unknown young man, snickering.

The shopkeepers grew dumb. The gangsters smirked. Sixty-year-old Manya, midwife to Slobodka's gangsters, having put two fingers to her mouth, whistled so sharply that her neighbors were startled.

"Manya, you aren't at work," Benya said to her. "Take a deep breath."

The young man who brought this shocking news was still bursting with laughter.

"They left the precinct, about forty of them," he told the story, jabbering. "They went out for a roundup. They hadn't even gone fifteen steps when the precinct was already on fire. Run, take a look, if you want to."

But Benya forbade the guests to go look at the fire. He and a couple of his cohorts set out. The precinct was properly on fire on all four sides. Policemen, their buttocks jiggling, were running up and down smoky stairways, throwing small file cabinets out of windows. The prisoners scattered in the commotion. The firemen were bursting with fervor, but there turned out to be no water in the nearest hydrant. The chief of the precinct—the same broom that sweeps clean—stood on the sidewalk on the opposite side of the street chewing his mustache, which was curling into his mouth. The new broom stood motionless. Benya, passing by the chief, saluted him in a military manner.

"To your health, Your Excellency," said Benya sympathetically. "What can you say about such misfortune? What a nightmare . . . "

He stared at the burning building, then he shook his head and smacked his lips: "My, my, my . . . "

. . . .

When Benya returned home, the lights in the courtyard were already dimming, and in the sky a new day was dawning. The guests had left, and the musicians were dozing, having rested their heads against the necks of their basses. Only Dvoira alone had no intention of going to bed. With both hands she directed her frightened husband to the door of their honeymoon suite. She looked at him carnivorously, like a cat that holds a mouse in her mouth and ever so lightly tries it with her teeth.

1921

Translation by Timothy Westphalen

Notes to the translation are on page 580.

RESOURCES

Primary Text

Babel', Isaak. "Korol'." *Izbrannoe.* Moscow: Khudozhestvennaia literatura, 1966, pp. 159–64.

Secondary Sources

Literary and Cultural Studies

Babel', Isaac. *The Collected Stories.* Ed. and trans. Walter Morison. Intro. Lionel Trilling. Cleveland: Meridian Books, 1969.

Carden, Patricia. *The Art of Isaac Babel'.* Ithaca: Cornell University Press, 1972.

Ehre, Milton. *Isaac Babel.* Boston: Twayne, 1986.

Falen, James. *Isaac Babel: Russian Master of the Short Story.* Knoxville: University of Tennessee Press, 1974.

Friedberg, Maurice. "Bábel, Isaák Emmanuílovich (1846–1941)." In *Handbook of Russian Literature,* ed. Victor Terras. New Haven: Yale University Press, 1985, pp. 31–33.

Hallett, R. *Isaac Babel.* New York: Fredrick Ungar, 1973.

Mendelson, D. *Metaphor in Babel's Short Stories.* Ann Arbor, MI: Ardis, 1982.

Ozmitel', E.K. *Sovetskaia satira. Seminarii.* Moscow–Leningrad: Prosveshchenie, 1964.

Drama and Theater

Piat' rasskazov I. Babelia. Director, E. Kucher. Composer, Sh. Kallosh. Scene design, B. Karafelov. Taganka Theater, premiere 1981. In *Russian Literary Theatre: Ten Plays at the Taganka Theatre.* NJR Video, 1984. Video recording of Taganka adaptation of Babel's "Odessa Stories."

Music

Tsyganova, Vika. "Povest' o Sare i Bene." In *Klubnichka.* Moscow, 1994.

Film

Benia Krik. Director, V. Vil'ner. Odessa: VUKFU Odessa Studio, 1926.
The Teamster and the King. Director, Vladimir Alenikov. Cast: Armen Dzhigarkanian, Irina Kozanova, Roman Kartsev. Distributed by RAES, 1991.

28

~Sergei Esenin~

Farewell, my friend, farewell . . .

Farewell, my friend, farewell.
Dear friend, you're in my heart.
The predetermined parting
Promises reunion ahead.

Farewell, my friend, without handshake or word,
Don't grieve and knit your brow—
In life death's nothing new,
But life's, of course, no greater novelty.

1925

Translation by Nicholas Rzhevsky

RESOURCES

Primary Text

Esenin, Sergei. "Do svidan'ia, drug moi, do svidan'ia." *Sobranie sochinenii v piati tomakh. Stikhotvoreniia i poemy 1924–1925.* Vol. 3. Ed. G.I. Vladykin et al. Moscow: Khudozhestvennaia literatura, 1961–62, p. 138.

Secondary Sources

Literary and Cultural Studies

Bristol, Evelyn. *A History of Russian Poetry.* New York: Oxford University Press, 1991, pp. 225–48.
Davies, Jesse, ed. *Esenin: A Biography in Memoirs, Letters and Documents.* Ann Arbor, MI: Ardis, 1982.
Glad, John. "Esénin, Sergéi Aleksándrovich (1895–1925)." In *Handbook of Russian Literature,* ed. Victor Terras. New Haven: Yale University Press, 1985, p. 131.
Markov, V. *Russian Imagism, 1919–1924.* Giessen: W. Schmitz, 1980.

Music

Timchenko, Nikolai. *Pesni na stikhi Esenina.* Melodiia, n.d.

29

~Ilya Ilf and Evgeny Petrov~

The Twelve Chairs

Part I, Chapter XIV
"The Union of the Sword and the Plow"

When a woman ages, she may encounter much unpleasantness: her teeth may fall out, her hair may thin and turn gray, her breathing may become labored, her weight may balloon or she may be overcome by extreme thinness, but her voice will never change. It will stay the same as when she was a schoolgirl, a bride, or a mistress of some young Casanova.

That is why, when Polesov knocked at the door and Elena Stanislavovna asked, "Who is there?" Vorobianinov shuddered. The voice of his mistress was the same as in 1899, before the opening of the Paris Exhibition. But, having entered the room and squinting from the light, Ippolit Matveevich saw that not a trace remained of her former beauty.

"How you've changed!" he said spontaneously, in spite of himself. The old woman threw herself at him. "Thank you," she said. "I know what you risked in coming to me. You are still the same magnanimous knight. I'm not asking why you came all the way from Paris. You see, I'm not curious."

"But I certainly did not come from Paris," said Vorobianinov, perplexed.

"My colleague and I arrived from Berlin," corrected Ostap, nudging Ippolit Matveevich's elbow. "Discussions aloud on the subject are not recommended."

"Ah, I am so glad to see you!" squealed the fortuneteller. "Come here, into this room . . . And you, Viktor Mikhailovich, forgive me, but won't you drop by in half an hour?"

"Oh," noted Ostap. "The first date! Difficult moments! Allow me to depart as well. May I go with you, my dear Viktor Mikhailovich?"

The metalworker trembled with joy. Both left for Polesov's apartment, where Ostap, sitting on what was left of the gate belonging to House No. 5

of Poleshinskii Lane, began spewing phantasmagoric ideas regarding the salvation of the motherland for the benefit of the overwhelmed and solitary craftsman-with-motor.[1]

They returned in an hour and found the old people completely mushy.

"And do you recall, Elena Stanislavovna?" said Ippolit Matveevich.

"And do you recall, Ippolit Matveevich?" said Elena Stanislavovna.

"It seems the psychological moment for supper has arrived," thought Ostap. And he said, interrupting Ippolit Matveevich, who was reminiscing about the City Government elections, "In Berlin, they have a strange custom: people eat so late there you don't know if they're having early supper or late dinner."

Elena Stanislavovna came to life, shifted her rabbit eyes away from Vorobianinov, and slowly dragged herself into the kitchen.

"And now action, action, and more action!" said Ostap, lowering his voice to the level of complete illegality.

He took Polesov by the hand.

"The old woman won't let us down? Is she reliable?"

Polesov folded his hands as if in prayer.

"Is this your political creed?"

"Always," Polesov answered ecstatically.

"You are, I hope, of the Kirill persuasion?"[2]

"Yes, sir."

Polesov snapped to attention.

"Russia won't forget you!" barked Ostap.

A pastry in his hand, Ippolit Matveevich listened with growing confusion, but there was no holding back Ostap. He was carried away. The Great Wheeler Dealer was inspired. He was in the state of bliss that precedes an above-average scam. He strutted through the room like a porpoise.

He was found in this elevated state by Elena Stanislavovna, as she with great difficulty dragged in a samovar from the kitchen. Ostap gallantly jumped to her side. In one motion he took the samovar from her and placed it on the table. The samovar whistled. Ostap decided to act.

"Madam," he said, "we are happy to view you as . . . "

Actually, he did not know whom he was happy to view her as. He had to start over. Of all the pompous expressions of the tsarist regime, only "graciously deigned to order" came to mind. But that did not suit the occasion. Therefore, he began in a businesslike fashion, "This is top secret! A matter of government security!"

Ostap pointed at Vorobianinov.

"Who do you think this powerful old man is? Don't even try to guess.

You simply cannot know. This is—a giant of thought, the Father of Russian Democracy, and a personage close to the Emperor."

Ippolit Matveevich rose up to his full magnificent stature and absent-mindedly looked around. He did not understand a thing, but, knowing by experience that Ostap Bender never spoke without a purpose, he remained silent. Polesov was trembling from everything going on around him. He stood with his chin raised toward the ceiling, in the pose of a man preparing to embark on a ceremonial parade. Casting a frightened look at Ostap, Elena Stanislavovna sat down in a chair.

"Are there many of our sympathizers in the city?" asked Ostap straight out. "What's the atmosphere like?"

"In the presence of the absence . . . " said Viktor Mikhailovich and began explaining his troubles in a confused manner. He touched on the janitor from Building No. 5, a lout who thought too highly of himself, sheet metal measuring three-eighths of an inch, a tram, and so on.

"Good!" exclaimed Ostap. "Elena Stanislavovna! With your help we want to link up with the city's best people, driven underground by cruel fate. Whom can we invite?"

"Whom can we invite! Perhaps, Maksim Petrovich, with his wife?"

"Without his wife," corrected Ostap. "Without his wife! You will be the sole pleasant exception. Whom else?"

In the course of the discussion, which Viktor Mikhailovich joined in a businesslike manner, it became clear that it was possible to invite the very same Maksim Petrovich Charushnikov, the former speaker of the City Council, who now miraculously could be numbered among the ranks of Soviet workers, as well as Diadiev, the owner of Express Packaging, Kisliarskii, the chairman of the Odessa baking company Moscow Bagels, and two young people who had no last names but were still completely reliable.

"In that case, I ask you to invite them immediately to this little meeting, under the veil of greatest secrecy."

Polesov said, "I'll rush over to Maksim Petrovich's, after Nikesha and Vladia. And you, Elena Stanislavovna, be so good as to go to Express Packaging for Kisliarskii." Polesov galloped off. The fortuneteller looked at Ippolit Matveevich with admiration and also left.

"What is this all about?" asked Ippolit Matveevich.

"It is about," answered Ostap, "you being a bit slow."

"Why?"

"Because! Forgive a vulgar question: How much money do you have?"

"What kind of money?"

"Any kind. Including silver and copper."

"Thirty-five rubles."

"And you were planning to cover all the expenses of our enterprise with this amount?"

Ippolit Matveevich was silent.

"Here's the deal, my dear patron. You seem to understand me. For an hour you will have to be a giant of thought and a personage close to the Emperor."

"Why?"

"Because we need working capital. Tomorrow is my wedding. I am not a beggar. I want to have a banquet on this momentous day."

"But what do I have to do?" groaned Ippolit Matveevich.

"You have to keep quiet. Sometimes look important, puff up your cheeks with air."

"But, after all, this is . . . a scam."

"Says who? Does Count Tolstoy say that? Or maybe Darwin? No. I am hearing this from the lips of the person who only last night planned to break into Gritsatsueva's apartment and steal the poor widow's furniture. Don't think about it. Remain silent. And don't forget to puff up your cheeks."

"But why get involved in such a risky business? Somebody could turn us in."

"Don't worry about it. I don't take unnecessary risks. It will be carried out in such a manner that no one will catch on. Let's have some tea."

While the conspirators were eating and drinking and the parrot was cracking open sunflower seeds the guests arrived. Nikesha and Vladia came in with Polesov. Viktor Mikhailovich hesitated to introduce the young people to the giant of thought. They sat down in the corner and observed the Father of Russian Democracy eating cold veal. Nikesha and Vladia were completely mature dolts. Each of them was about thirty. It was apparent they were very pleased to have been invited to the meeting.

The former speaker of the City Council Charushnikov, a hefty old man, shook Ippolit Matveevich's hand for a long while and kept looking into his eyes. Under Ostap's supervision the city elders began to exchange reminiscences.

Having given them a chance to converse, Ostap turned to Charushnikov, "In which regiment did you serve?"

Charushnikov started to sputter.

"I . . . I didn't serve at all, so to speak, because the sacred trust of society obliged me to run for office."

"Are you a nobleman?"

"Yes, I was."

"I hope you still are? Be strong. Your help will be required. Did Polesov tell you? We'll get help from abroad. The hitch is public opinion. Absolute secrecy regarding the organization! Be vigilant!"

Ostap chased Polesov away from Nikesha and Vladia and asked with authentic severity, "In what regiment did you serve? You will have to serve the Fatherland. Are you noblemen? Very good. The West will help us. Be strong. Absolute secrecy for depositors, that is, for the organization! Be vigilant!"

Ostap was in full swing. It appeared as if the deal were coming together. After he was introduced to the owner of Express Packaging by Elena Stanislavovna, he took him aside, proposed that he stay strong, inquired about the regiment he served in, promised cooperation from abroad and absolute secrecy for the organization. The owner of Express Packaging first felt a strong desire to run away as fast as he could from the conspirators' apartment. He considered his firm to be much too respectable to take part in a risky affair. But after looking at Ostap's agile figure he began to vacillate and to think, "What if! . . . Although everything depends on the way it's put together."

Friendly conversation around the table came alive. Those who had been told about the sacred conspiracy kept the secret religiously and talked about city news.

Last to arrive was Mr. Kisliarskii, who, never having belonged to a regiment or been a nobleman, after a short conversation with Ostap, immediately understood what was afoot.

"Be strong," said Ostap instructively. Kisliarskii promised.

"You, as a representative of private capital, cannot remain deaf to the moans of the people."

Kisliarskii became sad with compassion.

"Do you know who that is, sitting there?" asked Ostap, pointing at Ippolit Matveevich.

"Of course," answered Kisliarskii. "That is Mr. Vorobianinov."

"That," said Ostap, "is a giant of thought, the Father of Russian Democracy and a personage close to the Emperor."

"At best, two years in solitary confinement," thought Kisliarskii, beginning to tremble. "Why did I come here?"

"A secret union of the sword and the plow!" whispered Ostap ominously.

"Ten years," flashed through Kisliarskii's mind.

"Nonetheless, you can leave. But I am warning you, we have a long arm."

"I'll show you, you son of a bitch," thought Ostap. "I won't let you go for less than a hundred rubles."

Kisliarskii turned to stone. Just this afternoon he had peacefully eaten a delicious meal—chicken gizzards and bouillon with nuts—and did not know anything about this terrifying "Union of the Sword and the Plow." He stayed: The "long arm" produced an unfavorable impression on him.

"Citizens!" said Ostap, opening the meeting, "Life dictates its own laws, its own cruel laws. I won't speak about the aim of our gathering—you are all familiar with it. The aim is sacred. We hear moans all around us. From every end of our huge country there are cries for help. We have to extend the hand of help, and we will extend it. Some of you work for the government and eat bread and butter, while others of you engage in seasonal and privy enterprises and eat sandwiches with caviar. Both the one and the other sleep in their own beds, covered with warm blankets. Only little children, homeless children, are without a home. These flowers of the street, or as the proletarians of cerebral labor put it, these flowers on the asphalt, deserve a better lot in life. We, gentlemen of the jury, have to help them. And we, gentlemen of the jury, will help them."

The speech of the Great Wheeler Dealer elicited different feelings among the audience. Polesov did not understand his new friend, the young guardsman.

"What children?" he thought. "What do children have to do with it?"

Ippolit Matveevich did not even try to understand. He had given up on everything long ago and sat quietly puffing his cheeks.

Elena Stanislavovna was getting depressed.

Nikesha and Vladia were looking at Ostap's vest with great devotion.

The owner of Express Packaging was extraordinarily satisfied. "Nicely put," he thought. "Under such conditions one can even give money. In case of success, one gets the credit. If it doesn't work out, then I'll be their third cousin twice removed. I was helping the children, and that's that."

Charushnikov exchanged a meaningful glance with Diadiev and with full respect for the conspiratorial agility of the speaker continued to roll small balls of bread around the table.

Kisliarskii was in seventh heaven.

"What a genius," he thought. It seemed to him he had never loved homeless children as much as that evening.

"Comrades!" continued Ostap. "Help is needed urgently. We must extract the children from the powerful grasp of the street, and extract them we will. Let us help the children. Let us remember that children are the flowers of life. I invite you to make your donations right now to help the children, only the children, and no one else. Do you understand me?"

Ostap took a receipts book from his breast pocket.

"Please, make your donations. Ippolit Matveevich will confirm my authorization in the matter."

Ippolit Matveevich took a deep breath and nodded. At this moment even the slow-witted Nikesha and Vladia and the bustling metalworker himself understood the secret meaning of Ostap's allegories.

"In order of seniority, gentlemen," said Ostap. "Let's start with the esteemed Maksim Petrovich."

Maksim Petrovich fidgeted around and gave barely thirty rubles.

"I'd give more in better times!" he announced.

"Better times will come soon," said Ostap. "However, that does not help the homeless children, whom I represent at the present moment."

Nikesha and Vladia donated eight rubles.

"That's very little, young men."

The young men blushed.

Polesov ran home and brought back fifty rubles.

"Bravo, hussar!" said Ostap. "For a lone hussar with a motor, that's enough for the first time. What does our merchant class have to say?"

Diadiev and Kisliarskii haggled for a long time and complained about the rate of economic averaging. Ostap remained firm.

"In the presence of Ippolit Matveevich himself, I consider these discussions superfluous."

Ippolit Matveevich nodded. On behalf of the children, each merchant sacrificed two hundred rubles.

"All in all," proclaimed Ostap, "four hundred and eighty-eight rubles. Oh! Only twelve rubles to make it even."

Elena Stanislavovna, who had been building up her courage for a long time, went to the bedroom and brought out the necessary twelve rubles from her purse.

The rest of the meeting was disorganized and bore a less solemn character. Ostap began to have a good time. Elena Stanislavovna was totally worn out. The guests gradually went their own ways, parting respectfully with the organizers.

"You will be notified of our next meeting," said Ostap in parting. "It's top secret. Aid to children should remain secret . . . in your own interest."

After hearing these words, Kisliarskii got the urge to give another fifty rubles, as long as he would not have to come to any more meetings. He could hardly keep himself from acting on the impulse.

"Well," said Ostap, "let's get moving. I hope you, Ippolit Matveevich, will take advantage of Elena Stanislavovna's hospitality and stay overnight.

Incidentally, it will be good for us and the conspiracy to part for a while. As for me, I'm off."

Ippolit Matveevich desperately winked at Ostap, but Ostap pretended not to notice and went outside.

After walking a block, Ostap remembered that five hundred honestly earned rubles lay in his pocket.

"Coachman!" shouted Ostap loudly. "Take me to the Phoenix!"

"Okay," said the coachman.

Without hurrying he drove Ostap to the closed restaurant.

"What's this? Closed?"

"Due to the first of May."

"Damn it! Plenty of money, and nowhere to have fun. Well, on to Plekhanov Street. You know it?" Ostap decided to see his fiancée.

"What was the street named before?" asked the coachman.[3]

"I don't know."

"So, which way do we go? I don't know either."

Nevertheless, Ostap ordered him to drive and to look for it. For about an hour and a half, they went round and round the empty city, questioning night watchmen and policemen. One of the policemen hemmed and hawed and finally informed them that Plekhanov Street was none other than the former Governor Street.

"Oh, yes! Governor Street! I know Governor Street well. I've taken fares to Governor's for twenty-five years."

"So, take one now!"

They arrived at Governor Street, but it turned out to be Karl Marx Street, not Plekhanov Street.

The enraged Ostap renewed the search for the lost Plekhanov Street but did not find it.

The pale dawn illuminated the face of a rich martyr who had not been able to have a good time.

"Take me to the Sorbonne!" he shouted. "And you call yourself a coachman! Don't even know Plekhanov Street!"

The palace of the widow Gritsatsueva shone. At the head of the table sat the tramp king, the son of a Turkish citizen. He was elegant and drunk. The guests were noisy.

The young bride was no longer young. She was no younger than thirty-five. Nature had lavishly endowed her. She had everything: watermelon breasts, a nose like the blunt side of an axe, rouged cheeks, and a powerful nape. She adored and very much feared her new husband. That's why she called him not by his first name, and not even by his

patronymic, which she never found out anyway, but by his last name—
Comrade Bender.

Ippolit Matveevich was sitting again on the cherished chair. In the
course of the wedding dinner he bounced up and down on it to test for a
firm spot. Sometimes he succeeded in feeling it. Then he would grow
fond of everyone, and he would begin to shout furiously to the newlyweds,
"Bitter!"[4]

Ostap declaimed, gave speeches, and made toasts the whole time. They
drank to the enlightenment of the people and to the irrigation of Uzbekistan.
After that the guests began to go their own ways. Ippolit Matveevich hung
back in the entry way and whispered to Bender, "So, don't delay. They are
there."

"Listen, you extortionist," the drunken Ostap answered. "Wait for me in
the hotel. Don't go anywhere. I may be back at any minute. Pay the hotel
bill. Everything must be ready. Adieu, Field Marshal! Wish me good
night."

Ippolit Matveevich wished him good night and left for the Sorbonne to
worry.

At five in the morning Ostap appeared with the chair. Ippolit Matveevich
was overcome with emotion. Ostap placed the chair in the middle of the
room and sat down.

"How did you pull it off?" Vorobianinov finally uttered.

"Very simple, the way it's done in good families. The widow was sleeping
and dreaming. Would've been a pity to wake her up. 'Don't wake her at
dawn.'[5] Alas! I had to leave my beloved a note: 'Leaving for Novokhopersk
to give a talk. Don't wait dinner on me. Yours, Suslik.' And I grabbed the
chair from the dining room. There's no tram at this early hour, so I rested
on the chair along the way."

Purring, Ippolit Matveevich threw himself at the chair.

"Quiet," said Ostap. "We have to act without any noise."

He pulled out a pair of pliers from his pocket, and the work commenced.

"Did you lock the door?" asked Ostap.

Pushing the impatient Vorobianinov away, Ostap carefully opened up the
chair, trying not to damage the flowery English chintz.

"This material is not available anymore. We must preserve it. There's a
shortage of goods these days, and nothing you can do about it."

All this brought Ippolit Matveevich to a state of extreme aggravation.

"Ready," Ostap said softly.

He lifted the cover and began to rummage around the springs with both
hands. A vein popped out on his forehead.

"Well?" Ippolit Matveevich kept repeating in different tones. "Well? Well?"

"Well yourself," irritatedly answered Ostap. "One chance in eleven. And this one . . . " He carefully foraged through the chair and concluded, "And this one isn't it."

He rose up to his full height and began to dust his knees. Ippolit Matveevich threw himself at the chair. There weren't any diamonds. Ippolit Matveevich's arms hung down. But Ostap was as optimistic as before.

"Now the percentages have improved."

He paced around the room.

"It's okay! This chair cost the widow more than it cost us."

From his hip pocket Ostap took out a golden brooch with glass pieces, a hollow gold bracelet, half a dozen golden spoons, and a tea strainer.

In his grief Ippolit Matveevich did not grasp that he had become party to an ordinary theft.

"Trivial stuff," noted Ostap. "But you'll agree I couldn't abandon my beloved without some remembrances of her. However, let's not waste any time. This is still just the beginning. The end is in Moscow. And the furniture museum is not some old widow. It's going to be a lot tougher out there."

The duo stuck the remnants of the chair under the bed. After counting the money (the total with the contributions for the children turned out to be five hundred thirty-five rubles), they set off for the station to catch a train to Moscow.

They had to travel by carriage through the whole town.

On Co-op Street they saw Polesov, who was running like a frightened antelope along the sidewalk. The janitor from Building No. 5 was chasing him down Pereleshinskii Lane. Turning the corner, the duo was able to see the janitor catch Viktor Mikhailovch and begin pounding him. Polesov shouted, "Help!" and "Lout!"

Up to the departure of the train, they sat in the lavatory, afraid of meeting a beloved woman.

The train carried the friends away to the noisy capital. They leaned toward the window . . .

Ostap patted the sullen Vorobianinov on the back.

"Don't worry about it, old man! Don't be sad! The meeting continues. Tomorrow evening we'll be in Moscow."

Translation by Timothy Westphalen and Nicholas Rzhevsky

Notes to the translation are on page 580.

RESOURCES

Primary Text

Il'f, Il'ia, and E. Petrov. *Dvenadtsat' stul'ev.* Kiev: Radianskii pis'mennik, 1957, pp. 116–28.

Secondary Sources

Literary and Cultural Studies

Brown, Deming. *Soviet Russian Literature since Stalin.* Cambridge: Cambridge University Press, 1978.
Maguire, Robert A. *Red Virgin Soil: Soviet Literature in the 1920s.* Princeton: Princeton University Press, 1968.
Ozmitel', E.K. *Sovetskaia satira. Seminarii.* Moscow–Leningrad: Prosveshchenie, 1964.
Terras, Victor, "Ilf, Ilyá and Petróv, Evgény." In *Handbook of Russian Literature,* ed. Victor Terras. New Haven: Yale University Press, 1985, p. 198.

Film

Dvenadtsat' stul'ev (The Twelve Chairs). Director, Leonid Gaidai. Georgia: Gruziiafilm, 1971.
Ekhali v tramvae Il'f i Petrov (Ilf and Petrov in a Tram). Director, I. Titov. Cast: I. Smoktunovskii, E. Leonov, O. Tabakov, R. Bykov. Mosfilm, 1967. Adaptation of stories with participation of leading Soviet actors.
Zolotoi telenok (The Golden Calf). Director, Mikhail Shveitser. Mosfilm, 1969.

30

~Mikhail Sholokhov~

Virgin Soil Upturned

Chapter 7, Book 1

Andrei Razmetnov and his group came to see Frol Damaskov while he was having lunch with his family. Sitting at the table were Frol himself, a small, frail oldster with a pointed beard and a torn left nostril (he had disfigured his face in childhood falling off an apple tree, thus his nickname, "Tornyi"); his wife, a portly and imposing old woman; his son Timofei, twenty-two years old; and his daughter—a girl ready for marriage.

Timofei, like his mother imposing and good-looking, got up from the table. With a cloth he wiped the bright lips under his youthful fluffed mustache, narrowed his insolent, protruding eyes, and with the devil-may-care attitude of the best accordion player and favorite of young women in the village, pointed with his hand:

"Come in and sit down, cherished powers on high."

"We don't have time to sit down." Andrei took out a piece of paper from his file folder. "The Council of the Poor has issued a resolution to evict you, citizen Frol Damaskov, from your home and to confiscate all your belongings and livestock. So finish your meal and move out. We're going to write up an inventory of all the belongings right now."

"What's this?" Throwing down his spoon, Frol got up.

"We are destroying you as a kulak class." Demka Ushakov explained.

Frol went to the living room, creaking his solid, leather-soled boots, and brought back a piece of paper.

"Here's an official statement. You yourself signed it, Razmetnov."

"What statement?"

"That I fulfilled my grain obligations."

"Grain has nothing to do with it."

"So why are you driving me out of my house and confiscating my property?"

"The Council of the Poor made a resolution, I already told you."

"There are no such laws!" Timofei shouted sharply. "It's plain and simple robbery! Father, I'll ride to the Regional Executive Committee right now. Where's the saddle?"

"You can walk there, if you want. I won't give you a horse." Andrei sat down at the end of the table and took out a pencil and paper.

Frol's torn nose swelled with blood and his head began to shake. He sat down on the floor exactly where he was standing and was barely able to control his swollen, darkened tongue.

"Ssson's . . . Sons of bitches! Rob! Butcher!"

"Father, get up, for the love of Christ!" The girl began to cry and pulled up her father, grabbing him under the arms.

Frol straightened, stood, lay down on the bench, and from then on listened without taking any part as Demka Ushakov and the tall, bashful Mikhail Ignatenok dictated to Razmetnov:

"An iron bed, with white knobs, a bedspread, three pillows, also two wooden beds . . . "

"A cupboard with dishes. Should I list each dish? The hell with it!"

"Twelve chairs, one tall chair with a back. An accordion with three rows."

"I'm not giving you the accordion!" Timofei grabbed it out of Demka's hands. "Get off, cross-eyes, or I'll break your nose!"

"I'll smash yours so your own mother won't recognize it!"

"Ma'am, let's have the keys to the trunks."

"Don't do it, Mother. Let them break them open if they have such rights."

"Do we have the right?" asked Demid Molchun, showing some life. Molchun was famous for speaking only at moments of the most extreme necessity and for otherwise working silently, having a smoke silently with Cossacks gathered together during a holiday, sitting silently in meetings, and only rarely answering someone's questions while smiling guiltily and pitifully.

The wide-open world was full of excessive loud noises for Demid. They flooded life to the edges; without ceasing, even at night, they prevented one from listening to the quiet, they disturbed that wise silence with which the steppe and forest are sometimes full around autumn. Demid did not like the human clamor. He lived by himself at the edge of the village, he was a hard worker and the strongest man in the district. But fate somehow marked him with abuses, misused him like an orphan. For five years he worked for Frol Damaskov, then married and went off to his own household. He barely had time to settle in when his place burned down. Another fire a year later left him one plow standing in the yard and still smelling of smoke. And soon his wife left him, after declaring: "I've lived with you two years and haven't heard you say two words. No, you better go live alone! One could have more fun with a hermit in the forest. You're likely to drive me crazy. I've already started talking to myself . . . "

She had been getting used to Demid up until then. The first months, it's true, she cried, kept annoying her husband: "Demid, dear Demid! Say something to me. Just say something." Demid would only smile a quiet childish smile and scratch his hairy chest. And when his wife's pestering became unbearable he would say in a deep bass voice, "You're a magpie, pure and simple!" and leave. For some reason, Demid was taken to be a proud and sly man, one of those who "keeps things to himself." Perhaps it was because all his life he kept away from loud people and blaring sounds?

That was why Andrei jerked back his head after hearing the deep thunder of Molchun's voice ring out over him.

"Rights?" he asked again, looking at Demid as if seeing him for the first time. "We have the right!"

Taking bearish steps and getting the floor dirty with his worn boots, Demid went to the living room. Smiling, he moved Timofei out of the doorway with his arm as easily as a twig, went past the cupboard and its dishes clanging mournfully from his steps, and approached the chest. He squatted down, twisted the heavy lock with his fingers. In a minute the lock, its hasp broken, was lying on the chest, and Arkashka Menok looked Molchun over with unconcealed amazement and exclaimed in wonder:

"I'd trade my strength for yours any day."

Andrei had trouble keeping up as he wrote the inventory. From the living room and the hall, Demka Ushakov, Arkashka, and Aunt Vasilisa—the only woman in Andrei's group—shouted out, vying with each other in different voices.

"One woman's fur coat, from the Don!"

"A sheepskin coat!"

"Three pairs of new boots with galoshes!"

"Four pieces of canvas!"

"Andrei! Razmetnov! You won't get all this stuff out, even on a cart! There's calico, and black satin, and all kinds of other . . . "

On the way to the front of the house Andrei heard a girl's plaintive cries in the side room, joined by her mother's shouts, and the reasonable, persuasive voice of Ignatenok. Andrei threw open the door.

"What's the matter here?"

Swollen with tears, the homeowners' snub-nosed daughter was crying in a frenzy, leaning on the door. Close by, her mother darted about clucking, while Ignatenok, red in the face and smiling in embarrassment, tried to pull off the girl's skirt.

"What are you doing!?" Andrei said, not grasping what was going on, and choking with rage he gave Ignatenok a violent push. Ignatenok fell on his back, kicking up his long legs in their ragged footwear. "Everything's based on politics for us! We're attacking the enemy and you're pawing girls in corners?! I'll have you charged with . . . "

"Wait a minute, you!" Ignatenok in fright jumped up from the floor. "What's she to me? Some dreamboat! Paw her? Look, she's put nine skirts on! I tried to prevent it and you start off pushing . . . "

Only then Andrei saw that the girl had dragged a bundle of clothing out of the living room and under cover of the ongoing commotion had indeed managed to put on a bunch of wool dresses. Strangely sluggish, huddled in the corner, she was pulling down a hem, confined by the many clothes restricting her movement. Seeing her wet, rabbit-red eyes, Andrei felt disgust and pity. He slammed the door and said to Ignatenok:

"Don't touch her! The hell with whatever she managed to get on, but take the bundle of clothes."

The inventory of household goods was coming to an end.

"The keys to the storehouse," Andrei demanded.

Frol, black like a charred stump, waved his hand.

"There are no keys!"

"Go break it down," Andrei ordered Demid.

Demid went off to the storehouse, jerking an iron bolt out of a cart on the way.

The five-pound lock was overcome thanks to an axe, but with difficulty.

"Don't chop the lintel! It's our storehouse now, so treat it like you own it. Easy! Easy!" Demka advised the wheezing Molchun.

They began to weigh the grain.

"Maybe we can prepare it right away? There's a large sieve in the bin," suggested Ignatenok, drunk with happiness.

He was made fun of, and they continued to joke while pouring the heavy wheat into measuring vessels.

"There's two hundred poods here for breadmaking yet," said Demka Ushakov, up to his knees in grain.[1] Using a shovel he tossed the wheat toward the bin opening, grabbed it with his hand, and let it fall through his fingers . . .

"Look at it! Black gold it is, only you can see it was just on the ground: See, the spots."

Arkashka Menok and one other fellow were making themselves at home in the storage area. Arkashka stroked his small, light brown beard and pointed to the bull's manure with bits of undigested corn sticking out of it.

"Is it any wonder they can work? They eat pure grain, while we have a hard time in the peasant association even getting hay."

Out of the storehouse came lively voices, laughter, aromatic bread dust, at times a strongly worded curse ... Andrei returned to the house. The mother and daughter had gathered cast iron utensils and dishes into a sack. Frol, like a dead man with fingers crossed on his chest, was now lying on the bench in his stocking feet. Timofei, quiet now, glanced up in hatred and turned away to the window.

In the living room Andrei saw Molchun squatting down. He wore Frol's new leather boots. Not seeing Andrei enter, he scooped honey with a table-spoon out of an iron bucket and ate in sweet delight, squinting, smacking his lips, and dribbling honeyed drops on his beard ...

Translation by Nicholas Rzhevsky

Note to the translation is on page 580.

RESOURCES

Primary Text

Sholokhov, Mikhail. *Podniataia tselina*. Moscow: Khudozhestvennaia literatura, 1960, pp. 51–56.

Secondary Sources

Literary and Cultural Studies

Brown, Edward J. *Russian Literature since the Revolution*. New York: Collier, 1963, pp. 179–89.

Clark, Katerina. *The Soviet Novel: History as Ritual*. Chicago: University of Chicago Press, 1981.

Dunham, Vera. *In Stalin's Time: Middleclass Values in Soviet Fiction*. 2nd ed. Durham: Duke University Press, 1990.

Ermolaev, Herman. *Mikhail Sholokhov and His Art*. Princeton: Princeton University Press, 1982.

Mathewson, Rufus. *The Positive Hero in Russian Literature*. New York: Columbia University Press, 1958.

Struve, Gleb. *Russian Literature under Lenin and Stalin, 1917–1953*. Norman: University of Oklahoma Press, 1971.

Drama and Theater

Pogodin, Nikolai. *Sobranie dramaticheskikh proizvedenii v piati tomakh*. Vol. 3. Moscow: Iskusstvo, 1960, pp. 85–172.

Film

Podniataia tselina (Virgin Soil Upturned). Director, Iulii Raizman. Mosfilm, 1939.

Tikhii Don (The Quiet Don). Director, Sergei Gerasimov. Cinematographer, Wulf Rapaport. Design, Boris Dulenko. Music, Iurii Levitin. Gorky Studio, 1957.

31

∽Mikhail Zoshchenko∽

Crime and Punishment
A Comedy in One Act

Cast of Characters

GORBUSHKIN, *Director of a Cooperative Enterprise*
MRS. GORBUSHKIN, *his wife*
SENYA, *the wife's brother*
BANANOV, *a dealer*
NEIGHBOR
UNKNOWN MAN
RED ARMY SOLDIER
DRAYMAN

(The play can be performed by four actors.)

GORBUSHKIN's *apartment. A table. A painting on the wall. A lamp hanging under a silk lampshade.* GORBUSHKIN *and* MRS. GORBUSHKIN *are drinking tea from a samovar.* GORBUSHKIN *is glancing through a newspaper.*

GORBUSHKIN: *(Reading)* Oho ... That's how it is ... Well, well, well. I never thought ...

MRS. GORBUSHKIN: What is it already?

GORBUSHKIN: *(Reading)* I can't believe it, can't believe it ... Well, well, well. Yes sir, that's how it is. I never thought ...

MRS. GORBUSHKIN: Will you explain clearly what's the matter?

GORBUSHKIN: Uh, uh, uh, well, well, well, I never thought ... mu, mu, mu.

MRS. GORBUSHKIN: I am literally beginning to feel ill from your mooing. Well, what is it?

GORBUSHKIN: What it is is the death sentence for stealing government property.

MRS. GORBUSHKIN: What's that got to do with you? What have you been stealing?

490

GORBUSHKIN: Did I say I had anything to do with it? You're so stupid! All I said was generally speaking, capital punishment for stealing.

MRS. GORBUSHKIN: So what have you been stealing? Big deal! Brings home some piece of garbage once a year and now he can't bear to read the papers—afraid of capital punishment.

GORBUSHKIN: I am speaking generally. I am merely noting, look, a revolutionary decree has been published.

MRS. GORBUSHKIN: Decree, big deal! Other administrators bring stuff home by the truckload, every day, so there's no place to put it.

GORBUSHKIN: And I don't bring things home . . . according to you I'm off smelling roses somewhere? You're so stupid! *(Pointing to different objects in the room)* And what's this? And how about this? And look at what you're wearing? *(Again reads the newspaper)* My, my, my.

MRS. GORBUSHKIN: So you brought a little bit from the office. That's no sin. Other people sell the things they get and you don't see them reading the newspaper and moaning and groaning.

GORBUSHKIN: How about the sugar? I sold the sugar. *(Again reads the newspaper)* Oh my, oh my, my, my, my.

(The doorbell rings. Conversation is heard off stage)

MRS. GORBUSHKIN: Someone's at the door.

GORBUSHKIN: Who can that be this early? Maybe it's your brother, the scoundrel. *(Hides the breakfast cheese)*

MRS. GORBUSHKIN: My brother was planning to come later.

GORBUSHKIN: Oh, it must be Bananov. He's brought me the money . . . for the sugar. Uh, uh, uh.

MRS. GORBUSHKIN: *(Drops her fork)* No, it's not him. When someone drops a fork it's a sure sign the next visitor will be a woman. I really believe in that superstition.

(RED ARMY SOLDIER enters. MRS. GORBUSHKIN cries out. GORBUSHKIN, pouring tea, forgets to shut off the samovar. Both panic and are dumbfounded)

RED ARMY SOLDIER: Excuse me, citizens. Don't be afraid. I'm here from the District Attorney. Who is Citizen Gorbushkin . . . Which one of you?

MRS. GORBUSHKIN: There he is, that's him, Gorbushkin.

RED ARMY SOLDIER: Then be so kind as to accompany me. The District Attorney ordered it be done at once. Here's the summons.

MRS. GORBUSHKIN: The District Attorney?

GORBUSHKIN: Oh me, oh my, oh me, oh my. *(With trembling hands takes the summons. Reads)* Rum and onions. I can't make it out, the letters are skipping around. Rum at once . . . rr . . . s . . . s . . . su . . . su . . . summons . . . summons . . .

MRS. GORBUSHKIN: Summons?!

GORBUSHKIN: I told you, I told you . . . and you didn't believe me . . . *(Looks at the newspaper)* Oh my, oh my, oh my . . . *(Paces around the room)*

RED ARMY SOLDIER: We're ordered to be there by ten.

GORBUSHKIN: *(Dressing rapidly, shoves arm into wrong sleeve)* Oh my, oh my.

MRS. GORBUSHKIN: Take some leftovers at least. Take a paper bag.

GORBUSHKIN: *(Buttoning the top button of his overcoat to the bottom button-hole)* I'm rrr . . . rr . . . ready. Take me away, comrade. *(*GORBUSHKIN *and* RED ARMY SOLDIER *exit)*

MRS. GORBUSHKIN: In the name of all the saints, what's happening? *(Paces about the room, takes a packet out from behind a painting on the wall, hides it again)* What am I to do with this? *(Telephone rings)* What's that ringing again? Ah, yes, hello . . . it's me . . . hello . . . Brother is that you? Grisha, he's been, you know . . . No, worse . . . Yes, yes . . . Only right away. I don't know . . . I don't know anything. Just come right away. *(Again takes the packet from behind the painting)* Now where can I put this? *(Exits running)*

*(*BANANOV, *the dealer, enters)*

BANANOV: Oh yes, the low-life, not bad at all! And he complains, the son of a bitch. Money, on the table he wants. Although he stole the sugar himself—and I'm supposed to pay in his place! It's a shame, that's what it is. *(Coughs)* And he makes you wait for half an hour. *(Sits down on a chair)* Look at all the groceries, look at the groceries piled up! Mama mia! What's he do, gobble it day and night! . . . And I'm supposed to bring money. *(Walks up to the table. Eats, looking around carefully)* And such tyrants get letters. *(Reads the summons)* "Immediate action required . . . to Citizen Gorbushkin . . . You are requested to appear at once as a witness in the case of Shchukin. Prosecutor Kemin." Isn't that something, they want a character like that for a witness . . . Maybe I shouldn't have come here . . . He can come get it himself. *(Goes to the exit. Returns)* Would you look at all the groceries! *(Eats again, again goes to the exit, again returns, takes a piece of bread and puts butter on it. Stuffs it into his mouth)*

*(*MRS. GORBUSHKIN *enters carrying the packet)*

MRS. GORBUSHKIN: *(Frightened)* Oh! Who is it? Who is it?

BANANOV: *(Eating the bread)* Kmm, kmm . . .

MRS. GORBUSHKIN: Who is it? I'll scream.

BANANOV: *(Swallowing the bread)* Kmm . . . Excuse me . . . Wait a minute . . . I'll explain everything . . . There's something stuck in my throat.

MRS. GORBUSHKIN: What are you doing here?

BANANOV: Excuse me. I'm choking on something, some kind of spastic twitch . . . I'm here to see Mr. Gorbushkin, Bananov . . . But since he's . . .

MRS. GORBUSHKIN: So you know . . . Yes, yes, Mr. Gorbushkin has been arrested.

BANANOV: Arrested! What d'you mean arrested? . . . Well . . . I'd better go then . . . I thought it was something completely different. I thought he was a witness in some case . . .

MRS. GORBUSHKIN: A witness? What kind of witness?

BANANOV: You know that happens there sometimes . . . You start out a witness, and then you're not . . . that happens often . . . I'd better go . . . since he's arrested. *(Rapidly exits)*

MRS. GORBUSHKIN: *(Puts a chair on the table, climbs up and hides the packet on the lampshade)* Up here, maybe that's the place to hide it.

*(*NEIGHBOR *enters. He loudly clears his throat)*

Who is it? Who's that?

NEIGHBOR: Well, Anna Vasilievna, what are you scared of? Don't you recognize your own neighbor?

MRS. GORBUSHKIN: Oh, it's you. Excuse me.

NEIGHBOR: Excuse me, why are you climbing up the ceiling?

MRS. GORBUSHKIN: Oh, you know, just to see what's going on, up here.

NEIGHBOR: Yes, what's going on can get you climbing up the wall. I saw your husband being taken away. So I decided to stop in and console his wife. Was there a search yet?

MRS. GORBUSHKIN: *(Agitated)* A search? No, there was none.

NEIGHBOR: Then there will be.

MRS. GORBUSHKIN: My God, will there really?

NEIGHBOR: What do you think? Do you remember Shchukin? The one who was stealing. There was a search and they say total confiscation of all property.

MRS. GORBUSHKIN: Total confiscation?

NEIGHBOR: Stop worrying already. I've come especially to calm you down. You are, so to say, a woman in her flowering years ... You can still be appealing. Someone, perhaps, may still marry you. Anything can happen. You'll make out.

(SENYA, MRS. GORBUSHKIN*'s brother, enters*)

SENYA: *(Hurriedly)* What is it? Well? What's the matter? *(To the* NEIGHBOR) What's this?

MRS. GORBUSHKIN: That's our neighbor.

NEIGHBOR: I decided to stop in to calm her down a bit. I saw the rascal being taken away. So I thought, she's too agitated now ... I'll go and calm her down.

SENYA: What's the matter, I'm asking you?

MRS. GORBUSHKIN: I don't know myself, brother.

SENYA: Stop it with your women's stuff, 'I don't know.' What did he have?

MRS. GORBUSHKIN: I'm at a loss myself. What he had. Of course he had. He had sugar, soap ... Probably, of course ... who knows ...

SENYA: That's not good. That's really bad. We have to think of something quick.

NEIGHBOR: As I understand it, they can confiscate everything now.

SENYA: What? Confiscate? That's what I said. We have to act quickly. You have to sell everything at once. *(Pulls at the carpet on which* NEIGHBOR *and* MRS. GORBUSHKIN *are standing. Rolls it up)*

MRS. GORBUSHKIN: Brother, do we really have to sell everything?

NEIGHBOR: As I understand it, you have to sell everything to the bare walls. I'll take the sugar myself, as an example.

SENYA: The sugar's not for sale. I'm taking it. *(Picks up the telephone)* Hello. Seven, sixteen, thirty, two ...

NEIGHBOR: Then how about some of the textile goods?

SENYA: *(To* MRS. GORBUSHKIN) Sis, quick, show him the overcoat and the suits. The suits will fit him just right. Only quickly. Quickly!

(MRS. GORBUSHKIN *shows the suits.* NEIGHBOR *examines them closely*)

NEIGHBOR: Suits, of course, aren't very interesting. One wants something more, something more lasting. How much do you want for the whole lot of secondhand objects?

SENYA: *(Speaking on the telephone)* Hello, Fedor Palich? Yes, it's me ... What? Yes, that's it exactly. Everything is for sale. A total quick sale. Well, there's certain circumstances. Yes, the bureaus too. And the paintings, yes, the paintings. What? Whose brushes? What brushes? I don't think there are any brushes. *(Looks at the paintings)* No, the painting is without brushes. An ordinary frame, and no brushes, you know. What? Oh, that. *(To* MRS. GORBUSHKIN) He's talking about some brushes.[1]

MRS. GORBUSHKIN: *(Angrily)* What brushes? I don't have any brushes.

SENYA: Hello. The widow doesn't have any brushes. What? Oh, that. Hhm. *(To his sister)* He's asking, whose brushes? Who are the painters?

MRS. GORBUSHKIN: What brushes? There aren't any brushes.

NEIGHBOR: No, that's how the earlier bourgeois class used to express themselves in a humanist fashion: whose brush. That is, who painted the paintings? That's real funny, swear to God.

MRS. GORBUSHKIN: Who knows who painted them.

SENYA: The names. He's asking about the names. Only quick.

MRS. GORBUSHKIN: I can't think of it now. Some name with "oy." Or, wait, maybe "akh."

NEIGHBOR: Akhov? Chekhov?

SENYA: *(To telephone)* The name begins in "akh."

MRS. GORBUSHKIN: No, wait, maybe it's "ay."

SENYA: It begins in "ay." Ayvazovsky?[2] Yes, that's the one. Ayvazovsky. On one painting there's a beautiful dry birch grove—forty meters or so of dry birch logs, and on the other, I'm sorry, there's plain water. Three hundred no less for the birch grove, and we can talk about the water later. So we're waiting for you, Fyodor Palich.

NEIGHBOR: Well, I'm taking this stuff here, Anna Vasilievna. And stop worrying about your spouse. I always treat such matters calmly. Such things never scare me. As long as it's not capital punishment, I say to myself. Capital punishment is indeed hard to take, and anything else we can manage.

SENYA: Has he paid you? Don't let him distract you with all that talk.

NEIGHBOR: I paid, I paid. Don't worry. *(Exits)*

SENYA: Give me the money. Why are you holding it?

MRS. GORBUSHKIN: That's all right . . . I'll hold on to it for a while.

SENYA: We have to turn over everything here in a hurry. We need to go full speed ahead. This one will take the furniture. The other one—the bureaus. Him—the suits. I'll take something too. I'll do my best for you, as much as I can. I'll help any way I can.

MRS. GORBUSHKIN: Well, thank you, brother. Only what's happening? All our property is disappearing right before my eyes!

SENYA: Oh sister, you don't understand anything. When someone's arrested in such an important case, the government, perhaps, has suffered innumerable losses. We can't waste a minute. We have to act forcefully. Like real Bolsheviks. And if someone comes, we don't have anything. The wife is sitting on a cot in total poverty. But look how you're dressed! Look how you're dressed! You've piled so much on you're like a camel. Put on a black dress, something indigent. Sell everything else. Where are you shoving that bundle, give it to me.

(MRS. GORBUSHKIN exits. UNKNOWN MAN
[secondhand furniture dealer] enters)

Fyodor Palich! It's good to see you, etc. Please, have a look at the furniture. Only, please hurry.

UNKNOWN MAN: Well. I can buy this . . . Well. Paintings. *(Looks at them through his fist)* This too . . . How much do you want for all this junk?

SENYA: There's still a wonderful lady's bedroom set.

UNKNOWN MAN: *(Looking through the open door)* That too. This too. How much wholesale for the entire house? How about three.

MRS. GORBUSHKIN: *(Enters wearing rags)* Oh, oh, three. How cheap he is, and he won't take it home. Three!

UNKNOWN MAN: All right, then, I'll give you four—and that's it. *(Takes down the paintings, places the chairs on the table)*

SENYA: Take it, sister, take it. Every minute is precious for us. Write him a receipt.

MRS. GORBUSHKIN: My God! How can this be happening? How can it? *(Writes receipt, takes the money)*

UNKNOWN MAN: I'll send a horse right away. *(Exits)*

SENYA: Send the horse as quick as possible . . . In the Bolshevik manner. Sister, speed is of the essence. You know my character. I never panic. But I know how to get things done. We have to turn everything over in rapid tempo.

MRS. GORBUSHKIN: Of course, I understand. I'm fully aware of your point of view. Only I'm sorry for our property. Look, now I won't even have anything to sit on in my own apartment.

SENYA: That's right, the apartment! You bought it for ten thousand. We have to turn over the apartment also. *(Picks up the telephone)* Hello, zero,

zero, zero, fifteen. Hello, it's me, me. An apartment, two rooms. The builder himself. *(To his sister)* Will you stop grabbing me? *(Speaking into the phone)* No, the furniture, unfortunately, has been sold already. The suits too. No, that's all been sold. The widow's sold everything. So come over for the apartment.

(NEIGHBOR *enters in a new, very large suit)*

NEIGHBOR: I'm afraid the suit is a little large on me. What do you think?

SENYA: Perfectly fine fit.

MRS. GORBUSHKIN: Fits you very nicely.

NEIGHBOR: No, I feel it's too big.

SENYA: Where do you think it's big? *(Squeezes the back of the suit together)* I think it's even a little tight on you.

NEIGHBOR: *(Almost in tears)* Where is it tight, I ask you?

SENYA: It's obvious it's tight. You can't even take a deep breath.

MRS. GORBUSHKIN: It looks very nice on him.

NEIGHBOR: No, you know, there's something wrong. The shoulders are tight too. No, it's too tight. I can feel it's too tight.

SENYA: Well, you know, you're really acting strange. You just said it was too big.

NEIGHBOR: Did I say too big? No, I said, too tight. That's exactly what I said, it's too tight. I even have difficulty breathing.

SENYA: You don't make any sense. *(Releases the suit)* How can it be tight when the material lies so evenly? If anything it's too big.

NEIGHBOR: Maybe it is too big. Who the hell knows. I swear to God it's too big.

SENYA: There's nothing tight about it. Look how it molds your figure. You don't know yourself what you want.

MRS. GORBUSHKIN: He doesn't know what he wants. He's just acting strange.

NEIGHBOR: *(Almost in tears)* Then at least I'll take the lampshade too. As a bonus. Such lampshades interest me a little.

SENYA: Take the shade. Only quickly, quickly. Make your feet fly.

(NEIGHBOR *climbs up on the table and takes off the lampshade)*

MRS. GORBUSHKIN: What's going on right in front of me? Why are you clambering up on the table, you devil?

NEIGHBOR: My apologies. *(Moves to exit with the lampshade and picks up two chairs on the way)*

SENYA: Put the chairs back where you got them. The furniture has all been sold.

NEIGHBOR: My apologies.

SENYA: The étagère is also sold. Don't grab things with your hands. Everything here has been sold. The only thing left is the apartment.

NEIGHBOR: I'd take the apartment, if I could pay it off gradually. I've never stopped admiring your apartment.

MRS. GORBUSHKIN: Friends, countrymen! What is going on? And I, for example, where am I supposed to live?

SENYA: Ah, hell! That's true. Where will the widow live?

NEIGHBOR: In an extreme case I can allow her a corner of my apartment.

SENYA: Write a receipt. Or better let me write it. You just sign here. Don't paw me. *(NEIGHBOR leaves with the lampshade and receipt)* Now, I think, that's everything. The other one's going to take the furniture, you can relax.

MRS. GORBUSHKIN: I don't understand what's happening. What if I get a summons? What am I to say?

SENYA: If you get a summons then you'll just say there's nothing here.

MRS. GORBUSHKIN: Or maybe I better tell them I'm staying with my brother?

SENYA: Don't even think of it! With your brother! Don't mention me directly at all. Forget about me directly. Like I don't exist. Oh, my God. Hell! They'll ask who the relatives are and off they'll go. Perhaps, sister, you'd like to get married? Can you find a spouse, I mean, can you get married quickly, ah? Only quickly.

MRS. GORBUSHKIN: How's that again?

SENYA: Then you'd be in seventh heaven. No property, all alone, the husband's supporting you, and so on. Is there some idiot you can think of?

MRS. GORBUSHKIN: Brother, what are you saying?

SENYA: Only quickly, quickly. Do you have someone?

MRS. GORBUSHKIN: How could I?

SENYA: For instance, how about the one that was here—the neighbor. What do you think, will he get married? Call him, quickly. Quickly, quickly!

MRS. GORBUSHKIN: Really, what's happening? How can ... There, he's already coming.

NEIGHBOR: I swear to God, I won't take the suits. Everyone's laughing.

SENYA: Will you stop sniveling? Instead, I'd like to ask you, why do you come to visit my sister so often? That will only give her a bad reputation.

NEIGHBOR: What do you mean, often? I only stopped in once during the whole month, to console the woman.

SENYA: "Console the woman." We know all about these consolations. And he dares to lie! Came in only once. He's been here three times in my presence alone. You're giving her a bad reputation. And if you like her, then just say so.

NEIGHBOR: What do you mean like her? Take it easy now.

SENYA: I said, if you like my sister, then take her and marry her.

NEIGHBOR: Did I say, did I say, I liked her?

SENYA: Yes, you just said it.

NEIGHBOR: Me? You know . . . Me, me, all I mentioned was the suits. And it was exactly the opposite. I said I didn't like the suits.

SENYA: No, don't try to fool me, and just go marry her if you like her. Only quickly, quickly. In record time.

NEIGHBOR: *(Almost crying)* But spare me! Why should I get married? I really don't understand you.

MRS. GORBUSHKIN: If he really doesn't want to, then there's no point discussing it.

SENYA: What do you mean, he doesn't want to? He wants to, only he's embarrassed.

NEIGHBOR: I swear to God, I don't want to. I really don't understand you. Spare me, please! I didn't say anything to you. Why are you pushing me around?

SENYA: Oh, he's got to say something. So say, like this, I want to get married. I'm not stopping you from speaking up.

NEIGHBOR: No, I really don't understand. I don't want to . . . I don't want to get married. Why should I suddenly do something stupid like get married? Why are you pestering me, for heaven's sake?

MRS. GORBUSHKIN: There's really nothing else to be said.

SENYA: Such an interesting woman! I really don't understand him. If you don't have good taste then come out and tell us instead of fooling people.

NEIGHBOR: I, am not fooling anyone. I have taste. Only, I say . . .

SENYA: You have taste! Don't make me laugh. Such a glorious, interesting woman. And look at her structural qualities! No, I can see you don't understand anything about women.

NEIGHBOR: No, I understand . . . I'll admit this one's, somewhat interesting. Only I . . . I really don't know, how one can . . .

SENYA: She has a good, straight way of walking. Another woman will walk like a camel, and this one places her feet evenly. One, two, one, two.

NEIGHBOR: I understand that, I admit it. Of course, I like her, I have good taste, but only, how can one, spare me . . .

SENYA: Sister, go to him. Take him by the hand.

NEIGHBOR: How can one . . . wait . . . go easy now! I'm dumbfounded . . .

SENYA: More's the reason, you can always get a divorce, and I don't know what else there is to talk about.

NEIGHBOR: Well, if I can get a divorce—so be it, I will get married.

SENYA: Of course you'll get married. Only quickly, quickly. Sis, run this very minute to the Bureau of Registration and get a divorce . . . And at the same time try to get rid of some of the kitchen utensils there. Kiss him.

MRS. GORBUSHKIN: What's happening? *(They kiss,* MRS. GORBUSHKIN *exits)*

SENYA: You see, you were sniveling, and now look what a wife you got for yourself.

NEIGHBOR: No, I only said . . .

SENYA: There's nothing to be said. Just do it and get married.

NEIGHBOR: Wait a minute, wait a minute. All right, so I'm married. Then why did I buy the suits from her? How about that?

SENYA: That's what you'll wear on your honeymoon.

NEIGHBOR: But I paid money for them, and since I'm getting married it seems I could have gotten them for nothing anyway. Does this mean I bought them from myself? No, you know, I don't agree under these conditions.

SENYA: But you bought them first, and then you got married. Why are you confusing the issue? You're only muddling everything.

NEIGHBOR: But how can that be, I beg your pardon! No, I don't agree under those conditions. If I am getting married then the suits are mine anyway. Give me back the money. Or I won't get married.

SENYA: Here, try getting it back—give him back the money. My sister may be divorced by now. Consider—isn't she a woman, and very self-conscious? And you allow yourself to say you won't get married!

NEIGHBOR: But, but . . . I paid a deposit for the apartment also. How can . . . No, I swear to God, I won't do it . . . I . . . I . . .

SENYA: What are you getting upset about? All right, I'll give you back half.

(DRAYMAN enters)

DRAYMAN: Is this the furniture to be taken?

SENYA: That's it, that's it.

NEIGHBOR: And the furniture! Why are you selling the furniture then? Why have you sold my furniture? Don't touch my furniture! I swear to God, I won't marry.

SENYA: So why did you stretch it out for so long? You only brought shame on the woman with your behavior. If you had gotten married earlier, the furniture would have remained yours.

NEIGHBOR: How could I earlier? You only told me now, this very minute, that I should get married.

SENYA: And why didn't you think of it on your own? Now you have no one to blame but yourself.

NEIGHBOR: But, but, I swear to God.

SENYA: Oh, get lost! Look, the bride is coming.

NEIGHBOR: Anna Vasilievna, what is this? I don't understand. Stop them from touching our furniture.

SENYA: The furniture has been sold. There's nothing to talk about. *(To his sister)* So, did you get divorced? Only answer quickly.

MRS. GORBUSHKIN: I got divorced. And I sold the kitchen utensils to our neighbors.

NEIGHBOR: *(Whining)* What, the kitchen utensils? Why are you selling my kitchen utensils? And what are we supposed to eat out of?

SENYA: *(To his sister)* What a bastard your bridegroom turned out to be. We've done such a good job of selling and he's still unhappy, howling like an owl. And to top it off I don't feel well today. I have a headache.

MRS. GORBUSHKIN: What's there for us to be happy about?

NEIGHBOR: That's right! Make him give us our money back.

SENYA: All right already. Shut up. I said I'll give you half. *(To DRAYMAN)* This too. Take it as well.

NEIGHBOR: I feel as if I'm in a fog. I don't understand anything.

SENYA: At least go to your bride. Don't stand there like an idiot.

MRS. GORBUSHKIN: Why are you shouting at him? You see, you've scared the man completely. *(Walks up to NEIGHBOR. They exchange tender remarks. They kiss)*

(GORBUSHKIN *enters. He is slightly tipsy. He sings and dances*)

GORBUSHKIN: *(Singing)* Silver bells, silver bells, tell of the times in my youth . . .

MRS. GORBUSHKIN: Grisha!

GORBUSHKIN: *(Does not notice the state of the room)* They were very courteous. Very. We apologize, they said, that we didn't send the summons by mail. We needed you very quickly as a witness. Aha, I say, of course, that's why I came, to be a witness. I say, silver bells, silver bells . . . So what's the case in which I'm to be a witness? They answer, and so politely, elegantly: Tell us, they say, what you know about Shchukin. In a short time, they say, he's managed to steal everything. As you please, I say. I take a chair, pull it up to the table like this . . . *(In fright looks around the half-emptied room)* What is this, I say, what is this?

(SENYA *exits carefully on tiptoe*)

MRS. GORBUSHKIN: This, this . . . we thought . . . this, we, Grigory Ivanovich . . .

NEIGHBOR: I feel as if I'm in a fog.

GORBUSHKIN: *(Shouting)* What's this? What's going on in my apartment?

(DRAYMAN *enters*)

DRAYMAN: Is that everything?

(All three stand dumbfounded)

Curtain

Translation by Nicholas Rzhevsky

Notes to the translation are on page 580.

RESOURCES

Primary Text

Zoshchenko, Mikhail. "Prestuplenie i nakazanie." *Uvazhaemye grazhdane.* Moscow: Knizhnaia Palata, 1991, pp. 497–508.

Secondary Sources

Literary and Cultural Studies

Brown, Edward J. *Russian Literature since the Revolution.* New York: Collier, 1963, pp. 231–37.

Fitzpatrick, Sheila, Alexander Rabinowitch, and Richard Stites, eds. *Russia in the Era of NEP.* Bloomington: Indiana University Press, 1991.

Maguire, Robert A. *Red Virgin Soil: Soviet Literature in the 1920s*. Princeton: Princeton University Press, 1968. For literary climate of Zoshchenko's early works, although not on Zoshchenko himself.

McLean, Hugh. "Belated Sunrise: A Review Article." *SEEJ* 18 (1974): 406–10.

Moldavskii, D. *Mikhail Zoshchenko: Ocherk tvorchestva*. Leningrad: Sovetskii pisatel', 1977.

Scatton, Linda. *Mikhail Zoshchenko: Evolution of a Writer*. Cambridge: Cambridge University Press, 1993.

Film

Ne mozhet byt' (It Can't Be). Director, L. Gaidai. Mosfilm, 1975. Based on Zoshchenko's works and including film adaptation of *Crime and Punishment*.

32

~Osip Mandelstam~

We live without feeling . . .

We live without feeling the land under us,
Our words can't be heard ten steps away,
Yet when the smallest talk takes place,
The Kremlin mountaineer comes up always.
His thick fingers are fat as worms,
His words are as crushing as heavy weights,
Huge cockroach eyes laugh
And his boot tops shimmer.

Thin-necked leaders gather around him.
He plays with the services of semi-humans.
Some whistle, some miaow, some whine,
He alone shouts and pokes them in the chest.
Like throwing horseshoes, he bestows decrees,
Hitting some in the groin, some in the brow or eye.
Every execution is a feast for him
Him—with his broad chest of an Ossete.

November 1933

Translation by Vera Dunham

RESOURCES

Primary Text

Mandel'shtam, Osip. "My zhivem, pod soboiu ne chuia strany." *Sochineniia v dvukh tomakh*. Vol. 1. Moscow: Khudozhestvennaia literatura, 1990, p. 197.

Secondary Sources

Literary and Cultural Studies

Brown, Clarence. *Mandelstam*. Cambridge: Cambridge University Press, 1973.
Brown, C., ed. and trans. *The Prose of Osip Mandelstam*. Princeton: Princeton University Press, 1967.
Broyde, Stephen. *Osip Mandelstam and His Age: A Commentary on the Themes of War and Revolution in His Poetry, 1913–1923*. Cambridge: Harvard University Press, 1975.
Harris, J.G. "Mandelshtám, Ósip Emílievich (1891–1938)." In *Handbook of Russian Literature*, ed. Victor Terras. New Haven: Yale University Press, 1985, pp. 27–73.
Mandelstam, Nadezhda. *Hope Against Hope: A Memoir*. Trans. Max Hayward. New York: Atheneum, 1970.
———. *Hope Abandoned*. Trans. Max Hayward. New York: Atheneum, 1974, 1977.
Struve, Nikita. *Osip Mandelstam*. London: Overseas Publications Interchange, 1988.

Music

Pugacheva, Alla, i gruppa Retsital. "Ia bol'she ne revnuiu." *Kak trevozhen etot put'*. 2 records. Melodiia, 1983.

~Anna Akhmatova~

The Last Toast

I'm drinking to my ravaged hearth,
My life's ill-fated path,
To loneliness that stays with us,
And to you I raise my glass.

To lies on lips disloyal to me,
To deathly cold eyes,
To this world so full of cruelty,
To God's not saving us.

1934

Translation by Yelena Posina

RESOURCES

Primary Text

Akhmatova, Anna. "Poslednii tost." *Stikhotvoreniia i poemy.* Ed. F.Ia. Priima. Leningrad: Sovetskii pisatel', 1977, p. 198.

Secondary Texts

Literary and Cultural Studies

Chukovskaia, L. [*Zapiski ob Anne Akhmatovoi.*] *The Akhmatova Journals.* Trans. M. Micholski, S. Rubashova, Peter Norman. New York: Farrar, Strauss and Girowic, 1994.

Haight, Amanda. *Anna Akhmatova: A Poetic Pilgrimage.* New York: Oxford University Press, 1990.

Film

Lichnoe delo Anny Akhmatovoi (The Personal File of Anna Akhmatova). Director, S. Aranovich. Lenfilm, 1989.

For additional secondary sources, see above, p. 442.

~Daniil Kharms~

Makarov and Peterson

No. 3

MAKAROV

Here, this book speaks of our wishes and their fulfillment. Read it and you'll understand how vain wishes are. You'll also understand how easy it is to grant someone else's wish and how difficult one's own.

PETERSON

You said something extremely fancy. Only Indian Chiefs talk like that.

MAKAROV

This book is such, that one has to talk about it very exaltedly. I take off my cap just thinking about it.

PETERSON

And do you wash your hands before touching it?

MAKAROV

Yes, one must wash one's hands.

PETERSON

You should wash your feet, too, just in case.

MAKAROV

That was not very smart—in fact, it was pretty crude of you.

PETERSON

Well okay, so what sort of book is this?

MAKAROV

Its title is secret . . .

PETERSON

Hee! Hee! Hee!

MAKAROV

This book is called MALGIL.

(PETERSON *is silent*)

MAKAROV

My God! What's this? Peterson!

PETERSON'S VOICE

What happened? Makarov! Where am I?

MAKAROV

Where are you? I can't see you!

PETERSON'S VOICE

And where are you? I can't see you either! . . . And what are these spheres?

MAKAROV

Oh! What should I do? Peterson, can you hear me?

PETERSON'S VOICE

Yes! But what happened? And what are these spheres?

MAKAROV

Can you move?

PETERSON'S VOICE

Makarov! Do you see these spheres?

MAKAROV

What spheres?

PETERSON'S VOICE

Let me go! . . . Let me go! . . . Makarov! . . .

   (*Silence.* MAKAROV *is horrified, then he grabs the book and opens it*)

MAKAROV

(*Reads*) " . . . Gradually man loses his form and becomes a sphere. And having become a sphere, man loses all his desires."

Curtain

Translation by Rama Sohonee

RESOURCES

Primary Text

Kharms, Daniil. "Makarov i Petersen." *Sluchai*. Moscow: Mezhdunarodnaia assotsiiatsiia "Mir kul'tury" Fortuna, 1993, p. 33.

Secondary Sources

Literary and Cultural Studies

Gibian, George. *Russia's Lost Literature of the Absurd: A Literary Discovery*. Ithaca: Cornell University Press, 1971.

Drama and Theater

Kharms, Charms, Shardam! ili Shkola klounov. Predstavlenie iskliuchitel'no dlia legkomyslennykh liudei v trekh sharakh, dvukh molotkakh. Director, Mikhail Levitin. Moscow Theater "Ermitazh." Moscow: Glavnoe upravlenie kul'tury ispolkoma Mossoveta, April 21, 1982.

35

~Anonymous~

Chapayev Anecdotes

Petka sees Vasily Ivanovich digging a hole.

"Vasily Ivanovich, why are you digging a hole?"

"Furmanov wants me to join the party. So I need a head shot photograph, from the shoulders up."

"But why such a deep hole?"

"Well, I'll be photographed on a horse y'see."

Petka and Vasily Ivanovich are escaping from White soldiers. They see a well and jump into it.

Vasily Ivanovich says, "Petka, do the echo."

The White soldiers reach the well and one of them says, "There's no one here."

Petka: "There's no one here. There's no one here."

Another White soldier says, "Maybe they ran ahead?"

Petka: "Maybe they ran ahead? Maybe they ran ahead?"

The White soldier: "Maybe we should chuck in a stone?"

Petka: "Maybe they ran ahead? Maybe they ran ahead?"

A peasant died, and he ended up in a strange place, neither Heaven nor Hell. He sees Rasputin, Stalin, Sherlock Holmes, Doctor Watson, and others around him. And all of them are periodically rotating on their axes. The peasant asks God, "What are they up to?"

"Oh, whenever an anecdote is told about any of them, the person rotates once," God answers.

"And what about those two spinning tops?"

"Those aren't tops. That's Chapayev and Petka."

In the Museum of the Revolution a guide was showing a group of tourists the exhibits. They came to Vasily Ivanovich Chapayev's skeleton.

"And what is this little skeleton next to him?" a small boy asked.

"That, little boy, is Chapayev's childhood skeleton."

Translation by Rama Sohonee

RESOURCES

Primary Texts

Furmanov, Dmitrii. *Chapaev. Krasnyi desant. Miatezh.* Leningrad: Lenizdat, 1967.
Ivanova, O., ed. *Anekdoty i tosty.* Moscow: Aurika, 1994.

Secondary Sources

Literary and Cultural Studies

Brown, Edward J. *Russian Literature since the Revolution.* New York: Collier, 1963, pp. 150–61.
Ermolaev, Herman. *Soviet Literary Theories, 1917–1934: The Genesis of Socialist Realism.* Berkeley: University of California Press, 1963.
Gladovskaia, L.A. *Seminarii.* Leningrad: Leningradskii universitet, 1957.
Lunacharskii, A.V. *Stat'i o sovetskoi literature.* Moscow: Prosveshchenie, 1971.
Segall, Helen. "Fúrmanov, Dmítry Andréevich (1891–1926)." In *Handbook of Russian Literature,* ed. Victor Terras. New Haven: Yale University Press, 1985, p. 161.

Film

Chapaev. Director, Sergei and Georgii Vasiliev. Photography, Aleksandr Sigaev. Design, I. Makhlis. Music, Gavriil Popov. Lenfilm, 1934.

36

~Mikhail Bulgakov~

The Master and Margarita

Chapter 12
"Black Magic and Its Exposure"

A small man with a pear-shaped crimson nose and wearing a yellow bowler full of holes, checkered trousers, and lacquered shoes pedaled out onto the Variety Theater stage on an ordinary two-wheel bicycle. He made a circle to the strains of a fox trot and then let out a victorious howl, which made the bicycle rear up. After riding on one back wheel, the man flipped over upside down and while cycling managed to unscrew the front wheel and send it into the wings, after which he continued his journey on one wheel, turning the pedals with his hands.

On a high metal pole with a seat on top and with one wheel, a plump blonde wearing tights and a little skirt covered with silver stars rode out and began to ride in circles. Meeting with her, the man would utter welcoming cries and with his foot remove the bowler from his head.

Finally, a little boy of about eight with the face of an old man drove in and darted between the grown-ups on a tiny two wheeler with a huge automobile horn.

After performing several loops, the whole company, accompanied by the alarming beat of an orchestra drum, rolled to the very edge of the stage, and the spectators in the front rows gasped and leaned back because it looked as if the entire threesome with their vehicles was going to crash into the orchestra.

But the bicycles stopped at the very moment when the front wheels already threatened to slip into the abyss onto the heads of the musicians. The cyclists jumped down from their bicycles with a loud cry of "Hey!" and took their bows, while the blonde blew kisses to the audience and the infant trumpeted funny sounds on his horn.

Applause shook the building, a blue curtain appeared from both sides and hid the cyclists, the signs indicating "Exit" in green lights by the doors went out, and white spheres flared like the sun in the trapeze web under the dome. Intermission, before the last part of the show, had begun.

The only person not in the least interested in the wonders of bicycle technique demonstrated by the Juli family was Grigory Danilovich Rimsky. He sat in total isolation in his office and bit his thin lips as tremors kept passing across his face. Likhodeev's extraordinary disappearance now compounded the absolutely unforeseen disappearance of the administrator Varenukha.

Rimsky knew where he had gone, but he had gone and ... he had not returned! Rimsky shrugged his shoulders and whispered to himself:

"What for?"

And, how strange: for a serious man of affairs such as the business manager it was, of course, the simplest of matters to call the place where Varenukha had gone and to find out what had happened to him, but until ten o'clock in the evening he could not force himself to do so.

At ten o'clock, however, after literally coercing himself, Rimsky picked up the receiver and immediately discovered his telephone was dead. A messenger reported that the rest of the telephones in the building were also out of order. For some reason, this turn of events, unpleasant, of course, but hardly something supernatural, completely unnerved the business manager and at the same time made him happy: he no longer had to make the call.

At the moment when the red lamp above the business manager's head lit up and began to blink announcing the beginning of intermission, a messenger entered and declared that a foreign talent had arrived. For some reason, the business manager was unpleasantly affected by this, and now, gloomier than a storm cloud, he proceeded backstage to receive the visitor because there was nobody else to greet him.

Under various pretexts, curious people were peeping into a large dressing room off a corridor where the warning buzzers were already clamoring. They included magicians in bright robes and turbans, a skater in a white knitted jacket, a comedian pale from powder, and a makeup man.

The visiting celebrity awed everyone with his frock coat of unprecedented length and marvelous cut and also by coming in wearing a black half-mask. But most surprising of all were the magician's two companions: a lanky checkered fellow wearing a cracked pince-nez, and a fat black tomcat who entered the dressing room on his back legs, sat down without any compulsion on the sofa, and squinted at the bare makeup lamps.

Rimsky tried to put a smile on his face, which only made it sour and nasty looking, and he bowed to the silent magician sitting next to the tomcat on the sofa. There was no handshaking. However, the free-and-easy checkered fellow made his own introductions to the business manager, recommending himself as "their assistant." This circumstance surprised the business manager and again in an unpleasant way: decidedly nothing had been mentioned in the contract about any assistant.

Very unwillingly and drily, Grigory Danilovich asked the checkered fellow who had been dumped on him about the whereabouts of the talent's equipment.

"You are a gem, of celestial proportions, invaluable Mister Director," the magician's assistant answered in a quivering voice. "Our equipment is always with us. Here it is! Ein, zwei, drei!" And twirling his gnarled fingers before Rimsky's eyes, he suddenly pulled out of the tomcat's ear Rimsky's own gold watch with its small chain, which until now had been in the business manager's vest pocket under a buttoned jacket with the chain run through a loop.

Rimsky involuntarily grabbed at his stomach, those present gasped in amazement, and the makeup man, looking in from the doorway, grunted in approval.

"Your watch? Please take it," the checkered fellow said with a free-and-easy smile, and on his dirty palm he offered Rimsky's own property to the dumbfounded manager.

"Don't sit on a trolley next to that sort of fellow," the comedian whispered quietly and merrily to the makeup man.

But the tomcat managed something better than the gag with the watch. Unexpectedly getting up from the sofa, he walked on his hind legs to a table under the mirror, pulled out the cork from a decanter with his front paw, poured water into a glass, drank it, replaced the cork, and wiped his whiskers with a makeup rag.

This time nobody even gasped. They only opened their mouths and the makeup man whispered in admiration:

"That's class!"

At this point the buzzers sounded anxiously for the third time and everyone, in a state of excitement and anticipating an interesting act, rushed out of the dressing room.

A minute later, the lights dimmed in the auditorium, the footlights blazed up and emitted a reddish reflection on the bottom of the curtain, and in an illuminated gap before the audience appeared a stout man, joyful as a child, with a shaven face, in a rumpled evening jacket, and unwashed linen. This was the master of ceremonies, Georges Bengalsky, well known to all of Moscow.

"And so, citizens," Bengalsky said, smiling with the smile of an infant, "appearing before you . . ." At this point, Bengalsky interrupted himself and began to speak with a different intonation. "I see the size of the audience has increased again for the third part of the show. Half of the city is here! Not long ago I met a friend and asked him, 'Why don't you come see us? Yesterday we had half the city here.' And he answered me: 'But I live in the other half!' " Bengalsky paused, expecting an outburst of laughter, but since nobody laughed he continued. "And so, we present a famous foreign artiste, Monsieur Voland, and his seance of black magic! But, you and I under-stand"—at this point Bengalsky smiled wisely—"that magic does not exist in reality and that it is nothing but superstition, and that Maestro Voland simply is highly skilled in the technique of magic tricks, which will become apparent in the most interesting part of the act, that is, the exposure of this technical side, and since we all together support both what is technical and its exposure, let us now welcome Monsieur Voland."

After uttering all this nonsense, Bengalsky put both hands together palm to palm and in a welcoming manner waved them in the opening of the curtain, as a result of which it parted to the sides, rustling quietly.

The entrance of the magician with his lanky assistant and the tomcat, who came out on stage on his hind paws, delighted the audience a great deal.

"An armchair," Voland quietly ordered, and that very instant, one could not tell how or from where, an armchair appeared, on which he sat. "Tell me, my dear Fagot," Voland inquired of the checkered fellow, who apparently had another name as well as "Koroviev," "doesn't it seem to you the Moscow inhabitants have changed significantly?"

The magician looked out at the audience, which was subdued and stunned by the appearance of an armchair out of thin air. "Exactly so, sire," Fagot-Koroviev answered in a low voice.

"You're right. The inhabitants have changed a great deal, on the sur-face I mean to say, as has the city itself, by the way. Not to mention the way they dress, but now you have these—what do you call them—trolleys, automobiles . . ."

"Buses," Fagot respectfully suggested.

The audience listened attentively to this conversation, expecting it to be the prelude to a magic trick. The wings were crowded with performers and stagehands, and the tense pale face of Rimsky could be seen among them.

The facial expression of Bengalsky, who had sequestered himself at the side of the stage, began to show bewilderment. He raised an eyebrow slightly and, taking advantage of a pause, said:

"The foreign artiste expresses his delight with Moscow, which has devel-oped technologically, as well as with Muscovites." At this point Bengalsky smiled twice, the first time to the orchestra rows, the second to the gallery.

Voland, Fagot, and the tomcat turned their heads in the direction of the master of ceremonies.

"Did I really express delight?" the magician asked Fagot.

"Not at all, sire, you did not express any delight at all," the latter replied.

"So what is this man talking about?"

"He is lying, plain and simple!" the checkered assistant reported loudly to the whole theater and, turning to Bengalsky, added, "I congratulate you, citizen, fibber!"

A light shower of laughter came down from the gallery, and Bengalsky gave a start and stared wide-eyed.

"But I'm interested, of course, not so much in automobiles, telephones, and all the . . ."

"Implements," prompted the checkered one.

"Absolutely true, thank you," the magician said slowly in a heavy bass. "What interests me is the much more important question: whether these citizens have changed inwardly."

"Yes, that is the most important question, sir."

In the wings, people began to exchange glances and to shrug their shoulders, Bengalsky stood red-faced, and Rimsky was pale. But at this point, as if he had guessed the growing sense of uneasiness, the magician said:

"However, we're talking away, my dear Fagot, while the audience is getting bored. Show us something simple for a start."

The auditorium stirred in relief. Fagot and the tomcat went to opposite sides of the proscenium. Fagot snapped his fingers and cried out in a devil-may-care manner:

"Three, four!" He caught a deck of cards out of the air, shuffled it, and sent it flying in a streamer to the tomcat. The tomcat grabbed the streamer and tossed it back. The satin snake snorted, Fagot opened his mouth like a baby bird, and swallowed it whole, card after card.

Then the tomcat took his bows, shuffling his right rear paw and provoking unbelievable applause.

"That's class, class!!" people shouted out in admiration backstage.

And Fagot pointed his finger at the orchestra seats and announced:

"The deck, dear citizens, is now in the seventh row in the possession of Citizen Parchevsky exactly between a three ruble note and a summons in the matter of paying alimony to Citizen Zelkova."

The audience in the orchestra seats stirred, began getting up, and finally some man, whose name was indeed Parchevsky and who was crimson with amazement, extracted cards from his wallet and began to poke the deck into the air not knowing what to do with it.

"Keep it as a memento!" Fagot shouted. "Yesterday after dinner you did say life in Moscow would be absolutely unbearable without poker."

"It's an old trick," could be heard in the gallery. "The guy from the orchestra is their stooge."

"You suppose so?" shouted Fagot, squinting at the gallery. "In that case you too are one of us because it's in your pocket!"

Movement in the gallery and a delighted voice could be heard.

"It's true! He has it! Here, here . . . Hold on! It's money!"

The people in the orchestra turned their heads. In the gallery, some confused citizen discovered a pack in his pocket tied up in the bank manner, with an inscription on the cover: "One thousand rubles."

Neighboring members of the audience clamored around as he picked in amazement at the label with his fingernail, trying to find out whether the rubles were real or some type of magic money.

"Swear to God! They're real! Ten ruble notes!" Joyous shouts could be heard from the gallery.

"Play such a card trick on me," some fat fellow in the middle of the orchestra seats asked merrily.

"Avec plaisir," Fagot responded. "But why you alone? Everybody will participate with enthusiasm!" And he commanded: "I ask you to look up. One!" A pistol appeared in his hand. He shouted: "Two!" The pistol jerked upward. He shouted: "Three!" There was a flash, a booming noise, and immediately, from under the dome, white pieces of paper money began falling into the hall, swirling between the trapezes.

They twisted and turned, they were swept to the sides, pushed to the gallery, thrown into the orchestra and onto the stage. In a few seconds, the now heavy shower of currency reached the chairs and the audience began to catch the paper notes.

A hundred hands went up, the spectators looked through the bank notes at the lit stage, and they saw the most genuine and authentic watermarks. The smell also left no doubt: it was the smell, incomparable in its charm, of freshly minted money. At first gaiety and then amazement enveloped the entire theater. The word "rubles, rubles" rang out from all sides, and one could hear cries of "Oh, oh," and joyful laughter. Some people were already crawling in the aisle, groping under the seats. Many stood on the chairs to catch the twisting, capricious pieces of paper.

Perplexity gradually appeared on the faces of policemen, and the performers began to push out of the wings without ceremony.

In the first tier a voice was heard: "Why are you grabbing? That's mine! It was floating to me." And another voice: "Don't push or I'll show you how to push!" And suddenly there was the sound of a slap. The helmet of a policeman immediately appeared in the first tier, and someone was escorted out.

In general, the excitement grew more and more, and it's impossible to say how it would all have ended had Fagot not put a halt to the rain of money by suddenly blowing into the air.

Two young men, having exchanged meaningful and merry glances, left their seats and headed directly into the buffet. In the theater, the hubbub continued, the eyes of everyone in the audience glittered with excitement. Yes, yes, it's impossible to say how it would all have ended had not Bengalsky found the inner strength to act. Trying to get firm control of himself, he rubbed his hands as was his habit and began to speak in his most resonant voice:

"Citizens, we have just witnessed an instance of so-called mass hypnosis. It is purely a scientific experiment, which proves as nothing better that miracles and magic do not exist. Let us now ask Maestro Voland to reveal this experiment to us. Citizens, you will now see how this alleged money disappears as quickly as it appeared."

Then he began to applaud, but completely alone, and as he applauded a confident smile played on his face, although his eyes completely lacked this confidence and more likely expressed a mute appeal.

The audience was not pleased with Bengalsky's speech. There was total silence, which was interrupted by the checkered Fagot.

"This again is an instance of so-called lying," he announced in a loud, reedy tenor. "The paper notes, citizens, are real!"

"Bravo!" a bass voice abruptly bellowed from above.

"By the way, this fellow"—Fagot pointed to Bengalsky—"is becoming tiresome. He is meddling all the time when nobody asks him, he is spoiling the performance with his misleading remarks! What should we do with him?"

"Off with his head!" somebody said sternly in the gallery.

"What did you say? How's that?" Fagot immediately responded to this offensive suggestion. "Off with his head? What an idea! Behemoth!" he shouted to the tomcat. "Do it! Ein, zwei, drei!"

And an unprecedented thing happened. The black cat's fur stood on end and he gave a heart-rending meow. Then he contracted into a ball, jumped like a panther straight to Bengalsky's chest, and from there leaped to his head. Purring and with swollen paws he seized hold of the master of ceremonies' thin head of hair, and after a wild screech, tore off the head from its stout neck in two twists.

Twenty-five hundred people in the theater cried out as one. Blood spurted in a fountain upward from the torn arteries and poured down

Bengalsky's shirt front and jacket. The headless body somehow absurdly paddled its legs and sat down on the floor. Women's hysterical cries could be heard in the auditorium. The tomcat handed the head to Fagot, the latter lifted it by the hair and showed it to the audience, and the head cried out in anguish to the whole theater:

"A doctor!"

"Are you going to keep up your nonsense?" Fagot sternly asked the crying head.

"I won't, ever again," the head said hoarsely.

"For God's sake, don't torture him," a female voice from a loge suddenly rose above the uproar, and the magician turned toward it.

"So, citizens, should we forgive him? Is that it?" Fagot said to the auditorium.

"Forgive him, forgive him!" resounded at first individual and mainly female voices, which then merged into one chorus with male ones.

"What are your wishes, sire?" Fagot asked the masked one.

"Well," he responded lost in thought, "they are as people are. They like money, but this was always so . . . Humanity loves money, in whatever form it might be, whether it's skin, paper, bronze, or gold. So they're frivolous . . . all right . . . but compassion sometimes beats in their hearts . . . they're ordinary people . . . in general they remind me of those from the past . . . only the housing question has spoiled them, . . ." and he loudly ordered: "Put the head back on."

The tomcat, after taking cautious aim, plopped the head on the neck, and it fit exactly in place, as though it had never been gone. Most important, no scar whatsoever remained on the neck. With his paws the tomcat brushed off Bengalsky's shirt front and jacket and every trace of blood disappeared from them. Fagot lifted the sitting Bengalsky to his legs, stuffed a pack of ten ruble notes into the pocket of his tail coat, and saw him off the stage with the words:

"Get lost! It's more fun without you."

The master of ceremonies, looking back in confusion and swaying, got only as far as the fire post and became ill there. He mournfully cried out:

"The head, my head!"

Rimsky ran up to him among the others. The master of ceremonies cried, tried to catch something out of the air with his hands, and mumbled:

"Give me back my head! Give the head back! Take my apartment, take my paintings, just give me back my head!"

A messenger ran for a doctor. An attempt was made to place Bengalsky on a sofa in the dressing room, but he fought back and became violent. It was necessary to send for an ambulance. When the unfortunate master of ceremonies was taken away, Rimsky ran back to the stage and saw that new wonders were taking place on it. By the way, at this moment, or perhaps a little earlier, the magician disappeared together with his faded armchair, and moreover, it should be said, the audience absolutely did not notice, engrossed as it was in the extraordinary things Fagot was doing.

And Fagot, having sent the abused master of ceremonies on his way, announced the following to the audience:

"Now that we're rid of this obnoxious specimen, let's open a ladies' shop!"

And immediately the stage floor was covered with Persian rugs, huge mirrors sprang up lit from the sides by greenish lights, and between the mirrors showcases, and the audience, happily bedazzled, saw different colors and styles of Parisian dresses in the showcases. The dresses were in one showcase and in another appeared hundreds of women's hats with and without feathers, with and without buckles, hundreds of shoes—black, white, yellow, leather, satin, suede—with small straps, and with sequins. Among the shoes appeared small boxes, and light played against the sides of crystal perfume bottles in them. There were mountains of ladies' bags made out of antelope hide, suede, silk, and in their midst whole piles of small long embossed golden tubes with lipstick.

The devil knows how, but a redheaded girl in a black evening gown appeared next to the showcases and smiled in the manner of a shopkeeper; she would have been fine in all respects if she had not been spoiled by a grotesque scar on her neck.

Fagot, smirking sweetly, announced that the shop was ready to exchange old dresses and shoes for Parisian styles and Parisian shoes, absolutely free of charge. The same applied, he added, to ladies' bags, perfume, and so on.

The tomcat began to shuffle his hind paw, then his front one, at the same time making some type of gestures characteristic of porters who open doors.

The girl, although she was somewhat hoarse, began singing out sweetly; she mispronounced her r's and was hard to understand, but judging by the faces of women in the orchestra seats, what she offered was very alluring.

"Guerlain, Chanel No. 5, Mitsuki, Narcissus Noir, evening dresses, cocktail dresses . . ."

Fagot twisted and turned, the tomcat bowed, the girl opened the glass showcases.

"Be our guest!" Fagot yelled. "Don't be embarrassed or stand on ceremony."

The audience stirred, but for the time being nobody made up their minds to go up on stage. Finally, some brunette emerged from the tenth row of the orchestra and, smiling to suggest that she decisively did not care and generally did not give a damn, went up the side ramp to the stage.

"Bravo!" exclaimed Fagot. "I welcome the first customer! Behemoth, an armchair! Let us begin with shoes, madame."

The brunette sat in the armchair, and Fagot immediately dumped out a whole mound of shoes onto the carpet in front of her.

The brunette took off her right shoe, tried on a violet one, stamped her feet on the carpet, and examined the heel.

"But will they be too tight?" she asked, deep in thought.

Fagot, offended, exclaimed:

"How can you! How can you!" and the tomcat meowed from the insult.

"I'll take this pair, monsieur," the brunette said with a dignified air, putting the second shoe on as well.

The brunette's old shoes were thrown away behind a dressing room curtain, and she herself followed them there accompanied by the redheaded girl and by Fagot, who carried several model dresses on his shoulders. The tomcat bustled about, assisted, and for the sake of appearing more important hung a tapemeasure around his neck.

After one minute, the brunette came out from behind the curtain in such a dress that a sigh rolled through all the orchestra seats. The brave woman, having become amazingly beautiful, stopped in front of the mirror, shrugged her exposed shoulders, touched the hair on her forehead, and bent backward, trying to see her back.

"The shop asks you to accept this as a souvenir." Fagot said and gave the brunette an open box with a perfume decanter.

"Merci," the brunette answered haughtily, and she went down the ramp into the stalls. As she walked by, members of the audience sprang to their feet to touch the perfume box.

Then all hell broke loose and women poured from all sides onto the stage. In the midst of the hubbub, laughter, and sighs, a masculine voice was heard: "I won't permit you!" Then a feminine one: "You tyrant, petty bourgeois. Don't break my arm!" The women disappeared behind the dressing room curtain, left their dresses there, and came out in new ones. A whole row of women sat on stools with gilded legs and energetically stomped on the rug with newly shod feet. Fagot got down on his knees and wielded a shoe horn; the tomcat grew fatigued carrying piles of handbags and shoes, dragging himself back and forth from the shop windows to the stools. The young woman with the disfigured neck kept appearing and disappearing, and finally began jabbering away solely in

French, and the wonder of it all was that all the women instantly understood her, even those among them who did not know a single word of the language.

Everyone was astonished by a man who wormed his way onto the stage. He announced that his wife had a cold and that as a result he was requesting something be given her through him. As proof that he was indeed married, the citizen was ready to present his passport. The concerned husband's announcement was met with loud laughter. Fagot shouted that he trusted the man as he trusted himself, even without a passport, and he handed the citizen two pairs of silk stockings. The tomcat added a small jar of pomade from himself.

Latecomers struggled to get onto the stage, and from it flowed a stream of fortunate women, in ball gowns, in pajamas decorated with dragons, in austere business suits, in little hats pulled over one brow.

Then Fagot announced that because of the late hour the store would close exactly in one minute until the next evening, and an unbelievable commotion broke out on the stage. The women hastily grabbed shoes without trying them on at all. One of them, like a whirlwind, flew behind the dressing room curtain, threw off her own suit there, and took possession of the first thing that turned up, a silk robe decorated with an enormous bouquet; in addition, she managed to grab two bottles of perfume.

Precisely in one minute, a pistol shot rang out, the mirrors disappeared, the showcases vanished, and the stools and the carpets faded away into the air together with the dressing room curtain. The last to disappear was the very tall pile of old dresses and shoes, and the stage again became austere, empty, and bare.

And at this point, a new player intruded in the action.

A pleasant, sonorous, and very persistent baritone was heard from Loge No. 2:

"Nevertheless, it is desirable, citizen performer, that you immediately expose the techniques of your tricks to the audience, and especially the trick with paper money. The return of the master of ceremonies to the stage is also desirable. The audience is worried about his fate."

The baritone belonged to none other than the evening's honored guest, Arkady Apollonovich Sempleyarov, the president of the Acoustical Commission of Moscow Theaters.

Arkady Apollonovich was in the loge with two women: one, expensively and stylishly dressed, was getting on in years; the other, dressed rather simpler, was young and pretty. The first woman, as soon became evident when the police report was being written, was Arkady Apollonovich's spouse, and the second was his distant relative, a beginning actress who showed promise, who hailed from Saratov, and who was now living in the apartment of Arkady Apollonovich and his wife.

"I'm sorry!" Fagot answered. "My apologies, but there is nothing to expose here. Everything is clear."

"No, I beg your pardon! An exposé is absolutely necessary. Without it your brilliant act leaves a painful impression. The audience masses demand an explanation."

"The audience masses," Sempleyarov was interrupted by the insolent jester, "haven't seemed to say anything. But out of respect for your highly respected wishes, Arkady Apollonovich, I will indeed present an exposé. Permit me, however, one more short trick?"

"Why not?" Arkady Apollonovich replied in a patronizing manner. "But definitely with an exposé."

"I obey, I obey. And so, allow me to ask, where were you yesterday evening, Arkady Apollonovich?"

At this inappropriate and even, indeed, ill-mannered question, the expression on Arkady Apollonovich's face changed, and changed dramatically.

"Yesterday evening, Arkady Apollonovich attended a meeting of the Acoustical Commission," Arkady Apollonovich's wife declared very haughtily. "But I don't understand what that has to do with magic."

"Oh, madame," Fagot confirmed. "Of course you don't understand. You are entirely in the dark regarding the meeting. After he left for the aforesaid meeting, which by the way, was not scheduled yesterday at all, Arkady Apollonovich let his chauffeur go near the building of the Acoustical Commission on Clear Ponds"—the entire theater grew deadly quiet—"then took a bus to Yelokhovsky Street to visit an actress of a regional traveling troupe, Militsa Andreevna Pokobatko, and he spent approximately four hours in her company."

"Oy!" someone's suffering voice exclaimed in the total silence.

Arkady Apollonovich's young relative, however, suddenly burst into low-pitched and dreadful laughter.

"Now I understand," she exclaimed, "and I suspected it long ago. Now it's clear to me why that inept woman got the role of Luisa!"

And, suddenly brandishing a short and thick violet umbrella, she struck Arkady Apollonovich on the head.

The despicable Fagot (and Koroviev in the same person) cried out:

"There you are, respected citizens, an example of the exposé so persistently sought by Arkady Apollonovich."

"You wretched creature, how did you dare touch Arkady Apollonovich?" his wife asked in a terrible voice, rising up in the loge to her full gigantic height.

A second short burst of demonic laughter overcame the young relative.

"If anyone does," she answered laughing, "it's me who has the right to touch him!" And the dry crack of an umbrella rang out a second time, bouncing off the head of Arkady Apollonovich.

"Police! Arrest her!" Arkady Apollonovich's wife screamed in such a frightful voice that many hearts in the audience turned cold.

And at this point, moreover, the tomcat jumped out to the proscenium and suddenly bellowed to the whole theater in a human voice:

"The show is over! Maestro! Hit it, the march!!"

The unhinged conductor, not realizing what he was doing, waved his baton, and the orchestra did not begin playing, did not even blare out, or even strike up, but specifically, according to the tomcat's revolting expression, hit out some kind of unbelievable march, totally unique in its jauntiness.

For a moment it seemed as if one could hear under southern stars in a *café chantant* the bygone words—hard to understood, half-discernible, but bold—of this march:

> His Excellency loved
> Birds that were tame
> And took under his wing
> Pretty women just the same

But perhaps these were not the words at all, and they were other extremely indecent ones performed to the identical music. This is not important, but what is is that the Variety, after everything that had happened, turned into something akin to the Tower of Babel. The police rushed to Sempleyarov's loge; curious onlookers climbed onto the rails, diabolical outbursts of laughter could be heard, and mad cries were drowned out by the golden clanging of cymbals from the orchestra.

And suddenly, one could see, the stage was empty and the swindler Fagot and the insolent tomcat Behemoth had dissipated into thin air, disappeared, just as the magician in the armchair with faded upholstery had disappeared earlier.

1929–1940

Translation by Howard Blue and Nicholas Rzhevsky

RESOURCES

Primary Text

Bulgakov, Mikhail. *Master i Margarita. Sobranie sochinenii v piati tomakh.* Vol. 5. Moscow: Khudozhestvennaia literatura, 1990, pp. 115–29.

Secondary Sources

Literary and Cultural Studies

Milne, Lesley. *The Master and Margarita: A Comedy of Victory*. Birmingham: Birmingham Slavonic Monographs, 1977.

————. *Mikhail Bulgakov: A Critical Biography*. Cambridge: Cambridge University Press, 1990.

Proffer, Ellendea. *Bulgakov: Life and Work*. Ann Arbor, MI: Ardis, 1984.

Smeliansky, Anatoly. *Is Comrade Bulgakov Dead? Mikhail Bulgakov at the Moscow Art Theater*. New York: Routledge, 1993.

Wright, A. Colin. *Mikhail Bulgakov: Life and Interpretation*. Toronto: University of Toronto Press, 1978.

Theater and Drama

Liubimov, Yury. *A Stage Adaptation of "The Master and Margarita."* London: Overseas Publication Interchange, 1985. Play.

Master i Margarita. Adapted by V. D'iachina and Iu. Liubimov. Director, Iu. Liubimov. Scene design, M. Annist, S. Barkhin, D. Borovskii, Iu. Vasiliev, E. Stenberg. Musical score, E. Denisov. Premiere 1977. In *Russian Literary Theater: Ten Plays at the Taganka*. NJR Video. Video recording of Taganka adpatation.

Film

Beg (Flight). Director, A. Alov and V. Naumov. Cast: Aleksei Batalov, Mikhail Ulianov, Evgenii Evstigneev. Mosfilm, 1975.

Dni Turbinykh (The Days of the Turbins). Director, V. Basov. Mosfilm, 1993.

Ivan Vasil'evich meniaet professiiu (Ivan Vasil'evich Changed His Profession). Director, L. Gaidai. Gruziiafilm, 1975.

Sobach'e serdste (A Dog's Heart). Director, V. Bortko. Lenfilm, 1988.

37

~Boris Pasternak~

Hamlet

The roar is stilled, I enter the makeshift stage.
Leaning slightly against the open door
I try to discern in the echoes of the age
The things my lifetime holds in store.

Against me is set the darkness of the night,
A thousand binoculars strewn along its ray.
Oh Abba, Father, I stand before Thy sight,
If it can be done, then take this cup away.

I love the stubborn grand design you have in mind
And I have consented to play my part.
But the drama that is played now is of a different kind
And for this once, please let me depart.

But the order of the acts will be as He sees
And the inevitable end of the road will not yield.
I am alone, everything drowns in the hypocrisy of the Pharisees.
Passing through life is not like crossing a field.

1959

Translation by Joanna Radwanska-Williams

RESOURCES

Primary Text

Pasternak, Boris. *Doktor Zhivago*. Ann Arbor: University of Michigan Press, 1958, p. 532.
Pasternak, Boris. *Doktor Zhivago*. Moscow: Zemlia i Fabrika, 1964.

Secondary Sources

Literary and Cultural Studies

Davie, Donald, and Angela Livingstone, eds. *Pasternak: Modern Judgements*. London: Macmillan, 1969.
Erlich, Victor, ed. *Pasternak: A Collection of Critical Essays*. Englewood Cliffs, NJ: Prentice Hall, 1978.
Fleishman, Lazar. *Boris Pasternak: The Poet and His Politics*. Cambridge: Harvard University Press, 1990.
Gifford, Henry. *Pasternak: A Critical Study*. Cambridge: Cambridge University Press, 1977.
Levi, Peter. *Boris Pasternak*. London: Hutchinson, 1990.
Livingstone, Angela, ed. *Pasternak on Art and Creativity*. Cambridge: Cambridge University Press, 1985.
Mallac, Guy De, *Boris Pasternak: His Life and Art*. Norman: University of Oklahoma Press, 1981.

Drama and Theater

Shakespeare, William. *Gamlet* (Hamlet). Taganka Theater. London: Odeon, 1984, 1971. Recording of production that begins with Pasternak's "Hamlet" read by Vladimir Vysotskii.

Audio recording

Boris Pasternak Reads His Work. Read by Boris Pasternak. Distributed by RAES, n.d.

38

~Vladimir Vysotsky~

Morning Exercise

Take a deep breath, put your arms wide,
Do not hurry, three and four!
Cheer of spirit is a must and grace is prized.
Generally strengthening,
And in the morning sobering
If you're still alive, then do your exercise!

If you are in your apartment
On the floor, three and four!
All the movements must be done correctly.
Outside influences eschew
Learn to like all that is new
Take deep breaths 'til you're exhausted!

Viral colds increase by scores
Through the whole world, three and four!
And more illnesses can be felt.
If you're sick—death will ensue!
Something else that you must do—
Vigorously rub yourself to keep your health.

If you are already tired, up and down, get up, sit down
For the Arctic and Antarctica have no timidity!
It's been proven by Ioffe
That for cognac and for coffee
You can substitute sporting activity.

It's forbidden to converse—
You must squat until it hurts
Better not be gloomy or frown balefully!
If your strength begins to flag

Wipe yourself with any rag,
And apply a water treatment carefully!

By dreadful news we're not undone,
We commence in place to run.
Benefiting rookies even at that pace.
Beautiful—look at them running
No one leading, no one lagging!
All are equal as we run in place.

1968

Translation by Alexander Burry

RESOURCES

Primary Text

Vysotskii, Vladimir. "Utrenniaia gimnastika." *Sobranie stikhov i pesen.* Vol. 1. New York: Apollon Foundation and Russica, 1988, pp. 259–60.

Secondary Sources

Literary and Cultural Studies

Blinov, Valery. "Vysótsky, Vladímir Semyónovich (1938–80)." In *Handbook of Russian Literature,* ed. Victor Terras. New Haven: Yale University Press, 1985, p. 516.
Leonidov, P. *Vladimir Vysotskii i drugie.* New York: "N'iu Iork," 1982.
Smekhov, V. *Taganka. Zapiski zakliuchennogo.* Moscow: Polikom, 1992.
Vishevsky, Anatoly. *Soviet Literary Culture in the 1970s: The Politics of Irony.* Gainesville: University of Florida Press, 1993, pp. 43–57.

Music

Vysotskii, Vladimir. *Na kontsertakh Vladimira Vysotskogo.* 10 records. Melodiia, 1987–90.
———. *100 pesen Vladimira Vysotskogo: pesennik.* Kiev: Muzychna Ukraina, 1990.

39

~Fedor Abramov~

Wooden Horses

1

The arrival of old Milentyevna, Maxim's mother, was a constant topic of conversation in the house. Her visit was not only discussed but prepared for as well.

Maxim himself, for instance, who like most men without children was rather indifferent about household matters, did not straighten up once during his last day off from work; he rearranged the stones in the bath shed, fixed the hedges around the house, splintered the spruce logs that had been lying under the windows since spring, and, finally, in total darkness laid out boards near the porch—so that mornings his mother would not have to wade in grass heavy with dew.

Maxim's wife, Evgeniya, was even more industrious. She washed and scraped everything clean—in the living quarters, in the side rooms, in the loft—put down bright, colorful throw rugs, polished the ancient lead washstand basin and bowl till they shone.

Generally speaking, it was no secret for me that a new person would shortly appear in the house. And still the old woman's arrival was like an unexpected blow.

When the rowboat with Milentyevna and her younger son, Ivan, with whom she lived, was approaching the village shore, I was laying down my net on the other side.

It was already fairly dark, fog covered the shore, and I could guess what was happening, using my ears more than my eyes.

The welcome was noisy.

First to run to the river, of course, was Zhuka, the neighbor's small dog with an unusually resonant bark, who always runs out after hearing the noise of a motor; then, a familiar iron ring clanged and echoed like a bell, that was Maxim, who slammed the gates after dashing out of his house; then, I heard Evgeniya's thin, tearful voice: "Oh, oh! Who have we here . . . !" Then, more and more voices, old Mara, old man Stepan, Prokhorov. In general, it seemed all of Pizhma was welcoming Milentyevna, and probably at that moment I alone cursed her arrival.

For a long time, for many years, I had wanted to find such a place, where everything would be available, hunting, fishing, mushrooms, and berries. And without fail it had to be deadly quiet, without those obnoxious street radios that are now popular in most villages and that blare from early morning to late night, without that iron clatter of cars, which had driven me insane in the city as well.

In Pizhma I had found all this and more.

A small village of seven houses, on a large river, surrounded by woods, isolated spruce groves with forest game, joyful pines, and mushrooms. All to enjoy, if one was not lazy.

I was not, it is true, lucky in regard to the weather; it was a rare day without rain. But I was not downcast. I found something else to pass the time: my landlord's house.

Oh, what a house it was! It had four different living quarters alone: the winter hut, the summer hut, the loft with a carved small balcony, and a side room. In addition, there was a sunny outer room with stairs to the porch, and a storage room, and an enclosed area under the overhang some fifteen meters long—they used to drive a pair of horses in there—and below it a yard with various flocks and animal sheds.

And so, when the owners were not home (and in the daytime they were always at work), I had no greater pleasure than to wander about this wondrous house. To wander barefoot, without hurrying. Lazily. To feel the past not only with heart and mind but with the very soles of my feet.

Now, with the arrival of the old woman, these excursions around the house were over and done with; I was sure of it. And my museum activities— so I called the process of gathering the old peasant utensils and vessels strewn about the house—had also come to an end. How could I drag out some dusty birch vessel and examine it closely under the nose of the house's old mistress? As for other habits and small pleasures to which I had become accustomed, such as falling in bed during the middle of the day and lighting up a cigarette, they were now totally out of the question. Forget it. Don't even think of it! The old woman's on the premises.

2

I sat for a long time in the rowboat drawn up to the shore.

The fog had already spread over the river like cloth, so that a small flame lit in the house on the other side seemed to be a muddy yellow spot; the stars had already fallen out in the sky (yes, everything suddenly, the fog and the stars), and I still sat and sat and worked myself up.

They called me. Maxim himself called me, Evgenyia called me, and I gritted my teeth and—not a word. For a while I entertained the idea of floating away for the night to Rusikha—a large village four kilometers away, three downriver—but I feared getting lost in the fog.

And so I sat in the boat, like a glum owl, and waited. Waited for the light to go out on the other side, in order to postpone meeting the old woman for a short period of time, till tomorrow, till morning.

I do not know how long I sat in the rowboat; perhaps two hours, perhaps three, and perhaps even four. In any case, according to my calculations, in that time one could have eaten a meal and drank more than once, and meanwhile they did not even think of dousing the flame on the other side, and the yellow spot continued to shine like a beacon in the fog.

I wanted to eat, after coming back from the forest and in a hurry to fish I had not had lunch; I began to shiver, from the damp, from the night cold; and finally—I was not going to sit there till I expired, after all—I picked up the oar.

The flame on the other side helped me beyond measure. Using it for orientation, without wandering in the fog, I rather easily crossed the river, then as easily went up the path, past the old bath shed and the garden, to the house.

The house, to my great surprise, was quiet, and but for the bright flame in the window one could have thought everyone was already asleep.

I stood around for a while listening under the windows and decided to go up to my quarters without going into the house.

But I had to go in, after all. For in opening the gate I made such a noise with the iron ring that the entire house shook from the clang.

"He's been found?" I heard a voice from the stove. "Thank God, then. And I've been lying here hoping nothing's happened."

"And what could happen?" Evgeniya said with irritation. It seemed she also was not asleep. "She put out that light for you," she said, indicating a lamp standing on the windowsill behind a broad iron bed. "So the lodger won't get lost in the fog. The lodger is a child, you see. As if he himself doesn't know what's what."

"Well, you know, anything can happen," the old woman answered again from the stove. "One time my husband spent all night rowing on the river and barely made it to the shore. It was the same kind of fog."

Evgeniya, groaning and grimacing, began to get up from bed to feed me, but I was hardly capable of eating then. In all likelihood, I was never so ashamed in my life, so ashamed of my thoughtless anger, and without daring to look up to the stove where the old woman slept, I walked out of the house.

3

In the morning, I usually got up early, as soon as the people downstairs began to move about.

But today, although the old wooden house clamored and trembled in each of its logs and beams, I forced myself not to get up until eight. At least today I would not wrong an old person, who, naturally, would want to rest after her journey.

How great was my surprise when, after coming down from my loft, I saw only Evgeniya in the house.

"So where are the guests?" I did not ask about Maxim, who, after his days off, would stay an entire week in the tar and log factory where he worked.

"The guests have come and gone," Evgenyia answered in a gay, rapid patter. "Ivan went home. I'm surprised you didn't hear the motor rattling; and Mother, she, of course, went to look for mushrooms."

"For mushrooms? Milentyevna went to pick mushrooms?"

"And why not?" Evgeniya glanced at the old clock, decorated with grass designs, hanging on the front wall next to a cherry dish cupboard. "She left before five. As soon as it grew light."

"Alone?"

"Did she go alone? Of course, alone. What do you think! How many years have I lived here? Eight, probably. Not a year has passed that she hasn't come to visit us at this time. She finds everything. Each and every type of mushroom, and berries. She's the joy of Nastya's life." At this point, Evgeniya in a feminine gesture glanced around quickly and began whispering. "Nastya only stays with Ivan because of her. I swear! She said it herself in the spring when she took Ivan to town to cure his drinking. She cried bitter tears. 'I wouldn't torture myself for one more day with him, that brute, if I weren't sorry for Mother.' Yes, that's Milentyevna for you," Evgeniya said not without pride, picking up a poker. "Maxim and I come to life when she visits."

And that was true. I never before saw Evgeniya so lively and quick on her feet. Usually in the mornings she stomped around the house in old worn slippers and cotton-quilted vest, moaning, groaning, and complaining about the aches in her legs and spine. Her life, as in general the life of all the village women whose youth coincided with the war years' hard labor, had not been an easy one. Carrying only a staff she walked her river from its source to the end thirteen times.

Now, I could not take my eyes off Evgeniya. It was as if some miracle had happened, as if she had been sprinkled with the waters of life. The iron poker did not move but danced in her hands. The stove's heat flickered on her dark youthful face, and her black round eyes, so dry and stern, now gently smiled.

I was also caught up by some unexplainable burst of exuberance. I quickly splashed water on my face, thrust my feet into rubber boots, and ran outside.

The fog was dreadful—only now I understood it wasn't curtains that were turning the windows white. The river and banks were immersed. Even the tops of the fir trees on the other side could not be seen.

I imagined elderly Milentyevna wandering now with a box somewhere beyond the river in this damp and cold fog, and I ran off to the shed to splinter wood in case the bathhouse would have to be warmed up for the chilled old woman.

4

I ran out to the river three times that morning, and Evgeniya probably just as many times, and we still did not notice when Milentyevna came back. She arrived suddenly, while Evgeniya and I were having breakfast. I do not know whether the porch gate was open, or whether Evgeniya and I were too engrossed in our conversation, only suddenly the door swung back and I saw her—tall, wet through, with her hem folded back in the peasant manner, holding two large birch boxes full of mushrooms.

Evgeniya and I jumped up from the table to take the boxes. Milentyevna herself, walking somewhat unsteadily, went to the bench next to the stove and sat down.

She was tired, of course, as was evident from her gaunt, delicate face, soaked to a pale tint by the ever-present fog, and from the noticeable trembling of her head. At the same time, what blessed contentment and quiet happiness were reflected in her blue, slightly closed eyes. The happiness of an old person who had labored well, to the fullest, and who again and again had proven to herself and to everyone that her life on this earth was still not useless. And here I remembered my late mother, whose eyes at times would shine and sparkle with the same contentment, when she, after working in the meadows or reaping fields to the point of exhaustion, would return home late at night.

Evgeniya, oohing, aahing, and droning, "What a grandmother we have! Here we're sitting, stuffing ourselves while she's done all that work," launched into vigorous action. Action appropriate for a model daughter-in-law. She brought in a light small tub from the side room, it had been steamed clean, prepared beforehand for salting the mushrooms, ran to the

storage room for salt, picked fresh fragrant currants in the garden, and when
Milentyevna, after resting for a short time, went to change in the other
room, began folding up the bright floor mats in the center of the house to
prepare a place for the salting.

"You think she's going to eat and drink now?" Evgeniya said, as if
explaining to me why her mother-in-law's breakfast was not her first priority.
"Not for anything in the world! She's of the old school. Don't even think of
food if the mushrooms aren't done yet."

We sat, crowded together leg to leg, right on the bare floor. Around us
flickered the sun's rays, the aroma of mushrooms mixed with the house's
warmth, and it was so gratifying, so agreeable, to watch old Milentyevna,
who had changed into a dry printed cotton dress, to see at work her dark,
veined hands, which she would intermittently immerse first in a box, then
the tub, then an enameled pot with salt. The old woman, of course, did the
salting herself.

The mushrooms were a select group. Without hurrying and with great
care I would take one from the box and each time, before beginning to
clean, would lift it to the light.

"So you haven't seen such gold before?" asked Evgeniya. Her question
had a hidden edge to it, clearly hinting at my rather meager contributions
from the forest. "See, you walk in the same forest and there's no good
mushrooms for you. Don't be surprised. She's been friends with that spruce
grove beyond the river from her wedding night. Those mushrooms almost
killed her."

I looked uncomprehending at Evgeniya: What specifically did she mean?

"Oh?" she said, extremely surprised. "Haven't you heard? How her
husband fired a rifle at her? Well, well, Mother, tell us how it all happened."

"What's there to tell," sighed Milentyevna. "What doesn't happen
between one's kin."

"Between kin . . . but this kin almost killed you!"

"If it's almost it doesn't count."

Evgeniya's dark dry eyes grew round with fury.

"I don't know, Mother, you . . . Now everything's upside down. Perhaps
you'll say now nothing happened? Perhaps, even, your head didn't start
trembling after that?"

With the back of her hand Evgeniya pushed back a strand of escaped hair
behind a small ear with a red berry earring and, apparently deciding that
nothing satisfactory could be elicited from her mother-in-law, began the
story herself.

"Milentyevna was shoved into marriage at sixteen. She probably didn't
even have breasts then. I didn't, swear to God, at that age. And then did

they worry what a young girl's life would be like? Her very own father got worked up about married life and a husband. There's only one young man in the house, you'll live like a princess. And what could you expect when the whole village was brim full of savages?"

"Well, perhaps not the entire village," Milentyevna objected.

"Don't defend them! Don't defend them! Anyone will tell you. Savages. Even I remember. They'd show up on holidays in our village—a horde, a real horde. All together—married, unmarried. With beards, without. They'd stroll around, yelling, bothering everyone on the street, spoiling the air—firing shots all over the place. And at home, behind closed doors, it was even worse. Each one had some kind of crazy fixation, some tomfoolery. One would run around in a woman's *sarafan*, another—Martynko-Chizhik it was—would always go for water to the river on skis. In summer, in the heat, he also would put on a fur coat, inside out. And Isaak Petrovich, that one imagined himself to be an archpriest. I heard tell he would wait till night, light a candle in the front of the house, put on some blue decorated material—a woman's *sarafan*—and he'd walk from house to house singing psalms. Isn't that so, mother? I'm not making it up?"

"No one's without sin," Milentyevna answered, sidestepping.

"Without sin! What kind of sins could you have had at sixteen to be shot at with a rifle? No, it was just in their blood. Living forever in the forest and far from people, like it or not, you're going to run wild and go crazy. And they threw a girl of sixteen into that sort of animal lair. Live or die—it's up to you.

"Well, Mother here decided that the very first thing was to win over her mother-in-law and father-in-law. To be nice to them. And how did one win over old people in those days? Work.

"And so while newlyweds pass the time being loving and tender the first night, Vasilisa Milentyevna got up before dawn and went off across the river after mushrooms. You picked yours in autumn, didn't you, mother?"

"Probably autumn," Milentyevna answered, not very willingly.

"Not probably, but that's when it was," Evgeniya said with conviction. "There's hardly any mushrooms in the forest during summer, and you picked an entire boxful in an hour or two. You couldn't roam around the forest, could you, when your husband was waiting?

"And so our Milentyevna returns from the woods. Happy. Not one puff of smoke could be seen above the entire village, everyone is still asleep and she already has mushrooms. So, she thinks, they'll praise me. And they really praised her. She just crossed the river and took a step or two out of the boat—and bang, a shot in the face. The stern husband greeting his young wife . . ."

The veins on old Milentyevna's thin, wrinkled neck grew taunt like ropes, her bent back straightened out—she wanted to stop the trembling, which had noticeably worsened. But Evgeniya saw nothing of this. She herself, no less than her mother-in-law, suffered the events of that distant morning, known to her from the stories of others, and the blood intermittently flooded in waves to and from her dusky face.

"God, God saved Mother from death. Is it far or not from the garden to the bathhouse? And Mother came up straight to the bathhouse when he raised the gun to her, and probably his hand trembled after drinking the night before, or he would have killed her right there. There's shotgun pellets still in the bathhouse door. Have you seen them?" Evgeniya turned to me. "Have a look, have a look. Where do you think my husband, when he first brought me here, where do you think he took me before anything else? To show off his dwelling? To brag of the wealth he accumulated? No, to the dark bathhouse. 'That's how my father,' he says, 'educated my mother.' That's the kind of forest demon he is. And they're all, all like that here. Each and every one has a place in jail specially reserved for him."

I saw Milentyevna's growing distress over our conversation; our brusque insistence was disagreeable to her. On the other hand, how could one resist this totally engrossing and unusual narrative? And I asked:

"But what was the reason for all that?"

"The shooting?" Evgeniya liked to call everything by its proper name. "That was because of Bald Vanyka. You see, he, the wood demon, God forgive me it's not right to talk about one's father-in-law like that, woke up in the morning and started looking. Where did you sleep, Mother? In the room off the porch? He feels with his hand, here, there—no one. Runs outside. And there she is, the young wife. Coming from beyond the river. And he went crazy. Aha, he thinks, so that's how it is, went to Bald Vanyka? For a date?"

Milentyevna had apparently managed to bring herself under control by then and asked, not without a hint of the sardonic:

"And you also happen to know what your father-in-law was thinking?"

"Why shouldn't I know? No need to make up something everyone knew. Bald Ivan would get drunk and say, 'Boys and girls, I'm a citizen of two villages: my body is home and my soul is in Pizhma.' He would talk like that till the day he died. He was a handsome man.

"No two ways about it. Mother had a flock of suitors. They wanted her for her beauty. Look, even now, one could marry her off." Evgeniya flattered her mother-in-law and smiled, I think, for the first time during her narrative.

Then, simpering somehow, squinting and shifting one joyless black eye, she said playfully:

"And you, Mother, don't have anything to be proud of either. No matter how young, you still should have understood why they marry you. Whatever, but not, I think, to go looking for mushrooms the first night . . . "

Oh, how Milentyevna's quiet blue eyes flashed out then! As if a thunderstorm had passed outside the window, as if a red-hot cannonball had exploded there.

Evgeniya immediately became flustered, she looked down, and I too did not know where to look. For some time everyone sat silent, taking particular care to clean debris off the mushrooms.

Milentyevna was the first to give voice to reconciliation. She said:

"Today I was already remembering my life. While I was walking in the forest, my mind all the time was taking the road back. I'm on my seventh decade now . . . "

"The seventh since you left for married life in Pizhma?" I wanted to clarify.

"Yes, although I didn't leave but was shoved out," Milentyevna said with a slight smile. "She told the truth: I had no adolescence. And according to the way people think now, I didn't love my husband . . . "

"So there," exclaimed Evgeniya, not without a triumphant note of gloating. "She's admitted it! And each time I open my mouth everything I say is wrong."

"Well, if you saw at a live spot, even an old tree creaks," in an even more conciliatory spirit said Milentyevna.

The mushrooms were running out.

Evgeniya, placing the empty box on her knees, began picking in the debris left from the mushrooms, finding berries, wet bilberries that were overripe and large red ones that were just right. She was still affronted, although from time to time she cast curious glances at her mother-in-law, who again began speaking of the past.

"Old people like to praise old times," said Milentyevna in a soft, deliberate voice, "but I don't. Now people are educated, they can stand up for themselves, while we didn't know freedom from childhood. I was married off—now you can't even say it without laughing—thanks to a fur coat and a shawl."

"Really?" Evgeniya exclaimed in extreme agitation. "And no one ever told me that."

There was nothing left of her former anger. The peasant woman's greedy curiosity, deeply ingrained in her personality, triumphed over all other emotions, and her eager gaze fixed on her mother-in-law.

"So," said Milentyevna, "our father was building, putting up a large house, every kopek was needed, and here I was growing up. It would dishonor him for a daughter to go out merrymaking without a new fur coat and shawl, so he could not resist when marriage brokers came from Pizhma and said, 'We'll take her without a coat or shawl . . . ' "

"And where were your brothers?" Evgeniya could not resist and once again interrupted. "Mother had good brothers. They loved her so much. Would treat her as careful as a lit candle. She was already married, and they themselves had a full house of children and still helped their sister."

"My brothers," said Milentyevna, "were in the forest then. Chopping trees for timber."

Evgeniya briskly nodded her head.

"Well, then it's clear enough. I couldn't figure it out, why such brothers, first among the villagers—Mother came from a well-off family—didn't intercede for their beloved sister. And that's what it was—they weren't home when you were being married off."

After this sally, Evgeniya, having discovered more and more details she did not know earlier, again took over the conversation. The end result was that Milentyevna's soft voice soon fell totally silent.

Evgeniya suffered the ancient drama of her mother-in-law with her entire being.

"A calamity, what else could it be!" She waved her hands about. "Her brothers found out about it, their sister's husband had shot her, and they came galloping on horses. With rifles. 'One word, Sister, and his soul belongs to God.' They were tough. Strong—they could bend a bear in half, not to mention people. And then Mother told them: 'Aren't you ashamed, my dear brothers, to make such a fuss for no reason, to upset good people. Our young husband was trying his rifle, for hunting, and you imagined God knows what . . . '

"That's how wise and smart she was! And at sixteen!" Evgeniya looked with pride at her stooped mother-in-law. "No, if Maxim raised his hand to me I couldn't control myself. I would take him to court and put him away where he belongs. And she shakes her head and tells her brothers off. 'Why are you interfering? Do you have a head on your shoulders? Once I've put on a married woman's kerchief, it's too late to turn back. I have to learn to live here as best as I can.' That's the twist she gave the whole matter."

Evgeniya suddenly sobbed. She was, after all, basically a kind person.

"Well after that her father-in-law only stopped short of kissing her feet. Think about it. It could have ended in a flat-out killing. The brothers were angry like anything—they could have done away with Miron without a second thought. I was small then, and I don't remember Onika Ivanovich well, but the old people remember even now. Wherever he came from, whatever trip he returned from, he always would have a gift for his daughter-in-law. And when he'd get caught up in some drinking party and his friends would try to persuade him to stay over, he'd say: 'No, fellows, I won't stay. I'm off for home. I miss my Vasilisa the Beautiful.' Whenever he drank he would call her Vasilisa the Beautiful."

"So he did," said Milentyevna with a sigh, and it seemed to me her old, perceptive eyes grew moist.

Apparently Evgeniya noticed also. She said:

"There is, there is something good to remember Onika Ivanovich by. He may have been the only real human being in the whole village. For they're all Urvays here—in Pizhma everyone has the surname of Urvaev.[1] And Miron Onikovich, my father-in-law, was also an Urvay. And how. You know how someone else in his place would have behaved after what happened? Quiet like a mouse. While he was so contrary—always finding fault in everything."

Milentyevna raised her head. She seemed to want to defend her husband, but Evgeniya had worked herself up again and did not give her a chance to open her mouth.

"No, no, there's no reason to pretty him up. Everyone knows what he was like. If he was so great, why didn't he let you out of Pizhma for ten years? Mother hadn't been anywhere—not to visit her parents, or to any holiday celebration. She would spin yarn at nights alone rather than with the girls. That's what devilish jealousy it was.

"What's there to say"—Evgeniya waved her hand—"he found fault with everything. Tell me, please, is the wife to blame if all the children look like her, and not the father, and he found fault even with that. 'Whose little doves are scattered about the table?' he would demand of Mother when drunk. And what right did he have to ask? He himself was dark and ugly, looked like a piece of rotting wood, his face covered with scars from smallpox, as if sheep had marked him up with hoofs. He should have been glad, he should have thanked God every night, the children didn't look like him . . ."

I do not know whether Milentyevna disliked the manner in which her daughter-in-law treated her past, or if she, as a peasant woman of the old school, was unaccustomed to sitting around idle for a long time, but she abruptly got to her feet, and our conversation broke off.

5

Maxim's house is the only one in Pizhma that stands with its front facing the river's current; all the others stand with their backs to the water.

Evgeniya, who was not particularly indulgent when it came to Pizhma inhabitants, explained matters simply:

"Urvays! They stuck out their filthy behinds to spite people."

But there was a different reason for building that way, of course—it was that Pizhma is located on the south side of the river, and how could one turn away from the sun, rare as it is in these forest areas?

I loved this small, quiet village . . . I was especially enchanted by the Pizhma houses—big log homes with wooden horses on the roofs.

Incidentally, a house decorated with a small horse is not rare in the North. But I had never seen a village in which each home had one. And in Pizhma each one did. If you walked on the sill of a narrow grass path, which had been the village road when there were more inhabitants, seven wooden horses would look at you from the skies.

"Before, we had more of them. You could count a wooden herd of twenty," noted Milentyevna walking next to me.

The old woman had surprised me again and again in the past twenty-four hours.

After breakfast I thought, old as she was, she would first think of rest, some peace and quiet. And she got up from the table, crossed herself, brought a birch box from the side room, and began tying straps out of an old linen towel to it.

"Where are you off to, grandmother? Not the forest again?" I showed my curiosity.

"No, not the forest. I have a notion to see my oldest daughter in Rusikha," Milentyevna said, expressing herself in the old-fashioned way.

"And what's the box for?"

"The box is because I'll go to the forest tomorrow morning, if everything's all right. When the women go to milk cows they'll give me a ride. Only, you see, I can't lose any time. They only let me go for a little while this time, for a week."

Evgeniya, who was getting ready for work and had not interfered in our conversation up till then, could not resist at this point.

"Tell us about it, how they only let you go for a while. That's how it is every time. She can't rest, can't sit without doing something. If it was up to me I'd lie down for the whole day. Do you think people are born only to work like they're possessed from morning till night?"

I offered my services to accompany Milentyevna to the embarkment; if the ferryman was drunk again the old woman would need someone to help her.

But Milentyevna found helpers in addition to me. As we approached the stable, an old half-wrecked shed in the field on the edge of the village, Prokhor Urvaev came charging out, roguishly whistling and giddyapping. He was driving a clattering, unoiled cart harnessed to Thunder, the only live horse in Pizhma.

At one time, it could be assumed, this Thunder was everything a steed should be; now, due to old age, he looked like a walking skeleton enclosed in an excess of putrid hide, and if anyone could still make this skeleton shake his old bones to life it was Prokhor—one of the three men left in Pizhma.

Prokhor, as usual, was tipsy—he gave off a strong aroma of cheap cologne.

"Aunt, Aunt," he shouted driving up. "I remembered you. I've been on duty with Thunder waiting since morning because I knew you'd have to go to the embarkment. Ain't that right, Aunt, Prokhor made no mistake?"

Milentyevna did not refuse her nephew's services, and the cart, with her and Prokhor aboard, was soon on its way rolling along a green harvested meadow toward the distant, yellow sand beach and the embarkment.

I returned home.

Evgeniya had already gone. She was in the field helping the women harvest peas, and now I too should have occupied myself—I had an unattended net out beyond the river, and a walk in the forest would have been all to the good; it was uncertain when we would have another such agreeable day.

Instead, I entered the empty house, stood undecided next to the threshold, and went into the enclosed area under the overhang.

Maxim had introduced me to this part of the house the very first day (initially I had intended to sleep in the straw shed), and I remember actually exclaiming out loud when I saw what was there. It was an entire peasant museum!

A horned pitchfork, a *krosna*—a home weaving loom, a spindle, a decorated spinning wheel from Mezeni, a skutching device, all kinds of boxes and baskets, twined out of thin pieces of oak, birch bark, and roots, birch bread containers, bask vessels, unpainted wooden cups, taken to distant harvests in earlier times, a candle holder, salt shakers in the form of ducks, and many, many more, different types of vessels, appliances, and work implements, all heaped into one pile, like unneeded debris.

"All this junk should be thrown out," said Maxim, as if justifying himself to me, "it's good for nothing now. But somehow I can't bring myself to do it. My parents used them to feed themselves . . ."

From then on, a day seldom passed when I did not look into this part of the house. And not because these obsolete relics were unknown to me—I myself had come out of this wood and birch bark kingdom. New to me was the beauty of the whittled wood and bark. That was what I had not noticed previously.

My mother had not put down the birch tumbler during her entire life, the very same tumbler used for preparing flax, but had I ever noticed it was itself the color of flax, the same gentle, idle-lusterless color with a silver sheen? And the bread box of birch bark. How could I forget its golden glow? It appeared on our table each time like the long-awaited sun. And I only remembered what was in it and when.

And so everything I picked up, everything I saw—the old rusted sickle with a handle polished to a fine gloss, the soft cup that appeared to be copper but was whittled out of solid birch—all opened up a special world of beauty to me. Beauty, in the Russian manner, that was not striking, even diffident, created with axe and knife.

But today, after I had made the acquaintance of the old mistress of this house, I discovered one other thing for myself.

Today, I suddenly came to understand that not only the axe and the knife stood at the origins of this beauty. The main polish and sharpening of all these tumblers, sickles, pestles, and wooden plows (yes, there was an old, antedeluvian Andreevna model standing bowlegged in a dark corner) took place in the field and meadow. Peasant calluses had buffed and polished them.

6

The following day it began to rain in the morning, and I again stayed home.

Like the day before, Evgeniya and I, thinking Milentyevna would come back any minute, did not sit down to the table for a long time.

"She shouldn't wander far off today," said Evgeniya. "She's not a small child."

But the time passed, the rain did not stop, and on the other shore—I did not leave the window—still no one appeared . . .

"I don't know, I don't know what to think," Evgeniya said, shaking her head despondently. "She must have gone to Bogatka, no less. What a stubborn old woman! It's useless to tell her anything. How can a person her age go tramping about the forest in this rain."

Covering her face with her tanned hands pressed together at the fingertips, she looked at the river and said with even more conviction:

"She's skipped off, skipped. No two ways about it. Last year it was the same: we're waiting, waiting, eyes red from watching, and she went off to her Bogatka."

I knew of Bogatka—a grazing area two or three miles from Pizhma upriver—but I had never heard it to be rich in mushrooms and berries, and I asked Evgeniya to explain.

As was her habit when matters seemed perfectly clear to her, her dark eyes grew round.

"What for! What mushrooms in Bogatka? Maybe now there are; everything's overgrown by forest, but before it was all sown meadows there. Onika Ivanovich, Mother's father-in-law, alone brought in up to a hundred wagons of hay. And so she walks there every year—Bogatka was her doing. She was the instigator of the whole thing. Before Mother came to Pizhma no one even knew the name. Livestock and more livestock—that's all there was in these parts."

Evgeniya tossed her head at the village.

"You saw the wooden horses on the roofs? How many are there? You won't find so many anywhere in all of Russia. And tell me, how often were gates painted? Only the rich peasants, some bigwig in the village would do it, while here in Pizhma they're all painted. Walking on the other side of the river one could get scared to death, at times, when the sun was setting. It would look like all of Pizhma was on fire. And, see, that all came out of Bogatka, Milentyevna found them a gold mine there."

I still did not understand what gold mine Evgeniya had in mind. What was truth and what was fiction in her story?

A dense smoke coming out of the side room forced us to move to the small window. We sat down on a bench, under a small perch holding dry birch switches of the modern type.

After coughing from the smoke, Evgeniya obtained some relief by roundly cursing her husband—what a great job he did of arranging the bricks!—then for good measure passed on to the other village inhabitants.

"They're all Urvays here! I praised Onika Ivanovich yesterday to humor Mother, but to tell you the truth he was one, too. For sure. Even when he got on in years he used to make his old woman put on the best things at night. People usually like to dress up when going out or on holidays, but he insisted she dress in silk at night. That's the kind of man he was. And is that what a gray-haired peasant should be thinking about when the whole house, wherever you look, is full of cracks and holes? Mother, it was Mother who made them into human beings," Evgeniya said with conviction. "All the Urvays prospered thanks to her."

"How so?"

"How she made human beings out of them? Oh, thanks to Bogatka. Thanks to clearing the forest. The North from centuries past has depended on clearing. Whatever fields one cleared and dug up, that's how much bread and cattle one had. And Milenty Egorovich, her father, was the best at clearing in Rusikha. Four grown sons—you know how much muscle that was!

"In Pizhma, on the other hand, everything was upside down. Their main thing was hunting and fish, no worrying about the soil. Whatever was dug up, cleared by their grandfathers, that's what they lived off. Sometimes they didn't even have enough bread to last till the new year. When animals were plenty in the forest, true enough, then they had a great time. But when the woods were empty, then they went hungry as owls.

"And so, Mother lived like that, suffered it for a while, and decided it wasn't right. The soil had to be worked. Her father-in-law already had a soft spot in his heart for her. From that first honeymoon night. So she started working on him: Father, we have to use our heads, Father, let's live off the soil . . .

"All right. Whether he agreed with his daughter-in-law or not, most important he didn't stand in her way. Mother called her brothers: This is how it is, my dear brothers, help your sister. Everyone knows they would do anything for her. They picked the right plot, cleared the forest—some of it they chopped down, some they burned off—and sowed wheat that same autumn.

"And that's when the Urvays began scratching their heads. To their grief the wheat sprang up—almost as tall as the fir trees. You know how it grows after a fire is set. So hunting was over, goodbye to fishing. They picked up their axes.

"And how they worked! I myself don't remember, I was too small, but mother told us she saw them working in that Bogatka. I'm walking through the forest, she said, looking for a cow, she said, and suddenly there's a fire, and such a huge fire, she said, that it reached the sky. And men are galloping naked around this fire. I couldn't move at first, said Mother, couldn't take a step; they're wood demons, I thought, no one but. And they were Urvays. In clearing the forest they took off their shirts so as not to get hot. They also wanted to save the cloth; those were different times than now.

"And how they tortured the children! Now and then, my Maxim starts remembering it all, and I can't believe my ears. How can someone tie up a child with a rope like a dog? And they tied them up. They'd pour some milk into a cup, put it on the floor, and the child could crawl around tied to the rope all day, while mama and papa were at work. They were afraid, you see, the children would start a fire in the house.

"That's how crazy the Urvays were," Egeniya emphasized once again. "And what could you expect? They hadn't worked for years, all they did was shoot at birds, so you can imagine how much energy they had built up.

"Oh, Mother, Mother. She wanted what was best, and instead brought misfortune. They were dekulaked, when the kolkhozes started up . . ."

I did not ooh and aah at these words. Who today is surprised by the old, old story of chips that fly when a forest is chopped down!

Evgeniya, however, did not like my lack of response. She interpreted it as indifference and said, with a voice full of indignation:

"There's no respect for the past nowadays. Everything's been forgotten—how the kolkhozes were begun, how people starved during the war. I don't blame the young people; the young, clear enough, want to live a little, they don't have time for looking back, but now even the old women are different somehow. Look at them in Rusikha when they go get their pensions, one fatter and healthier than the next. Their own children, those who lost their lives in the war, are long gone, and all they think of is how to live a bit longer and to hope there's no war. And that their fields and meadows are overgrown with forest they don't care at all. They're well fed. The pension's regular like clockwork.

"I asked old Mara once how she could take it? Didn't it bother her? Before, I said, you saw the fields from your window and now there's only bushes. She laughs: 'That's good, girl, the firewood is closer at hand.' Can you imagine an old person thinking like that? She's an Urvay in skirts, a pure Urvay. My Maxim is of the same sort. He'd be laughing and joking in the middle of a flood."

Evgeniya fell silent for a moment, then sighed deeply.

"No, I'm some kind of mutant by the likes of today. All I do is worry and irritate myself. I'm all nerves. But my mother-in-law really breaks my heart. Look what happened! You work your fingers to the bone, and you're the one to blame. That's how it was. 'If it was only me,' says Mother, 'that's nothing, that I could bear. But what about putting the curse on other people.'"

"What people?"

Evgeniya quickly turned to me. Her dark unblinking eyes again flared up.

"Five families were destroyed. During the Civil War they already got a barnful of grain out of each one of them, and by the time of the kolkhozes they really went to town. And to top it off, here are the Urvays being their usual selves. It all came together. Had they kept quiet and laid low maybe they wouldn't have been touched—who knows what started it. They came to sign them up for the kolkhoz and their answer was, 'We'd rather not. We already have a kolkhoz as it is.' So the authorities threw a fit, took a dislike to them. Four of the men were brought back, it's true, and my father-in-law, Mother's husband Miron Onikovich, came back, although he was sick by then, but as for Onika Ivanovich, he himself never returned.

"What a calamity, what a calamity it was! When Mother told us about it I wished she hadn't. I couldn't help crying."

Evgeniya noisily blew her nose and wiped her eyes with her handkerchief.

"Just think how things sometimes turn out in life. Mother was pounding rye in the field where they prepared the grain when lightning struck them. Yes, in the field." She nodded, after thinking for a moment. "She was happy. God again has given us bread, she was thinking. It was good, big rye, maybe she hadn't seen any like it all her life. And suddenly a girl runs up: 'Mother, run home quick. They're taking Father and Grandfather.'

"And I myself knew, Mother said, that I had to run. There was no fooling around then, one-two and it was good-bye forever, but, she says, my legs gave out. I couldn't move. So, she says, I crawled to the gate on my knees. It was frightening. It was her fault, you see, they had to settle accounts. If she hadn't talked her father-in-law into clearing the forest, who would have bothered with the Urvaevs, poor as they always were?

"Her father-in-law did her in, not by scaring her but with kindness. She was ready for anything, ready for all sorts of abuse—you know what people are capable of at such moments—and she suddenly sees her father-in-law get on his knees. And in front of all the good people he says: 'Thank you, Vasilisa Milentyeva, that you made us into decent human beings. And don't think,' he says, 'that there is a grudge in our hearts against you. Till our last breath we will bless the day you came into our lives.' "

Evgeniya broke out crying and finished her story choked by tears.

"And Mother never did say goodbye to Onika Ivanovich. She fell in a dead faint."

7

Milentyevna returned from the forest after three in the afternoon; she was totally exhausted. But she came back with mushrooms. With a heavy birch box that creaked as she walked . . .

8

The mushrooms this time were unexceptional red *russulas*, old flat ones, gray *konki*, and, most important, they were unprepossessing in appearance. The birch box was full of some kind of wet hodgepodge, half of which was debris.

Based on this evidence, perceptive Evgeniya came to a rather cheerless conclusion.

"What a calamity," she said. "Our Milentyevna's sick. I've never seen her bring home mushrooms like these."

She sighed meaningfully.

"There you are, there you are. Mother, too, is showing her age, and before I thought she was made of steel. Nothing could keep her down. Oh, considering her life what's strange is not that she can't keep up sometimes but how she's managed to survive till now. Her husband—something happened to his head—tried to shoot himself three times. How's one to live through that? She buried her husband and—bam, the war. Two sons were killed outright, the third, my man, disappeared for God knows how many years without a word, and then Sanyushka put a noose on Mother's neck . . . Look how much suffering she's accumulated for her old age. It'd be too much for ten people, and it's all on one pair of shoulders."

"Sanyushka's her daughter?"

"Her daughter. Don't you know?" Evgeniya put aside the kitchen knife with which she had been cleaning the mushrooms. "Mother had twelve children, and only six are left alive. Marfa is the oldest daughter, the one who was married off to Rusikha, then came Vasily and Egor—both disappeared in the war—then my husband, then Sanya, and then that drunk, Ivan.

"Milentyevna saw her sons off to war, and in a year it was Sanya's turn. They took her east to move logs. Just like being drafted . . . Oh, she was a beauty! I don't think I've seen anyone like her all my life. Tall, white-white skin, a braid down her entire back to the knee. Everyone said she took after her mother, and maybe she was even more beautiful. And quiet, like still water. Not like our kind, the no-good scoundrels. And being quiet is what did her in. She met up with some low-life, and he got her pregnant.

"I'm not at all surprised it turned out that way, not at all. Someone who spent all his life at home with parents and never saw anything can act surprised, while I left home for the forest at thirteen—and I saw everything there was to see.

"Sometimes you'd come back to the barracks at night from the woods, barely moving your feet. While they, the devils, wouldn't be tired at all from their work pushing pencils all day, and they'd goggle at you. You couldn't take off your shoes or try to change—before you'd know it they'd drag you into some corner . . . .

"And so, perhaps, Mother's Sanya met up with a devil like that. How could she resist him? If she had had some bite to her she could have sent him where he belonged, but as it was she didn't even know what to say. I remember she came to us in Rusikha before the war on a holiday—blushing she was. The women couldn't take their eyes off her, she was like some angel, and the fellows in awe followed her around like a mob. And on top of it, perhaps, Mother warned her when she was getting ready to go: You can lose whatever you want, Daughter, only bring home your maidenly honor. That's how they were told then, in good families.

"I don't know, I don't know how it all happened. Don't ask Mother about it, she'll become your worst enemy."

Evgeniya listened, then began speaking in an impassioned whisper.

"She wanted to hide it from people. They say she didn't let anyone come close to her dead daughter. Mother took her out of the noose herself, washed the body herself, and put her in the grave herself. But how could you hide a big belly from everyone? The same girls who were with her back East said it all. Sanya, they said, started swelling up right before our eyes, and Efimko, the driver, also noticed. 'Sanya, it seems you're in that way,' he said. And how could Sanya be that way when she was off to the Last Judgment. Well now, Daughter, look your own mother in the eye and tell her how you played loose with your honor among strangers.

"And so she, misery itself, came home and didn't dare take a step past the porch. She sat down on the stoop and stayed there like that all night. And when it started to get light, she ran off to the fields. She couldn't look at the day without shame, not to mention her mother."

Evgeniya again stopped to listen and alertly raised her curved black eyebrows.

"Probably sleeping. Maybe she'll sleep it off yet. I asked her," she said whispering again just in case, "didn't you suspect anything, as a mother? 'I did,' she said. 'That night I went out to the side room three times and asked who was on the porch. And when it got light I felt a sudden pain in my heart. Like with a knife.' She told me that openly. And she told me how she found the boots on the porch.

"Think what sort of girl she was. I'm dying, destroying my young life, but I remember my mother. You know yourself how it was with shoes in the war. We would be barefoot sometimes at the log embarkment, while ice hurled down the river. And here's Sanyushka saying goodbye to life, but she doesn't forget her mother, her mother's her final worry. She goes barefoot to her death. And those were the steps Mother followed running to the threshing field. It was already late in the year, the next day was Protection of the Holy Mother—every small toe could be seen in the snow.[2]

"She ran, and when she got there what could she do? Sanyushka was already cold, hanging on a woven belt, and over on the side there was her jacket neatly folded and a warm kerchief on top: Please wear it, my dear, remember me, my sad life . . ."

The rain outside did not stop. The old iridescent windows in their frames sobbed as if alive, and it seemed to me that there, beyond the windows, someone was quietly crying and making a rasping sound.

Evgeniya, as if reading my mind, said:

"I'm really scared of living in this house. No more sleeping alone for me. I'm not Mother. In the winter, when the moaning begins in all the stoves and pipes and the ring on the porch begins to clang, you can go crazy. At first I tried to convince Maxim to live at home. What's so different in other parts? And now, perhaps, I too have had enough. In the winter there isn't even a road to reach people. We have to go to Rusikha on skis."

9

Milentyevna stayed in bed for two days, and Evgeniya and I began to think seriously of calling for a medic. We also decided to notify her children of her illness.

Fortunately, however, nothing of the sort was necessary. On the third day, Milentyevna herself got up from the stove. And she not only got up but managed to walk to the table without our help.

"How are you, grandmother? Better?

"I don't really know. Maybe I'm not completely better, but I have to go home today."

"Home? Today?"

"Today," Milentyevna answered calmly. "My son Ivan's due to come for me today."

Evgeniya was no less taken aback by the news than I.

"Why should Ivan come in such a rain? Look what's going on outside. You're not thinking clearly, Mother. You haven't even picked enough mushrooms yet."

"The mushrooms can wait, while it's a school day tomorrow. Ekaterina goes to school."

"So it's because of Ekaterina you're going?"

"I have to. I gave my word."

"To whom? To whom did you give your word?" Evgeniya even choked from astonishment. "Mother, sometimes, you really say things. She gave Ekaterina her word! All of Ekaterina is no larger than your big thumb. A little snot-nosed thing. She was here in the spring. She'd hide somewhere in a corner and you could never find her."

"No matter what she's like, I have to go if I promised." Milentyevna turned toward me. "My granddaughter is a nervous child, and she's unlucky with her eyes, she squints. And on top of it, the woman next door decided to scare the girl: 'Why are you letting your grandmother out of the house,' she says. 'Can't you see how old she is? She might even die on the way.' My poor little one burst into tears. She wouldn't let go of her grandmother all night."

Milentyevna stayed all day in front of the window waiting for her son to arrive at any moment. She had on her boots and a warm wool scarf and held her small bundle under her arm, to make sure there would be no delay because of her. But Ivan did not come.

And then toward evening, when the old clock struck five, Milentyevna suddenly announced to us that since her son had not come she would go herself.

Evgeniya and I exchanged horrified glances. Outside there was rain, the windows in their frames were swollen with water, she herself was completely sick, and cars that could give her a ride on the main road beyond the river were rare. It was suicide, sure death . . . That's what her decision meant.

Evgeniya tried to dissuade her mother-in-law as best as she could. She tried to frighten her, she cried, she begged. I too, of course, did not remain silent.

Nothing helped. Milentyevna was firm. She did not raise her voice, did not argue with us, but silently, shaking her head, threw her coat on, tied up her small bundle with her things again, looked around her home, saying goodbye to it . . .

And at that moment, for the first time, perhaps, I came to understand how the young Milentyevna conquered the Pizhma bestiary. No, not only with her gentleness and endless patience, but also with determination, and her flint-hard character.

I alone accompanied the sick old woman across the river. Evgeniya became so upset she could not even go out on the porch.

The rain did not stop. The river had noticeably swelled up in the last few days, and we were carried two hundred meters or so beyond the log usually used for landing boats.

The worst, however, awaited us in the woods, when we came out onto the forest path. One splished and splashed on this path even in dry weather, and can you imagine the conditions after three days of solid rain?

So I walked ahead, pushed through the stirring swamp with my walking stick, grabbed at wet bushes, and each moment expected it to happen, expected the old woman to go down . . .

But, thank God, all ended well. Milentyevna, leaning on her reliable friend, a light aspen staff, walked out on the road. And she not only walked out but got into a truck.

Of course, we were fantastically lucky in regard to that truck. It was some kind of a miracle, no less, no more. For just as we approached the road, the sound of a motor suddenly rang out.

In a frenzy, shouting ferociously as if attacking someone, I threw myself forward. The truck stopped . . .

Unfortunately, there was no place in the cab next to the driver. His wife was sitting inside holding a newborn baby in her arms. But Milentyevna did not take a second to think whether to go or not in an open lorry.

The back of the truck was huge, with tall welded sides, and she dove into it as if into a well. For a long time, under the dark overhang of the pines closely pressing onto the road from both sides, I saw a swaying white spot.

That was Milentyevna in the truck, bouncing back and forth over the pits, bumps, and ruts and waving her kerchief to me in parting.

10

After Milentyevna's departure I did not remain in Pizhma even three days more because everything suddenly became tiresome, everything now seemed to be some kind of a game, and not real life: my aimless hunting in the forest, my fishing, and even my sacred rituals with the peasant past.

I was irresistibly drawn to the large and noisy world. I wanted to work, to do some good for others. To do what was and will be done to her last hour by Vasilisa Milentyevna, that old peasant woman, obscure yet magnificent in her deeds, from the remote depths of the Northern forest.

I left Pizhma on a warm sunny day. Steam rose from the drying log buildings. And steam rose from old Thunder, standing unmoving like a log next to a wagon at the stable.

I called to him in passing.

Thunder stretched out his neck in my direction but did not give voice to anything.

And equally silent, hanging their heads from the plank roofs, the wooden horses saw me off. An entire herd of wooden horses, fed by Vasilisa Milentyevna.

And I suddenly wished, to the point of tears, to the point of a painful shudder in my heart, to hear their neighing. At least once, at least in a dream if not in reality. That youthful resonant neighing with which they had filled these forest domains in the past.

1969

Translation by Nicholas Rzhevsky

Notes to the translation are on page 580.

RESOURCES

Primary Text

Abramov, Fedor. "Dereviannye koni." *Trava-Murava. Povesti i rasskazy.* Moscow: Sovremennik, 1982, pp. 4–30.

Secondary Sources

Literary and Cultural Studies

Brown, Deming. *Soviet Russian Literature since Stalin.* Cambridge: Cambridge University Press, 1978.
Lahusen, Thomas, ed., with Gene Kuperman. *Late Soviet Culture: From Perestroika to Novostroika.* Durham: Duke University Press, 1993.
Parthé, Kathleen. *Russian Village Prose: The Radiant Past.* Princeton: Princeton University Press, 1992.
Vishevsky, Anatoly. *Soviet Literary Culture in the 1970s.* Gainesville: University of Florida Press, 1993.

Drama and Theater

Dereviannye koni. Adapted by F. Abramov and Iu. Liubimov. Director, Iu. Liubimov. Scene design, David Borovskii. Music, N. Sidel'nikov. Premiere, 1974. In *Russian Literary Theatre: Ten Plays at the Taganka Theatre.* NJR Video, 1984. Video recording of the Taganka production of *Wooden Horses.*

Film

Proshchanie (The Farewell). Directors, L. Shepitko and E. Klimov. Based on the novel by V. Rasputin. Distributed by RAES, 1983.
Kalina krasnaia (The Red Snowball Tree). Director, Vasilii Shukshin. Mosfilm, 1974.

1. "The Tale of Igor," pages 11–20

1. Boyan: in all likelihood a bard who lived in the latter half of the eleventh century.

2. Yaroslav ("the Wise"): prince of Kiev (1019–1054); Mstislav the Brave (d. 1036): prince of Tmutorokan, brother of Yaroslav; Rededia: prince of the Kasogs, ancestors of the Circassians; Roman the Handsome: prince of Tmutorokan, son of Sviatoslav, slain in 1079 by the Polovtsians, Turkic-speaking nomads (modern Kumans), who merged into the Mongol Golden Horde in the thirteenth century.

3. Most likely Vladimir I, later Saint Vladimir (956–1015): grand prince of Kiev, who made Christianity Russia's official religion in 988; Igor, the hero of the tale, died in 1202.

4. Troyan: most likely pagan deity, or Trajan, Roman emporor (98–117).

5. Grandson: "heir," or "descendant" of Veles, Russian pagan god of cattle.

6. Bui Tur, "wild bison, ox," further "Yar Tur," fierce bison." Vsevolod, Igor's brother, died in 1196.

7. Div: pagan god in form of a bird; Surozh: town on the south shore of Crimea (now Sudak); Korsun (Chersonesus): Byzantine town in Crimea, near Sevastopol.

8. Idol of Tmutorokan: Polovtsian idol.

9. Oleg, prince of Chernigov (d. 1115), further "son of Woe-Glory": grandfather of Igor, responsible for much feudal strife and mentioned later in this context.

10. Gzak, Konchak: Polovtsian khans who made raids into Russia.

11. Kaiala River: tributary of the Donets.

12. Stribog: ancient Russian god of the winds.

13. Igor and Vsevolod's father Sviatoslav (d. 1164) reigned in Chernigov, town south of the Desna River, principal city of Igor's domain.

14. This is an unclear passage and subject to scholarly debate, but the Yaroslav in question is probably Yaroslav the Wise. Boris, son of Viacheslav, was killed with his cousin Oleg (see note 9) and died in 1078 fighting other Russians in response to the "offense to Oleg."

15. Sviatopolk: son of Iziaslav, killed in the same battle as Boris, conveyed his father's body for burial in St. Sophia Cathedral, center of Russian Christianity in Kiev.

16. Dazhbog: Russian pagan god of thunder and lightning.

17. Karna: personification of regret and sorrow; Zhlia: lamentation for the dead, keen, possibly related to *zhalet'*, to regret.

18. Kobiak: Polovtsian khan who was taken prisoner during the campaign launched by united Russian forces under Sviatoslav's leadership in 1184.

19. Bus: unknown, probably a Polovtsian khan; Sharukan, Kuman Kahn: grandfather of Konchak, defeated by the Russians.

20. Moguts, Tatrans, Shelbirs, Topchaks, Revugs, and Olbers: nomadic tribes of Turkic origin that had settled in the Chernigov princedom and fallen under the influence of the Russians.

21. Vladimir: son of Gleb, slain in 1187; Rimov: a city on the Sula River, was ravaged by the Polovtsians.

22. Vsevolod: prince of Vladimir-Suzdal (d. 1212).

23. *Nogata, rezana*: small coins.

24. Rurik: prince of Novgorod and of Kiev, son of Rostislav (d. 1215); David: Rurik's brother (d. 1198).

25. Osmomysl Yaroslav of Galicia (1152–1187): father of Yaroslavna, Igor's wife. Osmomysl, his nickname, probably means "eight-witted" and could refer to his intelligence.

26. Saltans: Nabokov optimistically suggests "At sultans," but meaning is uncertain.

27. Roman (d. 1205), Mstislav (d. 1226): princes of Volynia.

28. Ros and Sula Rivers: tributaries of the Dnieper.

29. Ingvar, Vsevolod: princes of Volynia.

30. Pereiaslavl: town on the Trybezne River.

31. Polotsk: town on the western Dvina River.

32. Iziaslav: prince (d. 1162).

33. Vseslav: prince of Polotsk, ruler of Kiev in 1068 (d. 1101).

34. Belgorod: town near Kiev.

35. Nemiga: a river, location of a great battle (1067) in which Vseslav was defeated. Location of Dudutki has not been estabished.

36. Hors: possibly Russian pagan god of the sun.

37. Olvur: Igor's servant.

38. Prince Rostislav, drowned in 1093 crossing the Stugna, a tributary of the Dnieper.

39. Borichev: located on the Dnieper in Kiev; the Church of the Holy Virgin of Pirogoshch was built in 1132.

2. "Boris and Gleb," pages 21–32

1. Many variants of this manuscript give "the Month of July, on the 24th day" as the date preceding the title of the work; see D. Abramovich, *Die altrussischen hagiographischen Erzählungen und liturgischen Dichtungen über Die Heiligen Boris und Gleb* (Munich: Wilhelm Fink, 1967), p. 27.

2. The introductory sentence seems to refer to Isaiah 65:23: "They shall not labour in vain, nor bring forth for trouble; for they are the seed of the blessed of the Lord, and their offspring with them."

3. The date of Volodimir's (Saint Vladimir) baptism is given variously as 987 or 988.

4. Perhaps because of an oversight on the part of the author, only eleven sons are identified. More curious, however, is the fact that the names given in this work do not agree with those found in the *Primary Chronicle (The Russian Primary Chronicle: Laurentian Text*, trans. and ed. S.H. Cross and O.P. Sherbowitz-Wetzer, Cambridge, MA: Medieval Academy of America, 1953, p. 207), where we read, "For he [Vladimir] had twelve sons: Vysheslav, Izyaslav, Yaroslav, Svyatopolk, Vsevolod, Svyatoslav, Mstislav, Boris, Gleb, Stanislav, Pozvizd, and Sudislav." That Vladimir had been a polygamist before his conversion there is no doubt. He is believed to have had at least seven wives before his marriage to Anna and, after her death in 1011, to have remarried. The ensuing conflict among the many sons of Vladimir after his death was in part due to the lack of brotherly ties among them and the considerable tension in the relations among the differing family groups. As concerns Boris and Gleb, it would seem that they were illegitimate, since strict chronology would have Boris and Gleb born after around 990, hence after Vladimir's Christian marriage. However, it is possible that their youth may have been exaggerated in the legends. It is interesting to note that there is a tradition that has Gleb as the son of Anna.

5. The Pechenegs—also called Patzinaks in Byzantine sources—were a nomadic Turkic people. During much of the tenth century they controlled lands between the Don and the lower Danube and commanded the trade route from Rus' to the Crimea. In their relations with the Russes they were at times allies, but more often enemies and a continual menace. According to the chronicles, they first attacked Rus' in 915. As a result of the rapprochement between Rus' and Byzantium in 988, a protracted and bitter war ensued between them and Rus'. In 1036 they were routed by Jaroslav the Wise of Kiev and moved off to the lower reaches of the Danube, where they mounted raids against Bulgaria, Macedonia, and Byzantium. In the twelfth century they merged partially with the Polovtsy (Kumans), encountered by Prince Igor, and in the thirteenth century with the Mongols (Tatars).

6. This is not a verbatim quotation from Proverbs 4:3.

7. Prince Volodimir (Vladimir/Vasilij) died July 15, 1015. There is hardly any doubt as to Vladimir's personal devotion to Christianity once baptized. Despite his pagan beginnings and pre-Christian excesses, he accepted his new faith with the greatest sense of responsibility: He saw to the Christianization of the people, built churches, promoted education, and practiced charity. Indeed, his banquets and hospitality became legendary and were recorded for posterity by the popular imagination in the *byliny* (epic folk songs), where he is the "beautiful/dear sun" (*krasnoe solnyshko;* see D. Čiževskij, *History of Russian Literature from the Eleventh Century to the Baroque*, The Hague: Mouton, 1960, p. 73). To the new Christian nation as a whole, he was their baptizer, their great preceptor, who brought the Russian people to regeneration in Christ. For this the Russian Church bestowed the dignity of sainthood upon him.

8. Berestovo, an estate near Kiev that belonged to Prince Vladimir.

9. Conveying the body of a deceased person on a sledge was part of the burial ritual of ancient Russia.

10. The entire passage from James 4:6 reads: "But he giveth more grace. Wherefore he saith, God resisteth the proud, but giveth grace unto the humble."

11. The Slavic text refers only to a fragment of 1 John 4:20, which reads: "If a man say, I love God, and hateth his brother, he is a liar: for he that loveth not his brother whom he hath seen, how can he love God whom he hath not seen?"

12. This passage contains only a part of the first sentence from 1 John 4:18. The entire biblical verse is: "There is no fear in love; but perfect love casteth out fear: because fear hath torment. He that feareth is not made perfect in love."

13. The allusion here is to Genesis 43:29: "And he [Joseph] lifted up his eyes, and saw his brother Benjamin, his mother's son, and said, 'Is this your younger brother, of whom he spake to me?' And he said, 'God be gracious unto thee, my son.' "

14. This passage is elliptic and omits the verb "said," which I have added.

15. It would appear that there is a confusion of grammatical number in this passage, all the more so since several variant readings give the expected form.

16. The entire passage from the Ecclesiastes 1:2 reads: "Vanity of vanities, saith the Preacher, vanity of vanities; all is vanity."

17. The allusion in this passage appears to be 1 Peter 1:22: "Seeing ye have purified your souls in obeying the truth through the Spirit unto unfeigned love of the brethren, see that ye love one another with a pure heart fervently."

18. Part of this quotation of the words of Christ is taken from Mark 8:35 and part from John 12:25: "For whosoever will save the life shall lose it; and he that hateth his life in this world shall keep it unto life eternal." Compare also Luke 17:33.

19. The Slavic passage is elliptic. For the sake of clarity, I have made the additions that are found in the translation.

20. Vyšegorod (Vyšgorod), a town just north of Kiev.

21. This passage refers to Isaiah 59:7–8: "Their feet run to evil, and they make haste to shed innocent blood: Their thoughts are thoughts of iniquity, wasting and destruction are in their paths. The way of peace they know not; and there is no judgment in their goings: they have made them crooked paths: whosoever goeth therein shall not know peace."

22. The L'to (Al'ta), a river that flows into the Trubež River southeast of Kiev.

23. The martyr-saint Nikita (Nicetas) was, like Boris, a soldier. Because he was preaching Christ among his fellow Goths at a time of fierce persecution of Christians, he was seized by the Visigothic chieftain Athanaric—one of the most zealous of the persecutors—tortured, and burned at the stake. He died in 372. The martyr-saint Vjačeslav (Wenceslas), the prince of the Czechs, died at the hands of his brother Boleslav in 929. Like Boris, he fell victim to a brother's political ambitions. According to the legend, the martyr-saint Barbara converted to Christianity against the will of her pagan father. For this he turned her over to the Roman governor of Bithynia, Martianus, to be dealt with by the law. Unable to make her renounce Christianity, he returned her to her father, who had offered to strike off his daughter's head. She died on December 4, 306. It is of interest to note that, according to the legend, as soon as she was beheaded, her father was struck by lightning. As a result, she is prayed to in storms; and she became the patron saint of artillery.

24. This passage seems to allude to 2 Timothy 4:7: "I have fought a good fight, I have finished my course, I have kept the faith."

25. Boris is actually chanting the opening lines from Psalm 22:16 and from Psalm 22:12. Cf., "For dogs have compassed me: the assembly of the wicked have enclosed me: they pierced my hands and feet," and, "Many bulls have compassed me: strong bulls of Bashan have beset me round."

26. There is a confusion of grammatical number in this sentence, viz., a first-person plural form rather than the first-person singular.

27. The reference in this passage is to 1 Corinthians 13:7 and 13:5: "[Charity] beareth all things, believeth all things, hopeth all things, endureth all things"; and "[Charity] Doth not behave itself unseemly, seeketh not her own, is not easily provoked, thinketh no evil. . . ."

28. This is not a verbatim quotation from Psalm 44:22. See also Romans 8:36.

29. This passage alludes to Psalm 55:12: "For it was not an enemy that reproached me; then I could have borne it: neither was it he that hated me that did magnify himself against me; then I would have hid myself from him. . . ."

30. The repetition of prepositions—in the present case, "between" (*mežju*)—is a type of tautology more frequently found in the oral tradition.

31. This is not a verbatim quotation from Acts 7:60.

32. The first day of each month in the Roman calendar was called calends. From this day, the days of the preceding month were counted backward to the Ides, which were on the fifteenth of March, May, July, and October, and on the thirteenth of every other month. In this system, both the calends itself and the day in question were counted when calculating time. Counting the first of August as the first day of the calends, the twenty-fourth of July—the day of Boris's death—was the ninth day before the calend (the first) of August. Boris died in the year 1015.

33. Compare this phrase with Luke 22:3.

34. In this monologue, Svjatopolk is paraphrasing various verses from Psalm 69.

35. In the oral tradition, particularly the *byliny*, a horse stumbling beneath its rider appears as an ill omen. It is curious that such an element—considered by many to be a mythological pagan survival—should have found its way into a work of this type.

36. The Smjadin' is a river in the Smolensk region.

37. Jaroslav (1036–54), who became known as Jaroslav the Wise, was to be the only

survivor among the sons of Vladimir of the fraternal struggle that lasted from 1015 to 1036. His reign, one of the most brilliant periods of Kievan Russia, saw the blossoming of Russian spirituality and culture. He was a great builder (churches, monasteries, the golden gate of Kiev) and played a significant role in the artistic, cultural, and literary development of Russia. He proved also to be a capable military commander and wise lawgiver. Predslava (Peredslava) was the daughter of Vladimir and Rogneda, hence Jaroslav's sister.

38. In the original text the suggested image of *syrorězanie* is obvious in Slavic; I have not been able to find a more precise English equivalent than "butchery."

39. This passage paraphrases parts of Luke 21:12 and 16, respectively.

40. In order to make this passage clearer, I have added the words "in your thoughts" to refer to the commitment the assassins had made once they located Gleb. The Slavic is rather elliptical.

41. Gleb met his death approximately six weeks after his brother.

42. This is not a verbatim quotation from Psalm 9:17.

43. This is not a verbatim quotation from Psalm 37:14–15.

44. This is not a verbatim quotation from Psalm 52:1–5.

45. The Slavs customarily buried their dead in hollowed-out tree trunks.

46. This is not a verbatim quotation from Psalm 34:20.

47. Other manuscripts of this work begin the concluding sentence with an apostrophe to Boris and Gleb, "O my brothers!" which makes the shift of appeal from the Lord to Boris and Gleb much smoother. See Abramovich, *Die Altrussischen Hagiographischen Erzählungen*, p. 46.

48. The number of "clashes" should not be taken literally since trebling is a common device in works of this type.

49. For the sake of clarity, I have added the noun "troops" to the translation.

50. The concluding sentence is also a stylistic formula that is reserved for the death of pagan or impious princes. Invariably mention is made of the grave that still exists and the evil stench issuing therefrom.

51. The allusion here is to Genesis 4:24: "If Cain shall be avenged sevenfold, truly Lamech seventy and sevenfold."

52. Julian, or Flavius Claudius Julianus, was Roman emperor from A.D. 361 to 363. He was surnamed the Apostate because of his renunciation of Christianity. In the expedition against the Persians in March 363, he was fatally wounded in battle.

3. "The Life of Alexis, Holy Man of God," pages 33–39

1. Honorius (A.D. 384–423) and Arcadius (A.D. 377–408) were the sons of the Roman emperor Theodosius the Younger, to whom he left the Roman Empire at his death in 395. Honorius inherited the western half of the empire and Arcadius the eastern half. Some later Russian versions of the text refer to the emperors as Theodosius the Younger and Arcadius (which would mean the events mentioned took place prior to Theodosius's death in 395, during the period when Theodosius and Arcadius jointly ruled the empire) or only mention Arcadius. There is some confusion as to whether the events actually took place in Rome or in the "New Rome" (Constantinople), which was often referred to as Rome and its inhabitants as Romans.

2. 3:00 P.M.

3. The exact dates of St. Alexis are not known, but he lived during the last half of the fourth century and the first half of the fifth century A.D.

4. Includes all liturgical, scriptural, theological, spiritual, dogmatic, historical, and dogmatic learning.

5. In some editions "and his golden belt" is added.

6. Identity and dates unknown. Western and later Russian versions of the *Life of Saint Alexis* say Innocent I, pope of Rome, A.D. 401–17.

4. *The Life of Avvakum*, pages 46–77

The information included in these annotations is drawn from a variety of sources, but above all from the copious, valuable notes contained in A.N. Robinson's edition of the *Life*.—K.B.

1. The honorific rank of archpriest (*protopop*) was the highest open to the married "white" (as opposed to the monastic "black") clergy; common Russians often considered an archpriest equal in rank to a bishop. His duties might include serving as rector of the principal church in a city, as supervisor of the clergy in a small district, or as vicar to a bishop. The name Avvakum is the Russian form of Habakkuk.

Avvakum uses the Old Russian term for confessor, "spiritual father" (*duxovnyj otec*), and it figures significantly in his traditional understanding of the sonship of believers and the fatherhood of God. Consequently, this "charge," standing at the beginning of the holograph of the second redaction of the *Life* and written in Epifanij's own hand (see photograph in Robinson, p. 141), is intended to justify an autobiographical undertaking that otherwise would violate the medieval literary norm of authorial self-deprecation and humility. Choice of a confessor was a private matter for each believer; earlier, Ivan Neronov, sometimes called the father of the Russian reformation, and the notable Stefan Vonifat'ev, the tsar's confessor and Neronov's close associate, had both served Avvakum in this capacity.

The volume containing the holograph of the third redaction of the *Life* also includes, as a separate item, Avvakum's famous defense of vernacular Russian: "This is written by the sinful hand of the Archpriest Avvakum, according to the exhortation and blessing of his confessor, the Elder Epifanij. And if that spoken here is simple, you who read and listen must not rebuke, for the Lord's sake, our simple speech, as I love my native Russian tongue. I am not used to beautifying my speech with verses philosophic, as God listens not to our beautiful words but desires our deeds. Paul writes, 'Though I speak with the tongues of men and angels but have not love, I am nothing' [1 Corinthians 13:1]. Here is plenty for you to ponder: not in Latin, nor in Greek, nor in Hebrew, nor in any other tongue does the Lord seek our speeches, but He desires our love together with the other virtues. So I don't bother about eloquence or belittle my Russian tongue. But forgive me, sinful man that I am, and God will forgive and bless all you servants of Christ. Amen." It must be emphasized here, of course, that Avvakum is not advocating use of the vernacular in the liturgy during divine worship.

The opening lines of the *Life* are a deliberate revision of a very familiar prayer read at the beginning of the Psalter; the "good works," which, according to this prayer, ought to crown the reading of the psalms, are here transformed into the deeds of Avvakum's life.

2. Simeon, Archbishop of Tobol'sk and Siberia, came from Avvakum's Upper Volga area. On August 2 (August 12, new style), 1654, a full eclipse of the sun occurred in Russia. Since Avvakum wrote his *Life* some twenty years later, he may have forgotten the precise times and sequence of events.

3. Nikon, more than any other man, was responsible for the liturgical reforms that led to the schism and made him Avvakum's most hated adversary. The lives of these spokesmen for the opposing camps seem almost fatefully intertwined. Nikon, of mixed Russian-Mordvinian blood, was born (1605) in the village of Val'demanovo, only a few miles from Avvakum's village of Grigorovo; during the late 1640s the two men acquired influence as members of the "Zealots of the Ancient Piety" (*Revniteli drevnego*

blagočestija), otherwise known as the "Lovers of God" (*Bogoljubcy*). Unlike Nikon, however, Avvakum was not a member of the tsar's inner circle of religious advisers. They were sent into exile in the Russian North simultaneously after decisions of the Ecumenical Council of 1666–67 went against them. Both were products of the religious vitality and fervor in the Russian Northeast that flared and faded as Russia moved toward the secular eighteenth century.

Rising from peasant to Patriarch of All Russia, Nikon had a spectacular career by any standard. At age twelve he entered the Makar'evskij Yellow Water Monastery but left it at age twenty without taking his vows. He married and served for a time as a parish priest, but when his children died he convinced his wife to take the veil, while he became a monk in the small Anzerskij Monastery on the White Sea. Later he moved to the Koževozerskij Monastery, again near the White Sea, where his piety, intelligence, energy, administrative talent, charismatic personality, and perhaps imposing stature (he was six feet six inches tall) soon brought him to the attention of ecclesiastics in Moscow. He became after 1646 an energetic, effective member of the Lovers of God and rose in a matter of six years to the patriarchate, in part because of his great influence on the tsar. It was only after his elevation that Nikon's ambition and lust for power became increasingly apparent. However, he announced six years later (1658) that he was laying down the burden of his office and retreated to the Voznesenskij Monastery (this after a campaign of insults engineered by the tsar). A quixotic attempt in 1664 to regain his past power failed. The Ecumenical Council of 1666–67, summoned in part to find a new patriarch and deal with Nikon, deposed him and sent him into exile. Legends quickly spread regarding his great works in his solitary exile; he not only accomplished healings but apparently built an island retreat in a lake with stones carried to the shore by hand. He died while returning to Moscow in 1681, in possession of a partial pardon from the imperial court.

The image "vials of his wrathful fury" has its source in that most revered of eschatological books in seventeenth-century Russia, the Apocalypse (cf. Revelations 16:1). The plague raged in Moscow and other Russian cities from July to December 1654; over half the population of Moscow perished (i.e., over 150,000 persons).

4. This eclipse occurred twelve, not fourteen, years after the first eclipse, on June 22 (July 2, new style), 1666. The Lovers of God and other religious zealots had long expected apocalyptic events in 1666 (666 is the number of the Beast of the Apocalypse), so this celestial event inevitably produced a strong impression. (Avvakum uses the old Russian calendar in his *Life*; the year 1666 was thus 7174, but he was certainly aware of the new calendar. See S. Zenkovsky, *Staroobrjadchestvo*, pp. 97–98, 154). In addition, Avvakum notes the hour during which the eclipse began, for it recalls the Crucifixion and attendant eclipse, which also began in the sixth hour (Matthew 27:45).

Avvakum was unfrocked and anathematized in the Moscow Kremlin's Cathedral of the Assumption on May 13, 1666. By order of Tsar Aleksej Mixajlovič he was imprisoned two days later in the Nikol'skij Monastery in Ugreša, near Moscow. The eclipse occurred some weeks after these events.

5. Grigorovo is located to the southeast of old Nižnij Novgorod. An old tax record book describes Grigorovo in the seventeenth century: "The village consists of three groups of buildings, and between them there is a spring. In the village there is the wooden Church of Sts. Boris and Gleb," in which Avvakum's father served.

6. The Russian word translated here as "feats of piety" is *podvig*. Like other medieval Russian writers, Avvakum uses it often, but it is difficult to translate consistently. For Avvakum it never implies a single feat but rather a lifestyle characterized by spiritual heroism. The term is bound up with his understanding of life as spiritual struggle: to be saved one must make a *podvig* of one's life.

7. Sexual temptation of future saints was a hagiographical tradition, and Avvakum resists it in a traditional manner. For example, in the *Prologue* (a popular collection of edifying stories that came to Russia from Byzantium) there is a tale about an Egyptian hermit monk who responds to a similar temptation by burning his fingers in an oil lamp. The Order for Confession directed confessors to demand detail regarding sexual transgressions from those come to confess, so Avvakum is not implying the young woman was in any way to blame for his lust. Indeed, the Order for Confession asserted that true repentance was impossible without tears, so her weeping is a sign of her sincerity.

8. "Eyes of the heart" is a literal translation from the Russian, which has its biblical source in Ephesians 1:18. English translations of the Bible vary here (e.g., "eyes of understanding" [King James Version]; "inward eyes" [New English Bible]; "eyes of the heart" [Revised Standard Version]).

9. Cf. Psalm 116:3 (Psalm 114 in the Russian Bible).

10. Less is known about the biography of Archpriest Stefan Vonifat'ev than is the case with other important figures among the Lovers of God. Like Avvakum, who revered him, he was born in the area of Nižnij Novgorod; he later became Archpriest of Moscow's Cathedral of the Annunciation and Tsar Aleksej Mixajlovič's personal confessor during the early period of his reign (1645–52), when the ideal of the Third Rome, of Holy Russia, dominated the latter's political and social ideas. Vonifat'ev's powerful influence upon the young tsar unquestionably contributed to the atmosphere of energetic piety at court, and during these years he was the principal figure in the vital area of religious policy. He was especially close to Ivan Neronov, and he played a leading role in the inner circle of the Lovers of God.

Ivan Neronov, sometimes called the father of the Russian reformation, was a seminal figure in the religious awakening that occurred in Russia toward the middle of the seventeenth century. He was born in 1590 or 1591 in the Monastery of St. Savior's, in the village of Lom near the northern Russian town of Vologda. The village, like many others in the area, grew up around this small, isolated monastery (*skit*) built by pioneering monks who desired the simple, elemental peace and austerity of the forests for their ascetic devotional life. Neronov must have grown up in contact with such men, and he acquired their ascetic fervor and simplicity. Nevertheless, like the other Lovers of God, Neronov did not wish to withdraw from the world like a monk to save his own soul, this despite his close association as a young man with Dionisij, archimandrite of the St. Sergius–Trinity Monastery in Zagorsk, in the early seventeenth century the most important center of Russian religious and cultural life. In 1649 he became archpriest of the Kazanskij Cathedral (St. Basil's) in Red Square. By 1651 he and his friends, the Lovers of God, were "at the helm of the Church," in Zenkovsky's apt phrase. Neronov protested vehemently and publicly against Nikon's initial reforms and in 1653 was exiled to the North. He escaped his supervised exile and fled, first to Solovki, then back to Moscow, where Vonifat'ev and others concealed him. During the next decade Neronov gradually became reconciled to the reforms, apparently owing to his fear of schism. Consequently, leadership of the Old Belief devolved automatically upon the fiery and uncompromising Avvakum. Although Avvakum deeply regretted Neronov's truce with the "apostates," he never condemned him publicly as did other Old Believers.

The year was 1647, the period when Vonifat'ev and Neronov were working closely together. Tsar Aleksej Mixajlovič's great interest in religious reform suggests why they introduced Avvakum to him.

11. Avvakum is here referring to *skomoroxi*, itinerant minstrels with trained bears and other animals who provided ordinary Russians with a favorite form of entertainment during the Middle Ages. Such entertainments were condemned by the Church for their pagan origins and content and for the impious carnival atmosphere they fostered. The

use of musical instruments could hardly recommend the *skomoroxi* to churchmen, who viewed such devices as dead metal and wood, of this earth, associated with carnality, and alien to the only true living instrument, the unaccompanied human voice employed in divine worship. The Lovers of God took vigorous action against the *skomoroxi* and their audiences, for the tsar gave full support to this repression, giving ecclesiastics the right to fine, imprison, and even exile those who attended such frolics. (An episode in Tarkovsky's film *Andrei Rublev* deals with a similar, earlier harsh treatment of the minstrels.—N.R.)

12. Šeremetev (d. 1659) was a boyar and for many years a leading figure at the Russian court. He had been governor in Nižnij Novgorod during the 1630s, so Avvakum had undoubtedly known of him long before this unfortunate confrontation. Churchmen associated shaving of the beard with loss of the image of God. Although the practice had long been spreading through the upper classes, its heretical nature had recently been reaffirmed by the Church.

13. Cf. Psalm 22:9 (21:10 in the Russian Bible). Filipp (1507–1569) [the notorious churchman of Sergei Eisenstein's film *Ivan the Terrible.*—N.R.] was the Boyar Fëdor Kolyčev before entering holy orders. He participated in a palace plot and subsequently fled to the Soloveckij Monastery, where he eventually became father superior. In 1566 he was elevated to Metropolitan of All Russia, but his opposition to Ivan the Terrible's *Opričnina* (personal troops) and denunciations of his atrocities finally led to his murder on Ivan's orders. The *Prologue* contains an apocryphal tale about the death of Zacharias, father of John the Baptist and a priest in Jerusalem. When Herod ordered the death of all male children under two years of age, Zacharias's wife Elizabeth hid the baby John. Herod ordered Zacharias executed in the Temple, in the manner of a sacrificial animal. Stefan was the first bishop of Perm and a successful missionary among the Komi. His *Life* relates an episode in which he and a Komi sorcerer agreed to test the truth of their conflicting religions by plunging into a river through a hole in its ice; the one returning from the bottom alive would be in possession of the true faith. The sorcerer ultimately avoided the test by fleeing. Avvakum obviously uses this story rather loosely in the present context.

14. These are the words of the Prodigal Son (Luke 15:18).

15. Cf. Proverbs 3:34 and James 4:6 (*Poslanie Iakova*, "The Epistle of Jacob," in the Russian Bible).

16. Avvakum fled to Moscow from Lopatišči for the second time no later than March 1652. Jur'evec was a small market town and still exists. Avvakum was in charge of the town's main church, to which ten other small churches were subordinate.

17. Archpriest Daniil's problems and their origins were similar to Avvakum's. The local priests in Kostroma had allied with the common people and a group of *skomoroxi* and had beaten him repeatedly and severely, causing him to flee to avoid death. Avvakum arrived in Kostroma between June 1 and June 3, 1652, approximately one week after these events.

18. Metropolitan Kornilij, an acquaintance of Avvakum's (d. August 17, 1656).

19. Nikon moved quickly after his elevation to neutralize his former associates, the Lovers of God, whose influence had deprived Patriarch Iosif of any effective power. The Chamber of the Cross is the reception hall in the Patriarch's Palace, which is located in the Kremlin. Here the patriarch conducted his daily business and performed the Mass. Here Avvakum disputed with the leaders of the Church in 1666 after his second arrest and imprisonment, and here he and Nikon were both condemned in 1667.

20. The instruction was sent on February 21, 1653, the first day of Lent. Avvakum refers here to St. Basil's Cathedral (the familiar name in English) as the "Kazan Church"; the Kazanskij Cathedral is the original name of the great cathedral in Red Square that has come to be known as the Cathedral of Basil the Blessed (Xram Vasilija

Blažennogo) or the Cathedral of the Protection of the Holy Theotokos (Pokrovskij Cathedral).

21. Nikon began his reforms boldly—or stupidly—since obeisances and especially the technique of crossing oneself were matters of fundamental ritualistic importance. What is more, the Stoglav Council of 1551 had reaffirmed the traditional Russian manner of crossing oneself, with two fingers. Nikon took the unheard of step of announcing these changes at the beginning of Lent, the most revered fast, and on his own authority, without benefit of a Church council. The pious, conservative archpriests, who were accustomed to figuring prominently in all decisions affecting the Church, were shocked.

22. An old center of learning, the Čudovskij (Miracle) Monastery is located in the Moscow Kremlin and was founded in 1356. It was under the direction of the patriarch.

23. Another religious leader born in the Upper Volga area, Pavel had only recently been elevated to the office of bishop (October 17, 1652). He was the only chief prelate to defend the old ritual, and at the Church Council of 1654, in the presence of both Nikon and Makarios, patriarch of Antioch, he objected to the changes made in the obeisances performed during the Prayer of Efrem Sirin. Pavel was arrested and exiled, first to the Paleostrovskij Monastery on Lake Onega, then to the Xutynskij Monastery near Novgorod. Later he was brutally flogged and burned by Nikon's agents.

24. Neledinskij was a high-ranking associate of Nikon's, which indicates that considerable importance was attached to the arrest of the still youthful Avvakum. These events occurred on August 21, 1653, and they halted Avvakum's public defiance of the hierarchy. After he had returned to Moscow from accompanying Neronov into exile, Avvakum attempted to take the latter's place at St. Basil's by claiming it was Neronov's command. He was turned away, of course, and began to hold vigils in a shed attached to Neronov's house.

25. The Andronikov or Spas-Andronikov Monastery (named after its first father superior) was founded around 1360; it is located on the Yauza River, on the outskirts of Moscow near the Rogožskaja *zastava*.

26. Avvakum wished, of course, to bow to the east, according to tradition.

27. Avvakum's description of this miracle resembles passages in Acts (5:19 and 12:7–9), wherein angels appear in prisons to assist the apostles.

28. On September 1, 1653, Nikon ordered Avvakum and his family into exile, to the Lena River. However, on the September 16 the tsar eased the archpriest's punishment by sending him only as far as Tobol'sk, the administrative center for Siberia. Besides his wife, Avvakum traveled with sons Ivan (9 years), Prokopij (5 years), newborn Kornilij, daughter Agrafena (8 years), and his niece Marina. Travel to Tobol'sk and back to Moscow usually required twelve weeks in the winter; Avvakum's slow journey was caused by the muddy autumn roads and the obvious difficulties of traveling with small children. The family and their escort arrived in Tobol'sk during the last week of December 1653.

29. Archbishop Simeon was an energetic administrator who did much to strengthen the Church in Siberia. He brought more priests into the region and obtained patriarchal approval in 1652 to appoint archpriests both to the regional ecclesiastical center, the Cathedral of St. Sofija in Tobol'sk, and to the city's Cathedral of the Ascension. The latter is the post to which Avvakum refers. An instruction from the tsar also directed Simeon to give Avvakum ecclesiastical duties, as he was still a consecrated priest.

30. Avvakum lived in Tobol'sk from December 1653 to June 29, 1655.

31. When Archbishop Simeon left for the Moscow Council of 1654, Struna was one of two officials left in charge of ecclesiastical administration in Tobol'sk.

32. Metropolitan Pavel was one of the most vigorous opponents of the Old Believers. During the eight-year hiatus after Nikon's retirement, he often performed the patriarch's duties, and he was a principal organizer of the Ecumenical Council of 1666–67 that finally deposed Nikon. Deacon Afanasij served in the Kremlin's Cathedral of the Assumption.

33. Archbishop Simeon reported to Moscow that a woman and her daughter had petitioned him regarding the rape of the girl by her father, and that Struna had dismissed the peasant and ordered the women whipped "without mercy." The archbishop chained Struna in the bakery of a monastery but the latter escaped, fled to the two local military commanders, and denounced not only Avvakum but the archbishop as well for torturing him and for protecting "the exiled archpriest." Struna took advantage of the continual political tug-of-war between the civil and the ecclesiastical authorities in Tobol'sk over their respective jurisdictions. Even though Struna was subject to the ecclesiastical court, the commanders refused to return him to the archbishop.

34. Pëtr Beketov had served with honor in Siberia for many years, as Russia extended its area of influence and control ever to the east. He had recently arrived in Tobol'sk after a difficult and dangerous mission entrusted to him by Avvakum's future nemesis, Afanasij Paškov. His assignment as Struna's guardian was standard procedure, as informers customarily received protection while their denunciations were being investigated. Nikon was sympathetic, and in 1656 he pardoned Struna. In addition, he soon denied Archbishop Simeon the right to celebrate the Mass, perhaps because of his collaboration with Avvakum in the Struna affair.

35. In 1655, Tsar Aleksej Mixajlovič was away on his Polish campaign and Nikon had virtually a free hand in Moscow, as he was empowered to rule in the name of the tsar's young son Aleksej as well as in his own. After the Church Council of 1655 had finally ratified his reforms, he acted swiftly, apparently in the conviction that he no longer had to await the results of the investigation of the charges brought against Avvakum by Ivan Struna. In the name of Aleksej he ordered Avvakum and his family on to the east, to the Lena River, as he had originally done before the tsar intervened.

36. The path covered by Avvakum's journey in the east is over 18,000 kilometers in length. Daurija was the name used in the seventeenth century to denote the geographical area to the east of Lake Baikal, which includes the basins of the Šilka, Argun, Seya, Amur (in part), Sungari, and Ussuri rivers. Avvakum remained in the western regions of this vast territory.

37. Afanasij Paškov (d. 1664) was the great-grandson of Grigorij Paškevič, a Pole who came to Russia during the reign of Ivan the Terrible. Paškov's long career included service at court, in the city of Moscow, and a military command in the Far North (in the area of the Mezen River) before he was sent to Yenisejsk as military commander. In 1655, I.P. Afinkov arrived as the new military commander of the city, bringing at the same time Paškov's appointment as commander in the "new land of Daurija." Paškov's task included the subjugation of local princes, collection of large tribute in furs, and discovery of valuable metals (if any) and of arable lands in the river valleys. He was also to build in the East a church with two altars, one dedicated to Metropolitan Aleksej and the other to the humble St. Aleksej, Man of God, whom we have already encountered (Aleksej was the name of the tsar and his son). Archbishop Simeon was directed to send two priests and a deacon to serve in the East; he assigned Avvakum to one of these positions. Preparations for the expedition took more than a year (1655–56).

38. A prame (also pram or praam) is a lightweight, flat-bottomed boat, traditionally propelled by sail or oars; it is thus similar in design to the *doščenik*, a type of boat widely used by Russian forces in Siberia. However, "prame" is not a precise translation, because the *doščenik* is larger, a good one being capable of carrying thirty persons or up to five tons of cargo.

39. The Šamanskij Rapids are located on the Angara at a point where the river is divided by a rocky island. They are about three and one-half miles in length and extremely violent, with waves reaching twelve to thirteen feet in height.

40. Avvakum's laconic description of the lands around the Angara only hints at their

rugged majesty and harshness. Avvakum apparently heard local legends about great snakes, for in fact only smaller species live in the area. However, the other fauna mentioned substantiate his memory of detail, as the birds and animals noted almost certainly reflect personal observation. It is likely that he refers here to the following fauna native to the Lake Baikal area: the gray goose, the red duck or *ogar'*, the Siberian raven, the white-collared or white-breasted Daurian jackdaw, the East Siberian fish eagle, the Russian falcon, the Siberian gyrfalcon, the mountain pheasant, the whooper swan, the Siberian roe deer, the Siberian forest deer, the elk, the wild boar, the Altai mountain goat, and the wolf.

41. The *čexan* ("command axe") was a single-bitted weapon used both in combat and as an emblem of rank. Despite Paškov's reputation for violence, his personal participation in Avvakum's flogging was an unacceptable breech of "propriety," even by the seventeenth century's savage standards. Paškov remained silent on this point in his report to the tsar regarding Avvakum's punishment, but Archbishop Simeon denounced him vehemently in a letter to the tsar (1658): "Afanasij Paškov . . . with his own hands beat Avvakum with his command axe. . . . He beat him about the head with his command axe and completely shattered his head; and from this flogging Archpriest Avvakum lay for a long time as if dead." Some four years later Tsar Aleksej cited this event as his reason for stripping Paškov of his Siberian command. A man about to be flogged with the knout was customarily stripped to his thighs; the knout consisted of a short wooden handle and a flexible leather shaft with a leather loop or metal ring at the end, to which was attached a wide, stiff rawhide "tail" bent lengthwise in such a way that the rough edges tore the skin and flesh. Sometimes the tail had sharp metal gouges attached to its striking end and edges.

42. The Angara's Padun Rapids consist of seven cascades, of which three are the largest; the roar of the broiling water passing through them can be heard for miles around. At present the great Bratsk hydroelectric station is located at this point in the river. The word "gates" was a local term used to describe the navigable passages past the rapids (one of these passages was "the old gates").

43. Cf. Hebrews 12:5–8.

44. The Bratsk fortress was located not far from the present-day city of Bratsk, near the confluence of the Angara and Oka rivers. Avvakum was imprisoned from approximately October 1 to November 15, as St. Philip's Fast comprises the six weeks before Christmas.

45. Hostages were taken by Russian military leaders, usually from prominent families among native tribes, in order to force payment of "imperial taxes." Such taxes, or more accurately, tribute, consisted for the most part of furs.

46. Paškov's force moved out early in May 1657. His original orders were to journey to the north of Lake Baikal and into Daurija. Paškov had decided before leaving Yenisejsk that his boats and supplies were too heavy for this northern route. So he continued up the Angara to Lake Baikal, crossed it, and proceeded up the Selenga River. The journey to the Xilok River through this tortuous, mountainous terrain required approximately two weeks. At the mouth of the Xilok, Paškov's force abandoned the large prames and built small, bargelike boats. Avvakum does not mean that he spent two summers on the Xilok. After moving up the Xilok to Lake Irgen, Paškov's troop abandoned their boats and carried their supplies over a long portage to the Ingoda River. The following spring and summer they moved down the Ingoda.

47. Lake Baikal is 1,525 feet above sea level; Lake Irgen (one of several small lakes in a swampy upland separating the Lake Baikal and Amur River basins), 3,640 feet. Paškov arrived at Lake Irgen during October 1657 and rebuilt the fortress there before beginning the winter portage to the Ingoda.

48. Large numbers of logs were cut on the Ingoda and used in approximately 170 rafts, each carrying two or three persons downstream to the Šilka River. There the logs were used to build two forts. Avvakum's journey was in its fourth year, as he claims: in summary, during the summer of 1655 he journeyed from Tobol'sk to Yenisejsk, where he wintered; during the summer and fall of 1656 he moved from Yeniseisk to the Bratsk fortress, where he spent the winter; during the spring, summer, and fall of 1657 he traveled from the Bratsk fortress to Lake Irgen; during the winter he hauled supplies over the portage to the Ingoda; and in the spring of 1658 he struggled down this river.

49. Paškov arrived at the mouth of the Nerča, a tributary of the Šilka, early in June 1658, and built a fort there to replace one earlier erected by Beketov and Urasov and destroyed by local tribes. The terrain in this general area is forest steppe and, in some areas, arid *chernozem* (black earth) steppe. Avvakum later claimed that Paškov caused more than five hundred people to starve to death. Robinson considers this figure to be only slightly exaggerated. Starvation began when needed supplies did not arrive from Yeniseisk.

50. Avvakum probably means a "pine-bark porridge," the term he uses in his tale of the little black hen.

51. These were Avvakum's youngest sons, Kornilij and the infant born on the way to Tobol'sk; the latter's name is unknown.

52. This passage combines Jeremiah 9:1 with a line from the Service for the Presentation of Christ in the Temple, one of the twelve great Orthodox holidays (February 2), known as Candlemas or Feast of the Purification of the Virgin in the Roman Catholic Church. The latter passage reads as follows: ". . . rain warm tears upon me that I might weep for my soul, which I have wickedly sullied."

53. One pood equals 36.11 pounds.

54. Agrafena was living with her sisters Akulina and Aksin'ja, while her mother and brothers Prokopij and Ivan were imprisoned nearby in a covered pit. The third and youngest son Afanasij was apparently living with his sisters.

55. Cf. Matthew 24:13 and Mark 13:13.

56. This biblical citation (Matthew 27:24) was one of Avvakum's favorites, as he uses it rather often to describe energetic but futile actions.

57. *The Christian's Pilot* (Kormčaja) is a collection of ecclesiastical legislation and rules that came to Russia from Byzantium via Serbia at the beginning of the thirteenth century. It was published in Moscow in 1650 and again, with Nikon's emendations, in 1653. Avvakum apparently carried a copy of this very large volume (undoubtedly the first edition) into exile, for we later read that he gave it to a friend upon beginning his return to Russia.

58. The schism created serious problems in the continuing administration of Communion among Old Believers: Can a priest consecrated after the Nikonian reforms administer the Eucharist? (see Zenkovsky, *Staroobrjadchestvo*, especially pp. 424–27). That Avvakum gave advice concerning Communion in his *Life* is not surprising, as he was frequently queried on this issue. "Host" here translates *zapasnyj agnec*, communion bread consecrated in a church but used elsewhere. Generally Old Believers used bread consecrated only in unreformed churches, which meant it was increasingly difficult to obtain over time.

59. This is a prayer recited by the priest and the deacon before the altar in the sanctuary prior to receiving the Sacrament.

60. The "priest of darkness" refers to Sergij, an adherent of Nikon's reforms and Avvakum's opponent. He was the recognized ecclesiastic in Paškov's force, although Avvakum obviously did not admit his legitimacy.

61. After Paškov's death in 1664, his wife Fëkla Simeonovna moved into the Moscow

Kremlin's Voznesenskij Convent, where she later took the veil and served as mother superior from 1673 to her death in 1685. Likewise, her daughter-in-law Evdokija Kirillovna took the veil in this convent prior to her death, and she was buried there by Avvakum.

62. In folk tradition, Cosmas and Damian were considered to be protectors of fowl.

63. Ecclesiastical law forbade sorcery of any kind, for in principle it was equivalent to worship of pagan divinities. Nevertheless, both the government and the Church received reports from Siberia that not only the natives but Russians resorted to sorcerers, especially in healing the sick. Priests were required to ask women during confession whether they had visited sorcerers or brought them into their homes. Practitioners of sorcery were punished with flogging, exile, and death by fire. The Russian verb here (*šamanit´*) is formed on the noun *šaman*. The shaman was the central figure in the religions of most Siberian tribes, for he was at once priest, healer, and prophet. Shamans among the Buryat Mongols and the Tungus often prophesied the outcome of important undertakings, preceding this with the sacrifice of an animal and sometimes basing their predictions on the pattern of fissures in the shoulderblade of a burned ram. Later descriptions of the behavior of a shaman exercising his prophetic powers substantiate the accuracy of Avvakum's remarks—the first such description on record. For example, the nineteenth-century scholar D. Banzarov wrote that the shaman first chants prayers in a sitting position, beating a drum with increasing force until, at the appropriate moment, he "rises, leaves the drum, and begins to dance, leap about, spin, beat himself, all the while chanting incantations and howling frightfully, so that foam flows from his mouth."

64. Avvakum refers here to the entire period of his acquaintance with Paškov, 1655 to 1664, the year of the latter's death.

65. Owing to frequent attack by local tribes, it was generally very dangerous for Russians to travel along Siberian rivers without a heavily armed escort. The situation was much more serious in the spring of 1662, for a general uprising of Bashkirs, Tatars, Chuvash, Kalmyks, Cheremis, and other tribes was occurring. It was led by Devlet-Kirei, who rose against Russia in hopes of resurrecting the Siberian kingdom of his grandfather, Kuchum Khan.

66. Execution by impalement was not an institution in Russia, but it was utilized in the seventeenth and early eighteenth centuries.

67. The identity of this "servant of Christ," whom Avvakum addresses several times, is unknown. Possibly he refers to the Afanasij to whom the Elder Epifanij addressed his *Life*.

68. See Joshua 2.

69. Ksen´ja was the second child born to Avvakum and Markovna in Siberia; Ksen´ja is a diminutive form of Aksin´ja.

70. To this point Avvakum has not made direct reference to Nikon's interdict. This defiant assertion of its spuriousness is important: it is part of the archpriest's rationalization for assuming leadership in the Old Belief in the narration to follow.

71. Pëtr, Aleksej, and Iona were all metropolitans. Pëtr (1305–26) moved the center of the Russian church from Vladimir to Moscow during the period when Grand Prince Ivan Kalita was consolidating the Muscovite state. Aleksej (1354–78), distinguished by his erudition, was the tutor of the young Dmitrij Donskoj. Iona was metropolitan of Moscow from 1448 to 1461. All were canonized. Representatives of both the official Church and the Old Belief appealed frequently to the authority of these metropolitans in the course of their doctrinal disputes.

72. Some of the highest mountains on Lake Baikal are located along Avvakum's route back to Russia; they reach heights of 5,000 feet above lake level. They are remarkable for their singular configurations, which indeed are reminiscent of medieval walled towns or monasteries.

73. Avvakum was the first Russian writer to remark upon the flora around Lake Baikal as well as on the many varieties of fish in it. The types of fish he mentions specifically are of considerable commercial importance. For example, the Siberian sturgeon ranges in weight from 65 to 255 pounds and in the past reached 450 pounds; the amul salmon can exceed 6 pounds, while the whitefish may weigh 17–18 pounds. The large taimen salmon is more often encountered in the Selenga and Angara rivers, and the sterlet is found in the Angara, not in Baikal. The seals in Baikal reach a body weight of 280 pounds. In our time no sea lions live in the lake, but Robinson speculates (p. 258) that they may have been there in the seventeenth century.

74. The series of similes struck by Avvakum between man and beasts is traditional; for example, St. John Chrysostom remarks in his *Marguerite* (a book known to Avvakum): "For when thou art angered, thou brayest like an ass, like a horse dost thou neigh at women; thou dost gorge thyself like a bear, fattening thy body like an ox. . . Thou ragest like a serpent . . . thou dost hate men like a lynx and provokest enmity like an evil devil." The final line ("Forgive me . . .") is borrowed from the declaration of assurance made by priests prior to hearing confession, in which the penitent is told that his confessor is also a sinner.

75. Cf. 1 Corinthians 7:27.

76. Avvakum refers here to the winters of 1662–63 and 1663–64.

77. Avvakum's exile lasted approximately ten years and eight months, as he left Moscow in September 1653 and returned sometime between February and May 1664.

78. Avvakum arrived in Tobol'sk near the end of June 1663. The town of Verxoturie marked the border of Siberia; in 1663 it was caught in the middle of the uprising of the Siberian tribes. Kamynin, a *stol'nik* in rank, was commander in Verxoturie during the period 1659–64. His close association with the Borovskij Pafnut'ev Monastery enabled him to give aid and comfort to Avvakum later, when the archpriest was imprisoned there.

79. Fëdor Rtiščev (1626–1673) was one of the most attractive personalities of his time; a close associate of Aleksej Mixajlovič's and an influential figure at court, he was an energetic member in the inner circle of the Lovers of God prior to the elevation of Nikon. The evidence indicates he was a man who combined genuine learning and piety, a warm and vigorous personality, and an active concern for the welfare of others.

80. The murmanka was an official parade hat; it had a high, flat crown with a fur band that had the appearance of ear flaps. It was normally made of velvet or brocade.

81. Robinson is probably correct in stating that Avvakum's refusal to become the confessor of leading state functionaries and, above all, of the tsar was the turning point in his career (p. 261). Acceptance of this position would certainly have been contingent upon Avvakum's accepting the reforms. Refusal signaled his assumption of leadership in the Old Belief opposition.

82. Rodion Matveevič Strešnev (d. 1687) was a childhood friend of Aleksej Mixajlovič's. He had the tsar's special trust and served as an intermediary during the latter's conflicts with both Nikon and Avvakum.

83. St. Simeon's Day: the date was September 1, 1664.

84. Luk'jan Kirillov was archpriest of the Cathedral of the Annunciation and the tsar's confessor. Later his relations with Avvakum changed; the Deacon Fëdor writes: "I gave the Confessor the petition about Avvakum, about his freedom, and in a mighty rage he threw it in my face." One hundred rubles was a great deal of money, equal, for example, to Arsenios the Greek's salary during the first two years of his work in the Church's printing house.

85. Feodos'ja Morozova née Sokovnina and her sister Evdokeja were among the best-known representatives of the Old Belief during the early stages of the schism. They

were born into the highest ranks of the aristocracy, and they moved freely in the inner circles of the Russian court (Morozova was a close friend and associate of the empress). Married to a man already old and soon widowed, Morozova met Avvakum upon his return from Siberia and fell under the influence of his powerful personality. Her household was reorganized in the manner of a convent, and its rooms were soon crowded with nuns and beggars. Morozova cared for the needy personally, cleaning the open sores of beggars, eating with them from the same pot, and walking the streets of Moscow in poor clothes, distributing alms and clothing made with her own hands to the poor. She practiced traditional mortifications of the flesh such as wearing a hair shirt, and, not surprisingly, she eventually took the veil in secret. Morozova's deep commitment to Avvakum and to the Old Belief aroused the ire of influential members of her family, but the pressure they brought to bear failed to alter her convictions.

During the period of Avvakum's second exile, trial, and imprisonment, she gave him constant moral and material support. In 1669 the empress died, and Morozova lost her chief defender àt court. When the tsar remarried, she refused to fulfill her rightful—and obligatory—duties in the ceremonies. Soon thereafter (November 16, 1671) she and her sister were arrested, fettered, and cast into prison. Neither argument, nor bestial tortures including the rack, nor the death of her son, nor the loss of her vast wealth succeeded in bending Morozova. Her courageous resistance and terrible suffering understandably embroiled the court and deepened the schism, for the Muscovite masses loved her and were beginning to stir ominously. (V.I. Surikov's famous painting of Morozova being transported through Moscow on a drag sled, defiantly holding her hand aloft, her fingers in the traditional conformation, refers to this period of what came to be considered her passion.) Such audacity was not easily tolerated; she was swiftly condemned and a pit was prepared for her execution by fire. The tsar's sister Irina pleaded with her brother, and Morozova received a temporary reprieve. She and her sister Evdokija were transported to Borovsk, imprisoned in harsh conditions, and starved. Evdokija died there in her sister's arms (September 11, 1675), while Morozova died on November 2, 1675. Avvakum's relations with Morozova were characteristically erratic. He rejoiced in and glorified her courage and loyalty to the Old Belief, and he cherished her martyrdom. His laments upon her death are still deeply moving to read. However, the few occasions that Morozova dared to disagree with him on minor issues evoked a less positive response.

86. Nikon went into voluntary retirement in 1658, but technically he was still patriarch. Avvakum's petition to the tsar in 1664 was an effort to influence this complex, confused situation. Certainly the good will he had encountered at court gave him cause to believe his suggestions might have some effect.

87. The "fool in Christ" (*jurodivyj*) was an important cultural type in medieval Russia (see introduction to part I). The term referred to people either mentally unbalanced or retarded, whose bizarre behavior was understood as an outward manifestation of the movements of mysterious spiritual forces to which they were privy. Thus, they were often respected as prophets and generally believed to be especially favored by God. Avvakum obviously distinguished such people from unfortunates suddenly become deranged; the latter were possessed by devils. Aleksej Mixajlovič apparently shared these views, for numbers of such fools were always living in and near his residences, fully supported by him. This may explain why Avvakum sent Fëdor to the tsar with his letter; the chances that it would be received by the tsar personally were improved by its bearer's "foolishness." Avvakum began to attract fools in Christ upon his return from Siberia, and one can scarcely doubt that they greatly enhanced the apocalyptic qualities of his public image and the impact of his preaching. Fëdor was his favorite, and Avvakum returns to him more frequently in his *Life* than to any other representative of

the Old Belief. Their friendship began in Great Ustiug during Avvakum's return from Siberia and ended with Fëdor's execution by hanging at Mezen (March 1670), Avvakum's first place of exile in the Far North.

88. The Red Terrace served as the parade entrance to the palace.

89. Prior to his Siberian exile, Avvakum had drawn worshipers away from St. Basil's. The complaints against him then by priests were repeated now, but this time by prelates. Avvakum had succeeded in attracting large numbers of Muscovites, who abandoned their usual spiritual mentors.

90. Pëtr Mixajlovič Saltykov was an important administrator. At this time he was in charge of Ukrainian affairs, but he also played a role in ecclesiastical matters. He was given responsibility for guiding the investigation regarding the consequences of Nikon's sudden retirement.

91. Mezen is a small town located on the right bank of the Mezen River, which flows northward into the White Sea. Avvakum and his family were sent from Moscow to Pustozersk on August 29, 1664.

92. Avvakum's return to Moscow (March 1666) was one element in Aleksej Mixajlovič's preparations for the Ecumenical Council of 1666–67. He was determined to protect the Nikonian reforms, to replace the quixotic and autocratic Nikon as patriarch, and to isolate and silence those in opposition. If entirely successful, he would bring clarity to the murky situation in the Church, at the same time bringing under control those religious forces that were threatening to fragment Russian national life. Avvakum was initially allowed considerable freedom of movement in Moscow, and he spent two days with Morozova discussing the faith and how they should "suffer for the Truth." He then went to the Kremlin's Cathedral of the Assumption and presented himself to "Metropolitan Pavlik" (a disparaging diminutive form of "Pavel"), showing that he had "voluntarily come to his torments."

93. The Borovskij Pafnut'ev Monastery was founded in 1444; since the sixteenth century it had been a fortress surrounded by a stone wall with towers. Avvakum was imprisoned there from March 9 to May 12, 1666. Metropolitan Pavel directed Father Superior Parfenij to afflict Avvakum in an effort to compel his reconciliation with his enemies. However, Morozova was able to supply him with food and other necessities, and he did not yield.

94. Paraphrase of Luke 9:55.

95. The disputation with the bishops took place in the Chamber of the Cross on May 13, 1666. Later the same day Avvakum was defrocked in the Cathedral of the Assumption.

96. The Deacon Fëdor (or "Feodor" in the traditional ecclesiastical spelling) was one of the leading writers and teachers of the Old Belief. He was arrested on December 9, 1665, during the repressions that preceded the Ecumenical Council. After Fëdor was imprisoned at Ugreša with Avvakum, he recanted and reconciled himself to the reforms—but only briefly. His action here can only be attributed to hunger, exhaustion, and perhaps worry about his family, for when he was subsequently sent to the Pokrovskij Monastery he escaped to his home, gathered his wife and children, and fled. After renewing his opposition, he was apprehended, arrested, and, after having his tongue cut out, sent to Pustozersk to join Avvakum, Epifanij, and Lazar (February 1668). After the death of the aged Archpriest Nikifor, these four became the famous, and notorious, prisoners of Pustozersk, whose prolific writings fueled the fires of schism until they died together in 1682.

97. The Patriarch's Court was located in the Kremlin, extending away from the northwest side of the Cathedral of the Assumption. Nikon enlarged the court and constructed a new patriarchal residence there with passages connecting it with the palace of the tsar. The Monastery of St. Nikola was located about nine miles to the northeast of

Moscow, on the left bank of the Moscow River. According to tradition, it was founded by Dmitrij Donskoj to commemorate the Russian victory over the Tatars at Kulikovo Field in 1380. It was situated near the village of Ostrovo, where the tsar often retreated to rest. Consequently, Aleksej Mixajlovič often visited the monastery. The prisoners were sent there on May 15, 1666.

98. Avvakum was confined at St. Nikola's from May 15 to September 3, 1666. Once again, Morozova managed to supply him with necessities.

99. Avvakum perhaps exaggerates Vorotynskij's allegiance to the Old Belief. He was the tsar's first cousin and frequently accompanied him on both military campaigns and journeys. Almost certainly he spoke for the tsar earlier in reprimanding Morozova during her torture, which he witnessed, at least in part.

100. Prince Ivan Ivanovič Xovanskij the Elder (1645–1701), a member of the noble Russian family who inspired Mussorgsky's *Khovanschina*, was not altogether consistent in his support of the Old Belief. His flogging (around 1670) caused him to abandon the old rituals in his public life, and he rose in the state service in subsequent years. However, his real sympathies never changed, and he finally died in prison, having been implicated in the plot organized by the printer G. Talickij, who printed pamphlets aimed at fomenting rebellion against the "Antichrist," Peter the Great. Isaiah was the butler of Boyar P.N. Saltykov. According to Semën Denisov, Isaiah convinced his master to stand firm in the Old Belief. The tsar allegedly saw Saltykov crossing himself in the ancient manner and placed blame on the butler, who was arrested, interrogated, tortured, and finally burned.

101. Avvakum was taken from the Monastery of St. Nikola on September 3, 1666, and he arrived at the Pafnut'ev Monastery two days later to begin his second imprisonment there. He remained until April 30, 1667. By order of the tsar he was to be closely supervised; no one was to be admitted to see him, nor was he to be given writing materials. Nevertheless, Morozova managed to supply his needs.

102. Smoking and trading in tobacco were criminal offenses punishable by death. Tobacco was of foreign origin and thus immediately suspect; the Old Believers referred to it as "the Devil's incense." Musical instruments were forbidden in church, of course, where only the living human voice could rightfully lift up praise to God. Early in Aleksej Mixajlovič's reign, in 1649, six carriages of musical instruments were burned in Moscow. Associating the Greek hierarchs with either tobacco or musical instruments was another emblematic proof of their heretical views. In mentioning the metropolitan of Gaza, Avvakum has in mind the Greek Paissios Ligarid (1610–78), who was, judging from the available evidence, a cynical opportunist and adventurer.

103. A paraphrase of Romans 14:4.

104. Ilarion (d. 1673) grew up in a village near Avvakum's native place, Grigorovo, and as young men they were friends. But later he became a close associate of Nikon's and strongly supported his arguments regarding the primacy of ecclesiastical power. Avvakum's antipathy is thus predictable.

105. The tale of Fëdor's escape from prison is modeled on a similar story involving the Apostle Peter, in Acts 12:7–10.

106. The town Great Ustiug is located on the left bank of the Suxona River. In the 1670s it consisted of approximately a thousand households. Travelers to or from Siberia generally passed through it.

107. Avraamij proved to be one of the most tenacious and courageous spokesmen for the Old Belief. Considered yet another fool in Christ, he was the only one of this particular group of Old Believers to leave a body of writings. He was author of, among other texts, *A Mighty Christian Shield of Faith Against the Armies of Heresy*; this compilation of Old Believer writings, extracts from the patristic literature, and his own

work developed an especially pessimistic eschatology. He was strongly inclined to view the year 1666 as the watershed between Moscow the Third Rome and the beginning of the reign of the Antichrist. He openly denounced the tsar as a "dishonorable heretic and the new apostate of the Orthodox faith . . . and the new torturer and persecutor of the saints in Russia" (Nikon had retired). Such declarations could easily be viewed as a treasonous summons to anarchy in troubled times, and Avraamij was eventually burned during the winter of 1671–72.

108. On November 2, 1666, Paissios, patriarch of Alexandria, and Makarios, patriarch of Antioch, arrived in Moscow amid great pomp and splendor for the beginning of the Ecumenical Council. The Greek Church lay prostrate before the Turks and was compelled to look to the northeast, to Orthodox Moscow, for support. The council began on December 1, 1666. After the condemnation of Nikon and the elevation of Ioasaf II, it turned to the matter of the schism, and on May 13, 1667, it anathematized the old rituals.

109. This is a paraphrase of Psalm 51:15 (50:16 in the Russian Bible).

110. Palestine was an inclusive term used to denote all the southern and eastern Orthodox churches and peoples.

111. The conception of Moscow as the Third Rome is apparent in these remarks. It is the basis for both the contention and the supporting argument that follow. Avvakum contends that the Old Believers are the sole repository of unsullied Orthodoxy. If they are indeed heretics as claimed, then earlier tsars and all the old Russian saints must have been heretics as well. Within the narrow confines in which theological argument was conducted in this era, there was no satisfactory response to this argument, and it therefore became dear to the hearts of the schismatic polemicists.

112. These recognized authorities were especially valued by the Old Believers because it was possible to argue on the basis of their writings, or writings attributed to them, that they taught Christians to make the Sign of the Cross with two fingers. Meletius died in 381, Theodoret's dates are approximately 386–457, and Peter was active during the second half of the twelfth century. Maksim was educated in Italy but came to Russia in 1518 and remained there to his death in 1556.

113. Avvakum refers to the Stoglav Council, which convened in February 1551.

114. After defeating the city of Kazan in 1555, Ivan the Terrible established the Kazan eparchy and made Gurij (c. 1500–1563) its first archbishop. Varsonofij (1495–1576) was Gurij's close associate; both were canonized in 1595. While living with Ivan Neronov in Moscow, Avvakum served in "the Kazan Church" (i.e., St. Basil's, the church built by Ivan the Terrible and named for the holy fool to whom the victory over Kazan was credited); Avvakum therefore considered these saints his protectors. The term "Bearer of the Sign" (*znamenonosec*) refers to the highest rank of monastic ascetics, who wore large crosses on their mantles and cowls.

115. Cf. Acts 18:6 and Luke 9:5. The statement, "Better one, . . ." has its source in the apocryphal book known in the Latin Bible and Greek manuscripts as the Wisdom of Jesus, Son of Sirach (16:3). It is likely that "Seize him!" echoes Luke 23:18 in the old Russian translation of the Bible used by Avvakum; the passage describes an event during the condemnation of Christ.

116. Avvakum refers to the Greek prelate Dionysios, an archimandrite from the complex of monasteries on Mount Athos. He came to Russia in 1655, and because of his fluency in Russian he served as translator for Patriarchs Paissios and Makarios in 1666–67. He was author of a tract that condemned old Russian rituals as heresies that had grown out of ignorance; it served as a guide for the Greek patriarchs during the Ecumenical Council.

117. A condensation of Hebrews 7:26.

118. A slightly rephrased citation of 1 Corinthians 4:10.

119. Evfimej was a man of considerable learning, having mastered Greek, Latin, Polish, and Hebrew, so Nikon installed him in 1652 as a proofreader in the Church's printing house.

120. The Sparrow Hills were renamed the Lenin Hills in the Soviet period. They are located to the southwest of central Moscow and are the site of Moscow State University.

121. Lazar became Avvakum's close friend and remained one of his staunchest supporters. In 1665–66, Elder Epifanij wrote a "book" dedicated to exposing the heresies in the Church, placing much of the blame on the tsar. He journeyed to Moscow with his work and gave it to the tsar during the council. He was arrested and convicted. His close association with Avvakum began soon thereafter.

122. See, for example, John 18: 13–14, 24, 28.

123. The prisoners were taken to the Sparrow Hills on June 17, 1667, then moved into a horse barn in the Andreevskij Monastery, which was located at the base of the hills. Nearby was the Savvin Settlement, in the immediate vicinity of the Convent of St. Savva, which had been joined since 1649 to the Novodevičij Convent.

124. The tsar made a sustained effort to convince Avvakum and his comrades to recant even after their conviction and excommunication, and these visits by Jurij Lutoxin, Artemon Matveev, and Dementij Bašmakov were only part of this effort. The failure of these negotiations must have disappointed Aleksej Mixajlovič, for the goals of the Ecumenical Council remained partially unrealized as long as these schismatics continued in their stubborn resistance. Jurij Lutoxin was steward of the tsar's estate near the village of Izmajlovo; he was one of the sovereign's trusted agents. Artemon Sergeevič Matveev (1625–1682) was a boyar who enjoyed the tsar's special trust. His wife was born in Scotland, an incidental fact that reflected his Western sympathies. Dementij Minič Bašmakov (1618–1705) was one of the tsar's closest administrative associates. His chief responsibility was for the Chancellory of Secret Affairs, which often figured prominently in matters that were technically concerns of the patriarch and his administration. The principal function of this chancellory was to keep the central administration under surveillance and to investigate cases of wrongdoing.

125. Avvakum refers to the fall of Byzantium to the Turks in 1453.

126. On August 26, 1667, Avvakum, Lazar, Epifanij, and Nikifor were exiled to Pustozersk by order of the tsar. They left Moscow on August 30 and arrived in Pustozersk on December 12. The Pustozersk fortress, approximately a hundred miles from the Artic Ocean, was established in 1499 at the mouth of the Pečora River. In 1679 there were ninety households there consisting of over six hundred persons; there was also the commander's house, a customshouse, and the prison. The land there is tundra— frigid, barren and treeless, inhospitable. According to Robinson, in 1961 only three houses remained standing. Avvakum wrote his autobiography in Pustozersk and remained there for the last fifteen years of his life. He was burned at the stake with his fellow exiles in 1682.

127. Avvakum has in mind his Fourth and Fifth Petitions to the tsar. The former (1669) reported the death of Nikifor and requested that two of his sons be released from Moscow to live with their mother in Mezen; the latter (1669) he called his "final sorrow-laden supplication to you . . . from my dungeon, as from my grave."

128. *The Answer of the Orthodox* was written in the name of all four prisoners at Pustozersk; it was a lengthy compilation of theological and polemical materials divided into the two parts indicated by Avvakum: a formal "answer" to the Nikonians; and a discussion of the defilements wrought by the new books and attendant heresies. It was intended as a kind of manual, a textbook and a guide for Old Believers everywhere in Russia. The text was sent to Mezen before September 1669. Deacon Fëdor requested Avvakum's son Ivan to have it copied "in a good hand" and to send it to the rebel monks

at Solovki and to Moscow, where it arrived in fact near the close of 1669. The new mutilations visited upon the prisoners at Pustozersk in April 1670 were in large measure reprisals for this intransigent, rebellious book.

129. Cf. Matthew 26:75, Mark 14:72, Luke 22:62.

130. Elagin had been the ranking official in Mezen between 1661 and 1663, so he knew local conditions there. He was a reliable strong-arm man for the tsar, as he had served in the royal bodyguard. His mission was important, because Mezen had become the principal communications link between Pustozersk and Moscow. By interrupting this correspondence, Tsar Aleksej hoped to calm the restless capital and isolate the inflammatory Pustozersk schismatic leadership.

131. Lazar's public mutilation took place on April 14, 1670. The barbarous punishments had practical significance. Removing a heretic's tongue was a means of terminating his preaching of heresies, while chopping off part or all of his right hand might end their written propagation. In Russia the latter punishment also made the "heretical" crossing with two fingers impossible.

132. The term "angelical image" translates *sxima*, a Greek borrowing that denoted the highest rank among monks; it was reserved especially for hermits. The rank had two degrees, and Epifanij had received the lesser before he left Solovki for the northern forests.

133. Mutilation followed by regeneration of the amputated member(s) is an old hagiographical device, the obvious purpose of which is to demonstrate God's approval of the stand taken by any particular martyr.

134. "Pilate" is Elagin.

135. Cf. Mark 16:15–16.

136. Here again Avvakum suggests the official Church has been polluted by the Greeks, who have been defiled by the Islamic Turks. The wave of terror that enveloped Old Believers after 1667 gave Avvakum substantial grounds for invoking the Islamic notion of a holy war.

137. Cf. Matthew 7:18.

138. Cf. Daniel 3.

139. Cf. Proverbs 22:28.

140. Paraphrase of Psalm 115:1 (113:9 in the Russian Bible).

141. Cf. 2 Corinthians 11:6.

5. "Felicity," pages 91–98

1. Khlor: from an allegorical work, "The Tale of Tsarevich Khlor," written by Catherine II (here "Felicity") and intended for the moral education of her grandson, the future Alexander I.

2. *Murza*: Eastern form of address for a wise man or someone of noble birth.

3. Parnassus's steed is Pegasus in Greek mythology, Zeus's winged horse, associated with poetic creativity. Derzhavin is noting that Catherine prefers not to write poetry.

4. Catherine disliked mysticism and its social manifestations in seances and secret societies such as Masonic lodges.

5. Yet another symptom of eighteenth-century Orientalism, the East often referred to Masonic lodges.

6. The *murza* of this passage is Prince Grigory Potemkin (1739–1791); Derzhavin's historical reference is his role in the spread of the Russian empire. Other noblemen satirized further in the habits noted by Derzhavin are A.G. Orlov, P.I. Panin, S.K. Naryshkin, and A.A. Viazemsky.

7. A serf orchestra composed of hunters' horns.

8. *Svaika*: a game similar to ring toss. The exploration in question is the popular amusement of hunting for head lice.

9. Heroes of popular literature translated from Western sources in the seventeenth century and transposed into *lubok* fairy tales.

10. From Psalm 116.

11. A reference to the characters Lentiag (Mr. Idle) and Briuzga (Mr. Whiner) used by Catherine in her fairy tale to satirize Potemkin and Viazemsky.

12. Reference to Catherine's government reform of 1775 and the division of Russia into provinces.

13. Derzhavin's self-reference.

14. Catherine's response both in 1767 and 1779 to her legislature's initiative.

15. Fourth century B.C. Greek rhetorician, nicknamed "Homer's scourge" for his ridicule of the latter's epics. Known for being witty and spiteful.

16. Derzhavin is hinting at the harsh reign of Empress Anna (1730–40).

17. Among other such court merriments, Derzhavin's likely reference is the wedding of Anna's court jester and the wedding night spent by the bride and groom in an ice palace constructed for the occasion. The event later became a part of popular Russian fiction in Ivan Lazechnikov's *Ice House* (1835).

18. Tamerlane (1336–1405): Tatar conqueror of much of Central Asia, ruler of Samarkand (1369–1405), and another historical source of Russian Oriental generalizations.

19. Croesus: king of Lydia, c. 550 B.C., famous for wealth and vanity.

7. "Poor Liza," pages 104–17

1. Simonov Monastery: Moscow, founded in 1370 by St. Feodor.

2. Danilov Monastery: founded in the thirteenth century by Prince Daniil, son of Alexander Nevsky.

3. Sparrow Hills: present-day site of Moscow University.

4. Kolomenskoe: village south of Moscow, site of a residence of the tsars, the Church of the Ascension, the Church of the Kazan Mother of God, and the Church of St. George.

5. The Simonov Monastery was deserted from 1771 to the middle 1790s due to a plague outbreak in Moscow.

6. Hebe: in Greek mythology, goddess of youth and spring, cupbearer to the gods.

7. Cynthia: in Greek mythology, goddess of the moon (Artemis).

8. Pushkin's Notes to "The Bronze Horseman," pages 118–31

1. Algarotti said somewhere: "Petersbourg est la fenêtre, par laquelle la Russie regarde en Europe."

2. Mickiewicz described in beautiful verses the day preceding the Petersburg flood (in one of his best poems, "Oleszkiewicz"). The only pity is that this description is not accurate; there was no snow, and the Neva was not covered with ice. Our description is more faithful, although it lacks the bright coloring of the Polish poet.

3. See the description of the monument in Mickiewicz. It is borrowed from Ruban, as Mickiewicz himself observes.

10. "Taman," pages 136–46

1. These "Black Sea Cossacks" (not to be confused with the other Cossacks mentioned in the book) were descendants of Ukrainians removed by the Empress Catherine II

from beyond the cataracts of the Dniepr to the Kuban region in order to repel the incursions of Caucasian and Turkish tribes.

2. Gelendzhik: a port on the small bay of the Black Sea about 80 miles southeast of Taman, in the extreme northwest corner of the Caucasus. Taman village is a small port in Taman Gulf, an eastern inlet of the Kerch Strait, about 250 miles northwest of Suhum.

3. The hallway (or covered porch) of the second, smaller cottage.

4. "Then the eyes of the blind shall be opened . . . And the tongue of the dumb shall sing" (Isaiah 35:5–6). The revised Standard Version of 1952 adds "for joy."

5. The word used here is *valuni* (sing. *valun*), which means "boulders," not "breakers," as indicated by the context. Lermontov's odd application of the word may have been influenced by a similarity to *volni* or *vali* (German, *Wellen*), "waves," "billows." These *valuni* reappear as breakers on p. 181 [in Mihail Lermontov, *A Hero of Our Time*, translated by Vladimir Nabokov in collaboration with Dimitri Nabokov, Garden City, NY: Doubleday Anchor, 1958], in a special poetical metaphor that links up the end of Lermontov's "Princess Mary" with the "Taman" seascape.

6. Ruins of an ancient Greek colony in the vicinity northeast of Taman village.

7. The Russian epithet *nechisto* implies some devilry; the "evil" shades into the "uncanny" and "haunted." "There is something wrong about this place." *Nechisto*, in all its absolutely literal sense, means "not clean," which is the way Pechorin first interprets it. It is interesting to note that the Cossack corporal practically repeats line 15 of Zhukovsky's *Undina* (see note 8).

8. A buoyant and frisky maiden meant to be eerie, a changeling of mermaid origin, well known to Russian readers from Zhukovsky's adaptation in unrhymed dactylic verse (1833–36) of a romance by the German writer La Motte Fouqué (*Undine*, 1811).

9. *Yunaia Frantsia*, in the Russian text. The *Jeune-France* was the Parisian dandy of 1830 who copied the London dandy of 1815. The movement (not to be confused with a later political organization, 1848) had but few repercussions in the literature of the period 1830–40. Eccentricity of language and manners, detestation of bourgeois smugness, a desire to scandalize people, and the like marked this rather sterile post-romanticist fad.

10. A reference to the fey Italian girl in Goethe's romance *Wilhelm Meisters Lehrjahre* (1795–96). Lermontov knew French perfectly, German passably, and seems to have had a little more English than his master in poetry and prose, Pushkin (1799–1837).

11. Pechorin borrows this epithet from Pushkin's novel-in-verse *Eugene Onegin* (Five, XXXIV, 9), where Onegin gives Tatiana a "wondrously tender" look.

12. Borrowed from the poem *Le Déjeuner,* by the French elegiast Millevoye (1782–1816):

> *Un long baiser . . .*
> *Vient m'embraser de son humide flamme.*

13. Pechorin's description of the girl's attire is romantically vague. That kerchief or scarf was not her *only* garment.

11. *Boris Godunov,* pages 161–235

1. Nikolai Karamzin (1766–1826): historian and author of *The History of the Russian State,* which provided a rich source of historical material for Pushkin.

2. Irina was the sister of Boris Godunov and wife of Tsar Fedor.

3. Maliuta-Skuratov (d. 1573), Ivan the Terrible's right-hand villain. Vladimir

Monomakh (r. 1113–25): grand prince of Kiev and progenitor of the Moscow line of grand princes.

4. According to legend and *The Primary Chronicle,* Rurik was a Varangian who migrated in A.D. 862 to Novgorod and the land of Rus. Often considered to be the founder of the Russian state.

5. A reference to the Varangians and to Rurik.

6. A reference to specific icons that were believed capable of miracles, the Mother of God of Vladimir and the Mother of God of the Don.

7. After the death of Fedor, Godunov's sister Irina retired to this convent, now in the south of Moscow.

8. Ivan III (r. 1462–1505) and Ivan IV (r. 1533–84).

9. The Angel-Tsar: Fedor (r. 1584–98).

10. Monastery near Moscow.

11. Grigory is based on Grigory Otrepyev, widely believed to be the real name of the first False Dmitry (there were three such pretenders). He was crowned tsar in Moscow in 1605 and was killed in 1606. Pimen is a fictional character.

12. Reference to the democratic town council of medieval Novgorod.

13. Tatar capital on the Volga River. See notes 19 and 23.

14. Metropolitan Job (1589–1605): friend of Godunov and the first Muscovite patriarch.

15. Godunov's daughter Ksenia was to marry Duke John of Denmark in 1602; however, the intended bridegroom fell ill and died.

16. An ironic utterance (which can be paraphrased as, "What a fine kettle of fish this is!") derived from the one day in the year, the holiday of St. George, when peasants in medieval Russia could change landlords and households. Found frequently on subway walls during Yury Andropov's tenure in the Kremlin and when *Boris* was in rehearsal in Moscow. Yury is a Russian form of George.

17. The character of Afanasy Mikhailovich Pushkin is probably based on Pushkin's ancestor Ostafy Mikhailovich Pushkin, who was sent to Siberia in 1601. Gavrila Grigor'evich Pushkin (d. 1638), Afanasy Mikhailovich's nephew and a supporter of Dmitry in the play, fascinated the writer with his conspiratorial talents.

18. Sigismund III (1566–1632): king of Poland.

19. That is, the son of Prince Andrei Kurbsky, the hero of Kazan. After a distinguished career in the Russian military, Kurbsky went over to the Polish army in 1564. His subsequent written correspondence with Tsar Ivan IV is significant for both its historical and literary value.

20. Reference to Pskov, birthplace of Olga, wife of Grand Prince Igor of Kiev (913–45) and mother of Sviatoslav (962–72), for whom she acted as regent (945–62).

21. Stephen Bathory (r. 1575–86): king of Poland.

22. The muse crowns glory, and glory—the muse.

23. Kazan fell to Ivan IV and Kurbsky in 1552.

24. Let's go.

25. What, what?

26. What does *Orthodox* mean? . . . Damn ruffians, vile bastards! Damnation, sir, I am completely enraged. One could say they have no arms for fighting but only legs for running away.

27. It's disgraceful.

28. Damnations a thousand times over! I won't move a step more. Once begun the matter must be finished. What do you say, sir?

29. You're right.

30. Hell! Things are getting hot! That devil of a Pretender, as they call him, is a nasty piece of goods. What do you think, sir?

31. Oh, yes!

32. Look, look! There is action at the enemy's rear. It must be the brave Basmanov who has attacked.

33. I believe so.

34. Here are our Germans! Gentlemen! . . . Sir, order them to form rank and, hell's fire, let us attack!

35. Very good. Halt! . . . March!

36. God is with us!

12. "The Queen of Spades," pages 236–58

1. Comte de Saint-Germain (1710–1780): alchemist, adventurer, and member of French high society.

2. *Jeu de la reine:* queen's card game.

3. Zorich, Semen Gavrilovich: one of Catherine the Great's favorites and a passionate gambler.

4. "You decidedly seem to prefer chambermaids." "What can one do? They are fresher." The epigraph was provided to Pushkin by Denis Davydov.

5. *Vis-à-vis,* here "a dancing partner."

6. "You write four-page letters to me, my angel, faster than I can read them."

7. Elisabeth Vigée-Lebrun: French painter (1755–1842).

8. "A man with no morality or religion!"

9. "Neglect or pity."

10. "In the style of the royal bird."

11. *Attendez:* "no more bets."

12. The Obukhovsky Hospital treated the poor.

13. "The Overcoat," pages 259–84

1. In Russia during the nineteenth and early twentieth centuries there were many divisions ("departments") of various government institutions, the State Council, the Senate, and the ministries.

2. According to the Table of Ranks introduced by Peter the Great, Akaky Akakievich is a titular councillor, a rank of the ninth class.

3. *Bashmak* in Russian is "shoe." There are various sources and explanations for Gogol's use of the name "Akaky," ranging from the purely scatological to yet another Russian kenotic prototype, the sixteenth-century St. Akaky. In Greek the name means "slow to take offense."

4. Names for the newborn were frequently chosen from the church calendar marking the birthdays of saints. The ones mentioned are extremely uncommon and sound as comical to the Russian ear as they might to English speakers.

5. Rank of the fifth class.

6. Once again, although without a tail, the statue of Peter I and the subject of Pushkin's poem included in this volume.

7. Privy, actual, and court councillors; ranks of the third, second, and seventh classes, respectively.

8. Nevsky Prospect: the main street in Petersburg.

9. Collegiate registrar, fourteenth, and lowest, civil rank; government secretary, a rank of the twelfth class and not a definite position in the service.

10. Kalinkin Bridge: a stone drawbridge across the Fontanka River (a tributary of the Neva), built 1780–89.

11. Kolomna: at the time of the story, a quiet suburb on the bank of the Fontanka. The setting for Pushkin's frolicsome "Little House in Kolomna," well known to Gogol.

12. Obukhov Bridge: a stone drawbridge across the Fontanka.

14. "Bezhin Meadow," pp. 285–302

1. Rolling-room or dipping-room: the name for the place in paper factories where the paper is baled out in vats. It is located next to the mill itself under the wheel. (Turgenev's note)

2. In Russian, *Lisovshchiki:* workers in the paper factory who press and flatten the paper. (Turgenev's note)

3. The keep: in our region, the name given the place where water runs over the wheel. (Turgenev's note)

4. Form: the net used to scoop out paper. (Turgenev's note)

5. Split-grass: in folk tales, magic grass that opens any lock or bolt.

6. Parents' Saturday: according to old Russian custom, a Saturday in October dedicated to the memory of deceased parents.

7. Heavenly apparition: name given by peasants in our region to a solar eclipse. (Turgenev's note)

8. Trishka: the superstition about Trishka probably goes back to legends of the Antichrist. (Turgenev's note)

15. "The Meek Woman," pp. 303–37

1. *Faust,* scene III, "Ein Teil von jener Kraft, die stets das Böse will und stets das Gute schafft . . . "

2. *La Perichole:* operetta by Jacques Offenbach (1819–1880).

3. John Stuart Mill (1806–1874). The reference continues Dostoevsky's criticism of utilitarianism evident in *The Diary of a Writer, Crime and Punishment,* and other works.

4. Sennaya Square: located in one of the more disreputable districts of St. Petersburg.

5. The bridge was so named due to its proximity to the house of the chief of police. Located on Nevsky Prospect.

6. Dostoevsky stayed in Boulogne-sur-Mer in 1862.

7. Alain Lesage's *L'Histoire de Gil Blas de Santillane* (1715–35): part of the picaresque literary tradition that influenced Gogol's *Dead Souls* and other works of serious Russian humor.

8. Open trials were introduced during the 1860s as part of the judicial reforms that Dostoevsky both criticized in *The Diary of a Writer* and used to telling effect in *The Brothers Karamazov.*

16. "Lefty," pages 338–67

1. A *skaz* is a tale, but the term is used also to designate Leskov's narrative technique. See Hugh McLean's remarks in *Handbook of Russian Literature,* ed. Victor Terras, New Haven: Yale University Press, 1985, p. 420.

2. Alexander Pavlovich: Alexander I participated in the Congress of Vienna (1814–15), which established new borders after the war with Napoleon.

3. Platov, Matvei Ivanovich, Count (1751–1818): leader (*ataman*) of the Don Cossacks, near-legendary participant in the 1812 war against Napoleon. After the conclusion of peace, he escorted Alexander I to London.

4. Probably a play on the Italian city of Calabria with a candelabra thrown in.

5. At the beginning of the nineteenth century there was a sugar factory in Petersburg owned by Ya.N. Molvo.

6. Bobrinsky Factory: sugar refinery of Count A.A. Bobrinsky in Kiev in the 1830s.

7. "Father Fedot" was not an invention. Before he died in Taganrog, the Emperor Alexander Pavlovich had his last confession with Father Alexei Fedotov-Chekhovsky, who afterward was called "Confessor to His Majesty" and who liked to make much of this purely chance occurrence. This Fedotov-Chekhovsky is probably the legendary "Father Fedot" [Leskov's note].

8. Reference to the 1825 Decembrist revolt.

9. Count Kiselvrode: play on Count Karl Vasilievich Nesselrode (1780–1862), minister of foreign affairs (1822–56).

10. Kleinmikhel, Pyotr Andreevich, Count (1793–1869).

11. Skobelev, Ivan Nikitich (1778–1849): general and commandant of the Peter and Paul Fortress beginning in 1839.

12. Martyn-Solsky: play on Martyn Dmitrievich Solsky (1798–1881), military doctor.

13. Chernyshev, Aleksandr Ivanovich (1786–1857): minister of war (1827–52).

17. "Holstomer," pages 368–99

1. M.A. Stakhovich: a playwright from whom Tolstoy took the idea of his story.

2. Smetanka: from *smetana* (sour cream), the name of a white Arabian stallion given to Count Orlov by the sultan of Turkey and the sire of a breed of Orlov trotters.

3. "Fritz, bring another box, there are two." The host's German is grammatically incorrect.

4. Holstomer is made up of two words *holst* (canvas, cloth) and *merit'* (to measure). The name implies the horse's stride is suitable in length and regularity for measuring rolls of cloth, thus the frequent English translation "Yardstick."

18. "The Lady with the Lapdog," pages 407–21

1. A reference to the 1917 revision of the Cyrillic orthography.

2. Dimitry used instead of the common Dmitry here suggests affectation.

3. Gurov switches at this point to the familiar form of address.

4. Also *solyanka:* dish of meat, fish, or mushrooms, and cabbage.

5. *The Geisha:* operetta by English composer Sidney Jones, 1896.

24. "Verses about Moscow," pages 447–48

1. Transliteration for "forty times forty."

2. Moscow is built on seven hills.

26. *Petersburg,* "The Escape," pages 451–54

1. Sink: *opustit'sia.* In Russian, however, both a reflexive "to lower oneself" and "to degenerate," with connotations of the very close *opustet',* to empty, or to become desolate.

2. The Russian navy was almost completely destroyed at Tsushima during the Russian-Japanese War of 1905; the Kalka River was the site of a much earlier defeat by Tatars in 1223.

3. Kulikovo Field: the site of a Russian victory over the Tatars in 1380, as important for historical symbolism as Borodino.

27. "The King," pages 466–72

1. *Krik:* in Russian, "scream" or "shout."
2. Big Fountain: a resort in the Odessa region.
3. *Katsap:* derogatory Ukrainian term for "Russian."
4. See the toasts in Ilf and Petrov's "The Union of the Sword and the Plow."

29. *The Twelve Chairs,* pages 474–84

1. Polesov is an inept repairman whose botched jobs include the gate on which Ostap is sitting and a motor that looks perfect but does not run.

2. Part of the anti-Bolshevik forces supported Grand Duke Kirill Vladimirovich.

3. That is, before the 1917 revolution. Ilf and Petrov are satirizing the confusing changes in names mandated by political considerations.

4. "Bitter!": a Russian toast at weddings calling for a kiss between the newlyweds.

5. Ostap sings a popular romance composed by A.E. Varlamov (1801–1851) and based on Afanasy Fet's 1842 poem.

30. *Virgin Soil Upturned,* pages 485–89

1. Pood: a Russian unit of measure equal to approximately thirty-six pounds.

31. *Crime and Punishment,* pages 490–503

1. Brush: used in Russian to indicate a particular painter.

2. Ivan Ayvazovsky: popular Russian painter of seascapes. See the introduction to Part V.

39. "Wooden Horses," pages 529–52

1. Evgeniya creates an untranslatable pun combining the surname Urvaev and the word *urvat',* "to snatch, grab."

2. Protection of the Holy Mother is celebrated October 14 (October 1 on the Julian calendar) in the Russian Orthodox Church.

~Selected Bibliography~

Literary and Cultural Studies

Barricelli, Jean-Pierre, ed. *Chekhov's Great Plays: A Critical Anthology*. New York: New York University Press, 1981.

Besançon, Alain. *Le Tsarevitch immolé*. Paris: Plon, 1967.

Billington, James H. *The Icon and the Axe: An Interpretive History of Russian Culture*. New York: Vintage Books, 1966.

Benz, Ernst. *The Eastern Orthodox Church: Its Thought and Life*. New York: Anchor Books, 1963.

Bethea, David M., ed. *Pushkin Today*. Bloomington: Indiana University Press, 1993.

Brown, Deming. *Soviet Russian Literature since Stalin*. Cambridge: Cambridge University Press, 1978.

Brown, Edward W. *A History of Russian Literature of the Romantic Period*. 4 vols. Ann Arbor, MI: Ardis, 1986.

Broyde, Stephen. *Osip Mandelstam and His Age: A Commentary on the Themes of War and Revolution in His Poetry. 1913–1923*. Cambridge: Harvard University Press, 1975.

Chizhevsky, Dmitry. *History of Nineteenth-Century Russian Literature*. Ed. Serge Zenkovsky, trans. R.N. Parker. Vol. 1, *The Romantic Period*, Vol. 2, *The Realistic Period*, Nashville, TN: Vanderbilt University Press, 1974.

————. *History of Russian Literature from the Eleventh Century to the End of the Baroque*. The Hague: Mouton, 1960.

————. *Russian Intellectual History*. Trans. John C. Osborne and Martin P. Rice. Ann Arbor, MI: Ardis, 1978.

Emerson, Caryl. *Boris Godunov: Transpositions of a Russian Theme*. Bloomington: Indiana University Press, 1986.

Erlich, Victor. *Russian Formalism: History–Doctrine*. 3rd ed. New Haven: Yale University Press, 1981.

Ermolaev, Hermann. *Soviet Literary Theories, 1917–1934: The Genesis of Socialist Realism*. Berkeley: University of California Press, 1963.

Fedotov, G.P. *The Russian Religious Mind*. New York: Harper Torchbooks, 1960.

Fennel, John. *Early Russian Literature*. Berkeley: University of California Press, 1974.

Fitzpatrick, Sheila, Alexander Rabinowitch, and Richard Stites, eds. *Russia in the Era of NEP*, Bloomington: Indiana University Press, 1991.

Fleishman, Lazar. *Boris Pasternak: The Poet and His Politics*. Cambridge: Harvard University Press, 1990.

Florovsky, Georges. *Collected Works of Georges Florovsky*. Belmont, MA: Nordland, 1972.

Frank, Joseph. *Dostoevsky: The Seeds of Revolt, 1821–1849*. Princeton: Princeton University Press, 1976.

————. *Dostoevsky: The Years of Ordeal, 1850–1859*. Princeton: Princeton University Press, 1983.

————. *Dostoevsky: The Stir of Liberation, 1860–1865.* Princeton: Princeton University Press, 1986.

————. *Dostoevsky: The Miraculous Years, 1865–1871.* Princeton: Princeton University Press, 1995.

Gibian, George. *Russia's Lost Literature of the Absurd: A Literary Discovery.* Ithaca: Cornell University Press, 1971.

Hingley, Ronald. *Russian Writers and Society in the Nineteenth Century.* 2nd ed. London: Weidenfeld and Nicolson, 1977.

Janecek, Gerald. *The Look of Russian Literature: Avant-Garde, Visual Experiments 1900–1930.* Princeton: Princeton University Press, 1975.

Kalbouss, George. *A Study Guide to Russian Culture:* Needham Heights, MA: Ginn Press, 1991.

Kelly, Catriona. *A History of Russian Women's Writing, 1820–1992.* Oxford: Clarendon Press, 1994.

Lenhoff, Gail. *The Martyred Princes Boris and Gleb: A Sociocultural Study of the Cult and the Texts.* Columbus, OH: Slavica, 1989.

Likhachev, D.S. *Chelovek v literature drevnei Rusi.* 2nd ed. Moscow: Nauka, 1970.

————. *Poetika drevnerusskoi literatury.* Leningrad: Akademiia Nauk SSSR, 1967.

————. *"Slovo o polku Igoreve" i kul'tura ego vremeni.* Leningrad: Khudozhestvennaia literatura, 1985.

————. *Velikoe nasledie: klassicheskie proizvedeniia literatury drevnei Rusi.* Moscow: Sovremennik, 1975.

————, ed. *Vzaimodeistvie literatury i izobrazitel'nogo iskusstva v drevnei Rusi.* Moscow–Leningrad: Nauka, 1966.

Leong, Albert, ed. *Oregon Studies in Chinese and Russian Culture.* New York: Peter Lang, 1990.

Lunacharskii, A.V. *Stat'i o sovetskoi literature.* Moscow: Prosveshchenie, 1971.

Madariaga, Isabel de. *Russia in the Age of Catherine the Great.* New Haven: Yale University Press, 1981.

Malia, Martin. *Alexander Hertzen and the Birth of Russian Socialism, 1812–1855.* Cambridge: Harvard University Press, 1961.

Mathewson, Rufus. *The Positive Hero in Russian Literature.* New York: Columbia University Press, 1958.

Markov, Vladimir. *Russian Futurism: A History.* Berkeley: University of California Press, 1968.

Meyendorff, John. *Byzantium and the Rise of Russia: A Study in Byzantio-Russian Relations in the Fourteenth Century.* Cambridge: Cambridge University Press, 1981.

Miliukov, Pavel. *Outlines of Russian Culture.* Philadelphia: University of Pennsylvania Press, 1942.

Mirsky, D.S. *A History of Russian Literature.* Ed. Francis J. Whitfield. New York: Knopf, 1949.

Mochulsky, K.D. *Dostoevsky, His Life and Work.* Trans. Michael Minihan. Princeton: Princeton University Press, 1967.

Nakhimovsky, Alexander D., and Alice Stone. *The Semiotics of Russian Cultural History: Essays by Iurii M. Lotman, Lidiia Ia. Ginsburg, Boris A. Uspenskii.* Introduction by Boris Gasparov. Ithaca: Cornell University Press, 1985.

Novaia volna: Russkaia kul'tura i subkul'tury na rubezhe 80–90 gg. Comp. N.I. Azhgikhina. Moscow: Moskovskii rabochii, 1994.

Novitskaia, E.L., ed. *O Dostoevskom. Tvorchestvo Dostoevskogo v russkoi mysli 1881–1931 godov.* Moscow: Kniga, 1990.

Obolensky, Dimitri. *The Byzantine Commonwealth: Eastern Europe, 500–1453.* Crestwood, NY: St. Vladimir's Seminary Press, 1982.

Ozmitel', E.K. *Sovetskaia satira. Seminarii.* Moscow–Leningrad: Prosveshchenie, 1964.

Panchenko, A.M. *Smekhovoi mir drevnei Rusi.* Leningrad: Nauka, 1984.

Parthé, Kathleen. *Russian Village Prose: The Radiant Past.* Princeton: Princeton University Press, 1992.

Poggioli, Renato. *The Poets of Russia, 1890–1930.* Cambridge: Harvard University Press, 1960.

Riasanovsky, Nicholas. *A History of Russia.* New York: Oxford University Press, 1984.

Rice, Martin P. *Valery Briusov and the Rise of Russian Symbolism.* Ann Arbor, MI: Ardis, 1975.

Rogov, E.N. *Atlas istorii kul'tury Rossii.* Moscow: Krug-Rapid-Print, 1993.

Rybakov, B.A., ed. *Ocherki russkoi kul'tury XVIII veka.* 4 vols. Moscow: MGU Press, 1988.

Seduro, Vladimir. *Dostoevsky in Russian and World Theatre.* North Quincy, MA: Christopher, 1977.

Segal, Harold. *The Literature of Eighteenth-Century Russia.* 2 vols. New York: Dutton, 1967.

Shklovsky, Victor. *Mayakovsky and His Circle.* Trans. Lily Feiler. New York: Dodd & Mead, 1972.

———. *Sobranie sochinenii.* Moscow: Khudozhestvennaia literatura, 1973–74.

Smelianskii, Anatolii. *Nashi sobesedniki.* Moscow: Iskusstvo, 1981.

Terras, Victor. *A History of Russian Literature.* New Haven: Yale University Press, 1991.

———, ed. *Handbook of Russian Literature.* New Haven: Yale University Press, 1985.

Todd, William Mills. *Fiction and Society in the Age of Pushkin: Ideology, Institution and Narrative.* Cambridge: Harvard University Press, 1986.

———. *Literature and Society in Imperial Russia, 1800–1914.* Stanford: Stanford University Press, 1978.

Valency, Maurice. *The Breaking String: The Plays of Anton Chekhov.* New York: Schocken Books, 1966.

Venturi, Franco. *Roots of Revolution: A History of the Populist and Socialist Movements in XIX Century Russia.* London: Weidenfeld and Nicolson, 1960.

Walicki, Andrzej. *A History of Russian Thought from the Enlightenment to Marxism.* Stanford: Stanford University Press, 1979.

Ware, Timothy. *The Orthodox Church, Intellectual History and Philosophy.* New York: Penguin Books, 1993.

Weber, Harry B., et al., eds. *The Modern Encyclopedia of Russian and Soviet Literature.* Gulf Breeze, FL: Academic International Press, 1977–.

Weidle, Wladimir. *Russia: Absent and Present.* Trans. A. Gordon Smith. New York: Vintage Books, 1961.

West, James. *Russian Symbolism. A Study of Vyacheslav Ivanov and the Russian Symbolist Aesthetic.* London: Methuen, 1970.

Zenkovsky, V. *A History of Russian Philosophy.* 2 vols. New York: Columbia University Press, 1953.

Ziolkowski, Margaret. *Hagiography and Modern Russian Literature.* Princeton: Princeton University Press, 1988.

Anthologies of Literature

Afanas'ev, A.N. *Narodnye russkie skazki v trekh tomakh.* Moscow: Nauka, 1984.

Alexander, A.E. *Russian Folklore: An Anthology in English Translation.* Belmont, MA: Nordland, 1975.

Brown, Clarence, ed. *The Portable Twentieth-Century Russian Reader.* London: Penguin, 1993.

Fedotov, G.P. *A Treasury of Russian Spirituality.* New York: Harper & Row, 1965.

Gibian, George, ed. *The Portable Nineteenth-Century Russian Reader.* New York: Penguin, 1993.

Glad, John, and Daniel Weissbort, eds. *Russian Poetry: The Modern Period.* Iowa City: University of Iowa Press, 1978.

Green, Michael, ed. and trans. *The Russian Symbolist Theatre: An Anthology of Plays and Critical Texts.* Ann Arbor, MI: Ardis, 1986.

Guterman, Norbert, trans. *Russian Fairy Tales.* Folkloristic commentary by Roman Jakobson. New York: Pantheon Books, 1975.

Karlinsky, Simon, and Alfred Appel, Jr., eds. *Russian Literature and Culture in the West: 1922–1972.* 2 vols. *TriQuarterly* 27–28 (Spring–Fall 1973).

Kelly, Catriona, ed. *An Anthology of Russian Women's Writing 1777–1992.* New York: Oxford University Press, 1994.

Lawton, Anna, ed. *Russian Futurism through Its Manifestoes, 1912–1928.* Trans. Anna Lawton and Herbert Eagle. Ithaca: Cornell University Press, 1988.

Luker, Nicholas, ed. *From Furmanov to Sholokhov: An Anthology of the Classics of Socialist Realism.* Ann Arbor, MI: Ardis, 1988.

MacAndrew, A.R. *Nineteenth-Century Russian Drama.* New York: Bantam Books, 1963.

———. *Twentieth-Century Russian Drama.* New York: Bantam Books, 1963.

Pachmuss, Temira, ed. and trans. *Women Writers in Russian Modernism.* Urbana: University of Illinois Press, 1978.

Proffer, Carl and Ellendea, eds. *The Silver Age of Russian Culture: An Anthology.* Ann Arbor, MI: Ardis, 1975.

Proffer, Carl R., et al., eds. *Russian Literature of the Twenties: An Anthology.* Ann Arbor, MI: Ardis, 1980.

Rydel, Christine, ed. *The Ardis Anthology of Russian Romanticism.* Ann Arbor, MI: Ardis, 1984.

Art and Architecture

Alpatov, M.V. *Etiudy po istorii russkogo iskusstva.* Moscow: Iskusstvo, 1967.

Anderson, Roger, and Paul Debreczeny, eds. *Russian Narrative and Visual Art: Varieties of Seeing.* Gainesville: University of Florida Press, 1994.

Bowlt, John E., ed. and trans. *Russian Art of the Avant-garde: Theory and Criticism.* New York: Thames and Hudson, 1988.

Brumfield, W.C. *A History of Russian Architecture.* New York: Cambridge University Press, 1993.

Chernevich, Elena. *Russian Graphic Design, 1880–1917.* New York: Abbeville Press, 1990.

Dembo, H.G., ed. *Gosudarstvennyi Russkii Muzei. Al'bom reproduktsii.* Moscow–Leningrad: Izobrazitel'noe iskusstvo, 1959.

Dodge, Norton, and Alison Hilton. *New Art from the Soviet Union: The Known and the Unknown.* Washington, DC: Acropolis Books, 1977.

Elliot, David. *New Worlds: Russian Art and Society, 1900–1937.* New York: Rizzoli, 1986.

Gerasimov, Iu.K., ed. *Russkaia literatura i izobrazitel'noe iskusstvo, XVIII–nachalo XX veka.* Leningrad: Nauka, 1988.

Grabar, Igor, V. Lazareva, and V. Kemenova, eds. *Istoriia russkogo iskusstva.* Moscow, Akademiia nauk SSSR, 1953.

Hamilton, G. *The Art and Architecture of Russia*. 3rd. ed. New York: Penguin, 1983.

Iablonskaia, M. *Women Artists of Russia's New Age, 1910–1935*. New York: Rizzoli, 1990.

Kirichenko, E.I. *The Russian Style*. London: Laurence King, 1991.

Lodder, Christina. *Russian Constructivism*. New Haven: Yale University Press, 1983.

Milner, John. *A Dictionary of Russian and Soviet Artists*. Woodbridge, Suffolk: Antique Collector's Club, 1993.

Norman, John O., ed. *New Perspectives on Russian and Soviet Artistic Culture*. New York: St. Martin's Press, 1994.

Ocheretiansky, Alexander. *Literature and Art of Avant-garde Russia (1890–1930)*. Newtonville, MA: Oriental Research Partners, 1989.

Roman, G.H., and Virginia H. Marquardt, eds. *The Avant-garde Frontier: Russia Meets the West, 1910–1930*. Gainesville: University of Florida Press, 1992.

Rowell, Margit. *Art of the Avant-garde in Russia: Selections from the George Costakis Collection*. New York: Solomon R. Guggenheim Museum, 1981.

Sarab'ianov, D.V. *Russian Art from Neoclassicism to the Avant-garde, 1800–1917: Painting–Sculpture–Architecture*. New York: Abrams, 1990.

Sokolova, Natalya, ed. *Selected Works of Russian Art*. Leningrad: Aurora, 1976.

Suslov, Vitaly, ed. *Great Art Treasures of the Hermitage Museum, St. Petersburg*. New York: Abrams, 1994.

Talbot Rice, Tamara. *A Concise History of Russian Art*. New York: Praeger, 1967.

Valkenier, Elizabeth K. *Ilya Repin and the World of Russian Art*. New York: Columbia University Press, 1990.

Vasil'ev, V.N., ed. *Pamiatniki russkoi kul'tury pervoi chetverti XVIII veka*. Leningrad-Moscow: Sovetskii khudozhnik, 1966.

Volodarsky, V., *The Tretyakov Gallery Painting*. Leningrad: Aurora, 1981.

Vostretsova, L., et al. *Soviet Art, 1920's–1930's: Russian Museum, Leningrad*. New York: Abrams, 1988.

Wood, Paul. *The Great Utopia: The Russian and Soviet Avant-garde, 1915–1932*. New York: Abrams, 1994.

Drama and Theater

Green, Michael, ed. and trans. *The Russian Symbolist Theatre: An Anthology of Plays and Critical Texts*. Ann Arbor, MI: Ardis, 1986.

Karlinsky, Simon. *Russian Drama from Its Beginnings to the Age of Pushkin*. Berkeley: University of California Press, 1985.

Komissarzhevsky, Victor, ed. *Nine Modern Soviet Plays*. Moscow: Progress, 1977.

Mikhailova, Alla, ed. and Yuri Koplyov, trans. *Classic Soviet Plays*. Moscow: Progress, 1979.

Noyes, George Rapall, ed., and trans. *Masterpieces of Russian Drama*. 2 vols. New York: Dover, 1960–61.

Poliakova, E. *Teatr L'va Tolstogo*. Moscow: Iskusstvo, 1978.

Rudnitsky, Konstantin. *Russian and Soviet Theatre: Tradition and the Avant-Garde*. London: Thames and Hudson, 1988.

———. *Russkoe rezhisserskoe iskusstvo 1908–1917*. Moscow: Nauka, 1990.

Segal, Harold B. *Twentieth–Century Russian Drama: From Gorky to the Present*. Baltimore: Johns Hopkins University Press, 1993.

———, ed. and trans. *The Literature of Eighteenth-Century Russia: An Anthology of Russian Literary Materials of the Age of Classicism and the Enlightenment*. 2 vols. New York: Dutton, 1967.

Senelick, Laurence, ed. and trans. *Russian Dramatic Theory from Pushkin to the Symbolists*. Austin: University of Texas Press, 1981.

Slonim, Mark. *Russian Theatre from the Empire to the Soviets*. Cleveland: World, 1961.

Varneke, Boris V. *History of Russian Theatre: Seventeenth through Nineteenth Century*. Trans. Boris Brasol. New York: Macmillan, 1951.

Music

Abraham, Gerald. *On Russian Music*. New York: Scribner, 1939.

Campbell, Stuart, ed. *Russians on Russian Music, 1830–1880: An Anthology*. Cambridge: Cambridge University Press, 1994.

Leonard, R. *A History of Russian Music*. London: Jarrolds, 1956.

Newmarch, Rosa. *The Russian Opera*. Westport, CT: Greenwood Press, 1972.

Pokrovsky, Boris, and Yury Grigorovich, eds. *The Bolshoi Opera and Ballet at the Greatest Theatre in Russia*. Trans. Daryl Hislop. New York: William Morrow, 1979.

Roberts, Peter. *Modernism in Russian Piano Music: Scriabin, Prokofiev and Their Russian Counterparts*. Bloomington: Indiana University Press, 1993.

Ridenour, Robert. *Nationalism, Modernism, and Personal Rivalry in Nineteenth-Century Russian Music*. Ann Arbor, MI: UMI Research Press, 1981.

Seaman, Gerald. *History of Russian Music*. Oxford: Oxford University Press, 1967.

Swann, Alfred. *Russian Music and Its Sources in Chant and Folk Songs*. New York: Norton, 1973.

Taruskin, Richard. *Opera and Drama in Russia as Preached and Practiced in the 1860s*. Ann Arbor, MI: UMI Research Press, 1981.

Terry, Walter. *Ballet Guide*. New York: Popular Library, 1977.

Vasina-Grossman, V.A. *Istoriia russkoi sovetskoi muzyki*. 3 vols. Moscow: Gosudarstvennoe Muzykal'noe Izdatel'stvo, 1959.

Film

Aumont, Jacques. *Montage Eisenstein*. Trans. L. Hildreth, C. Penley, and A. Ross. Bloomington: Indiana University Press, 1987.

Birkos, Alexander. *Soviet Cinema: Directors and Films*. Hamden, CT: Archon Books, 1976.

Dondurei, Daniil. *Film, TV, Video in Russia: 94*. Moscow: Progress, 1994.

Eagle, Herbert. *Russian Formalist Film Theory*. Ann Arbor: Department of Slavic Languages and Literatures, University of Michigan, 1981.

Eizenshtein, Sergei. *Immoral Memories*. Trans. H. Marshall. London: Owen, 1985.

Galichenko, Nicholas. *Glasnost—Soviet Cinema Responds*. Austin: University of Texas Press, 1991.

Katz, Ephraim. *The Film Encyclopedia*. New York: Harper Perennial, 1994.

Kenez, Peter. *Cinema and Soviet Society, 1917–1953*. Cambridge: Cambridge University Press, 1992.

Lary, Nikita. *Dostoevsky and Soviet Film*. Ithaca: Cornell University Press, 1986.

Lawton, Anna. *Kinoglasnost: Soviet Cinema in Our Time*. Cambridge: Cambridge University Press, 1992.

———. ed. *The Red Screen: Politics, Society, Art in Soviet Cinema*. London–New York: Routledge, 1992.

Leyda, Jay. *Kino: A History of the Russian and Soviet Film*. New York: Macmillan, 1960.

Slater, Thomas J., ed. *Handbook of Soviet and East European Films and Filmmakers.* Westport, CT: Greenwood, 1992.

Sokolov, I.V., ed. *Istoriia sovetskogo kinoiskusstva zvukovogo perioda.* Moscow: Goskinoizdat, 1946.

Taylor, Richard, and Ian Christie, eds. *Inside the Film Factory: New Approaches to Russian and Soviet Cinema.* New York: Routledge, 1991.

Turovskaya, Maya. *Tarkovsky: Cinema as Poetry.* London: Faber and Faber, 1989.

Youngblood, Denise. *Movies for the Masses.* Cambridge: Cambridge University Press, 1992.

————. *Soviet Cinema in the Silent Era, 1918–1935.* Austin: University of Texas Press, 1951.

Zemlianukhin, Sergei, and Miroslav Segida, comps. *Catalogue: Russian Films: 1991–1994.* Moscow: Dubl'-D, 1994.

Zhdan, V., ed. *Kratkaia istoriia sovetskogo kino.* Moscow: Iskusstvo, 1969.

Nicholas Rzhevsky (Ph.D. Princeton, 1972) is an associate professor of Russian at the State University of New York at Stony Brook. He is the author of *Russian Literature and Ideology* (1983) and editor of *Dramaturgs and Dramaturgy* (with E.J. Czerwinski, 1986), *Media→←Media* (with Caryl Emerson, 1990), and *The Cambridge Companion to Modern Russian Culture* (forthcoming). His articles on Russian literature and culture have appeared in such publications as *Encounter, Modern Drama, The Nation, New Literary History*, and *Slavic Review.* On the creative side of the arts, Rzhevsky wrote the English-language version of Dostoevsky's *Crime and Punishment* directed by Yury Liubimov at London's Lyric Hammersmith Theatre.